ARTIFICIAL INTELLIGENCE, SIMULATION, AND MODELING

REVIEW BOARD

The editors would especially like to thank the dedication, time, and effort of the Editorial Review Board.

ARTIFICIAL INTELLIGENCE, SIMULATION, AND MODELING

Edited by

Lawrence E. Widman
Division of Cardiology, Department of Medicine
The University of Texas Health Science Center at San Antonio
San Antonio, Texas
and Cardiology Service
Audie L. Murphy Memorial Veterans' Hospital
San Antonio, Texas

Kenneth A. Loparo
Department of Systems Engineering
and Center for Automation and Intelligent Systems Research
Case Western Reserve University
Cleveland, Ohio

Norman R. Nielsen
Information Industries Division
SRI International
Menlo Park, California

WILEY

A WILEY-INTERSCIENCE PUBLICATION

JOHN WILEY & SONS

New York • Chichester • Brisbane • Toronto • Singapore

Library of Congress Cataloging-in-Publication Data

Artificial intelligence, simulation, and modeling/edited by Lawrence
  E. Widman, Kenneth A. Loparo, and Norman R. Nielsen.
    p. cm.
    "A Wiley-Interscience publication."
    Includes bibliographies and index.
    ISBN 0-471-60599-9
    1. Artificial Intelligence. 2. Computer simulation. I. Widman,
Lawrence Edward, 1950– . II. Loparo, Kenneth A. III. Nielsen, N.
R. (Norman R.)
  Q335A78783 1989
  006.3--dc19   88-30282
                                       CIP

Printed in the United States of America

10 9 8 7 6 5 4 3 2 1

CONTRIBUTORS

Pierre Belanger   Department of Electrical Engineering, McGill University, Montreal, Quebec, Canada H3A 2K6

Kurt M. Berger[1]   Department of Systems Engineering and Center for Automation and Intelligent Systems Research, Case Western Reserve University, Cleveland, Ohio 44106

Charles Chiu   Department of Physics and Artificial Intelligence Laboratory, The University of Texas at Austin, Austin, Texas 78712

Bruce D'Ambrosio   Department of Computer Science, Oregon State University, Corvallis, Oregon 97331-4602

Renato De Mori   School of Computer Science, McGill University, Montreal, Quebec, Canada H3A 2K6; and Centre de recherche informatique de Montreal, Montreal, Quebec, Canada H3G 1N2

Paul A. Fishwick   Department of Computer and Information Sciences, University of Florida, Gainesville, Florida 32611

Mark S. Fox   Intelligent Systems Laboratory, The Robotics Institute, Carnegie Mellon University, Pittsburgh, Pennsylvania 15213-3890

Peter Friedland   Knowledge Systems Laboratory, Department of Computer Science, Stanford University, Stanford, California 94305

Shoshana L. Hardt   Department of Computer Science, State University of New York at Buffalo, Buffalo, New York 14260

Nizwer Husain[2]   Intelligent Systems Laboratory, The Robotics Institute, Carnegie Mellon University, Pittsburgh, Pennsylvania 15213-3890

Peter D. Karp   Knowledge Systems Laboratory, Department of Computer Science, Stanford University, Stanford, California 94305

E. J. H. Kerckhoffs   Faculty of Mathematics and Informatics, Delft University of Technology, 2628 BL Delft, The Netherlands

H. Koppelaar   Faculty of Mathematics and Informatics, Delft University of Technology, 2628 BL Delft, The Netherlands

---

[1]Present address: Charles Stark Draper Laboratory, Inc., 555 Technology Square, Cambridge, Massachusetts 02139.
[2]Present address: Intellicorp, 1975 El Camino Real West, Mountainview, California 94040-2216.

Donald W. Kosy   The Robotics Institute, Carnegie Mellon University, Pittsburgh, Pennsylvania 15213

Mark A. Kramer   Department of Chemical Engineering, Massachusetts Institute of Technology, Cambridge, Massachusetts 02139

Benjamin Kuipers   Department of Computer Sciences, The University of Texas at Austin, Austin, Texas 78712

Kenneth A. Loparo   Department of Systems Engineering and Center for Automation and Intelligent Systems Research, Case Western Reserve University, Cleveland, Ohio 44106

Pertti Lounamaa   Nokia Corporation Research Center, P.O. Box 780, Helsinki, Finland SF-00101

Malcolm McRoberts[3]   Intelligent Systems Laboratory, The Robotics Institute, Carnegie Mellon University, Pittsburgh, Pennsylvania 15213-3890

Robert M. O'Keefe   Department of Decision Sciences and Engineering Systems, Rensselaer Polytechnic Institute, Troy, New York 12180-3590

Olayiwola O. Oyeleye   Department of Chemical Engineering, Massachusetts Institute of Technology, Cambridge, Massachusetts 02139

Robert Prager   CAE Electronics Ltd., St. Laurent, Quebec, Canada H4L 4X4; and School of Computer Science, McGill University, Montreal, Quebec, Canada H3A 2K6

Y. V. Reddy   Intelligent Systems Laboratory, The Robotics Institute, Carnegie Mellon University, Pittsburgh, Pennsylvania 15213-3890; and Artificial Intelligence Laboratory, Department of Statistics and Computer Science, West Virginia University, Morgantown, West Virginia 26506

J. P. Rice   Knowledge Systems Laboratory, Department of Computer Science, Stanford University, Stanford, California 94305

Jeff Rothenberg   The RAND Corporation, Santa Monica, California 90406-2138

Sergio Ruiz-Mier[4]   Center for Intelligent Manufacturing Systems, Purdue University, West Lafayette, Indiana 47907

Joseph Talavage   Center for Intelligent Manufacturing Systems, Purdue University, West Lafayette, Indiana 47907

H. J. van den Herik   Department of Computer Science, Faculty of General Science, University of Limburg, 6211 LM Maastricht, The Netherlands

---

[3]Present address: McDonnell Douglas Astronautics Company, Kennedy Space Division, Technical Services Company, P.O. Box 21233, Kennedy Space Center, Florida 32815.
[4]Present address: P.O. Box 1615, La Paz, Bolivia.

Lawrence E. Widman Division of Cardiology, Department of Medicine, The University of Texas Health Science Center at San Antonio, San Antonio, Texas 78284; and Cardiology Service, Audie L. Murphy Memorial Veterans' Hospital, San Antonio, Texas 78284

Bernard P. Zeigler Department of Electrical and Computer Engineering, University of Arizona, Tucson, Arizona 85721

Guoqing Zhang[5] Department of Electrical and Computer Engineering, University of Arizona, Tucson, Arizona 85721

[5]Present address: Zycad Corporation, 1380 Willow Road, Menlo Park, California 94025.

PREFACE

This book is the product of a very typical phenomenon in scientific circles—the chance remark or encounter that leads to a whole sequence of events. In our case, a chance remark at a bull session one Sunday in the Spring of 1986 led to the assembly of this book.

David Helman and Lawrence Widman were ruminating on the state of the world when David noticed an announcement for the first Workshop on AI and Simulation to be held in conjunction with the Fifth National Conference on Artificial Intelligence in Philadelphia. David had just signed a contract to edit an interdisciplinary book in the fields of artificial intelligence, cognitive science, and philosophy. He suggested that Larry undertake the editing of a similar book related to AI and simulation. One thing led to another, and David and Larry attended the workshop. A sample of speakers, whose work might form the framework of a review of the nascent field of AI and simulation, were consulted. Each of the potential contributors responded favorably to the invitation, and the germ of an idea began to grow.

Ken Loparo was invited to join the venture and the search for a publisher undertaken. The goals and structure of the book were established, contributors identified, invitations extended, and the book began to take shape. The publisher introduced Norman Nielsen to the editors. His insights proved to be so helpful that he was invited to become a co-editor when for reasons of time David's interests were drawn away last year.

The field of AI has much to offer the world of simulation, and vice versa. Accordingly, we have organized the contributions in this book to address both points of view, examining the field from the perspective of

- traditional simulationists who seek greater representational flexibility and ease of use which AI techniques can provide and
- computer scientists with a symbolic computing background who seek greater power and realism which rigorous simulation techniques can provide.

To this end, we have divided the book into three parts. The first part contains eight chapters that discuss the theoretical underpinnings of AI and simulation. The second part contains three chapters that discuss the application of simulation techniques to current research problems in AI, while the third part contains eight chapters that discuss the application of AI methods to the needs of simulationists and simulation users.

ix

In designing and assembling this book, we have assumed a broad audience with interests ranging from AI to simulation and experience ranging from little to extensive. Accordingly, we have included a fairly comprehensive introductory chapter that that seeks to provide a framework for the remaining 19 chapters. It provides

- a brief history of AI and of simulation,
- a concise introduction to the basic concepts of each discipline,
- a survey of the current literature related to the intersection of these two disciplines, and
- an introduction to each of the book's parts and the chapters therein.

Many people have contributed to the development of this book over the two years that it has been in gestation. First and foremost, of course, are the authors, without whose contributions this book would not have been possible. They were a marvelous group to work with, and we owe them a special debt of gratitude. Not only have they patiently borne our requests for repeated revisions, but they have modified their manuscripts in order to achieve a degree of uniformity in the scope and depth of the material presented.

Credit must also be given to Professor David Helman of Case Western Reserve University. Not only did he plant the seed that gave rise to this book, but he nurtured the emerging seedling as well. Truly, his spirit is imprinted on this book.

Finally, we would like to credit our editor, Diane Cerra, Wanda Cuevas, Jenet McIver, Robert Hilbert, and the entire Wiley team. Not only did they have faith in our vision of what one day might become a book, but they actively guided and supported us in that endeavor.

May you enjoy the fruits of everyone's labors and find that the material is of assistance to you in understanding the growing field of AI and simulation and in carrying out your work.

LAWRENCE E. WIDMAN
KENNETH A. LOPARO
NORMAN R. NIELSEN

San Antonio, Texas
Cleveland, Ohio
Palo Alto, California

CONTENTS

ARTIFICIAL INTELLIGENCE, SIMULATION, AND MODELING

1 Artificial Intelligence, Simulation, and Modeling: A Critical Survey

LAWRENCE E. WIDMAN

Division of Cardiology
Department of Medicine
The University of Texas Health Science Center at San Antonio
San Antonio, Texas
and
Cardiology Service
Audie L. Murphy Memorial Veterans' Hospital
San Antonio, Texas

and KENNETH A. LOPARO

Department of Systems Engineering
and Center for Automation and Intelligent Systems Research
Case Western Reserve University
Cleveland, Ohio

1 MOTIVATION AND OVERVIEW

The growing cross-fertilization of ideas between the fields of artificial intelligence (AI) and simulation has stimulated increasing interest in both the simulation and the artificial intelligence communities. This interest is evidenced by the inauguration of special sessions on artificial intelligence at the major simulation conferences in 1985 and in the increasing number of papers in similar sessions, which rose 150% between 1985 and 1986. Also in 1985, the first (stand-alone) Working Conference on "AI and Simulation" in Europe was held at the University of Ghent (Belgium) [46]. In the artificial intelligence community, the National Conference on Artificial Intelligence held its first Workshop on Artificial Intelligence and Simulation in 1986.

The motivations for workers in each field differ. Simulationists find that simulation software is weak: Users demand more realistic models, more support for the novice, and better assistance with extracting information from large amounts of data. These requirements are evolutionary, not revolutionary: For many years, simulation programs have been written in general-purpose procedure-oriented languages such as FORTRAN. Complex but common tasks such as integration algorithms for continuous simulation, statistical data-processing routines, and queuing procedures for discrete simulation were rewritten for each application [49]. Subsequent steps in the development of contemporary simulation practice are described in Section 2.2. Adoption of artificial intelligence technology is but one more step toward user-friendly, powerful simulation software.

Artificial intelligence workers find that their programs break down when dealing with real-world problems: They have difficulty in reasoning about time-varying phenomena and in predicting the behavior of complex probabilistic systems. These limitations prevent expert systems from achieving their full potential in planning, diagnostic, advisory, and similar applications that require a flexible and robust understanding of the behavior of realistically complex problems.

In this chapter, we review the current status of each field in this regard and set forth a conceptual framework for understanding the current literature on the interface between simulation and artificial intelligence. This introductory chapter has four purposes:

- to review briefly the histories of the two fields,
- to provide a tutorial on the basic concepts in each,
- to highlight the areas in which each field is expected to augment the other in practical systems during the next decade, and
- to introduce the chapters that follow in this volume.

In an area in such rapid flux as this, it is virtually impossible to survey the entire pertinent literature. We have therefore attempted to select representative projects that illustrate the major aspects of the field as we see it. We hope that the conceptual framework we present here will serve as a guide to the reader as new work emerges.

2   HISTORIES OF ARTIFICIAL INTELLIGENCE AND OF SIMULATION

The evolutionary paths of artificial intelligence and simulation have only recently begun to converge. AI began as an outgrowth of research in cognitive psychology and mathematical logic. Until recently, the focus has been on explanation of the workings of the mind and the construction of general-purpose problem-solving algorithms. In contrast, simulation developed from the need to study and understand complex time-varying behaviors exhibited by real physical systems. It is not surprising, therefore, that the world views of the two fields differ considerably.

The world view of artificial intelligence favors abstraction, generality, and elegance. The world view of simulation favors practical utility, precision, and reliability. The cultural forces separating the two communities have begun to subside, however, as a consequence of falling computing costs, increasing demands by sophisticated users for improved software performance, increasing access of inexperienced end users to sophisticated computers, and increasing connectivity between databases and machines. In what follows we review the historical development of each field and suggest that in fact the differences between them are more apparent than real.

2.1   Artificial Intelligence

The origins of artificial intelligence lie in the earliest days of machine computation [38]. In 1843, Lady Ada Augusta Byron, the daughter of the poet Lord Byron and patroness of

Charles Babbage, raised the question whether Babbage's proposed analytical engine, the first programmable computing machine, might "think." In her honor, the U.S. Department of Defense has named its new standard language Ada. It was not long after Babbage that researchers tackled problems such as solving puzzles, playing chess, and translating texts from one language to another [6, Vol. I, pp. 4–5]. During World War II, Norbert Wiener and John von Neumann set forth the principles of "cybernetics" in connection with the realization of complex decision and control functions on machines.

Although not called "artificial intelligence" at the time, much work was done on machine translation in the early 1950s, resulting from discussions between Andrew Booth and Warren Weaver in the late 1940s. In those early years, the seeds of natural-language understanding were sown, and it is from this that knowledge representation eventually developed.

It was not until 1956 that artificial intelligence began as a separate aspect of computer science at the now-famous Dartmouth conference [15]. The central distinction of the new field was its concentration on the nonalgorithmic character of intelligent human activity [6, Vol. I, pp. 5–6] (see Section 3.1.1).

The evolution of knowledge-based programming can be divided into four overlapping eras:

- The 1950s and 1960s, the era of general problem solvers. Initially, attempts were made to find algorithms that would exhibit intelligence by solving problems without large amounts of a priori information. Considerable success was achieved in game playing, such as in checkers, chess, and backgammon. Projects concerned with commonsense problems and problems requiring specific expertise were less successful.

- 1965–1970, the early era of expert programs [39]. These programs were motivated by the recognition that specific knowledge was necessary for high performance on problems requiring specific expertise. The early successful projects included DENDRAL and a precursor of MACSYMA. DENDRAL has developed into a commercial product that assists chemists in elucidating complex chemical structures. MACSYMA is now a commercial product that assists engineers and scientists in the symbolic solution of complex mathematical equations.

- 1970–1980, the growth era of expert systems [39]. These programs, many designed for medical applications, refined methods for dealing with the complexity and uncertainty of real-world problems. MYCIN, a program that assisted physicians in diagnosis and treatment selection for blood infections, and R1/XCON, a program that configures complex equipment orders, first demonstrated the utility of the production rule methodology that underlies many current expert systems. Expert levels of performance were also demonstrated by medical systems including PIP and ABEL, for kidney disorders; CASNET, for glaucoma; PUFF, for lung test interpretation; and INTERNIST/CADUCEUS, for general internal medicine. Work on XCON and the latter three projects continues today.

- 1975–present, the era of expert system-building languages (shells). The earliest expert system shells were EMYCIN, EXPERT, and a precursor of OPS5. The first two consisted of the reasoning machinery used in MYCIN and CASNET. Subsequently, a large number of academic and commercial expert system shells have been developed [110] and are widely used.

The future is widely bruited to be the era of "fifth-generation" intelligent programming environments [25]. These environments will contain embedded expert systems in order to improve user friendliness and program functionality. The reader may form his or her own judgments on the potential for these environments. The authors feel the odds are good that expert system technology will result in large evolutionary changes in the practice of modeling and simulation.

2.2 Simulation

The first "simulation" machines were mechanical and performed mathematical operations such as integration, differentiation, and multiplication using a combination of gears and mechanisms. These mechanical computing devices were replaced by electronic machines consisting of an arrangement of active and passive circuit elements that implemented the same types of mathematical operations. The term "analog computer" was coined because electrical circuit elements were used to simulate all types of systems. Analog simulators are parallel computing devices and can be used in a real-time mode if so desired.

The development of digital, or sequential, computing machines provided an alternate avenue for simulation and offered greater reliability and accuracy. The implementation of numerical analysis procedures in digital computing machines was the first step toward the development of the general-purpose digital simulators that exist today.

The use of digital computers to simulate otherwise intractable systems began shortly after programmable computers became available after World War II. The evolution of simulation software can be divided into five periods [74]:

- 1955–1960, the era of custom programming. Each application required rewriting of all necessary software.
- 1960–1966, the first-generation simulation languages. Guided by K. D. Tocher's General Simulation Program, the first versions of GPSS, SIMULA, CSL, SIMSCRIPT, and GASP were introduced. These packages form the foundation for today's simulation software. SIMULA was the first object-oriented language. GASP was the first hybrid language allowing mixed modeling of discrete and continuous systems.
- 1967–1970, the second-generation simulation languages. Primarily these were revised versions of the first-generation languages. Also, the publication in 1967 of the "CSSL Report" for continuous system simulation languages established the equation-oriented approach as standard.
- 1971–1978, the era of new features for existing languages. Interactive features appeared early in this period [61].
- 1979–present, the transition period from programming to model development. This period reflects a change in the paradigm for the simulation process. Whereas previously the focus was on writing the program that performed the simulation, the focus has now become the model underlying the program. The use of graphic

display interfaces and of development environments such as TESS also grew during this period.

Contemporaneous with this trend to view simulation primarily as a problem in modeling, computer languages in general evolved to highly specialized and abstract levels. Five generations of general languages are also recognized [100]: first, machine language; second, assembly languages; third, general-purpose higher-level languages such as FORTRAN; fourth, user interaction (natural-language interface, graphics, etc.), specialized (spreadsheets, simulation languages, etc.), and application-generator languages; and fifth, intelligent languages. The goal for fifth-generation languages is that they include the knowledge of the expert programmer so that the user can write programs for his or her needs without having programming expertise.

Thus, the trend toward incorporating expert system technology into simulation software can be seen as a natural continuation of a tradition of writing and executing flexible and accurate simulation programs in ever more conceptual, easy-to-use languages.

This trend is consistent with the shift from analog to digital computing machines. During this transition, many of the problems that plagued analog computation, such as time scaling and magnitude scaling to avoid saturation of the active amplifier components, did not appear to be important for digital simulation. Instead, problems related to numerical stability and numerical accuracy in digital simulations became prevalent. Experienced modelers who understood the physical system being simulated were needed to tune the simulation parameters, to streamline the implementation to achieve more accurate and reliable simulation results, to analyze the simulation output, and to adjust model parameters in response to the simulation output. Intelligent simulation languages are a step in this direction to provide assistance to novice users.

3   TUTORIAL ON BASIC CONCEPTS

3.1   Artificial Intelligence

The definitions of "artificial intelligence" programs are many. We choose to define them as programs that perform tasks that, if performed by a human being, would be considered intelligent. These programs obviously run on digital computers, just as do ordinary programs. Admittedly, they can be applied to a wide range of tasks for which conventional programs are ill-suited, such as robotic control, natural-language understanding, knowledge-based image processing, strategic game playing, automatic theorem proving, and reproducing the expertise of human experts. What, then, makes them distinct as a group? Their distinctive character lies in their overall architectures and the ways in which knowledge is represented and reasoned about.

3.1.1   *What Is Unique about Artificial Intelligence Programs?*

Symbolic versus Numeric Computing   A fundamental characteristic that distinguishes artificial intelligence methods from numerical methods is that the basic unit of computation in AI is a symbol rather than a number. This difference is not sufficient to distinguish AI programs, however. Other types of programs, such as compilers and database retrieval systems, also process symbols and yet are not generally regarded as using AI techniques.

Neural nets, in contrast, depend on strictly numerical computation for acquiring and using knowledge (see Section 3.1.3). Whether the neural net technology will be considered part of "artificial intelligence" is not yet clear.

Algorithms for Problem-solving A second characteristic of AI programs is that the behavior of the program is not described explicitly by the algorithm. The sequence of steps followed by the program is influenced by the particular problem presented to it: The program specifies how to find the sequence of steps needed to solve the given problem (declarative programming). In contrast, non-AI programs generally follow a well-defined algorithm that specifies explicitly how to find the output variables for any given input variables (procedural programming).

A procedural program for selecting an optimum drug prescription might, for example, compute the quantity of drug and interval between doses using a formula adjusted for the patient's age, weight, kidney and liver function, and severity of illness. A declarative program for selecting the best of several antibiotics to administer when the exact infecting organism is not known, in contrast, might assemble a list of possible organisms using a knowledge base of frequent and/or serious organisms found in the involved part of the body, the particular part of the hospital, and the specific underlying condition of the patient. Based on this list, the program would select a combination of antibiotics that have a high likelihood of curing all the likely and/or serious organisms that might be responsible for the patient's condition.

Thus, the conclusions of the declarative program are not fixed by the program but instead are determined partly by the intermediate conclusions reached by the program during its consideration of a specific problem. Note that object-oriented languages such as SMALLTALK-80 share this property and have been characterized as exhibiting an "artificial intelligence" character [60].

At the deepest level, of course, AI programs are procedural because they are ultimately translated into and executed as binary code. From this perspective, one could argue that the declarative nature of the artificial intelligence program lies in the level at which the user chooses to view the implementation of the program [78]. For our purposes, we consider as artificial intelligence those programs implemented using problem-solving techniques generally considered declarative. Some of these have been described in the preceding.

Other typical AI problem-solving methods developed by artificial intelligence researchers or borrowed from other fields include:

- *Dependency-directed backtracking,* in which the conclusions of a line of reasoning based on a plausible but incorrect assumption can be altered in an efficient manner when an inconsistency is found.
- *Problem decomposition,* in which the original problem is separated into distinct and more easily solved subproblems.
- *Generate-and-test,* in which some or all possibilities consistent with information at hand are enumerated, and the list is then shortened by ruling out possibilities on the basis of new information.

- *Heuristic search,* in which the search is limited to a small subset of a very large universe of possibilities on the basis of external information.
- *Inductive inference,* the process of hypothesizing general rules from examples.
- *Least-commitment strategies,* in which assumptions are made in as general a form as possible and are made specific only when a commitment must be made.
- *Logical deduction,* in which relationships are found that are not explicit in the knowledge base.
- *Metareasoning,* the use of knowledge about the reasoning process to assist in problem solving.

Knowledge-based Reasoning   A third characteristic of AI programs is that they incorporate facts and relationships about the part of the real world, or "knowledge domain," in which they operate. Unlike non-AI programs for specific purposes, such as accounting and scientific calculations, however, AI programs can distinguish between the reasoning program, or "inference engine," and their given knowledge, or "knowledge base." Because the knowledge base is explicit and distinct from the inference engine, the program can reason about its own knowledge as well as about the input data (facts). Reasoning about knowledge rather than about the domain is termed "metareasoning" [70], based on "metaknowledge" (knowledge about knowledge).

For example, a vision recognition system may have a knowledge base of shapes and their corresponding identities. Among the shapes might be an animal with certain features characteristic of an elephant. If the program would encounter an image with these features but much smaller in size, it might hypothesize (a) an error in calibration of the vision system, (b) the existence of an unknown new animal, or (c) the existence of a new class of shape, "toy elephant" [15, p. 153]. In the last hypothesis, the program would apply its knowledge of the existence of toy objects to explain a discrepancy between its knowledge base and its data.

In another example, a diagnostic program may have several rules of thumb that, given similar data, reach similar conclusions. If the inference engine contains a control algorithm that chooses among the rules by such characteristics as the number of data elements required in the premise and specificity of conclusions, the program can examine only one or a few "best" rules and thus reduce its computational burden.

The terms "expert systems" and "knowledge-based systems" are commonly used to describe the subfield of AI that deals with reproducing the behavior of human experts given a problem within their specialties. This class of programs is discussed further in what follows. It should be noted that, strictly speaking, knowledge-based systems include AI programs that incorporate external knowledge but do not attempt to mimic expert behavior. In this chapter, however, we follow the looser, more widely used meaning of the term.

Applicability to Ill-Structured Problems and Data   A fourth characteristic of AI programs is that they deal effectively with ill-structured problems. In contrast, non-AI programming techniques typically cannot be applied to such problems. Problems may be ill-structured if the algorithms needed to solve them cannot be given explicitly or if the data for a particular problem are not complete or cannot be specified precisely [76]. An example of the first type of problem is resolution of conflicts in goal-oriented tasks such as planning. In this class of problems, the inference engine (the knowledge-independent section of the program) decomposes the problem iteratively into achievable subgoals and uses the knowledge base to achieve the subgoals. It then synthesizes the subgoal solutions to reach an overall solution. When the subgoals impose conflicting requirements, the solution is ill-structured. The reader is referred to Georgeff and Lansky [33] for a discussion of planning strategies.

An example of the second type of problem is the diagnostic task in real-world systems [17]. An approach frequently taken is to devise an uncertainty calculus, a knowledge base that generates all possibilities consistent with available constraints, and a data structure that allows parallel reasoning. The available data are used as constraints, and all possibilities consistent with the data are considered initially. When possible, the knowledge base is used to generate new constraints that limit further the possibilities. The uncertainty calculus allows each possibility to be assigned a likelihood of being true. The "answer" is selected from the hypotheses found to be most likely true.

Consider, for example, an airplane with four engines, two on each wing. If an observer sees that at least one of the two engines on one wing has failed but that the airplane is still moving under adequate power, one possible conclusion is that the local mechanisms that are common to the functioning of the engines on one wing are suspect but that global mechanisms common to all four engines (such as the central fuel supply) are not. Each suspect mechanism is given its own data structure for the purpose of proving or refuting its role in the observed engine failure. If it is known that certain local mechanisms are redundant and therefore effectively global, they are exonerated and removed from the suspect list. If probabilities can be assigned to each of the suspect mechanisms, the potential diagnoses can then be ranked in order of likelihood.

Other classes of problems to which artificial intelligence techniques have been applied include robotics, natural-language understanding, knowledge-based image processing, strategic game playing, and automatic theorem proving.

Explanation and Justification of Results   The credibility of expert programs frequently depends on their ability to explain their conclusions. This is true of human consultants also. Thus, AI programs must maintain data structures that allow explanation and justification of the program's conclusions.

The operation of most diagnostic expert systems follows logic similar to that which human operators would use because their design is based on the accumulated intermediate conclusions reached at each step in the diagnostic procedure. An explanation of the reasoning of the program can be reproduced by listing, for each stage in the decision process, the intermediate conclusions reached, the list of failures exonerated, those that are still potential candidates, the reasoning that led to the most current list of conclusions, and the final diagnosis.

3.1.2   Expert Systems

The discipline known as artificial intelligence includes many fields, such as robotics, natural-language understanding, machine vision, character and speech recognition, and machine learning. The area that is currently having the greatest impact outside the university research setting, however, is that of expert computer systems.

Expert systems, or knowledge-based systems, are programs that reproduce the behavior of a human expert within a narrow domain of knowledge. Examples include programs for diagnosing infections of the blood (MYCIN) [12], interpreting seismic data in geological exploration [18, 23], and configuring complex equipment orders [66]. The expert system field has, over the past decade, proven useful in the commercial sector for reducing costs, improving the performance of inexperienced personnel, and improving quality control. This success has resulted in user demands for more sophisticated and reliable expert systems.

When Is Expert System Technology Useful?   The types of problems to which expert systems have been applied include [26, 39, 107]:

- *Control*   Performing real-world interventions to achieve desired goals.
- *Design*   The making of specifications to create objects that satisfy particular requirements.
- *Debugging or Diagnosis*   The process of fault finding in a system (or determination of a disease state in a living system) based on interpretation of potentially noisy and incomplete data.
- *Instruction*   Teaching new concepts and information to nonexperts.
- *Interpretation*   Analysis of data to determine their meaning.
- *Monitoring*   Continuous interpretation of signals and the setting of alarms when intervention is required.
- *Planning*   Creation of programs of actions that can be carried out to achieve goals.
- *Prediction*   Forecasting the course of the future from a model of the past and present.
- *Repair*   Prescription of real-world interventions to resolve problems.

Criteria have been developed that help decide whether a particular area of knowledge is suitable for development of an expert system [115]:

- The knowledge required is well circumscribed.
- There exist people who are acknowledged experts in the area.
- The experts can find high-quality solutions to a typical problem in minutes or hours, while nonexperts cannot achieve equally good solutions or require much more time to do so.
- A timely solution of the problem has high value.
- There is little or no requirement for commonsense reasoning.
- The knowledge base is stable: Once the knowledge is extracted from human experts, it can be used with little modification for a substantial time period.

Knowledge Representation   Expert systems typically consist of a knowledge base, which includes all expert knowledge available to the program, and an inference engine, which contains the control structure that enables the program to use the knowledge base.

The software technology for expert systems has matured to the point that most widely used expert systems are based on one or two methods of knowledge representation and one or more control algorithms. The major strength of these standard methods is the ability to deal with empirical and with uncertain data.

The Production Rule Representation   The standard knowledge representation methods are production rules and frames. Each has advantages and disadvantages [6, pp. 190–199, 216–222]. In the production rule representation, knowledge is expressed as modular units of knowledge in the form of if–then, or condition–action, or situation–action rules. The *if* premises, or "situations," of the rules consist of data obtained from the user, databases, sensors, and/or intermediate conclusions reached by other rules. The *then* conclusions, or "actions," consist of intermediate or final conclusions. Frequently, the conclusions are associated with "confidence factors," which reflect an informal estimate of the probability that the conclusion is true if the premises of the rule are met. The advantages of the production rule representation include modularity, uniformity, and naturalness for the appropriate type of knowledge. The disadvantages are inefficiency of program execution resulting from the modular, uniform design and opacity to explanation of program logic.

The Frame Representation   In the frame representation, knowledge is expressed as values or procedures stored in a series of "slots" that together constitute a "frame." Each frame constitutes an assertion or hypothesis that is either valid or invalid in the context of the problem. Slots may contain the assertion that is true if the frame proves valid; a list of antecedent assertions that must be true for the frame to be valid; references to procedures for acquiring and evaluating information; lists of confirmed and denied assertions; pointers to other frames to be considered if the given frame proves either valid or invalid; and simple data. Inclusion criteria (the *if* premises of production rules) and exclusion criteria are represented by the list of assertions required for the frame to be valid. The conclusion (the *then* action of production rules) of the frame is the assertion that is true if the frame is valid.

The advantages of the explicit data structure in the frame representation are the provision of a context for expecting and interpreting new data and the simplification of the reasoning control structure. In production rule systems, it is frequently necessary to introduce screening clauses and interdependencies into the rules to ensure that the rules fire in a reasonable order. This problem is obviated in the frame representation, in which slots are evaluated only in the context of appropriate frames [3].

In one carefully studied system in which a specific expert knowledge base was first developed in pure production rule representation, it was found that the same knowledge could be represented equally well in a mixed production rule–frame representation [3] and in a pure frame representation [104].

Representation of Quantities: The Quantity Space   Representation of quantities is an important aspect of knowledge representation in the context of simulation. The term "quantity space" refers to the set of all values allowed for a given class of variables. In numerical simulation, for example, values for continuous variables are taken from the strictly ordered, infinite set of real numbers: the quantity space is the set of real numbers. In contrast, classical qualitative simulation frequently allows only three values, namely "increased," or positive; "normal," or zero; and "decreased," or negative. Semi-quantitative quantity spaces are those that permit only a finite number of values at one time. Numerous semi-quantitative formulations have been proposed; three are described in the chapters by D'Ambrosio, by Karp and Friedland, and by Widman in this book.

Reasoning Control Structure: The "Inference Engine"   The standard control algorithms for the preceding knowledge representations are forward and backward "chaining." These may be best understood by visualizing a directed graph that connects all possible input data to all possible output conclusions. Intermediate points, or nodes, in the graph represent intermediate conclusions.

Backward chaining is a method for starting with a desired goal, or output conclusion, such as "find the best antibiotics for any infections this patient may have." It proceeds by identifying subgoals, such as listing all possible antibiotics and then selecting among them iteratively until the available data permit specific answers to be achieved. In the classic MYCIN production rule system, the top level "goal rule" could be stated as [101, pp. 104–105]

IF

1. There is an organism that requires therapy, and
2. Consideration has been given to the possible existence of additional organisms requiring therapy, even though they have not actually been recovered from any current cultures

THEN: Do the following:

1. Compile the list of possible therapies that, based upon sensitivity data, may be effective against the organisms requiring treatment, and
2. Determine the best therapy recommendations from the compiled list

OTHERWISE: Indicate that the patient does not require therapy.

In this example, subgoals included "decide whether the patient has a significant infection," "decide where the infection is and what the infecting organism is," and "decide which antibiotics would be best for the responsible organisms." The answers are then percolated up toward the original goal.

In forward chaining, reasoning proceeds from input data. For example, observing that "the temperature in the reactor coolant is too high" might lead to checks on the level of coolant in the reservoir, adequacy of coolant pump function, and adequacy of function of the heat exchange mechanism.

CONTROL IN PRODUCTION RULE SYSTEMS   Both types of control algorithm can be implemented with both production rule and with frame knowledge representations. In the production rule representation, backward chaining is implemented by identifying all rules whose conclusions can yield the desired information: The premises of these rules are then made subgoals that are investigated in turn. Forward chaining is implemented by repeatedly surveying the set of rules. As new conclusions become available, additional rules are fired until the initial data and accumulated intermediate conclusions result either in a stalemate or in the firing of the highest level rules. The control of the order of firing of individual rules affects the efficiency of production-rule-based reasoning. Strategies for controlling production rule reasoning include metarules, interpreter-based logic to prevent endless reasoning loops in which the premises of rules include consequences of their own conclusions, screening clauses to ensure dependencies between rules, and self-referencing rules that have the same parameter in both the premise and the conclusion [101].

CONTROL IN FRAME-BASED SYSTEMS   In the frame representation, reasoning control can be implemented as an agenda of assertions that are examined for validity in their order of appearance on the agenda [104]. If an assertion is found to be valid, the assertions of which it is suggestive are placed on the agenda in positions reflecting the degree of belief (see "confidence factor" in what follows) in the given assertion and the measure of suggestivity in the subsequent assertions. If an assertion is found to be invalid, complementary assertions can likewise be placed on the agenda. If an assertion cannot be evaluated because some of its antecedent assertions are unknown, those assertions are placed on the agenda in positions determined by their measure of importance and the agenda level of the original assertion.

The problem of reasoning control is somewhat more manageable because the flow of logic, the order in which the questions are asked, and whether a given question is asked are all determined at the level of the frame rather than at the level of a production rule. Since the frame represents a conceptual hypothesis while the production rule represents a conceptual rule of thumb, frame-based reasoning can model more closely the hypothesis-driven logic humans frequently use [3].

Backward and forward chaining can be implemented in the frame representation by varying the selection of assertions placed on the agenda initially and by varying the magnitudes of the measures of suggestivity and of importance that determine the subsequent ordering of the agenda. Thus, if high-level goals are selected initially and subgoals are always placed at the top of the agenda, goal-directed depth-first "backward-chaining" behavior will occur. In contrast, if low-level data assertions are selected initially and the assertions suggested by them are always placed below them on the agenda, data-driven breadth-first "forward-chaining" behavior will occur.

Reasoning under Uncertainty   A major strength of these algorithms is their ability to deal with uncertainty. Uncertainty can arise from noisy, unavailable, or incorrect data and incomplete or self-contradictory expert knowledge. Uncertainty is quantified by associating a "confidence factor," analogous to a probability, with each datum and each rule. These confidence factors are combined to yield confidence factors for each intermediate conclusion and, ultimately, for each final hypothesis and recommended action. The mathematical validity of the various confidence factor methods is controversial. It is clear, however, that they succeed in providing adequate system performance in areas in which formal probability data are not available.

Emerging Expert System Technology   The expert system technology described in the preceding is termed "first generation" because it is based on methods used in the first successful expert systems. It is characterized by empiric associations between premises and conclusions in the knowledge base. Limitations in this technology include

- inability of the knowledge representation to represent accurately time-varying and spatially varying phenomena,
- poor program performance when presented with a problem outside its range of expertise (the "cliff" performance degradation effect),
- inability of the program to detect specific gaps in the knowledge base,
- difficulty for human knowledge engineers to acquire knowledge from experts reliably, particularly when more than one expert is used,
- difficulty for human knowledge engineers to ensure consistency in the knowledge base, and
- inability of the program to learn from its errors.

Some of the limitations in first-generation expert system technology are addressed in "second-generation" and "third-generation" expert programs. It should be noted that only first-generation expert systems are in widespread applied use. The systems described next are, for the most part, research tools.

The second-generation expert systems use model-based reasoning: Expert knowledge is contained primarily in a model of the expert domain rather than a set of empiric rules of thumb. These systems have not yet reached maturity because of the difficulty in doing symbolic inference in complex models. It is with respect to this issue that simulation technology may prove invaluable (see Section 4).

Third-generation expert systems focus on learning or model parameter tuning from examples. In this context, "learning" implies an acquired ability to classify specific instances or examples. The relationship to the act of learning new concepts requires further exploration at the research level. That is, current learning algorithms do not attempt to infer causality: They classify, or "learn," based on blind correlation of new examples with previously analyzed examples. There are two fundamental approaches to learning from examples: the induction method and the exemplar method. In the induction method [14, 58], specific instances are generalized to form a representative prototype. Each prototype represents all pertinent characteristics of a class of instances. The program then stores the prototypes and applies them to new instances. A failure by the program results in modification of one or more prototypes.

In the exemplar method [5], all specific instances are indexed and retained. New instances are compared with the previous cases and a "similarity metric" is computed that describes how similar the new cases are to the previous ones. The new instances are then identified on the basis of similarity to previous cases.

3.1.3   Neural Networks

Artificial intelligence programs are increasingly incorporating a nonsymbolic method called "neural networks" [65, 95]. This technology is discussed here because it appears to be quite powerful in certain tasks that fall in the domain of AI, such as classification and pattern recognition.

Neural network technology is based on the concept of "learning" by an aggregation of a large number of very simple *processing elements*. Each element consists of an output gate that has a real value. This value may be binary (either on or off) or continuous. Each element has one or more inputs from other elements, which have the same type of values. The unique aspect of the neural network concept is that the response of each element to its inputs is determined by a flexible set of *weighting coefficients*. Each input is associated with one weighting coefficient. The relationship between the inputs, when modified by the weighting coefficient, and the output value is determined by an output function of the designer's choice. Commonly used output functions are the threshold function, the sigmoid function, and a modified threshold function in which the value of the element is zero if the inputs fall below a threshold but increases continuously as the inputs rise above the threshold.

The elements in the network can be arranged in a variety of interconnection architectures. Commonly used element architectures include interconnections from each element to every other in the network (full interconnection), stratification in layers with feed-forward or topology-preserving design, and cellular.

The neural network learns by modifying its sets of weights and/or threshold characteristics in response to the correctness of its classification. Correct classifications reinforce (increase) the weights that led most strongly to the final result. Incorrect classifications do the opposite. There are many types of weight adjustment algorithms, or "learning rules."

The performance of a given neural network depends critically on the appropriate selection of design in each of the preceding categories as well as of initial values for the weights and the sequence of processing of elements [86]. The performance also depends on the availability of a sufficient number of examples from which the network can learn before it is tested. At this time, no single best design for neural networks has been identified.

Neural network technology has proven to be very effective in pattern recognition tasks such as handwriting recognition and modeling of seemingly serial human behavior such as touch typing and verb conjugation and may provide an important new tool for tasks that require learning by the program.

Two major limitations of the neural network approach are that the network cannot be "told" facts, as can conventional expert systems, and that "knowledge" in the network is not easily available to the user. Unlike a symbolic AI system, the neural network elements cannot "explain" their numeric weighting factors. This latter limitation can be partially overcome by examining the weights of a mature network to characterize the strengths of the relationships between inputs and outputs.

3.1.4 AI Programming Languages

AI programming has traditionally been done in the LISP language [121] in the United States and in the PROLOG language [19] in Europe and the Far East. While convenient for their specialized purpose, these languages are not unique in being able to support AI programming. Several large and complex expert computer programs have been written in FORTRAN [57], and LISP-to-C converters are now becoming more popular because C is faster and more widely available on standard microcomputers and general engineering work stations. It is likely true, however, that LISP and PROLOG environments are better for AI developmental programming because of the specialized facilities they provide than are more conventional language environments.

3.1.5 Introductory Literature

For a general introduction to artificial intelligence concepts, the reader is referred to Charniak and McDermott [15], Schapiro [97], and Winston [120]. A comprehensive encyclopedia, the *Handbook of Artificial Intelligence* [6], has been issued in three volumes to date, and a fourth volume is in the planning stages [27]. A large number of AI data structures and reasoning algorithms have been developed for a variety of classes of problems. The reader is referred to Brachman and Levesque [9], Nilsson [81], and Webber and Nilsson [116] for general surveys. Expert system technology is reviewed by Hayes-Roth, Waterman, and Lenat [40]. The extensive experience with production rules and related methodologies accumulated during the seminal MYCIN project at Stanford University is reviewed in the volume edited by Buchanan and Shortliffe [12]. Some issues involved in selecting an expert system shell for developing one's own expert system are discussed by Szolovits [110].

3.2 Simulation

3.2.1 What Is Simulation?

Computer simulation is the problem-solving process of predicting the future state of a real system by studying an idealized computer model of the real system. Simulation experiments are usually performed to obtain predictive information that would be costly or impracticable to obtain with real devices. Typical applications would include determining the optimum capacity and layout of a factory, the optimum number of tellers in a bank, the best mix of reactants to maximize production of a given product, and the most energy-efficient design for a reactor. Ultimately, information gained from simulation experiments contributes to decisions about the real system modeled by the simulation.

Simulation models resemble mathematical (analytic) models in that both have the same purpose and both utilize mathematical relationships. However, the simulation model captures the change in the status of the system by focusing on the behavior of individual components of the system. In contrast, analytic models deal with the aggregate system behavior directly [98]. Simulation models are necessary because only rarely can complex real systems be described adequately by closed-form, analytic equations.

Building and using a simulation model is a skilled process requiring expertise in a number of theoretical fields including statistics, systems analysis, and numerical analysis. As well, practical rules of thumb and experience are needed to use simulation as an effective tool [83, 96]. For these reasons, each of the steps in the simulation process is suitable for expert system development, as described in Section 4.

There are two major types of simulation: continuous and discrete. Continuous simulation predicts the behavior of systems described by differential equations, such as thermal, mechanical, analog electrical, and fluid devices. Discrete simulation predicts the behavior of event-driven systems, such as manufacturing plants, message traffic on networks, and purposeful movements of people such as in bank queues. Typically, these systems use stochastic processes to model unknown influences on the system. Discrete simulation also is used to simulate intelligent agents such as opposing military command centers, competing commercial organizations, and espionage–counterespionage networks.

3.2.2   The Simulation Process

In what follows we review the major steps in performing a simulation. In many current simulation models, the programs involved in the various steps are integrated together. Some more recent languages, however, distinguish among the model, the experiment, and the output analysis. The latter organization promotes clarity of understanding and simplicity of program modification.

Model Development   As noted by Zeigler in his seminal work [123], the elements of a model for a particular problem may be organized into a hierarchy. His formulation includes five levels:

- the "real system," a source of potentially observable data;
- the "experimental frames," a set of limited circumstances under which the real system could potentially be observed or manipulated;
- the "base model," a comprehensive model capable of accounting for the behavior of the real system in all possible experimental frames;
- the "lumped model," a simplification of the base model that remains valid in the experimental frames of interest; and
- the "computer model" which implements the lumped model in a particular programming language on a particular machine.

Note that the model cannot represent the real system completely: It always represents an idealized approximation. The simulationist must ensure that the approximation is adequate for the desired simulations.

For example, in the simulation of the operation of an electric power system, the complexity of the system necessitates simplification in the modeling process. Generally, a family of models is developed. Each member model in the family is derived by imposing certain restrictive assumptions on the operating conditions of the system. Decomposition methodologies, such as temporal or functional decomposition, can be used to facilitate the modeling process. The simulationist must be sure that the appropriate model is used for each of the various operating conditions in order to guarantee accurate results.

Models for simulation may be categorized according to several aspects corresponding to the major types of simulation already described. The independent variable(s) may be continuous or discrete: In the discrete case, the state of the model changes discretely and is constant at intermediate points. Inputs and outputs may be continuous or discrete: Systems described by differential or difference equations typically have continuous variables, while systems described by automata typically have discrete variables. Changes in the model state may occur continuously or discretely: Differential equations describe continuous phenomena while event-driven phenomena such as queuing are represented by discrete-event models. Parameters and relationships may be stationary (deterministic) or may vary randomly according to a given probability distribution (stochastic).

The goal of the simulationist is to identify those features of the real system that must be represented in the lumped model, then to build and validate the lumped model. The form in which a model is specified is as a network of components. Each of the components is specified as a "black box" with inputs and outputs, with explicit functions for calculating the outputs given the inputs. Frequently, the black-box mathematical functions contain parameters, such as coefficients for difference equations or the type and specifications of random distributions. These parameters must be measured, if possible, or estimated.

Model Calibration An important aspect of the model-building task is model calibration, or matching of outputs predicted by the model with output values observed in the real physical system being modeled. The models can take several different forms: input–output, state–space, parametric, or nonparametric. Model calibration is a formidable task and often involves detailed experiments in the real physical system to provide appropriate data for the calibration process. For parametric models, the techniques of parameter estimation can be used to calibrate the model. The basic idea is to use input–output data from the real physical system to adjust the parameters of the model based on given model-fitting criteria such as minimum mean squared error between the model and the system outputs given the same inputs. Nonparametric models require identification of a causal or functional relationship between inputs and outputs based on available input–output data.

For stochastic parameters, a probabilistic model is required. Depending on the problem, the probabilistic model can be based on the physics of the system, such as a Brownian motion model for particle interaction, or can be derived from system data, such as a Poisson process model for customers arriving at a bank teller window. The parameters for the random distributions in the models must be specified. Preferably, the parameters are measured in the real system in the experimental frames of interest.

When the parameters cannot be measured directly, they also must be estimated. The estimation task can be guided by heuristics [45], making them suitable for expert system guidance. An example is the beta distribution, in which the time duration of an activity is empirically assessed by eliciting from an expert the minimum, maximum, and most likely durations.

Model Implementation and Verification When the model has been specified, it can be translated into a computer programming language. The translation process may involve additional assumptions and approximations and introduces an additional risk of error.

The process of checking the program to ensure that it represents the model faithfully is called "model verification."

Once the model has been implemented and verified, it is ready for validation and then use in performing simulation experiments. It is assumed to represent completely the variables and relationships that determine those aspects of the system that are of interest to the users of the simulation. As noted in the preceding, no model can or should incorporate all possible system variables and relationships. This limitation does, however, require that the simulation process undergo continuing oversight to ensure that the model is used only in the verified operating region.

Model Validation When the model has been specified, it must be checked to make sure it represents the real system accurately and completely within the application domain and for the purpose intended. This process is called "model validation."

Simulation Experiment Design The simulation experiment is the process by which the user "asks" questions about the real system being simulated. The simplest question is of the form "What will happen if the model parameters are set to the following values?" For example, "What would happen to inventory costs and average shipping time if we implemented a just-in-time supply ordering system?" Another type of question is the comparison: "What would happen to our average and maximum order fulfillment times if we added another drill press versus if we added another lathe?"

More difficult questions involve optimization of one or more parameters. For example, "What combination of heat and pressure gives optimum yield in this reaction?" This question requires the simulationist to specify guidelines for the ranges of heat and pressure to be studied and the interval by which each parameter should be varied. Frequently, experience allows the guidelines to be chosen expertly. For example, previous experience may have shown that certain parameter values are more critical than others so that the parameters must be varied more slowly near the critical points.

Optimization experiments involving stochastic models are more complex because the answers must be shown to be statistically valid. For example, "What is the best number of tellers to have at this branch for a given number, frequency, and patience factor of clients and a given cost per teller?" In addition to selecting the range and variation interval for each of several parameters, the simulationist must choose the length and number of simulation runs that will be necessary to achieve statistically reliable answers at reasonable computational cost.

Other goals of simulation include performance evaluation, sensitivity analysis, establishing functional relationships, and studying transient behavior [99].

Simulation Oversight Practical simulation is a labor-intensive task. Frequently, in addition to the validation runs, other initial runs are made to see how the model behaves in the particular operating region of interest and to double-check that the behavior corresponds with the known behavior of the real system. Often, a compromise is made between model complexity and simulation accuracy during validation over the entire operating region or envelope. For more restricted use, additional tuning is often required, and oversight throughout the entire simulation may be necessary. In continuous simulation, for example, a variety of mathematical algorithms are available for integrating the differential equations in the model. The equations may be "stiff" (some dependent variables change rapidly with small changes in the independent variables while others change slowly, and simulation over a long time period is required; or there may be large variations in the time-dependent behavior, such as modes of response in a linear system) only in certain operating regions, or the particular algorithm chosen may fail to converge at certain points in the simulation. The simulationist must often evaluate the simulation output and choose the best algorithm for each stage of the simulation. The same is true for stochastic simulations, during which the simulationist must ensure that adequate samples are collected to test for statistically significant output results.

Output Analysis Once the simulation experiment is completed, its output must be analyzed. Did the model in fact act in a reasonable manner? If optimization was desired, was it clearly reached, or did oscillation around a local maximum or minimum occur? In retrospect, would a different selection of parameters for the model or for the experiment have been better? This analysis requires experience in simulation and a clear understanding of the goals of the end user.

Once the simulation output is accepted as reasonable, it must be analyzed for its content. If several options are being compared, which of the discriminant parameters show most clearly the best choice? If no clear choice emerged, which of the parameters best illustrate the trade-offs? If a multistage process is being analyzed, what step(s) act as bottlenecks to limit the throughput of the overall process?

Output Explanation, Interpretation, and Decision Support Frequently, the end user is a decision maker who does not have the technical background to perform the actual simulation. The simulationist must communicate the results of the simulation in as nontechnical a format as possible and in terms that allow the data to be used productively in making decisions. If the user expected results different from those produced by the simulation, the simulationist must be able to justify the results of the model. Ultimately, whether the simulation is accepted by the user rests on the credibility developed during the simulation process and during the communication of the simulation output to the user.

3.2.3 Simulation Languages

The programming languages available for simulation include the general-purpose programming languages such as FORTRAN, COBOL, PL/1, C, and Pascal. Specialized languages have evolved for certain types of simulation. Simulation of continuous variable dynamic systems is supported by DYNAMO, CSMP, ACSL, SYSL, and many others. Discrete-event simulation is supported by process-oriented languages such as GPSS and SIMSCRIPT II.5, event-scheduling languages such as early SIMSCRIPT, and object-oriented languages such as SIMULA, Q-GERT, SOL, ASPOL, and SMALL-TALK-80. As the limitations of these languages have become more apparent, hybrid languages combining features of several types of simulation have become available. The most notable examples are SLAM II and SIMAN, in which the process view is dominant. Implementation of artificial intelligence features in the standard commercial simulation languages is not yet available. We expect that they will become available within the next several years because of the growth of interest in them within the simulation community.

3.2.4 Introductory Literature

There are many excellent introductory texts to the simulation field. Discrete simulation is well covered by Bulgren [13] and Neelamkavil [75]. Continuous simulation is discussed by Korn and Wait [51] and by Roberts et al. [91]. A thorough discussion of modeling techniques may be found in Spriet and Vansteenkiste [106]. And the classic text on the theoretical basis for simulation modeling is Zeigler [123].

4 GROWTH AREAS

In this section, we expand on the concepts outlined in the preceding to highlight the aspects of each field that are likely to benefit from the technology of the other. The examples chosen for citation have all been reported to be implemented in working programs.

4.1 Artificial Intelligence

This section discusses how simulation technology can be adapted to improve the performance of artificial intelligence systems. We start with a more general discussion of adapting numerical techniques to the needs of expert systems.

4.1.1 Coupling Symbolic and Numeric Computing

A fundamental problem in AI research is how to allow AI programs to use standard numerical algorithms. The problem arises because AI programs tend to work with symbolic quantities. Yet, if they are to prove useful in practical systems, they must be able to reach conclusions as precise as humans. This issue has been explored most thoroughly in the area of expert systems for applications involving complex models and was the subject of a recent symposium [53].

From the point of view of the AI knowledge engineer, it is useful to think of two levels of coupling: shallow and deep [50]. It should be noted that this usage of the terms "shallow" and "deep" differs from the usage in describing expert system knowledge bases. In that usage, "shallow" refers to empiric, associational representation of relationships while "deep" refers to causal, usually model-based representations. The usage in the context of coupling of symbolic and numeric computing is described next.

In shallow coupling, the expert system treats the numerical algorithms as black boxes to be called as needed. For example, the KAOS expert system [73], developed at NASA Ames Research Center to assist in route planning of a flying astronomical observatory, uses production rules to create a list of possible routes meeting specified observational objectives. The system uses numerical routines to generate partial routes starting at a given location, time, and sequence of objects to be observed and to determine, for a given aircraft location and date, the times when the desired objects will be visible. Another example, the ALADIN alloy design system developed at the Carnegie-Mellon University [44], uses an expert system to determine the ranges for several alloy design parameters and then uses regression equations to determine the optimal exact value for each parameter.

In deeply coupled systems, the expert program has access to a knowledge base describing the numerical routines. This additional information enables it to select the best routine for a given task, to interpret the output of the routine in light of known limitations of the routine, and perhaps to modify the numeric routine to match better the needs of the problem at hand. This class of systems is best exemplified by simulation assistants known as "intelligent front ends." These are described in Section 4.2.

In addition to shallow and deep coupling, we feel it may be useful to define "very deep" coupling to denote programs in which there is no distinction between the symbolic and numerical databases. For example, the dynamic systems model of the human cardiovascular system developed by Widman [117] represents the parameters of the model in terms of symbolic building blocks that can be translated directly into differential equations (or the analogous difference equations, in the finite-difference calculus [36]). These equations can then be integrated numerically by standard algorithms to answer "what if" questions about the consequences of initial model states. Because it is represented symbolically, the same model can be used by a heuristic search algorithm to identify possible model faults (diseases) that can account for observed abnormalities of the system [118].

The distinction of shallow, deep, and very deep coupling applies also to the coupling of expert systems with numerical simulation algorithms. Two general uses for simulation in expert systems are deep model-based reasoning and verification of expert system conclusions.

4.1.2 Deep Model-based Reasoning

As discussed, the production rule and frame-based knowledge representations now used widely in commercial expert systems have major limitations. Many workers feel that the best way to overcome these limitations, particularly the issues of temporal and spatial reasoning, truth maintenance, and the "cliff" performance degradation effect, is to build symbolic models of the expert domain inside the expert system.

Expert reasoning with symbolic models has not yet been widely used despite its evident usefulness. The obstacles lie in two general types of models that are frequently required to describe real-world physical systems: continuous models containing interacting feedback loops and discrete stochastic models containing interacting probability distributions (conditional dependencies). Purely symbolic algorithms capable of accurate reasoning with such models have been very difficult to develop; it may be that coupled numerical or stand-alone semi-quantitative simulation-based algorithms may prove to be more powerful. In particular, numerical and semi-quantitative simulation can handle *time* as an independent variable much more flexibly than can available symbolic methods.

Multiple Feedback Loops in Continuous Systems Continuous systems are those described by differential equations. Examples are thermal, electrical, mechanical, and fluid devices. Feedback loops are sets of causal relationships in which a change in a given variable, after possibly being modified, becomes part of the driving impetus that affects future changes in the variable. The feedback loop paradigm is essential to modeling of control algorithms.

The expert system gains two advantages by having ready access to accurate simulations of continuous systems: (1) temporal reasoning and (2) unmasking of faults that have been hidden by the symptoms of another fault.

A major limitation of current expert systems is that few can work in time-dependent domains. First-generation expert systems do not know how to reason about time-varying systems, particularly those with multiple feedback loops. This is a major limitation because many systems of practical interest do exhibit complex time-varying behavior.

The masking problem was resolved in the special case of kidney acid–base disorders by Patil [87] by computing the quantitative effect of an identified fault using closed-form analytic equations. The finding that an identified fault did not account entirely for a measured abnormality allowed the expert system to infer that a second fault was present and then to identify it. Very deeply coupled simulation algorithms might allow the masking problem to be solved in the general case.

Some expert systems have used black-box numerical simulations to reason about the behavior of these systems [11, 111]. Black-box simulation packages are, by definition, completely opaque to the expert system: It has no way to know how the answers it receives were obtained, what their limitations may be, and what factors would lead to different answer. For these reasons, there is considerable interest in enabling expert systems to work with models of complex systems at a very deep level of coupling.

The artificial intelligence approach to very deeply coupled, model-based simulation of continuous systems to date has been purely qualitative. An absolute minimum of quantitative detail is used. The argument advanced against using standard numerical simulation is that, in expert systems, the detailed information needed to set up and run a numerical simulation is not available. The qualitative approach to date has taken a position on the other end of the qualitative–quantitative spectrum by avoiding virtually all quantitative information.

In the qualitative reasoning method, the quantity space, or the universe of allowed variable values, is quantized into a discrete set of values. Usually, only three values are allowed (greater than zero, zero, and less than zero). In some formulations, additional landmark values may be added during the reasoning process [54]. Landmark values reflect qualitative limits, such as the maximum height reached by a thrown ball before it begins to return toward earth.

The models used in qualitative reasoning are constrained to represent only the direction, but not magnitude, of influence of independent variables on dependent variables. Thus, if two independent variables affect a given dependent variable in opposite directions, it is not possible to determine which variable, if either, dominates. This situation, according to the "influence resolution rule," is handled by "branching," or considering all three possibilities in parallel.

There have been two major goals of the classical qualitative reasoning approach: to infer the behavior of devices from their structural descriptions and to infer their behavior from abstractions of the differential equations that describe them. Related to these are the problems of diagnosis of faults and verification of the behavior of specific designs. Despite considerable effort [7], it has not been possible to use purely qualitative methods to model complex continuous systems [55]. The reason appears to be that qualitative models of complex systems (i.e., with multiple feedback loops) generate intractable branching. That is, there are so many opportunities for interaction of variables that the task of considering all possibilities becomes very time consuming. Further, the qualitative method provides no way to distinguish which of the many possible outcomes produced by the qualitative simulation actually corresponds to the behavior of the system under study.

Three new purely qualitative approaches have been proposed. They are based on the following:

1. Segmentation of the model by time scale to reduce its complexity so that changes on a shorter time scale are assumed to occur instantaneously relative to changes on a longer time scale. Thus, confusing interactions between them do not occur [56]. This method, while standard in the numerical domain [16], does not resolve the difficulty with qualitative complex models in many cases.

2. Specification of complex functional behavior using an external knowledge base. Hardt [37] uses a two-level expert system to infer diffusion behavior in three-dimensional geometric structures. This approach avoids ambiguous computations by encoding analytic functional forms in the superficial expert system and the deep model-based expert system.

3. Derivation of additional constraints from the model. Oyeleye and Kramer, in Chapter 13, describe a systematic approach to the derivation of additional causal and noncausal constraints from the structure of the model, thus reducing considerably the number of possible behaviors the program must consider.

Recently, a number of authors have suggested approaches to this problem using semi-quantitative information. The intention is that by increasing the number of discrete variables in the quantity space and by allowing relative ordering of influences in the model, it may be possible to avoid all branching while retaining the ability to model systems using imprecise or incomplete data.

1. *Fuzzy Relational Influences* D'Ambrosio [21] extends pure qualitative simulation by introducing quantized, semi-quantitative weights ("sensitivities") to the digraphs representing the model. Also, an increased number of values are introduced into the quantity space.

   The central issue of ambiguity arising from opposing influences is approached by automatic identification of opposing relationships. These are labeled as requiring more precise specification of sensitivities. For these relationships, the effect of each input (influencing variable) on the influenced variable is computed as the geometric mean of the value of the influencing variable and the sensitivity of the relationship between the two variables.

   D'Ambrosio also introduces two other features: The quantity space is maintained at its original number of discrete values by aggregating adjacent, newly computed values, and the sensitivities are used as parameters of a standard fuzzy relational influence algorithm. The algorithm has been tested successfully on a model of about 70 variables describing about a dozen processes in a chemical reaction furnace (B. D'Ambrosio, 1987, personal communication).

2. *Close-Enough Symbolic Differential Equation Models* Widman [117] adopts a real-valued quantity space and a quantized set of digraph weights to construct

close-enough models of the system under study. The concept is that while the critical model parameters needed to avoid ambiguity and guarantee correct simulation may not be known precisely, they may be known well enough to achieve the desired goals. In the test system with 46 variables including 4 state variables and 12 feedback loops, only 33% of all model weights are specified explicitly, using half as many distinct values. The advantage to this approach is that the use of a real-valued quantity space, numerical weights, and standard integration algorithms guarantees that the model will not perform incorrectly because of unanticipated flaws in the simulation algorithm.

As demand for improved performance by qualitative reasoning programs increases, we expect that one or more of these approaches will become more widely used. Other approaches may follow from the comprehensive review of generic methods for qualitative modeling that have been used during the evolution of classical quantitative modeling and simulation [28].

Interacting Probability Distributions in Discrete Stochastic Systems   The use of formal probabilistic reasoning in expert systems has been limited because of the difficulty in obtaining accurate conditional probability data for real systems. Even when some probability data are available, they rarely include the combinations of variables needed to avoid the often unrealistic assumption of conditional independence of the variables.

Two interesting approaches, one based on simulation, have appeared. Cooper [20] has derived algorithms for calculating the bounds on formal probability values given causal relationships among related variables. In a follow-up on Cooper's work, Pearl [88] uses stochastic simulation to infer the behavior of complex, nondecomposable probabilistic causal models. In causal models in which stochastic variables influence each other in complex relationships, propagation of probabilities is complicated by dependencies within the model. In stochastic simulation, random-variable values are assigned to a given scenario, and their consequences computed. By observing the outcome in a large number of scenarios, the behavior of the model can be inferred. It should be noted that the convergence of these algorithms may be very slow in some cases.

The use of simulation allows the expert system to reason correctly about very complex models. We expect that this approach will find wider use.

4.1.3   Verification of Expert System Conclusions

Simulation may be used to verify expert system reasoning either as a refinement of the expert knowledge base or as a double-check on it. In the first case, for example in a design problem, the expert system would select reasonable bounds for each of the parameters in a simulation model. The simulation would then be used, for example, together with optimization routines, to select the best values for each of the parameters under study. This would be an extension of the procedures implemented in the ALADIN system [44] discussed in the preceding in which the system selects likely parameter values and then refines them through a regression procedure.

Another use of simulation in design problems is selection among competing candidates. Simulation is a widely used technique for comparing competing designs and selecting the "best" for a given application. An example is the expert system reported by Rozenblit et al. [92], which uses expert system methods to design alternative local area network configurations given building blocks and constraints. A simulation is used to decide which design is preferred.

Simulation can also be used as a double-check on the expert program in tasks such as fault identification or planning, in which the system concludes that a given problem exists or a given sequence of actions will lead to a desired goal. The simulation model can predict values for other key variables in the system to ensure that they do in fact fall in acceptable operating ranges. This approach is illustrated by the "redesign" system of Simmons and Dixon [103], which starts with an "almost right" mechanical design, invokes an expert system to suggest modifications that might improve the design, and then uses qualitative simulation to show that the suggestions actually do improve the design without interfering with other constraints or requirements in the design. An expert power system planner tested in Japan [31] uses production rules to recommend changes intended to remove overload conditions from power networks. It then uses a simulation program and a system of algebraic equations to check that the transient and steady-state network behavior will be satisfactory after the recommended changes are made.

4.1.4 Summary

The role of simulation in artificial intelligence programs will likely be primarily in deep reasoning and verification of predictions about complex systems. To accomplish very deep coupling of symbolic and numeric simulation, the current difficulties with qualitative simulation must be resolved.

4.2 Simulation

In the previous section, we considered how simulation concepts relate to issues in artificial intelligence. In this section we discuss how AI concepts may be useful in simulation, but we focus particularly on expert system methodology. Expert system techniques, which are introduced at some length in Section 3.1.2, are used to mimic the behavior of human experts within a well-defined, usually narrow range of human knowledge.

4.2.1 Introduction

Building and using a simulation model is a skilled process requiring expertise in a number of theoretical fields including statistics, systems analysis, and numerical analysis. As well, practical rules of thumb and experience are needed to use simulation as an effective tool [83, 96]. For these reasons, each of the steps in the simulation process is suitable for expert system assistance.

In what follows we consider each of the steps in the simulation process separately. An important trend, however, is the development of intelligent simulation environments, which are integrated software packages that provide assistance with one or more of these steps as part of a user-friendly simulation support system. The best developed appears to be the Knowledge-Based Simulation (KBS) system [90] discussed below. Another is the

SES system [1], which provides user-friendly graphical input of the model components together with rule-based validation and consistency checking, a goal-driven experimental design driver, and statistical packages. A microcomputer-based expert simulation model builder [49] uses an icon-based graphical interface for model specification and a rule-based consistency checker to detect missing or incorrectly connected components. The program then translates the model into a standard simulation language.

In support of combining AI and simulation tasks, several new languages and environments have been developed that allow the programmer to move easily between the numeric and symbolic domains. For example, the STAR language [8] allows the symbolic program to access FORTRAN data directly and allows FORTRAN programs in turn to access its data structures. The Jade environment [113] supports the development of distributed software in any combination of five languages (Ada, C, LISP, PROLOG, and SIMULA). These new facilities ease the programmer's task by allowing selection of the best language for each task in the numeric–symbolic interface.

4.2.2   Individual Steps in the Simulation Process

In the following we consider systematically the classes of interaction of expert systems with the simulation process, and review examples when available.

Model Development   There are three major modes by which expert systems can improve simulation performance: expert assistance to novice users, improved modeling representations for numerical simulation of the real system being modeled, and reduction in the computational burden of simulation.

Expert Assistance to Novice Users   There are two ways in which expert systems can help inexperienced users: in specifying a particular model and in selecting the best available model for a particular simulation goal. Several systems have been reported that assist the novice user in specifying models. Typically, they use graphical interfaces on which the user positions icons representing model components. The systems use expert system technology to check that all necessary components are present and are correctly connected. The models are then translated into standard simulation languages. Four examples are the Simulation Environment System (SES) [1], the ECO system for ecologists [72], an existing commercial AI shell [77], and a microcomputer-based system [49]. Natural-language interfaces have also been described [29].

When several predefined models are available, the user is faced with the problem of deciding which is best for the type of question and range of operating conditions to be studied. This too is a task suitable for expert system assistance [47, 114]. The second mode, described next, is much more fundamental to the simulation process because it affects both new and experienced simulationists.

IMPROVED MODELING REPRESENTATIONS OF THE REAL SYSTEM   Improved representations of the real system under study may be more important in the long run than expert assistance to the user but may also take longer to develop. The problem here is that current simulation methods cannot represent well (1) complex decision making, such as that required to model intelligent agents, man-in-the-loop systems, organizational objectives and goals, political and economic entities, and military strategy and tactics, or (2) uncertain or incomplete models and/or data, such as are frequent in both engineering and managerial domains. Current simulation programs use decision tree and decision matrix logic for the first purpose: These have inherent limitations [24]. Uncertainty is currently represented by probability distributions even though formal probabilities may not be the best description in all cases.

By placing expert system modules in the simulation model itself, these complex "objects" can be modeled more accurately, and thus the simulation process itself can be made more reliable. The experimental network simulation language SIMYON, for example, combines elements of goal-directed inference and procedure-oriented programming (in LISP) with object-oriented and discrete-event simulation features to allow the model to use production rule knowledge representations to model complex behaviors of individual objects [93, 94]. An interesting example of this concept is the use of an expert system inside a simulation model for representing the behavior of agents in labor–management negotiations [2]. The use of semi-quantitative components in models may allow improved performance in operating regions outside the experimental frames for which reliable data are available.

REDUCTION IN THE COMPUTATIONAL BURDEN OF SIMULATION   When the goal of a series of simulation experiments is verification of a proposed set of design steps, the precise calculation of all numerical values of all model variables may not be necessary. In this subset of simulation experiments, extensive calculation can sometimes be replaced by qualitative simulation to bracket values between known landmarks if the bracket ranges are usefully narrow. Qualitative simulation provides, in addition to a savings in computational cost, explicit tracking of dependencies among variables. Thus, the designer can ascertain the degree to which a set of inputs affect a given output without having to perform a formal numerical sensitivity analysis.

For example, the qualitative simulation system for semiconductor fabrication of Mohammed and Simmons [69] evaluates a recipe of linear fabrication steps intended to transform silicon wafers into integrated circuits. It allows input parameters to be specified by constraints (e.g., a time period "long enough to remove completely the outer layer"). Relying on the serial nature of the fabrication process, it uses scalar landmark values in partially ordered quantity spaces to represent the effects of constrained actions on the model state. The expert knowledge is represented by production rules linking conditions in the model with effects or actions on it. The output of the simulation is threefold: the steps necessary to fabricate the product, the geometry of the fabricated product, and a dependency history that shows explicitly the fabrication steps that contributed to each element in the final product.

Parameter Estimation: Assistance with Statistical Design   Statistical advice is useful for novices faced with tasks such as estimating model parameters and testing input data for goodness of fit. An example of expert systems for this purpose is the EDA statistical advisory program [91], which combines symbolic and numerical computing to advise novice users of large statistical software packages on the best statistical procedures to use for their purposes. Knowledge-based systems can also be used to estimate parameter values from field observables [89]. The use of expert systems in statistical practice is itself a growing interface field [32].

Model Validation and Verification   The validation and verification of models are expert tasks for which pragmatic rules can be formulated [13, Chapter 5; 96]. Expert systems, in addition to providing advice on model debugging, can implement the advice, for example by testing the model automatically with data designed to stress the model at key points. Also, expert systems can analyze the erroneous results of test simulations to pinpoint likely sources of error [42].

Separately from providing advice on numerical debugging techniques, expert systems can construct parallel qualitative models from high-level descriptions of the system and use them to obtain constraints on acceptable simulation results. These constraints can then be used with sets of test input data to help assure that the model has been encoded correctly. Also, the expert system might offer advice on the proper choice of inputs for validation and verification runs.

Simulation Experiment Design: Assistance with Statistical Design   There are three roles that expert systems can play in helping the user design the simulation experiment: (1) critiques based on general statistical and simulation principles, (2) critiques based on specific domain knowledge, and (3) critiques based on previous experience with the particular model selected for use.

CRITIQUES BASED ON GENERAL PRINCIPLES   The design of the simulation experiment depends on the purpose(s) for which it is being done. There can be a variety of such purposes, including performance evaluation, comparison, prediction, sensitivity analysis, optimization, establishing functional relationships, and studying transient behavior [99]. Since design of the simulation experiment is relatively easily achieved by the expert, not easily achieved by the novice, and has a high economic value, it is an ideal task for expert system support.

An example of such an advisory system is TRANS [84], a system that advises students on experimentation with transactional flow models. It helps select which objects (resources, transactions, and activities) are interesting candidates for possible experiments and what statistics should be collected given a certain design objective.

CRITIQUES BASED ON SPECIFIC DOMAIN KNOWLEDGE   The design of a simulation model frequently requires a detailed knowledge of constraints and relationships found in a particular domain or in a particular system in a domain. Mistakes in building models can be avoided by providing suitable critiques during model design. The use of augmented transition networks in generating knowledge-based plan critiques in natural language has been developed by Miller [68] in the medical domain.

CRITIQUES BASED ON PREVIOUS EXPERIENCE WITH THE SAME MODEL   As expert systems become more adept at learning from experience (see Section 3), they will be able to advise the user when the proposed simulation is unlikely to work and/or to add new information. Such advice could potentially save considerable time and expense, particularly when groups of workers share the same model for similar purposes.

An example of this type of system is the ANLYZ expert system for large-scale numerical computations in the field of plasma physics [34]. This system indexes each simulation run by the ranges over which the parameters were varied, the initial guesses for the state variable values, indications of the quality of simulation outcome, and qualitative descriptors of the changes in state variables during the simulation. It uses heuristic search techniques to select, from a large number of previous simulation runs, those that are "similar" to the proposed new run. It then presents its findings to the user, who can decide whether or not to modify the proposed new simulation conditions.

Simulation Oversight: Ongoing Analysis of Accumulated Error and/or Statistical Validity During the simulation run, the data being generated need to be examined to make sure that adequate statistics are being collected, in stochastic models, or that satis- factory algorithms are being used, in continuous models. An example of an embedded expert system for simulation oversight is in SMPACK for continuous simulation [122], which selects the initial step size and algorithm, monitors the simulation to detect performance, and selects automatically a better algorithm when necessary. Haddock [35] has described a statistics expert system embedded in a simulation generator environment to reduce the likelihood that naive users will reach the wrong conclusions because of errors in statistical analysis.

Output Analysis: Assistance with Optimization, Selection of Key Variable Changes A key requirement for expert simulation environments is the capacity to assist the user in modifying the model to achieve the simulation goals. For example, if a manufacturing model is used to decide how to reduce the frequency of delays due to insufficient goods on hand, the system could determine the order in which model parameters ought to be modified to achieve the goal most rapidly and then proceed to do so. Of all the simulation steps, this is the most knowledge intensive because it requires the system to have both an understanding of the workings of the model and a knowledge of general simulation methods.

This complex task has been addressed by the Knowledge-Based Simulation system (KBS), under development at Carnegie Mellon University since 1981. In its current implementation [30, 90], this system has the following components for analysis of simulation output:

- an expert system for evaluating how well a given simulation run approximates the desired goals, taking into account the possibility of conflicting constraints;
- an introspection mechanism that monitors the simulation run to determine causal relationships;
- a causal path analysis module that uses the causal relationships determined by introspection to determine the best causal model and to quantify the sensitivities of the output parameters to controllable input parameters;
- an expert system that suggests changes in the model to achieve simulation scenarios closer to the desired goals. The sensitivities determined by causal path analysis are incorporated into this expert system to improve its quantitative performance;
- an expert system for running the model automatically, making changes as needed to approach the desired goals; and
- an expert system for interpreting user requests for goal-oriented simulation output.

In the detailed example of automatic analysis of data described in their chapter [30], the goal-oriented question was "How can we minimize stockouts while maintaining low distribution overhead." As part of this question, the program needed to know how to minimize stockouts. A prototype rule was available that stated, "If the goal is to minimize Stockouts and Average-Inventory is low and Stockouts are high and Production-Rates can be monitored, Then increase the Production-Rate."

This was a vague rule. However, after running the simulation and determining the sensitivity of stockouts to production rate, the rule could be modified to: "If the goal is to keep Stockouts below 40% and Average-Inventory is less than 30 and Stockouts are in the range 40–50% and Production-Rate can be altered, Then increase Production-Rate by 23.38 · (Stockouts – 40)." This rule, with others for minimizing distribution overhead, was then run automatically several times to show how close the user's model could come to the desired goal.

A similar goal-driven system has been reported for flexible manufacturing system design [67]. As simulation models become more symbolic, the need for introspection and causal path analysis should decrease. When the abstracted model can be expressed in terms of explicit causal relationships, the information for these steps can be found by inspection. Note that the existing KBS model is "causal" and "deep" in the sense that relationships among the objects in the simulation are represented. Clearly, however, the factors that are important at a higher level of abstraction, such as the sensitivity of stockouts to production rate in the example, are not represented explicitly in the basic simulation model.

These systems will have a major impact on the way simulations are used by organizational decision makers. Together with natural-language interfaces and automation of the other steps in the simulation sequence, they have the potential to allow the decision makers to communicate their needs directly to the system.

Output Display, Explanation, and Interpretation   Once a simulation is successfully completed, it is still necessary to extract the information needed to answer the questions for which the simulation was done. Currently, this is a task requiring considerable expertise, primarily in the real system under study, but to some extent also in simulation methodology.

OUTPUT DISPLAY   Simulations generate much more data than they do information. In an interesting expert system for intelligent display control based on neural network technology [64], a three-layer neural network monitors the states of sensors (layer 1), icon control units (layer 2), and diagram control units (layer 3) in a model of a steam engine. The units in the two control layers compete (within each layer) for display on the user's screen: Only actively changing units are displayed. The neural network "learns" the normal behavior of each object it monitors and the preferences of the user for information display in various model states. The network then displays only those objects that the user desires to see and/or have changed in value from their "normal" values.

Selection of pertinent trends and data for review by the decision maker can also be performed by goal-oriented artificial intelligence programs, which can provide perspective from similar cases, help to define further questions, and help plan new simulation experiments that address unresolved issues. Automated assistance is particularly valuable in data overload situations such as military command/control [10, 108] and equivalent medical decision-making environments [22, 102], and large management information systems [71].

OUTPUT EXPLANATION   There have been several efforts made to enable explanation programs to answer questions about the simulation output. Helman and Bahuguna [41] describe generic classes of explanation taken from the philosophy of explanation together with a model-based implementation that answers users' questions. Kosy [52] describes a program that, given the symbolic form of the equations in a financial model, generates explanations at several levels of detail to account for discrepancies between the simulation output and the user's expectations. In the expert system field, Lehnert et al. [59] and Swartout [109] have described explanation programs based on story scripts and production rule systems, respectively. As simulation models begin to incorporate expert programs to represent the real system under study, these latter methods will become increasingly useful.

OUTPUT INTERPRETATION   In some cases, the final results of simulation will move directly into expert systems for analysis. This is the expected mode for intelligent monitoring systems as well as for complex analysis systems. Thus, there may prove to be little distinction between expert systems for selecting display variables relevant to the user's objectives and the systems that interpret the variables.

4.3   Summary

In summary, we expect that expert system technology will play two major roles in the simulation process:

- It will make the software more user-friendly, so that the nonspecialist will be able to use sophisticated simulation models correctly and productively.
- It will enable the simulationist to build more realistic, robust models that will yield more reliable, useful results.

5   OVERVIEW OF THE BOOK

This volume is divided into three sections: conceptual bases for artificial intelligence and simulation, reasoning by simulation in AI systems, and applying AI to enrich simulation. We have divided the chapters to provide a balance but would not argue that the selected arrangement is unique.

5.1   Conceptual Bases for Artificial Intelligence and Simulation

Both the simulationist and the expert system worker are concerned with representing, in computer code, an external reality. This section of the book is concerned with issues in the construction of models that are common to both application areas. We also include here the introductory chapters on semi-quantitative modeling and on parallel computing.

5.1.1   Conceptual Aspects of Modeling

One of the pioneers of the modern era of model-based simulation, Zeigler, and his associate Zhang continue their work [124] on the theory of modeling of complex real systems by presenting a formal representation of the system entity structure. This formulation is a unified knowledge representation combining structural and functional representations. It permits provably correct manipulation of complex hierarchical models, which can then be translated automatically into simulation code. In Chapter 2, Zhang and Zeigler present mathematical aspects of this representation and illustrate its usefulness in practical applications of simulation of multifaceted hierarchical models.

On a more general note, Rothenberg (Chapter 3) considers thoughtfully the goals and limitations of classical modeling paradigms and suggests approaches based on artificial intelligence methods to overcome them. His points are illustrated by examples taken from the experience of the RAND Corporation, one of the early leaders in the integration of artificial intelligence and simulation.

Fishwick (Chapter 4) considers the process of abstraction itself: How several models of the same phenomenon, all at differing levels of detail, can be related usefully to each other. This is an important issue in the practical problem of developing useful multilevel models. He reviews extensively the literature on abstraction and describes a program, the HIRES Simulation system, which implements his theory in the domain of scene animation.

5.1.2   Semi-Quantitative Simulation: An Alternative to Qualitative Simulation

Three chapters propose semi-quantitative approaches to simulation. D'Ambrosio (Chapter 5) builds on the semi-quantitative properties of linguistic variables to develop a framework for representing the relative strengths of competing influences within the model as parameters of fuzzy-set functions. His chapter describes the theoretical basis for this framework and an example.

Widman (Chapter 6) proposes the use of normalized real-valued coefficients, derived empirically by parameter estimation, to weight competing relationships in the model and thus avoid ambiguity during simulation. The advantage over ordinary numerical modeling is that the accuracy required of the parameters is much less. The parameters need be estimated only with accuracy to distinguish the relative influences of the competing relationships. This approach is applied to simulation of continuous systems whose structure is well understood but whose parameters and operating region are known only approximately. His chapter, based in the medical domain, describes the use of approximate, close-enough dynamic systems models for diagnosis of faulty systems and for prediction of the consequences of faults and proposed treatments for them. It includes examples taken from a complex model of the human cardiovascular system.

Karp and Friedland (Chapter 7) describe new work on the problem of modeling complex systems in which some components are well understood and some are not. Choosing a problem in the domain of bacterial molecular biology, they describe algorithms for mathematical calculations using expert interpretations of operands of widely varying precision from purely qualitative to purely quantitative. Their chapter discusses the use of quantitative knowledge for solving the envisionment branching problem and the development of less precise representations of functional relationships for use when precise knowledge is not available in the context of a problem in the domain of molecular biology.

5.1.3   *Parallel Treatment of Simulation Systems and Knowledge-based Systems*

Kerckhoffs, Koppelaar, and van den Herik (Chapter 8) discuss the role of parallel processing in real-time intelligent simulation, where knowledge-based systems are assumed to interact continuously with simulation systems. In real-time applications, both categories of systems have to meet strict response requirements. Modeling such integrated systems and implementing them efficiently on appropriate multicomputers are complex and difficult tasks with which experience is just beginning to grow. The authors first describe what an advanced intelligent simulation environment might look like, providing a framework within which various research scenarios, including artificial intelligence and parallel processing, can be planned. Then, they introduce and review the literature on parallel processing in simulation and AI, concentrating on knowledge-based systems for problem solving and reasoning. From the results obtained in their own HYDRA project, described in the chapter, and from reports by other workers, they conclude that parallel realizations of conventionally formulated "expert" production systems yields disappointingly little speed-up and that new formulations with increased inherent parallelism are needed.

Rice (Chapter 9) addresses directly the issue of disappointing results from attempting parallel implementations of AI systems. After enumerating characteristics of AI programs that distinguish them from the conventional programs that do work well when in a parallel environment, he describes experiments with the Poligon system. Poligon is an experimental system designed to represent, in a simulated parallel architecture, the Blackboard System AI methodology [79, 80]. The experimental task is in the domain of real-time interpretation of passive radar signal data. As with the preceding chapter, the overall conclusion is that parallel processing, as tested, yields only modest increases in speed. Specific aspects of this conclusion are discussed in detail.

5.2   Reasoning by Simulation in AI Systems

The chapters in this section are concerned with the theory of methods for symbolically representing and reasoning about deep models. The parallel section (Section 5.3.1) houses a chapter that is practically oriented and deals with a deep model of a real-world system. Deep models have not been analyzed well by the symbolic logic algorithms common to other areas of artificial intelligence, and there is increasing interest in using simulation concepts for relating structure to function and for predicting the behavior of systems represented by symbolic models.

The classical qualitative simulation approach is discussed by one of its pioneers, Dr. Benjamin Kuipers. Kuipers begins Chapter 10 with a lucid explanation of the motivation for qualitative simulation as a tool for reasoning about the structure and behavior of complex systems. He describes the operation of his simulation package, QSIM, in a medical domain and shows the ability of the classical qualitative simulation approach to reach correct and understandable conclusions.

Chiu (Chapter 11) proposes a "domain map" approach to qualitative analysis of algebraic models, similar to the thought processes of expert physicists. His method operates on the symbols of the equations that constitute the model but retains a real-valued quantity space. It yields the critical values of variables: those values at which the behavior of the model changes qualitatively. An important step in his approach is the replacement of algebraic functions by monotonic functions. This enables one to reason qualitatively about the system in question. His chapter describes the method and its application to a problem in classical physics.

Hardt (Chapter 12) focuses on the important problem of choosing a frame of reference for modeling a particular problem. This concept is commonly used in theoretical domains but is difficult for the naive user to apply to sophisticated problems. The chapter discusses the issues of identifying, characterizing, and implementing novel frames of reference in the domain of three-dimensional diffusion. Her implementation, DUNE, uses problem decomposition to apply a two-level knowledge base to problems in three-dimensional material diffusion. It gains the efficiency of compiled knowledge when appropriate, yet retains the flexibility of model-based reasoning when necessary. The heuristics in the knowledge base are formulated in the frame of reference of an expert in the domain, which is demonstrably different from that of the nonexpert.

5.3   Applying AI to Enrich Simulation

There are several development areas for artificial intelligence technology, particularly expert system technology, in support of the simulation task. The contributors to this section discuss improved modeling tools, including nonnumerical simulation methods, a new application in the control system field, and integrated support environments for simulation users, including integrated programming languages and explanation systems for interpreting simulation output.

5.3.1   Qualitative Simulation

The behavior of realistic models under varying conditions can be complex, and exhaustive simulation to detect all important behaviors can be expensive. One alternative is the use of qualitative and semi-quantitative simulation to obtain, at reduced cost, useful approximations of model behavior. As well, these approximations often can be expressed and explained more easily to the user. Classical qualitative simulation and alternative approaches based on semi-quantitative simulation are discussed in Sections 5.2 and 5.1.2, respectively.

Classical qualitative simulation has proven most successful in modeling very simple systems. The contribution by Oyeleye and Kramer (Chapter 13) is concerned with making qualitative simulation more robust and useful in describing real-world systems. They describe a general method for imposing additional constraints on classical qualitative reasoning algorithms. Their motivation is that the failure of classical qualitative simulation, which results from its consideration of an excessive number of possible behaviors, can be overcome by making explicit use of additional constraint information that is implicit in the system model. They have implemented their techniques in the chemical engineering domain and show a very clear improvement in qualitative simulation performance without use of a semi-quantitative quantity space.

5.3.2 Embedding Simulation in AI Programming Environments

The process of building a simulation model and using it effectively can be daunting to the naive user. This is especially true when traditional simulation projects must be encoded in AI languages to integrate AI methods as fully as possible into the model. The next three chapters illustrate the use in simulation of languages supporting AI methods.

O'Keefe (Chapter 14) has developed a tool for discrete-event simulation based in the PROLOG language. In the introduction to his chapter, he reviews the general issues in building simulation models in artificial intelligence programming environments. Focusing on discrete-event simulation, he then describes practical aspects of building traditional discrete-event simulation models in PROSS, his PROLOG-based simulation tool.

The classic paper of Ruiz-Mier and Talavage (Chapter 15) is reprinted for its lucid literature review and description of their hybrid language, SIMYON, which integrates object-oriented programming, logic programming, and the discrete-event approach to systems modeling. Their chapter reviews the origins of methodologies for simulation modeling, object-oriented programming, logic programming, and hybrid languages for building models, describes SIMYON and its underlying language CAYENE, and provides two examples in the manufacturing environment.

For the continuous simulation user, Lounamaa (Chapter 16) has developed an object-oriented modeling language for dynamic systems simulation built on top of the Common LISP language. Named SLICL, it permits the user to execute models incrementally and directly in this widely used artificial intelligence programming language. His chapter considers benefits and trade-offs in developing specialized object-oriented representation languages for modeling purposes in the LISP environment.

5.3.3 AI in Control of Complex Systems

Conventional control system design methodologies are, for the most part, based on detailed mathematical models of the physical system to be controlled. In most instances only approximate system models, with limited ranges of applicability, are available for the design process. Current operating control systems supplement the lack of detailed mathematical process knowledge with operating experience. Hierarchical control structures are an effective means of integrating both quantitative and qualitative process knowledge.

The general issue of control design is an important application of modeling and simulation. Berger and Loparo (Chapter 17) discuss some relevant methodologies from AI and learning and knowledge-based systems to the control of complex and uncertain systems. Assuming minimal a priori knowledge of the system, a hierarchical learning controller is proposed. Initial simulation studies indicated better performance than comparable controller designs on an unstable, multioutput nonlinear dynamic system, the pole (and cart) balancing problem.

5.3.4   *Applying AI to Enhance Simulation Tools*

The highest level of integrated simulation support is the environment level. Fox, Husain, McRoberts, and Reddy (Chapter 18) review their past eight years of research on codification of simulation expertise for management of the simulation life cycle. Their Knowledge-Based Simulation (KBS) tool for intelligent decision support, designed to answer what-if questions for the primary corporate decision maker, also embodies techniques for modeling complex systems. Their chapter describes in detail the architecture and logic of the KBS tool and its use of expert system technology to support the simulation user.

Kosy (Chapter 19), in an applied system, has developed relatively simple yet powerful model-based algorithms for interpreting user questions and providing appropriate explanations of the output from a simulation of the financial history of a manufacturing organization. The method is also applicable to other domains characterized by continuous variables, sampled periodically, which are related by known algebraic relationships.

Prager, Belanger, and De Mori (Chapter 20) address the issue of troubleshooting simulation models. This task includes verification of the model by comparison with data from the real system and improvement (tuning) of the model by adjusting appropriate parameters to improve its performance. Their chapter describes the problem domain, aerodynamic simulation, and how expert system methods can be used interactively to assist the user in the troubleshooting task.

6   SUMMARY AND CAUTIONARY NOTE

This chapter has focused on how each of the two fields, artificial intelligence and simulation, can complement each other. It is well to remember that they have fundamental similarities as well. These have been articulated by Kerckhoffs and Koppelaar [48]: Both are meant to represent knowledge and expertise about a system and its behavior in a specific domain. Both describe and use measures of uncertainty. Flow control in both depends on logical decisions, for example forward and backward reasoning in expert systems and next- and previous-event scheduling in discrete-event simulation. Finally, expert reasoning from first principles in deep causal models is akin to the simulation process. These similarities may offer useful perspectives for further research on integration of these fields.

On a cautionary note, it is also well to consider the risks inherent in the new technologies of expert simulation environments and powerful expert computer programs. As these tools improve, they will be used increasingly by naive users. Just as the microcomputer brought vastly improved access to calculations such as spreadsheet-based budgeting and planning, it also removed the technical expert from the computation loop. Subsequently, there were instances in which unsophisticated users placed undue faith in the conclusions of erroneously programmed spreadsheets, with considerable adverse economic consequences.

With the tools discussed in this book the trend will continue. Technically naive decision makers will rely increasingly on automated simulation-based advice, training of critical personnel will be based at least in part on simulation rather than on field experience [82, 112], and policy decisions concerning major projects [4] will be made using large simulation models that may be too large for then-current software engineering techniques to manage and debug effectively. As scientists and engineers, it is our responsibility to include quality control as a major system specification and to ensure that expert systems for this purpose achieve high design priorities [85].

ACKNOWLEDGMENTS

The authors would like to thank the following for valuable criticisms of the manuscript:

Drs. François Cellier, Bruce D'Ambrosio, David H. Helman, Peter Karp, Paul Luker, Norman Nielsen, Robert O'Keefe, and Bernard P. Zeigler.

The work of the first author was supported in part by the American Heart Association, Texas affiliate by Grant-in-Aid 87G-379, the Veterans Administration Research Service, San Antonio, Texas; and by the National Institutes of Health, Division of Research Resources by PHS Grant 5 P41 RR00785-14.

The work of the second author was supported in part by the NASA Lewis Research Center, Grant NAG3-788, and the Center for Automation and Intelligent Systems at Case Western Reserve University.

REFERENCES

1. H. H. Adelsberger, U. W. Pooch, R. E. Shannon, and G. N. Williams, "Rule Based Object Oriented Simulation Systems," in P. A. Luker and H. H. Adelsberger (Eds.), *Intelligent Simulation Environments. Proceedings of the Conference on Intelligent Simulation Environments, 23–25 January 1986, San Diego, California,* Society for Computer Simulation, San Diego, CA, 1986, pp. 107–112.

2. S. V. Ahamed and E. G. Roman, "Extension in the Application of Expert System Concepts to Labor Management Negotiations," *Proceedings of the 1985 Summer Simulation Conference, Chicago, Illinois,* Society for Computer Simulation, San Diego, CA, 1985, pp. 702–703.

3. J. S. Aikins, "A Representation Scheme Using Both Frames and Rules," in B. G. Buchanan and E. H. Shortliffe (Eds.), *Rule-Based Expert Systems: The MYCIN Experiments of the Stanford Heuristic Programming Project.* Addison-Wesley, Reading, MA, 1984, pp. 424–440.

4. S. C. Bankes and P. K. Davis, "Models of Strategic Decisionmaking Imbedded in a Game-Structured Simulation," *Proceedings of the 1986 Summer Simulation Conference, Reno, Nevada,* Society for Computer Simulation, San Diego, CA, 1986, pp. 743–747.

5. E. R. Bareiss, B. W. Porter, and C. C. Wier, "Protos: An Exemplar-based Learning Apprentice," in R. Michalski and Y. Kodratoff (Eds.), *Machine Learning,* Vol. 3, Morgan Kaufmann, Los Altos, CA, 1988.

6. A. Barr and E. A. Feigenbaum, *The Handbook of Artificial Intelligence,* William Kaufmann, Los Altos, CA, 1981 (Vol I), 1982 (Vols II and III).

7. D. G. Bobrow (Ed.), *Qualitative Reasoning about Physical Systems,* MIT Press, Cambridge, MA, 1985.

8. G. C. Borchardt, "STAR: A Computer Language for Hybrid AI Applications," in J. S. Kowalik (Ed.), *Coupling Symbolic and Numerical Computing in Expert Systems,* Elsevier, The Netherlands, 1986, pp. 169–177.

9. R. J. Brachman and H. J. Levesque (Eds.), *Readings in Knowledge Representation,* Morgan Kaufmann, Los Altos, CA, 1985.

10. M. M. Broadwell and D. M. Smith, "Interfacing Symbolic Processes to a Flight Simulator," *Proceedings of the 1986 Summer Simulation Conference, Reno, Nevada,* Society for Computer Simulation, San Diego, CA, 1986, pp. 751–755.

11. J. S. Brown, R. R. Burton, and J. de Kleer, "Pedagogical, Natural Language and Knowledge Engineering Techniques in SOPHIE I, II and III," in D. H. Sleeman and J. S. Brown (Eds.), *Intelligent Tutoring Systems,* Academic, London, 1982, pp. 227–282.

12. B. G. Buchanan and E. H. Shortliffe, *Rule-Based Expert Systems: The MYCIN Experiments of the Stanford Heuristic Programming Project,* Addison-Wesley, Reading, MA, 1984.

13. W. G. Bulgren, *Discrete Event Simulation,* Prentice-Hall, Englewood Cliffs, NJ, 1982.

14. J. G. Carbonnell, R. S. Michalski, and T. M. Mitchell, "An Overview of Machine Learning," in R. S. Michalski, J. G. Carbonell, and T. M. Mitchell (Eds.), *Machine Learning: An Artificial Intelligence Approach,* Vol. I, Morgan Kaufmann, Los Altos, CA, 1983, pp. 3–23.

15. E. Charniak and D. McDermott, *Introduction to Artificial Intelligence,* Addison-Wesley, Reading, MA, 1985.

16. R. C. Y. Chin, G. W. Hedstrom, and F. A. Howes, "Considerations on Solving Problems with Multiple Scales," in J. U. Brackbill and B. I. Cohen (Eds.), *Multiple Time Scales,* Academic, 1985, pp. 1–27.

17. W. J. Clancey, "Heuristic Classification," *Artificial Intelligence,* **27**:289–350, 1985.

18. J. G. Cleary, L. L. Kramer, and M. P. Wingham, "Knowledge-Based Systems for the Interpretation of Seismic Data," in J. S. Kowalik (Ed.), *Coupling Symbolic and Numeric Computing in Expert Systems,* Elsevier Science, The Netherlands, 1986, pp. 231–246.

19. W. F. Clocksin and C. S. Mellish, *Programming in Prolog,* Springer-Verlag, New York, 1984.

20. G. F. Cooper, "A Diagnostic Method that Uses Causal Knowledge and Linear Programming in the Application of Baye's Formula," *Computer Methods and Programs in Biomedicine,* **22**:223–237, 1986.

21. B. D'Ambrosio, "Extending the Mathematics in Qualitative Process Theory," *Proceedings of the Sixth National Conference on Artificial Intelligence,* Morgan Kaufmann, Los Altos, CA, 1987, pp. 595–599.

22. W. R. M. Dassen, W. P. S. van Braam, K. den Dulk, H. J. J. Wellens, E. D. Smith, L. Sasmor, and P. P. Tarjan, "Expert Systems and Compiler Techniques for Intelligent Implantable Cardiac Pacemakers," *Proceedings of the 1986 Summer Simulation Conference, Reno, Nevada,* Society for Computer Simulation, San Diego, CA, 1986, pp. 410–414.

23. R. Duda, J. Gaschnig, and P. Hart, "Model Design in the Prospector Consultant System for Mineral Exploration," in D. Michie (Ed.), *Expert Systems in the Microelectronic Age,* Edinburgh University Press, Edinburgh, 1979, pp. 153–167.

24. S. A. Erickson, "Fusing AI and Simulation in Military Modeling," in E. J. H. Kerckhoffs, G. C. Vansteenkiste, and B. P. Zeigler (Eds.), *AI Applied to Simulation. Proceedings of the European Conference at the University of Ghent, February 25–28, 1985, Ghent, Belgium,* Society for Computer Simulation, San Diego, CA, 1986, pp. 140–150.

25. E. A. Feigenbaum and P. McCorduck, *The Fifth Generation. Artificial Intelligence and Japan's Computer Challenge to the World,* New American Library, New York, 1984.

26. E. A. Feigenbaum, P. McCorduck, and P. Nii, *The Rise of the Expert Company,* Times Books, New York, 1988.

27. E. A. Feigenbaum, personal communication, March 24, 1988.

28. P. A. Fishwick, "Qualitative Simulation: Fundamental Concepts and Issues," *Proceedings of the Society for Computer Simulation Multiconference on AI and Simulation, San Diego, California,* Society for Computer Simulation, San Diego, CA, 1988, pp. 25–31.

29. D. R. Ford and B. J. Schroer, "An Expert Manufacturing Simulation System," *Simulation,* **48**:193–200, 1987.

30. M. S. Fox, N. Husain, M. McRoberts, and Y. V. Reddy, Chapter 18, this volume.

31. R. Fujiwara and T. Sakaguchi, "An Expert System for Power System Planning," in E. J. H. Kerckhoffs, G. C. Vansteenkiste, and B. P. Zeigler (Eds.), *AI Applied to Simulation. Proceedings of the European Conference at the University of Ghent, February 25-28, 1985, Ghent, Belgium,* Society for Computer Simulation, San Diego, CA, 1986, pp. 174–177.

32. W. A. Gale, *Artificial Intelligence and Statistics,* Addison-Wesley, Reading, MA, 1986.

33. M. P. Georgeff and A. L. Lansky (Eds.), *Reasoning about Actions and Plans. Proceedings of the 1986 Workshop,* Morgan Kaufmann, Los Altos, CA, 1987.

34. N. T. Gladd and N. A. Krall, "Artificial Intelligence Methods for Facilitating Large-Scale Numerical Computations," in J. S. Kowalik (Ed.), *Coupling Symbolic and Numerical Computing in Expert Systems,* Elsevier Science, The Netherlands, 1986, pp. 123–136.

35. J. Haddock, "An Expert System Framework Based on a Simulation Generator," *Simulation,* **48**:45–53, 1987.

36. R. W. Hamming, *Numerical Methods for Scientists and Engineers,* 2nd ed., Dover, New York, pp. 211–223.

37. S. L. Hardt, "On the Power of Qualitative Simulation for Estimating Diffusion Transit Times," *Proceedings of the 1986 Winter Simulation Conference, Washington, D.C.,* Society for Computer Simulation, San Diego, CA, 1986, pp. 460–463.

38. R. D. Hawkins, "Artificial Intelligence from the Systems Engineer's Viewpoint," in W. M. Holmes, *Artificial Intelligence and Simulation,* Society for Computer Simulation, San Diego, CA, 1985, pp. 10–25.

39. F. Hayes-Roth, D. A. Waterman, and D. B. Lenat, "An Overview of Expert Systems," in F. Hayes-Roth, D. A. Waterman, and D. B. Lenat (Eds.), *Building Expert Systems,* Addison-Wesley, Reading, MA, 1983, pp. 3–29.

40. F. Hayes-Roth, D. A. Waterman, and D. B. Lenat (Eds.), *Building Expert Systems,* Addison-Wesley, Reading, MA, 1983.

41. D. H. Helman and A. Bahuguna, "Explanation Systems for Computer Simulations," *Proceedings of the 1986 Winter Simulation Conference, Washington, D.C.,* Society for Computer Simulation, San Diego, CA, 1986, pp. 453–459.

42. T. R. Hill and S. D. Roberts, "A Prototype Knowledge-based Simulation Support System," *Simulation,* **48**:152–161, 1987.

43. W. M. Holmes, *Artificial Intelligence and Simulation,* Society for Computer Simulation, San Diego, CA, 1985.

44. I. Hulthage, M. D. Rychener, M. S. Fox, and M. L. Farinacci, "The Use of Quantitative Databases in Aladin, an Alloy Design System," in J. S. Kowalik (Ed.), *Coupling Symbolic and Numerical Computing in Expert Systems,* Elsevier Science, The Netherlands, 1986, pp. 209–216.

45. W. D. Kelton, "Input Data Collection and Analysis," *Proceedings of the 1984 Winter Simulation Conference, Dallas, Texas, 1984,* Society for Computer Simulation, San Diego, CA, pp. 91–95.

46. E. J. H. Kerckhoffs, G. C. Vansteenkiste, and B. P. Zeigler, *AI Applied to Simulation. Proceedings of the European Conference at the University of Ghent, February 25–28, 1985, Ghent, Belgium,* Society for Computer Simulation, San Diego, CA, 1986.

47. E. J. H. Kerckhoffs and G. C. Vansteenkiste, "The Impact of Advanced Information Processing in Simulation: An Illustrative Review," *Simulation,* **46**:17–26, 1986.

48. E. J. H. Kerckhoffs and H. Koppelaar, "Knowledge Bases in Simulation," in *Advances in Systems, Control and Information Engineering.* Systems and Control Encyclopedia, Pergamon, first supplement, in press.

49. B. Khoshnevis and A.-P. Chen, "An Expert Simulation Model Builder," in P. A. Luker and H. H. Adelsberger (Eds.), *Intelligent Simulation Environments. Proceedings of the Conference on Intelligent Simulation Environments, 23-25 January 1986, San Diego, California,* Society for Computer Simulation, San Diego, CA, 1986, pp. 129–132.

50. C. T. Kitzmiller and J. S. Kowalik. "Symbolic and Numeric Computing in Knowledge-Based Systems," in J. S. Kowalik (Ed.), *Coupling Symbolic and Numerical Computing in Expert Systems,* Elsevier Science, The Netherlands, 1986, pp. 3–17.

51. G. A. Korn and J. V. Wait, *Digital Continuous System Simulation,* Prentice-Hall, Englewood Cliffs, NJ, 1978.

52. D. W. Kosy and B. P. Wise, "Self-Explanatory Financial Planning Models,"*Proceedings of the AAAI-84, Austin, Texas,* Wm. Kaufmann, Inc., Los Altos, CA, 1984, pp. 176–181.

53. J. S. Kowalik (Ed.), *Coupling Symbolic and Numerical Computing in Expert Systems,* Elsevier Science, The Netherlands, 1986.

54. B. Kuipers, "Commonsense Reasoning about Causality: Deriving Behavior from Structure," *Artificial Intelligence,* **24**:169–204, 1984.

55. B. Kuipers, "The Limits of Qualitative Simulation,"*Proceedings of the Ninth International Joint Conference on Artificial Intelligence, Los Angeles, California,* Morgan Kaufmann, Los Altos, CA, 1985, pp. 128–136.

56. B. Kuipers, "Qualitative Simulation as Causal Explanation," *IEEE Transactions on Systems, Man, and Cybernetics,* **SMC–17**:432–444, 1987.

57. C. A. Kulikowski and S. M. Weiss, "Representation of Expert Knowledge for Consultation: The CASNET and EXPERT Projects," in P. Szolovits (Ed.), *Artificial Intelligence in Medicine,* Westview, Boulder, CO, 1982.

58. M. Lebowitz, "Not the Path to Perdition: The Utility of Similarity-Based Learning," *Proceedings of the Fifth National Conference on Artificial Intelligence, Philadelphia, Pennsylvania, 1986,* Morgan Kaufmann, Los Altos, CA, 1986, pp. 533–537.

59. W. G. Lehnert, M. G. Dyer, P. N. Johnson, C. J. Yang, and S. Harley, "BORIS—An Experiment in In-Depth Understanding of Narratives," *Artificial Intelligence,* **20**:15–62, 1983.

60. H. Lieberman, "Object Oriented Languages," in S. C. Schapiro (Ed.), *Encyclopedia of Artificial Intelligence,* Wiley, New York, 1987, pp. 452–456.

61. P. A. Luker and J. Stephenson, "Interactive Simulation—Ten Years On,"*Proceedings of the Summer Computer Simulation Conference, Washington, D.C., 1981,* Society for Computer Simulation, San Diego, CA, 1981, pp. 99–104.

62. P. A. Luker and H. H. Adelsberger (Eds.), *Intelligent Simulation Environments. Proceedings of the Conference on Intelligent Simulation Environments, 23–25 January 1986, San Diego, California,* Society for Computer Simulation, San Diego, CA, 1986.

63. P. A. Luker and G. Birtwistle (Eds.), *Simulation and AI. Proceedings of the Conference on*

AI and Simulation, 14–16 January 1987, San Diego, California, Society for Computer Simulation, San Diego, CA, 1987.

64. T. P. McCandless, "PDP Mechanisms for Intelligent Display Control," in P. A. Luker and H. H. Adelsberger (Eds.), *Intelligent Simulation Environments. Proceedings of the Conference on Intelligent Simulation Environments, 23–25 January 1986, San Diego, California,* Society for Computer Simulation, San Diego, CA, 1986, pp. 87–91.

65. J. L. McClelland, D. E. Rumelhart, and G. E. Hinton, "The Appeal of Parallel Distributed Processing," in D. E. Rumelhart and J. L. McClelland (Eds.), *Parallel Distributed Processing: Explorations in the Microstructure of Cognition,* Vol. I, MIT Press, Cambridge, MA, 1986, pp. 3–44.

66. J. McDermott, "R1: A Rule-based Configurer of Computer Systems," *Artificial Intelligence,* **19**:39–88, 1982.

67. J. M. Mellichamp and A. F. A. Wahab, "An Expert System for FMS Design," *Simulation,* **48**:201–208, 1987.

68. P. L. Miller, *Expert Critiquing Systems: Practice-Based Medical Consultation by Computer,* Springer-Verlag, New York, 1986.

69. J. Mohammed and R. Simmons, "Qualitative Simulation of Semiconductor Fabrication," *Proceedings of the Fifth National Conference on Artificial Intelligence, Philadelphia, Pennsylvania, 1986,* Morgan Kaufmann, Los Altos, CA, 1986, pp. 794–799.

70. E. Morgado, "Meta-Knowledge, Meta-Rules, and Meta-Reasoning," in S. C. Schapiro (Ed.), *Encyclopedia of Artificial Intelligence,* Wiley, New York, 1987, pp. 598–603.

71. J. G. Moser, "Integration of Artificial Intelligence and Simulation in a Comprehensive Decision-Support System," *Simulation,* **47**:223–229, 1986.

72. R. Muetzelfeldt, A. Bundy, M. Uschold, and D. Robertson, "ECO—An Intelligent Front End for Ecological Modeling," in E. J. H. Kerckhoffs, G. C. Vansteenkiste, and B. P. Zeigler, *AI Applied to Simulation. Proceedings of the European Conference at the University of Ghent, February 25–28, 1985, Ghent, Belgium,* Society for Computer Simulation, San Diego, CA, 1986, pp. 67–70.

73. P. R. Nachtsheim, W. B. Gevarter, J. C. Stutz, and C. P. Banda, "A Knowledge-Based Expert System for Scheduling of Airborne Astronomical Observations," in J. S. Kowalik (Ed.), *Coupling Symbolic and Numerical Computing in Expert Systems,* Elsevier Science, The Netherlands, 1986, pp. 217–229.

74. R. E. Nance, "Model Development Revisited." *Proceedings of the 1984 Winter Simulation Conference, Dallas, Texas, 1984,* Society for Computer Simulation, San Diego, CA, 1984, pp. 75–80.

75. F. Neelamkavil, *Computer Simulation and Modelling,* Wiley, New York, 1987.

76. A. Newell and H. A. Simon, *Human Problem Solving,* Prentice-Hall, Englewood Cliffs, NJ, 1972.

77. N. R. Nielsen, "The Impact of Using AI-based Techniques in a Control System Simulator," in P. A. Luker and G. Birtwistle, *Simulation and AI. Proceedings of the Conference on AI and Simulation, 14–16 January 1987, San Diego, California,* Society for Computer Simulation, San Diego, CA, 1987, pp. 72–77.

78. N. R. Nielsen, personal communication, April 4, 1988.

79. H. P. Nii, "The Blackboard Model of Problem Solving and the Evolution of Blackboard Architectures," *AI Magazine,* **7**:38–53, 1986.

80. H. P. Nii, "Blackboard Application Systems and a Knowledge Engineering Perspective," *AI Magazine,* **7**:82–107, 1986.

81. N. J. Nilsson, *Principles of Artificial Intelligence,* Tioga, Palo Alto, CA, 1980.

82. R. Novak, "Computer Simulation Replaces Live Ordnance in Air Combat Training," *Simulation,* **46**:251–253, 1986.

83. R. O'Keefe, "Simulation and Expert Systems—A Taxonomy and Some Examples," *Simulation,* **46**:10–16, 1986.

84. R. M. O'Keefe, "Advisory Systems in Simulation," in E. J. H. Kerckhoffs, G. C. Vansteen-kiste, and B. P. Zeigler (Eds.), *AI Applied to Simulation. Proceedings of the European Conference at the University of Ghent, February 25–28, 1985, Ghent, Belgium,* Society for Computer Simulation, San Diego, CA, 1986, pp. 73–78.

85. T. I. Oren, "Quality Assurance Paradigms for Artificial Intelligence in Modelling and Simulation," *Simulation,* **48**:149–151, 1987.

86. D. Palmer, Hecht-Nielsen Neurocomputer Corporation, personal communication, February 3, 1988.

87. R. Patil, "Causal Representation of Patient Illness for Electrolyte and Acid-Base Diagnosis," Technical Report MIT/LCS/TR-267, Laboratory for Computer Science, MIT, Cambridge, MA, 1981.

88. J. Pearl, "Evidential Reasoning Using Stochastic Simulation of Causal Models," *Artificial Intelligence,* **32**:245–257, 1987.

89. R. Reboh and T. Risch, "Syntel (TM): Knowledge Programming using Functional Representations," *Proceedings of the Fifth National Conference on Artificial Intelligence, Philadelphia, Pennsylvania, 1986,* Morgan Kaufmann, Los Altos, CA, 1986, pp. 1003–1007.

90. Y. V. R. Reddy, M. S. Fox, N. Husain, and M. McRoberts, "The Knowledge-Based Simulation System," *IEEE Software,* March 1986, pp. 26–37.

91. N. Roberts, D. F. Anderson, R. M. Deal, M. S. Garet, and W. A. Shaffer, *Introduction to Computer Simulation: The Systems Dynamics Approach,* Addison-Wesley, Reading, MA, 1983.

92. J. W. Rozenblit, S. Sevinc, and B. P. Zeigler, "Knowledge-Based Design of LANs using System Entity Structure Concepts," *Proceedings of the 1986 Winter Simulation Conference, Washington, D.C., 1986,* Society for Computer Simulation, San Diego, CA, 1986, pp. 858–865.

93. S. Ruiz-Mier, J. Talavage, and D. Ben-Arieh, "Towards a Knowledge-Based Network Simulation Environment," *Proceedings of the 1985 Winter Simulation Conference, San Francisco, California,* Society for Computer Simulation, San Diego, CA, 1985, pp. 232–236.

94. S. Ruiz-Mier and J. Talavage, "A Hybrid Paradigm for Modeling of Complex Systems," *Simulation,* **48**:135–141, 1987.

95. D. E. Rumelhart, G. E. Hinton, and J. L. McClelland, "A General Framework for Parallel Distributed Processing," in D. E. Rumelhart and J. L. McClelland (Eds.), *Parallel Distributed Processing: Explorations in the Microstructure of Cognition,* Vol. I, MIT Press, Cambridge, MA, 1986, pp. 45–76.

96. R. G. Sargent, "A Tutorial on Verification and Validation of Simulation Models," *Proceedings of the 1984 Winter Simulation Conference, Dallas, Texas,* Society for Computer Simulation, San Diego, CA, 1984, pp. 115–121.

97. S. C. Schapiro (Ed.), *Encyclopedia of Artificial Intelligence,* Wiley, New York, 1987.

98. J. W. Schmidt, "Introduction to Simulation," *Proceedings of the 1984 Winter Simulation Conference, Dallas, Texas,* Society for Computer Simulation, San Diego, CA, 1984, pp. 65–73.

99. R. E. Shannon, "Artificial Intelligence and Simulation," *Proceedings of the 1984 Winter Simulation Conference, Dallas, Texas,* Society for Computer Simulation, San Diego, CA, 1984, pp. 3–9.

100. R. E. Shannon, R. Mayer, and H. H. Adelsberger, "Expert Systems and Simulation," *Simulation,* **44**:275–284, 1985.

101. E. H. Shortliffe, "Details of the Consultation System," in B. G. Buchanan and E. H. Shortliffe (Eds.), *Rule-Based Expert Systems. The MYCIN Experiments of the Stanford Heuristic Programming Project,* Addison-Wesley, Reading, MA, 1984, pp. 78–132.

102. J. H. Siegel and B. Coleman, "Computers in the Care of the Critically Ill Patient," *Urologic Clinics of North America,* **13**:101–117, 1986.

103. M. K. Simmons and J. R. Dixon, "Reasoning about Quantitative Methods in Engineering Design," in J. S. Kowalik (Ed.), *Coupling Symbolic and Numerical Computing in Expert Systems,* Elsevier Science, The Netherlands, 1986, pp. 47–57.

104. D. E. Smith and J. E. Clayton, "Another Look at Frames," in B. G. Buchanan and E. H. Shortliffe (Eds.), *Rule-Based Expert Systems. The MYCIN Experiments of the Stanford Heuristic Programming Project,* Addison-Wesley, Reading, MA, 1984, pp. 441–452.

105. F. N. Springsteel, "A Multilevel Expert System for Exploratory Data Analysis," in J. S. Kowalik (Ed.), *Coupling Symbolic and Numerical Computing in Expert Systems,* Elsevier Science, The Netherlands, 1986, pp. 295–306.

106. J. A. Spriet and G. C. Vansteenkiste, *Computer-aided Modelling and Simulation,* Academic, New York, 1982.

107. M. Stefik, J. Aikins, R. Balzer, J. Benoit, L. Birnbaum, F. Hayes-Roth, and E. Sacerdoti, "The Organization of Expert Systems, a Tutorial," *Artificial Intelligence,* **18**:135–173, 1982.

108. S. D. Stewart, "Expert System Invades Military," *Simulation,* **46**:69–70, 1986.

109. W. R. Swartout, "XPLAIN: a System for Creating and Explaining Expert Consulting Programs," *Artificial Intelligence,* **21**:285–325, 1983.

110. P. Szolovits, "Expert Systems Tools and Techniques: Past, Present and Future," in W. E. L. Grimson and R. S. Patil (Eds.), *AI in the 1980s and Beyond. An MIT Survey,* MIT Press, Cambridge, MA, 1987, pp. 43–74.

111. S. N. Talukdar, E. Cardozo, L. Leào, R. Banares, and R. Joobbani, "A System for Distributed Problem Solving," in J. S. Kowalik (Ed.), *Coupling Symbolic and Numerical Computing in Expert Systems,* Elsevier Science, The Netherlands, 1986, pp. 59–67.

112. R. D. Teichgraeber, "General Dynamics Simulation and Artificial Intelligence Integration Testing," *Proceedings of the 1986 Summer Simulation Conference, Reno, Nevada, 1986,* Society for Computer Simulation, San Diego, CA, 1986, pp. 748–750.

113. B. Unger, A. Dewar, J. Cleary, and G. Birtwistle, "A Distributed Software Prototyping and Simulation Environment: Jade," in P. A. Luker and H. H. Adelsberger (Eds.), *Intelligent Simulation Environments. Proceedings of the Conference on Intelligent Simulation Environments, 23–25 January 1986, San Diego, California,* Society for Computer Simulation, San Diego, CA, 1986, pp. 63–71.

114. G. C. Vansteenkiste, "New Challenges in System Simulation," *Proceedings of the 1985 Summer Simulation Conference, Chicago, Illinois,* Society for Computer Simulation, San Diego, CA, 1985, pp. 692–695.

115. J. Walters and N. R. Nielsen, *Crafting Knowledge-based Systems,* Wiley, New York, 1988.

116. B. L. Webber and N. J. Nilsson (Eds.), *Readings in Artificial Intelligence,* Morgan Kaufmann, Los Altos, CA, 1981.

117. L. E. Widman, "Expert System Reasoning about Dynamic Systems by Semi-Quantitative Simulation," *Computer Methods and Programs in Biomedicine,* **29**:95–113, 1989.

118. L. E. Widman, "Knowledge-based Fault Identification and "What If" Simulation in Symbolic Dynamic Systems Models," *Proceedings of the Society for Computer Simulation Multiconference on AI and Simulation, San Diego, California,* Society for Computer Simulation, San Diego, CA, 1988, pp. 89–94.

119. L. E. Widman, Chapter 6, this volume.

120. P. H. Winston, *Artificial Intelligence,* 2nd ed., Addison-Wesley, Reading, MA, 1984.

121. P. H. Winston and B. K. P. Horn, *LISP,* 2nd ed., Addison-Wesley, Reading, MA, 1984.

122. G. Xiong and A. Song, "An Expert System for Dynamic System Simulation," in E. J. H. Kerckhoffs, G. C. Vansteenkiste, and B. P. Zeigler (Eds.), *AI Applied to Simulation. Proceedings of the European Conference at the University of Ghent, February 25–28, 1985, Ghent, Belgium,* Society for Computer Simulation, San Diego, CA, 1986, pp. 106–110.

123. B. P. Zeigler, *Theory of Modelling and Simulation,* Wiley, New York, 1976.

124. B. P. Zeigler, *Multifacetted Modelling and Discrete Event Simulation,* Academic, New York, 1984.

PART I
Conceptual Bases for Artificial Intelligence and Simulation

2 The System Entity Structure: Knowledge Representation for Simulation Modeling and Design

GUOQING ZHANG[1] and BERNARD P. ZEIGLER
Department of Electrical and Computer Engineering
University of Arizona
Tucson, Arizona

1 INTRODUCTION

An enriched framework capable of utilizing both kinds of knowledge representation schemes, deriving from AI (artificial intelligence) approaches and from dynamic systems, is motivated by the recognition that each in itself is incomplete [18]. Inspired by system-theoretic concepts originating in simulation methodology, the suggested framework marries frame-based concepts for representing system structure with dynamic model-based formalisms for representing system behavior.

We begin by reviewing current concepts of knowledge representation in artificial intelligence and simulation modeling, viewing them in a common perspective. This is followed by a brief overview of the system entity structure knowledge representation framework. The heart of the chapter is contained in the fourth section, where a formalization of the entity structure is given which is oriented to proving completeness, correctness, and irredundancy of two transformations which support the use of the structure for automated construction of models. The final section briefly discusses applications of the entity structure in knowledge-based simulation.

2 REPRESENTATION SCHEMES AND KNOWLEDGE

A representation scheme (Figure 1) is a means of representing reality in computerized form. Each representation adhering to the pattern laid down by the scheme consists of four kinds of features or slots. Operations are procedures which can create, modify, and destroy representations or their components. Questions are procedures that can be used to interrogate the representation to get answers. Operations and questions are internal features of the representation in that they are meaningful independently of outside reality. However, a representation is not useful as a thing onto itself but only in reference

[1]Present address: Zycad Corporation, 1380 Willow Road, Menlo Park, California 94025.

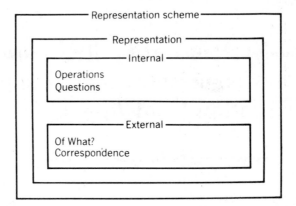

Figure 1. Representation scheme.

to something else. Thus the third feature of a representation is the designation of what it purports to represent. Finally, there must be a means of putting into correspondence the features of the representation with the reality it claims to represent.

Having a representation of an entity is obviously not enough to claim knowledge about that entity. Somehow we would like to say the representation becomes knowledge just in case the representation is accurate; that is, we define knowledge as valid representation. A homomorphism is a correspondence between the states of a pair of objects which is preserved under all relevant operations, a relationship that can be depicted by commutative diagrams such as that in Figure 2. (See Zeigler [16] for a detailed discussion in the context of systems theory, modeling, and simulation.) Applied to the present context, we see that the correspondence in question should associate states of the real world entity with those of its representation in such a way that when we ask a question about the entity, we get the same answer from the representation that we would get by making a corresponding observation on the entity. The states of the entity and its representation will stay in correspondence if for each real-world action that changes the entity state, there is a corresponding operation which updates the representation state accordingly.

Thus we say that a system knows about an entity if it has a valid representation of the entity; that is, a homomorphism exists between the representation and the entity itself. It follows that valid dynamic models constitute a form of knowledge just as do valid AI schemes. A system can learn about an object by generating and validating representations or models of it. Some fundamental systems theory is applicable: the epistemological hierarchy [5] provides levels of system specification at which knowledge may be acquired as well as conditions under which validation is possible [16].

There is much interest in combining AI and simulation methodologies. The AI knowledge representation schemes go beyond classical model formalisms in allowing dimensions of representation [2] such as inference of new knowledge, associative and other access to existing knowledge, matching of patterns, and metaknowledge. Although such schemes can organize much of the knowledge about systems that cannot be represented with dynamic formalisms, they are not adept at representing the

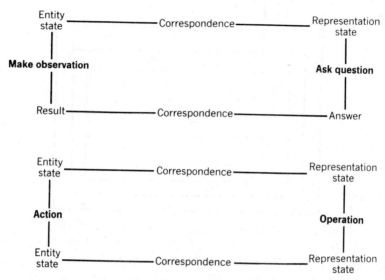

Figure 2. Correspondence relationship.

dynamics intended by the latter. Thus, there needs to be a paradigm whose scope of representation includes both classical and AI schemes. This is an area of research with at least two sources of inspiration. One stems from the hypothesis that for a computer to reason about physical systems, it must have more of a qualitative and commonsense representation than exists in the classical modeling formalism [2, 8]. However, in attempting to capture commonsense knowledge about physical systems, qualitative modeling may drastically coarsen the state descriptor space from the real numbers to small discrete sets. Accordingly, much ambiguity arises in generating the behavior (reasoning) of such models. Recent approaches to qualitative modeling use symbolic means to summarize dynamic system behavior rather than to derive it [3, 9, 10].

Another source of inspiration for a wider paradigm comes from computer simulation. Here the world views of discrete-event simulation have been found to be highly compatible with the representation schemes of AI [6]. Object-oriented programming can be viewed as providing a computational basis for knowledge representation by allowing the programmer to associate methods with objects organized in taxonomic classes. Such methods can perform operations on the global object state (the ensemble of its slots) and invoke each other by passing messages. Already in 1965, the discrete-event simulation language SIMULA introduced class inheritance and association of both procedures and data structures with class instances. It is not surprising, therefore, that languages are being developed to express both the dynamic knowledge of discrete-event formalisms and the declarative knowledge of AI frame paradigms (see [4] and other articles in the volume in which it appears).

2.1 System-theoretic Representation

These developments led us to seek a more fundamental basis for the marriage of AI and dynamic paradigms. The basis we shall propose here draws its inspiration from the systems theory view of the world (reviewed by Pichler, [7]) and stems from the system-theoretic representation of simulation models for multifaceted modeling methodology [16].

System theory distinguishes between system structure (the inner constitution of a system) and behavior (its outer manifestation). Regarding structure, the theory has given us the concept of decomposition (i.e., how a system may be broken down into component systems) and coupling (i.e., how these components may be combined to reconstitute the original system). Thus decomposition and coupling should be fundamental relations in a knowledge representation scheme. System theory, however, has not focused itself on a third fundamental kind of relation, taxonomic, which concerns the admissible variants of a component and their specializations, exhibited, for example, by the generalization hierarchy of frames.

Regarding system behavior, we distinguish between causal and empirical representations. By empirical representation we refer to actual records of data (time history of variable values) gathered from a real system or model. Causal relationships are integrated into units called models which can be interpreted by suitable simulators to generate data in empirical form.

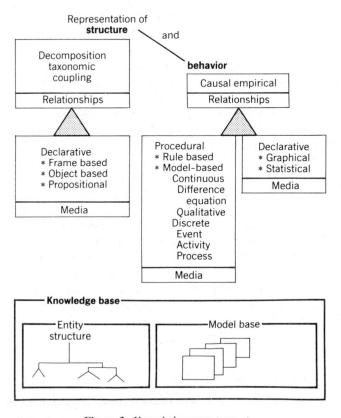

Figure 3. Knowledge management.

As a step toward a complete knowledge representation scheme, we propose the framework illustrated in Figure 3. We combine the decomposition, taxonomic, and coupling relationships in a representation scheme called the system entity structure [16], a declarative scheme related to frame-theoretic and object-based representations. The model base contains models which are procedural in character, expressed in classical and AI-derived formalisms mentioned earlier. This scheme is not complete since it does not deal with the fine-grained causal relations from which models are synthesized nor with the empirical raw data. The first should be the focus of a major research effort while the second is essentially available in database technology. The entities of the entity structure refer to conceptual components of reality for which models may reside in the model base. Also associated with entities (as with other object types we shall discuss) are slots for attribute knowledge representation.

3   THE SYSTEM ENTITY STRUCTURE/MODEL BASE

The knowledge base framework just introduced is intended to be generative in nature; that is, it should be a compact representation scheme which can be unfolded to generate the family of all possible models which can be synthesized from components in the model base. As shown in Figure 4, the user, whether human or artificial, should be a goal-directed agent which can interrogate the knowledge base and synthesize a model using pruning operations that ultimately reduce the structure to a composition tree. This

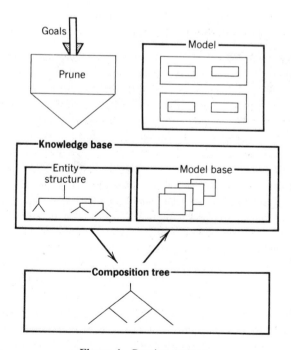

Figure 4.   Pruning process.

contains all the information needed to synthesize a model in hierarchical fashion from components in the model base.

We review some fundamental entity structure concepts that are discussed in greater detail elsewhere [16, 18]. An entity may have several aspects, each denoting a decomposition and therefore having several entities. Associated with aspects are coupling specifications involving their entities. In pruning, eventually one aspect is selected for each nonatomic entity (to be described later).

Whereas the entity–aspect relation conveys decomposition knowledge, the entity–specialization relation represents taxonomic knowledge. Specializations (classification schemes) also have several entities. Specializations can be thought of as partitions; the product of two partitions forms a finer partition whose blocks are the intersections of the originals. In pruning, when one entity from a specialization is selected, it inherits the substructure (slots, aspects, and remaining specializations) of its parent. The selected entity also replaces the parent in any coupling specifications involving the latter. Specializations may form a hierarchy analogous to those of semantic nets [18, 19].

A multiple entity represents the set of entities all of the same type. This is the extension of the class as opposed to its intension (class definition). Such a multiple entity always has an aspect depicted with three vertical lines, which is its multiple decomposition into the individual entities of the same type. Class variables, carrying aggregation and distribution information, are associated with the multiple entity, whereas instance variables, belonging to each instance of the class, are associated with the entity.

3.1 DEVS-Scheme Simulation Environment

The preceding knowledge representation framework underlies DEVS-Scheme, a general-purpose environment for constructing hierarchical discrete-event models [17, 19]. DEVS-Scheme is written in the PC-Scheme language which runs on IBM-compatible microcomputers and under a SCHEME interpreter for the TI-Explorer. DEVS-Scheme also serves as an interface to existing simulation systems. To illustrate the entity structure concepts, we show how such an interface organizes the modules of a continuous simulation package called TRNSYS [21] for which an extensive set of routines for greenhouse microclimate modeling is available. Such routines are selected, modified if needed, and coupled together by the modeler to meet current objectives. DEVS-Scheme writes a file containing such specifications to drive the TRNSYS simulation executive. The modeler can thus work with the entity structure pruning interface to construct a model rather than writing directly an extensive set of coupling specifications in an obscure numerical coding.

Figure 5 is a simplified entity structure representation of the TRNSYS simulation framework. The TRNSYS_SYSTEM consists of MODULEs (a multiple entity). Each MODULE has a specialization SYSTEM_TYPE and an aspect MODULE_DEC (decomposition). Three of the many types of modules that have been developed are shown: SOLAR_WATER_HEATING_SYSTEM, AIR_FLOW_SYSTEM, and COOLING_SYSTEM; these are represented as entities of SYSTEM_TYPE (specialization). The

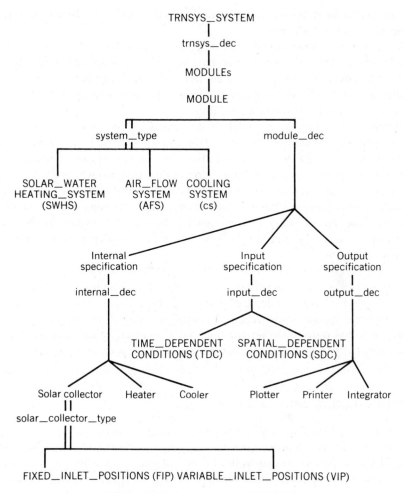

Figure 5. Entity structure for TRNSYS.

MODULE_DEC has three entities: INPUT_SPECIFICATION, INTERNAL_SPECIFI-
CATION, and OUTPUT_SPECIFICATION, representing the components of a MOD-
ULE specification. Each of these has its own decomposition as shown. The components
of such decompositions may have further specializations, one of which is shown for
SOLAR_COLLECTOR.

As indicated in the preceding, such an entity structure is pruned by the modeler and
then transformed by DEVS-Scheme into a file which drives the TRNSYS simulation
system. Selected routines in the model base are retrieved and coupled together
according to the specifications attached to the MODULE_DEC aspect. Two transformations of the entity structure are important in supporting the pruning process.

The result of applying the first transformation (I) to the entity structure of Figure 5
is illustrated in Figure 6. The resulting entity structure explicitly represents the entity

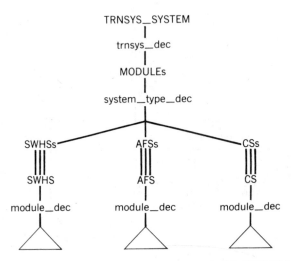

Figure 6. Transformation I on TRNSYS_SYSTEM_TYPE (SYSTEM_TYPE).

MODULE as decomposed into the multiple entities SOLAR_WATER_HEATING SYS-
TEMs, AIR_FLOW_SYSTEMs, and COOLING_SYSTEMs. In pruning, the modeler
can now select any number of each of the latter module types to construct a model. Each
module has the same decomposition as represented by MODULE_DEC as before.
MODULE_DEC has several occurrences each of which carries the same properties, an
illustration of the uniformity axiom [16].

Applying Transformation II to the original entity structure yields the result shown
in Figure 7. The resulting entity structure represents the situation where the choice of
FIXED_INLET_POSITION(FIP) is considered from the SOLAR_COLLECTOR_TYPE
specialization. Two kinds of MODULE result: those in which FIP replaces its parent
SOLAR_COLLECTOR and those for which this choice is removed from consideration.
These are denoted MODULE@FIP and MODULE~FIP@VIP, the latter indicating that
the only remaining choice in this case, VARIABLE_INLET_POSITION (VIP), has
been selected.

Transformation I applies whenever there are specializations directly under a
multiple decomposition while Transformation II applies whenever specializations are
separated by at least one aspect from an enclosing multiple decomposition. Both
transformations are needed to reduce an entity structure to pure form, that is, where all
specializations have been removed. Both transformations apply recursively, and
cooperatively, to a structure to enable such reduction to be accomplished. Note, for
example, that Transformation I may be applied three times to the structure in Figure 5
to expand each of the SYSTEM_TYPE MODULEs to comprise the two forms of
SOLAR_COLLECTOR configurations. For example, AIR_FLOW_SYSTEM@FIP is
the MODULE type for modeling air flow which contains a fixed inlet position solar
collector.

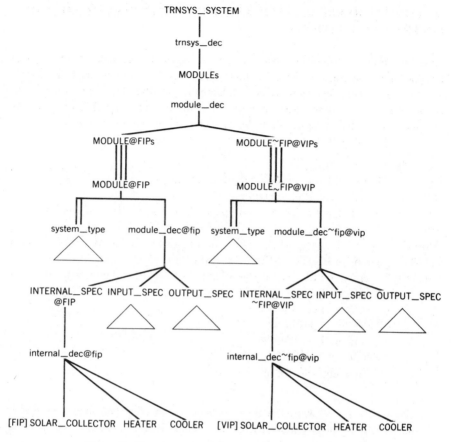

Figure 7. Transformation II on TRNSYS_SYSTEM (FIP).

Aspects and specializations of an entity structure also possess constraint specifications which restrict the choices of configurations. More detailed treatment of this topic is available elsewhere [11, 14].

In the ensuing sections we develop a formalization of the entity structure for the purposes of rigorously characterizing its properties. In particular, we shall employ the formalization to consider the following questions concerning Transformations I and II.

Completeness   Are Transformations I and II sufficient to convert any entity structure containing multiple entities and specializations into pure form?

Correctness   Do these transformations preserve the knowledge embedded in the original entity structure?

Redundancy   Are these transformations redundant, in that one can sometimes achieve the same effect as the other?

4   FORMAL REPRESENTATION OF THE ENTITY STRUCTURE AND ITS TRANSFORMATIONS

Although the entity structure has been visually represented as a treelike structure, it can be coded into other forms which can coherently convey the information it bears. In this section, we present a set-theoretic formalization that is both rigorous and amenable to proofs of correctness of transformations we shall discuss. The formalization provides an alternative to that presented by Belogus [1] more suited to these purposes.

We shall employ the following notation:

ES	Entity structure in formal representation
(ES)	Treelike visual presentation of an ES
ENTITY	Set of all entities in ES; multiple entity marked as special kind of entity
SPEC	Set of all specializations in ES
ASPECT	Set of all aspects in ES; multiple decomposition noted as the special aspect
ITEM	Union of ENTITY, SPEC, and ASPECT
(ent a b)	Element of ES, where ent belongs to ENTITY, a belongs to SPEC or ASPECT, b is subset of ENTITY
×	Operator of cross product
*	Operator of power set
∪	Operator of set UNION
−	Set operator of DIFFERENCE
==	Sign of equivalence of entity structures

If ELE = (a b c) ∈ ES, we define three element selectors (ent, type, and sub) on ELE such that a, b, and c can be extracted from ELE, that is, ELE.ent = a, ELE.type = b, and ELE.sub = c.

4.1   Definition of Entity Structure

An entity structure, also called a system entity structure, is a set of triples defined over ENTITY × { SPEC ∪ ASPECT } × (ENTITY)*. This primary definition, along with some restrictions, constitutes the formal definition for an entity structure. The restrictions are addressed later.

Figure 5 depicts an example (ES) tree structure. Sets mentioned in the preceding are:

```
ENTITY  = { TRNSYS_SYSTEM, MODULEs, MODULE, .... }
ASPECT  = { TRNSYS_DEC, MODULE_DEC, .... }
SPEC    = { SYSTEM_TYPE, SOLAR_COLLECTOR_TYPE }
ES      = { (TRNSYS_SYSTEM, TRNSYS_DEC, MODULEs),
            (MODULEs, |||, MODULE), (MODULE, MODULE_DEC,
            {INTERNAL_SPECIFICATION, INPUT_SPECIFICATION,
            OUTPUT_SPECIFICATION}) ... }
ITEM    = ASPECT ∪ SPEC ∪ ENTITY
```

We give special treatment to the multiple-entity concept. Let ES={S} where S.ent is a multiple entity. ES is thus the compact form to represent the countable set of entity structures { ESi | i is a nonnegative integer, ESi is an entity structure, ESi = {Si | Si.ent=[i]S.ent}. Here Si.ent is no longer a multiple entity, Si.type=[i]S.type is an aspect but not a multiple decomposition, Si.sub = {Sij | j ∈ {1,..,i}, Sij = [i][j]S.ent which is derived from Si.ent}. Figure 8 shows how ES is unfolded to ESi's in general. A specific example is also provided where eight modules are specified for a multiple entity, MODULEs.

We define the following operations and functions on ES to clarify the formal definition of entity structure concepts:

1. ASPECT_OF: A function mapping ENTITY → ES*: For any e ∈ ENTITY, ASPECT_OF(e) = { s | s ∈ ES; s.ent = e; s.sub ∈ ASPECT }. In (ES), ASPECT_OF(e) is viewed as the set of aspects hanging from e.

2. SPEC_OF: A function mapping ENTITY → ES*: For any e ∈ ENTITY, SPEC_OF(e) = { s | s ∈ ES; s.ent = e; s.type ∈ SPEC }. In (ES), SPEC_OF(e) is viewed as the set of specializations hanging from e.

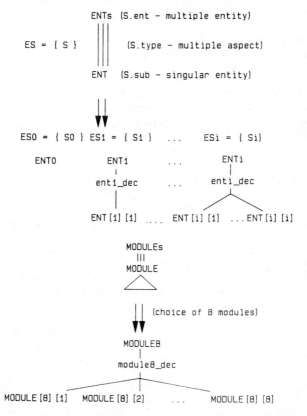

Figure 8. Unfolded multiple entity ES = {S}.

In Figure 5,

```
ASPECT_OF(MODULE) = { (MODULE, MODULE_DEC,
{INPUT_SPECIFICATION, OUTPUT_SPECIFICATION,
INTERNAL_SPECIFICATION }) },
SPEC_OF(MODULE) = { (MODULE, SYSTEM_TYPE,
{COOLING_SYSTEM,
SOLAR_WATER_HEATING_SYSTEM, AIR_FLOW_SYSTEM})}.
```

3. DIRECT_REACHABLE: A function mapping ITEM $\rightarrow$ ITEM*. If ent and pat are in ITEM, pat $\in$ DIRECT_REACHABLE(ent) only if there exists (ent, pat, B) $\in$ ES or (A, ent, B) $\in$ ES such that pat is in B, where A is in ENTITY and B is a subset of ENTITY. In the tree representation, a child is directly reachable from its parent.

As an example in Figure 5, DIRECT_REACHABLE(OUTPUT_DEC) = { PLOTTER, PRINTER, INTEGRATOR }.

4. REACHABLE: A function mapping ITEM $\rightarrow$ ITEM*. It produces a subset of ITEM in such a way that for any ENT in ITEM, REACHABLE(ENT) contains DIRECT_REACHABLE(ENT), and for any X in DIRECT_REACHABLE(ENT), REACHABLE(X) is a subset of REACHABLE(ENT).

In Figure 5, since all items are reachable from the root, we have REACHABLE(TRNSYS_SYSTEM) = ITEM.

5. REST: A function mapping ES$\rightarrow$ES*. For any s $\in$ ES, REST(s) = ASPECT_OF(s.ent) $\cup$ SPEC_OF(s.ent)-{s}. This function collects any element e in ES, except the given one, such that e.ent = s.ent.

6. PARENTS: A function defined as ENTITY $\rightarrow$ ES*. For any e $\in$ ENTITY, PARENT(e) = {t | t $\in$ ES; e $\in$ t.sub}. In (ES), PARENTS(e) is viewed as the set of the items from which e hangs.

7. PATH: A function mapping ITEM $\times$ ITEM $\rightarrow$ (ITEM*)*. For any two entities from ITEM, x and y, PATH(x,y) is the set of sequences in ES from x to y. A sequence $(A_1 A_2 ... A_n)$ is a path from x to y in (ES) if A_i is in DIRECT_REACHABLE(A_{i-1}) for i in {2 .. n}, and A_1 and A_n are the two given items x and y, respectively. If y is not in REACHABLE(x) $\cup$ {x}, PATH(x,y) = { }. Each sequence in PATH(x,y) constitutes a different occurrence of y, for which a unique name can be constructed by concatenating the elements of the sequence. For any a $\in$ ITEM, considering PATH(ROOT,a), we have a way to get a unique global name for such item occurrence in the (reachable part of the) entity structure (ROOT will be defined next).

As an example in Figure 5, PATH(MODULE,AFS) = { (MODULE SYSTEM_TYPE AHS)}.

8. ROOT: A function mapping ITEM $\rightarrow$ ITEM*. For any y $\in$ ENTITY, if there is no x $\in$ ITEM such that PATH(x,y) < > { }, then ROOT(y) equals y, otherwise ROOT(y) equals ROOT(x). Thus, ROOT(y) is the set of items from which y is reachable, but themselves are not reachable from any other item. In the case of Figure 5, ROOT(MODULE) = ROOT(PLOTTER) = TRNSYS_SYSTEM.

9. SELECT[E]: A function mapping ES → ES*. Given t ∈ ES, t.type ∈ SPEC, and E ∈ t.sub, we get SELECT[E](t) as follows:

```
SELECT[E](t) = SELECTremain[E](t) ∪ SELECTinherit[E](t) ∪
               SELECTparent[E](t).
```

where,

```
SELECTremain[E](t) ={ s | s is a triple; there exists s1
                     in ASPECT_OF(E) ∪ SPEC_OF(E), such
                     that
                         s.ent = [E]t.ent,
                         s.type = s1.type,
                         .sub = s1.sub }
SELECTinherit[E](t) = { s | s is a triple; there exists
                       s1 in REST(t), such that,
                       s.ent = [E]s1.ent, s.type =
                       s1.type, s.sub = s1.sub }
SELECTparent[E](t) = { s | s is a triple; and there
                      exists an s1 in PARENTS(t.ent),
                      such that,
                      s.ent = s1.ent,
                      s.type = s1.type,
                      s.sub = s1.sub - {t.ent} ∪
                      {[E]t.ent} }
```

As viewed in (ES), SELECT[E] is an operation which represents the result of replacing a general entity E, by a sub-type, that is, an entity in one of its specializations. The three suboperations correspond, respectively, to revising the name of the subtype to show its lineage (since the general entity is removed), carrying out the inheritance of structure, and connecting the parents of the general entity to their new child. This operation is central to our formalization of entity structure pruning concepts. It will operate locally in the sense that it affects only those items that are reachable from t.type. Some detailed descriptions of SELECT operation and the following SPLIT operation can be found in [12].

10. SPLIT: A function mapping ES → ES*. Given t ∈ ES, t.type ∈ SPEC, t.sub = { A1, A2, ... An}, and n is a positive integer.

```
SPLIT(t) = { ESi | i∈{1 .. n}; ESi = ES ∪ SELECT[Ai](t)
             - REDUNDANT(t) - REMAIN[Ai](t) }.
```

Here,

```
REDUNDANT(t) = { t } ∪ REDUNDANTparents(t)
               ∪ REDUNDANTinherit(t),
```

```
REMAIN[Ai](t) = { s | s is a triple; s ∈ ASPECT_OF(x) ∪
SPEC_OF(x); x ∈ ENTITY; x ∈ REACHABLE(t.type) -
             REACHABLE(Ai) - {Ai} and number of
             elements in PATH(t.type, x) = number of
             elements in PATH(ROOT(t.type), x) },
             REDUNDANTparents(t) = PARENTS(t.ent),
             REDUNDANTinherit(t) = REST(t).
```

SPLIT replaces a specified entity with each of the subtypes in its specializations. It calls upon SELECT to perform these replacements and makes sure that redundant elements are eliminated from the resulting set of entity structures. As the name implies, SPLIT produces a set of entity structures, each of which comes from the selection of one entity from the given specialization by means of the SELECT operation.

11. DENOTATION, abbreviated as D, is an operation: ES* →ES*, ES → ES, or ITEM → ITEM. For ESS = {ES1, ES2, ...}, where ESS ∈ ES*, we have D(ESS) = {D(ES1), D(ES2), ...}. If ESi = { Si1, Si2, ...}, then we have D(ESi) = { D(Si1), D(Si2), ... }, where D(Sij) = Sij, if Sij.type is in ASPECT and is not a multiple decomposition; if Sij.type is a multiple aspect, Sij stands for an infinite number of countable entity structures to which SPLIT can apply recursively; D(Sij) will be further defined in an axiom given later if Sij.type is in SPEC.

DENOTATION is essential in defining the equivalence of two entity structures at the levels of entity structure, substructure, and item (entity, aspect, or specialization). Accordingly, DENOTATION is defined over multiple levels.

5   RESTRICTIONS

We now impose some restrictions on the definition of the entity structure in such a way that its desired properties can be rigorously defined:

Restriction 1   For any E ∈ ITEM, E is not in REACHABLE(E). This ensures that a tree (having no loops) is formed as viewed in (ES).

Restriction 2   For any s ∈ ES and t ∈ ES, if s.type = t.type, then t.sub must be the same as s.sub, regardless of what t.ent and s.ent are.

Restriction 3   For any s and t ∈ ES, if s.ent = t.ent, then ASPECT_OF(s.ent) = ASPECT_OF(t.ent) and SPEC_OF(s.ent) = SPEC_OF(t.ent).

Restriction 4   We require that ROOT(x) always equals ROOT(y) for any x and y in ITEM. This is called the *Unique root property*. Also we require the root be in ENTITY.

Restriction 5   For any S ∈ ES, if S.ent is a multiple entity, S.type must be a multiple decomposition, and vice versa. In either case, S.sub contains only one individual entity (or singular entity).

From the definition of entity structure, along with these five restrictions, we can derive the fundamental properties of entity structure, stated as axioms [16]. They are:

1. *Uniformity*   All occurrences of an item have the same substructure (in the tree form, the substructure of an item is the subtree hanging from it). For any two triples s and t in ES, if s.ent = t.ent, then we have REACHABLE(s.ent) = REACHABLE(t.ent), and for any e REACHABLE(s.ent), PATH(s.ent, e) = PATH(t.ent, e). Restriction 1 ensures this property.

2. *Strict Hierarchy*   No occurrence of an item has another occurrence of the same item in its substructure. Restriction 1 ensures this property.

3. *Alternating Mode*   Entities alternate with aspects and specializations in successive levels. For any e1 and e2 in ITEM, if e1 $\in$ DIRECT_REACHABLE(e2), and e1 $\in$ ENTITY, then e $\in$ SPEC $\cup$ ASPECT. If e2 $\in$ ENTITY, then e1 $\in$ ASPECT $\cup$ SPEC. This property is implied by the definition of ES.

4. *Valid Brothers*   No two occurrences of the same item are brothers. For any s and t $\in$ ES, if s.ent = t.ent and s.type = t.type, then s = t. This can also be derived from the combination of restrictions 1–4.

In addition to the standard properties just derived, we need new axioms to characterize the preservation properties of the transformations to be introduced. First we provide a concept of EQUIVALENCE of entity structures which will serve to formalize their semantics as it relates to the transformations.

Two entity structures are equivalent if they generate the same set of entity structures up to isomorphism by applying sequences of SPLIT operations and then the DENOTATION. Let ES1 and ES2 be two sets of entity structures. We have

```
ES1 == ES2 iff
D((SPLIT)*(ES1)) = D((SPLIT)*(ES2))
```

where (SPLIT)*(E) is the set of entity structures that result from applying all finite sequences of operation, SPLIT. The following axioms will serve to make DENOTATION a matter of definition.

We identify four elementary axioms as follows:

Axiom 1   Equivalence by flattening and deepening,
Axiom 2   Empty aspects,
Axiom 3   Empty specializations,
Axiom 4   Equivalence of specialization.

Axiom 1   Flattening and Deepening   As illustrated in Figure 9, flattening is a transformation of an entity structure that reduces the depth of the tree by eliminating a level. In Figure 9a, entity M is decomposed into components A1, ... , An, which are in turn decomposed into more elementary ones {Aij ...}. The flattened version in

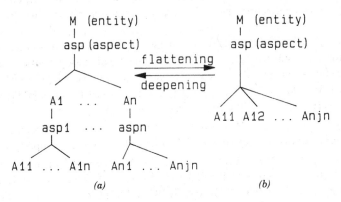

Figure 9. Flattening and Deepening.

Figure 9b has only one level of decomposition in which M is decomposed in the { Ai j },
the intermediate level having been eliminated. The axiom states that we will regard the
original and flattened structures as equivalent.

Let t be in ES, and t.sub = { Ai | i in {1 ... n} and n is a positive integer}.
Correspondingly, for each Ai, there exists a ti such that ti.ent = Ai. Besides, t.type and
ti.type are members in ASPECT.

Let E1 = { t } ∪ { ti | i in {1... n} }
    E2 = { s | s is a triple,
            s.ent = t.ent,
            s.type = t.type,
            s.sub = t1.sub ∪ ... ∪ tn.sub }
Then D(E1) = D(E2).

Note that from the definition of EQUIVALENCE , we also have E1 == E2.

Axiom 2   Empty Aspect   As shown in Figure 10, an aspect having no other entities
as its components has no use in the entity structure and thus can be replaced with any
other nonexistent aspect.

Let E1 = { t } where t.type is in SPEC and t.sub = { }.
Let E2 = { s } where s is a triple, s.ent = t.ent, s.type is not in ASPECT and is the
    permittable name for ASPECT.

By permittable it is meant that its appearance obeys the definition of entity structure.

Then D(E1) = D(E2). This also implies E1 == E2.

Axiom 3   Empty Specialization   This axiom can be explained by referring to
Figure 10, as in the case of empty aspect, with ASPECT replaced by specialization.

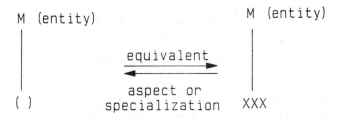

Figure 10. Empty aspect/specialization.

Axiom 4   Equivalence of Specialization   A specialization of an entity represents the possible replacements for this entity. This axiom assures such a feature: Let E1 and E2 be two sets of entity structures. E1 = { { t } } where t.type is in SPEC, t.sub = {e1, ... , en} and n is a positive integer and E2 = { {ti} | ti.ent = [t.ent]ei, i in {1 ... n}, ti.type can be any permittable and nonexistent aspect, ti.sub = { } }.

Then D(E1) = D(E2). This also implies E1 == E2.

These axioms play important roles in proving the correctness of the pruning operations, especially the transformations to be discussed.

The strict hierarchy and uniformity axioms endow entity structures with a natural scheme for naming different occurrences of the same item. The following property is based on a minimal path name assignment [16].

5.1   Unique Naming Property

Any occurrence of an item in ITEM can be given a unique name to distinguish it from any other occurrences of the same item.

In the following discussion, we will always assume there is a unique name associated with each item occurrence.

5.2   Formal Definition of Transformations on Entity Structures for Pruning

Recall that transformations support the pruning of entity structures having multiple decompositions. Two such operations were defined. Transformation I deals with the case where there is a specialization directly under the multiple decomposition context. Transformation II, on the other hand, works on the subtree below an aspect of a singular entity (called its context) of a multiple decomposition.

Let ES denote an entity structure and TES be the result of transforming it; ES and TES are called the original and transformed structures, respectively. We now provide formal definitions of Transformations I and II.

Transformation I   As depicted in Figure 6, Transformation I changes a specialization hung on a singular entity to a decomposition which has a set of multiple entities as its subcomponents. These components are derived from the component entities of the given specialization.

Let ES = { t1, t2 }, t1.ent is a multiple entity of ENTITY,

t1.type is a multiple aspect of ASPECT,

t1.sub contains the single entity relative to t1.ent,

t2.ent is in t1.sub,

t2.type is in SPEC,

t2.sub = { Mi | i is in {1 ... n} and n is a positive integer }

Thus we have TES = { S, S1, ... , Sn } where

S.ent   = t1.ent, an entity (not a multiple entity),

S.type = t1.type, an aspect (not a multiple aspect),

S.sub = {Mi's | i in {1 ... n}, Mi's is the multiple entity derived from Mi }

Si.ent = Mi's,

Si.type is a new and permissible multiple aspect,

Si.sub contains Mi only.

Transformation II   We use the symbol @ to express the meaning of "choosing" and ~ to state "excluding." For instance, GENERAL@ELEMENT means the entity ELEMENT is chosen from a specialization and ELEMENT is in REACHABLE(GENERAL) of the entity structure before applying this transformation. Similarly, GENERAL~ELEMENT means the entity ELEMENT is removed from a specialization and ELEMENT is in REACHABLE(GENERAL) as above. In both cases, the entities GENERAL@ELEMENT and GENERAL~ELEMENT are called transformed entities.

Let ES = { T0, T1, ... , Tn, S } and given E in S.sub,

T0.ent is a multiple entity of ENTITY,

T0.type is a multiple aspect of ASPECT,

T0.sub contains only a single entity relative to T0.ent,

T1.type is in ASPECT,

Ti.ent is in (T_{i-1}).sub for i in {1 ... n},

S.ent is in Tn.sub,

S.type is in SPEC.

Transformation II acting on E results in the transformed entity structure TES as follows:

TES = TESchoosing $\cup$ TESexcluding,

where

TESchoosing = { C, C0, ...,Cn },

TESexcluding = { R, E0, ...,En },

C.ent = T0.ent,

C.type = T0.type,

C.sub = { M@Es, M~Es | M = M@Es_mult, a permissible new aspect },

C0.sub = { M@E },

Ci.ent = Ti.ent@E,

Ci.type = Ti.type@E,

Ci.sub = Ti.sub − { T_{i+1}.ent } ∪ { T_{i+1}.ent@E } for i in {1 … n}.

Note that, T_{n+1} = S and S.ent@E is replaced by [E]S.ent.

R.ent = S.ent~E,

R.type = S.type~E,

R.sub = S.sub − { E },

E0.ent = M~Es,

E0.type = M~Es_mult, a permissible new aspect,

E0.sub = { M~E },

Ei.ent = Ti.ent~E,

Ei.type = Ti.type~E,

Ei.sub = Ti.sub - { T_{i+1}.ent } ∪ {T_{i+1}.ent~E} for i in {1 … n}.

Here R.sub may be an empty set. If such a case arises, we can further optimize Transformation II by making TESexcluding empty and C.sub have M@Es only.

5.3 Proof of Properties of Transformations

Having formal definitions of the transformations enables us to consider the properties of completeness, correctness, and redundancy.

5.4 Redundancy

To show that these transformations are not redundant, we note that they always apply in mutually exclusive circumstances. In contrast to Transformation II, Transformation I does not affect any aspect directly hanging from a singular entity. Moreover, it deletes one specialization from the entity structure and introduces no extra aspects to a singular entity, though more branches may be created. Similarly, Transformation II does not affect any specializations applying to singular entities. Since they operate in different contexts and achieve distinct effects, the transformations are not redundant.

5.5 Completeness

We can show that Transformations I and II applied recursively and cooperatively are sufficient to convert any entity structure containing multiple entities and specializations into pure form, that is, to eliminate all specializations in the context of multiple decompositions. Any entity structure has only a finite number of specializations, and because Transformations I and II are mutually exclusive, we can apply these transformations to an entity structure with the following algorithm for transformations:

WHILE(there is a spe in SPEC, spe is under multiple
    decomposition context) DO
    IF (Transformation I is applicable)
    THEN DO it
    ELSE IF (Transformation II is applicable)
       THEN DO-IT;

At each application of Transformation I we eliminate a specialization under a singular entity, while in each application of Transformation II a specialized entity in the context of a singular entity is eliminated. However, the number of specializations does not strictly decline. It can be shown that the time complexity of the algorithm is $O(NL^N)$, where N is the number of specializations (in SPEC) under all multiple decompositions and L is the maximum number of specialized entities in the specializations. We conclude that the preceding algorithm always terminates in a pure entity structure. The exponential character of the algorithm is not surprising in view of the combinatorial nature of the pruning process. Clearly, pruning must be supported by a heuristic process [14].

5.6 Correctness

We now show that Transformations I and II applied as in the foregoing algorithm preserve the knowledge embedded in the original entity structure. There are two formal properties to be considered here. The first is recoverability, that is, that ES is always recoverable from TES. The second is equivalence, that is, that ES and TES have the same denotation under application of all SPLIT operations, $D(SPLIT^*(ES)) = D(SPLIT^*(TES))$. Recoverability assures that no knowledge is lost in a transformation, while equivalence guarantees that the transformed entity structure has the same meaning (as defined by the denotation mapping) as the original.

5.7 Recoverability

To show that ES can be recovered from TES is equivalent to showing that the transformations are one-to-one mappings, or invertible with respect to their domains. Inspection of the changing digraph for each transformation easily reveals a method to define the inverse transformation corresponding to Transformations I and II, respectively (Figure 6 for transformation I, Figure 7 for transformation II).

5.8 Equivalence

To show that ES and TES are equivalent, we must apply none, one, or more SPLIT operations to each and then show that the two sets of entity structures have one-to-one correspondence in meaning. In this chapter, we sketch only the proof process for Transformation I.

5.8.1 Equivalence of ES and TES

Let ES = { t1, t2 } and TES = { S, S1, ... , Sn } as in the definition of Transformation I. We apply DENOTATION to ES (first to t1). The result is

D(ES) = { D(ESm) I m is any nonnegative integer, ESm is as described before when the formal definition of entity structure is presented}.

Noted that ESm = { T, T1, ...,Tm }, where

T.ent	=	t1.ent, an entity (not a multiple entity),
T.type	=	t1.type, an aspect (not a multiple aspect),
T.sub	=	{ t1.ent[1], t1.ent[2], ... , t1.ent[m] },
Ti.ent	=	t1.ent[i], for i in {1 ... m},
Ti.type	=	t2.type, for i in {1 ... m},
Ti.sub	=	t2.sub, for i in {1 ... m}.

The first three equations come directly from the definition of multiple decomposition and the rest are derived from the name expansions such that t2 of ES can fit correctly into ESm.

SPLIT can now be applied to ESm to get a new set of entity structures with no more specializations. As a matter of fact, SPLIT can be called m times in order to eliminate all specializations (all Ti.type) in ESm to get the pure entity structures. Because of Axiom 4, the denotation on specialization, each time SPLIT is called upon we can get n pure entity structures. We name any one of the resulting pure entity structures ESm2 in SPLITm(ESm). We can assume ESm2 = {R}, where

R.ent = T.ent,

R.type = T.type,

R.sub = { [Mji]Ti.ent I i ∈ {1 ... m}, Mji is from Ti.sub, and j ∈ {1 ... n}}.

These three equations are directly derived from the definition of SPLIT in simplified form.

Among all [Mji]Ti.ent in ESm2, we assume ki copies are made from Mi when applying the SPLIT operation. Consequently, we have the conditions that (1) all the ki's are nonnegative integers and (2) k1 + ... + kn = m. The order of elements in R.sub can thus be arranged in such a way that all [M1]Tj.ent comes first, followed by [M2]Tj.ent, and so forth. Here [Mk]Tj.ent stands for [Mkj]Tj.ent in the original form. Figure 11 shows ESm2 in a tree-like structure.

Now we we consider the case of D(TES). With the above ki's, we can make Si's with

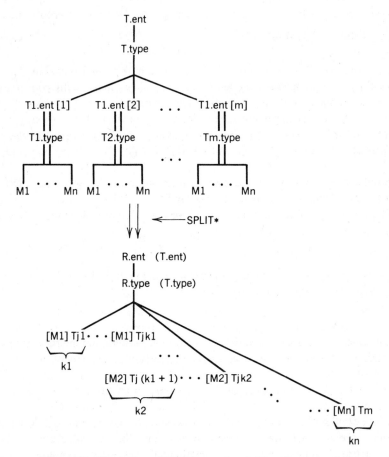

Figure 11. Illustration of SPLIT operation (in Transformation I).

ki copies of the element in Si.sub. Any one of the resulting entity structures can be shown as:

TES1 = { S, TS1, …,TSn } where for i in {1… n},
    TSi.ent = Si.ent, an entity (not a multiple entity),
    TSi.type = Si.type, an aspect (not a multiple aspect),
    TSi.sub = { [Mi]j | j ∈ {1 … ki}, Mi in Si.sub }.

By applying Axiom 1 to TES1, we have the final entity structure TES2 = { E }, where

E.ent = S.ent, an entity (not a multiple entity),
E.type = S.type, an aspect (not a multiple aspect),
E.sub = T1.sub ∪ … ∪ Tn.sub.

{ [M1]1, ... [M1]ki,

....

[Mm]1, ... [Mm]km }.

By comparing TES2 with ESm2, we are sure that they are equivalent since two entity structures have the same models as the components and with the same structure as a whole. In other words they have the same denotation.

So we conclude that any denoted entity structure from D(ES) obtained by applying SPLIT and DENOTATION can find an equivalent denoted entity structure from D(TES), also by applying SPLIT and DENOTATION. Thus D(ES) is included in D(TES).

Similarly, we can prove that D(TES) is included in D(ES). So we have D(ES) = D(TES). By definition of equivalence, we say ES == TES.

The correctness of Transformation II can be proved rigorously in the same way as Transformation I.

6 APPLICATIONS OF THE KNOWLEDGE FRAMEWORK: MULTIFACETED MODELING

The multifacetted modeling methodology [16] helps to deal in a coherent manner with the multiplicity of facets entailed in large-scale modeling and simulation applications. Design and synthesis of self-sufficient, ecologically stable habitats capable of supporting humans offers a state-of-the-art example of such applications. The following discusses several facets to which the system entity structure/model base knowledge representation scheme is relevant.

The entity structure provides a means of organizing the possible configurations of a system to be designed. Just as in the design of conventional artifacts, the design of a self-sufficient habitat must select combinations of components—biome ecosystems, plants and animals, and planting and harvesting schedules—that mutually support one another in achieving the goals of the system. Rozenblit [12] describes how pruning of the entity structure for a system design domain serves as a basis for the generation of families of design models which can be simulated and evaluated relative to the design objectives.

As a backdrop for design and decision making, a simulation environment must be able to support rapid development of various models at different levels of abstraction/ aggregation and oriented toward diverse objectives [16, 20]. To obviate having to start from scratch each time a model is needed, models may be kept in an organized library called a model base. The system entity structure organizes models in such model bases so that they can readily be retrieved and employed at the command of the designer/ decision maker or a computerized assistant. An environment of this kind for the domain of local area network design is described by Sevinc and Zeigler [13].

This approach requires that the model base be populated by models in modular form enabling hierarchical assembly and disassembly. Conventional discrete-event simulation languages are not well suited to these demands. The successful development of

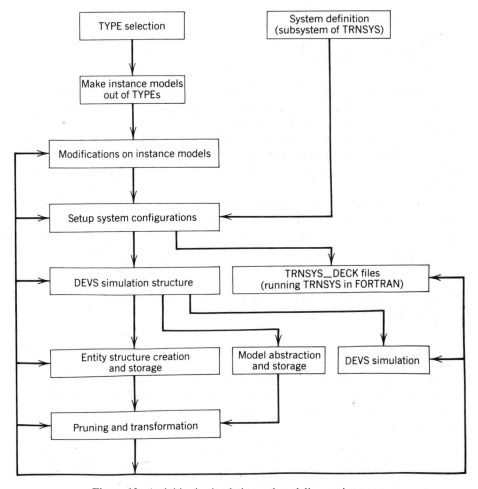

Figure 12. Activities in simulation and modeling environment.

DEVS-Scheme, mentioned earlier, shows that hierarchical, modular construction of models can be conveniently realized in object-oriented, LISP-based programming systems. Figure 12 depicts the kinds of activities supported by the DEVS-Scheme interface to TRNSYS, a simulation model base supporting design of habitat microclimate management. Such activities include definition and modification of TRNSYS model types, specification of coupling relations (system configurations), and translation to TRNSYS simulation executable files. Moreover, facilities are also provided to automatically derive entity structures from model specifications and amalgamate them into a single entity structure [16]. Thus a modeler can define and simulate models, place them into a model base, and later prune the entity structure to reuse them in new configurations.

An important consideration in the design of self-sufficient habitats is that, unlike a well-understood engineering domain, many of the conditions encountered and questions which are raised are novel, and knowledge is lacking. In this "ill-defined systems" context, it is especially important to employ extensive cross-checking of computations (e.g., the predictions of models at various levels of aggregation). As has been indicated, organization of these models is facilitated by the entity structure.

The system entity structure representation serves as a framework upon which to organize the vast amounts of data to be collected for observation and analysis of habitat operation. The data can be pigeon-holed in slots organized first according to the entities representing conceptual components of the real system and then in the various levels of aggregation represented in the entity structure.

Data collected and stored in an archiving system compatible with the entity structure facilitates the calibration and validation of models. Since the data is organized by entity and by level of aggregation, it directly relates to models in the model base that are organized according to the same scheme. Since real-system data and model-generated data can be readily compared, the basis exists for automatic model calibration and validation.

A self-sufficient habitat is expected to encounter many new kinds of deviant behaviors, such as gas imbalances and plant epidemics, that must be dealt with in a timely manner. Simulations to discover corrective actions and predictions of their effects will play a major role in such failure management. Availability of models at various levels of aggregation will once again be crucial in such procedures. Coarse models with fast simulation characteristics may be employed to develop initial responses in crisis situations. More accurate, dissagregated models may then be employed to validate and refine the initial responses or indeed to abort them in favor of better considered responses. Organization of these models is facilitated by the system entity structure.

7   CONCLUSIONS

Viewing reality as composed of systems, we have proposed a framework in which both system structure and behavior are knowable by a computer. System structure, in the form of decomposition, taxonomic, and coupling relationships, are represented in the system entity structure, a generative frame-based scheme. System behavior is encoded in a base of models, represented by procedural formalisms, of classical or recent vintage. We have presented a set-theoretic formulation of the system entity structure which allows us to rigorously characterize its important transformations. Applications of the system entity structure to simulation-based design, modeling, and operation of self-sufficient habitats illustrate the use of the knowledge representation framework.

ACKNOWLEDGMENTS

Research reported herein was partially supported by National Science Foundation grants DCR8407230 ("Distributed Simulation of Hierarchical, Multicomponent Models") and CCR8714148 ("Intelligent Simulation Environment for Advanced Computer Architecture").

REFERENCES

1. D. Belogus, "Multifacetted Modelling and Simulation Methodology: A Software Engineering Implementation," Doctoral Dissertation, Weizmann Institute of Science, Israel, 1983.
2. D. G. Bobrow, *Qualitative Reasoning about Physical Systems*, MIT Press, Cambridge, MA, 1985.
3. S. H. Hardt, "Aspects of Qualitative Reasoning and Simulation for Knowledge Intensive Problem Solving," in M. S. Elzas, T. I. Oren, and B. P. Zeigler (Eds.), *Modelling and Simulation Methodology: Knowledge Systems*, North-Holland, Amsterdam, in press.
4. P. Klahr, "Expressibility in ROSS, an Object-oriented Simulation System," in G. C. Vansteenkiste, E. J. H. Kerckhoffs, and B. P. Zeigler (Eds.), *Artificial Intelligence in Simulation*, SCS Publications, San Diego, CA, 1986.
5. G. J. Klir, *Architecture of Systems Problem Solving*, Plenum, New York, 1985.
6. R. O'Keefe, "Simulation and Expert Systems— A Taxonomy and Some Examples." *Simulation*, **46**(1):10–16, 1986.
7. F. Pichler, "Dynamic Systems Concepts," Source-Book, in R. Trappl (Ed.), *Cybernetics and Systems Research*, Hemisphere, Washington, DC, 1985.
8. R. Rajagopalan, "The Role of Qualitative Reasoning in Simulation," in G. C. Vansteenkiste, E. J. H. Kerckhoffs, and B. P. Zeigler (Eds.), *Artificial Intelligence in Simulation*, SCS Publications, San Diego, CA, 1986.
9. Y. V. Reddy, M. S. Fox, and N. Husain, "Automating the Analysis of Simulations in KBS," *Proceedings of the SCS Multiconference*, SCS Publications, San Diego, CA, 1985.
10. Y. V. Reddy, M. S. Fox, N. Husain, and M. McRoberts, "The Knowledge-Based Simulation System," *IEEE Software*, pp. 26–37, March, 1986.
11. J. W. Rozenblit, S. Sevinc, and B. P. Zeigler, "Knowledge-based Design of LANs Using System Entity Structure Concepts," in J. R. Wilson, J. O. Hendriksen, and S. D. Roberts (Eds.), *Proceedings of the Winter Simulation Conference, Washington, DC*, SCS Publications, San Diego, CA, 1986.
12. J. W. Rozenblit, "A Conceptual Base for Knowledge Based System Design," Doctoral Dissertation, Wayne State University, Detroit, 1985.
13. J. W. Rozenblit and B. P. Zeigler, "Design and Modelling Concepts," in R. Dorf and S. Nef (Eds.), *Encyclopedia of Robotics*, Wiley, New York, 1987.
14. J. W. Rozenblit and Y. Huang, "Constraint-driven Generation of Model Structures," *Proceedings of the Winter Simulation Conference, Atlanta, GA,* pp. 604–611, SCS Publications, San Diego, CA, 1987.
15. S. Sevinc and B. P. Zeigler, "Entity Structure Based Design Methodology: A LAN Protocol Example,'" *IEEE Transactions on Software Engineering*, **14**(3):375–383, February 1988.
16. B. P. Zeigler, *Multifacetted Modelling and Discrete Event Simulation*, Academic, London, 1984.
17. B. P. Zeigler, "DEVS-Scheme: A Lisp-based Environment for Hierarchical, Modular Discrete Event Models," Technical Report AIS-2, CERL Laboratory, Department of ECE, University of Arizona, Tucson, AZ, 1986.
18. B. P. Zeigler, "Knowledge Representation from Newton to Minsky and Beyond," *Applied Artificial Intelligence*, **1**:87–107, 1987.

19. B. P. Zeigler, "Hierarchical, Modular Discrete Event Modelling in an Object Oriented Environment," *Simulation Journal,* **49**(5):219–230, November 1987.

20. B. P. Zeigler and T. I. Oren, "Multifacetted, Multiparadigm Modelling Perspectives: Tools for the 90s," in *Proceedings of the Winter Simulation Conference,* pp. 708–712, *Washington, DC,* SCS Publications, San Diego, CA, 1986.

21. Solar Energy Laboratory, *TRNSYS Manual,* Solar Energy Laboratory, University of Wisconsin at Madison, December 1983.

3 The Nature of Modeling

JEFF ROTHENBERG

The RAND Corporation
Santa Monica, California

1 INTRODUCTION

Modeling is one of the most fundamental processes of the human mind. Yet it is often misunderstood in ways that seriously limit our ability to function coherently and effectively in the world. The use of inappropriate models (or the inappropriate use of modeling itself) is responsible for countless disasters of personal, technological, and historical proportions. Modeling is the quintessential human conceptual tool. Yet it is rarely examined from a theoretical point of view and therefore rarely mastered.

This chapter attempts to define modeling precisely. It surveys the kinds of models human beings use and discusses their motivations, advantages, and limitations. It places simulation in this context and surveys various kinds of computerized simulation. It then discusses artificial intelligence in the broadest terms, highlighting a few of its most relevant aspects, and attempts to show how AI can contribute to—and how it depends on—modeling. Finally, it suggests that the traditional view of simulation is too narrow and should be expanded to encompass more of modeling, leading to "knowledge-based simulation." This is illustrated in terms of ongoing research at The RAND Corporation.

2 OVERVIEW OF MODELING

Modeling in its broadest sense is **the cost-effective use of something in place of something else for some cognitive purpose.** It allows us to use something that is simpler, safer, or cheaper than reality instead of reality for some purpose. A model *represents* reality for the given purpose; the model is an abstraction of reality in the sense that it cannot represent all aspects of reality. This allows us to deal with the world in a simplified manner, avoiding the complexity, danger, and irreversibility of reality.

Modeling underlies our ability to think and imagine, to use signs and language, to communicate, to generalize from experience, to deal with the unexpected, and to make sense out of the raw bombardment of our sensations. It allows us to see patterns, to appreciate, predict, and manipulate processes and things, and to express meaning and purpose. In short, it is one of the most essential activities of the human mind. It is the foundation of what we call intelligent behavior and is a large part of what makes us human. We are, in a word, **modelers:** creatures that build and use models routinely, habitually—sometimes even compulsively—to face, understand, and interact with reality.

Using an inappropriate model to deal with reality can do considerable harm. How many patients were killed by Medieval bloodletting who might otherwise have recovered? How many children have been locked into Procrustean roles by models such as *girls are not good at math* or *boys are not intuitive?* How many computer programs do the wrong thing correctly? These are all cases of using incorrect or inappropriate models. There are even cases where using any model at all is inappropriate. For example, relating to someone in terms of a model precludes the comprehension and appreciation of the richness and unpredictability that distinguish living beings from rocks and tractors.

In order to avoid inappropriate choices and uses of models, it is vital to formulate a clear definition of what a model really is, what constitutes a good, appropriate model, and how to judge when using a particular model (or *any* model) is justified.

3   OTHER MODELS OF MODELING

Before developing our own definition, it is useful to discuss some of the literature on modeling. The subject is as broad as human intellectual endeavor itself since modeling is the intellect's tool of choice. At one extreme lie fundamental points of view on how we approach reality, tracing their roots to Plato and Aristotle. For example, Kant contends that reality in and of itself (the "noumenon") is unknowable and that the "forms of our perception" constitute what is effectively an inherent and unavoidable modeling process (though he does not use this term) that separates us from the noumenon [25]. A survey of this subject would amount to a synopsis of much of philosophy, which is beyond the scope of this chapter.

At another extreme, formal model theory in mathematical logic defines the semantics of a propositional language as a "model" that specifies what can be concluded validly from what [13]. Model theory (despite its name) is somewhat esoteric to the discussion at hand, in that it focuses on formal properties of one particular kind of model (i.e., logical) rather than on modeling as a whole [49].

Of greater relevance is the literature on the application of specific modeling techniques in application areas such as systems analysis and decision support. These discussions tend to be concrete enough to be relevant to real-world modelers while being abstract enough to provide insight into modeling in general.

From this applied perspective, modeling is often seen as a way of gaining control over the world [47] or of making decisions or answering questions about the world [7, 11, 14, 18, 23, 33, 35, 39, 43, 46]. It is widely recognized that the purpose of a model must be understood before the model can be discussed [12, 33]. The purposes to which models may be put are frequently categorized as being either *descriptive* (describing or explaining the world) or *prescriptive* (prescribing optimal solutions to problems) [14, 34, 39]. Prescriptive uses of a model are sometimes further distinguished from *normative* uses (such as identifying feasible goals or standards [18]) and from *idealization* (allowing the construction of hypothetical, ideal entities that illuminate real-world phenomena [21]). Specific uses of models include projection (conditional forecasting), prediction (unconditional forecasting), allocation and derivation (e.g., of expected demands for resources or services [18]), as well as hypothesis testing, experimentation, and explanation [21].

Models are generally assumed to have an analogous or imitative relationship to some real-world phenomenon or system, though this assumption is often only implicit. Even where explicit, this assumption usually remains vague and intuitive [18, 33, 46]. Since most work in modeling is carried out for a particular purpose within a particular application domain, most discussions touch only lightly on abstract modeling issues before elaborating specific techniques.

Some writers [18, 39, 46, 50] point out that models can be characterized in many alternative ways, but most suggest categorizations specific to the application areas under consideration. Models may be characterized in terms of their form, their relationship to reality, their purpose, the way they interact with their users, the way they are used, their assumptions about the certainty of their data (i.e., deterministic vs. probabilistic models), their treatment of time (static vs. dynamic and continuous vs. discrete-state models), the kinds of questions they can answer, the kinds of answers they give, and so on.

It is tempting to try to describe models in terms of their form, but the definition of form is subjective. For example, models can be described as physical or symbolic; however, physical (i.e., material) models are sometimes divided into "iconic" (or "schematic" [18]) and "analog" models, whereas symbolic models may be thought of either as strictly mathematical [7, 14, 18, 34] or as nonmaterial (i.e., including conceptual, or "mental," models) [21, 33, 39].

Furthermore, the physical–symbolic dichotomy is sometimes extended to include disparate terms, thereby subverting a simple material–immaterial interpretation. For example, simulation [14] or role playing (i.e., "gaming") [18] may be added to the categories "physical" and "symbolic," producing heterogeneous classification schemes. In addition, many terms have multiple meanings in the literature; for example, "iconic" may include physical models of houses, engineering drawings, and maps [7, 27, 34], or it may be restricted to the former meaning (physical miniatures), while a different term (e.g., "analog" [24], or "physical" model [18]) is used to include things such as maps. On the other hand, the term "analog" may be used to denote a physical model that uses analog processes such as water or electrical flow to model dynamic phenomena [7, 27, 34].

Mathematical models can themselves be classified as continuous versus discrete and as deductive (proceeding from a priori knowledge or axioms), inductive (generalizing from observed behavior), or pragmatic (relying on a means–end oriented engineering approach) [47]. Analytical techniques (for which closed-form solutions exist, permitting optimization) are sometimes contrasted to numerical techniques [7]. Because of their formality, analytical techniques are seen as capable of representing only limited aspects of the real world [46]. Explicit computerized models (as compared to implicit mental models) are seen as having potential advantages including rigor, accessibility, comprehensiveness, logic, and flexibility [33, 39].

Mathematical modeling encompasses the use of qualitative interaction (or "impact") matrix techniques such as Leopold matrices as well as numerical optimization techniques [22]. In addition to optimization (or "mathematical programming") based on network theory, PERT, calculus, and so on, there are a wide range of stochastic techniques drawn from areas including queuing theory and inventory theory, as well as general statistical techniques including multivariate analysis (factor, principle component, discriminate analysis, etc.), statistical inference, and decision theory [34]. Finally, no discussion of real-world modeling can ignore the issues of data availability, reliability, quality, and relevance [18, 22, 23].

There is little consensus on how simulation relates to modeling, or even what the word "simulation" means. It is either thought of as (1) a way of using models that is more general than any particular kind of model [14, 18, 23, 27, 39] or (2) a specialized kind of model that makes use of a particular subset of the available modeling techniques [7, 9, 22, 24, 34]. Nevertheless, there is some consensus that simulation is a dynamic, imitative kind of modeling [9, 14, 18, 24, 27] that tends to be a technique of "last resort" used to model phenomena that are poorly understood or for which more rigorous techniques are unavailable [9, 22].

The following discussion attempts to synthesize a coherent definition of modeling and simulation.

4 DEFINITION OF MODELING

Precisely what do we mean by modeling? Modeling is a way of dealing with things or situations that are too "costly" to deal with directly (where "cost" is interpreted in the broadest sense). Any model is characterized by three essential attributes:

1. *Reference:* It is *of* something (its *"referent"*).
2. *Purpose:* It has an intended cognitive *purpose* with respect to its referent.
3. *Cost-effectiveness:* It is more *cost-effective* to use the model for this purpose than to use the referent itself.

To *model,* then, is to represent a particular referent cost-effectively for a particular cognitive purpose.[1]

The referent and purpose of a model must be well defined; otherwise all three criteria become meaningless. For example, a video game need not represent anything real; there may be some video games based on models (e.g., flight simulators), but most are "pseudo-models." The notion of a "game" implies an *incidental* relationship to reality, or the fabrication of a "pseudo-reality." It is tempting to "back-project" a pseudo-model into a corresponding pseudo-reality, thereby becoming convinced that the pseudo-model is a bona fide model [44]. However, in addition to being misleading, this process is also indeterminate, since the modeling abstraction cannot be reversed deterministi-

---

[1]Verbal forms such as "modeling" and "to model" are used here to denote the entire enterprise of building and using models. Some authors reserve these forms for the process of developing a model as opposed to using one [23]; however, this usage precludes saying that a model "models" its referent. Terms such as "model building" will be used here to achieve this distinction.

cally. Even if a purpose and cost-effectiveness criterion are fabricated for a pseudo-model, the fact that it can be back-projected into any number of equally possible pseudo-realities makes it worthless as a model.

The referent of a model need not actually exist, but it must be objectively testable in order to serve as "reality" for the model. It is reasonable to model a fictitious or hypothetical reality (e.g., the psyche of Oedipus, the terrain of Camelot, or the flight characteristics of a proposed airplane), but only if the referent has some objective form against which the validity of the model can be verified.

The purpose of a model may include comprehension or manipulation of its referent, communication, planning, prediction, gaining experience, appreciation, and so on. In some cases this purpose can be characterized by the kinds of questions that may be asked of the model. For example, **prediction** corresponds to asking questions of the form *"What if . . . ?"* (where the user asks what would happen if the referent began in some initial state and behaved as described by the model). This is analogous to applying "if–then" rules in the forward direction (i.e., "forward chaining").

On the other hand, **goal-directed** questions are concerned with finding an initial state or condition of the referent (along with constraints or conditions of the model itself) that can lead to a given result. This is analogous to the use of if–then rules in the backward direction (i.e., "backward chaining") or to mathematical optimization techniques.

There are also **definitive** questions that ask whether certain states, conditions, or actions are *ever* possible for the referent. These correspond to proving assertions about the referent by using the model. Finally, there are **explanatory** questions that seek to explain the behavior of the referent by showing how some state is reached or what the referent's reasons are for acting in a certain way.

Even an exhaustive list of such questions could not characterize all possible purposes of a model. A model may be intended for appreciation of its referent, in which case its user may not ask any questions of it at all. The purpose of a model is constrained only by the ingenuity of its builder and user.

It is impossible to evaluate—or intelligently use—a model without understanding its purpose. Calling something "a model" of its referent without further qualification makes it impossible to know which aspects of the referent are being modeled and which are not. No model can faithfully reproduce *all* aspects of its referent (since only the referent itself can do this). Therefore, without specifying its intended purpose, it is almost impossible to prevent using a model for purposes for which it may be highly inappropriate. This can have dire consequences if decisions and actions are based on false predictions or understanding. Similarly, it is imperative to have a clear statement of the intended purpose of a model before trying to build it. Otherwise it is impossible to decide which aspects of the referent must be modeled and with what fidelity.

Yet knowing a model's purpose is not enough. It must also be more cost-effective to use the model for the given purpose than to use its referent, either because it is impossible to use the referent directly or because using the referent would be dangerous, inconvenient, or (generally) expensive in some relevant coin. This cost-effectiveness criterion is central to the notion of modeling. Without it, there is never any reason to use a model in place of its referent. The cost-effectiveness criterion of a model must be known in order to judge the model's value.

Judging the cost-effectiveness of a model requires answering two questions: "What does it claim to buy?" and "Does it buy this?" In addition, building a model requires asking two prior questions: "Is this the most appropriate thing to be bought by the proposed model?" (i.e., "Is this the most appropriate cost-effectiveness criterion on which to base the proposed model?") and "Will the model's cost-effectiveness pay for the cost of building it in the first place?"

The cost-effectiveness criterion is a kind of Occam's razor for modeling: It allows models of equal power to be compared and evaluated. However, whereas Occam's razor applies the criterion of *simplicity* (or "parsimony"), here the costs to be compared and evaluated are stated explicitly as part of the cost-effectiveness criterion. Since the criterion is *not necessarily* simplicity, it follows that a model is not necessarily simpler than its referent. A model may actually be *more complex* than its referent if in so doing it satisfies some valid cost-effectiveness criterion other than simplicity.

Since a model cannot be identical to its referent, it is always an *abstraction* of its referent in the sense that it can never be completely faithful to it. The fact that a model may be more complex than its referent implies that abstraction does not necessarily result in simplification, as is usually assumed. Although we sometimes appear to model something by using the thing itself, this always involves using the referent in some unusual way or restricted mode that offers some advantage over using it directly (an example of this is the modeling of human behavior by asking human subjects how they would act in hypothetical situations).

The criteria of **purpose** and **cost-effectiveness for that purpose** together determine which features of the referent must be modeled (and with what accuracy) and which features can be ignored. These criteria provide a complete functional characterization of a model. In addition, they determine a number of key "pragmatic" characteristics such as who the intended users of the model are and how the results of using the model must be presented in order to be usable (i.e., understandable) by those users. These can be thought of as **interface** issues: For a model to fulfill its stated purpose cost-effectively, it must be appropriately *useful to* and *usable by* its intended users.

There is also the pragmatic issue of how a model is to be maintained. This depends on how likely the model is to change and evolve over its lifetime, how extensible it needs to be, and who will be maintaining it. Accounting properly for these **maintenance** issues requires that the *purpose* of the model allows for its evolution over its entire projected lifetime and that its *cost-effectiveness criterion* considers the cost of maintaining it over this lifetime.

5   MODELS, SYMBOLS, AND REPRESENTATIONS

The preceding definition clarifies what are often blurred distinctions, namely, those among models, symbols, and representations. A **representation** can be *any* use of something in place of something else. It *need not* (though it *may*) have a purpose or a cost-effectiveness criterion. That is, a model is a special kind of representation. Similarly, **names** and **symbols** are representations but are not models.

To some extent these distinctions depend on how something is used. A model may be used degenerately as a symbol for the thing it models: For example, the formula $E = mc^2$ is a mathematical model for the relationship between energy and mass, but the formula has become a popular symbol for all of Einstein's work and even modern physics as a whole. Similarly, an object may be usable as a model whether or not it was intended as one. The megalithic structure at Stonehenge may be interpreted as an astronomical model [19], but it is unlikely that that was its intended purpose [10].

6 EXAMPLES OF DIFFERENT TYPES OF MODELS

There are many ways of modeling a given thing or phenomenon, including physical analogs, closed-form mathematical representations, conceptual metaphors, linguistic formalisms, simulation, and many others. A given model (of any of these types) has strengths and weaknesses depending on its fidelity, utility, "computational cost" (i.e., the amount of work required to use the model), and pragmatic considerations including its suitability for various kinds of users and its maintainability. Whereas a given type of model may *tend* to have certain characteristics (e.g., physical analogs tend to be more static and harder to modify than mathematical models), there are no invariant rules about which types of model display which strengths and weaknesses. Some examples will make this more concrete.

A street map is a physical analog that provides some kinds of information (such as connectivity) but usually not others (such as elevation). It can answer some kinds of questions easily (such as "Can I get from A to B?") while others (such as "How long is the shortest route from A to B?") may require considerable computation [3]. It is used for comprehension, communication, and planning; its cost-effectiveness derives from the difficulty of comprehending the layout of a city directly. It is relatively inflexible and hard to "maintain" either by the cartographer who creates it or by its user, who can at most add annotations to it.

Mathematical models come in many flavors. The darling of modern physics is the theory called quantum electrodynamics (QED), which describes the quantum mechanics. This model has achieved unprecedented accuracy of prediction over a range of dozens of orders of magnitude in scale [37]. However, it is relatively inaccessible and incomprehensible to all but physicists, and the cost of using it is relatively high even for the most mathematically astute and computationally well armed.

Formal logic has made great strides in recent years, with the advent of efficient algorithms for the constructive proof of certain restricted classes of assertions [4, 40]. This has resulted in a new generation of computer programming languages, typified by PROLOG [48]. Models based on these formalisms have a compelling similarity to the "natural logic" of everyday language. For example, it is easy to write a PROLOG program that defines intuitive models of the relationships in a family and then to ask questions such as "Who are John's sisters, cousins, and aunts?" Unfortunately, such models are relatively opaque to all but PROLOG programmers.

Conceptual metaphors are models consisting of ideas that shape the way we think about reality [16]. They introduce the intentional fiction that the referent is similar to some other better-known object or phenomenon. For example, the development of mechanical clocks had a profound influence on literary, philosophical, and religious models of the universe. Similarly, the simplistic view of the atom as a miniature solar system provides comprehension, though it has poor predictive power. Closer to home, the metaphor of the human brain as a computer is one of the driving motivations for AI. Conceptual models such as these form the paradigms that shape the thought of science and society as a whole [31].

Simulation is a form of modeling whose purpose is usually comprehension, planning, prediction, and manipulation. It can be defined broadly as a behavioral or phenomenological approach to modeling; that is, a simulation is an active, behavioral analog of its referent. The essence of simulation is that it unfolds over time. It models sequences and (possibly) timings of events in the real world. Simulation is a *process* in which a model of *any* kind is used to imitate (some aspect of) the behavior of its referent. Simulation is a kind of *modeling* rather than a kind of model. It denotes an action (process) rather than a thing. However, the term is often used as a modifier of "model" (i.e., "simulation model"), with the word "model" itself often being omitted in such cases (e.g., when speaking of a "weather simulation"). Nevertheless, what is meant in these cases is the *use* of a model *as* a simulation.

Simulation is generally used to answer what-if questions. It can also be used to answer questions of causality by generating a sequence of events from which one can attempt to infer what caused what. As traditionally conceived, simulation works only in this "forward" direction: The user "winds it up" and lets it run to see what happens.

In some cases, one type of model may evolve or transmute into a different form. For example, there is some evidence that writing may have evolved from the use of physical analogs [42]. This putative evolution highlights the difficulty of distinguishing too sharply between physical analogs and symbols.

7 CHOOSING AMONG TYPES OF MODELS

The three criteria of reference, purpose, and cost-effectiveness provide complete functional and pragmatic requirements for a model. But given a purpose with respect to some reality and a measure of cost-effectiveness, what determines which type of model should be used?

Most of the trade-offs among the types are in terms of pragmatic issues (flexibility, extensibility, and suitability to different user groups) rather than among their functional abilities to fulfill various purposes cost-effectively. Furthermore, these pragmatic trade-offs are often relative; for example, differential equations may be comprehensible to mathematicians, whereas intricate physical analogs may be more comprehensible to those with well-developed mechanical intuition. Conceptual metaphors have the advantage that they are immaterial and therefore require no apparatus for their use; in addition, they tend to be relatively simple and therefore accessible to a large community of users. Yet the lack of substance limits their computational power and may make them *inaccessible* to users who find abstractions hard to grasp. In contrast, physical analogs are highly tangible but therefore have limited accessibility and may be difficult to modify and maintain.

Even with strong pragmatic constraints, the choice of which type of model to use is rarely determined by the requirements. The preferences and convenience of the model builders and users may ultimately dictate one type over another, but there are often several viable alternatives.

The following sections concentrate on one particular form of modeling—namely, computerized simulation—not because it is *best* but because of its relevance in the context of this book.

8   COMPUTER SIMULATION

Implementing a simulation as a computer program results in unsurpassed flexibility; the malleability of the programming medium means that in principle (acknowledging the difficulty of producing programs without bugs) it is possible to refine, evolve, and extend a computer-based simulation in ways that are difficult to match in any other medium. Modern programming environments also facilitate the development of modular data and program code that (again, ideally) allow new simulations to be built using pieces of existing ones.

Computer simulation can be divided into **analytic** and **discrete-state** approaches. The analytic approach brings the power of mathematical analysis to bear on problems that can be understood or approximated analytically. For example, in cases where the reality being modeled can be accurately described by a set of differential equations (as in the flow of heat over a surface), analytic solutions of those equations can be used to generate the time-dependent behavior required for simulation.

Though closed-form solutions are often mathematically elegant, this very elegance may make them cryptic and incomprehensible. By reducing reality to an abstract mathematical relationship, they may obscure the understanding that is being sought. There are also cases in which analytic solutions are known, but feasible means of computing these solutions are not available. Nevertheless, analytic simulations are indispensable in many situations, particularly when dealing with complex physical phenomena involving vast numbers of relatively small and relatively similar entities whose individual interactions are relatively simple and whose aggregate interactions obey the "law of large numbers" (i.e., permit statistical treatment). In such cases, analytic models often represent at least one form of "complete" understanding.

There remains a large class of problems, however, that are not well enough understood to be handled analytically, that is, for which no formal mathematical solutions exist. These problems usually involve small to large (but not "vast") collections of interacting entities each of whose behavior is understood reasonably well in isolation and whose low-level, pairwise interactions with each other are known but whose high-level, group interactions are not well understood. The strategy of discrete-state simulation is to encode the known low-level interactions and "run" the resulting simulation in the hope that the overall behavior of the system will approximate that of its referent and (ideally) that higher-level interactions will reveal themselves.

Time is dealt with in discrete-state simulations as a succession of separate "states" in which entities interact; time advances discretely, either in fixed "ticks" of a simulated clock (referred to as "time-based" simulation) or whenever something significant happens (referred to as "event-based" simulation).

Discrete-state simulation can be viewed as a last resort for modeling certain kinds of intractable problems. Its power lies in its ability to reveal high-level patterns of interaction that cannot be recognized in other ways. It is often possible to enumerate and describe a collection of entities and their immediate interactions without knowing where these interactions lead; if this knowledge is encoded in a discrete-state simulation and the behavior of the resulting model is observed, deeper understanding will often emerge.

9   A MODELING PERSPECTIVE ON AI

Artificial intelligence is one of the frontiers of computer science. It has traditionally been concerned with problems that have not yet yielded to solution by "conventional" means. The quest for computer intelligence has two distinct motivations, which might be referred to (guardedly) as "modeling" and "engineering." The modeling approach seeks to model the way we perform tasks that require intelligence; it therefore attempts to identify problems that we recognize as requiring intelligence, and it seeks to elucidate the mechanisms we employ in our own solutions of those problems. The engineering approach, on the other hand, is concerned with producing systems that solve useful problems, regardless of whether their solutions require "intelligence" or involve mechanisms parallel to our own.

The modeling approach to AI begins from a psychological or philosophical departure point: Given a conceptual theory of intelligence, can we embody that theory in a computer model? Computer models make such theories concrete, allowing them to be tested, validated, and refined. The modeling approach to AI therefore views the implementation of computerized models as a key technique for understanding intelligence. In addition, these models often suggest novel mechanisms that may become part of the conceptual theory itself. It is this kind of feedback that has led to the popular conception of the brain as a computer. In addition, insights gained from AI models (as often from their failures as from their successes) have contributed to major theoretical revisions in areas ranging from linguistics to cognitive psychology.

The engineering approach to AI has a different departure point: Since computers are not organisms, why not use them to their best advantage to try to solve useful problems, without worrying about whether they are solving them the way we would? This approach works in symbiosis with the modeling approach; when a given model fails to work, sound engineering often suggests a solution. While these solutions are sometimes ad hoc, they may reveal flaws in the conceptual theory that engendered the model, thereby suggesting revisions to the theory. The engineering approach to AI has the sometimes frustrating attribute that whenever it succeeds in solving a problem (or even approaches success), its results tend to be appropriated by "conventional" computer science or engineering, with the result that AI receives no credit for the eventual solution. This has occurred repeatedly in AI's history (examples include list processing, character recognition, speech synthesis, and demons), contributing to the only partially facetious adage that "AI never *solves* any problem—by *definition*."

AI has made many contributions to computer science and software engineering. It is arid to try to distinguish too sharply between what is AI and what is not; at any given time there are a set of unsolved problems in computer science to which AI has laid claim. Often these problems are also attacked from other quarters of computer science, and it is not always easy to assign credit for the solutions that eventually emerge. It is sufficient to note that AI has had some part in solving—or is currently attempting to solve—a number of problems that have direct bearing on simulation and modeling. Of particular relevance are the object-oriented programming paradigm, demons, planning, search techniques, taxonomic inference via inheritance hierarchies, forward and backward chaining, qualitative reasoning, truth maintenance, proof procedures for formal logic, neural nets, and the representation of spatial and temporal phenomena, uncertainty, plans, goals, and beliefs.

The next section can only hint at some of the most important areas of overlapping research and cross-fertilization between AI and simulation.

10   AI IN SIMULATION AND SIMULATION IN AI

The term "simulation" is traditionally taken to mean only a very specific kind of modeling. Having gone to the trouble of encoding the requisite knowledge for building a simulation, one should attempt to derive the maximum benefit from this knowledge. That is, in addition to "running" the simulation to answer what-if questions, one should be able to utilize the full range of inferencing, reasoning, and search methods that are available in AI. This broad view of simulation is referred to as **knowledge-based simulation.**

There is a well-entrenched tendency to view simulation narrowly as a way of making predictions by running an encoded behavioral model. The major impact of AI on simulation should be to encourage simulation to make use of other kinds of modeling as well: The result will still be a phenomenological model but one that can take full advantage of additional modeling techniques to answer questions that are of interest to its users. This natural, though long-overdue, extension of simulation can be referred to as **beyond "what-if."**

Discrete-state simulation has derived great benefit from many of the techniques developed in AI. The object-oriented paradigm, though it first appeared in SIMULA [8], owes its present state of refinement to AI language efforts such as SMALLTALK [17] and ROSS [32]. The object-oriented approach to discrete-state simulation has many advantages despite its shortcomings [41]. For example, the appropriate use of inheritance hierarchies (or lattices) greatly simplifies the specification of a complex simulation, producing highly comprehensible models [29]. Searching and planning techniques developed in AI should make it feasible to simulate the behavior of human decision makers in environments involving "command and control," while backward chaining should help answer questions about how to achieve a given result. Techniques for representing goals and beliefs should help build simulations that can explain the behavior of simulated entities.

Analytic simulation has tended to look to mathematics rather than AI for its methods, but here too there are possibilities on the horizon. One example is recent work at the RAND Corporation in sensitivity analysis (a sorely neglected problem in simulation), which uses AI techniques to represent and propagate sensitivity information through a computation. This avoids the need to recompute sensitivity for every nested function call whenever some higher-level function is perturbed to probe its sensitivity to changes in its parameters. We also foresee the use of symbolic algebra programs such as REDUCE [20] to apply expert algebraic manipulation to analytic functions within a simulation.

AI programs have a long history of using models as sources of internal expertise. An early example is Gelernter's geometry machine [15], which embedded a model of a geometry student's diagram and used a "diagram computer" to test hypotheses against this internal diagram. The geometry machine's stated motivation was to solve problems generally considered to require intelligence; here the "engineering" approach converged with the modeling approach in choosing a solution based on a model of how we ourselves solve geometry problems; being inveterate modelers, we use a model (i.e., a diagram).

Another classic example of an embedded model in an AI system is SOPHIE [5], which taught electronic circuit diagnosis by means of an interactive dialog. In order to allow students to ask hypothetical questions (e.g., "What would happen if I measured the voltage across points A and B?"), SOPHIE used a simulator of the electronic circuit being diagnosed. Here the simulator was treated as a source of expertise about electronic circuits. The AI program that conducted the dialog with the student did not attempt to know all the answers to all possible questions the user might ask; instead, it answered those questions by consulting its internal model of reality, that is, running its embedded simulation.

It is generally acknowledged that in order to exhibit more than superficial intelligence, AI systems must make use of "deep structures," or models of reality such as those described in the preceding. Simple action–response rules can produce programs that perform impressively up to a point, but beyond that point there is no escaping the need to imbue programs with real "understanding" of the world, at least within their domains. The way to provide such understanding is to endow a program with a model of the world that it can use to answer a wide range of unanticipated questions arising from its need to act (or reply to queries) appropriately in that world. These ideas are discussed further in the next section.

11   KNOWLEDGE-BASED SIMULATION AT THE RAND CORPORATION

A number of research efforts are currently attempting to blend AI and simulation in a new discipline called **knowledge-based simulation.** In order to elaborate the ideas of the previous section, the following describes our current research in this area at the RAND Corporation.

Artificial intelligence and simulation have been major areas of research at RAND for many years [30]. The work of Newell, Shaw, and Simon at RAND in the 1950s [36] was one of AI's earliest successes and defined many areas that continue to be focal points for AI research. More recently RAND's research in expert systems produced the languages RITA [1, 2] and ROSIE [26, 45] as well as several expert system applications (including LDS [51], TATR [6], and SAL [38]). Similarly, RAND's long history of simulation research produced the SIMSCRIPT language [28] as well as both theoretical and experimental results in game theory and Monte Carlo simulation. RAND began applying AI to simulation in the late 1970s and early 1980s. The development of the object-oriented ROSS language clearly demonstrated that AI could benefit simulation technology. The knowledge-based simulation project continues this tradition.

The goal of the KBSim project is to make simulations both more powerful and more comprehensible by (1) allowing modelers to build, validate, evolve, and maintain more powerful and realistic simulations that model a wider range of relevant phenomena and (2) allowing users to interact with these simulations in ways that provide deeper understanding of the phenomena being modeled. Making simulations more powerful requires extending the kinds of modeling they can perform and the kinds of questions they can answer (as discussed in the preceding). Making simulations more comprehensible requires developing techniques for what we call **intelligent exploration and explanation,** that is, allowing users to modify both the model and the course of events in a simulation and making the simulation explain its behavior in useful ways. Our context is the object-oriented, discrete-state simulation of objects in a geographical setting.

This research has spawned a number of distinct tasks, the first of which involves reasoning about simulation behavior. This includes being able to ask goal-directed questions, questions about whether or how an initial state can produce a desired result, questions about the possible values of variables in a simulation, questions about the interactions of objects or factors, questions about the goals of an object, and questions about why an object performed an action. The inability of current discrete-state simulations to answer such questions derives from limitations in their representational and inferential capabilities stemming from the fact that knowledge is represented implicitly in procedural code and is therefore not amenable to inference. Support for reasoning requires representing the behavior of objects in ways that allow the use of automated reasoning techniques (such as forward and backward chaining) and integrating these with other forms of inference, such as those based on the use of object taxonomies.

In addition to the explicit use of reasoning, it is important to allow implicit reasoning based on multiple relations. Complex simulations require the representation of multidimensional relationships among objects, such as "A is *a-kind-of* B," "A is *a-part-of* B," "A is *in-control-of* B," "A is *in-communication-with* B," or "A is *near* B." It is vital for the simulation user to be able to define relations freely, examine the state of the simulation in terms of these relations, and modify them dynamically. Most object-oriented systems support only minor variations of the "class–subclass" (also called "IS-A" or "taxonomy") relation along with a corresponding "inheritance" mechanism to maintain taxonomic relationships (i.e., specialized inferential support for the class–subclass relation). We are attempting to provide a true multiple-relation environment in which different kinds of relations are supported by appropriate specialized inference mechanisms and to provide a general facility to allow the simulation developer to define new relations with appropriate inferential support.

In order to be comprehensible to users, simulations must make intelligent use of highly interactive graphics interfaces. These should allow graphic querying of the simulation state; being able to roll the simulation back to a previous state, change a parameter, and rerun the simulation; saving multiple simulation states for later analysis and comparison; being able to build or modify simulation scenarios graphically; and being able to build or modify simulation objects graphically (e.g., defining and exercising new behaviors graphically). We have defined a highly interactive graphics environment of this sort that emphasizes the ease of manipulating simulation objects, minimizes redundant display updating, and facilitates animation of sequences of events (i.e., "causal chains"). We are also investigating the use of graphically interactive diagrams or pictorial representations of relations, which users can display and edit graphically.

Sensitivity analysis is one of the great abandoned areas of simulation. Yet without it there is no guarantee that the results of a simulation would not be drastically different if some small change were made to some initial parameter. Sensitivity analysis is also important for indicating which parameter values are the most important to verify (by real-world means) for a simulation to be valid and believable.

The straightforward approach to sensitivity analysis requires running a simulation many times, perturbing individual parameters to see how the results differ. This is prohibitively expensive in most cases, as a consequence of which it is rarely done. Our research seeks to provide a means of doing computationally feasible sensitivity analysis in a simulation environment, utilizing a new approach that propagates and combines the sensitivities of composite functions through a computation. Viewing a simulation as a top-level function that invokes many levels of nested subfunctions, most of these invocations normally involve a relatively small number of distinct subfunctions, each of which is called many times. For example, a sine function may be called thousands of times in computing the geographical positions of objects. Normally, perturbing a top-level parameter involves executing the top-level function several times, each time executing the nested sine function thousands of times. Our approach instead computes a representation of the sensitivity of the sine function the first time it is executed and propagates this sensitivity information through the computation rather than recomputing it each time it is needed.

Another major shortcoming of current simulation models is their inability to vary the level at which they are aggregated (also referred to as their "resolution"). It is generally necessary to choose a desired level of aggregation in advance and design a simulation around that level. Changing this level typically requires considerable reprogramming of the simulation; changing it under user control or dynamically is generally unthinkable. The fact that the level of aggregation of a model gets "frozen in" early in its design is a major impediment to the reusability of models and the utility of simulation in general. Users should be able to vary the level of aggregation of a simulation and to indicate which aspects of the model are of particular interest, running those aspects of the simulation disaggregated while running peripheral aspects at higher levels of aggregation. Users should also be able to run highly aggregated simulations to identify interesting cases and then examine those cases in more detail by rerunning them disaggregated. Our goal is to develop a methodology for building simulations whose level of aggregation can be varied either statically or dynamically, as appropriate to the user's purpose. This requires mechanisms for representing "vertical slices" of objects in an aggregation hierarchy and for allowing interactions between objects at different levels of aggregation. It is also necessary to address problems of inconsistency that can arise between different levels; that is, running a simulation at an aggregated level should produce results that are consistent with the results of running the same simulation at a disaggregated level.

In order to model real-world environments that include human decision makers, we are attempting to build simulations that embed models of intelligent agents possessing varying degrees of awareness, authority, initiative, intelligence, and so on. This also requires hierarchical planning so that, at each level, plans will be translated into objectives for agents at the next lower level.

Finally, there are a number of "pseudo-objects" or phenomena that are not modeled well by the current object-oriented paradigm. For example, terrain, roads, rivers, and weather defy easy representation by conventional object-oriented means. These pseudo-objects seem to require representations and manipulations that are different from those used for more compact objects, either because they traverse or interpenetrate other objects (without actually being "part" of them) or because they are best described by continuous models (such as partial differential equations). We are exploring a number of AI techniques to represent such pseudo-objects and their interactions.

The preceding gives a brief summary of our current research in this area. The wedding of AI and simulation is still in progress; its consummation promises to be of great value to both fields of endeavor.

12 SUMMARY AND CONCLUSION

Modeling is one of the foundations of intelligence and is an essential aspect of being human. It is nothing short of the primal lever with which we move the earth to suit our needs. However, the creation and use of models is so instinctive that we rarely analyze it or question its appropriateness. This chapter has attempted to define modeling precisely in order to provide a framework within which models can be compared and evaluated according to the three criteria of reference, purpose, and cost-effectiveness. This should make it possible to design and choose more effective models, avoid inferior ones, recognize pseudo-models, and acknowledge that the use of *any* model may sometimes be inappropriate.

Simulation is a powerful modeling strategy for understanding complex phenomena. Artificial intelligence provides new techniques that will infuse simulation with unprecedented power. At the same time, simulation has a great potential for contributing to AI, providing phenomenological models that can be used by reasoning programs as a deep source of expertise about the world. Some of the most exciting potentials of this new marriage of disciplines are exemplified by current research in knowledge-based simulation at the RAND Corporation.

It is apparent that the future of civilization depends, at least in part, on our ability to devise new and more effective tools for making intelligent decisions. Whatever form these tools may take, they must necessarily be based on appropriate models of ourselves and our reality. It is perhaps not too much to ask—or at least to hope—that the informed use of AI and simulation may play a major role in producing these vital tools. It is in any case clear that current developments in this area will greatly enhance the efficacy of simulation as a means of understanding the world.

REFERENCES

1. R. H. Anderson and J. J. Gillogly, "RAND Intelligent Terminal Agent (RITA): Design Philosophy," The RAND Corporation, R-1809-ARPA, 1976.

2. R. H. Anderson, M. Gallegos, J. J. Gillogly, R. B. Greenberg, and R. V. Villanueva, "RITA Reference Manual," The RAND Corporation, R-1808-ARPA, 1977.

3. R. H. Anderson and N. Z. Shapiro, "Design Considerations for Computer-Based Interactive Map Display Systems," The RAND Corporation, R-2382-ARPA, 1979.

4. W. Bibel, *Automated Theorem Proving,* Viewweg, Braunschweig, 1982.

5. J. S. Brown, R. R. Burton, and J. DeKleer, "Pedagogical, Natural Language and Knowledge Engineering Techniques in SOPHIE I, II, and III," in D. Sleeman and J. S. Brown (Eds.), *Intelligent Tutoring Systems,* Academic, New York, 1982, pp. 227–282,.

6. M. Callero, D. A. Waterman, and J. R. Kipps, "TATR: A Prototype Expert System for Tactical Air Targeting," The RAND Corporation, R-3096-ARPA, 1984.

7. A. J. Catanese, *Scientific Methods of Urban Analysis,* University of Illinois Press, Champaign, IL, 1972.

8. O. J. Dahl and K. Nygaard, "Simula—An Algol-Based Simulation Language," *Communications ACM,* **9,** 671–678, 1966.

9. N. C. Dalkey, "Simulation," in E. S. Quade and W. I. Boucher (Eds.), *Systems Analysis and Policy Planning: Applications in Defense,* Elsevier, New York, 1968.

10. G. Daniel, "Megalithic Monuments," *Scientific American,* **243**(1):78–90, 1980.

11. M. Davis, S. Rosenschein, and N. Shapiro, "Prospects and Problems for a General Modeling Methodology," The RAND Corporation, N-1801-RC, 1982.

12. G. W. Evans, G. F. Wallace, and G. L. Sutherland, *Simulation Using Digital Computers,* Prentice-Hall, Englewood Cliffs, NJ, 1967.

13. A. M. Frisch, "Using Model Theory to Specify AI Programs," *Proceedings of the International Joint Conference on Artificial Intelligence (IJCAI' 85),* Morgan Kaufmann, Los Altos, CA, 1985.

14. S. I. Gass and R. L. Sisson, *A Guide to Models in Governmental Planning and Operations,* U.S. Environmental Protection Agency, Washington, DC, 1974.

15. H. Gelernter, "Realization of a Geometry Theorem-proving Machine," *Proceedings of an International Conference on Information Processing,* UNESCO House, Paris, 1959, pp. 273–282.

16. G. Gentner and A. L. Stevens (Eds.), *Mental Models,* Erlbaum, Hillsdale, NJ, 1983.

17. A. Goldberg and A. Kay, "Smalltalk-72 Instruction Manual." Report SSL 76–6, Xerox PARC, Palo Alto, CA, 1976.

18. M. Greenberger, M. A. Crenson, and B. L. Crissey, *Models in the Policy Process,* Russell Sage Foundation, New York, 1976.

19. G. S. Hawkins, *Stonehenge Decoded,* Doubleday, New York, 1965.

20. A. C. Hearn, "REDUCE User's Manual, Version 3.2," The RAND Corporation, CP78, 1985.

21. B. W. Hogwood and L. A. Gunn, *Policy Analysis for the Real World,* Oxford University Press, New York, 1984.

22. C. S. Holling, *Adaptive Environmental Assessment and Management,* Wiley, New York, 1978.

23. P. W. House and J. McLeod, *Large-Scale Models for Policy Evaluation,* Wiley, New York, 1977.

24. W. P. Hughes, *Military Modeling,* The Military Operations Research Society, Inc., Alexandria, VA, 1984.

25. I. Kant, *Prolegomena to Any Future Metaphysics,* Liberal Arts, New York, 1950.

26. J. R. Kipps, B. Florman, and H. A. Sowizral, "The New ROSIE Reference Manual and User's Guide," The RAND Corporation, R-3448-ARPA, 1986.

27. P. J. Kiviat, "Digital Computer Simulation: Modeling Concepts," The RAND Corporation, RM-5378-PR, 1967.

28. P. J. Kiviat, R. V. Villanueva, and H. M. Markowitz, *The Simscript II Programming Language,* Prentice-Hall, Englewood Cliffs, NJ, 1968.

29. P. Klahr, "Expressibility in ROSS: An Object-Oriented Simulation System," *AI Applied to Simulation, Proceedings of the European Conference at the University of Ghent,* Society for Computer Simulation, San Diego, CA, 1986, pp. 136–139.

30. P. Klahr and D. A. Waterman, "Artificial Intelligence: A Rand Perspective," in *Expert Systems Techniques, Tools and Applications,* Addison-Wesley, Reading, MA, 1986, pp. 3–23.

31. T. S. Kuhn, *The Structure of Scientific Revolutions,* University of Chicago Press, Chicago, IL, 1962.

32. D. McArthur, P. Klahr, and S. Narain, "ROSS: An Object-Oriented Language for Constructing Simulations," The RAND Corporation, R-3160-AF, 1984.

33. D. H. Meadows, J. Richardson, and G. Bruckmann, *Groping in the Dark,* Wiley, New York, 1982.

34. Meta Systems, Inc., "Systems Analysis in Water Resource Planning," Water Information Center, Inc., 1971.

35. M. Minsky, "Matter, Mind and Models," in *Proceedings of the IFIP Congress 65,* Spartan, Washington, DC, 1965, pp. 45–49.

36. A. Newell, J. C. Shaw, and H. Simon, "Empirical Explorations with the Logic Theory Machine," in *The Proceedings of the Western Joint Computer Conference,* Institute of Radio Engineers, New York, 1957.

37. H. R. Pagels, *The Cosmic Code,* Bantam, New York, 1983.

38. J. Paul, D. A. Waterman, and M. A. Peterson, "SAL: An Expert System for Evaluating Asbestos Claims," in *The Proceedings of the First Australian Artificial Intelligence Congress,* Melbourne, 1986.

39. E. S. Quade, "Modeling Techniques," in H. J. Miser and E. S. Quade (Eds.), *Handbook of Systems Analysis,* North-Holland, Amsterdam, 1985.

40. J. A. Robinson, "Logic Programming—Past, Present and Future," in *New Generation Computing,* Vol. 1, Springer-Verlag, New York, 1983, pp. 10–124.

41. J. Rothenberg, "Object-oriented Simulation: Where Do We Go From Here?" *Proceedings of the 1986 Winter Simulation Conference, Washington, DC,* ACM, New York, 1986, pp. 464–469.

42. D. Schmandt-Besserat, "The Earliest Precursor of Writing," *Scientific American,* June 1978, pp.50–59.

43. H. A. Simon, et al., "Scientific Futures: Selected Areas of Opportunity," Report of the Research Briefing Panel on Decision Making and Problem Solving, National Academy of Science and Engineering, Washington, DC, 1986.

44. B. C. Smith, personal communication, 1986.

45. H. A. Sowizral and J. R. Kipps, "ROSIE: A Programming Environment for Expert Systems," The RAND Corporation, R-3246-ARPA, 1985.

46. R. D. Specht, "The Nature of Models," in E. S. Quade and W. I. Boucher (Eds.), *Systems Analysis and Policy Planning: Applications in Defense,* Elsevier, New York, 1968.

47. J. A. Spriet and G. C. Vansteenkiste, *Computer-aided Modeling and Simulation,* Vansteenkiste (University of Ghent, Belgium), Academic, New York, 1982.

48. L. Sterling and E. Shapiro, *The Art of Prolog,* MIT Press, Cambridge, MA, 1986.

49. A. Tarski, "The Concept of Truth in Formalized Languages," in *Logic, Semantics, and Mathematics,* Oxford at the Clarendon Press, New York, 1956.

50. W. E. Walker, J. M. Chaiken, and E. J. Ignall (Eds.), *Fire Department Deployment Analysis,* North-Holland, Amsterdam, 1979.

51. D. A. Waterman and M. A. Peterson, "Models of Legal Decisionmaking," The RAND Corporation, R-2717-ICJ, 1981.

4 Process Abstraction in Simulation Modeling

PAUL A. FISHWICK

Department of Computer and Information Sciences
University of Florida
Gainesville, Florida

1 INTRODUCTION

The incorporation of "abstraction" into the study of processes has a long history; its importance within simulation is notable especially when we consider the potential complexities of modeling very large discrete and continuous systems. The breadth of simulation modeling is sufficient to warrant a cross-fertilization of "abstraction" and "aggregation" definitions. Unfortunately, due to the wide diversity of discussions on abstraction in modeling, we often lack a cohesive theory or methodology that links the concepts together. Figure 1 shows some of the areas that use abstraction in process modeling. Our primary goal is to attempt to bridge the gaps somewhat by presenting a more comprehensive view of *process abstraction*. This presentation will consist of an enumeration of techniques for defining abstraction as it relates to process modeling. An emphasis will be placed on creating formal definitions for the methods of abstraction and on elucidating those definitions within the context of an application involving the motion of several articulated figures.

Before proceeding further, we need to establish a definition for process abstraction. Informally, process abstraction is defined as a method for transforming one process description into another, more abstract description. In Section 2, we create a formal definition, but for the moment we digress so that the proper foundation is formed. Abstraction of a process will inevitably involve a reduction in model components and interactions along with the reduction in behavioral complexity of the model when simulated. The term "aggregation" can conceptually be considered as a subset of "abstraction." By clustering or amalgamating process components together (namely, *aggregation*), we are performing a type of abstraction. Abstraction, however, is generally thought of as a slightly more flexible term that does not necessarily rely solely on clustering. To avoid confusion in terminology and for the sake of consistency, we shall talk of process abstraction rather than process aggregation. Another reason for choosing the term "abstraction" rather than "aggregation" is to contrast the work

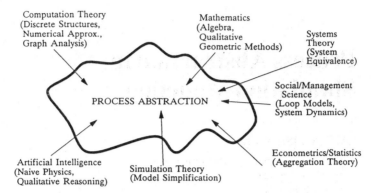

Figure 1. Applications using process abstraction. Copyright 1988 IEEE.

against "data abstraction." Why is it important to study the abstraction of process descriptions and models? Some points are offered:

- An abstract model is usually less computationally complex than the base model. As long as the trade-off between complexity and data sufficiency is a favorable one, the abstract model becomes useful.
- The abstract model is easier to understand than the base model in most cases. Since an abstraction involves a reduction in process component(s), the model is more easily created and modifiable.
- The creation of an abstract model permits us to build a library of different models that represent the same process. This "library" will take the form of a network in a subsequent section. This gives the simulationist (for simulation models) or the psychologist (for mental models) a common ground for communication.
- In many cases, the library of models for one process represents an evolutionary path for the modeling process: Processes often are modeled using simple methods at first and more complex methods later as (1) more knowledge is gained by the simulationist and (2) validation helps to prune away inferior models.

The study of process abstraction is as important to study as the areas of data abstraction and object abstraction, which have received wide attention in the computer science literature. Methods for data abstraction, in particular, are important in programming languages when defining data types. Object abstraction methods have been employed in geometry and computer graphics.

The overall motivation for the study of process abstraction came from the need to unify various methods of abstraction in process modeling that appear in many different disciplines. Zeigler's formalization of simulation models [52, 51, 49] and discussions of applications [50, 48] serve as good starting points for formal discussions of process abstraction. Foo [20] defines a set of concepts for homomorphic simplification of systems using general algebras. Much of this recent formal work was spurred by the earlier work in mathematical systems theory [46, 47, 30]. There is also other work in econometrics and statistics (specifically aggregation theory [44, 27]) that is of direct importance. On the other hand, we have the more qualitative approaches. These approaches, such as systems dynamics [21, 22] and qualitative reasoning [8], rely on abstract process modeling techniques and "more intuitive" methods for modeling. In a recent paper, we provide some concerns and issues [18] arising from the use of qualitative models. Also, there have been various studies in the "geometry of behavior [1]" and loop analysis [41] that include qualitative analyses of phase portraits. The analyst, for instance, may identify regions of stability and instability for an n-variable dynamic system by identifying geometric characteristics inherent within portraits. The identification procedure is based upon sound mathematical definitions for stability. We must constantly consider trade-offs in simulation complexity and especially model validation before deciding on the correct method (quantitative vs. qualitative) to use when abstracting processes [18]. There is one point that is of paramount importance when considering approaches: Formal methods have tended to concentrate on the *mapping problem* between an arbitrary number of abstraction levels while the more informal, qualitative methods tend to concentrate, not on mapping, but instead on defining a certain high level of abstraction for a process. Validating a formal model is therefore somewhat more straightforward if we have a valid base model and a valid homomorphic mapping. Validating a qualitative model is more difficult since the base model, if any, is not mentioned specifically.

2   A FORMAL FOUNDATION

2.1   Abstraction Network

We define an *abstraction network* (denoted $\mathcal{A}$) as follows:

$$\mathcal{A} = [S, \varphi]$$

where S is the set of systems (or models) representing the same process at different levels of abstraction. Therefore $S = \{S_i\}$, where any given S_i represents an abstraction level. The set of possible abstraction relations φ induces a partial ordering over S. Here, $\varphi = \{\rho_i\}$, where any given ρ_i represents a method of abstraction (or "abstraction relation"). All relations ρ and combinations (within φ thereof) are defined to be nonreflexive, antisymmetric, and transitive. We restrict ourselves to partial orderings since a definition of process abstraction in terms of a network might imply a circularity in $\mathcal{A}$ (e.g., it would then be possible to say that S_i was an abstraction of S_j and vice versa). On the other hand, we do not restrict ourselves to a total ordering since it is possible that two models might not be related—in this case, the two S_i's would be considered at similar (or unknown) levels of abstraction. We denote that S_i is an abstraction of S_{i+1} in one of three ways:

1. *Graph form*, $S_{i+1} \rightarrow S_i$.
2. *Relational form*, $\rho_i(S_{i+1}, S_i)$.
3. *Infix notation*, $S_{i+1} \prec S_i$.

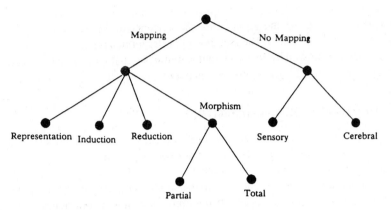

Figure 2. A taxonomy for process abstraction. Copyright 1988 IEEE.

The symbol in method 3, $\prec$, matches any $\rho_i \in \varphi$. Method 2 is the only complete notation since it defines the specific abstraction relation; however, it is often convenient to represent that model A is less abstract than model B as follows: $A \prec B$. In some cases, we may simulate a system before applying a method of abstraction to yield a new system. We denote the behavior of system S when simulated for some time duration as $\beta(S)$. It is sometimes necessary to differentiate between asynchronous (β_A) and synchronous (β_S) simulation of model components. For instance, we might form an abstract mapping between a cellular automaton (*CELL*) and a finite-state automaton (*FSA*) by possibly simulating *CELL* and then subsequently creating an abstract mapping based on abstraction method ρ_i, yielding $\rho_i(\beta(CELL), FSA)$.

Before discussing various methods for linking given S_i's using an abstraction relation $\rho_i \in \varphi$, we provide a taxonomy for process abstraction methods. Figure 2 illustrates the taxonomy. In the following definitions, we consider an abstraction mapping to occur between a less abstract system S_{i+1} and a more abstract system S_i.

2.2   System

A system is denoted S_i such that $S_i \in C^m$, where C is the set of components for a system. We denote $S_i = <c_{i1}, c_{i2}, ..., c_{im}>$ as an m-valued system specified at abstraction level i. The c's are the individual components. All processes can be defined within such a definition. An example would be a simple *input-output* relation defining a system $S = <I, O, R>$, where I is the set of input segments, O is the set of output segments, and R is the set of valid relations using members of the sets.

Recall that S is the set of all systems. We then define several functions that will be used by certain abstraction methods. First, we define $\tau_1: S \rightarrow T_1$ and $\tau_2: C \rightarrow T_2$ to be "type 1" and "type 2" functions, respectively. $\chi: S \rightarrow 2^{C^1}$ is the "category" function. An example for T_1 is the set {*finite-state-automaton, cellular-automaton, petri net, turing-machine*}. The second type of function refers to the component types. The set for T_2 might equal {*variable, function, relation, parameter*}. The category function describes a system in terms of a collection of categories. For instance, {*frequency, order*} may be useful when ascribing properties to a system such as an *FSA*. Specifically, any *FSA* with a given input string has the two properties of frequency (i.e., relative frequency of transitions to certain states) and order (the sequence of transitions).

We now proceed to define each method of abstraction in Sections 2.3–2.9. Section headers will be followed by an acronym in parentheses that will be used subsequently when illustrating the complete abstraction network.

2.3   Abstraction by Representation (*REP*)

Perhaps the simplest and most utilized form of process abstraction is "abstraction by representation." Simply stated, this type of abstraction is characterized by the fact that the abstraction S_i "represents" S_{i+1} in another form. By representing S_{i+1} in abstract form S_i, we identify the complexity of S_{i+1} with the notational convenience of S_i. The most important aspect of representational abstractions is that they are often purely structural and lack any abstract behavioral characteristics of their own; in fact, the abstract model's behavior is defined in terms of the functionality associated with the detailed model. Programming languages use this form of abstraction to encode procedural hierarchies using key words such as *procedure, function, or subroutine*. The representational notation *quicksort (list)*, for instance, means absolutely nothing until we descend the hierarchy to locate *quicksort*'s procedural (or functional) definition. We can also consider digital logic hierarchies; representational abstraction has long been used in digital logic simulation [12]. Consider Figure 3. We see that the behavior (or semantics) for the circuit shown in Figure 3 is completely defined at the lowest abstraction level where the functionality of AND, OR, and NOR gates are well known. There are some noteworthy points concerning the digital logic hierarchy in Figure 3:

- The circuit is purely for example purposes and does not reflect an actual design.
- Level S_1 is shown in the figure. Level S_2 can be formed from S_1 by substituting components C_i inside S_1. Level S_3 can be formed in a similar manner.
- The inputs and outputs are shown using varying line thicknesses that refer to the "bit width" at that abstraction level. Level S_1 uses widths of 3 bits, level S_2 uses 2 bits, and S_3 uses 1 bit.

The high levels of abstraction serve to simplify the more detailed layers. Genesereth [23], within the context of fault diagnosis, terms this "structural abstraction." We should note that it would be possible to assign behaviors to the more abstract layers if desired, although we have not done so. Behaviors for high abstraction levels in digital circuits can be defined equationally, or even in a tabular, relational form. However, if we did assign behaviors directly to high levels, then we would still refer to representational abstraction since, from a behavioral viewpoint, the levels would be identical $(\forall i \ [\beta(S_{i+1}) = \beta(S_i)])$.

2.4   Abstraction by Induction (*IND*)

Abstraction by inductive inference between $S_{i+1} \to S_i$ refers to "coalescing" several $c_{(i+1)j}$'s from system S_{i+1} into a more compact system S_i. The size of S_i will therefore be

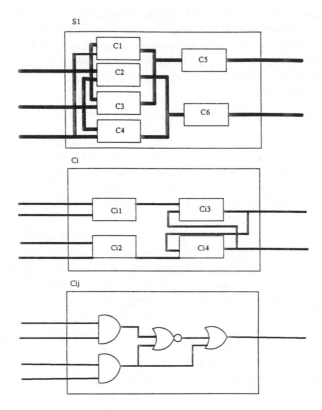

Figure 3. A digital logic hierarchy. Copyright 1988 IEEE.

much less than the size of S_{i+1} ($|S_i| \ll |S_{i+1}|$). Assumptions: $\forall c_{(i+1)j}$, $c_{(i+1)k}$ involved in the induction, $\tau_2(c_{(i+1)j}) = \tau_2(c_{(i+1)k})$. As an example, imagine that we have a system defined as a set of binary states as follows: $S = <1, 0, 1, 1, 0, 1, 1, 0, 1, 1, 0, 1>$. First note that $\forall i \, [\tau_2(c_i) = \text{state-variable}]$. We can therefore inductively infer that the sequence $1,0,1$ recurs four times. This recurrence can be abstracted into a finite-state machine or a recurrence equation.

Angluin and Smith [5] provide a survey of the theory and methods associated with inductive inference. Since inductive inference methods can be used in machine learning [33], there has been work by Andreae [4] in using induction as a basis for learning procedures from examples. Also, Dufay and Latombe [13] use inductive learning methods to generate robot task descriptions. Weld [45] defines a method of reasoning about cyclic behavior by inducting aggregate production rules (which he terms "continuous processes") from sequences of events.

2.5 Abstraction by Reduction (*RED*)

Abstraction by reduction involves reduction in a set-theoretic sense. That is, we can abstract $S_{i+1} \rightarrow S_i$ using one of two methods: (1) $S_i \subset S_{i+1}$ or (2) $\chi(S_i) \subset \chi(S_{i+1})$. The first method can be used, for instance, to abstract a system defined by a set of equations. We can abstract the original set by choosing a subset of equations that are "representative" of the entire set. Clearly, we shall be concerned with a level of tolerance associated with variable ranges and the relative importance of variables in the system of equations. The second method can be used when we determine that one model is an abstraction of another by virtue of the category function. If an *FSA* system has attributes of frequency and order, then it is possible to create an abstract model that displays just one of those attributes. A probability density function is an example of such an abstraction.

2.6   Total Systems Morphism (*TSM*)

A total systems morphism is best defined by Zeigler [51]. Informally, a total systems morphism for a *structured system specification* is a complete mapping between all $c_{(i+1)j}$ to c_{ij} in S_{i+1} and S_i, respectively. The important aspect of this morphism is that it is a structure- and behavior-preserving homomorphism. All corresponding system components are of equal types ($\forall j [\tau_2(c_{(i+1)j}) = \tau_2(c_{ij})]$) and the systems themselves are of equal types $[\tau_1(S_{i+1}) = \tau_1(S_i)]$. In terms of formalism, the total systems morphism is best defined in terms of traditional algebraic concepts; it is natural to consider a process abstraction to be generated as a result of homomorphic mapping. We should note, though, that the resulting abstraction S_i will not necessarily reflect an "intuitive" sense of abstraction even though it is behaviorally equivalent (under the mapping) to S_{i+1}. We should also note that homomorphisms are ideal for representing abstraction on systems defined as discrete structures (such as directed graphs); however, homomorphic functions contain less utility for systems defined as continuous functions and systems. Abstractions of processes defined as continuous functions are often based on geometric considerations (where a curve or surface portion is approximated with a simpler geometric entity).

2.7   Partial Systems Morphism (*PSM*)

A partial systems morphism between S_{i+1} and S_i is defined *most generally* as a verifiably correct algorithm that accepts S_{i+1} as input and produces S_i as output. It is defined *more specifically* as a set of morphisms between *some* components; all relations and functions are not necessarily preserved during mapping.

The definition for this type of process abstraction seems very open ended; however, we include it within our taxonomy for the sake of completeness, especially when we consider certain graph algorithms such as those to determine strongly connected components in an arbitrary directed graph [2], interval analysis [3], and other topics within program flow analysis [35]. Graph grammars can also be used to create abstract systems from less abstract ones. If our model is represented as a graph, $S = <V, E>$, then such algorithms and procedures will be useful in creating abstractions. It is possible that such a method will not preserve all relations and functions; it may operate only on the structure and not the behavior of the process graph, for instance. Nevertheless, we view such procedures as playing an important role in process abstraction.

In structuring abstraction networks, we may also use the notation *SM* to simply denote a systems morphism without specifying whether it is "total" or "partial."

2.8   Sensory Abstraction

An abstraction can be created on the basis of visual validation of the model. Of our five senses, we consider the visual sense to be most amenable to abstraction; that is, when we view an animated scene, we sense that a particular visual sequence is reflective of an abstract model of the corresponding real-world system. In any event, we shall concentrate on the visual sense even though process abstraction in terms of audiological response along with the other senses is also important. This definition of abstraction has been heavily used in computer graphics literature. In Section 5 we discuss an application of process abstraction using animation of the "dining philosophers" [11] (referred to as **DP**) model.

Within the computer graphics literature we find many examples of abstract process modeling. Dynamic models of fire [42] by particle systems, for instance, have been demonstrated to provide the viewer with realistic sequences of both fire and explosions over time. The concept of the particle system described by Reeves defines attributes of particles such as position, vector of motion, and lifetime. In many respects a particle system might be formally defined as a type of three-dimensional cellular automaton [14]. The important note is that the particle system approach represents an abstract modeling approach to a physical system that is highly complex; modeling of fire by differential and flow equations might be more accurate but would be far more complex in terms of both model building time and simulation time.

Work in computer graphics over the last two decades has always relied on abstract methods when modeling motion [6, 34]. Psychological factors are important when considering the *perception of motion* rather than simply the actual motion at the lowest level of abstraction. Methods of animation, in particular [32, 31], have often employed techniques for producing realistic scenes using fairly ad hoc methods. The criterion for validation is the *visual realism* associated with the use of such a technique. Statistical validation is rarely performed; usually it is deemed sufficient to (1) compare the technique with previous methods and clearly define the proposed extension and (2) present the method to large audiences (such as animated films at a computer graphics conference). If the method is visually stunning and impressive in its realism to peer reviewers, then it is considered a valid abstraction of the real system.

2.9   Cerebral Abstraction

The section title "cerebral" is meant to capture those abstraction methods that deal with modeling intuitive processes at high levels of abstraction. A critical question is "Are there any constraints on how we can define a mental model [24] of a process?" If we cannot place constraints on a definition for a "qualitative" model, then clearly *any* model can be considered qualitative. This is clearly an unsatisfactory situation. We consider two methods for abstract, mental modeling: system dynamics and qualitative reasoning and simulation.

Within the scope of simulation, Forrester's systems dynamics [21, 22] emphasis is appropriate when discussing abstract modeling methods. The systems dynamics approach to simulation [43] is predicated on constructing causal graphs with feedback loops. It has been used in many disciplines, especially the social and management sciences. The primary virtue of the approach is one of simplicity. It is fairly easy for the novice, for instance, to create simulation models and then subsequently use them to perform analyses and then possibly compare results against the observable data (if it exists). Often, the modeling process begins with informal models that may resemble the causal graphs in system dynamics. There have been continuing debates about the merit of such an approach, especially in light of the problem of model validation. Nordhaus [36], for instance, cites problems with the overly general nature of Forrester's approach; the model may be too general to provide the simulationist with accurate results and feedback.

Within the domain of artificial intelligence literature of the past decade there has been recent interest in the areas of "naive physics [25]" and "qualitative reasoning/ simulation [8]" to develop thought models associated with device behavior. A central theme connected with the qualitative reasoning work is to provide some means of (1) creating an abstract process model, (2) applying an analysis procedure to the model to create a causal model, and (3) provide an explanation feature to describe the nature of the device. Various partitions of $\mathcal{R}$ (the real-number system) are often used when defining "quantity spaces." The most common partition involves a mapping $h: \mathcal{R} \rightarrow \{-, 0, +\}$. Qualitative reasoning research is much newer than systems dynamics research and is just beginning to come under closer scrutiny [29]. The goals of both systems dynamics and qualitative reasoning are quite similar. They both strive to provide abstract methods for defining processes. Systems dynamics is oriented toward the human analyst whereas qualitative reasoning is geared toward a complete autonomous environment where a program/machine is able to simulate "reasoning" about device behavior given a minimal amount of structural information.

3   AN EXAMPLE ABSTRACTION NETWORK

If we choose the "dining philosophers" [11] as an example physical process, then we can define a network $\mathcal{A}$ composed of the following individual abstractions: ·

1. $\mathcal{A} = [S, \varphi]$.
2. $S = \{FREQ, FLOW, PNET_1, PNET_2, FSA, DATA, EQN_1, EQN_2\}$.
3. $\varphi = \{REP, IND, RED, TSM, PSM, SM\}$.
4. Network node definitions: *FREQ*, frequency of eating activity; *FLOW*, simple *representation* of **DP**; *PNET*'s, Petri nets defining resource contention and synchronization, *FSA*, finite-state machine representing a simple synchronization mechanism for **DP**; *DATA*, a table of events or states; and *EQN*'s, equations of spline motion for all degrees of freedom associated with the articulated figures.

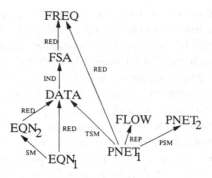

Figure 4. Abstraction network for DP. Copyright 1988 IEEE.

5. Network arc definitions: *REP* denotes abstraction by representation: *IND* and *RED* represent abstraction by induction and reduction, respectively; and *SM*, *TSM* and *PSM* represent system morphism, total system morphism and partial system morphism, respectively.

Figure 4 displays $\mathcal{A}$ given the definitions and systems at each abstraction level. In reference [19] we define the complete network; however, in the following section we define a subset of the total number of abstraction levels and mappings. The level *DATA* is an abstraction of **DP** defining the process as a set of states over time:

1. $S = <\{S^{(i)}\}>$.
2. $S^{(0)} = (1, 0, 1, 0, 0)$.
3. $S^{(1)} = (0, 1, 0, 1, 0)$.
4. $S^{(2)} = (0, 0, 1, 0, 1)$.
5. $S^{(3)} = (1, 0, 0, 1, 0)$.
6. $S^{(4)} = (0, 1, 0, 0, 1)$.
7. $S^{(5)} = S^{(0)}$.
8. $S^{(6)} = S^{(1)}$, and so on until $S^{(9)}$ is reached.

The state $(x_0, x_1, x_2, x_3, x_4)$ refers to philosophers that are eating ($x_i = 1$) and philosophers that are not eating ($x_i = 0$). The sequence of data $(S^{(0)}, \dots, S^{(9)}$ would typically be obtained by observing the process from a perspective (or within a given experimental frame [51]) and then defining the process as the data itself. We illustrate the other levels in Figures 5 through 7. Note that for PNET$_1$ (Figure 6) and PNET$_2$ (Figure 7) the places and transitions are labeled counterclockwise (using two concentric passes) starting with p_0 and t_0, respectively.

3.1 *DATA* → *FSA*, $\rho = IND$

A process defined by a set of states, variable values, or other type of homogenous data can often be abstracted using inductive inference [5]. In process description *DATA*, we are given a set $S^{(i)} = (x_0, \dots, x_4)$. Note that $\forall\, i, j[\tau_2(S^{(i)}) = \tau_2(S^{(j)})]$ so that induction is

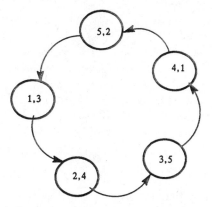

Figure 5. *FSA*. Copyright 1988 IEEE.

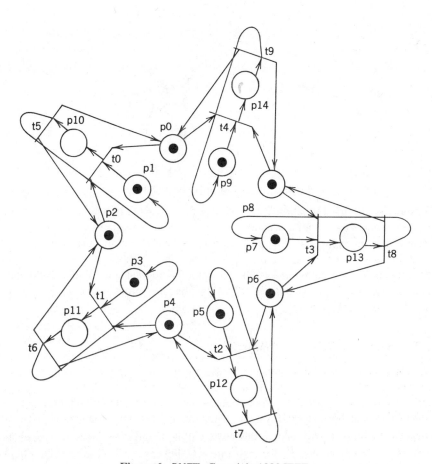

Figure 6. *PNET₁*. Copyright 1988 IEEE.

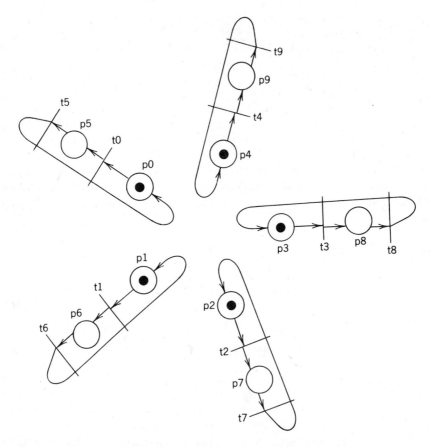

Figure 7. *PNET$_2$*. Copyright 1988 IEEE.

feasible. We define a function h such that $h(x_0, ..., x_4) = (X, Y)$, where $X = i+1$ for the first $x_i = 1$ and $Y = i+1$ for the second $x_i = 1$. The general constraints on the **DP** process ensure that no more than two philosophers will be simultaneously eating. After applying h to *DATA*, we arrive at a sequence of "states" (shown in the *FSA* in Figure 5) that can be induced using a method of inferring regular grammars [5]. We have chosen to let the (X,Y)'s be outputs of *FSA*; labeling the automaton using (X,Y) would also have been appropriate.

3.2 *PNET$_1$ → PNET$_2$, ρ = PSM or TSM*

We can produce abstract models from less abstract, base models by using a systems morphism [51]. This is a natural algebraic method for system simplification that attempts to preserve behavior. We define the method for total system morphism first and then explain how a partial system morphism might also be produced. *PNET$_2$* is an abstract model of *PNET$_1$*. We define such a systems morphism since $\tau_1 (PNET_1) = \tau_1(PNET_2) = $ *petri-net*. Let *PNET$_1$* = <P, T, I, O> and *PNET$_2$* = <P', T', I', O'>. First to map the place sets, define a morphism $h_1: P^\infty \rightarrow P'^\infty$ such that

1. $h_1(\{p_0, p_1, p_2\}) = \{p'_0\}$.
2. $h_1(\{p_2, p_3, p_4\}) = \{p'_1\}$.
3. $h_1(\{p_4, p_5, p_6\}) = \{p'_2\}$.
4. $h_1(\{p_6, p_7, p_8\}) = \{p'_3\}$.
5. $h_1(\{p_8, p_9, p_0\}) = \{p'_4\}$.

Define morphism $h_2 : T \rightarrow T'$ such that $\forall i\, [h_2(t_i) = t'_i]$. We now note that morphisms h_1 and h_2 are structure-preserving homomorphisms in the sense that functions I' and O' are both defined as $\forall t_i \in T,\ p_i \in P\ [I'(h_2(t_i)) = h_1(p_i)]$, and $\forall\ t_i \in T,\ p_i \in P[O'(h_2(t_i))\ = h_1(p_i)]$, respectively. To make the morphisms behavior preserving as well, we must ensure that $PNET_2$ is a proper subset of $PNET_1$ in terms of state behavior. We therefore concern ourselves with the marker function for places (μ). Let us first list the valid states for $PNET_1$:

1. (1, 1, 1, 1, 1, 1, 1, 1, 1, 1, 0, 0, 0, 0, 0).
2. (0, 0, 0, 1, 0, 0, 0, 1, 1, 1, 1, 0, 1, 0, 0).
3. (1, 1, 0, 0, 0, 1, 0, 0, 0, 1, 0, 1, 0, 1, 0).
4. (0, 1, 1, 1, 0, 0, 0, 1, 0, 0, 0, 0, 1, 0, 1).
5. (0, 0, 0, 1, 1, 1, 0, 0, 0, 1, 1, 0, 0, 1, 0).
6. (0, 1, 0, 0, 0, 1, 1, 1, 0, 0, 0, 1, 0, 0, 1).

Due to the constraints imposed by the resources, these six states are the only ones that can be associated with $PNET_1$. We must now derive a function m that maps the marker counts for places in the domain of function h_1 (listed above) to some particular value. It is also essential that a transition sequence be found for $PNET_2$ that will give us the specified state trajectory. Specifically, we choose the function as follows: $m(\{\mu(p_i),\ \mu(p_j),\ \mu(p_k)\}) = \mu(p_j)$. The i, j, and k refer to the values given for the place indices in the domain of the preceding function h_1. Such an m will yield the following newly defined states for $PNET_2$:

1. (1, 1, 1, 1, 1, 0, 0, 0, 0, 0).
2. (0, 1, 0, 1, 1, 1, 0, 1, 0, 0).
3. (1, 0, 1, 0, 1, 0, 1, 0, 1, 0).
4. (1, 1, 0, 1, 0, 0, 0, 1, 0, 1).
5. (0, 1, 1, 0, 1, 1, 0, 0, 1, 0).
6. (1, 0, 1, 1, 0, 0, 1, 0, 0, 1).

We must now determine a transition sequence that uses these states and the structure of $PNET_2$. Finding the transition sequence can be done by starting with each preceding state and determining which transition(s) in parallel ($t_0, \ldots, t_9$) in $PNET_2$ that will yield other valid states. Such a sequence is $(t_0, t_2) \rightarrow (t_1, t_3) \rightarrow (t_2, t_4) \rightarrow (t_3, t_0) \rightarrow (t_4, t_1)$, where (t_i, t_j) means that transitions t_i and t_j fire simultaneously. The preceding state set is closed under these firings.

The homomorphisms h_1 and h_2 in conjunction with the reduced state set provide us with $PNET_2$ as a simplified, structure- and behavior-preserving system for $PNET_1$. The methods used justify a relationship of TSM. Note that we can also create a partial system morphism (PSM) by using the homomorphisms to preserve structure, and *ignoring* the marker counts, this yields the nonpreservation of behavior of $PNET_1$. Note that without the m function, $PNET_2$} could be in any one of 32 (i.e., 2^5) states; by fixing the transition firing sequence, we limit the number of states to 6.

3.3 $\beta_S(PNET_1) \rightarrow DATA, \rho = TSM$

If we assume that $PNET_1$ is *synchronous* (denoted by behavior β_S), then the Petri-net transitions will fire in exactly the same sequence for a simulation. This sequence is a permutation of the set of transitions. The Petri-net states are the same as in the last example, so we can create a systems morphism as follows:

1. $h(0, 0, 0, 1, 0, 0, 0, 1, 1, 1, 1, 0, 1, 0, 0) = (1, 0, 1, 0, 0)$.
2. $h(1, 1, 0, 0, 0, 1, 0, 0, 0, 1, 0, 1, 0, 1, 0) = (0, 1, 0, 1, 0)$.
3. $h(0, 1, 1, 1, 0, 0, 0, 1, 0, 0, 0, 0, 1, 0, 1) = (0, 0, 1, 0, 1)$.
4. $h(0, 0, 0, 1, 1, 1, 0, 0, 0, 1, 1, 0, 0, 1, 0) = (1, 0, 0, 1, 0)$.
5. $h(0, 1, 0, 0, 0, 1, 1, 1, 0, 0, 0, 1, 0, 0, 1) = (0, 1, 0, 0, 1)$.

Here, h is simply a mapping to the last five place values:

$$h(p_0, p_1, \ldots, p_{10}, p_{11}, p_{12}, p_{13}, p_{14}) = (p_{10}, p_{11}, p_{12}, p_{13}, p_{14})$$

4   HIRES: A MULTILEVEL SIMULATION LANGUAGE

4.1   Overview

The development of abstraction mappings is often determined in conjunction with running an actual simulation on a process. By combining experimental results obtained through simulation with already defined formalisms, we can efficiently study a process at multiple levels of abstraction. Unfortunately, most simulation languages currently in use such as SIMSCRIPT [28] and SLAM [40] do not offer methods for defining a process using multiple viewpoints. Some languages, such as SLAM [40] do offer combined discrete and continuous modeling facilities. This is a step in the right direction, but it is not comprehensive enough to study the effects of process abstraction in sufficient detail. For these reasons we chose to implement a new language called HIRES (HIerarchical REasoning System) [17]. We digress briefly to discuss terminology. The term "hierarchical reasoning" is used since it implies that a number of reasoning levels have been used to *develop* a complete abstraction network to be used for simulation. It is also possible that the *output* of a multilevel simulation model could be termed "reasoning," especially at the higher abstraction levels. Whether more mathematical models (such as equational models) strictly represent "a form of calculation"

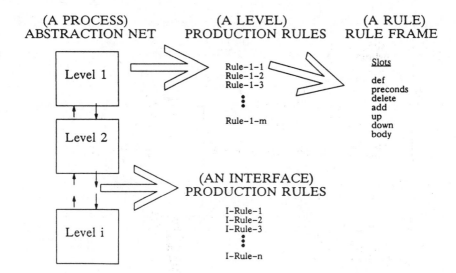

Figure 8. HIRES model structure: *PROCESS → LEVELS→ RULES*. Copyright 1988 IEEE.

or whether less mathematical models (such as causal graphs) represent "a form of reasoning" is a moot point: Cogent arguments could be presented that blur the distinction.

HIRES is a general-purpose simulation language with features that aid in the creation and simulation of a multilevel model. One of the fundamental problems with creating a language that is able to model mappings between systems relates to the wide variety of system modeling methods. Systems that represent abstraction levels may be encoded as Petri nets, cellular automata, scripts, finite-state machines, flow graphs, and systems of equations. There are potentially an infinite number of techniques for defining a structure S and its components $<c_1, ..., c_j>$. The wide variety causes problems in *interfacing* or mapping between abstraction levels that may be encoded quite differently. In HIRES, we chose to solve this problem by using a global database and control primitives in the form of production rules [39]. Production rules are primitive yet powerful enough to model all of the aforementioned systems. Preprocessors are built into HIRES that permit one to easily specify a system in a high-level language. The "source" is passed through the preprocessor which outputs the "object" in the form of a set of production rules.

The simulationist creates a number of models and mapping procedures (see Figure 8) as input to HIRES. Figure 8 depicts the form of the model hierarchy, a set of rules possibly created as output from a preprocessor and a set of interface rules used strictly for mapping from one abstraction level to another. The simulationist then enters the interactive interface and simulates the model hierarchy. Note that HIRES allows for mapping from more abstract to less abstract models even though the theoretic background for this type of mapping will not be discussed in this chapter. Zeigler [51] discusses this type of mapping briefly. He discusses certain conditions called "justifying conditions" where such a reverse mapping may take place. We have also recently discussed the nature of *refinement* in simulation modeling [16]. Refinement may be viewed as the converse of abstraction: Methods are developed allowing for traversals

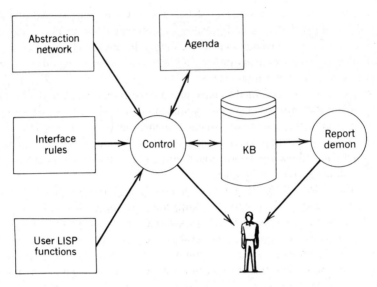

Figure 9. HIRES man-machine interface. Copyright 1988 IEEE.

from lumped models to base models. A sketch of the HIRES interfaces are shown in Figure 9. HIRES was written in Common LISP, developed on a DEC VAX minicomputer, and subsequently ported to a Symbolics LISP Machine. The HIRES "language" consists of a set of functions that can be input interactively or via command input files after starting the program. These functions are described in detail elsewhere [17] and categorized more generally in the appendix. In the following section we describe the essential methods emphasizing procedural and declarative rule interaction and processing.

4.2   The Architecture of HIRES

Sequencing is defined as the method used to order events for an abstraction level. We allow production rules to be fired using one of three possible methods: *procedural, declarative,* or *mixed mode.* In HIRES, each abstraction level is constructed using an event graph composed of a combination of procedural and declarative components. Note the bold arrows pointing upward and downward to adjacent levels of abstraction; it is possible at any point in the simulation to traverse levels using these links.

Procedural sequencing of events is supported by using the agenda capability portrayed in Figure 9. Events are scheduled either in a single global queue or in a local queue for a specific abstraction level. Each queue item is composed of the firing time, event name (i.e., rule name), and a list of assertions to be placed into the knowledge base just prior to firing. The procedural graph element is shown in Figure 10. *RULE1* schedules *RULE2* at absolute time t using two local assertions *a1* and *a2*.

Declarative sequencing occurs as an indirect consequence of matching preconditions against the knowledge base. This type of sequencing is commonly found in rule-

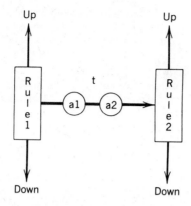

Figure 10. Procedural graph element. Copyright 1988 IEEE.

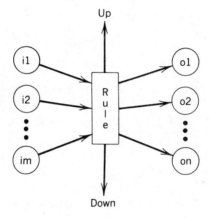

Figure 11. Declarative graph element. Copyright 1988 IEEE.

based systems [26]. Figure 11 illustrates the declarative graph element with preconditions, rule body, and postconditions. Mixed-mode sequencing is accomplished by
building event graphs whose components are a combination of procedural and
declarative elements. In certain instances, such an event graph is necessary. Consider
the problem of modeling an abstraction level using a Petri net [38, 37] whose transitions contain a time duration. Simple Petri nets can be constructed entirely from
declarative elements; however, when we add the concept of time duration, we must
include some kind of scheduling mechanism (i.e., using procedural elements). Mixing
procedural and declarative methods provides us with the necessary tools.

To some extent, we can view production rules as being the building blocks or
"assembly language" for our study of process abstraction. From this view we can create
metalevel processing capabilities that permit the mass creation of entire production
rule sets from a higher-order process definition. Certain abstraction levels within a
process net are likely to be constructed using models applicable to adequately defining
those levels. An example would be to use an ATN (augmented transition network) or

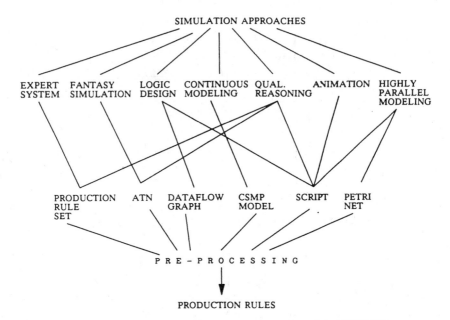

Figure 12. Network of simulation approaches. Copyright 1988 IEEE.

state machine for a high abstraction level or to use a CSMP [10] block model for a low abstraction level. Figure 12 depicts various simulation approaches and illustrates how we might define preprocessors that allow us to build the appropriate model for an abstraction level. Each of the HIRES preprocessors defines a method of translation from a high-level model to a graph composed of declarative and procedural elements. We consider two example translation techniques used to form the *script* and *timed data flow* preprocessors.

A script is defined by a table of actions; each **column** represents a separate physical object, and each **row** represents an instance in time. This type of process description can be found in many applications. Its primary virtue is its ability to represent concurrency among objects over time in a simple form. This simplicity is also a weakness since a script does not portray inherent synchronicity within a process (such as the ability to model an action that is dependent not only on time, but also on certain preconditions). We can translate a script process model into the necessary set of production rules by using only procedural primitives: For each column we set up a model where procedural primitives activate successive primitives (for each row in that column). Each object starts its first action at time zero (even though this can be an arbitrary value) and proceeds to "schedule itself" over time. When using a global event queue, all actions are synchronized over time.

Consider the problem of creating a process model represented by a data flow graph where each node takes a different amount of time. Such a graph is necessary to represent models that define processes such as electronic circuits (with propagation delays) and Petri nets whose transitions are time dependent. We can take advantage of mixed-mode sequencing in HIRES to form a graph composed of procedural and declarative ele-

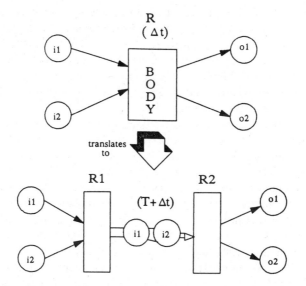

Figure 13. Translating a rule with duration. Copyright 1988 IEEE.

ments. The translation method is shown in Figure 13. We break down the conceptual timed rule *R* into two rules *R1* and *R2*. Rule *R1* fires through precondition satisfaction (i.e., declarative sequencing). Then *R1* schedules rule *R2* to fire at time $T + \Delta t$, where *T* represents the current simulation time. Note that the two input assertions are kept as local assertive data to be used when *R2* fires. Then *R2* fires at the specified time and proceeds as expected by executing the rule body and creating output assertions.

One can draw an analogy between the two created rules and the master–slave flip-flop used in logic design: The purpose of the new rule *R1* is to "lock the input values" for *R2* so that *R2* will fire with the original inputs and not the current inputs at the time of firing (which may be different). Therefore, to continue with the analogy, the inputs are permitted to "float" without causing problems.

This brings up another problem: If input assertions can change rapidly, what prohibits rule *R1* from firing again right after *R2* is scheduled. The implementation solves this problem by allowing the option of scheduling an event only if a duplicate does not already exist in the event queue. If a duplicate does exist, then the rule containing the scheduling function can be made to abort. This problem was first noticed when creating the dining philosophers simulation using the timed Petri net pre-processor.

4.3 Manual versus Automatic Control

We consider the problem of controlling the traversal of abstraction levels. HIRES allows for two modes of control operation: (1) The user may switch levels manually by interacting with an input device during simulation execution or (2) the user may explicitly specify simulation states where HIRES is to automatically switch abstraction levels. Such an explicit specification is accomplished using a simple form of logic programming in LISP. The simplest mechanism is to use a *manual* method. In this manner, we can manually weave through the abstraction net by direct commands to the simulator. We can choose to (1) stay on the current level of abstraction or (2) go up or down one level. We may also want to let the simulation run at a particular level and then manually control traversal through an asynchronous event routine bound to an input device (such as the keyboard). Then pressing control-D, for instance, will take us down a level while the simulation is running.

An automatic method for traversal can be accomplished by specifying portions of the process that should be simulated at a specified level. This method is "automatic" only in the sense that the user must predefine conditions that tell HIRES when to switch abstraction levels. The simulation run is not punctuated by manual interventions, but rather the run continues until completion while continuously checking conditions for level transfer. We have chosen to specify levels for simulation using a restricted form of first-order logic. For instance, let us consider a simulation of the **DP** process that produces an animated sequence as output. The abstraction level can be specified as a function of scene variables. This will be discussed in the next section.

Therefore, we can automatically control the simulation by relating abstraction levels to the current state of the knowledge base. It is useful to start a new simulation using *manual* mode and then subsequently progress to using *automatic* relations (with the HIRES function `.control`) that serve to help tune a simulation.

4.4 Sequential versus Parallel Flow

When previously discussing interfacing between levels, we noted the method by which the analyst could execute the process abstraction net by "weaving" through the levels. We term this execution flow as being *sequential* in nature: The net is executed via a sequential traversal while performing rule firings. We also consider the possibility of executing all abstraction levels in parallel (supporting a *parallel*-flow method). Clearly, if we decide to execute all abstraction levels in parallel, then we shall not need to utilize the interface rules since these rules exist solely to facilitate the bridging of abstractions.

5 AN APPLICATION: SCENE ANIMATION

5.1 An Overview

During the course of the research, two example models were produced: a four-level elevator model and a two-level model of **DP**. The elevator model includes levels for discrete-event simulation (with queues and resources), continuous simulation (a differential equation for vertical elevator motion, and two more abstract levels that serve as simplified models of the discrete level. The dining philosopher model has been discussed, and we shall continue to demonstrate the utility of HIRES with this model.

The initial application domain chosen by Fishwick [17] to illustrate benefits of process abstraction methods was in the area of scene animation with computer graphics techniques. This work is more completely defined in a recent paper [19]. Badler et al. [7] are constructing integrated methods for animating human figures of which "abstract simulation modeling" will play a part. More specifically, process abstraction can play an important role in both creating abstract process models and characterizing the general methodology associated with scene generation. The latter concept relates to the earlier notion of process abstraction relating directly to the "evolution of model construction." Animators will often want to start with abstract models, in terms of both geometric object abstraction [9, 15] and process abstraction. Animators will then gradually progress to finer modeling methods as the fundamental aspects of the animation are decided.

We can specify HIRES *control* functions that will automatically switch the level of abstraction based on current simulation state. We exploit this feature in animation by relating certain scene characteristics such as viewing angle and distance to level of abstraction. Let the level of abstraction (denoted by L) be $L \in \{1, 2\}$ for a two-level abstraction hierarchy consisting of the previously defined models $PNET_1$ and FSA. Recall that we have the following abstraction relationship based on the definitions:

$$PNET_1 \prec DATA \prec FSA$$

This implies, by transitivity of $\prec$ that $PNET_1 \prec FSA$. Thus, we let level 1 be FSA and level 2 be $PNET_1$. We can define an abstraction function f (encoded in HIRES as a `.control` function such that $L = f(\alpha, \Delta, \omega)$, where α and Δ represent the viewing angle and distance to the actual **DP** process and ω is a weight associated with **DP**. We assign weights since certain parts of a large scene may be more important to the simulationist or animator than others.

Let us say that we want to simulate at a low level (level 2) of abstraction whenever (1) the angle formed by the camera normal (center of projection) and the vector pointing to the center of the **DP** cluster (a minimal bounding box containing the polyhedral figures) is less than 60°, and (2) the distance to **DP** is less than 30 ft. Otherwise, we want to simulate at the high level (level 1) of abstraction. We define this in HIRES using the function call:

```
(.control 'automatic :level
   '((2 (and   (< (view-angle CAMERA-1 DP) (degrees 60))
              (< (distance CAMERA-1 DP) (feet 30))))
     (1 t)))
```

Figure 14 shows an aerial view of the five philosophers seated around a table with the virtual camera lens.

5.2   A HIRES Session

During the automatic execution of the simulation, we control the shifting from one abstraction level to another by using the control key $\hat{D}$ to move down the hierarchy and $\hat{U}$ to move up. We also use $\hat{B}$ once to break and list the contents of the knowledge base.

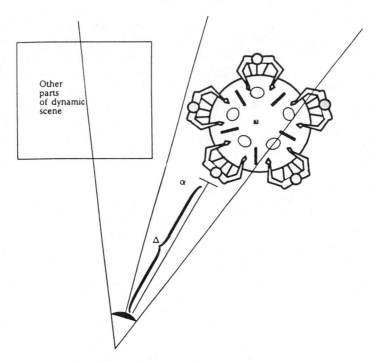

Other
parts
of dynamic
scene

α

Δ

Figure 14. Abstraction as a function of scene variables. Copyright 1988 IEEE.

We first note the LISP file that we load to specify the simulation environment
(phil.lsp):

```
(.ruleorder '((1 same)(2 prob)))
(.sequence '((1 production)(2 mixed)))
(.control 'automatic)
(.report-when 'after-rule)
(.simlevel 1)
(.trace 'off)
(.sim)
```

Function .ruleorder specifies that the five-state automaton will operate using
normal-rule firing (rules are fired in the same order in which they appear in the input
file). The Petri net transitions, however, use a probabilistic method of firing to ensure
fairness. Level 1 (the automaton) uses declarative sequencing whereas the Petri net
uses a combination of declarative and procedural sequencing. We choose to interrupt
the simulation dynamically so we choose automatic control. The report demon is
activated after a rule is fired. The initial simulation level is set at 1, the trace is turned
off, and simulation is initiated using .sim. Now we see an example session executed
in "automatic" mode using a D̂ to move down an abstraction level. In this sample
session, we have specified that each of the five philosophers takes 10 time units to eat:

```
$hires
+——————————————————-+
|   HIRES Simulation System |
|          Version 1.0      |
|          Paul Fishwick    |
+——————————————————-+
Please enter the application name.
(HIRES expects the files *.net, *.int, *.kb, and *.lsp)
: phil
Level 1 has 1 rule(s).
Level 2 has 20 rule(s).
There are 2 interface rule(s).
; Loading file USR1:[FISHWICK.HIRES.PHIL]PHIL.LSP;30
; .REPORT
; PRINT-TIME
; PETRI-PRECONDS
; PETRI-ADD
; ASSUMPTIONS-2-1
; ADD-2
; Finished loading USR1:[FISHWICK.HIRES.PHIL]PHIL.LSP;30

Hires> (load 'demo1)
; Loading file USR1:[FISHWICK.HIRES.PHIL]DEMO1.LSP;21
Trace turned OFF
Philosophers 2 and 4 are eating.
Philosophers 3 and 5 are eating.
Philosophers 4 and 1 are eating.
Philosophers 5 and 2 are eating.
Philosophers 1 and 3 are eating.
Philosophers 2 and 4 are eating.
Philosophers 3 and 5 are eating.
Philosophers 4 and 1 are eating.

- Changing to level 2 - (* note that ^D was pressed here *)


Time: 0.0 Philosopher 4 is not eating.
Time: 0.0 Philosopher 1 is not eating.
Time: 0.0 Philosopher 2 is eating.
Time: 0.0 Philosopher 5 is eating.
Time: 10.0 Philosopher 5 is not eating.
Time: 10.0 Philosopher 4 is eating.
Time: 10.0 Philosopher 2 is not eating.
Time: 10.0 Philosopher 1 is eating.
```

```
Time: 20.0 Philosopher 1 is not eating.
Time: 20.0 Philosopher 2 is eating.
Time: 20.0 Philosopher 4 is not eating.
Time: 20.0 Philosopher 4 is eating.
Time: 30.0 Philosopher 4 is not eating.
Time: 30.0 Philosopher 5 is eating.
Time: 30.0 Philosopher 2 is not eating.
Time: 30.0 Philosopher 3 is eating.
Time: 40.0 Philosopher 3 is not eating.
Time: 40.0 Philosopher 2 is eating.
Time: 40.0 Philosopher 5 is not eating.
```

In Figures 15–34 we present sample frames from a more extensive simulation of the dining philosophers on an Iris Workstation (made by Silicon Graphics, Inc.). In this simulation, we vary the time that each philosopher needs to perform the eating action. There are 10 frames shot at abstraction level 1 followed by 10 frames shot at level 2. Note that actions at level 2 "appear" more complex than actions at level 1 since the actions are generated from a less abstract model (the Petri net). In level 1, pairs of philosophers eat using the same time duration. In level 2, some philosophers will eat faster than others yielding a more "asynchronous" appearance.

Figure 15. Level 1, frame 1. Copyright 1988 IEEE.

Figure 16. Level 1, frame 37. Copyright 1988 IEEE.

Figure 17. Level 1, frame 43. Copyright 1988 IEEE.

Figure 18. Level 1, frame 46. Copyright 1988 IEEE.

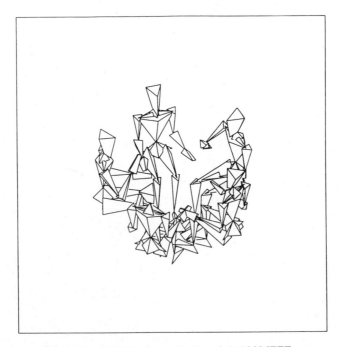

Figure 19. Level 1, frame 56. Copyright 1988 IEEE.

Figure 20. Level 1, frame 60. Copyright 1988 IEEE.

Figure 21. Level 1, Frame 71. Copyright 1988 IEEE.

Figure 22. Level 1, Frame 100. Copyright 1988 IEEE.

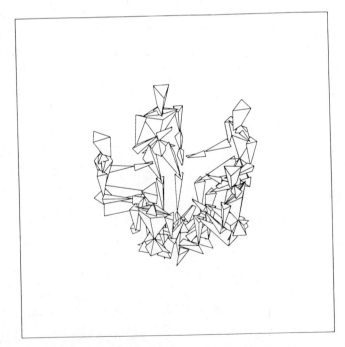

Figure 23. Level 1, Frame 150. Copyright 1988 IEEE.

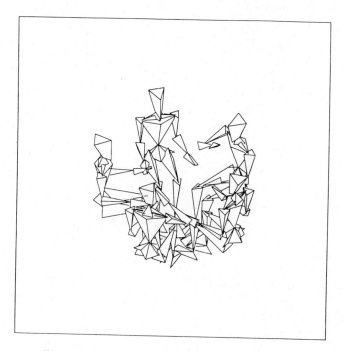

Figure 24. Level 1, Frame 259. Copyright 1988 IEEE.

Figure 25. Level 2, Frame 1. Copyright 1988 IEEE.

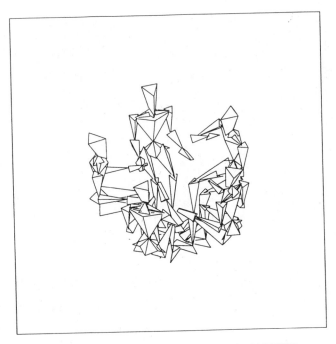

Figure 26. Level 2, Frame 35. Copyright 1988 IEEE.

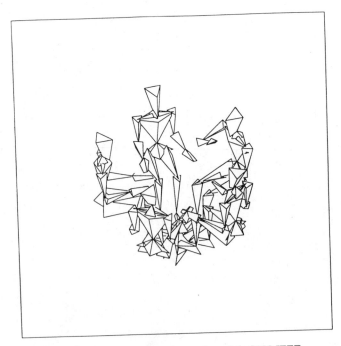

Figure 27. Level 2, Frame 106. Copyright 1988 IEEE.

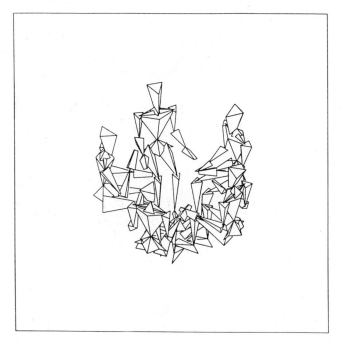

Figure 28. Level 2, Frame 121. Copyright 1988 IEEE.

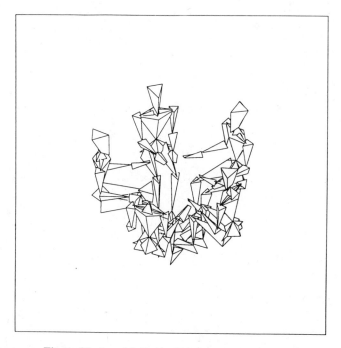

Figure 29. Level 2, Frame 195. Copyright 1988 IEEE.

Figure 30. Level 2, Frame 214. Copyright 1988 IEEE.

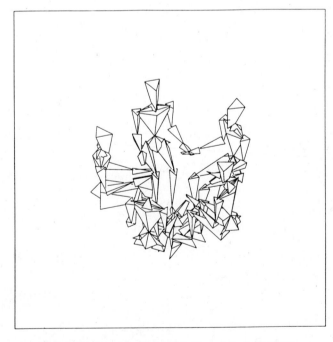

Figure 31. Level 2, Frame 290. Copyright 1988 IEEE.

Figure 32. Level 2, Frame 314. Copyright 1988 IEEE.

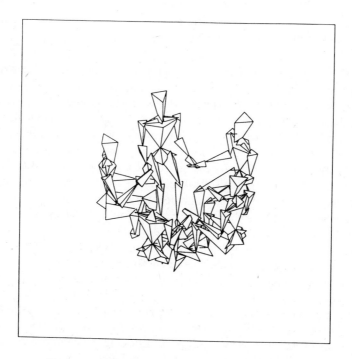

Figure 33. Level 2, Frame 330. Copyright 1988 IEEE.

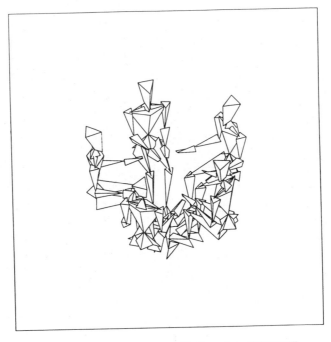

Figure 34. Level 2, Frame 387. Copyright 1988 IEEE.

6 CONCLUSIONS

We have discussed a formal foundation for a definition of process abstraction and have referenced work in various disciplines that contribute to this discussion. A process is defined not as a single-level model but instead as a partially ordered graph termed an *abstraction network*. Valid methods of abstraction have been enumerated. Methods defined using a definite mapping technique are essentially validated by the precise definition of the mapping function(s). Methods not defined using a mapping, such as those modeling methods in system dynamics, qualitative reasoning, and scene animation must rely on some type of statistic to illustrate the validity of the model. A sample statistic is an average (mean, median, or mode) for a sample of human observers that review the model. The dining philosophers process (**DP**) has been exclusively used so that the concepts of *methods of abstraction* and *abstraction network* could be explained clearly. The simulation language HIRES serves as a basis for experimenting with process abstraction concepts; capabilities are embedded within HIRES to allow for the use of traditional simulation methods (queues, random variates, continuous block model components) in addition to more abstract methods (production rules).

To properly assess the importance of a notion such as process abstraction, we demonstrated the use of HIRES in scene animation. Animation is treated simply as a form of simulation that involves a highly visual reporting mechanism. The reason that animation was considered useful to our work is twofold:

• *Animation helps in studying process abstraction.* This is due to the direct visual feedback one receives while dynamically switching abstraction levels for the process being simulated. The animation itself is not crucial to studying process abstraction; it is simply an auxiliary method (i.e., sensory) of validating abstract models.

• *Process abstraction helps in studying animation.* Abstraction methods can help reduce the complexity of scene animation. Also, abstraction methods may be used to study human visual motion perception.

This study is still continuing, and we hope to obtain interesting results in complexity analysis and the overall methodology in creating an animation from first principles. We believe that the study of process abstraction should be considered as important as, say, data abstraction in programming languages. There are many opportunities to extend and revise concepts already presented; the notion of process abstraction is to some extent orthogonal to other types of abstraction including geometric object abstraction [9, 15] and report abstraction. We hope to continue this work on abstraction by integrating these different abstraction types. Much more needs to be done to formalize these concepts and experiment with effective means for integration. Methods for researching *refinement* (the reverse direction of abstraction) are discussed elsewhere [16], and we continue to study this more completely as well.

The process of simulation modeling is evolutionary. First, we begin with informal models and gradually progress to more formal models as our knowledge increases. For this reason, it is important to capture and record the models associated with each layer of evolutionary stratification. Even though we are often completely aware of a detailed method for modeling a process, we choose a simplistic method (such as a causal graph), perhaps, if an issue in complexity or model comprehension arises. Sometimes, we shall not be aware of a more detailed model. In any event, all levels of abstraction can be maintained and related in the abstraction network; we should view processes and simulation as multifacetted [49] and multilayered. With an abstraction network at his or her disposal, a simulationist can make dynamic choices about levels while simulating. The multilayered modeling method will also tend to foster a more intense interdisciplinary approach to simulation.

APPENDIX: HIRES FUNCTIONS

After initiating a session, the user converses with HIRES by using certain LISP functions that are completely defined elsewhere [17]. In this appendix, we simply categorize and overview the functions that can be utilized during a HIRES session:

• *General Simulation* `.delta`, increment, decrement time slice; `.de-schedule`, deschedule an event from the event queue; `.dont-fire`, abort rule firing in the current rule; `.get-slot`, `.set-slot`, modify/obtain rule frame slots; `.loadapp`, `.loadint`, `.loadkb`, `.loadnet`, `.init`, set up the inputs for the simulation; `.schedule`, schedule an event; `.sim`, start simulation for a duration or while a condition is true.

- *Mode Setting* `.control`, control event firing (manual vs. automatic); `.empty-queue`, capability to empty abstraction level queues; `.event-queue-scope`, use a queue per abstraction level or one global queue; `.flow`, set simulation flow to sequential or parallel; `.report-when`, used by report demon to decide when to report simulation output; `.ruleorder`, specify conflict resolution strategy for rule firing; `.sequence`, maps rule firing method to each abstraction level (procedural, declarative, or mixed); `.simlevel`, set abstraction level for simulation; `.simtime`, set simulation time; `.trace`, set simulation trace on or off.

- *Uncertainty/Heuristic Knowledge* `.pand`, `.por`, AND/OR trees combined with probability factors.

- *Random Variates* `.random-define`, user-defined distribution; `.random-uniform`, uniform distribution; `.random-exp`, exponential distribution; `.random-normal`, normal distribution.

- *Utility Functions* `.dec`, `.inc`, `.dlist`, `.edt`, `.em`, `.for`, `.inc`, `.interval`, `.match`, `.output`, `.repeat`, `.time`, `.while`, general functions that help when using LISP. Some functions implement "Pascal-like" features in LISP.

- *Report Generation* `.report`, the report demon; `.filter-key`, use a key to filter knowledge base for potential simulation output; `.filter-levels`, filter by abstraction levels (i.e., output only certain level information independently of levels that are simulated); `.filter-match`, filtering by general matching; `.filter-time`, report information only for specified time interval; `.report-add`, report when asserting information to knowledge base.

- *Preprocessors* `.script`, generate script (table-driven) processes; `.flow-graph`, `.flow-graph-time`, generate graph-based processes; graphs are bipartite and can have duration times associated with "transition" elements; `.csmp`, `.csmp-params`, `.bang-bang`, `.constant`, cosine, `.dead-space`, `.divider`, `.exponential`, `.gain`, `.half-power`, `.integrate`, `.inverter`, `.jitter`, `.limiter`, `.logarithm`, `.magnitude`, `.multiply`, `.negative-clipper`, `.offset`, `.positive-clipper`, `.relay`, `.summer`, `.weighted-summer`; CSMP [10] primitives, `.petri`, `.petri-time`, generate Petri net and timed Petri net processes.

- *Representational Abstraction* Allow for processes to be organized in a representational hierarchy. `.flow-graph-sub`, `.flow-graph-time-sub`, `.csmp-sub`, `.petri-sub`, `.petri-time-sub`, methods for hierarchically representing preprocessors discussed in the previous item.

ACKNOWLEDGMENTS

The material for this chapter is based in part on a paper in the *IEEE Transactions on Systems, Man and Cybernetics*, **18**(1):18–39, January/February 1988. Certain parts have been reproduced by permission of IEEE.

The author wishes to thank Norman Badler at the University of Pennsylvania for discussions on process-related topics such as human motion representation and Bernard Zeigler of the University of Arizona for comments on the material presented in earlier drafts of this chapter. Many thanks also to the anonymous referees for taking their time to make valuable comments on drafts of the chapter.

REFERENCES

1. R. H. Abraham and C. D. Shaw, *Dynamics—The Geometry of Behavior*, vols. 1–3, Aerial, Santa Cruz, CA, 1982.

2. A. V. Aho, J. E. Hopcroft, and J. D. Ullman, *The Design and Analysis of Computer Algorithms*, Addison-Wesley, Reading, MA, 1974.

3. F. E. Allen and J. Cocke, "A Program Data Flow Analysis," *Communications of the ACM*, **19**(3):137–147, 1976.

4. P. M. Andreae, "Constraint Limited Generalization: Acquiring Procedures from Examples," in *Fourth National Conference on Artificial Intelligence, Austin, Texas, AAAI*, Kaufmann, Los Altos, CA, 1984, pp. 6–10.

5. D. Angluin and C. H. Smith, "Inductive Inference: Theory and Methods," *Computing Surveys*, **15**(3):237–269, September 1983.

6. N. I. Badler, "Temporal Scene Analysis: Conceptual Descriptions of Object Movements," Ph.D. Thesis, University of Toronto, Toronto, Canada, February 1975.

7. N. I. Badler, B. L. Webber, J. U. Korein, and J. Korein, "Positioning and Animation Human Figures in a Task-oriented Environment," *Visual Computer*, **1**:212–220, 1986.

8. D. G. Bobrow, *Qualitative Reasoning about Physical Systems*, MIT Press, Cambridge, MA, 1985.

9. J. H. Clark, "Hierarchical Geometric Models for Visible Surface Algorithms," *Communications of the ACM*, **19**(10):547–554, October 1976.

10. IBM, *IBM 1130 Continuous System Modeling Program, Program Description and Operations Manual*, IBM Program Information Department, Hawthorne, NY, sh20-0905 edition, 1976.

11. E. W. Dijkstra, "Cooperating Sequential Processes," in F. Genuys (Ed.), *Programming Languages*, Academic, New York, 1968.

12. M. H. Doshi, R. B. Sullivan, and D. M. Schuler, "Themis Logic Simulator—A Mix Mode, Multi-level Hierarchical, Interactive Digital Circuit Simulator," in *IEEE Design Automation Conference*, IEEE, New York, 1984, pp. 24–31.

13. B. Dufay and J. C. Latombe, "An Approach to Automatic Robot Programming Based on Inductive Learning," in *Robotics Research: The First International Symposium*, MIT Press, Cambridge, MA, 1984.

14. D. Farmer, T. Toffoli, and S. Wolfram (Eds.), *Cellular Automata: Proceedings of an Interdisciplinary Workshop*, North-Holland, Amsterdam, 1983.

15. S. Feiner, "Apex: An Experiment in the Automated Creation of Pictorial Explanations," *IEEE Computer Graphics and Applications*, **5**(11):29–37, November 1985.

16. P. A. Fishwick, "Automating the Transition from Lumped Models to Base Models," in *SCS Eastern Simulation Conference, Orlando, FL, April 1988*, Society for Computer Simulation, San Diego, CA, pp. 57–63.

17. P. A. Fishwick, "*Hierarchical Reasoning: Simulating Complex Processes over Multiple Levels of Abstraction,*" Ph.D. Dissertation, University of Pennsylvania, 1986.

18. P. A. Fishwick, "Qualitative Simulation: Fundamental Concepts and Issues," in *AI and Simulation: The Diversity of Applications*, The Society for Computer Simulation, part of the Society for Computer Simulation Multi-Conference, San Diego, CA, February 1988, pp. 25–31.

19. P. A. Fishwick, "The Role of Process Abstraction in Simulation," *IEEE Transactions on Systems, Man and Cybernetics*, **18**(1):18–39, January/February, 1988.

20. N. Y.-K. Foo, "Homomorphic Simplification of Systems," Ph.D. Thesis, University of Michigan, 1974.

21. J. W. Forrester, *Industrial Dynamics*, MIT Press, Cambridge, MA, 1961.

22. J. W. Forrester, *World Dynamics*, Wright-Allen, Cambridge, MA, 1971.

23. M. R. Genesereth, *The Use of Design Descriptions in Automated Diagnosis*, MIT Press, Cambridge, MA, 1985, pp. 411–436.

24. D. Gentner and A. Stevens, *Mental Models*, Erlbaum, Hillsdale, NJ, 1983.

25. P. J. Hayes, "The Naive Physics Manifesto," *Expert Systems in the Microelectronic Age*, University of Edinburgh Press, Edinburgh, Scotland, 1979.

26. F. Hayes-Roth, "Rule-based Systems," *Communications of the ACM*, **28**(9):921–932, September 1985.

27. Y. Ijiri, "Fundamental Queries in Aggregation Theory," *Journal of the American Statistical Association*, **66**(336):766–782, December 1971.

28. Consolidated Analysis Centers Inc., "SIMSCRIPT II.5 Reference Handbook," La Jolla, CA, 1972.

29. Y. Iwasaki and H. A. Simon, "Causality in Device Behavior," *Artificial Intelligence*, **29**(1):3–32, July 1986.

30. R. E. Kalman, P. L. Falb, and M. A. Arbib, *Topics in Mathematical Systems Theory*, McGraw-Hill, New York, 1962.

31. N. Magnenat-Thalmann and T. Daniel, *Computer Animation: Theory and Practice*, Springer-Verlag, New York, 1985.

32. N. Magnenat-Thalmann and T. Daniel, "Three-dimensional Computer Animation: More an Evolution than a Motion Problem," *IEEE Computer Graphics and Applications*, **5**(10):47–57, October 1985.

33. R. Michalski, J. G. Carbonell, and T. M. Mitchell, *Machine Learning: An Artificial Intelligence Approach*, Kaufmann, Los Altos, CA, 1983.

34. "Motion: Representation and Perception," paper presented at SIGGRAPH/SIGART Interdisciplinary Workshop, April 1983.

35. S. S. Muchnick and N. D. Jones, *Program Flow Analysis: Theory and Applications*, Prentice-Hall, Englewood Cliffs, NJ, 1981.

36. W. Nordhaus, "World Dynamics: Measurement Without Data," *Economic Journal*, **83**(332):1156–1183, 1973.

37. J. L. Peterson, *Petri Net Theory and the Modeling of Systems*, Prentice-Hall, Englewood Cliffs, NJ, 1981.

38. C. Petri, "Kommunikation mit Automaten," Ph.D. Thesis, University of Bonn, 196

39. E. Post, "Formal Reductions of the General Combinatorial Problem, *American Journal of Mathematics*, **65**:197–268, 1943.

40. A. A. B. Pritsker, *Introduction to Simulation and SLAM II*, Halsted, New York, 1986.

41. C. J. Puccia and R. Levins, *Qualitative Modeling of Complex Systems*, Harvard University Press, Cambridge, MA, 1985.

42. W. T. Reeves, "Particle Systems—A Technique for Modeling a Class of Fuzzy Objects, *ACM Transactions on Graphics*, **2**:91–108, 1983.

43. N. Roberts, D. Andersen, R. Deal, M. Garet, and W. Shaffer, *Introduction to Computer Simulation: A Systems Dynamics Approach*, Addison-Wesley, Reading, MA, 1983.

44. H. A. Simon and A. Ando, "Aggregation of Variables in Dynamic Systems," *Econometrica*, **29**(2), April 1961.

45. D. S. Weld, "The Use of Aggregation in Causal Simulation," *Artificial Intelligence*, **30**(1):1–34, October 1986.

46. A. W. Wymore, *A Mathematical Theory of Systems Engineering: The Elements*, Krieger, Melbourne, FL, 1977.

47. A. W. Wymore, *Systems Engineering Methodology for Interdisciplinary Teams*, Wiley, New York, 1976.

48. B. P. Zeigler, *Multifaceted Systems Modeling: Structure and Behavior at a Multiplicity of Levels*, Academic, New York, 1985, pp. 265–293.

49. B. P. Zeigler, *Multi-Facetted Modeling and Discrete Event Simulation*, Academic, New York, 1984.

50. B. P. Zeigler, *Simplification of Biochemical Reaction Systems*, Cambridge University Press, New York, 1980, pp. 113–145.

51. B. P. Zeigler, *Theory of Modeling and Simulation*, Wiley, New York, 1976.

52. B. P. Zeigler, "Towards a Formal Theory of Modelling and Simulation: Structure Preserving Morphisms," *Journal of the Association for Computing Machinery*, **19**(4):742–764, 1972.

5 Extending the Mathematics in Qualitative Process Theory

BRUCE D'AMBROSIO

Department of Computer Science
Oregon State University
Corvallis, Oregon

1 INTRODUCTION

Qualitative process (QP) theory [7] describes the form and structure of naive theories [8] about the dynamics of physical systems. A key component of QP theory is the qualitative mathematics used to represent values of continuous parameters and relationships between them. A research strategy for developing this mathematics has been to search for a qualitative mathematics capable of yielding significant results from a minimum of information about the situation being modeled. In the work described here, we ask a slightly different question: What kinds of information can we add to the base theory, and what new questions can we answer with this additional information? We examine a simple example that reveals two limitations in the current theory. First, the qualitative description of a situation is often ambiguous. Second, QP theory is of limited use in reasoning about the effects of adjustments to continuous control parameters. We then present an extension to the mathematics used in QP theory that improves its performance in both these areas. We begin with a review of QP theory.

1.1 Mathematics in QP Theory

The representation for a continuous parameter in QP theory is a *quantity*. A quantity has four parts:

1. the magnitude of the amount of the quantity,
2. the sign of the amount $\{-, 0, +\}$,
3. the magnitude of the derivative, and
4. the sign of the derivative.

The use of the sign as a significant qualitative abstraction is adopted from DeKleer [4, 5]. Magnitudes are represented in a *quantity space*. The quantity space for a number consists of all those amounts to which it is potentially related in the situation being modeled. The special value ZERO is always included in every quantity space and relates the quantity space representation with sign information.

Quantities are related to one another through *relations,* which can be either ordering relations, functional relations, or influences. Ordering relations include simple statements regarding the relative values of quantities, such as

```
level(p) = level(q)
pressure(p) Greater_than Zero
```

Functional relations are a qualitative analog of continuous monotonic functions whose domain and range are real numbers. The following states that the level of water in a container is qualitatively proportional to the amount in the container:

```
level(p) Q+ amount_of(p)
```

These are called qualitative proportionalities (Qprops). Qprops can be named, permitting the propagation of ordering information through separate instances of the same named relationship. The *process* is the mechanism of change in QP theory. A process acts to change a situation by *influencing* some parameter(s) of objects in the situation. An *influence* is similar in information content to a qualitative proportionality but affects the derivative of the range variable rather than its amount. For example, the primary effect of a fluid flow process is on the derivatives of the source and destination fluid quantities:

```
amount_of(destination) I+ flow_rate
amount_of(source) I- flow_rate
```

Qprops are often referred to as *indirect* influences since they provide pathways through which *direct* influences propagate.

Forbus's implementation of QP theory combines this basic domain information with an initial system description to perform measurement interpretation and envisioning. The initial description contains only a listing of the basic physical objects in the situation and need not identify any processes that may be active in that situation. These are automatically determined from descriptions of the conditions under which processes become active. The basic inferences performed are as follows:

1. *Elaboration*   All possible process instances that may occur in a situation are added to it.
2. *Process Structure Determination*   Selection from the set of possible process instances those subsets that are mutually consistent and consistent with the known facts about the situation. Each such subset is a partial description of one or more possible qualitative states of the physical system.
3. *Influence Resolution*   The set of influences on each situation parameter is closed for each possible process structure in an attempt to resolve the effect of the influences on the parameter.

EXAMPLE   135

4. *Limit Analysis*   Predictions are made regarding possible transitions out of
   each qualitative state.

For a detailed discussion of these inferences, see reference 7. We shall primarily be
concerned in this chapter with influence resolution and a modification of it we term
linguistic perturbation analysis. In addition, we briefly discuss extensions to process
structure determination for dealing with uncertain information. For a more detailed
discussion of these extensions, see reference 1.

2   EXAMPLE

We now analyze a hypothetical model of a typical continuous-flow industrial process
in order to demonstrate these steps and identify the capabilities and limitations of QP
theory. Figure 1 shows a simplified sketch of the process. Reactants in granular form
enter through the port at the top left (a material flow process) and are heated to reaction
temperature within the vessel (a heat flow process). When the reactants reach reaction
temperature, they undergo a state change (a reaction) in which they disappear and a
fluid product and an off-gas are created. The off-gas exits through the port at the upper
right (another material flow process). As the hot off-gas flows out of the reaction vessel,
heat is transferred to the cool incoming reactants (countercurrent heat flow). We shall
ignore the processes by which the product is extracted from the vessel and simply allow
it to accumulate at the bottom.

Our interest in a system such as this is in reasoning about it for purposes of process
control. Many forms of reasoning are needed for process control, from which we have

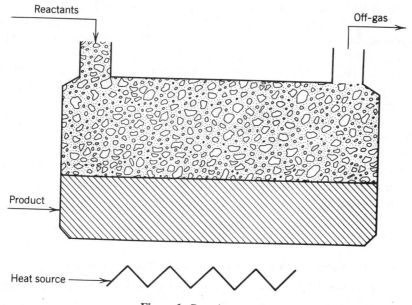

Figure 1. Reaction vessel.

selected two for initial investigation: measurement interpretation and prediction. Specifically, we would like to determine what might be happening in the system given some observations of selected measurable parameters (measurement interpretation) and to estimate the effects of possible control actions (prediction). These control actions typically are adjustments to independent continuous parameters.

A well-established mathematical theory, control theory, exists for reasoning about systems such as this. Unfortunately, it is not applicable in many situations for any of four reasons:

1. Observational data may be uncertain or incomplete.
2. Precise mathematical models of the underlying physical processes may be unavailable or too complex for efficient reasoning.
3. The results of mathematical modeling must be further interpreted before they can be used by human or automated control systems.
4. Mathematical models carry only part of the modeling burden. Specifically, they cannot conveniently account for the appearance or disappearance of objects in the situation being modeled, and do not account for the processes by which an appropriate model is formulated.

QP theory, on the other hand, can reason with incomplete data, is computationally tractable, allows for description of system processes in terms familiar to those who actually control such systems today, and can represent and reason about situations in which objects appear and disappear. For these reasons, QP theory offers the promise of significantly extending the scope of automated process control.

The four basic processes crucial to understanding of the system described in the preceding, basic heat flow, the reaction, material flow, and counter current heat flow, are described in detail elsewhere [1]. Given a suitable initial-state description, the first two QP inferences identify three possible states for the situation described: (1) that nothing is happening, (2) that the only thing occurring is that the reaction vessel is being heated, or (3) that all processes are active. The state of interest is the one in which all processes are active. The influence graph in Figure 2 illustrates a simplified version of the influences and qualitative proportionalities between variables in the state.

Using influence resolution, we can determine various facts about this state, such as (a complete output for the three cases is shown in Figure 3):

- If the heat input is increasing, the off-gas generation rate will be increasing also.
- If the incoming reactant temperature is decreasing, the off-gas temperature will be decreasing.

However, we cannot determine the following:

1. Is the product temperature increasing, decreasing, or constant?
2. If the heat input is increasing, is the off-gas exit temperature increasing or decreasing?

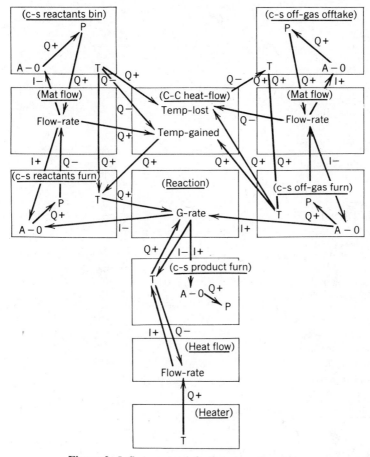

Figure 2. Influence graph for furnace active state.

3. If we increase the heat input a little, how much will the generation rate increase?
4. If the available observations do not uniquely identify a single state, which of the possible states is more likely?

These limitations are the result of ambiguity in the conclusions derived using QP theory.

3   AMBIGUITY IN QP THEORY

We identify two types of ambiguity in QP theory, *internal* and *external* ambiguity. Internal ambiguity occurs when the use of QP theory produces multiple descriptions of a single physical situation. External ambiguity is the dual of this, namely, when a single QP theory description corresponds to several possible physical situations that must be distinguished. Internal ambiguity is of two types. First, given a situation

Parameter	Influence Resolution	QPA (heater)	QPA (reactants)
P (reactants bin)	−	−	?
A (reactants bin)	−	−	?
T (reactants bin)	0	0	+
P (reactants furnace)	?	−	?
A (reactants furnace)	?	−	?
T (reactants furnace)	?	+	?
P (product furnace)	+	+	?
A (product furnace)	+	+	?
T (product furnace)	?	+	?
P (off-gas furnace)	?	+	?
A (off-gas furnace)	?	+	?
T (off-gas furnace)	?	+	?
P (off-gas offtake)	+	+	?
A (off-gas offtake)	+	+	?
T (off-gas offtake)	?	?	+
Temperature (heater)	0	+	0
Flow-Rate (reactants)	?	+	?
Flow-Rate (off-gas)	?	+	?
Flow-Rate (heat)	?	+	?
G-Rate (reaction)	?	+	?
Temperature-Lost	?	?	−
Temperature-Gained	?	+	−

Note:

1. "?" indicates an ambiguity in the QP analysis.

2. The two independent parameters are in **boldface.**

3. The value shown is the sign of the derivative.

Figure 3. Results of QP analysis of furnace.

description, there may be ambiguity about which of several possible states a system is in (e.g., given a leaky bucket with water pouring in, is the water level rising or falling?). Second, given a specific state, there may be ambiguity about what state will follow it (e.g., given a closed container containing water and a heat source heating the container, will it explode?).

External ambiguity is the inability to determine, on a scale meaningful to an external observer, the duration of a situation as well as the magnitude and intra-situation evolution of the parameters of the situation (e.g., how fast is the water rising? How long before the container explodes?)

These ambiguities are the result of four fundamental limitations in QP theory representations and inference mechanisms:

1. Inability to resolve conflicting functional dependencies. That is, if two influences on a parameter are of opposite sign, QP theory has no way to determine the resulting composite influence. This is caused by the weak representation for the functional form of dependencies, which captures only the sign but no strength information.

2. Inability to order predicted state changes. This results in the inability to determine which of several possible successor states will be the actual successor of a state. This is caused by lack of ordering information on change rates as well as lack of quantitative information on the magnitude of change needed for state change.

3. Inability to quantify, even approximately, parameters significant to external observers during times between major state transitions. This is caused by a weak model of *intra*-state situation evolution. Time, quantity values, and functional dependencies are all represented qualitatively in QP theory.

4. Inability to represent non-Boolean predicate and state possibilities. This prevents the system from distinguishing between states that are possible but highly unlikely and states that are highly likely.

Solving these problems requires extending QP representations to capture more information about the system being modeled. We have studied three classes of extensions: extensions to the quantity representations, the relationship representations, and the certainty representations. Specifically, we have developed an extension to QP theory that utilizes the following:

- *Belief Function Certainty Representations*   These will permit capture of partial or uncertain observational data and estimates of state likelihood.
- *Linguistic Descriptions of Influence Sensitivities*   To reduce undecidability during influence resolution.
- *Linguistic Characterizations of Parameter Values and Ordering Relationships*   To permit capture of partial or uncertain observational data and enable estimates of the effects of adjustments to continuous control parameters.

It should be noted that these are extensions, not replacement representations. This extension is orthogonal to the quantity space representation used in QP. The original quantity space representation is retained and is assumed in the examples presented in this chapter. These extensions reason at the appropriate level of detail for the kinds of control actions typically needed, draw the needed distinctions, are computationally tractable, and can reason with the imprecise or uncertain data typically available. In this chapter we concentrate on the second of these extensions, linguistic influence sensitivities, and present a way of annotating the relationship representation in QP theory to reduce ambiguity. Discussion of the integration of Dempster–Shafer belief functions with QP theory and the underlying ATMS can be found elsewhere [3]. A later section of this chapter also discusses our parameter value extensions and shows how they, in combination with the functional extensions, can be used to estimate the effects of potential control actions. Further details can be found in the literature [1]. See reference 11 for an alternate extended quantity representation.

4 LINGUISTIC INFLUENCE SENSITIVITIES

Basic QP theory cannot resolve the conflicting influences on the off-gas temperature parameter in our example. The influence resolution rule used by Forbus states that if opposite influences impinge on a single parameter, then the net influence on the parameter is unknown. In order to reduce the number of situations in which conflicting functional dependencies cannot be resolved, we extend QP theory functional descriptions with a linguistic influence sensitivity. Intuitively, this corresponds to distinguishing between first-order, second-order, and so on, dependencies. With this extension we can now address the second question unanswerable earlier: If we increase the heat input, will the off-gas temperature increase or decrease?

Forbus claims that if actual data about relative magnitudes of the influences is available, it can be used to resolve conflicts. We might attempt to achieve this by extending direct and indirect influences with a strength parameter. This is inadequate, however, for two reasons. First, the overriding influence may not be local. Information may have to be propagated through several influences before reaching the parameter at which it is combined. Second, various sources of strength information have varying scopes of validity. In the following sections we first identify two basic influence subgraphs responsible for the ambiguity in our example and argue that the ambiguity can be eliminated by annotating the subgraphs with influence sensitivity and adding additional situation parameters. We then present extensions to the influence resolution algorithm for utilizing the sensitivity annotations and finally describe a control structure for managing acquisition and use of annotation information.

4.1 Identifying Internal Causes of Conflict in Influence Graphs

We have identified two basic patterns of influences that account for the ambiguity previously encountered. These are the conflict triangle (Figure 4) and the feedback loop (Figure 5). The reason, for example, that the change in off-gas temperature in the offtake cannot be resolved is that there are two conflicting paths through which a single parameter (off-gas temperature in the reaction vessel) affects the target parameter. But the effect on temperature lost is in this case smaller than the direct effect on the offtake temperature and can be ignored. We can indicate this by adding to the influence arc an annotation indicating that temperature lost in countercurrent heat flow is relatively insensitive to off-gas temperature in the furnace (Figure 4b).

Another ambiguity in the QP theory analysis of the furnace is in the generation rate and associated variables. One of the causes of this ambiguity is the set of influences on product temperature shown in Figure 3. Since both the generation rate and heat flow rate are positive, the qualitative derivative of the product temperature is undecidable. This network is similar to one Kuipers [9] identifies as introducing a new *landmark value* not in the original quantity space for the product temperature. This new value

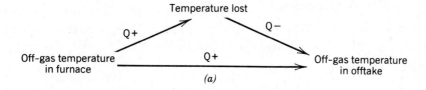

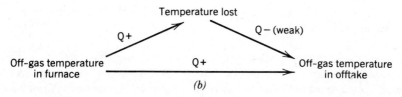

Figure 4. Conflict triangle.

represents an equilibrium value toward which the temperature will tend. Recognition of the existence of an equilibrium value permits resolution of the effects of the conflicting influences on product temperature, depending on the assumed ordering between the actual product temperature and the equilibrium value. Kuipers adds the equilibrium value to the set of fixed points in the quantity space for the original variable. We, however, add it as a *new parameter of the model* subject to influences similar to those of the original quantity. Thus, we can represent and reason about change in both the actual value and the equilibrium value in response to active processes. For example, if the actual temperature is only slightly sensitive to the heat flow rate but the equilibrium temperature is very sensitive, then we might conclude that the system will be slow in returning to equilibrium once perturbed. The extended influence diagram for the feedback loop is shown in Figure 5.

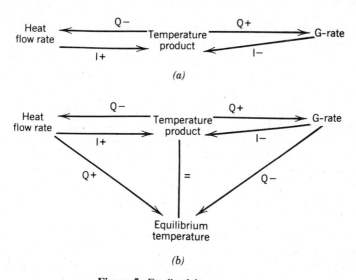

Figure 5. Feedback loops.

4.2   Sensitivity Annotations

An influence is a partial derivative of a controlled variable with respect to a controlling variable. In QP theory, computing a value for a controlled variable takes place in two phases:

1. All of the individual influences on the controlled variable must be identified, and the effect of each of these must be computed.
2. The various effects must be combined to determine the composite effect on the controlled variable.

This procedure relies on local propagation to perform influence resolution. If local propagation is to carry the burden of our extended influence resolution, then the propagated value must somehow be extended to represent the sensitivity information. The value being propagated in influence resolution is a quantity, and the representation used is sign abstraction. If we model influences as describing the normalized sensitivity of one variable to changes in another, then we can simply extend the quantity representation for the influence quantity and use a discrete scale of influence magnitudes. We then represent the actual value as a fuzzy set over this value space to model the imprecision in the available sensitivity information. The following observations lead us to choose a fuzzy-set representation for influence sensitivity annotations:

- A discrete representation matches well with the propositional-style reasoner underlying our implementation.
- The sensitivity is not always known with precision (recall our comment about lack of precise mathematical models).
- The sensitivity may not be constant over the range of the variables or may not be independent of the values of other parameters.

An alternate model is described elsewhere [10]. A major difference between their work and ours is our assumption that an annotation represents a normalized sensitivity. We show in the next section how this permits us to make semi-quantitative estimates, which we believe their system cannot do. While influence resolution using sensitivity annotations is conceptually simple, two questions arise. First, how can an appropriate discretization for the normalized change value (effect on one variable of changes in another; henceforth referred to as an influence value) be determined. Second, How are influence values to be propagated through annotated influences.

If we start with an n-level influence value discretization and an m-level sensitivity discretization, then after k influence propagation steps we seemingly might need an $(nm)^k$ influence value discretization to avoid information loss. This worst-case complexity can be avoided, however, by the following four observations:

1. We are only interested in the result at a resolution equivalent to the original n-level discretization.
2. Additional detail is only relevant when two annotated influences are being combined to aid in influence resolution if they conflict.

3. Rather than annotating all influences in a graph, we only annotate those necessary to disambiguate parameters of interest in a specific query. We can design the propagation algorithm to take advantage of this by treating an unannotated influence as an identity operator for influence values.

4. We use a fuzzy relational algorithm as the basic model for influence propagation. The basic fuzzy relational influence algorithm can be designed so that failure to maintain a fully detailed discretization only increases the ambiguity of the result rather than produce incorrect results (e.g., if the correct answer is 2.5 and our discretization for influence values contains only the values {1, 2, 3, 4, 5}, we can represent the answer as the set {2, 3}).

Given this, we model sensitivity annotations as parameters of a standard *fuzzy relational influence algorithm* [13]. We choose a fuzzy representation to allow simple modeling of the imprecision of these annotations.[1] We next detail the algorithms used to compute the consequences of this fuzzy sensitivity.

4.2.1   Computing Individual Influences

An influence of the form

```
(Influenced-variable Q+/- Influencing-variable,
Sensitivity)
```

is taken to specify a fuzzy relation between three amounts: C, the amount of the influencing variable; S, the amount of the influence sensitivity; and Iv, the influence value. The value of Iv can be computed as follows:

$$Iv = \Sigma_{C,S} \ [\min(\mu_C, \mu_S, \mu_Q)/Q_{Iv,C,S}(C, S)],$$

where $Q_{I,C,S}(C, S)$ is the relation providing a degree of membership for each possible value of Iv for each value of C and S. A short review of fuzzy notation is in order at this point: $\mu_x(y)$ is the degree of membership of element y in the fuzzy set denoted by x and can take on values in {0, 1}. When the argument is omitted, as in what follows, it is assumed that the element is obvious from context. For example, $\Sigma_C(\mu_C)$ is the sum of the degree of memberships of each element in the fuzzy set C. Also, the notation x/y typically means that y is a member of a set to degree x. The preceding formula then defines the set Iv to consist of all the values of the elements of the relation $Q_{Iv,C,S}$. Each value may appear more than once in Q. The degree to which it is a member of Iv is the maximum of the degrees of membership specified in each appearance. The degree of membership resulting from an appearance of a value in Q is the minimum of the degree of membership of the corresponding value of the influencing variable (C), the degree

---

[1] The underlying model we assume is of a set of independent, linear influences. Fuzzy-set models of sensitivities permit us to allow for the inaccuracies of this model.

of membership of the corresponding value of the sensitivity annotation (S), and the degree of membership of the value in $Q_{Iv,C,S}(C,S)$.

This relation ($Q_{Iv,C,S}$) can be customized when specific information is available. As a default, we use the following to generate the table, assuming influence value and sensitivity annotations are both represented on a $\{ ..., -2, -1, 0, 1, 2, ... \}$ scale[2]:

$$Q_{I,C,S}(C_j, S_k) = \text{sign}(C_j * S_k) * (\text{abs}(C_j * S_k)^{1/2}).$$

In cases where the result is not in the original discretization, we use the set representation described earlier. Thus, we get the following default relation table for a five-element discretization for sensitivities and influence values:

C/S	−2	−1	0	1	2
−2	2	$\{1, 2\}$	0	$\{-2, -1\}$	−2
−1	$\{1, 2\}$	1	0	−1	$\{-2, -1\}$
0	0	0	0	0	0
1	$\{-2, -1\}$	−1	0	1	$\{1, 2\}$
2	−2	$\{-2, -1\}$	0	$\{1, 2\}$	2

4.2.2 Combining Influences

Sensitivity annotations provide us with a means of estimating influence magnitudes, which are directly comparable. In what follows we show an algorithm for computing the combined effect of two influences. A rough translation is that an element is definitely a member of the set of possible values for the combined influence if that element is a member of the value sets for both input values or if it is a member of the value set for one input and a weaker element of the same sign is a member of the value set for the other input. Also, an element of the discretization may be an element of the result set under two conditions: first, if it is a member of the value set of one input and an element of the same magnitude but opposite sign is a member of the value set for the other input and, second, if an element of the same sign but greater magnitude is a member of one value set and an element of the opposite sign and greater magnitude is a member of the other value set. We formalize this algorithm as follows:

$$\mu = \left[\mu_{Iv_1}(i) \wedge \mu_{Iv_2}(i) \right] \vee \left\{ \vee_{j,|j|<|i|} \left[\mu_{Iv_1}(i) \wedge \mu_{Iv_2}(j) \right] \right\}$$
$$\vee \left[\mu_{Iv_1}(i) \wedge \mu_{Iv_2}(-i) \wedge \text{unknown} \right] \vee \left\{ \vee_{j,j>i} \vee_{k,k<-i} \left[\mu_{Iv_1}(j) \wedge \mu_{Iv_2}(k) \wedge \text{unknown} \right] \right\}.$$

Subscripts i, j, and k are assumed to be zero for no influence, increasing positive for positive-influence elements, and increasing negative for increasing negative-influence elements (e.g., −3, −2, −1, 0, 1, 2, 3 for a seven-element discrete scale, with −3 the strongest negative influence). The preceding is only half of the formula actually used.

[2] All the algorithms we present are independent of the actual discretization used. We typically use a five or seven-element discretization, that is, $\{-2, -1, 0, 1, 2 \}$ or $\{-3, -2, -1, 0, 1, 2, 3\}$.

Parameter	Standard Influence Resolution	Extended Influence Resolution
P (reactants bin)	–	–
A (reactants bin)	–	–
T (reactants bin)	0	0
P (reactants furnace)	?	0
A (reactants furnace)	?	0
T (reactants furnace)	?	+
P (product furnace)	+	+
A (product furnace)	+	+
T (product furnace)	?	0
P (off-gas furnace)	?	0
A (off-gas furnace)	?	0
T (off-gas furnace)	?	0
P (off-gas offtake)	+	+
A (off-gas offtake)	+	+
T (off-gas offtake)	?	–
Temperature (heater)	0	0
Flow-Rate (reactants)	?	–
Flow-Rate (off-gas)	?	–
Flow-Rate (heat)	?	0
G-Rate (reaction)	?	+
Temperature-Lost	?	+
Temperature-Gained	?	+

Figure 6. Comparison of results of influence resolution.

The actual relation is symmetrical in the two influences Iv_1 and Iv_2. Figure 6 shows a comparison of the results of standard and extended influence resolution procedures.

4.3   Annotation Management

In examining the sources of ambiguity in the reaction vessel example, we note that many of the annotations that could resolve the ambiguities are not universally valid. In fact, we identify four levels of validity for an annotation. These validity levels are determined primarily by opportunities in the implementation:

1. An annotation is *universally* valid when it can be incorporated directly into a view or process description and correctly describes the functioning of a particular influence in all situations in which an instance of the view or process participates. These are rare.

2. An annotation is *scenario* valid when it correctly describes the operation of a particular influence in a particular view or process instance for all qualitative

states in which the instance is active. Product temperature annotations in the example are an instance of this annotation type.

3. An annotation is *state* valid when it correctly describes the operation of a particular influence in a view or process instance only for a defined subset of the qualitative states of a system.

4. Annotation is *query* valid when it correctly describes the operation of a particular influence in a view or process instance only for a particular query. The conflict triangle annotation for determining off-gas temperature in the offtake is an example of this type of annotation.

The first type of annotation can simply be part of the basic view or process definition. The other three are added to the QP description of a scenario as needed during problem solving. A four-step algorithm extends the basic QP theory influence resolution algorithm:

1. Execute the basic influence resolution.

2. Check results for ambiguities in parameter values of interest. If all interesting parameter values are determined uniquely, then problem solving is complete.

3. Otherwise, search the influence graph for instances of ambiguity causing subgraphs. If one is found and the parameter for which it might create an ambiguity is ambiguous, then annotate the subgraph with influence sensitivity information if available.

4. Reexecute the basic influence resolution algorithm on the now annotated graph.

This algorithm assumes that the extended QP reasoner is embedded in a larger system that has or can obtain the necessary problem-specific information to resolve ambiguities. It provides a problem-directed way of selecting aspects of the larger system's problem-specific knowledge relevant to the query being processed.

5   LINGUISTIC PERTURBATION ANALYSIS

QP theory cannot directly answer quantitative questions about the effect of changes to independent parameters. Yet, many approaches to process control require a means to estimate the effects of hypothetical actions. The four basic deductions of QP theory do not directly address this problem, even on the qualitative level. However, a relatively simple extension of influence resolution does permit qualitative analysis of the impact of control actions. We use the influence graph for the state of interest and perform a qualitative form of classical small-signal or perturbation analysis. This analysis is based on de Kleer's IQ analysis [6].

Straightforward application of small-signal analysis yields qualitative estimates of the effects of control actions subject to the same limitations as the original QP deductions. Situations can arise in which it is impossible to determine whether a target parameter value will increase or decrease following a control action. Also, many of the control actions that must be reasoned about are adjustments to continuous-control parameters. Simple *increase* or *decrease* results are insufficient for reasoning about this kind of control. It is important to be able to estimate *how much* the increase or decrease will be.

The same functional characterizations used to extend influence resolution in the previous section can also remove much of the qualitative ambiguity. Also, these same annotations can be used to obtain linguistic estimates of change magnitudes. This results from our interpretation of function strength annotations as normalized sensitivities. By integrating these annotations with the linguistic quantity space extensions described in what follows, we can obtain complete semi-quantitative estimates of the effects of control actions. We call this complete procedure linguistic perturbation (LP) analysis. This section builds up the LP analysis algorithm step by step, starting with the simpler qualitative perturbation analysis.

5.1   Qualitative Perturbation Analysis

Classical small-signal analysis determines a delta for a target parameter given a delta for a control parameter. This change is determined by evaluating the partial derivative of the target with respect to the control parameter at the current value of the parameters and multiplying that value by the control delta. A simple qualitative version of this procedure would be to multiply a qualitative form of this partial derivative by the *sign* of the control delta. This is only valid as long as the change in the control parameter does not result in a change in the view and process structure for the situation. This is the qualitative equivalent of "small-signal" analysis. Therefore, a restriction on the application of this technique is that either the current view and process structure must not be dependent on any equality quantity conditions or, if it is, their validity must not be affected by the proposed change.

This procedure is simple to perform, and the partial derivatives are already represented as influences in the influence graph. De Kleer has developed a qualitative procedure for performing this computation, which he calls IQ analysis. A problem arises in determining the qualitative change values in de Kleer's confluence formalism, though, because arcs are undirected and he allows cycles in the influence graph. This requires a search to find a globally consistent solution, which he performs by introducing assumptions about unknown values, and backtracking as needed.

Forbus eliminates the possibility of cycles in QP theory by fiat, claiming that cycles violate intuitive notions of causality and are unnecessary [7]. The result of this simplification is that the search-intensive IQ algorithm of de Kleer reduces to the simple one-pass influence resolution algorithm of Forbus. An adaptation of this algorithm for qualitative perturbation analysis is shown in Figure 7. This algorithm uses the derivative of each quantity to store the delta. The basic difference between this and inference resolution is that we initialize certain derivatives to nonzero values.

However, while this algorithm is adequate for influence resolution, it is inadequate

```
(defun Simple-QPA (delta-list)
```
make a list of all quantities (amounts and first derivatives) in the situation, ordered by dependencies (this is the same as for influence resolution)

set the value of each quantity in the delta list to the value specified, set all others to unknown

For each quantity:
  If positive direct influences and no negative direct influences and no unknown direct influences, set its value to positive
  If negative direct influences and no positive direct influences and no unknown direct influences, set its value to negative.
  If both positive and negative direct influences, or any unknown direct influences, set its value to unknown.
If no direct influences, then:
  If positive indirect influences, and no negative or unknown indirect influences, set its value to positive.
  If negative indirect influences, and no positive or unknown indirect influences, set its value to negative.
  If both positive and negative indirect influences, set its value to unknown.
  Else set its value to zero.

Figure 7. Simple qualitative perturbation analysis algorithm.

for qualitative perturbation analysis. The problem is that the sign of the target parameter delta is not always the sign of the first derivative. It is the sign of the *lowest-order nonzero derivative*.[3] This fact renders the one-pass influence resolution algorithm only a partial solution to the problem of perturbation analysis. The graph of Figure 8 shows the problem.

Temp(x) – Q + → (Rate y) – I + → Amount(z)

$((D (Temp x)) > 0)$
$((D (Amount z)) ? 0)$

Figure 8. QP Sample influence graph and query.

A simple analysis of this diagram according to the preceding algorithm would lead one to conclude that $((D (Amount product)) = 0)$. However, the correct answer is $((D (Amount product) > 0)$. The reason is that while the first derivative is zero, the second derivative is positive. Therefore, assuming the change persists for a finite period of time, the eventual result will be a positive first derivative and therefore a positive delta. Increasing the temperature of the reactants will increase the amount of product produced over any nonzero time interval if all other factors are held constant. Information about second derivatives can be obtained from direct influences $(I+/I-)$ in QP theory.

[3] This depends critically on the state persisting for some nonzero time interval.

The inference sanctioned by QP theory, given that the amount of product is directly positively influenced by the generation rate, is that if the *amount* of the generation rate is positive, then in the absence of conflicting influences, the *derivative* of the product amount is also positive. However, we can make the same inference for the next higher-order set of values. That is, if the *first derivative* of the generation rate is positive, then in the absence of conflicting influences, the *second derivative* of the product amount is also positive. Combining this with the perturbation analysis rule that the result of perturbation analysis is the value of the lowest nonzero derivative, we conclude that the correct result for the example of Figure 8 is that the amount of product will increase since the second derivative is the lowest-order nonzero derivative. This is equivalent to treating selected direct influences ($I+$/$I-$) as indirect influences ($Q+$/$Q-$), thereby reintroducing loops into the influence graph and destroying the one-pass nature of Forbus's algorithm. A revised algorithm for QPA is shown in Figure 9. The key change to the previous algorithm is that once the previous one-pass algorithm is complete, the new algorithm searches for the earliest (in terms of the quantity dependency partial order) derivative that is zero and that has a nonzero second derivative. It then assigns that value to the first derivative, thus starting a new round of influence propagation. The procedure repeats until no such zero derivatives can be found. This is the algorithm used to derive the results shown in Figure 3. Notice that this algorithm uses the same basic procedures for computing individual influences and combining them that are used in influence resolution.

```
defun QPA (delta-list)
```
   Perform Simple-QPA as described earlier.
   Execute repeatedly until no further changes occur:
   For each quantity in the quantity list:
   If the quantity is a derivative and has a value of zero
   perform a higher-order derivative check and set its value according to the results.
   If the value is now not zero, mark a change has occurred.
   Also, if any changes have occurred on this pass through the quantity list, then
   re-execute normal influence check for this quantity.

```
defun high-order-deriv-check (quantity)
;;This function is only invoked on derivatives with a current
;; value of zero.
```

   Set the minus list to the list of direct negative influences
      (I– with positive derivative of influencing parameter,
      I+ with negative derivative of influencing parameter, or
      I+ or I– with unknown derivative of influencing parameter)
   Set the plus-list to the list of direct positive influences
   If the plus and minus lists are both empty, do nothing.
   If the plus-list is non-empty, and the minus list is empty, set the quantity value to plus.
   If the minus-list is non-empty, and the plus-list is empty, set the quantity value to minus.
   If neither list is empty, set the quantity value to unknown.

Figure 9. Revised qualitative perturbation analysis algorithm.

5.2   Extended Perturbation Analysis

The analysis described in the previous section is capable of deriving many useful results. Our furnace example has only two independent parameters, the temperature of the heat source and the temperature of the incoming reactants. Examination of the results of qualitative perturbation analysis shown in Figure 3 reveals that there are some indeterminacies in the analysis, though. The sources of these ambiguities have already been discussed in the previous section. By replacing the basic influence computation and combination algorithm of QP theory with the extended algorithm discussed in that section, we can eliminate those ambiguities. Figure 10 shows the results of extended QPA using the annotations described earlier and compares these results with the results of analysis without annotations. The figure follows the same format as those for influence resolution shown in the preceding section, and the same comments apply, except that the value shown is the computed delta. We compare results both for the increased heat query (labeled "heater") and the increased incoming reactant temperature query (labeled "reactants").

Parameter	QPA Heater	EQPA Heater	QPA Reactants	EQPA Reactants
P (reactants bin)	−	−	?	−
A (reactants bin)	−	−	?	−
T (reactants bin)	0	0	+	+
P (reactants furnace)	−	−	?	−
A (reactants furnace)	−	−	?	−
T (reactants furnace)	+	+	?	+
P (product furnace)	+	+	?	+
A (product furnace)	+	+	?	+
T (product furnace)	+	+	?	−
P (off-gas furnace)	+	+	?	+
A (off-gas furnace)	+	+	?	+
T (off-gas furnace)	+	+	?	−
P (off-gas offtake)	+	+	?	+
A (off-gas offtake)	+	+	?	+
T (off-gas offtake)	?	+	+	+
Temperature (heater)	+	+	0	0
Flow-Rate (reactants)	+	+	?	+
Flow-Rate (off-gas)	+	+	?	+
Flow-Rate (heat)	+	+	?	+
G-Rate (reaction)	+	+	?	+
Temperature-Lost	?	?	−	−
Temperature-Gained	+	+	−	−

Figure 10.   Extended QPA example summary.

5.3   Final Form: Linguistic Perturbation Analysis

QP theory is limited in the range of what-if or small-signal perturbation analysis questions it can answer by its restricted representations. We have seen that we can reduce the ambiguity in its analyses by adding additional functional characterizations and providing a semi-quantitative extension representation for influence magnitudes. In traditional small-signal analysis we can obtain an estimate of the final value of a target parameter by adding the computed delta to the initial value for the parameter. QP theory provides no representation for parameter magnitudes to which we can add a computed delta to obtain any meaningful result. The problem is that there is no information within the theory itself that permits us to establish any relevant distinctions beyond those already made in the quantity space, and these distinctions establish an ordinal, not a cardinal, scale. We can do more in reasoning about the consequences of change by providing an extension theory that can represent distinctions relevant to an *external agent*. We use a linguistic variable representation to meet this requirement. For our purposes, we simply consider a linguistic variable to be a possibility distribution over a discrete set of "interesting" values in some domain. For a more complete discussion, see reference 12.

Using linguistic variables as the needed quantitative representation of parameter magnitudes, we have developed a four-step procedure to perform a linguistic version of perturbation analysis. This procedure will need substantial amounts of situation-specific quantitative information, which could be obtained by default, by observation, or directly from the user. The procedure assumes that we are performing the perturbation analysis around some state for which we know the quantitative extension base values for both the source and target parameters. If we have not been able to establish these values either by observation or by influence resolution, then we assume that the extension base values are established by a correspondence provided to the system. The four steps are listed here and detailed in subsequent paragraphs:

1. Compute an input influence.
2. Propagate influence through an influence graph.
3. Convert computed influence into new a target parameter value.
4. Check the reasonableness of the result.

For the purpose of illustration, we follow the problem of estimating the effect on reaction rate and off-gas exit temperature if we increase the temperature of the heat source from low to medium. We assume that the extension base values are provided from observation. Computing the input influence is a knowledge-based process. We assume that the system has available a mapping function (parameter specific) that maps from an old and new input parameter value pair to an influence strength.[4] This mapping function can be expressed as a fuzzy relation between input values and

---

[4] A temperature increase from 90° C to 110° C might be a big or little change—there is no information internal to the theory that can be used to determine this. Since all parameters in a quantity space share a single value discretization, the number of discrete steps in the change does not directly provide this information.

influence magnitudes. Given a matrix IR specifying this mapping function, we can compute the influence equivalent of the delta as

Influence = New value $\odot$ *Current value* $\odot$ influence relation,

$$\mu_{Iv}(k) = \sum_{i,j} \mu_{new}(i) \wedge \mu_{old}(j) \wedge \mu_{IR}(i,j,k).$$

Propagating this influence through the view and process structure of the state uses the extended perturbation analysis algorithm described earlier. The coarseness of the influence representation needed is in general a function of the coarseness of the discretization of the goal parameter as well as the number of influence annotations made and their coarseness. We provide no procedure for computing this but assume the user has selected an appropriate discretization. In general, this must be maintained as relatively coarse: As it gets finer and finer, it approaches assuming a linear model, which is an invalid assumption in most cases. One problem arises, however, in using the extended qualitative perturbation analysis algorithm to estimate quantitative changes. Influence relations (I+/I–) are qualitative abstractions of equations with a temporal aspect [5]. In general, in order to obtain a quantitative estimate of the effect of propagating a delta through a direct influence, we must know *how long* the delta is in effect. We could ignore this problem in the qualitative analysis for three reasons:

1. The term *dt* is simply a scaling parameter that affects all direct influences proportionately and therefore does not affect their relative magnitudes when combining conflicting direct influences.
2. Most directly influenced variables, as we saw in Section 4, exist in feedback loops that control their values. When considering only the change in equilibrium due to a control action, time no longer need be considered. The amount of the shift in the equilibrium value is determined solely by the relative strengths of the direct and indirect influences in the feedback loops around the equilibrium variable.[5]
3. When combining direct and indirect influences for a parameter not in equilibrium, we can assume that the strength annotation on a direct influence is chosen to reflect its effect after some *nominal* time period.

The first and second of these three assumptions are still valid for quantitative (linguistic) analysis, but the third might not be. The extended qualitative perturbation analysis algorithm presented earlier must therefore be extended to scale influences propagated through direct influence arcs (I+/I-) by a user-specified time delta. However, in accordance with assumption 2, this must only be done for influences that are not part of feedback loops for variables in equilibrium. The example in Figure 11 does not incorporate this extension and must be viewed as estimating results for some standard nominal time delay after the change action is taken.

The next step is the inverse of the first step, combining the resulting influence with

---

[5] Note that while this argument and the previous one are each independently reasonable, each is based on assumptions that contradict the assumptions of the other!

Values prior to control action:

Domain for heater and product temperature (°C): 50, 100, 150, 200, 1000, 1500, 2000, 2500, 3000, 3500

Domain for generation rate (arbitrary mass units per minute): 100, 125, 150, 175, 200

Domain for off-gas temperature in offtake (°C): 100 200 300 400 500

Observations are expressed as D/S belief distributions over possible values:
```
[belief, plausibility]/value + [bel, plaus]/val + ...
```
for all values with plausibility > 0:

Temperature of heater: `[1, 1]/2500`

(Temperature of product): `[0,0.01]/1000 + [.84, 1]/1500 + [0, .01]/2000`

G-Rate: `[.95, .97]/125 + [.03, .05]/150`

(Temperature of c-s off-gas offtake): `[.95, .97]/200 + [.03, .05]/300`

Now do LP analysis—new heater temperature is one discretization element higher than before:
```
(lpa h new_value = [1, 1]/3000)
```

Estimates of system parameter values following control action:

(Temperature of heater): `[1,1]/3000`

(Temperature of product): `[0, .01]/1000 + [0, 1]/1500 + [0, 1]/2000 + [0, .01]/2500`

G-rate: `[0, 1]/125 + [0, 1]/150 + [0, 1]/175`

(Temperature (c-s off-gas offtake): `[0, 1]/200 + [0, 1]/300 + [0, 1]/400`

Figure 11. Linguistic perturbation analysis example.

the initial goal parameter value to obtain a final result. Assuming the influence relation (IR) is represented in matrix form, this inverse relation is straightforward to compute:

$$\mu_{new}(i) = \vee_{j,k}\,\mu_{influence}(k) \vee \mu_{old}(k) \vee \mu_{IR}(i, j, k).$$

Figure 11 shows the result of a linguistic perturbation analysis for a moderate increase in heater temperature. The system is able to make several interesting distinctions, such as the fact that while the temperature of the product in the furnace is unlikely to change much, the off-gas temperature in the offtake may change significantly. Such approximations are subject to substantial inaccuracy, and a person who attempts such rough estimates will try to verify their reasonableness somehow. We can do this by testing whether the results satisfy the quantity restrictions[6] for the state.

We can perform the reasonableness test in either of two ways. First, we can directly test whether the estimated value for the target parameter is within its quantity restriction. The restriction values are automatically derived by our implementation for each possible system state. Alternately, a more extensive test can be performed by estimating the final values of all parameters of the state and testing whether all parameter pairs satisfy all quantity conditions imposed on them by the state. This is a more restrictive test since testing each parameter in isolation may miss relational constraints of the state.

---

[6] A quantity restriction is the possibility distribution representing the union of all possible values the parameter can have in a particular system state.

5.4 Summary

In this section we have developed a technique for using QP theory to reason about the consequences of continuous-control actions within a qualitative state. Starting from the classical method of small-signal analysis, we developed a qualitative notion of small-signal analysis and extended the basic influence resolution algorithm of Forbus to perform this analysis. We then combined this basic algorithm with the quantitative extensions for parameter values developed earlier and presented a technique for estimating the effects of continuous-control actions within a qualitative state.

6 EVALUATION

Each of the preceding algorithms requires different information from the user and makes certain assumptions about the information provided that might limit the applicability of the algorithm.

Linguistic influence resolution derives its power from two sources, functional strength annotations and an appropriate discretization of the influence propagation parameter. We have already identified four classes of annotation: universal, system specific, state specific, and query specific. Of these, query-specific annotations are potentially the most troubling. While we have specifically excluded from consideration here the source of annotation information, it still remains to demonstrate that it is at least feasible that some external knowledge source could provide the required information. Recognizing that an annotation is appropriate requires that sufficient information be available at the time the annotation is requested. A query-specific annotation is requested when preliminary application of the influence resolution algorithm reveals an ambiguity in the result for some interesting parameter. At that time, several facts are available to aid the search for relevant query-specific annotations:

1. The subgraph causing the ambiguity can be recognized using graph-matching techniques.
2. The entry point of the change into the graph is readily identifiable by examining the change values of the nodes influencing subgraph nodes.
3. The component(s) that generated the subgraph can be identified as long as this information is recorded when the influence graph is constructed (the current implementation does not do this).

These facts seem to be exactly those that might be expected to trigger recognition of the relevant query-specific patch.

The second problem is the choice of an appropriate discretization for the influence parameter. This has been discussed earlier and shown not to be as critical as it might seem. The worst result of choosing too coarse a discretization is that some ambiguity remains in the final result that might have been eliminated. Also, a discretization finer than that of the control and observable variable values is only necessary when combining annotated influences, not when computing individual annotated influences. Thus, the minimum discretization needed to maintain full information grows more slowly than might be expected. We have obtained adequate results on the example used in this chapter using an influence discretization with the same coarseness as the discretization for functional strength annotations.

Finally, we note an implicit assumption that annotations are intended to resolve local ambiguities. There may be a danger when an influence computed using a strength annotation propagates outside the locale where it is valid and combines with an influence from another, unrelated annotation. It is partially for this reason that we have adopted the approach of only adding those annotations actually needed to resolve ambiguity rather than all possible annotations. This procedure has been sufficient for all examples studied so far. Should it turn out inadequate in other applications, another alternative would be to "age" influences, that is, to broaden or fuzzify them at each propagation step. This would serve to nullify the effect of strength annotations outside the immediate environment for which they are intended.

The second and more complex of the procedures we have described is linguistic perturbation analysis. It depends on the ability of the user to establish suitable discretizations for parameters of interest in addition to all of the information needed for linguistic influence resolution. It also places special demands on the functional annotations. These annotations must now describe quantized partial sensitivities of one parameter with respect to another. While this use of annotations is consistent with the use made by linguistic influence resolution (and in fact solves the problems created by propagation beyond local domain of applicability described in the preceding), it makes far more intensive use of the annotation mechanism. This therefore raises again, and even more strongly, the problem of establishing an appropriate discretization for the influence parameter. However, the same comments made earlier apply here: The only danger of an insufficient discretization is an increase in the ambiguity of the result. In fact, establishing a fairly coarse discretization can be a useful way to prevent overreliance on the linearity assumption inherent in LPA. Our development of the LPA algorithm depended on equilibrium assumptions. An extension of this to nonequilibrium situations is necessary. Finally, it is not yet clear that the use of the same annotations is valid when a direct influence is used to estimate a second derivative in the basic QPA algorithm.

7   SUMMARY

7.1   Review

We began this work with an interest in pursuing a symbolic, knowledge-based approach to the control of complex engineered systems. The work presented here has been based on two premises. First, we believe that the qualitative process (QP) theory offers potential for reasoning about the control of complex engineered physical systems, especially when they are poorly understood or the capability for making observations of the systems is limited. Second, we surmise that problem solving in this domain proceeds by an iterative process of building, applying, and patching models of the system under consideration.

On the basis of these premises we examined QP theory and found it severely limited in its present form. First, it is often unable to determine unambiguously the qualitative value of system parameters. Often, when information is available that could potentially serve to disambiguate results, there is no way to express the information within QP theory. Second, QP theory in its current form provides no facility for performing quantitative reasoning. Many of the tasks involved in the control of engineered systems involve adjustments of continuous-control parameters or estimation of effects relative to some scale external to the system under consideration. Both of these reasoning tasks require some form of quantitative capability.

In order to surmount these problems, we have developed a set of extensions to QP theory that reduce internal ambiguity and expand the scope of QP theory by providing an extension theory that can reason semi-quantitatively about consequences of external control actions. These extensions are based on the use of linguistic variables to represent the uncertain or imprecise system-specific information typically available to supplement models built from a domain theory. The extension set has three basic components:

1. A *linguistic quantity space*, which can represent partial information about quantity conditions and relate quantity orderings with linguistic descriptions of parameter magnitudes. These linguistic parameter values make user-relevant distinctions.
2. *Linguistic functional strength annotations* and an extension to the influence resolution algorithm that makes use of these annotations to resolve ambiguity.
3. *Linguistic perturbation analysis*, which builds on the preceding mechanisms and provides a way to estimate the effects of hypothetical control actions.

We have shown, at least for the example problem, that these extensions can be used to derive answers to several qualitative and quantitative questions that cannot be answered using basic QP theory. Specifically, we have demonstrated the following:

- the unambiguous determination of qualitative parameter values given linguistic functional strength characterizations (*linguistic influence resolution*) and
- the semi-quantitative estimation of the effects of adjustments to continuous control parameters (*linguistic perturbation analysis*).

7.2   Further Research

Much work remains to be done. Most importantly, the work described here must be extended to include limit analysis, the fourth basic deduction in QP theory. With semi-quantitative estimates of both parameter values and change rates, it should be possible to choose between possible future states that basic QP theory cannot disambiguate as well as estimate state durations.

Also, we have given only the briefest sketch of possible kinds of additional functional descriptions that could be used to reduce the ambiguity of the results of the basic QP theory deductions. Functional relationships often have a temporal character as well as relative strengths. What characteristics of relationships between continuous parameters of a situation do people observe? How are these characteristics remembered, and how are they used in problem solving?

This last question touches on another major research area, the subject of our second basic premise. What is the nature of the overall problem-solving architecture? What other kinds of knowledge are available during reasoning about physical systems besides domain theories of the kind representable in QP theory? How are they combined? We have suggested ambiguity-based model patching as one possible mechanism for interaction of different kinds of knowledge. There must be others.

ACKNOWLEDGMENTS

This research was performed while at the University of California Berkeley and FMC Corporation, and was supported in part by NASA Grant NCC-2-275 and NSF Grant IST-8320416. Support was also provided by FMC Corporation.

REFERENCES

1. B. D'Ambrosio, "*Qualitative Process Theory using Linguistic Variables*," Ph.D. Thesis, University of California, Berkeley, 1986.

2. B. D'Ambrosio, "Truth Maintenance with Numeric Certainty Estimates," in *Proceedings Third Conference on AI Applications, Kissimmee, Florida,* Computer Society of the IEEE, February, 1987, pp. 244–249.

3. B. D'Ambrosio, "A Hybrid Approach to Reasoning under Uncertainty," *International Journal of Approximate Reasoning,* in press.

4. J. deKleer, "*Causal and Teleological Reasoning in Circuit Recognition,*" Technical Report AI-TR-529, Artificial Intelligence Laboratory, Massachusetts Institute of Technology, October 1979.

5. J. deKleer and D. Bobrow, "Qualitative Reasoning with Higher Order Derivatives," in *Proceedings AAAI-84, Austin, Texas,* American Association for Artificial Intelligence, August 1984, pp. 86–91.

6. J. deKleer and J. Brown, "A Qualitative Physics Based on Confluences," *Artificial Intelligence,* **24**(1–3):7–83, December 1984.

7. K. Forbus, "*Qualitative Process Theory,*" Ph.D Thesis, Massachusetts Institute of Technology, July 1984.

8. P. J. Hayes, "The Naive Physics Manifesto," in D. Michie (Ed.), *Expert Systems in the Micro-Electronic Age,* Edinburgh University Press, Edinburgh, Scotland, 1979.

9. B. J. Kuipers, "Qualitative Simulation," *Artificial Intelligence,* **29**(3):289–338, September 1986.

10. M. Mavrovouniotis and G. Stephanopoulos, "Reasoning with Orders of Magnitude and

Approximate Relations," in *Proceedings AAAI-87, Seattle, Washington*, American Association for Artificial Intelligence, July 1987, pp. 626–630.

11. R. Simmons, "Commonsense Arithmetic Reasoning," in *Proceedings AAAI-86, Philadelphia, Pennsylvania*, American Association for Artificial Intelligence, August 1986, pp. 118–124.

12. L. A. Zadeh, "The Concept of a Linguistic Variable and its Application to Approximate Reasoning—I," *Information Science* **8**:199–249, 1975.

13. L. A. Zadeh, "Outline of a New Approach to the Analysis of Complex Systems," *IEEE Transactions of Systems, Man, and Cybernetics*, **3**(1):28–44, 1973.

6 Semi-Quantitative "Close-Enough" Systems Dynamics Models: An Alternative to Qualitative Simulation

LAWRENCE E. WIDMAN

Division of Cardiology
Department of Medicine
The University of Texas Health Science Center at San Antonio
San Antonio, Texas
and
Cardiology Service
Audie L. Murphy Memorial Veterans' Hospital
San Antonio, Texas

1 INTRODUCTION

The conflicting requirements for accuracy and flexibility in simulation models have stimulated exploration of new approaches to traditional simulation goals. This chapter is concerned with the broad area of systems dynamics models and describes a semi-quantitative approach that yields an important degree of flexibility in modeling while avoiding the incorrect solutions that frequently occur in classical qualitative simulation. This approach also increases the usefulness of system dynamics models by allowing them to be used without modification for fault diagnosis from first principles.

The dynamic systems methodology describes continuous systems, which are usually lumped-parameter and deterministic systems, in terms of functional building blocks. Such systems can be characterized by ordinary differential equations. Popularized by Forrester [13] in the 1960s, this methodology has been applied, for example, in domains such as economics, financial and government planning, corporate modeling, and biology [28]. The first step in building these models is, as usual, the selection of the variables of interest and identification of all other pertinent variables and relationships that affect the variables of interest. As in any modeling process, variable and relationship identification requires a balance between the comprehensiveness and cost-effectiveness of the resultant model.

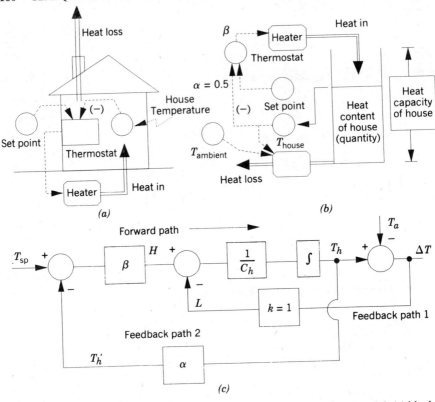

Figure 1. Toy example, heated house: (*a*) structural model; (*b*) functional model; (*c*) block diagram representation of model equations.

The result of the first modeling step is an unweighted influence graph in which the nodes represent the model variables and the edges represent unidirectional, cause-and-effect relationships. This influence graph is suitable for immediate qualitative simulation using a ternary quantity space consisting of the quantities "positive," "zero," and "negative." Since relative magnitudes cannot be represented in such a model, the qualitative modeling process stops here (subject to verification and validation). More accurate simulation models can be built by characterizing, as a second step, the numerical parameters of the model with precision sufficient to yield accurate simulation results. It is at this second step that the semi-quantitative approach begins.

The fundamental assumption of the semi-quantitative method, which must be satisfied by each application in which the method is used, is that the important insights to be gained from the simulation process are the degree and direction of change in the model variables. In contrast to traditional simulation models, a semi-quantitative model is not intended to predict accurately the absolute values that the model variables will assume over time. It *is* intended to predict correctly the direction in which each variable will change and to provide a correct partial ordering of the magnitude of change relative to other variables in the model. The benefits to the modeler of choosing these more limited simulation goals are two: reduced investment in building the model and availability of the model for diagnostic reasoning from first principles.

Applications for which a semi-quantitative approach would be appropriate might include an expert system that uses a symbolic model for causal reasoning, a computer-based productivity tool for informal "back-of-the-envelope" reasoning about proposed designs, and expert instruction systems. For the purpose of illustration, we consider in what follows the toy system of a heated house (Figure 1). Naturally, real-world applications would use much more sophisticated models, such as the one discussed in Section 4. The toy system is used only to make the basic concepts concrete and clear.

2 METHODS, ILLUSTRATED WITH AN EXTENDED EXAMPLE

In this section, we consider at length a toy system consisting of a heater, a house with imperfect insulation, and a proportional temperature controller (Figure 1). The purpose of this section is to illustrate the types of questions that this method can answer, the added concepts that semi-quantitative simulation brings to the problem, and the interaction between the symbolic and traditional numerical methods by which the goals of simulation are achieved.

In the model, the idealized heater functions continuously at variable output and has an infinite heat supply. Heat is lost through the surface of the house, including the windows and chimney, at a rate proportional to the temperature difference between the house temperature (T_h) and the ambient temperature (T_a) into an infinite heat sink. The first-order kinetics of heat loss constitutes one feedback loop (increased temperature differential increases heat loss, which decreases temperature). A second feedback loop connects the sensor (thermometer) through a proportional controller (thermostat) to the effector (heater). A single semi-quantitative parameter $\alpha = 0.5$ is introduced in the feedback path between the process and the controller as a sensor gain. It denotes the fraction of a temperature deviation from normal steady state, $[T_h(t) - T_h(normal)]/ T_h(normal)$, which will be corrected in a single simulation step.

As discussed in the next section, semi-quantitative parameters and variables are linguistic quantities mapped onto real numbers. The default, or implicit, value of "normal" maps onto unity for parameters and onto zero for variables. Thus, a parameter value of 0.5 represents a parameter that is less than the value one might expect in its location in the model, yet is still positive. Abnormal variables are normalized to their own normal values and then diminished by unity to minimize subtractive cancellation during digital simulation.

The parameter α, which has a different value from that of the default feedback gain of the first feedback loop (which is unity), represents a difference in influence that classical qualitative simulation representations cannot. The added power of this extended representation is that it allows semi-quantitative models to resolve unambiguously at a local level the opposing-influences problem that causes qualitative simulations to branch intractably in large models.

As shown in the figure, the model is represented in terms of symbolic building blocks. Each building block is equivalent to a differential equation. Thus, the model can be viewed equivalently as a standard numerical systems dynamics model and as a symbolic influence graph (Table 1). As illustrated in the toy model discussed in what

TABLE 1. Mapping of Model Building Blocks onto Difference Equations[a]

Name /Symbol	Equation	Functional Description
Level ▭	$Q_{k+1} = Q_k +$ $\{(\Sigma I_{k+1}^M -$ $\Sigma O_{k+1}^M) \cdot$ $\Delta t\}/RFT$ $C_{k+1} = \Sigma I_{k+1}^R$ Ratio $= Q_{k+1}/C_{k+1}$ $RFT = f$(filling times of inputs, emptying times of outputs)	*Quantity* is sum of material inputs and outputs, corrected by the relative flow time (RFT) relative to other material flows into and out of this variable, over the time period Δt. *Capacity* is the instantaneous measure of "size" relative to the variable's own normal capacity. *Ratio* is the ratio of current quantity to current capacity, analogous to pressure.
Rate ◯	$R_{k+1} = \Sigma\underset{\text{in Levels}}{I_{k+1}}$ $AQ_{k+1} = \Sigma_{i=1}^{\text{in Levels}}$ $(Q_{i,k+1}/RSI_i)$ $RQ_{k+1} = \Sigma_{i=1}^{\text{in Levels}}$ $(Q_{i,k+1})$	Rate variables (R) have no memory of their previous values: they are equal to the current values of their input variables. Two subtypes of rate variables, the absolute quantity and relative quantity, take inputs only from level variables. The absolute quantity (AQ) type corrects the quantity for the relative size of each level type input: it is a measure of absolute mass in the model. The relative quantity (RQ) does not consider the RSI. It is a measure of the degree of filling of a level relative to itself.
Regulator ⬠ or ▢	$RG_{k+1} = \Sigma I_{k+1}^R$	Regulator (RG) variables convert information into mass flow. Their values are material rates, but they are equal to the sum of their regulatory inputs. They are analogous to fluid pumps, whose outputs are set by their informational inputs.
Splitter SE ME ⇄ γ ⇄ F P	$P_{k+1} = \Sigma I_{k+1}^R$ $F_{k+1} = \Sigma I_{k+1}^M$ $SE_{k+1} = P_{k+1} + F_{k+1}$ $ME_{k+1} = F_{k+1} - \gamma$ $\cdot SE_{k+1}$	Splitter variables divide a material flow (F) into two separate flows, the main effluent (ME) and the side effluent (SE). The splitter concept is modeled after a fluid valve, in which valve position (P) determines the division of the incoming material flow (F). The factor γ is the dimensionless ratio of the normal SE flow to the normal ME flow in absolute units. it translates a relative change in SE into the corresponding reciprocal effect on ME.

[a]Key: Δt, time step from t_k to t_{k+1}; Q, quantity; C, capacity; I^M, material in; I^R, regulatory in; Q^M, material out; RSI, relative size index; $I = $ (weight of link) $\times$ (value of input variable).

follows, the model can be represented equivalently as a physical structure (Figure 1*a*), a functional diagram (Figure 1*b*), and a block diagram representation of the underlying equations (Figure 1*c*).

These two views, mathematical and structural-functional, can be used to ask what-if questions (numerical simulation) and why questions (diagnosis and explanation by symbolic reasoning).

2.1   Simulation

Simulation of dynamic systems can be used to answer questions that are too complex for intuitive analysis of the model. It is these systems that are difficult for current expert systems to reason about. Consider the question "What will happen to the initial rate of heat rise and to the steady-state temperature if the heater output is doubled or tripled?" The answers are not immediately apparent because of the interaction between the two feedback loops. The question can be answered in terms of relative quantities rather than absolute quantities. Therefore, parameters such as the actual thermal quantities of heat input and loss and the heat capacity of the house need not be characterized. Rather, these indifferent parameters can be assigned numerical values of unity, as can the baseline (normal steady-state) active parameters corresponding to the illustrated relationships in the model. In general, model parameters that are not specified explicitly are given the implicit, default values of "normal" (unity).

The baseline model is then simulated in the usual systems dynamics manner by translating it into its first-order differential equation equivalent, assigning initial conditions, and integrating the equations numerically over time. For convenience, the baseline variable values are set to zero by normalizing and subtracting unity: Negative numbers correspond to values below baseline for the individual variables. An example would be the variable

$$L(T) = \frac{L_{\text{absolute}}(t) - L(\text{baseline})}{L(\text{baseline})} - 1.$$

In general, model variables that are not specified explicitly are given the implicit, default values of normal (zero).

2.1.1   Example

As the first step in answering the question, the baseline curve is obtained by raising the set point to *High* to activate the heater. The semi-quantitative value *High* is a linguistic variable [6] whose numeric equivalent is chosen subject to the constraint that it be greater than zero. If the model is linear and contains no threshold values in the relationships between variables (which would make the model piecewise linear), the mapping between semi-quantitative variables and the real numbers is arbitrary. For convenience, we choose the value 1.0 so that a simple numerical integration algorithm will have acceptably small error with a default integration step size. The result of the baseline simulation is shown as the lowest curve (beta = 1) in Figure 2. Note that the rise

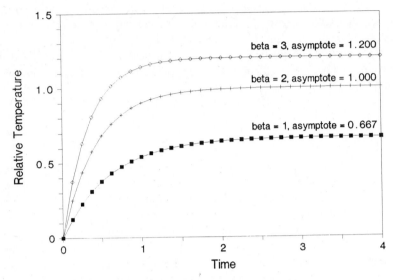

Figure 2. Simulation results for toy example

above baseline of the new steady-state temperature is only two-thirds of the rise of the set-point temperature above its normal steady-state value, reflecting the first-order effect of the heat loss relationship and the differential sensor gain coefficient α.

The parameter α represents the reduction of the sensitivity of the thermostat system by 50% from a baseline level: The temperature must change twice as much from its normal steady-state value to elicit the same heater response as it would if this parameter had a default value of unity. As noted in the preceding, this type of parameter is the key to resolving the ambiguities of conflicting influences that confound qualitative simulation of multifeedback systems. In this model, it allows representation of a difference between the sensitivities of the heater feedback path and the heat loss feedback path to changes in the temperature of the house and to changes in the gradient between the normalized house and ambient temperatures, respectively.

The what-if question is asked by modifying an appropriate parameter and repeating the simulation. Choosing the forward path from the controller to the effector, we increase the slope of the controller gain relationship β from unity to either 2.0 or 3.0. This slope models an increased heater response to a given house temperature deviation from the *Normal* value.

The analytic solution to this problem is shown in Equations 1–7, and the answers to the original question are shown in Table 2. Recall that all variables are normalized

TABLE 2. Relationship of House Temperature to Thermostat Gain, β

β	$T(\text{house})/T_{sp}$	$T(\text{sensed})/T_{sp}$
1	0.667	0.33
2	1.000	0.50
3	1.200	0.60

to their own normal, steady-state values, as described. Therefore, any nonzero variable value represents a deviation of that variable from its own normal value. The block diagram of Equations 1–3 is shown in Figure 1c:

$$L = k (T_h - T_a),$$ (1)

where T_h is house temperature, T_a is ambient temperature, $k = 1$ by default, and L is the rate of house heat loss. Then,

$$H = \beta (T_{sp} - \alpha T_h),$$ (2)

where β is the proportional control gain on the error term $(T_{sp} - \alpha T_h)$, T_{sp} is the set-point temperature, α is the feedback gain (sensor gain) relating T_h to the modified temperature T'_h sensed by the thermostat, and H is the rate of heat input into the house:

$$\frac{dT}{dt} = \frac{H - L}{C_h} = \beta T_{sp} - (1 + \alpha \beta)T,$$ (3)

where C_h is the heat capacity of the house and equals unity implicitly, $t \geq 0$, and $T(0)$ $= T_0$ is given. Following this, we have

$$T(t) := \{\beta T_{sp} - [\beta T_{sp} - (1 + \alpha \beta)T_0]e^{-(1 + \alpha \beta) t} \} / (1 + \alpha \beta),$$ (4)

$$\frac{dT}{dt} = [\beta T_{sp} - (1 + \alpha \beta) T_0]e^{-(1 + \alpha \beta) t},$$ (5)

$$\frac{dT}{dt}\bigg|_{t = 0} = \beta (T_{sp} - \alpha T_0) - T_0,$$ (6)

and

$$T(\infty) = \beta T_{sp} / (1 + \alpha \beta),$$ (7)

where $T(\infty)$ is the steady-state temperature.

The exact answers to the what-if question are (Table 2)

the rate of heat rise is proportional to β initially and then decreases as T approaches its new equilibrium value (Equations 5 and 6) and

the steady-state house temperature as a function of the set-point temperature T_{sp}, increases nonlinearly with β (Equation 7) and can exceed T_{sp} because the afferent limb gain α is less than unity [recall that heat loss is a first-order process, proportional to house heat T, but is not affected by changing the heating loop coefficients and that the thermostat senses only half (α) of any change in T].

The mapping of the model building blocks onto differential equations, or difference equations in the discrete form, is shown in Table 1. Note that all equations are linear, so that complicated behaviors cannot occur in this simple model. Nonlinear models can be constructed with the same formalism, but the modeler must be more cautious in verifying and validating it because of these risks [31]. This issue is discussed further in Section 2.1.2.

The semi-quantitative results are plotted in Figure 2. The asymptotic steady-state values are shown explicitly and correspond to the results in Table 2.

Thus, by modeling the qualitative structure of the system and the few active parameters that affect the desired response, results useful for inexact reasoning can be obtained with relative ease. Naturally, the choice of active parameters and their values requires judgment and experience.

2.1.2   Issues in Modeling of Complex Systems

It is important to realize that the semi-quantitative modeling task can be at least as challenging as that of numerical modeling. Two major issues are the choice of level of complexity to include in the model and the estimation of model parameters. The first issue is illustrated by the fact that the complexity of the toy model could have been reduced if the heat loss had been modeled as a zero-order process independent of temperature. Then, the model would have only one feedback loop, and there would be no need to include the parameter α.

Estimation of model parameters must include the understanding that complex systems can exhibit qualitatively distinct behaviors depending on the values of their parameters and the selection of initial-variable values [24, 34]. The mapping between behaviors and values can be displayed graphically as domain maps [see, for e.g., 3]. Clearly, the semi-quantitative method is constrained to work with systems that do not exhibit complex behaviors not known to exist a priori. For example, simple second-order linear systems can exhibit sigmoidal (overdamped) or oscillatory (underdamped) behavior; in the absence of a friction term, the amplitude of oscillation at the resonant frequency is unbounded. Nonlinear systems can change behavior dramatically in different regions of parameter space: The same system can exhibit steady-state, oscillatory, and chaotic behaviors depending on the choice of model parameters and initial values. This issue has not been widely discussed in the qualitative simulation literature, perhaps because qualitative methods have not been studied extensively with second- and higher-order systems.

Therefore, as noted in the introduction, model parameters must be estimated with accuracy sufficient to ensure correct qualitative model behavior. The contribution of the semi-quantitative quantity representation, as opposed to a numerical representation, is that the precision of estimation need not be more than required to provide correct qualitative behavior.

In contrast to classical qualitative simulation, the responsibility of ensuring that all possible model behaviors will be provided by the simulation rests on the modeler, not on the simulation machinery. In some cases, this means that a family of models will need to be developed, each containing a combination of parameters that is plausible given the available information about the real system and each representing one of the possible behaviors of the system.

These principles for semi-quantitative simulation are valid in the general case. Application to a more realistically complex model is discussed in Section 4.1.

2.2   Diagnosis

The process of diagnosis can be considered a heuristic classification task characterized by a domain-independent inference structure that systematically relates data to a pre-enumerated set of solutions [4]. Consider the question "Why is the house cold?" Intuitively, one suspects that the answer to this question is implicit in the model. Yet, Equations 1–7, which represent the system, would appear quite opaque to explanation. Previous approaches to the problem of diagnosis and explanation have included separate but parallel symbolic knowledge bases [2] and construction of precompiled fault tables that correlate individual faults with all the abnormalities associated with the faults [18, 29]. Both methods risk inaccuracy because the simulation and diagnostic knowledge bases are separate and may become inconsistent. The ABEL system [32] used the same deep model for both reasoning and explanation but was not used for simulation. Direct model-based diagnostic reasoning has been implemented in digital systems with binary value spaces [8, 14] and in analog systems with real-valued quantity spaces [11], but extension to systems with feedback has been difficult [8]. In general, very tight coupling of numerical and symbolic computing has been difficult to accomplish [19].

2.2.1   State-Space Search

For applications in which the semi-quantitative assumption is valid, the AI technique of state-space search by constraint propagation and generate-and-test allows diagnosis and explanation using the simulation model itself as the knowledge base [11, 37]. Some background may be useful. *Constraint propagation* refers to the inference of the value of an unknown variable when all the variables that determine the unknown's value are themselves known [9, 10, 36, 38]. Mathematically, this is similar to solving a system of linear algebraic equations by identifying equations containing exactly one unknown variable, solving those equations, and using the results iteratively to solve the system of equations. Symbolically, this can be viewed as a "value propagation" process. When the new value is "propagated," the "unknown" variable becomes "known" and can be used in turn to assign values to its successor variables. Thus, when an unambiguous path connects a subset of given variables with the remaining variables in a model, the entire model can be instantiated by constraint propagation. *Generate-and-test* is a two-part search process: First a set of possible solutions is generated; then this set is reduced, or "pruned," by eliminating possibilities to meet one or more constraints. *Hierarchical generate-and-test* is an important special case of the more general algorithm in which each possible solution is specified only partially. By eliminating impossible partial solutions, this powerful algorithm eliminates the entire classes of solutions that would have resulted from the expansion of the (eliminated) partial solutions [37].

2.2.2   Control Structure of the Semi-Quantitative Search Algorithm

The application of the technique of state-space search to semi-quantitative model-based diagnosis (vide infra) is as follows. The search starts with a single given value (selected arbitrarily from the set of given values). This value is propagated as far as possible through the model. Then, heuristic knowledge is used to *generate* a small set of possible behaviors for each suitable variable. Suitable variables are identified by "hypothesis generation" rules, which then generate semi-quantitatively distinct points in the quantity space for each variable. The distinction among the selected points is that each point represents a qualitatively distinct behavior of the system and its given constraints. Note that this definition is broader than a simple determination of the sign of the variable: If a threshold can be exceeded by the new, hypothesized value, then points must be selected on both sides of the threshold to ensure representation of all possible model behaviors. This is equivalent to selecting exactly one point for each variable from each distinct region of the domain map of the model [3].

The generation step thus operates at a local level to enumerate partial solutions of the model based on the given values, propagated values, and hypothesized values. These partial solutions can be *tested,* or *pruned,* by eliminating those that are inconsistent with constraints in the model or with other given variable values. For any partial solution, the search stops when it specifies consistent values for the entire model (a "complete" hypothesis), when it is found to be inconsistent (a "deleted" hypothesis), when it is identical to another partial solution (a "duplicate" hypothesis), or when none of the available constraint propagation or hypothesis generation rules generate new values for exploration (a "blocked" hypothesis). These concepts will be discussed in the context of the example in Figure 1.

A hypothesis of this project is that, by pruning inconsistent partial solutions early in their exploration, the search process can be made sufficiently efficient to permit model-based diagnosis. Data in support of this hypothesis are presented in Section 4.2.

2.2.3   Reasoning Mechanisms of the Search Algorithm

The constraint propagation and hypothesis generation algorithms are implemented as independent expert systems whose knowledge bases contain rules about the topology of weighted influence graphs. That is, the knowledge bases have no information about the specific domain of the system the model represents. They recognize topological patterns among the building blocks used to represent the model. Fault identification is done by comparing new value assignments, either from constraint propagation or from hypothesis generation, with a database of known faults and the labels by which they are called (the fault names).

There is a fundamental distinction between constraint propagation and hypothesis generation. Constraint propagation cannot tolerate ambiguity: It identifies linear dependencies containing exactly one unknown and solves for those unknowns. Hypothesis generation requires and resolves ambiguity: It identifies underdetermined linear dependencies for which reasonable hypotheses can be made. For each possible solution to the dependencies, it constructs a hypothesis with a value assignment to one or more of the unknown variables. Note that in many cases more than one hypothesis will be generated for each variable, reflecting the possibility of multiple regions along that variable's axis in the domain map of the system.

Constraint Propagation Rules An example of a constraint propagation rule is shown in Figure 3. Its premise is satisfied in any part of the model in which a successor variable and all but one prior variable, all being instantaneous variables, have assigned values such that the sum of the prior variables has an arithmetic sign different from the sign of the value of the successor variable. Its specified action is to assign a value to the single prior variable whose value is unknown. The new value is calculated arithmetically from the known values. When a negative or positive feedback relationship is present between the known successor variable and the other known prior variables, the calculated new value is moved further from or closer to *Normal*, respectively, by a multiplicative factor in order to anticipate the effect of inserting the new value into the model.

Note that this particular rule is not propagating values "forward," as in simulation, but rather "backward," as in diagnostic reasoning. The new value is assigned to one of the inputs to the (known) successor variable. Therefore, the operation of shifting the new value with respect to normal simply recognizes that the new value will be found, through negative or positive feedback, to have diminished or augmented effect, respectively, on the given successor variable. The shifting operation recognizes explicitly the well-known reduction in sensitivity to perturbations in forward-path variables in stable negative-feedback-regulated systems [24, pp. 60–61].

As an implementation note, finding the existence and sign of feedback between a given successor variable and its inputs in a linear systems model is a classic problem in feedback control theory. In the general case, it can be solved by Mason's general gain formula [34], which uses information about the directional linkages between variables and the gains associated with the linkages. This approach has been applied previously to a separate symbolic model in our testbed domain, the human cardiovascular system [27]. In the current system, the sign of feedback from a given variable to its own inputs is determined by the standard method of calculation of the return ratio [24, pp. 72–78]: The link from the inputs to the variable is broken, the inputs are set to *Normal*, and a token of unit value is applied to the variable. Simulation to steady state is then used to propagate the token to the inputs. These are then examined for sign and saved as a

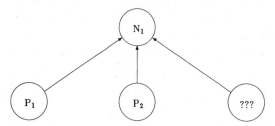

IF: the value of N_1, P_1, and P_2 are known, and the sign of $P_1 + P_2 \neq$ the sign of N_1
THEN:
(1) calculate the unknown value
(2) if P_1 or P_2 are affected by feedback paths (not shown) from N_1, worsen the calculated new value by factor α if the net feedback is negative, or improve it by factor $\frac{1}{\alpha}$ if the net feedback is positive (see text).

Figure 3. Example of a constraint propagation rule.

property associated with the variable. This process is performed twice at the time of model initialization for each instantaneous variable in the model with more than one input and at least one output, once with thresholds and time delays intact, and again with these set to zero. Both sets of return ratios are available to the inference engine.

Note also that the use of arithmetic does not itself require the use of real-valued variables since a calculus based on a finite number of linguistic variables could be constructed [6]. The advantage of using the real numbers is that the infinite resolution in a real-valued quantity space allows distinction of arbitrarily small differences among variable values. The usefulness of fine resolution in the quantity space is illustrated by the ability to use factors such as α to implement expected changes in the model state. Even though the quantities used for calculation are only semi-quantitatively accurate, they must still be as precise as possible: Even when quantities are "nearly" the same, their relative ordering must be preserved. Therefore, their magnitudes should be represented as precisely, if not as accurately, as possible.

Returning to the method of searching the state space, note that constraint propagation heuristics alone are insufficient for a complete diagnostic search. Many combinations of model topology and partial value assignments can be approached only by forming disjoint hypotheses. For these cases, "hypothesis generation" rules are used.

Hypothesis Generation Rules   The importance of hypothesis generation rules may be seen by considering that the state space of a real-valued model is infinite. For a pure qualitative model, with three possible values per variable, an N-variable model has a state space of 3^N points. Hypothesis generation rules identify the qualitatively distinct regions of the domain map of the model along the axis of one or more variables and select one point from each such region for the purpose of further search.

An example of a hypothesis generation rule is shown in Figure 4. This rule refers to a particular type of variable, the level. The level type is similar to Forrester's level [13] in that it represents a quantity that is the time integral of its inputs and outputs (the precise definition is given in Table 1). The rule states that in any part of the model in which the integrated part of a level variable (the quantity) is abnormal, there are two parallel possibilities. In one hypothesis, the inflow is proportionally abnormal with the same sign. In the other hypothesis, the outflow is proportionally abnormal with the opposite sign. The constant of proportionality β is equal to unity if no feedback relationship exists for the integrated quantity and is assigned a value between 0 and 1

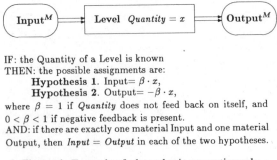

IF: the Quantity of a Level is known
THEN: the possible assignments are:
    Hypothesis 1. Input$= \beta \cdot x$,
    Hypothesis 2. Output$= -\beta \cdot x$,
where $\beta = 1$ if *Quantity* does not feed back on itself, and
$0 < \beta < 1$ if negative feedback is present.
AND: if there are exactly one material Input and one material
Output, then *Input = Output* in each of the two hypotheses.

Figure 4. Example of a hypothesis generation rule.

if there is a negative-feedback relationship. Further, if conservation of mass applies and if there is just one input and one output, the two flows for each hypothesis are constrained to be equal. An illustration of this rule is an overflowing sink: The water level will rise if the tap is running too fast or if the drain is clogged. If a strong, water-tight, elastic seal covers the sink, the pressure under the seal will eventually rise enough to equalize the two flows in either case.

Note that the constants of proportionality α and β in Figures 3 and 4 represent the relationship between the perturbing variable and the feedback-regulated variable. They model explicitly the reduced sensitivity to perturbation of systems containing negative-feedback regulation. The constant α models the reduction in sensitivity to a deviation from normal of the unknown input variable in Figure 3 by the multiplicative factor $1/\alpha$. When reasoning diagnostically from effect to cause or from regulated variable to perturbing variable, this factor is inverted to yield the multiplicative factor α. We choose the empiric value $\alpha = 1.25$, although other values greater than unity would also be satisfactory.

The constant β models the reduction in sensitivity of the flows in Figure 4 to a perturbation in the level quantity owing to negative regulation. Currently, it applies only if the level quantity regulates its outflow rate by negative feedback. This rule detects the presence of feedback by propagating a token from the quantity of the level variable, which is material, and checking whether the token reaches the informational input to the outflow rate. The current empiric value of β is 0.125, although other values less than unity would also be satisfactory.

Metarules: Rules about the Rules   A small set of metarules is used to inform the inference engine when to apply the conclusions of the constraint propagation and hypothesis generation rules. These rules cover special cases as, for example, those variables that may have nonnormal values only when they themselves are the primary fault variables.

Pruning of Inconsistent Hypotheses   Identification of inconsistencies uses sign information only. It does not use magnitude information explicitly because the semi-quantitative assumption does not allow specification of an error term within which all magnitude differences must fall.

The sign criterion is stringent, however, in models whose digraph representations have a large fan-in with inhomogeneous sign. That is, when a given variable typically is determined by several prior variables and when the prior variables typically affect the given variable both directly and inversely, the sign of the given variable will be correct only when the magnitudes of the prior variables are correctly ordered. Therefore, the requirement of correct sign for the given variable imposes a magnitude constraint on the prior variables. Note that this is precisely the type of model in which the classical qualitative simulation method tends to generate intractable branching.

Fault Identification   Specific faults are identified by comparing the new value assignments to model variables with a database of known model faults, as illustrated in Table 3. The table contains the linkage between the values that are consistent with

TABLE 3. Database of Known Model Faults

Fault Label	Fault Variable	Fault Value	Auxiliary Constraint
Broken heater	Heater	*Low*	Temperature is low
Runaway heater	Heater	*High*	Temperature is high
Cold weather	Heat loss	*High*	Temperature is low
Warm weather	Heat loss	*Low*	Temperature is high
Low set point	Set point	*Low*	Temperature is low
High set point	Set point	*High*	Temperature is high
Broken thermostat	Thermostat	*Low*	Temperature is low
Broken thermostat	Thermostat	*High*	Temperature is high

individual faults and the labels for the faults that are meaningful to the user. Additionally, it contains additional constraints that must be satisfied in order for each diagnosis to be valid.

When a particular hypothesis is identified as consistent with a given fault, it is copied to a duplicate new hypothesis. The original hypothesis is labeled with the fault name, so that it acquires the property of having an identified fault. The duplicate new hypothesis is used for exploration of those alternate paths in the search space in which the new value assignment is true but does not represent the given fault. For example, in the heated house, a low temperature may reflect a broken heater or, alternatively, a normal heater response to a broken thermostat. This construction of duplicate hypotheses is only one of several possible implementations of this tree search algorithm. We chose it to emulate our perception of the manner in which expert physicians diagnose problems in the complex testbed domain of cardiology.

2.2.4 Example: The Heated House

Consider the possible diagnoses for a house temperature of *Low* in the model in Figure 1. Following the precept of William of Occam, we assume that at most one fault is present in the model. This assumption is made in many model-based diagnostic reasoning systems [11] and can be avoided by accepting combinatoric enlargement of the number of possible explanations for a given malfunction [11, 35]. Further, we assume that the system is semi-quantitatively in steady-state, so that no variable will change its position in the quantity space with respect to *Normal* or with respect to any other model variable. This assumption can also be avoided at the cost of an enlarged number of possible hypotheses.

The application of the rules and fault table to the example in Figure 1 yields the trace shown in Table 4. The final set of hypotheses is set forth in Table 5. In this example, no instances of self-contradictory hypotheses requiring pruning occurred. Such an example is given in reference 40.

3 IMPLEMENTATION

The system described in this chapter has been implemented in Common LISP on a Symbolics 3640 computer. All figures and examples in the chapter have run success-

TABLE 4. Tracing of Diagnosis by Search of the Toy Model

Inference–Hypothesis Cycle	Current Hypothesis Focus	Premise(s) of rule	Action(s) of rule
1	—	*Low* temperature (T)	*Low* house ratio
	—	*Low* house ratio and unchanging capacity	*Low* house quantity
	—	*Low* house quantity	Hypotheses: *Low* heater, *High* loss
	1	*Low* heater, *Low* heat loss	Diagnosis: broken heater
	2	*Low* heater, *Low* heat loss	Dummy for further reasoning
	3	*High* loss, *High* heater	Diagnosis: cold weather
	4	*High* loss, *High* heater	Dumy for further reasoning
2	1	Established diagnosis	*Normal* set point (T_{sp})
	1	*Normal* T_{sp} and *Low* T	*High* thermostat
	1	Hypothesis 1 is complete	—
	2	*Low* heater	*Low* thermostat
	2	*Low* thermostat	Diagnosis: broken thermostat
	5	*Low* thermostat	Dummy for further reasoning
	5	*Low* thermostat and *Low* T	*Very Low* T_{sp}
	5	*Very Low* T_{sp}	Diagnosis: *Low* set point
	6	*Very Low* T_{sp}	Dummy for further reasoning
	6	Cannot proceed: hypothesis is blocked	
	5	Hypothesis 5 is complete	—
	2	Established diagnosis	*Normal* T_{sp}
	2	Hypothesis 2 is complete	—
	3	Established diagnosis	*Normal* T_{sp}
	3	*Normal* T_{sp} and *Low* T	*High* thermostat
	3	Hypothesis 3 is complete	—
	4	*Normal* T_{sp} and *Low* T	*High* thermostat
	4	Cannot proceed: hypothesis is blocked	

TABLE 5. Complete List of Consistent Hypotheses for Toy Example

Variable	Hypothesis No.					
	1	2	3	4	5	6
House heat						
Quantity	*Low*	*Low*	*Low*	*Low*	*Low*	*Low*
Capacity	*Normal*	*Normal*	*Normal*	*Normal*	*Normal*	*Normal*
Ratio	*Low*	*Low*	*Low*	*Low*	*Low*	*Low*
Heater	*Low*	*Low*	*High*	*High*	*Low*	*Low*
Heat loss	*Low*	*Low*	*High*	*High*	*Low*	*Low*
Temperature	*Low*	*Low*	*Low*	*Low*	*Low*	*Low*
Set point	*Normal*	*Normal*	*Normal*	—	*Very Low*	—
Thermostat	*High*	*Low*	*High*	*High*	*Low*	*Low*
Diagnosis	Broken heater	Broken thermostat	Cold weather	Blocked	Low set point	Blocked

fully in the current system. Numerical integration is performed using Euler's algorithm. Although more sophisticated algorithms such as the fourth-order Runge-Kutta algorithm could be used, they did not offer an advantage in this experimental system to compensate for their increased computational expense. In the current implementation of the system, there are 14 constraint propagation rules and 11 hypothesis generation rules.

4   RESULTS

This section shows an example of simulation with a complex testbed model, a study of the efficiency of the heuristic-guided model-based search algorithm for diagnosis in simple models, and a verification of the power of the diagnostic algorithm in the testbed model.

4.1   Complex Testbed Model: The Human Cardiovascular System

The methods described in this chapter are intended to be of general applicability. Frequently, however, proposed general methods prove unworkable when applied to realistically complex problems. Therefore, a testbed model of 46 variables, including 4 state (integrated) variables, was developed. Illustrated in Figure 5, it is a lumped-parameter, deterministic representation of the human cardiovascular system. It has been tested with simulations of a variety of single and multiple fault diseases [39]. The results of the simulations were verified by comparison with the standard medical literature [41]. One example, sudden weightlessness, is discussed here.

The effects of sudden transition to a weightless environment have been the subject of much study [26]. The salient clinical point is that all astronauts who have been in space for 9 hours or more are dehydrated when they return [16]. The current working hypothesis is that in the earth's gravitational field a significant proportion of blood in the body is pooled in the legs. In the weightless environment, this blood moves into the chest, raising pressures in the heart. The initial response of the heart to this volume load is to pump more blood out (Starling's law) with each stroke and also per unit time. Sympathetic tone decreases by reflex, with decreased systemic vascular resistance and pulse rate. The net result of the elevated atrial pressure is an increase in excretion of fluid, which begins over the next several hours and continues for several days until the circulating blood volume, as sensed by the heart, is normal. Thus, the astronaut adapts to the weightless environment. When he or she returns to earth, blood again pools in the legs and the astronaut becomes clinically dehydrated.

Data in humans are available from earth-bound tests, such as immersion in water up to the neck. Short-term (1–2 hour) experiments show the changes described: increases in cardiac output, stroke volume, atrial pressure, mean arterial pressure, and decreased pulse and systemic vascular resistance [17].

Data on the longer-term (days) are available from a monkey launched in the Biosatellite III flight [28]. Over several days, the animal excreted more water than he drank, and the central venous pressure, which had been elevated since launch, declined.

Simulation on the time scale of minutes, shown in Figure 6, predicts that the central venous pressure (CVP) rises rapidly, as does the cardiac output (CO), as the effective capacity of the veins shrinks. Urine output (UO) rises later, and the total blood volume is unchanged. The other variables mentioned in the preceding, (not shown), vary appropriately.

On the time scale of days, shown in Figure 7, the high urine output decreases the total blood volume and venous filling. The CVP declines along with the venous filling. Cardiac output decreases along with the CVP. Thus, the simulations are qualitatively correct on a variety of time scales, although the magnitudes are not absolutely correct.

4.2   Efficiency of the Heuristic-Guided Model-Based Search Algorithm

In any search algorithm, the goal is to reach the desired endpoints with a minimum of unnecessary exploration. In the semi-quantitative diagnostic algorithm, the objectives are the locations in N-space of all the diagnoses consistent with the given starting values. The search space size is 3^N, assuming that the domain map has at most three regions for each normalized variables (*Normal*, all positive values, and all negative values). In the presence of feedback and threshold relationships, there may be more regions for each variable. Thus, even small models have a large search space. The goal of the hierarchical generate-and-test state-space search algorithm is to identify all consistent diagnoses while considering a minimum number of inconsistent (partial) solutions. In this section, we consider the efficiency of search in a simple model.

The model is the heated house example illustrated in Figure 1. There are six variables, of which one is specified. The remaining search space has 243 possible hypotheses. The hypothesis set constructed by the diagnostic algorithm is listed in Table 5. The complete trace of the derivation of the hypotheses, showing the role of constraint propagation, hypothesis generation, and hypothesis duplication at the time of diagnosis, is shown in Table 4. The total number of hypotheses considered is six, including two blocked dummy copies of hypotheses 3 and 5. The pruning efficiency is $(243 - 6) / 243 = 97.5\%$. Since there are four distinct diagnoses, the maximum efficiency is $(243 - 4) / 243 = 98.4\%$. In another six-variable model [40], the pruning efficiency was 96.4%, compared with a maximum efficiency of 98.8%.

4.3   Complete Hypotheses in the Complex Model

The criterion for successful diagnosis of a model fault is assignment of values to all model variables such that (a) the faulty value has an abnormal value with sign consistent with the diagnosis and (b) all other variable assignments satisfy the constraints imposed by the model. At the simplest level, the second condition requires that the sign and partial ordering of the variable values be self-consistent. At a more rigorous level, it requires that all determinants (inputs to a given variable) combine to predict a value within some error threshold of the value actually assigned to that variable. The second criterion is stringent even in the simple case because it requires correct ordering of all variable values relative to each other. That is, the differences

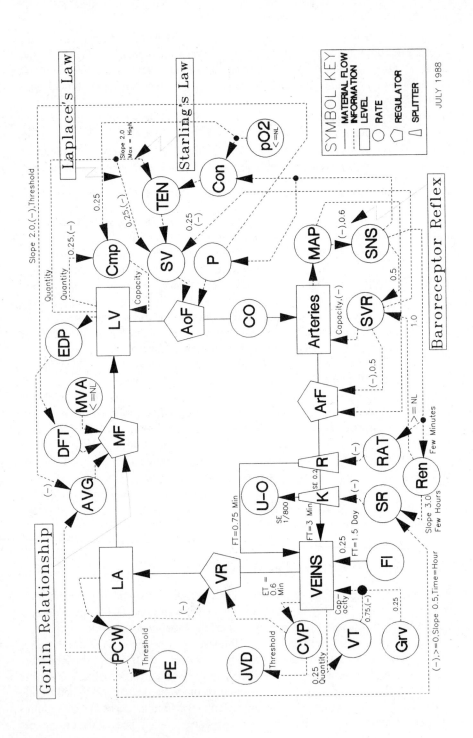

Gorlin Relationship

Laplace's Law

Starling's Law

Baroreceptor Reflex

SYMBOL KEY
- MATERIAL FLOW
---- INFORMATION
LEVEL
RATE
REGULATOR
SPLITTER

JULY 1988

176

KEY TO VARIABLES: **AoF:** aortic blood flow. **ArF:** arterial blood flow. **Arteries:** systemic arteries. **AVG:** atrioventricular (LA to LV) pressure gradient. **Cmp:** compliance of left ventricle. **CO:** cardiac output. **Con:** contractility of left ventricle. **CVP:** central venous pressure. **DFT:** diastolic filling time. **EDP:** end-diastolic pressure of left ventricle. **FI:** fluid intake. **Grv:** gravity. **JVD:** jugular venous distension. **K:** kidneys. **LA:** left atrium. **LV:** left ventricle. **MAP:** mean arterial pressure. **MF:** mitral valve flow. **MVA:** mitral valve area. **P:** pulse. **Pcwp:** pulmonary capillary wedge pressure. **PE:** pulmonary edema. **pO$_2$:** oxygen concentration (partial pressure) in blood. **R:** renal arteries. **RAT:** renal artery tone. **REN:** renin activity. **SNS:** sympathetic nervous system. **SR:** salt retention mechanisms. **SV:** stroke volume. **SVR:** systemic vascular resistance. **TEN:** fiber tension in left ventricle. **U-O:** urine output. **VEINS:** systemic veins. **VR:** venous return. **VT:** venous tone.

Not shown: myocardial variables. *Not modeled*: right atrium, right ventricle, shunts, valves, pericardium, pulmonary edema-oxygen link, parasympathetic nervous system. *Chamber size ratios*: veins, arteries, left atrium, left ventricle : 20, 10, 1, 1.

KEY TO RELATIONSHIP CODES: (−): Cause and Effect are inversely related. <number>: slope of linear relationship, Effect = slope · Causal Variable. <time value>: time lag from onset of change in Causal Variable to 100% transmission of Effect. {<, '≥**Normal**', '≤**Normal**', **or** >}: Effect is subject to the specified constraint. **Capacity:** The capacity of a Level variable to hold material. **ET:** emptying time, the time to deplete Level's Quantity at normal flow rates. **FT:** filling time, the time to fill Level's Quantity from Empty to Normal assuming other inputs and emptying are zero. The Emptying and Filling times determine the relative sizes of interconnected Level variables. **Quantity:** The amount of material in a Level variable. **Ratio:** the ratio of Quantity to Capacity in the Level variable type. **SE:** side-effluent ratio, the ratio of normal flow rate through the side port of a valve to the normal flow rate through its main port. **Threshold:** Effect = slope · (Causal Variable − Threshold), if Causal Variable is ≥ Threshold; otherwise, Effect = 0.

MAPPING OF VARIABLE TYPES ONTO DIFFERENCE EQUATIONS: See Table 1.

Figure 5. Simplified model of the human cardiovascular system.

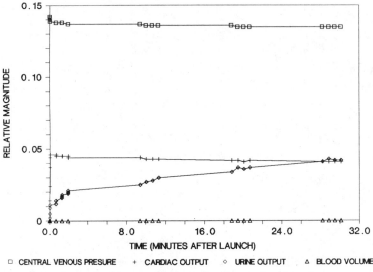

Figure 6. Low-gravity simulation (time scale, minutes).

between variables need not be correct, but the ordinal assignment of the variables when they are arranged from smallest to largest must be correct.

To test the ability of the diagnostic algorithm to meet these two criteria, a user-guided depth-first search was performed for a variety of diagnoses. The interaction with the user bypassed the state-space size problem by guaranteeing that the correct path was chosen at every decision point. By requiring an error of less than a small quantity for the second criterion in the preceding, the constraint propagation heuristics were observed to iterate to stability after initial values had been assigned to all

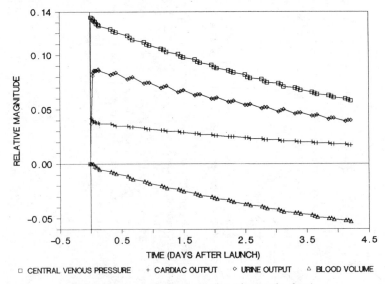

Figure 7. Low-gravity simulation (time scale, days).

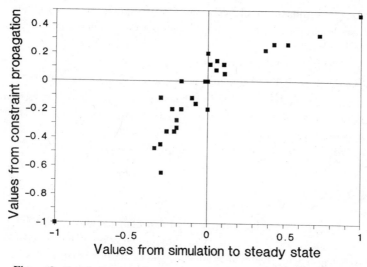

Figure 8. Results by simulation versus diagnostic search: mitral stenosis.

variables. Thus, they treated the differential equation model as a set of equality constraints and achieved stability by mathematical relaxation.

The results for two diagnoses compared with the "gold standard" results obtained by simulation with the identical model are displayed by scatter plots in Figures 8 and 9. The Pearson correlation coefficients between the values obtained for each variable by the search algorithm and by simulation for these two diagnoses were 0.88 and 0.89, respectively.

In summary, the methods described above can:

- Use the same model for both symbolic and numerical reasoning.

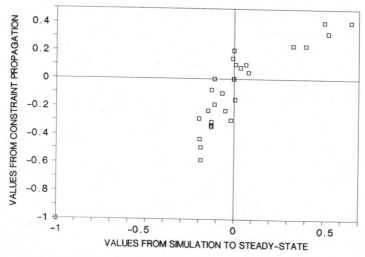

Figure 9. Results by simulation versus diagnostic search: congestive heart failure.

- Perform semi-quantitatively valid numerical simulation. The accuracy of the simulation is limited only by the accuracy of the estimated parameters in the model.
- Identify faults by model-based reasoning.
- Locate the faults in the N-dimensional semi-quantitative state space.
- Instantiate the model with a complete set of semi-quantitative values for each identified fault. The values in each instantiation correlate well with those obtained by steady-state simulation. These instantiations could thus be used for simulation of the effects of interventions (e.g., treatments) in each fault state.

5   DISCUSSION

This section includes four subsections: comparison of this method with previous work on qualitative simulation, comparison with previous work on model-based diagnostic reasoning, uses for semi-quantitative models, and directions for further work.

5.1   Qualitative Simulation

The semi-quantitative method described here shares several of the goals of qualitative simulation. Bobrow [1] describes six tasks for qualitative reasoning: simulation, envisionment, mental models, diagnosis, verification, and deducing functionality. He describes simulation as determining, starting with a structural description of some device or system and some initial conditions, a likely course of future behavior. Diagnosis is the problem of finding the change in an underlying structure that is responsible for the difference in its behavior from some specified desired behavior. Common to many qualitative reasoning systems are the principles of *compositionality* and *locality*. *Compositionality* requires that the system's behavior be derivable from the structure of the system. *Locality* requires that effects must propagate locally, through specified connections that may be considered causal. The semi-quantitative method is most similar to the work of Kuipers [22], who uses abstractions of differential equations and continuously differentiable functions to build a set of constraints. These qualitative constraints may then be used to predict the behavior of the system. Kuipers implemented his approach in a system called QSIM.

While powerful and general, the qualitative simulation method of Kuipers has found limited application in the modeling of real systems. We argue that the fundamental reason is the inability of pure qualitative simulation to represent semi-quantitative and quantitative information. This inability results in the inability to decide, on a local level, which of several competing inputs to a given variable will dominate and, as a result, the inability to predict the behavior of the system on a global level. Kuipers and others resolve this limitation by predicting a set of behaviors that includes the correct behavior(s); the remaining members of the set are spurious [21].

As described in the introductory chapter, there are several semi-quantitative approaches currently under investigation. Our approach differs in several ways from the qualitative one. Most fundamentally, the responsibility for correct modeling of the real system lies with the user, not with the simulation program. Because the behavior of real systems with multiple feedback loops can be quite complex [24, 34], the task of estimating parameters and initial conditions may be arduous. The advantage of a semi-quantitative method over a strictly numerical method is a reduction in the precision with which some of the parameters need be estimated.

In our approach, a mapping is constructed between model parameters and the real numbers, and model variables and the real numbers. Neither the parameters nor the variables are constrained to conform to the values found in the real system. They *are* constrained to be accurate enough to ensure correct model performance within the intended operating region of the model. Thus, in contrast to Kuipers's QSIM, the quantity space is shared between different variables. Time is treated as a continuous variable. Because numerical integration is used, individual time points appear to be discrete quantities. However, these may be obtained at arbitrarily close spacing by reducing the time step of the numerical integration algorithm.

As a practical matter, the building blocks used to represent models in our approach are linear. The causal links between variables are allowed to have threshold relationships and time lags, both of which interfere with the principle of superposition and therefore of linearity. The advantage of maintaining a linear, time-invariant model is the availability of powerful tools for analyzing the model, such as Mason's general gain formula and various methods for assessing stability. These issues were not pertinent in classical qualitative reasoning methods, perhaps because these methods were not able to work effectively with sufficiently complex models.

The use of linear building blocks does not imply the use of analytic solutions in parameterized form, as in the toy example. Although an analytic solution is convenient in simple systems, simulation is more useful for complex systems.

Turning again to qualitative simulation, it is notable that the use of sign consistency constraints on downstream variables to derive strong constraints on the magnitudes of upstream variables inverts the usual QSIM technique. Branching becomes an opportunity to further discriminate details about the system under study [7].

5.2 Model-based Diagnostic Reasoning

Algorithms for model-based troubleshooting have been under development for decades [11]. In almost all cases, they assume that at most one fault is present in order to avoid combinatoric explosion. The general approach is to target the components of the model in which the fault may lie using the known abnormal values or behavior and then to search within the components using the relationships among variables in the model. The abnormal values are passed, or "propagated," from variable to variable when no branching occurs along the propagation path. When branching does occur, separate hypotheses are generated and are then tested independently. The generated hypotheses define the leaves of a search tree. Testing of the hypotheses eliminates impossible hypotheses: This is called "pruning" the search tree. Pruning can be accomplished by finding contradictions within the hypothesis or between a hypothesis and external data.

Direct model-based diagnostic reasoning has been implemented in digital systems with large numbers of components and with binary quantity spaces [8, 14] and in analog systems with real-valued quantity spaces [11]. However, these reasoning programs have not been easy to extend to realistically complex systems.

The factors that limit model-based diagnostic reasoning include the feedback phenomenon, continuous variables, or real-valued quantity spaces [8]. The algorithm described here is designed for precisely this combination. As with other diagnostic systems that consider only single faults, it can be made to consider multiple faults at the cost of increased computational complexity [11, 35].

5.3   Uses for Semi-Quantitative Models

Four general areas are envisioned for the semi-quantitative approach: embedded expert systems in simulation models, simulation using models at varying levels of abstraction, temporal reasoning in expert systems, and model-based diagnosis in expert systems.

5.3.1   Embedded Expert Systems in Simulation Models

The systems dynamics method has often been applied to imperfectly understood domains. Presumably, all necessary parameters could be obtained to construct standard numerical models in these applications. As simulations of such domains are used more widely, it may be desirable to obtain a rough yet qualitatively accurate notion of the future state of a model. Semi-quantitative models can provide this information in return for a limited investment in parameter estimation.

For example, there is growing enthusiasm for modeling the behavior of intelligent agents by expert systems embedded within simulation models. Such agents might be expert robots in a factory simulation, man-in-the-loop systems, or the opposing command staffs in war game simulations. During the simulation, each such agent may have inexact but approximately correct information on which to base decisions. When these decisions can use qualitative knowledge of continuous systems, the semi-quantitative methods described here would be appropriate.

5.3.2   Simulation Using Models at Varying Levels of Abstraction

Detailed numerical simulation of complex systems can be very costly. For this reason, the modeling process frequently requires the abstraction of a group of unimportant lower-level variables into a single higher-level variable [43]. When the model is expressed in terms of equations, it can be very difficult to change the level of abstraction to meet changes in simulation objectives. Fishwick [12] discusses the issue of abstraction in detail. With semi-quantitative models for simulation and diagnosis, the symbolic nature of the semi-quantitative models eases the processes of abstraction and deabstraction, whether by empiric heuristics or by domain-independent identification of mathematically valid operations.

5.3.3   Temporal Reasoning in Expert Systems

Symbolic temporal reasoning about dynamic systems that include feedback relationships has not yet been handled in a general way [23]. The enthusiasm for classical qualitative simulation may reflect perception of a need for methods of reasoning about complex systems over time ("temporal reasoning" methods). Unfortunately, classical qualitative simulation have not proven useful for complex systems [21], although new approaches are being developed [30]. The semi-quantitative method provides the benefit of deterministic, branching-free, qualitative simulation at the cost of increased effort in model development, verification, and validation.

5.3.4   Model-based Diagnosis in Expert Systems

Model-based diagnosis or troubleshooting, when the domain is appropriate, has many advantages over alternate approaches. Unlike production rule methods, models are compact, easier to update, and less likely to have internal contradictions. Unlike precompiled fault tables, they can identify faults that may have been omitted from the fault tables and are less costly to update. Model-based diagnosis is likely to be less efficient than either production rule systems or precompiled tables, however. The literature in this area is cited in Section 2.2.

Not all domains are appropriate for model-based diagnosis. The earliest systems for model-based diagnosis used binary quantity spaces and domains without feedback, such as digital circuits. The major advances in such systems included dealing with large numbers of components and a variety of failure modes [8]. In contrast, the semi-quantitative method appears best suited for domains with relatively small numbers of variables but with large numbers of feedback loops.

An additional unsolved problem in expert temporal reasoning is that of reasoning on differing time scales. How does one distinguish short-term conditions from chronic conditions by model-based reasoning? The semi-quantitative diagnostic search algorithm may be helpful in this regard because it is able to ignore relationships in the model that require more than a specified length of time to occur. For example, if one wishes to reason about the very short-term effects of administration of an excess of fluids, the algorithm will ignore the compensatory reaction of the kidneys, which takes minutes to take effect. The requirement that the model be in "semi-quantitative" steady state is still satisfied because the model, when modified for very short-term reasoning, actually lacks the compensatory relationships in the kidney. This aspect of the diagnostic algorithm has not yet been explored in detail in the testbed system.

5.4   Directions for Further Work

One goal of this project is to delineate a general method for reasoning semi-quantitatively about dynamic systems. For any general method, it is wise to provide formal justifications, if possible, for the underlying assumptions. These are not yet available for the following points in this approach.

5.4.1   Mapping External Values into Semi-Quantitative Values

It is well known that the qualitative behavior of nonlinear models can be critically dependent on the precise values of key parameters [31]. Linear models can, of course, model nonlinear behavior within restricted operating regions. By restricting the semi-quantitative method to linear models, it is hoped that the accumulated error during simulation will be bounded by the error in parameter estimation. Empirically, it has been noted that homeostatic models are relatively insensitive to large errors in parameter estimation, even when they are nonlinear [15]. However, it would be desirable to find a rigorously correct algorithm for translating estimated parameters into the normalized values used in the semi-quantitative formulation. At this time, we are using an expert-system based user interface to select one or more internal values corresponding to a user-specified external value. The need for more than one internal value arises when the external value translates "near" a model threshold. In this case, it is frequently not possible to decide which side of the threshold the external value should fall on, and so multiple simulations to cover each possibility are necessary.

The issue of internal thresholds is a part of the more general question of representation of uncertainty within the model. In contrast to other model-based reasoning systems [11, 33], this system currently is deterministic. The rationale is that a calculus for propagation of informal probability measures is not well developed [5, 33], and that uncertainty can perhaps be better represented by conducting multiple simulation experiments, each of which represents one of the possible values of the uncertain parameters or variables. Thus, this system resolves the uncertainty issue by being equivalent to Monte Carlo simulation as the number of experiments with randomly selected values becomes large.

5.4.2   *Proof of Existence of Semi-Quantitative Models*

A fundamental assumption of this method is that the global behavior of a model will be correct if all local ambiguity of conflicting influences is resolved by proper weight assignments. That is, whenever several prior variables compete to determine a given variable, if the relative influences of the effects of the prior variables is always made clear by the parameters attached to each, then the model as a whole will always yield the correct qualitative behavior for the system. While it is true that the intractable branching of qualitative models arises from the impossibility of resolving this local ambiguity with pure qualitative quantity spaces, the converse is not necessarily true. Thus it would be desirable to prove that local resolution of ambiguity guarantees qualitatively correct model behavior.

5.4.3   *Proof of Complete Search*

The results presented in the preceding use empirically derived topology rules to propagate constraints and to delineate a complete set of semi-quantitative domain map regions. An example may show why a question arises on this point. The reader may have noticed the unintuitive restriction on the constraint propagation rule in Figure 3. This restriction that the sign of the consequent variable value be different from the sign of the sum of its known determinants results from the uncertainty in absolute magnitude of the quantities involved. For example, let the consequent variable have the value 0.5 and the sum of its known determining variables be 0.4. It may be that, after mathematical relaxation to steady state, the respective values will be 0.5 and 0.6 because of small changes in the variables, which sum to 0.6. Since this change in the sum cannot be predicted in advance, a critical value in the domain map must be presumed to be present along the axis of the unknown variable, and two parallel hypotheses must be made that assign opposite signs to the unknown variable's value.

At this time, the only proof that a suitable set of heuristics must exist lies in the fact that human experts can trace through very complex models. Further, other important methods also operate independently. The author knows of no general proof, for example, that the correct conclusions will always be reached by a production rule system with confidence factor uncertainty representation for an arbitrarily large rule base and an arbitrarily large number of conclusions. In fact, there is some evidence that deleterious interactions between individually good rules in a production rule system can degrade global performance [42].

5.4.4   Efficiency of Search

At this time, we have not yet constrained satisfactorily the diagnostic search process for the complex testbed model. Our strategy for improving the search is twofold. The first is to improve the diagnostic heuristics by identifying topologies permitting more restrictive conclusions. Also, we are exploring metapruning strategies that would link the high-level divergence point of an impossible hypothesis with the subsequent proof that one of its subsidiary hypotheses is inconsistent in a way that implicates the high-level divergence point. This strategy is based on the serial nature of connections in some models, in which the effect of a branching may not be evident until the value has been propagated through several intermediate variables.

6   SUMMARY

In this chapter, an approach to semi-quantitative modeling of continuous systems has been proposed. Building on the systems dynamics formalism for feedback systems, the approach provides model-based diagnosis with instantiation of the model for each identified model fault as well as for qualitatively correct simulation of models with minimally accurately estimated parameters.

An extended example illustrates the methodology in a toy system. The performance of the approach in a realistically complex model of the human cardiovascular system is demonstrated with examples of simulation and of user-directed diagnosis. The advantages of this approach for simulation using embedded expert systems, for ease of model abstraction, and for temporal reasoning and model-based diagnosis in expert systems have been described. Finally, current research problems with the approach are outlined. This approach may help to resolve some of the outstanding difficulties that prevent classical qualitative simulation from achieving practical usefulness.

ACKNOWLEDGMENTS

The author would like to thank the following for valuable criticisms of the manuscript: Drs. C. Chiu, B. D'Ambrosio, D. H. Helman, P. Karp, M. Kramer, W. Long, K. Loparo, N. Nielsen, R. Patil, J. Rozenblit, S. Sevinc, P. Szolovits, and B. P. Zeigler. This work was supported in part by the American Heart Association, Texas affiliate by Grant-in-Aid 87G-379, and by the National Institutes of Health, Division of Research Resources by PHS Grant 5 P41 RR00785-14.

REFERENCES

1. D. G. Bobrow, "Qualitative Reasoning about Physical Systems: An Introduction," in D. G. Bobrow (Ed.), *Qualitative Reasoning about Physical Systems*, MIT Press, 1985, pp. 1–5.

2. J. S. Brown, R. R. Burton, and J. De Kleer, "Pedagogical, Natural Language and Knowledge Engineering Techniques in SOPHIE I, II and III," in D. H. Sleeman, and J. S. Brown (Eds.), *Intelligent Tutoring Systems*, Academic, London, 1982, pp. 227–282.

3. C. Chiu, Chapter 11 of this book.

4. W. J. Clancy, "Heuristic Classification," *Artificial Intelligence*, **27**:289–350, 1985.

5. G. F. Cooper, "A Diagnostic Method that Uses Causal Knowledge and Linear Programming in the Application of Bayes' Formula," *Computer Methods and Programs in Biomedicine*, **22**:223–237, 1986.

6. B. D'Ambrosio, Chapter 5 of this book.

7. B. D'Ambrosio, personal communication, May 20, 1988.

8. R. Davis, "Diagnostic Reasoning Based on Structure and Behavior," *Artificial Intelligence*, **24**:347–410, 1984.

9. R. Dechter and J. Pearl, "Network-based Heuristics for Constraint-Satisfaction Problems," *Artificial Intelligence*, **34**:1–38, 1988.

10. J. De Kleer and J. S. Brown, "Theories of Causal Ordering," *Artificial Intelligence*, **29**:33–61,1986.

11. J. De Kleer and B. C. Williams, "Diagnosing Multiple Faults," *Artificial Intelligence*, **32**:97–130, 1987.

12. P. Fishwick, Chapter 4 of this book.

13. J. W. Forrester, *Industrial Dynamics*, MIT Press, Cambridge, MA, 1961.

14. M. R. Genesereth, "The Use of Design Descriptions in Automated Diagnosis," *Artificial Intelligence*, **24**:411–436, 1984

15. A. C. Guyton, T. G. Coleman, R. D. Manning, Jr., and J. E. Hall, "Some Problems and Solutions for Modeling Overall Cardiovascular Regulation," *Mathematical Biosciences*, **72**:141–155, 1984.

16. G. W. Hoffler, R. A. Wolthuis, and R. L. Johnson, "Apollo Space Crew Cardiovascular Evaluations," *Aerospace Medicine*, **45**:807–823, 1974.

17. S. K. Hong, D. R. Pendergast, J. A. Krasney, and J. R. Claybaugh, "Cardio-Renal Responses to a Simulated Gravity-Free State Induced by Water Immersion," *Sangyo Ika Diagaku Zasshi*, **7**(Suppl):205–214, 1985.

18. Y. Ishida, N. Adachi, and H. Tokumaru, "A Topological Approach to Failure Diagnosis of Large-Scale Systems," *IEEE Transactions on Systems, Man, and Cybernetics*, **SMC-15**:327–333, 1985.

19. C. T. Kitzmiller and J. S. Kowalik. "Coupling Symbolic and Numeric Computing in

Knowledge-based Systems," in J. S. Kowalik, (Ed.), *Coupling Symbolic and Numerical Computing in Expert Systems*, Elsevier Science, The Netherlands, 1986, pp. 3–17.

20. B. Kuipers and J. P. Kassirer, "Causal Reasoning in Medicine: Analysis of a Protocol," *Cognitive Science*, **8**:363–385, 1984.

21. B. Kuipers, "The Limits of Qualitative Simulation," *Proceedings of the Ninth International Joint Conference on Artificial Intelligence*, Kaufmann, Los Altos, CA, 1985, pp. 128–136.

22. B. Kuipers, "Qualitative Simulation," *Artificial Intelligence*, **29**:289–338, 1986.

23. J. C. Kunz, "Use of Artificial Intelligence and Simple Mathematics to Analyze a Physiological Model," Ph.D. Thesis, Stanford University, Stanford CA, 1984.

24. B. C. Kuo, *Automatic Control Systems*, Prentice-Hall, Englewood Cliffs, NJ, 1962.

25. J. D. Lebel, "System Dynamics," in F. E. Cellier (Ed.), *Progress in Modeling and Simulation*, Academic, New York, 1982, pp. 119–158.

26. M. N. Levy and J. M. Talbot, "Cardiovascular Deconditioning of Space Flight," *Physiologist*, **26**:297–303, 1983.

27. W. J. Long, S. Naimi, M. G. Criscitiello, and S. Kurzrok, "Reasoning about Therapy from a Physiological Model," *Proceedings of the Fifth World Congress on Medical Informatics MEDINFO 86, Washington, DC*, North-Holland, Amsterdam, 1986, pp. 756–760.

28. J. P. Meehan and R. D. Rader, "Cardiovascular Observations of the *Macaca nemestrina* Monkey in Biosatellite III," *Aerospace Medicine*, **42**:322–336, 1971.

29. J. Mohammed and R. Simmons, "Qualitative Simulation of Semiconductor Fabrication," *Proceedings of the Fifth National Conference on Artificial Intelligence, 1986, Philadelphia, PA*, Kaufmann, Los Altos, CA, pp. 794–799.

30. L. Oyeleye and M. Kramer, Chapter 13 of this book.

31. N. H. Packard, J. P. Crutchfield, J. D. Farmer, and R. S. Shaw, "Geometry from a Time Series," *Physical Review Letters*, **45**:712–716, 1980.

32. R. S. Patil, "Causal Representation of Patient Illness for Electrolyte and Acid-Base Diagnosis," Massachusetts Institute of Technology, Cambridge, MA, LCS TR-267, 1981.

33. J. Pearl, "Evidential Reasoning Using Stochastic Simulation of Causal Models," *Artificial Intelligence*, **32**:245–257, 1987.

34. C. L. Phillips and R. D. Harbor, *Feedback Control Systems*, Prentice-Hall, Englewood Cliffs, NJ, 1988.

35. R. A. Reiter, "Theory of Diagnosis from First Principles," *Artificial Intelligence*, **32**:57–95, 1987.

36. R. M. Stallman and G. J. Sussman, "Forward Reasoning and Dependency-Directed Backtracking in a System for Computer-Aided Circuit Analysis," *Artificial Intelligence*, **9**:135–196, 1977.

37. M. Stefik, J. Aikins, R. Balzer, J. Benoit, L. Birnbaum, F. Hayes-Roth, and E. Sacerdoti, "Basic Concepts for Building Expert Systems," in F. Hayes-Roth, D. A. Waterman, and D. B. Lenat (Eds.), *Building Expert Systems*, Addison-Wesley, Reading, MA, 1983, pp. 59–86.

38. G. J. Sussman and G. L. Steele, Jr., "CONSTRAINTS—A Language for Expressing Almost-Hierarchical Descriptions," *Artificial Intelligence*, **14**:1–39, 1980.

39. L. E. Widman, "Representation Method for Dynamic Causal Knowledge using Semi-

Quantitative Simulation," *Proceedings of the Fifth World Congress on Medical Informatics MEDINFO 86, Washington, DC*, North-Holland, Amsterdam, 1986, pp. 180–184.

40. L. E. Widman, "Knowledge-Based Fault Identification and 'What If' Simulation in Symbolic Dynamic Systems Models," *Proceedings of the 1988 Multiconference on AI and Simulation*, Society for Computer Simulation, San Diego, CA, pp. 89–94.

41. L. E. Widman, "Expert System Reasoning about Dynamic Systems by Semi-Quantitative Simulation," *Computer Methods and Programs in Biomedicine*, **29**:95–113, 1989.

42. D. C. Wilkins and B. G. Buchanan, "On Debugging Rule Sets When Reasoning Under Uncertainty," *Proceedings of the Fifth National Conference on Artificial Intelligence*, 1986, pp. 448–454.

43. B. P. Zeigler, *Theory of Modelling and Simulation*, Wiley, New York, 1976.

7 Coordinating the Use of Qualitative and Quantitative Knowledge in Declarative Device Modeling

PETER D. KARP and PETER FRIEDLAND

Knowledge Systems Laboratory
Department of Computer Science
Stanford University
Stanford, California

1 INTRODUCTION

The Molgen group at Stanford University is studying scientific theory formation in the domain of molecular biology. Our goal is to construct a computational system which can reproduce some of the discoveries and problem-solving strategies of Dr. Charles Yanofsky of the Stanford University Biology Department. Over the course of 15 years of research, Yanofsky and his colleagues discovered a novel mechanism of gene regulation in bacteria.

We are using the following framework to build a system to emulate this behavior. The system will begin with the initial theory of bacterial gene regulation which existed in the 1960s. Then, just as Yanofsky performed experiments whose results could not be predicted by the existing understanding of gene regulation, the system will predict the outcomes of certain experiments. When these predictions conflict with experimental results, the system will enter an iterative phase during which it determines which elements of its existing theory are incorrect, generates modifications to the theory, and is confronted with additional experiments which confirm or disconfirm the modifications.

Central to this framework is the existence of a theory of gene regulation which can make predictions and be reasoned about and modified. Our group has begun to apply the techniques of qualitative simulation (which we also term *declarative device modeling,* or *DDM*) as explored by de Kleer and Brown [2], Iwasaki and Simon [5], Forbus [3], Davis [1], Genesereth [4], and Kuipers [6] to the problem of expressing these theories. Most of these researchers are concerned with the properties of mechanical systems such as pipes, refrigerators, and bouncing balls. We are concerned with biochemical systems containing populations of interacting molecules. These physical systems are similar in that all are subject to a mathematical description, from which all qualitative modeling methodologies are derived. But because our simulations take place in a complex, real-world domain in which we desire close to expert-level predictions, we have identified limitations of the existing techniques in addition to those which have previously been identified [6].

In the domain of gene regulation we find that the form of the knowledge available for problem solving varies widely in its precision from quantitative to qualitative. One approach to dealing with this complexity would be to use an abstraction of the actual theory which reasons with the coarse type of qualitative information used by de Kleer and Brown. We built such a prototype system and found that its capabilities were far less sophisticated and interesting than those of an expert biologist because it lacked a significant amount of the knowledge which a biologist uses. While our current system does still abstract the actual theory to some degree, our goal has been to attempt to bring more diverse types of knowledge to bear on this simulation problem. This has led us to develop new techniques and representations for simulation which span a continuum from quantitative to qualitative.

The remainder of this chapter is structured as follows. First we discuss the biological problem in more detail so our motivations for this work become clearer. We then present our framework for simulation, which consists of representations for state variable values and for the interactions between state variables, and techniques for propagating values between variables. We compare related work to our techniques when it is relevant.

2 MOTIVATIONS

Charles Yanofsky studied the regulation of a set of genes in the bacterium *Escherichia coli* (*E. coli*). The cell translates this set of coregulated genes—called an *operon*—into enzymes in a two-step process (see Figure 1). The genes are first *transcribed* by a

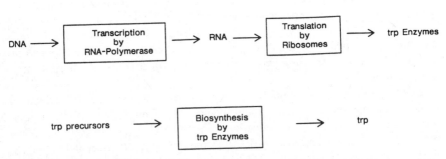

Figure 1. Important processes in regulation of tryptophan (trp) biosynthesis. Top sequence outlines steps of protein synthesis, in which enzymes which catalyze tryptophan biosynthetic pathway are produced from genes which encode them. Bottom sequence outlines production of tryptophan from chemical precursors via biosynthetic enzymes.

protein called *RNA-polymerase* into an intermediate template called *mRNA*. Next the cell machinery *translates* the mRNA into a set of enzymes using a molecule called a *ribosome*. These enzymes form a *biosynthetic pathway* which synthesizes the amino acid *tryptophan* (a building block of proteins) from other nutrients available in the cell. *E. coli* is able to regulate these genes through a negative-feedback mechanism such that they are only translated into mRNA when there is insufficient tryptophan in the cell's environment for its normal growth. Thus, the cell does not waste energy synthesizing these enzymes when it can absorb the required tryptophan from its environment. The first of the two known regulation mechanisms for the operon was discovered in the late

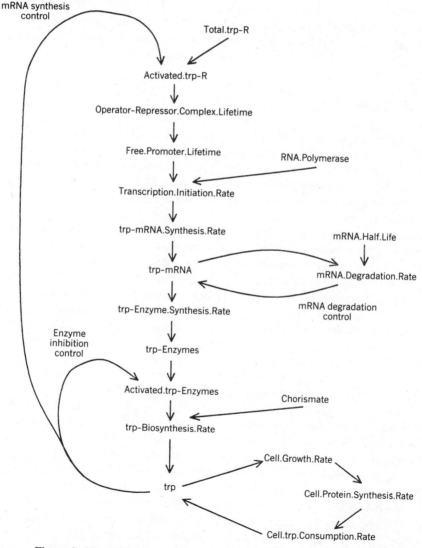

Figure 2. Network of state variables in trp system used in simulations.

1950s. When tryptophan is in excess, it binds to a *repressor protein*, which becomes *activated* and prevents transcription of these genes. Yanofsky discovered a second regulation mechanism in which the cell prematurely terminates the synthesis of mRNA if there is sufficient tryptophan in the cell for growth.

Figure 2 shows the network of state variables and their interactions which we have constructed for the biological domain. Our examples will focus on two molecular binding processes within this network. In the first, molecules of tryptophan bind to molecules of the protein *trp-repressor* to *activate* this protein. We thus refer to the amount of tryptophan present (the variable `trp`), the total repressor protein present (`Total.trp-R`), and the amount of activated protein (`Activated.trp-R`). Similarly, the molecule RNA-polymerase can repeatedly bind to a DNA site called a promoter when it is free, an event called *transcription initiation*. We thus refer to the amount of RNA-Polymerase, the `Free-Promoter.Lifetime`, and the `Transcription.Initiation.Rate`.

3   TECHNIQUES

In constructing this model of the biological domain, our first goal was to understand as much as possible about the problem-solving methodologies of our human experts. This process included extensive interviews with Yanofsky and our other collaborators and reviews of much of the relevant (and voluminous) scientific literature.

An important intermediate point in this process led us to develop the techniques discussed in this chapter. At this point, we the computer scientists possessed a logical understanding of the biological system. That is, we knew what objects existed in the system, what properties these objects had to have to interact in certain ways, and what new objects were created as a result of these interactions. However, it became clear that the biologists could make more specific predictions about the system than we could. For example, biologists can predict the amount of enzyme produced when the concentration of tryptophan is zero, or when it is at an equilibrium value, or when it is at or above a certain threshold value, or at some small constant times any of the latter two values (e.g., half or twice the equilibrium value). Thus, the biologists possessed quantitative information of the trp system which we had not yet acquired.

However, we knew that the biologists did not have a complete quantitative understanding of the system: Some state variables of the system had never been measured or were known very imprecisely or under a narrow range of conditions. And the functional dependencies between many state variables were not known precisely. In summary, the biologists' knowledge lay between the lower bound of our completely logical understanding of the system and the upper bound of a complete quantitative description of the system. We sought to understand just what knowledge the biologists had and how they employed it to predict the results of experiments.

In what follows we describe representations and reasoning techniques we developed to encode and utilize this knowledge. Like most other approaches to DDM, ours includes three components: a means of representing state variables of the system, a means of representing relationships between these state variables, and a means of reasoning about these state variables and relationships to produce a prediction and explanation of behavior. We describe our representations and simulation procedure and contrast our design with previous approaches.

We encode state variable values and dependencies between state variables using a combination of existing representations and representations which we have developed. It became apparent that multiple representations were necessary when we observed that biologists are often unable to determine the exact quantitative values of state variables or the precise mathematical relationships among the variables. But they are able to make several different types of statements about these values and relationships.

3.1   State Variable Representation

Our representation is designed to capture a variety of types of statements about the value of a variable. The value of a variable at a point in time during a simulation is called a *value-instance*, or *vin* for short. Each vin has a name based on the name of the associated variable. Several types of assertions can be made about the value of a vin, including:

- Assertions with respect to quantitative values, for example, `[trp = .001]`, `[trp < .005]`.
- Assertions with respect to other vins, for example, `[trp = trp.maximum]`, `[trp > trp.equilibrium]`.
- Relative assertions, for example, `[trp = 2 * trp.equilibrium]`, `[trp = trp.maximum - .0001]`.

Any combination of such assertions may be made about a given vin.

These representations are very similar to those in Simmons's quantity lattice [10] used in his modeling of geologic processes. The quantity lattice records assertions about many interrelated values. They are stored in a graph whose nodes are algebraic expressions and whose edges are relations. Queries to the quantity lattice test a given relation by finding paths between the two nodes in the query, and analyzing the paths to determine if the queried relation holds.

We have adopted a variant of his implementation and inference techniques. We use bi-directional search to find a path between two quantities in the lattice, which is an efficient search technique for this problem. We are using a subset of Simmons's techniques in that we can represent only relationships of the preceding forms, and not relationships between arbitrary expressions, for example, $[A + B > C + D]$. This simplifies the implementation and excludes the more computationally complex technique of constant elimination arithmetic. Thus far we have not required these types of inferences in our system. We have noted that it may often be necessary to describe a quantity using several intervals rather than only one since disjunctive information may be available. For example, the statement $[A \neq B]$ is really a disjunctive statement that $[(A < B) \vee (A > B)]$. Additional disjunctive information would give rise to additional intervals. We have not implemented this.

It is of interest that we independently arrived at such similar value representations from a completely different domain. This is empirical evidence of their utility and generality.

De Kleer and Brown have experimented with a qualitative physics in which a variable may have a value from the set $\{-, 0, +\}$. As mentioned, this representation is unable to express a host of important distinctions which we find to be necessary for producing expert-level predictions. Kuipers uses a less coarse representation called *landmark values*. These provide a way of naming values of interest which different variables may take and of maintaining partial ordering information among these values. Our value representations are a superset of both Kuipers's and de Kleer and Brown's.

Langlotz et al. [7] discuss the use of yet another type of value representation, namely, probability distributions. This technique encompasses all those discussed in the preceding since different probability distributions could be used to represent any of the mentioned types of value information. However, for our domain we see two drawbacks to its use: Its computational complexity may be prohibitive and it is not clear that it is possible to elicit such detailed information from experts. In addition, its representational power can draw much finer distinctions that we need to draw.

Generalizing from the preceding comparisons, we assert that the three dimensions described (computational complexity, ease of elicitation from experts, and required precision of the solution) are the crucial ones for describing a qualitative representation and for evaluating its applicability to a given task domain.[1]

3.2   Interaction Representations

Just as there is a range in the degree of precision with which we might know the value of a given variable, there is an analogous range in the precision with which we might know the mathematical relationship between two variables. Although some function does describe the interactions among a given set of state variables in the system, biologists may not have been able to determine the exact behavior of each function. But experiments and theory may provide some information about the properties of the function.

Thus we require a set of representations which allows us to represent the information we have about a function even if it is only approximate information. These representations of the function can differ in two orthogonal ways from the actual function: in precision and in accuracy. A less precise representation blurs the mapping from the function's inputs to its outputs, resulting in a more qualitative output but one which is not incorrect. A less accurate representation can produce a very precise, exact mapping from inputs to outputs but one which may be incorrect to some degree.

We consider relationships among variables to be complex concepts which are represented with several frames, within which all or only some slots may be filled. Relationships between each pair of interacting variables are represented with frames called *pairwise interactions*, which describe a unidirectional causal relationship between two variables. A pairwise interaction would describe the relationship between

---

[1]Curt Langlotz contributed to our understanding of the importance of these dimensions.

`Free-Promoter.Lifetime` and `Transcription.Initiation.Rate` by recording any of the following:

- the sign of the pairwise interaction
- whether it is monotonic
- the form of the functional relationship, for example, linear, higher polynomial, exponential, and unknown
- assertions about the sign or magnitude of the exponent for the polynomial or exponential function
- assertions about the sign or magnitude of the coefficient for the relationship

Frames called *functions* describe how a set of input variables combine to influence an output variable. All the combinations in our system are additive, multiplicative, or unknown. In addition, a function frame can reference one or more *mapping* frames (described in what follows), which describe the behavior of a function. A function would be used to describe how `RNA-Polymerase` and `Free-Promoter.Lifetime` combine to influence `Transcription.Initiation.Rate.`

Notice that if all the slots in the pairwise interaction and function units describing a given relationship are filled, we have the ability to describe a quantitative algebraic constraint. If the values of numeric constants are omitted, we are left with qualitative constraints. And if even less information is specified, we can represent even less precise interactions.

The motivation behind mappings is that even if we do not know the precise mathematical form of a function of several variables, we may know the value of the function at several points, and we should be able to make use of this information during a simulation. For example, a biologist may not know the precise relationship between the amount of tryptophan repressor present, the amount of tryptophan present, and the amount of activated repressor present (the repressor protein becomes activated by binding tryptophan). However, the biologist may know that repressor concentration varies over a small range of values and, within this range, for several concentrations of tryptophan, how much activated repressor exists. In fact, biologists have determined this information experimentally for three crucial values of tryptophan concentration and also know the approximate slope of the binding curve at these points.

A mapping frame is used to represent just this type of information for a function. A given mapping fixes all variables but two and lists a set of corresponding values of the free variables. A number of mappings may be used to describe different combinations of variables for one function or different parts of the domain and range of a function. We can specify that a mapping is monotonic and/or linear, which can aid in interpolating between points on the mapping. Mappings are similar to Forbus's *correspondences* [3], although mappings contain more information about the function they describe and are used in additional types of inference such as interpolation (described in what follows).

With these representational tools, we may express a piecewise linear approximation to a function. Biologists reason about enzyme kinetics in this way. Enzyme binding curves are often S-shaped, but biologists encode and reason about them as three linear segments.

The following mapping describes, at three different points, how the amount of `Activated.trp-R` varies with `trp` when `Total.trp-R` is at its normal concentration. It states, for example, that when `trp` is at its equilibrium concentration (a recorded value within the system), `Activated.trp-R` will be one half of `Total.trp-R`:

```
Clamped.Influences:   (Total.trp-R Total.trp-R.normal
Input.Variable:       trp
Output.Variable:      Activated.trp-R
Points:               ((0 0)
                          (equilibrium-trp-concentration
                              (Total.trp-R * .5))
                          (trp-excess-threshold Total.trp-R))
Monotonic:            T
Functional.Form:      UNKNOWN
Slope:                INCREASING
```

There is a potential consistency problem which results from describing the same function by pairwise interactions plus functions and by mappings. Nothing prevents one from asserting that a function is linear using one representation but the same function is quadratic using the other representation. Future research could derive rules for checking this consistency automatically.

De Kleer and Brown use "qualitative constraints" to represent the interactions among variables. These are abstractions of differential equations created by removing the constant coefficients (which become irrelevant given their space of values). For example, this equation describes a sum of pressure differentials: $[dP_{in,out} + dP_{out, s} - dP_{in, s} = 0]$. Kuipers uses similar qualitative constraints and, in addition, is able to state that one variable is a monotonically increasing or decreasing function of another variable. Iwasaki and Simon use arithmetic constraints which are very similar to de Kleer and Brown's.

Our relationships are unidirectional, unlike the constraint languages used by de Kleer and Brown and Iwasaki and Simon, which force one to write bidirectional relationships where one might not exist (e.g., the relationship between the position of an electrical switch and the flow of current). Such bidirectional relationships give rise to the problem of causal ordering described by Iwasaki and Simon [5].

Thus, all of the preceding representations are a subset of ours. Some are unable to express as detailed information as ours can (e.g., quantitative constraints), all are unable to represent the less precise interactions which we can, for example, "Y is proportional to the product of a monotonically increasing function of X plus a linear function of X_2."

Sacks [8, 9] has developed a qualitative reasoning system which uses a different approach. Rather than propagate values through a network of variables to derive a device's behavior, his system calls on Macsyma to symbolically solve the set of differential equations embodied by the network. Macsyma obtains an analytic description of the system's behavior over time. This solution is represented in a sufficiently declarative form that it can be explained and reasoned about by his system. This is an excellent approach when the closed-form solution can be obtained. However, our domain defies closed-form solution because of the complexity of some of the interactions within it and because some interactions are simply not known with enough precision (e.g., mappings) to be solved analytically.

3.3   Simulation

We are interested in simulating the behavior of the trp operon over a sequence of discrete time points. Thus, to simulate the state variable network in Figure 2, we first make assertions about the exogenous variables of the system such as the `Total.trp-R`, `RNA-Polymerase`, and initial `trp` concentrations. We then derive the values of all state variables at the next point in time by propagating these initial values through the interactions described by the state variable network. Predictions for subsequent time points are made by referring to exogenous variables and to the values of some variables at the previous time point. The following describes this process in more detail.

3.3.1   *A Framework for Predicting Device Behavior*

We predict device behavior using a variant of depth-first traversal of a digraph. The nodes of the graph are state variables, and edges link variables between which interactions have been defined (see Figure 2). The traversal algorithm maintains three sets of nodes: the sets K (variables with known values), U (variables with unknown values), and X (variables will become known on the next iteration). Prediction is accomplished using the following procedure:

1. Initialize all exogenous state variables by creating one vin for each state variable and storing the variable's initial value in this vin. Initialize K to this set of vins.
2. Create a new set of vins for each state variable's value on the next clock cycle. Set U to this set of vins.
3. Set X to all nodes in U adjacent to some node in K.
4. For all nodes x in X compute the value of x by propagating values of the state variables which influence x through the relevant interaction descriptions.
5. Set $K = K + X$, and $U = U - X$.
6. If U is not empty, go to step 3.

This procedure traverses the entire graph and is applied during each simulation clock cycle.

Three complications arise here. First, in step 3 it may be that values are not known for all the variables influencing the current x. If the value of an input variable has not yet been determined, we "backchain" through the graph, recursively attempting to determine the value of a *needed* variable from its inputs (which thus become needed variables), until we arrive at variables whose values are indeed known. This backchaining process will succeed as long as all exogenous variables (variables which are not influenced by any other variables) have values supplied for them. Variables will only lack values if the simulation was not initialized correctly.

The presence of cycles in the graph due to feedback loops in the system present a potential problem; without some care we might backchain around these cycles endlessly. We solve this problem by explicitly specifying that a given variable breaks a feedback loop. Backchaining must thus stop at this variable, and its value is computed from the values on the previous time point of the variables which influence it. Thus, we compute the current value of `Activated.trp-R` from the current value of `Total.trp-R` and the previous value of `trp`.

The second complication is that the propagation computation in step 3 is nontrivial. It is described in the section that follows.

Other researchers have used somewhat similar approaches. De Kleer and Brown predict device behavior using a combination of techniques. Normally they propagate qualitative values from one variable to another via constraints (essentially the same as our method) using an arithmetic they defined over these values. Their procedure may reach an impasse just as ours does if values for some variables have not yet reached the current constraint. At this point they use heuristics to guess a value for a variable. If such an assumption later violates a constraint, it can be retracted and a new assumption introduced. Because their value space is so small, only a small number of assumptions are syntactically possible at a given point.

Kuipers does not perform simulations by propagating values from one variable to another via constraints. Instead, he has rules for generating a set of allowable values which each variable can take on the next cycle of simulation. These generated values are then filtered according to several criteria, including the variable interaction constraints. In this manner he does not encounter the problem where de Kleer and Brown's propagation of values becomes stuck; he side-steps this problem by generalizing the technique de Kleer and Brown introduce to solve it: Kuipers *always* introduces new values as assumptions; the incorrect assumptions are then filtered out. We do not use this technique of introducing assumptions; when the system needs the value of a variable, it simply works backward through the network to derive the value. It seems unlikely that Kuipers's technique would work with our value representations; one would have to introduce and filter a huge set of quantitative assumptions. That is, Kuipers's technique works because his state variables may take on a very small possible set of values so it is computationally feasible to explicitly introduce assumptions that a variable takes on all values from this set. When this set is extended to include quantitative values representable by the quantity lattice, it becomes infinitely large.

The third complication in the preceding is that we wish to integrate the behavior of the system over a series of simulation clock cycles in order to infer its steady-state behavior in situations involving feedback loops. Does enzyme production reach an equilibrium, does it oscillate between two or more rates, or does it grow without bound? Previous researchers have tried three different approaches. First, de Kleer and Brown are concerned more with *detecting* that feedback is occurring than with producing a detailed prediction of the result of the feedback; for example, at what approximate point does negative feedback stabilize? Their coarse representation often gives rise to multiple, underdetermined types of feedback, which are reported to the user.

Second, Weld's aggregation technique [11] makes inductive inferences about the eventual behavior of the system by extrapolating from one or more short-term states of the system. This is a promising technique which we intend to apply to our domain; it will be interesting to see if it requires any modification to be used with our variable and interaction representations.

Third, Iwasaki and Simon [5] have applied the method of comparative statics to the analysis of feedback. This approach requires the user to state second-order differential equations which explicitly describe how the system changes over time and to solve these equations symbolically. This appears to be a promising approach, though it assumes that these second-order equations can in fact be stated and solved. Much work remains to be done in determining the strengths and weaknesses of these approaches.

3.3.2   Propagation

The second complication results from the rich value and interaction representations we employ. The propagation step requires us to evaluate an interaction description based on the values of its input variables (analogous to evaluating an algebraic expression). The problem is that we have several types of value representations and several types of interaction descriptions and thus quite a few different potential types of propagations to be performed. For example, in one case we might have to propagate the value [trp > trp.minimal] through the expression [activated.trp-R = trp * trp-R], and in another case we might have to propagate a quantitative value for trp through a mapping or through an interaction which is only known to be linear. In contrast, de Kleer and Brown have a 3×3 lookup table describing how to propagate values through the operations of multiplication, division, addition, and subtraction—a much simpler process.

We solve this propagation problem by identifying several important subclasses of the problem, defining procedures for solving these subclasses. Given that there are a number of combinations of a type of value to be propagated through a type of interaction, we have partitioned this set into a number of solvable instances. (However, there are cases where the value of the output variable is completely unconstrained.) Whenever a propagation step is to be performed, each class of inference is considered in the order that follows. All classes are considered since the information provided by one class will not necessarily be a subset of the information provided by another class. All classes are implemented as LISP procedures which query the quantity lattice to test the preconditions for the rule of inference and assert into the quantity lattice if the rule succeeds to store the propagated value. We now describe these classes and their associated rules.

Class 1: Quantitative Calculations   In this case the interaction in question is a quantitative arithmetic expression, for example, [A = 2B + C], and exact quantitative values are known for all the variables to be propagated. In this case we can perform a quantitative calculation, that is, we compute the value of A by doubling the value of B and adding the value of C.

Class 2: Using Mappings   Another case is to attempt to evaluate a function by evaluating mappings which are associated with it. First the system must determine that the mapping applies at all—that the fixed variables for this mapping have their required values (in the preceding example, it must be the case that [Total.trp-R = Total.trp-R.normal]). Next, if the current value of the input variable recorded is part of a recorded point in the mapping, we can set the output variable to the associated value from the mapping. So, if [trp = equilibrium-trp-concentra-tion], then we can assert that [Activated.trp-R = Total.trp-R * .5].

Class 3: Interpolating Mappings   A more complicated situation arises when a mapping point does not exist for the current value of the input variable. Using the previous sample mapping, we can compute Activated.trp-R when [trp = equilibrium-trp-concentration]. But what if we know that [trp = 4 * equilibrium-trp-concentration]? If we know that the mapping is mono-tonic, we can infer that [Activated.trp-R > .5 * Total.trp-R]. And if we know that this mapping represents a linear function with an intercept of zero, we can also infer that [Activated.trp-R = 4 * equilibrium-trp-concentra-tion] (quadrupling the input quadruples the output).

Class 4: Relative Calculations   Biologists often wish to compare the behaviors of a system under varying circumstances. For example, if the behavior of the system is known under a given concentration of tryptophan, trp_1, it may be desirable to predict the behavior at the concentration $[trp_2 = trp_1 * 2]$. Just as we interpolated a linear mapping in the preceding, if we have a number of interactions whose precise equations are not known but which are known to be linear with a Y-axis intercept of 0, we can compute values for variables in the new simulation run which are multiples of 2 (in this example) times the values in the old prediction. This class of inferences is very similar to class 3, but this class uses only information about the form of the equation, whereas class 3 also uses mapping information.

Class 5: Qualitative Calculations   When the preceding types of information are not available because of imprecise values or interactions or both, we attempt to apply the following inference rules to constrain the value of the output variable. For example, if we were attempting to evaluate an interaction which was a product of two variables, we could try to employ rule 4 that follows. These rules are also used in Simmons's quantity lattice [10]. In these rules, *rel* is one of $\{<, \leq, =, \neq, \geq, >\}$:

1. $(X \; rel \; Y)$ implies $(X - Y \; rel \; 0)$.
2. $(Y \; rel \; 0)$ implies $(X + Y \; rel \; X)$.
3. $(Y \; rel \; 0)$ implies $(X \; rel \; X - Y)$.
4. $((X \; rel \; 0) \wedge (Y > 0) \wedge (Y < 1))$ implies $(X \; rel \; X * Y)$.
5. $((X \; rel \; 0) \wedge (Y > 1))$ implies $(X * Y \; rel \; X)$.
6. $((X > 0) \wedge (Y > 1))$ implies $(X * Y > X)$.
7. $((X < 0) \wedge (Y > 1))$ implies $(X * Y < X)$.
8. $((X > 0) \wedge (Y < 0))$ implies $(X > X * Y)$.
9. $((X < 0) \wedge (Y < 0))$ implies $(X < X * Y)$.

For example, rule 5 states that if the program is attempting to evaluate the product of X and Y when X is known to be positive and Y is known to be greater than 1, then we can infer that their product is greater than X.

Class 6: Monotonicity Calculations   If we are evaluating a function which is known to be monotonic, at least over the relevant region of its domain, then analysis of its inputs may allow us to deduce whether the function increases, decreases, or remains constant with respect to its value at a previous time point. If all inputs remain constant or we can prove that the changing inputs cancel one another, then the function remains constant. And if the signs of all changing inputs are the same, then the function changes in the same direction as its inputs. For example, if in computing `Total.trp-R` one can prove that the current value of `Free.trp-R` is unchanged from a previous value and the current value of trp has increased over a previous value, then one can deduce that the current value of `Total.trp-R` is greater than the previous value. Other researchers have recognized this property of monotonic functions but have usually applied it in a much simpler context, that is, without such diverse information about values and interactions or value histories.

 Consider how this approach compares to that of de Kleer and Brown. Because they cannot represent values very precisely, they are often unable to resolve competing influences for example, the value of the sum $[dA + dB]$ is undefined if $[dA = -]$ and $[dB = +]$. At these times they generate branching predictions to model all possible behaviors of the device. This envisionment is an interesting and important ability, but experts are often able to resolve the ambiguity. When our system reaches such a condition, it instructs us to add more information to its knowledge base or to the problem statement, which our representation allows us to do.

4   AN EXAMPLE

Because our simulations involve a large number of variables and interactions and several different types of propagation, it is hard to demonstrate many of the system capabilities within the limited space here. However, we include the following example to provide a more concrete idea of how the system functions.

One important component of our simulation environment is a library of landmark values for variables: values of interest for the variables which are permanently stored in the system's quantity lattice. They might be of interest because they are extreme values or because they are mentioned in mappings. The library vins that follow, for example, describe three different transcription initiation rates which are related by multiplicative constants. When we describe a vin, we give its name followed by knowledge the system has about how it is related to other vins. Library vin names are often of the form `Variable.`*description*, while simulation value names are usually of the form `Variable.`*simulation-cycle*, for example, `trp.excess` and `trp.1`, respectively (the latter describes the value of `trp` on the first simulation cycle):

```
Transcription.Initiation.Rate.minimal
    (= (* Transcription.Initiation.Rate.maximal .0125)
    (= (* Transcription.Initiation.Rate.equilibrium
        .066667)
    (> 0)
```

```
Transcription.Initiation.Rate.maximal
   (= (* Transcription.Initiation.Rate.minimal 80))
   (= (* Transcription.Initiation.Rate.equilibrium 5.33))
Transcription.Initiation.Rate.equilibrium
   (= (* Transcription.Initiation.Rate.minimal 15))
   (= (* Transcription.Initiation.Rate.maximal .1875))
```

Figure 3. (*a*) Variable values for simulation cycle 1. Names of variables are in large font. Some of the information the system has about each variable is below it, in smaller font. (*b*) Variable values for simulation cycle 2.

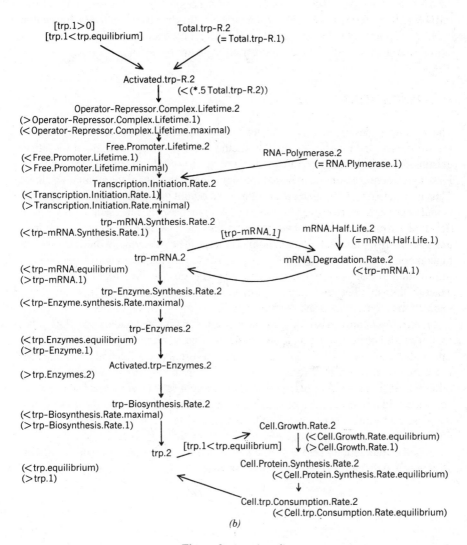

[trp.1>0]
[trp.1<trp.equilibrium]

Total.trp-R.2
    (= Total.trp-R.1)

Activated.trp-R.2
        ↓   (< (*.5 Total.trp-R.2))

Operator-Repressor.Complex.Lifetime.2
(> Operator-Repressor.Complex.Lifetime.1)
(< Operator-Repressor.Complex.Lifetime.maximal)

Free.Promoter.Lifetime.2
(< Free.Promoter.Lifetime.1)
(> Free.Promoter.Lifetime.minimal)

RNA-Polymerase.2
    (= RNA.Plymerase.1)

Transcription.Initiation.Rate.2
(< Transcription.Initiation.Rate.1)
(> Transcription.Initiation.Rate.minimal)

trp-mRNA.Synthesis.Rate.2
(< trp-mRNA.Synthesis.Rate.1)

[trp-mRNA.1]

mRNA.Half.Life.2
    (= mRNA.Half.Life.1)

trp-mRNA.2
(< trp-mRNA.equilibrium)
(> trp-mRNA.1)

mRNA.Degradation.Rate.2
    (< trp-mRNA.1)

trp-Enzyme.Synthesis.Rate.2
(< trp-Enzyme.synthesis.Rate.maximal)

trp-Enzymes.2
(< trp.Enzymes.equilibrium)
(> trp-Enzyme.1)

Activated.trp-Enzymes.2

(> trp.Enzymes.2)

trp-Biosynthesis.Rate.2
(< trp-Biosynthesis.Rate.maximal)
(> trp-Biosynthesis.Rate.1)

Cell.Growth.Rate.2
    (< Cell.Growth.Rate.equilibrium)
    (> Cell.Growth.Rate.1)

trp.2   [trp.1<trp.equilibrium]

Cell.Protein.Synthesis.Rate.2
    (< Cell.Protein.Synthesis.Rate.equilibrium)

(< trp.equilibrium)
(> trp.1)

Cell.trp.Consumption.Rate.2
    (< Cell.trp.Consumption.Rate.equilibrium)

(b)

Figure 3. *(continued)*

In Figures 3*a* and 3*b* we show what information has been derived about the value of every state variable on two successive cycles of a simulation. In the first cycle the system has been told that [trp.0 = 0], and it predicts that the bacterium begins to synthesize the trp enzymes and trp at a high rate. On the second cycle, the enzymes are synthesized at a lower rate, since trp begins to inhibit transcription to a small degree but trp is synthesized at a higher rate because more enzyme has accumulated. A number of mappings are used to compute the values of various interactions relative to values in the library.

Information about values in cycle 2 is recorded relative to values in cycle 1, so we know, for example, that `Transcription.Initiation.Rate` has decreased. Also in cycle 2, the system computes a value for `trp-mRNA.2` by combining the new mRNA synthesized in that cycle with the mRNA that has been degraded during that cycle. A mapping tells the system that since the concentration of mRNA is below its equilibrium value, synthesis is a stronger effect than degradation.

5   LIMITATIONS

The techniques described in this chapter have computed more precise simulations of the trp operon than earlier qualitative methods using less precise input data than existing numerical simulation methods employ. However, several limitations exist. First, the system contains no explicit representation of the rate of the simulation clock. Thus it is unable to determine the absolute total output of a process whose output accumulates over time. However, it should be possible to use the representations we have developed to make assertions about process rates which would let us infer, for example, that after 10 clock intervals of maximum synthesis, the trp enzymes would accumulate to their equilibrium levels. Second, it is possible to provide the system with too little information to make predictions of a desired precision. We have yet to determine the exact relationship between the precision with which state variable initial values and interactions are described and the expected precision of the simulation.

Finally, this approach to modeling the trp system has turned out to be too inflexible for our needs because of the static description of state variables and their interactions. The model we have developed is valid for only a certain experimental configuration. If a different experiment is to be simulated, with a mutant bacterium growing in a different medium, for example, a somewhat different set of state variables and interactions would be required. A more practical approach would be to specify what objects are present in a given experiment and let the system derive the state variable network dynamically from its knowledge of possible interactions between classes of objects, such as the interactions between an enzyme and the chemicals it reacts with. Our current research addresses all three of these issues.

6   SUMMARY

Our motivation for performing declarative device modeling comes from our goal of understanding and emulating the process of scientific theory formation. Scientific theories consist of both structural descriptions and functional knowledge which describe how structures interact with each other and with their environment. In a complicated, natural domain like regulatory genetics, it is rare that theories are described with complete, quantitative precision. Existing types of qualitative descriptions alone, however, do not suffice to capture the knowledge that scientists have about the tryptophan operon. Therefore, we have been motivated to develop methodologies by which a range of types of knowledge, from qualitative to quantitative, can be described and jointly utilized to simulate device behavior. These methodologies include representations for state variable values and for the mathematical interactions between state variables and reasoning processes for propagating state variable values through these interactions.

We have synthesized and extended the prior work of several others in this field. Our "devices," bacterial operons, regulatory proteins, and the like, are more complicated and less well understood than those which some of our colleagues have attempted to model, and we desire more precise predictions of their behavior. We are encouraged by the results presented in this chapter, but have yet to determine either the applicability of our methodology to other, equally complex domains or whether our representations of structural and functional knowledge that suffice for simulating and predicting behavior will be understandable and modifiable by the machine learning component of an integrated discovery system. These topics are the focus of our ongoing research work.

ACKNOWLEDGMENTS

The collaboration of Dr. Charles Yanofsky has been indispensable to this project. We thank Curt Langlotz, Reid Simmons, and Elisha Sacks for their comments on a draft of this chapter, and the biologist Dr. Robert Landick for sharing his expertise. This work was supported by NSF grant MCS83-10236. Computing facilities were provided by the SUMEX-AIM research resource through NIH grant 5P41 RR-00785 and through DARPA contract N00039-86-C-033.

REFERENCES

1. R. Davis, "Diagnostic Reasoning Based on Structure and Behavior," *Artificial Intelligence,* **24**(1–3):347–410, December 1984.

2. J. De Kleer and J. S. Brown, "A Qualitative Physics Based on Confluences," *Artificial Intelligence,* **24**(1–3):7–84, December 1984.

3. K. Forbus, "Qualitative Process Theory," (Technical Report TR-789), Massachusetts Institute Technology AI Lab, 1984.

4. M. R. Genesereth, "The Use of Design Descriptions in Automated Diagnosis," *Artificial Intelligence,* **24**(1–3):411–436, December 1984.

5. Y. Iwasaki and H. A. Simon, "Causality in Device Behavior," *Artificial Intelligence,* 3–32, 1986.

6. B. Kuipers, "The Limits of Qualitative Simulation," in *Proceedings of the Ninth International Joint Conference on Artificial Intelligence,* Kaufmann, Los Altos, CA, 1985.

7. C. P. Langlotz, L. M. Fagan, S. W. Tu, B. I. Sikic, and E. H. Shortliffe, "Combining Artificial Intelligence and Decision Analysis for Automated Therapy Planning Assistance," Technical Report KSL-86-3, Stanford University Knowledge Systems Laboratory, 1986.

8. E. Sacks, "Qualitative Mathematical Reasoning," Technical Report MIT/LCS/TR-329, Massachusetts Institute of Technology/LCS, 1985.

9. E. Sacks, "Qualitative Mathematical Reasoning," in *Proceedings of the Ninth International Joint Conference on Artificial Intelligence,* Kaufmann, Los Altos, CA, 1985.

10. R. Simmons, "'Commonsense' Arithmetic Reasoning," in *Proceedings of the Fifth National Conference on Artificial Intelligence,* Kaufmann, Los Altos, CA, 1986.

11. D. S. Weld, "The Use of Aggregation in Causal Simulation," *Artificial Intelligence,* **30**: 1–34, 1986.

12. C. Yanofsky, "Attenuation in the Control of Expression of Bacterial Operons," *Nature,* **289**:751–758, February 1981.

8 Toward Parallel Intelligent Simulation

E. J. H. KERCKHOFFS and H. KOPPELAAR
Faculty of Mathematics and Informatics
Delft University of Technology
Delft, The Netherlands

and

H. J. VAN DEN HERIK
Department of Computer Science
Faculty of General Science
University of Limburg
Maastricht, The Netherlands

1 INTRODUCTION AND OVERVIEW

In order to fully exploit the imminent prospects of modeling and simulation, besides modern methodologies and new simulation techniques, advanced information processing must be extensively incorporated in (complex) simulation studies (see, e.g., ref. 2). This chapter starts with an opinion on how advanced process control and simulation environments could look like (Section 2); in the proposal are integrated such techniques as parallel processing [17, 28], artificial intelligence [13, 18, 19, 22, 23], and database management [29, 30, 32]. Although the given conceptual outline is schematic and global and certainly lacks depth and detailed descriptions, it provides a framework within which relevant research directions can be planned. As far as parallel intelligent simulation environments are concerned, in Section 3 we summarize some relevant topics for further research, as they can be derived directly from the ideas previously outlined. Solving the problems around parallel implementation of simulation models (parallel languages, parallel algorithms, automatic scheduling, and synchronization), parallelizing knowledge-based systems, interconnecting (parallel) simulation systems and (parallel) knowledge-based systems running on a multicomputer, and so on, seem essential to us in the further development of really advanced simulation environments.

There indeed are several good reasons to investigate the various aspects of parallel treatment of simulation models and of knowledge-based systems as well as to study integrated numeric and symbolic systems running in a parallel processing environment. Simulation models range from simple to very complex, and the latter simply require high processing speeds and therefore number-crunching facilities. Moreover, real-time and faster than real-time solutions frequently ask for parallel execution of simulation models. Similarly, artificial intelligence (AI) is felt to require fast and powerful multicomputer hardware structures for real-world and/or simulation problems, where perception, decision making, problem solving, and so on, must take place and cooperate within demanding real-time constraints. This will be the case whenever the AI system must almost simultaneously recognize, gain control over, and/or interact with complex real-world and simulation objects as they move about and change.

A good example of knowledge-based systems gaining control over and interacting with real-world or simulation objects are knowledge-based controllers (see, e.g., ref. 7). Using intelligent systems for real-world process control is becoming an increasingly important application domain. Compared to conventional digital control systems, there are various reasons to employ knowledge-based controllers:

(a) The knowledge needed to control processes can be represented in a natural, explicit, adaptive, and easy-to-modify way.

(b) Symbolic processing may lead to entirely new control procedures (exploitation of symbolic data manipulation).

(c) Intelligent systems have proven to be able to deal with complex problems, incompleteness, uncertainty, and fuzziness (fuzzy control).

It is possible to replace the real-world process with software programs; that is, we can simulate the process. Simulations can serve useful purposes in developing the first general structure of the integrated system (knowledge-based controller linked to the real-world process concerned). Simulation would replace the often complex, expensive, and fault-prone input and output interfaces and related programs between the controller and process. It could also serve as a testbed within which precise, well-designed experiments might be run in order to check the controller with respect to its perfect working. Hence, in the simulation domain a knowledge-based system is controlling a simulation model to show, for example, a desired dynamic behavior by generating "on-the-fly" decisions about the model's input signals and/or changes in its parameter values.

In these (real-world or simulation) control applications the knowledge bases can contain process (or model) knowledge (such as the order of the process, the parameters with their values and variations, and nonlinearities), control technical knowledge (e.g., rules to control damping and overshoot), and heuristic knowledge based on past experiences (e.g., with respect to similar processes or models). Production rules [IF (conditions) THEN (actions)] are quite natural to represent control technical knowledge. In contrast to static knowledge-based systems that are merely used for consultation purposes, intelligent systems controlling real-world processes and/or simulation models should be able to operate in a (rapidly) varying environment. In real-time applications these dynamic knowledge-based systems are subject to strong speed requirements that could be met by employing multiprocessing techniques.

Combining the preceding arguments for parallel simulation models and parallel knowledge-based systems, the ultimate conclusion is to strive after a form of parallel intelligent simulation in which (parallel) simulation models and (parallel) knowledge-based systems can run concurrently on a multicomputer system and have continuously mutual exchange of information. This also might enable, at least in a few years, when the simulation of truly large real-world environments becomes feasible, having several intelligent systems embedded within a single environment; or it might enable the simultaneous exploration of various relevant alternative simulations (when, e.g., certainty factors in the knowledge-based control system cause the simulation to branch).

From the foregoing it is clear that the heart of this chapter will cover material on parallel simulation, parallelizing knowledge-based systems, and parallel holistic systems (the term "holistic system" is used to denote the configuration of a simulation model interacting with one or more knowledge-based systems). Rather than treating some specific subjects in extensive detail, it is our intention to give introductory reviews on these topics and to discuss globally what is going on without drawing already hard conclusions, for which in the authors' opinion it is still too early. In Section 4 we consider the evolution of simulation-oriented digital computers and especially the current emerging role of mini-supercomputers in parallel simulation. Subsequently, in Section 5 we comment on multicomputers applied to AI, architectures for holistic systems, and the (generally disappointing) attempts to parallelize standard "expert" production systems. The latter is illustrated on the basis of experimental results from the authors' own HYDRA project (see Section 6).

2 ADVANCED PROCESS CONTROL AND SIMULATION ENVIRONMENT: AN OPINION

2.1 Conceptual Outline

Figure 1 shows the conceptual outline of an advanced process control and simulation environment. For clarity, the various functions are tentatively supposed to be performed in separate processors.

A process computer (adapted to real-time data processing) is attached to the real-world system for in-line control purposes and for the on-line storage of measuring data from the process. Furthermore, in the configuration proposed a database management system (DBMS) dedicated to process control and simulation and based upon precise conceptual schemes and menu-driven application programs is incorporated for the off-line management of descriptive and quantitative information involved in the productivity control activities and (large-scale) simulations. Real-world measuring data and simulation experiment data—as well as information about the circumstances under which they have been obtained—are meant to be managed in this system. The quantitative data are delivered by the process computer and simulation computer (see next paragraph), while the user is expected to provide the descriptive information about the activities in both the real-world and simulation domain.

A simulation computer is included in the configuration to experiment on simulation models of the process concerned (or on models of related systems). In order to properly deal with complex, large-scale, real-time simulations, this computer should be a real number cruncher (multiprocessor). The knowledge-based system (KBS) processor in the configuration can serve as an intelligent preprocessor or postprocessor in both the real-world and simulation domain. Decision-making processes may be modeled by

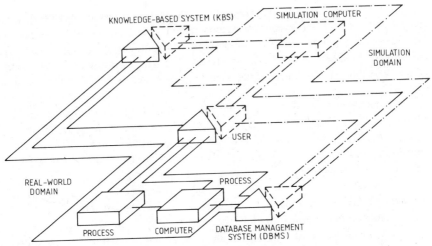

Figure 1. Process control and simulation environment.

knowledge-based expert systems running in this computer, or the KBS processor may be utilized in the intelligent control and analysis of the real-world and simulation processes, or it may assist the user in modeling, selecting algorithms, interpreting results, and so forth.

Although in Figure 1 the process control, simulation, database management, and knowledge processing are each assumed to be performed in separate (dedicated) processors, in practice several functions may well be shared in the same physical computer (see Section 2.2).

2.2   Practical Realization

The point here is how the functional outline of the process control and simulation environment as suggested in Section 2.1 can be practically realized (with a view to current and future computer developments). The central part of such an environment is proposed to be a (next-generation) computer capable of both parallel numeric and symbolic processing. (Instead of one central computer, one could also think of a configuration of different parallel architectures.) In this computer the large-scale and/ or time-critical scientific calculations, simulations, and symbolic processing are performed. For example, large-scale parallel simulation programs and parallel expert systems can run (simultaneously) in this computer.

The remaining functions (perhaps with the exception of process control) are proposed to be executed in network-based work stations that can communicate with the central parallel computer mentioned previously. At a work station, the complex parallel simulation programs and integrated parallel numeric–symbolic models, which require number- and symbol-crunching facilities and therefore are intended to run in the central computer, can be prepared. This should be possible in an adequate and user-friendly programming environment (e.g., the definitions of simulation models and simulation experiments are to be done in appropriate simulation languages, which of course implies the necessity of research to implementing models, written in a simulation language, on parallel computers). Small and not time-critical simulations (that do not necessarily need high-speed processing capabilities) can be directly performed in the work station. Also intelligent (not time-critical) advisory systems are supposed to run in the work station to provide the user assistance with respect to his or her real-world and simulation experiments. At the work station, the simulation analyst should have access to local and remote (dedicated) databases such as model bases, experimental frame bases, real-world experiment bases, and simulation experiment bases [32]. Furthermore, the work station must provide the simulationist with highly interactive tools as well as excellent graphical display and windowing facilities.

A first step toward a simulation environment as sketched in the preceding is being implemented at the University of Ghent (Belgium) in the framework of the AD10/ Apollo LAN (local area network) project. The number-crunching facilities for complex simulations are provided by an Applied Dynamics AD10 (peripheral) multiprocessor [4]. The host computer of this AD10 also serves as the process computer to control and sample real-world processes (in this case fermentation processes). A direct link exists from the AD10 to one of the Apollo work stations of the "DOMAIN" (Distributed Operating Multi Access Interaction Network) environment (see Figure 2), permitting, for instance, run time simulation graphics to be generated on the work station's display. A high-performance LAN connects the work stations. Intelligent advisory systems will run in the work stations to help the user in the modeling and simulation.

In the project mentioned, research efforts also have been devoted to implementing models specified in simulation languages on multiprocessors. A prototype of a CSSL (Continuous Systems Simulation Language), based upon CSSL-IV [26], is developed to run on the AD10. This prototype translates CSSL-IV models into MPS10, the modular programming language of the AD10. In this way models can be defined, tested, and adapted in CSSL-IV before being implemented and executed on the AD10.

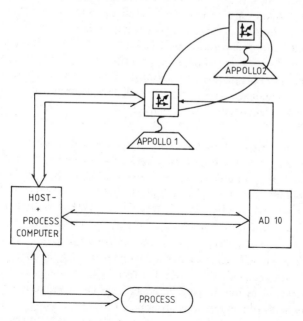

Figure 2. Simulation environment at University of Ghent.

3   RESEARCH SCENARIOS FOR ADVANCED SIMULATION

In Section 2, we presented the authors' personal views on an advanced environment for real-world experimentation and simulation. The proposed environment provides a framework within which significant research scenarios can be specified. In addition to the needed development and realization of parallel computer architectures, more adapted to simulation and AI applications (and integrated AI/simulation) than the ones currently in use, this framework reveals that in principle the general instrumentation of simulation must become considerably better, requiring a number of tools and techniques from different computer science subfields. Of course, one can agree or disagree with the framework as outlined in Section 2. But the feasibility of the following (not exhaustive) list of research scenarios around advanced simulation shall hardly meet any opposition.

(a) *Parallel Computer Architectures*   Up to now most simulation and AI programs have been designed to handle specific problems using serial algorithms for the serial computer. Because of the need for powerful multicomputer hardware structures, both the simulation researchers and AI researchers are increasingly turning to parallel processes. Although a number of multiprocessors do currently exist and are being used for simulation and AI, it is almost certainly the case that many of the most interesting and promising parallel architectures in both application domains have not yet been built or even designed. Research in new parallel architectures (both hardware and software) for simulation and AI and their combination, is certainly a significant research direction.

(b) *Parallel Simulation*   Adequate simulation-oriented parallel algorithms are needed, and sufficient expertise must be gained in simulation on mini-supercomputers of different architectures. It is remarked that parallel simulation can include much more than number crunching only: In properly performing methodology-based simulations the architectural features of parallel constructions may well be exploited (see Section 4.4). Simulation models and simulation experiments designed to run on a mini-supercomputer or peripheral array processor should preferably be defined in higher-level simulation languages. This implies the need of research with respect to implementing simulation languages on some of the existing multicomputer systems [1, 24]; see also Section 2.2.

(c) *Parallel Knowledge-based Systems*   High-speed demands are put on knowledge-based (expert) systems that are used for decision making on the fly in simulation environments. This requirement for fast reasoning capabilities can be met by more efficient algorithms and, above all, by parallel techniques. Consequently, the development of parallel knowledge-based systems running on parallel computer architectures seems to be an important issue in modern simulation and AI research.

(d) *Coupling (Parallel) Expert Systems and (Parallel) Simulation Models*   As said before, simulation models can be extended with knowledge-based expert systems to make them fit for decision making (on the fly). With a view to points (b) and (c), interesting research in this respect could be studying configurations in which a simulation model is running in one part of an array of processing elements while an expert system is (simultaneously) running in another part. Both (parallel) systems should be capable of continuously exchanging information, which implies the construction of appropriate (dynamic, numeric–symbolic) interfaces. In addition, adequate programming environments for such combined applications should be developed.

Some further significant research directions that, at least in the first instance, have no direct relations to parallel processing follow.

(e) *Simulation Information Systems*   One of the main activities peripheral to modeling, model implementation, and experimentation is the management of data involved in (especially large-scale) simulation studies. Therefore, research in simulation-oriented database management is of importance [29, 30]. In this respect we refer to research efforts to develop dedicated databases such as model bases, experimental frame bases, real-world experiment bases, and simulation experiment bases [27, 32].

(f) *Simulation Advisory Systems*   Advisory or advice-giving systems are expert systems that give useful advice on a particular topic following a short consultation. Since simulation itself is domain independent, a simulation advisory system may have to address an application domain as well as the "domain" of simulation. This generates a new set of problems not encountered by those expert systems that address a certain problem in a limited domain (e.g., medical diagnostic systems). Currently available expert systems are mostly applicable for some isolated problem areas in the modeling and simulation process. Research projects should be stimulated to develop advisory systems supporting the user in several modeling and simulation phases (see, e.g., ref. 20). In general, simulation advisory systems should have access to existing external (dedicated) databases [as meant in point (e)] designed to manage the quantitative and descriptive data from the modeling and simulation processes.

Most of the preceding instrumentation scenarios stem from the need to bypass conventional serial and procedural programming techniques. Without being exhaustive, in the subsequent sections we consider several aspects related to points (a)–(d) in more detail.

4   PARALLEL PROCESSING IN SYSTEMS SIMULATION

4.1   Evolution of Simulation-oriented Digital Computers

The simulation of (complex) continuous systems has been particularly influential in the evolution of special-purpose computer systems to attain higher computing speeds and performance. In this respect two major computer architecture innovations have permitted the circumventing of the von Neumann bottleneck in order to attain high speeds: parallelism and pipelining. The implementation of these techniques has resulted in some distinct families of high-speed digital computers including (pipeline-oriented) supercomputers, peripheral array processors, and multiprocessors [12, 14, 28].

The first supercomputer to become operational (in 1975) was the ILLIAC-IV, which consisted of an array of 64 processing elements, each containing an arithmetic–logic unit and local memory. During the mid-1970s the focus in the development of supercomputers shifted away from arrays of processing elements toward pipelining. Two major pipeline-oriented supercomputers, known as vector processors, of the 1970s were the Control Data Corporation STAR-100 and the Texas Instruments ASC (Advanced Scientific Computer). The first pipeline-oriented supercomputer to win widespread acceptance was the CRAY-1 developed by Cray Research and first installed in 1976. This machine was the trendsetter for many other supercomputers with a similar approach to high-speed computations, including the currently well-known products of Cray Research and ETA in the United States, and Hitachi, Fujitsu, and Nippon Electric in Japan.

In the late 1970s a new class of pipeline-oriented computing devices began to appear on the (signal-processing and simulation) market, called "peripheral array processors" or "attached array processors" [14, 21]. They are actually relatively small-scale vector processors and are intended to function as peripheral devices for sequential digital computers in order to attain high computing speed at a relatively moderate cost.

A few of the currently available machines achieve high speed by parallelism and pipelining in more dedicated applications. An example is the Applied Dynamics International AD10 and AD100, primarily useful for simulation of dynamic systems described by ODEs (ordinary differential equations) (see also Section 2.2). A particularly important phenomenon in the evolution of simulation-oriented digital computer systems was the appearance of mini-supercomputers in the mid-1980s: commercially available multiprocessing systems and relatively inexpensive vector processors, all with a favorable cost–performance ratio. An important subset of these mini-supercomputers shows the successful implementation of the MIMD (multiple instruction stream/multiple data stream) architecture concept (see Section 4.2), implying a (smaller or larger) network of identical processing elements (PEs). Examples are [15]:

ALLIANT, FX/8 : maximum 8 PEs;
AMETEK, SYSTEM 14: maximum 256 PEs;
ENCORE, MULTI-MAX: maximum 20 PEs;
INTEL, iPSC: maximum 128 PEs;
N-CUBE, NCUBE: maximum 1024 PEs.

Another subset of today's mini-supercomputers is based upon pipelining, and therefore these computers are more similar in architecture to the CRAY and other supercomputers. Computers of this category include

CONVEX COMPUTER CORPORATION, C-1;
FLOATING POINT SYSTEMS, INC., FPS 164, 264, and 364; and
SCIENTIFIC COMPUTER SYSTEMS CORPORATION, SCS-40.

Most of these systems employ a Unix-based operating system and are committed to providing compilers for the FORTRAN 77 and the C languages and sometimes for Pascal.

4.2   Classification of Multicomputers

Unfortunately, no fully satisfactory taxonomy of multiprocessors exists. However, it is possible to identify a number of fundamental design alternatives to support the classification of available multiprocessors.

4.2.1   Program Control

At the programming level multiprocessors can be distinguished in SIMD (single instruction stream/multiple data stream) and MIMD (multiple instruction stream/ multiple data stream) architectures [6]. The key point here is whether or not the processing elements contain their own control unit and therefore are or are not capable of executing their own stored program.

4.2.2   Manner of Data Exchange

A distinction is made between shared-memory systems (possibly provided with rapid-access or cache units) in which a common memory is successively recorded and read by the processing elements to pass information to each other and message-passing systems. In the latter, data to be exchanged are transmitted as messages between two processing elements.

4.2.3   Interconnection Structures

The major distinction to be considered in network topology is whether the interconnections are to be dynamic (reconfigurable network) or static [5]. Some authors (see, e.g., ref. 31) prefer as a major division in multicomputer architectures those showing or simulating a complete graph (i.e., every node is directly connected to each of the other nodes) and those having a point-to-point topology (i.e., every node has direct interconnections to a restricted number of other nodes).

In a dynamic interconnection network switches are provided to interconnect the processing elements (task-shuffle exchange, cross-bar switch). In static networks the processing elements are permanently connected to each other in one-, two-, or many-dimensional structures. Examples of static network topologies are (see Figure 3) the star, the ring, the nearest neighbor, the systolic array, and the hypercube [in a hypercube the number of processing elements, say, N, is made equal to a power of 2, and each processing element is directly connected to binary-log(N) neighbors]. The processing elements are mostly communicating via a bus connection, employing such techniques as token passing and time-sliced broadcasting.

The rapid increase in the size of multicomputers that can be built makes feasible a large variety of architectures (along with a set of hard problems in developing effective software). For potentially, a multicomputer can be built using any possible graph topology.

4.2.4   Parallelism Granularity

On the basis of the number of processing elements multiprocessors are generally said to be "small" (16 or less processing elements), "large" (from 16 to 1024 processing elements), or "massive" (more than 1024 processing elements).

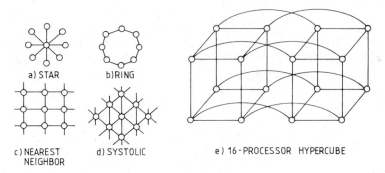

a) STAR

b) RING

c) NEAREST
NEIGHBOR

d) SYSTOLIC

e) 16-PROCESSOR HYPERCUBE

Figure 3. Some static network topologies.

4.2.5 System Software and Languages Supported

In the implementation of simulation models on multiprocessors and vector processors, the availability and quality of partitioning–segmentation–synchronization and vectorization supporting software play an emerging role. Since many of the early simulation programs were written in FORTRAN, multiprocessor systems and vector processors with efficient FORTRAN compilers are at the advantage. Moreover, there is an increasing demand for compilers for more modern languages such as Pascal, Ada, and C; also other dedicated high-level languages (e.g., continuous simulation languages) have been proposed and sometimes implemented [1, 4, 24].

4.3 Notes on Multiprocessor Fitness to Simulation

Regarding the reviews given in Sections 4.1 and 4.2, one might wonder which types of multiprocessor systems or topologies are best suited to simulation; which concept will gain the hegemony, parallelism, or pipelining and so on. We think that it is not very wise and moreover too early to deal with these kind of questions in depth. The MIMD architectures are obviously more powerful and allow more general numeric algorithms to be implemented than SIMD systems, but they also are more expensive and difficult to use efficiently, at least with today's operating systems and parallel algorithms. In the future the proper combination of "parallelism" and "pipelining" (large networks of pipeline processors with appropriate topologies) could largely satisfy the demands arising from complex simulation.

With respect to network topologies, a large or massive parallel computer consisting of an n-dimensional array of processors might be in many ways ideal to model an n-dimensional environment. This environment can be specified and carried out to whatever degree of detail the programmer chooses and the multicomputer can handle it. In particular, a three-dimensional array might well be the appropriate design for simulating three-dimensional environments. But such arrays are especially rich in links to nearby nodes and hence especially good for local operations; global distances (diameter) and global density are poor in arrays. It is currently not yet clear which (static or dynamic) point-to-point structures are best suited to simulations that also need more global operations. Hypercube structures may be feasible at the first glance. But we repeat what was stated in Section 3 [point (a)], that most likely many of the most interesting and promising parallel architectures have not yet been built or even designed.

In addition to the performances shown in benchmark simulation problems (see Section 4.4), in practice the system software and languages supported (as mentioned in Section 4.2.5) provide the major basis on which one chooses a specific multiprocessor. User environments are wanted in which, for example, a large virtual memory enables programmers to concentrate on their applications rather than on memory limitations of the programs or in which users are allowed to manage the work load on the system efficiently, permitting interactive users to remain productive even when large batch processing jobs are running on the system.

Furthermore, since many of the simulation programs have been written in FORTRAN, existing standard FORTRAN programs should be processed by the compiler preferably without any modifications to the source. The compiler of each supported language should produce an optimized parallel code that utilizes efficiently the parallel or pipeline processing capabilities; this implies the availability of optimizing, parallelizing, and/or vectorizing compilers. The following illustrative example demonstrates some of the vectorization methods as used in one of the commercially available pipeline-oriented mini-supercomputers (Convex C-1):

```
      DO 20 i=1,n
         b(i,1)=0
         DO 10 j=1,m
            a(i,j)=a(i,j)+b(i,j)*c(i,j)
10       CONTINUE
         d(i)=e(i)+a(i,1)
20    CONTINUE
```

In the first step the compiler uses its ability to vectorize across all nested loops and creates the following loops:

```
      DO 20a i=1,n
         b(i,1)=0
20a CONTINUE

      DO 20b i=1,n
         DO 10 j=1,m
            a(i,j)=a(i,j)+b(i,j)*c(i,j)
10       CONTINUE
20b CONTINUE

      DO 20c i=1,n
         d(i)=e(i)+a(i,1)
20c CONTINUE
```

The original outer loop is distributed over three loops 20a, 20b, and 20c. The loops 20a and 20c and the inner loop 10 can be vectorized directly. In the next step the compiler uses its ability to interchange loops on the second DO loop (20b):

```
      DO 10 j=1,m
        DO 20b i=1,n
          a(i,j)=a(i,j)+b(i,j)*c(i,j)
20b       CONTINUE
10    CONTINUE
```

The loops are interchanged to ensure processing on a so-called contiguous vector (i.e., the vector elements are stored in adjacent memory locations), which gives optimal processing speeds. The Convex FORTRAN compiler provides the user an easy-to-read summary comprising all relevant information about the performed vectorization activities.

4.4   Parallel Simulation

The term "parallel simulation" is used to mean simulation on computers with a parallel (pipeline) architecture. Users of such scientific digital computers are motivated to demand high processing speeds for two distinct reasons: the increasingly detailed representations required for more and more complex distributed parameter systems [characterized by PDEs (partial differential equations)] and real-time (or faster than real-time) simulations of complex lumped-parameter systems described by ODEs.

In the early 1980s centralized supercomputer facilities (such as the Cyber 205 and Cray-1, among others) were used for challenging complex simulations of systems characterized by PDEs and accessed remotely by scientists and engineers with large simulation problems to solve. The advent of mini-supercomputers may cause a fundamental change in this picture since currently these are generally marketed at a cost less than 10% of supercomputer prices and therefore may open the possibilities of decentralized use in many research groups and institutions.

Realistic performance comparisons and predictions are to be based upon benchmark (simulation) problems. For the simulation of systems characterized by PDEs, the treatment of sufficiently large sets of simultaneous linear algebraic equations (preferably with sparse characterizing matrices) on different computers may provide some performance indications. Relevant studies (however, for dense matrices) showed some mini-supercomputers reaching 5–20% of the performance of supercomputers, which results in a favorable cost–performance ratio [3]. No comprehensive benchmark studies have as yet been published dealing with solving ODEs on mini-supercomputers. A general remark is that based on the special characteristics of the mini-supercomputer and the complexity of the simulation problem (i.e., the number of state equations, the number of finite-difference or finite-element points, or the types of nonlinearities to be included), the user must be enabled to convey directives to the compilers to recognize parallelizable or vectorizable code in order to take maximal advantage of the mini-supercomputers' potentialities.

In addition to the aforementioned reasons to use multicomputers in (real-time) simulations of complex distributed or lumped-parameter systems, there can be other motivations for parallel simulation. In methodology-based interactive simulation the specific architectures of such multicomputer systems might well be exploited. Focusing the attention on MIMD arrays of processing elements, examples of this in model implementation and experimentation are [16, 17]

(a) exploitation of the one-to-one analogy realizable between a model structure and its physical implementation on a multicomputer,
(b) model composition by assembling components running on different processing elements (configuring excitable units), and
(c) interactive experimentation on model bases (e.g., multimodel output analysis after one single run).

5   PARALLEL PROCESSING IN THE AI DOMAIN

5.1   Parallelism and AI

The needs for high processing speeds—especially when real-time applications are involved—are found in vision perception software, decision support systems, problem-solving and reasoning systems, speech and language recognition systems, robot perceptual motor systems, and so on. In all but the simplest and most trivial problems these AI applications on conventional hardware suffer from slow processing capabilities. A major underlying reason for this is that most AI applications put demands on the supporting hardware that are completely different from those of conventional, procedural languages. Current computer hardware is generally directed to the support of procedural languages and numerical applications. In contrast, AI languages and applications use nonprocedural programming paradigms such as functional programming (LISP), logic programming (PROLOG, expert system inference engines), and object-oriented programming (SMALLTALK). The unpredictable recursion depth in functional programs and the search methods inherent in inference engines put strict demands on the required memory spaces and processing times that both grow exponentially with the size of the problem at hand.

Two general techniques are envisioned to accelerate the execution of AI applications:

(a) the use of heuristic and domain-dependent search algorithms to reduce the combinatorial explosion of the search space and
(b) the use of (possibly massive) parallelism.

In this chapter, we focus on the latter technique. Up to now various difficulties have prevented extensive use of parallel techniques in AI applications. To mention a few:

(a) Programmers predominantly think in a serial fashion. This behavior hampers the introduction of programming tools that employ programmer-specified concurrency (concurrent languages such as Occam, Ada, Modula-2, etc.). Consequently, automatic detection and exploitation of implicit parallelism is definitely needed.
(b) The semantics of AI languages might be changed by introducing parallelism. For example, the order in which the search trees in PROLOG programs are explored is strictly determined (depth first); this leaves little room for the introduction of parallelism in the search algorithm.

(c) Inference techniques (such as occur in PROLOG programs and expert systems) are known to generate extremely large and complex databases. Introducing parallelism may require these databases to be shared by multiple inference engines. Synchronizing simultaneous accesses to shared data causes a lot of overhead and hence reduces the potential gains of parallelism. The alternative of distributing the data and using a large number of communication paths poses severe problems of distributed coherence and access control.

Nearly all potential forms of parallelism in AI need further (fundamental) research before coming fully to fruition. At the programming level, for example, the feasibility of concrete parallel architectures to support parallel extensions of AI languages (PROLOG, SMALLTALK-80) can be studied. At the language implementation level, how well hardware (e.g., the development of accelerating language coprocessors) can support implicit forms of language parallelism, such as the functional parallelism in LISP, the potential AND/OR parallelism in PROLOG, the object parallelism in Pool-T, and the implicit parallelism in production systems and expert system shells, can be investigated. At the circuit level, the feasibility of (new) massively parallel hardware structures for knowledge processing can be explored (Boltzmann machines, neural networks, and connectionist architectures).

5.2 Multicomputers Applied to AI

Although generally a wide variety of architectures have been suggested for multicomputers (see Sections 4.1 and 4.2), only a few of these have been proposed for AI applications. Some multicomputers that have actually been built for AI purposes are, among others, the Aquarius PROLOG machine, the reconfigurable networks TRAC and PASM, and the Connection Machine. In ref. 31, multicomputer systems developed and/or used to handle AI problems are surveyed, and furthermore a variety of possible architectures are proposed that may appear to be more promising for AI. Parallel architectures under study by the AI community include a variety of structures ranging from small networks (applied to production-rule-based systems) to very large networks (for semantic memory searches and local operations on arrays of image pixels). The processors in the networks can be specialized to handle particular AI tasks.

In the remaining part of this chapter, we focus on the kind of AI applications that best fit our aims of intelligent simulation: problem solving and reasoning. Most attempts to develop computer programs for deductive problem solving and reasoning have in common the search in and manipulation of complex graphs of information and the use of list-processing languages such as PROLOG and LISP. Today a great deal of effort is going into the development of specialized hardware for list processing. The individual processor is carefully designed for the language and the type of problems it must handle. To achieve major increases in speed and power, these processors can be combined in networks [33]. The Japanese Fifth Generation Computer Project focuses on developing a computer capable of executing 1000 MLIPS (million logical inferences per second). This is generally envisioned as a gigantic PROLOG machine.

It is not clear how appropriate the three most widely proposed architectures are for problem solving [31]: A reconfigurable network is quite adaptable since it can be made to give the appearance of a complete graph topology. However, the cost is high, and the total size of the system is limited; hence these systems are slow. Hypercube computers are not felt to have an especially good topology for AI problems. Of the existing connection machines, one is a reconfigurable network and the other a hypercube. Thus the previous comments apply to them as well.

5.3   Limitations of Parallelized Standard "Expert" Production Systems

In this section we consider problem-solving and reasoning systems based on production rules (note our remark in Section 1 that production rules are quite natural to employ in, e.g., knowledge-based controllers).

In their original pure form, expert production systems use

    (a) sets of if–then production rules pertaining to conditions to be searched for in

    (b) a single common memory.

Pure production systems have no control structures (such as the ordering of rules and procedure calls) that specify how to move between productions. However, most systems are given a number of additional control capabilities. For executing pure production systems a multicomputer architecture with a star topology (all processors linked to a common memory) seems the best. Practically, however, such a system can only be built with a small number of processors. Bus, ring, or crossbar-based systems allow for a few more processors. However, the need for all of these to share a single memory and to choose a single production rule to fire results in major performance degradations.

In a sufficiently large multicomputer with an appropriate topology the production rules could become assigned to different processors. At the first glance, this is the truly parallel execution of a rule-based system. There are however two major problems. First, most expert systems are coded so that only a few productions can be expected to fire at a time. This suggests modifying the standard production systems by using a discrimination net to direct search for only those productions. Second, all processors will need to access common memory, leading to serious contention problems. For sufficiently small memories this might be handled by storing copies in each processor's memory, but updating these copies requires time and is error prone.

It turns out that parallelizing standard (pure) production systems yields disappointingly little speedup [8]; see, for instance, the HYDRA-2 results discussed in Section 6.2. Production systems with entirely different formulations and algorithms and hence much greater inherent parallelism should be explored in today's and future research.

5.4   Multicomputer Architectures for Holistic Systems

In holistic systems several intelligent functions are integrated and/or intelligent entities interfaced with conventional simulation models that simulate the surrounding real-world environments (see also Section 1). Modeling holistic systems entails such large and complex problems that we can today only begin to move in the direction of attempting to handle them. For tactical reasons we must start with simplifying the problems down to feasible size; but the art of tactical simplifications lies in the ability to successively remove the simplifying assumptions so that steady progress can be made toward the ultimate goal.

A possible approach to architectures that would best support such holistic systems is the development of general-purpose networks. These can be homogeneous structures, or to the extent that each separated function is best handled by a particular specialized system, it might be preferable to build a heterogeneous compound of specialized regions. (Heterogeneous) connection machines and (homogeneous) hypercubes are today possibly the most commonly considered point-to-point topologies for general-purpose AI [31].

With regard to those holistic systems that comprise intelligent systems interacting with simulation models, network topologies are obviously needed that could efficiently be used to simulate the environment within which the intelligent cognitive system must reside. As already said in Section 4.3, a large three-dimensional array may well be the most suitable structure to simulate the (three-dimensional) environment. The intelligent system could probably run efficiently on this array also, especially if each node in the array is designed to consist of a numerical-oriented processor and a processor dedicated to symbolic processing. An alternative might be to link the array to additional appropriate structures indicated for the intelligent system in such a way that good interaction would be possible between them.

6   THE HYDRA PROJECT AT DELFT UNIVERSITY OF TECHNOLOGY

6.1   Project Description

At Delft University of Technology (The Netherlands), the so-called HYDRA (HYpotheses Deduction through Rule Applications) project was launched a few years ago. Some of the major aims of this project are

(a) research in real-time (dynamic) knowledge-based systems with particular emphasis on the expected emerging role of parallel processing;

(b) fundamental research in possible architectures and performances of knowledge-based (expert) systems based on parallel processing;

(c) exploring the interaction of knowledge-based systems and simulation systems in a parallel processing environment;

(d) studying the use of vector processing in fuzzy reasoning; and

(e) general research with respect to parallelism and AI, running different AI applications on parallel computers.

For the research mentioned in the preceding we make use of a home-built MIMD parallel computer (Delft Parallel Processor DPP84) with 16 fully interconnected processing elements and especially an NCube/4+ parallel computer with a four-dimensional hypercube structure (16 nodes). The latter was recently donated by Shell Netherlands to the HYDRA project. We also have access to a pipeline-oriented mini-supercomputer, Convex C-1, located at the central computing center of the Delft University of Technology.

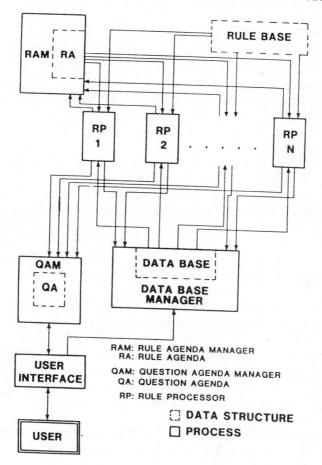

Figure 4. HYDRA-2 system concept.

With a view to the preceding list of research topics, it is clear that a part of the HYDRA activities fall—at least in the first instance—beyond the scope of this chapter. For example, our first research on the NCube/4+ computer was related to the design of a parallel knowledge-based optical character recognition system [9]. Currently, we are developing a user-friendly programming environment for the NCube/4+ system to deal with parallel numeric simulation models interacting with one or more (possibly parallel) knowledge-based systems.

Because of the recent availability of the NCube/4+ computer, rather than extensively overviewing the current state of the HYDRA project, we restrict ourselves to a description of the HYDRA-2 system (see Section 6.2). This system was one of the first PKB (parallel knowledge-based) system concepts that in the framework of the current project has been studied in depth [10, 11]. The HYDRA-2 example might be illustrative for the specific difficulties that arise when attempting to parallelize inference engines and for the resource contention problems that shared-data concepts meet when the data traffic becomes large; it illustrates the disappointingly small speedup achievable with parallelized, conventionally formulated standard expert production systems (see Section 5.3).

6.2 The Hydra-2 System

Figure 4 shows a schematic representation of the HYDRA-2 system. This concept implies an agenda-driven PKB system with a (parallelized) inference engine consisting of a RAM (rule agenda manager) and a number of concurrently operating RPs (rule processors). The RAM controls the rule agenda (RA), the latter containing the status and priority of each rule (according to some plain priority function). As soon as an RP is free, it consults the RA for the next rule (rule with highest priority number) to be processed. Whenever an RP can find neither a proof nor a disproof of a rule nor other rules in the rule base (RB) which might be of help, it sends a question to the QAM (question agenda manager). This QAM controls the QA (question agenda) and arranges the question queue (QQ), and it communicates with the user by means of the UI (user interface). Depending on the result of an RP, one or more of the following actions have to be executed: updating the DB (database), RA, and/or QA. The DB contains the (derived) facts, which are recorded under the control of the DBM (database manager). Table 1 shows how the various processes (DBM, RAM, RP, QAM, UI) make use of the diverse data structures (DB, RA, RB, QA, QQ); in Table 2 the communication between the processes is schematically represented.

In the first instance the HYDRA-2 system has been simulated on a conventional sequential computer. A parallel computer simulator program was built to enable measuring, among other things, run times and waiting times of the processes. To eliminate human effects in the performance-measuring experiments, the answers to questions posed to the user were automatically generated. In the following some (averaged) results are presented that were achieved using a rather small rule base (knowledge base of 162 rules and 70 hypotheses; mean branching factor 1.88; maximal depth of search graph 13).

Experiments were carried out with 1–15 RPs. In Table 3 the speedup and mean RP utilization, U (the subscript i in the formula refers to the ith RP);

$$U = \{\Sigma_i \text{ run time}_i \,/\text{total time}_i\}/\{\text{number of RPs}\},$$

are tabulated for the various numbers of RPs [11]. In the experiment considered, the optimal number of RPs (giving the highest speedup) is 3. The trend of the results

TABLE 1. How Processes Make Use of Data Structures in HYDRA-2

	Data Structure[a]				
Process	DB	RA	RB	QA	QQ
DBM	(W, D)	—	—	—	—
RAM	—	(W, D)	—	—	—
RP	(R, D)	(R, S)(W, D)	(R, S)	—	—
QAM	—	—	—	(R, D)	(W, S)
UI	—	—	—	(W, D)	(R, S)

[a]Symbols: (R, ✱), reading; (W, ✱), writing; (✱, D), direct access to data structure; (✱, S), sequentially following data structure.

TABLE 2. Communication between Processes in HYDRA-2

Sending Process	Receiving Process[a]					
	DBM	RAM	RPi	RPj	QAM	UI
DBM	—		*	*		
RAM		—	*	*		
RPi	×	×	—	*	×	
RPj	×	×	*	—	×	
QAM					—	*
UI	×				*	—

[a]Symbols: ×, communication; *, indirect communication.

presented is of course not amazing since the HYDRA-2 concept is essentially based upon a shared-memory approach, showing an expectation for the speedup behavior as qualitatively sketched in Figure 5.

When using more complex antecedents, the processing time for a single rule increases, and hence the shared resources of a process are less frequently utilized per unit of time. In order to roughly estimate the effect of complex antecedents, the processing of each antecedent of the rules could be artificially delayed. For this purpose the RPs were provided with a delay routine which can be set to 0 (no delay), 100, 200, 300, 400, 500, 1000, and 1500 units of 0.1 ms. Table 4 shows that the number of RPs in the optimal configuration (showing the highest speedup) increases with the delay factor [11]. From the indicated figures of the rule processor run times and idle times as well as of the system's total run times, we can conclude an increasingly better utilization of the RPs for larger delays. Comparatively, the run times of the RAM are

TABLE 3. Utilization Percentage and Speedup for Different Numbers of Processors

Number of RPs	Utilization (%)	Speedup
1	95.3	—
2	81.3	1.38
3	76.5	1.84
4	77.9	1.71
5	79.0	1.71
6	78.4	1.65
7	78.0	1.64
8	76.6	1.65
9	74.6	1.72
10	73.7	1.65
11	71.7	1.64
12	63.1	1.64
13	68.9	1.59
14	68.4	1.56
15	67.5	1.50

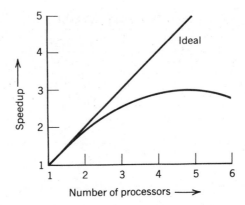

Figure 5. General trend of shared-memory multiprocessor speedup.

also taken up in Table 4; the speedup factors have not been indicated, but they appeared to increase from approximately 1.8 to 4.2 (for the largest delay factor).

The HYDRA-2 concept has also been implemented on the Delft Parallel Processor DPP84, notwithstanding the fact that this computer has been designed and up to now used entirely for numerical applications in a synchronized mode of operation [25]. In addition to the development of special software to handle asynchronous communications between processing elements, the HYDRA-2 concept has been slightly modified since the DPP84 is not a shared-memory system: Copies of the full database have been placed in the memory of each processing element acting as rule processor, and consequently a new data structure (database update agenda) has been introduced to keep each of the databases updated all the time. Figure 6 shows typical results obtained from several consultations with this DPP version of HYDRA-2 using different numbers of rule processors and different values for the above-declared delay factor [25]; these are in close correspondence with earlier simulation results. Note also that the DPP version of the HYDRA-2 concept essentially contains a star structure. Instead of the common database in the original HYDRA-2 system, now the database update agenda is placed in a central position; moreover, in both concepts the rule agenda and question agenda are centered as common resources.

TABLE 4. Optimal Configuration with Different Delay Factors[a]

Delay	Optimal Number of RPs	Run Time RP	Idle Time RP	Run Time RAM	Total Run Time
0	3	23,893	7,478	6,991	31,371
100	5	28,479	5,178	6,914	33,657
200	7	31,834	4,873	7,538	36,707
300	8	37,431	4,636	7,764	38,067
400	9	37,081	4,173	8,045	41,253
500	9	40,396	3,336	8,097	43,732
1,000	13	54,822	2,539	9,422	57,361
1,500	15	73,455	2,010	10,730	75,464

[a]Times in units of 0.0001 s.

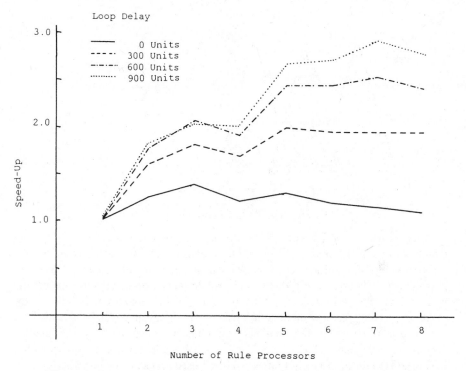

Figure 6. Typical performance results from DPP version of HYDRA-2 system.

Although quantitatively the speedup results shall certainly depend upon the kind of problems being dealt with, qualitatively the examples presented in the preceding seem to us representative and may give a reasonable indication about the order of magnitude of the speedup one might expect when using this kind of parallel expert system concept. The speedup achievable is modest unless perhaps the problems to be solved require really excessive work loads of the rule processors (e.g., if the evaluation of rules would demand extensive floating-point calculations).

From our experiments we also found that (inherent to the HYDRA-2 concept but dependent on the kind of problem to be solved) the number of questions directed to the user may considerably increase with a growing number of rule processors. Although appropriate algorithms can be implemented to reduce this effect (which, however, shall badly influence the speedup), a conclusion might be that the current concept is only feasible for consultations for which the number of all possible questions to the user is small.

As already said in Section 5.3, entirely different approaches to parallel knowledge-based (expert) systems have to be developed to attain appreciable speedups. One might wonder if the development of parallel expert systems of the kind presented in this section has made any sense. We think it does. The HYDRA-2 system is a parallel knowledge-based system anyway and hence is possibly feasible to be used in research experiments to test innovative ideas that do not necessarily depend on the system's speed (e.g., interfacing such parallel expert systems with parallel numeric simulation models, the latter, if needed, slowed down, both running on a multicomputer).

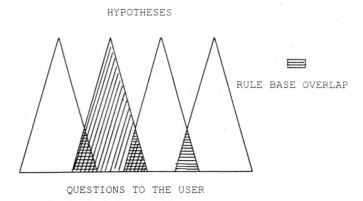

Figure 7. Partitioning a rule base.

Another use of the current HYDRA-2 or corresponding concept would be in combination with different techniques. Let us consider an illustrative example. The rule base could be partitioned into several independent parts with, in general, overlapping areas (see Figure 7). A possible approach to this partitioning is to separate the hypotheses and trace all facts to infer them. Taking into account that in the case of, for instance, certainty factors a number of N ($N>1$) hypotheses should all be investigated, various rule subbases can be simultaneously subject to concurrently operating inference engines. Say this technique would result in a speedup S. Then, the incorporation of several HYDRA-2 (like) systems, each being used to operate on one rule subbase, could result in an overall speedup of roughly sS, where s denotes the speedup of the HYDRA-2 system. Note that, in contrast to the HYDRA-2 concept, the approach of first partitioning the rule base is problem dependent and requires preanalysis.

7   CONCLUDING NOTE

There will come a time that it is feasible to implement, on an appropriate multicomputer, several large-scale intelligent systems that concurrently operate and interact with a complex simulated environment in a truly real-time mode. The obstacles and problems to solve on the way to advanced "parallel intelligent simulation" will be numerous and so complex that today we can only start attempting to handle them. This chapter intends to stimulate thinking and discussion about further research needed. For this purpose, various issues related to the parallel treatment of numeric simulation models and symbolic problem-solving and reasoning systems have been considered in (to the authors' opinion necessarily) global terms. It is left to the reader to draw his or her own conclusions.

REFERENCES

1.   D. Ariel, "CSSL-IV on the Cyber 205: A Study in Porting, Vectorization and Suitability," MSc Thesis, University of Calgary, Department of Computer Science, Calgary, 1986.

2. E. C. Deland, "Conceptual Models in Physiology, Where Are We?" in G. C. Vansteenkiste and P. C. Young (Eds.), *Proceedings of the IFIP WG 7.1 Working Conference on Modelling and Data Analysis in Biotechnology and Medical Engineering (Brussels 1982)*, North-Holland, Amsterdam, 1983, pp. XI–XVII.

3. J. J. Dongarra, "Performance of Various Computers Using Standard Linear Equations Software in a Fortran Environment," Mathematics and Computer Science Division, Technical Memorandum No. 23, Argonne National Laboratory, Argonne, IL, December 1985.

4. E. J. Fadden, "The System 10 Plus: Broader Horizons," in W. J. Karplus (Ed.), *Peripheral Array Processors*, Simulation Series, Vol. 14, No. 2, Society for Computer Simulation Int., San Diego, CA, 1984.

5. T. Feng, "A Survey of Interconnection Networks," in K. Hwang (Ed.), *Supercomputers: Design and Applications*, IEEE Computer Society Press, Silver Springs, MD, 1984.

6. M. J. Flynn, "Some Computer Organizations and Their Effectiveness," *IEEE Transactions on Computers*, **C-21**:948–960, September 1972.

7. J. C. Francis and R. R. Leitch, "ARTIFACT: A Real-Time Shell for Intelligent Feedback Control," in M. A. Bramer (Ed.), *Research and Development in Expert Systems*, Cambridge University Press, Cambridge, 1985, pp. 151–162.

8. A. Gupta, *Parallelism in Production Systems*, Pitman, London, 1987.

9. J. Henseler, H. J. van den Herik, E. J. H. Kerckhoffs, H. Koppelaar, J. C. Scholtes, and C. R. J. Verhoest, "Knowledge-Based Parallelism in Optical Character Recognition," in *Proceedings of the 1988 Summer Computer Simulation Conference, Seattle 1988*, Society for Computer Simulation Int., San Diego, CA, 1988, pp. 14–20.

10. H. J. van den Herik, E. J. H. Kerckhoffs, and H. Koppelaar, "Simulation of the Parallel Knowledge-Based System HYDRA," in R. Crosbie and P. Luker (Eds.), *Proceedings of the 1986 Summer Computer Simulation Conference, Reno 1986*, Society for Computer Simulation Int., San Diego, CA, 1986, pp. 972–977.

11. H. J. van den Herik, A. G. Hofland, J. Henseler, and C. R. J. Verhoest, "Parallel Processes in the Knowledge-Based System HYDRA," in *Proceedings of IMACS International Symposium on AI, Expert Systems and Languages in Modelling and Simulation, Barcelona 1987*, North-Holland, Amsterdam, 1988.

12. R. W. Hockney and C. R. Jesshope, *Parallel Computers*, Adam Hilger, Bristol, United Kingdom, 1981.

13. W. M. Holmes (Ed.), *Artificial Intelligence and Simulation*, Society for Computer Simulation Int., San Diego, CA, 1985.

14. W. J. Karplus (Ed.), *Peripheral Array Processors*, Simulation Series, Vol. 14, No. 2, Society for Computer Simulation Int., San Diego, CA, 1984.

15. W. J. Karplus (Ed.), *Multiprocessors and Array Processors*, Simulation Series, Vol. 18, No. 2, Society for Computer Simulation Int., San Diego, CA, 1987.

16. E. J. H. Kerckhoffs and S. W. Brok, "The Delft Parallel Processor DPP81: Properties and Utilization in Simulation and Related Fields." Systems Analysis, Modelling and Simulation," *Journal of Mathematical Modelling and Simulation in Systems Analysis*, **2**(3):175–208, 1985.

17. E. J. H. Kerckhoffs, "Parallel Processing and Advanced Environments in Continuous Systems Simulation," Ph.D. Thesis, University of Ghent, Ghent, 1986.

18. E. J. H. Kerckhoffs and G. C. Vansteenkiste, "The Impact of Advanced Information Processing on Simulation/An Illustrative Review," *Simulation*, **46**(1):17–26, 1986.

19. E. J. H. Kerckhoffs, G. C. Vansteenkiste, and B. P. Zeigler (Eds.), *AI Applied to Simulation*, Simulation Series, Vol. 18, No. 1, Society for Computer Simulation Int., San Diego, CA, 1986.

20. A. Lehmann, B. Knödler, E. Kwee, and H. Szczerbicka, "Dialog-oriented and Knowledge-based Modeling in a Typical PC Environment," in E. J. H. Kerckhoffs, G. C. Vansteenkiste, and B. P. Zeigler (Eds.), *AI Applied to Simulation*, Simulation Series, Vol. 18, No. 1, Society for Computer Simulation Int., San Diego, CA, 1986, pp. 91–96.

21. T. Louie, "Array Processors: A Selected Bibliography," *Computer*, September 1981, pp. 53–57.

22. P. A. Luker and H. H. Adelsberger (Eds.), *Intelligent Simulation Environments*, Simulation Series, Vol. 17, No. 1, Society for Computer Simulation Int., San Diego, CA, 1986.

23. P. A. Luker and G. Birtwistle (Eds.), *Simulation and AI*, Simulation Series, Vol. 18, No. 3, Society for Computer Simulation Int., San Diego, CA, 1987.

24. A. Makoui and W. J. Karplus, "ALI: A CSSL/Multiprocessor Software Interface," *Simulation*, 49(2):63–71, 1987.

25. R. R. Meijer and E. J. H. Kerckhoffs, "Implementation of a Knowledge-based Expert System on the Delft Parallel Processor DPP84," in *Proceedings of ESM88 (European Simulation Multiconference), Nice (France) 1988*, Society for Computer Simulation Int., European Office, Ghent, 1988.

26. R. N. Nilsen, *CSSL-IV Reference Manual*, Simulation Services, Chatsworth, CA, 1984.

27. T. I. Ören and B. P. Zeigler, "Concepts for Advanced Simulation Methodologies," *Simulation*, 32(3):69–82, 1979.

28. J. A. Spriet and G. C. Vansteenkiste, *Computer-Aided Modelling and Simulation*, International Lecture Notes in Computer Science, Academic, London, 1982.

29. C. R. Standridge, "Using the Simulation Data Language (SDL)," *Simulation*, 37(3): 73–81, 1981.

30. C. R. Standridge and A. A. B. Pritsker, "Using Data Base Capabilities in Simulation," in F. E. Cellier (Ed.), *Progress in Modelling and Simulation*, Academic, London, 1982, pp. 347–365.

31. L. Uhr, *Multi-Computer Architectures for Artificial Intelligence: Towards Fast, Robust, Parallel Systems*, Wiley, New York, 1987.

32. G. C. Vansteenkiste and E. J. H. Kerckhoffs, "Information Base Support in Simulation of Biological Systems," in D. J. Murray-Smith (Ed.), *Proceedings of the 1984 UKSC Conference on Computer Simulation, Bath, England, 1984*, Butterworths, London, 1984, pp. 198–218.

33. M. J. Wise, *Prolog Multiprocessors*, Prentice-Hall, Englewood Cliffs, 1987.

9 Problems with Problem Solving in Parallel: The Poligon System

J. P. RICE

Knowledge Systems Laboratory
Department of Computer Science
Stanford University
Stanford, California

1 INTRODUCTION

The domain of supercomputing has traditionally been very large regular problems. This has been driven by two main forces;

- A large class of important problems were soluble by existing programming technology but were intractable with "normal" processors (e.g., PDE solution, finite-element analysis, or simulation).
- Early programming languages focused on arrays as data structures, whose use could efficiently use the hardware available. This led to the idea of vector and array processors.

It is therefore by no means a coincidence that the sort of problems that tend to use existing supercomputers are those problems best suited to supercomputers.
The field is changing now, however. This is driven by two main forces:

- Developments in hardware technology now allow the development of multi-processor systems composed of large numbers of relatively simple processors, which are potentially more cost effective than existing super-complex supercomputer uniprocessors.
- Both hardware and software technologies have progressed to a point where a number of problems which have become soluble by means of symbolic programming would now like a slice of the speedup cake.

Symbolic computation has for a long time been accused of inefficiency. Recent developments in compiler and hardware technologies, however, have allowed the development of high-performance uniprocessor workstations for the execution of symbolic programs. These have shown that there is a large class of *artificial intelli-*

gence (*AI*) problems for which significantly greater computational resources will be needed to make these problems worth addressing. This has focused the attention of AI and symbolic programming research on the exploitation of parallelism.

The sort of problem currently applied to supercomputers is very crystalline [28] in nature. This means that a relatively small "inner loop" of the computation can be vectorized in order to exploit existing supercomputer hardware [15]. Similarly, such problems can often exploit parallelism at a finer grain in a systolic manner [16].

AI problems have none of these useful characteristics [17]. This chapter describes first what is meant by *Problem Solving* and how this relates to parallelism (Section 2). It goes on to describe *Poligon* [24], a system implemented in order to investigate the potential for speedup of a class of AI applications called "blackboard systems" through parallelism (Section 3). After this some preliminary experiments and what we have learned from them are discussed (Section 4).

2   PARALLELISM AND PROBLEM SOLVING

In this section we examine what is meant by Problem Solving, contrasting it with common supercomputing doctrine and concerns. This will show why it is that a different approach to parallelism than is taken by conventional programs is necessary in AI and also why it is so hard to achieve.

2.1   What Is Problem Solving?

Questions are never indiscreet. Answers sometimes are.
—Oscar Wilde, "An Ideal Husband"

"Problem solving" was often taken to refer to the process of searching a tree or graph of alternative solutions. "Knowledge" is that which allows the program to eliminate searching parts of the tree. For instance, a chess-playing program might have a tree made of all of the legal moves at any given point.[1] The term "knowledge" will always be used in this sense in this chapter. The application of strategic knowledge, such as knowledge about chess end games, to each generated node in the tree would point out to the system likely candidate paths to follow. The method of constructing all legal possibilities at any given leaf of a dynamically generated tree and then testing them to determine whether they are possibilities worth following is usually referred to as the *generate-and-test* method. It is an axiom of such systems that the more knowledge there is, the less blind search has to be done, and the more efficiently the tree is pruned.

The focus of much AI research is on the use of knowledge to reduce or obviate search. This is because such searches are expensive and combinatorial processes. The use of knowledge in this way might not be the best solution for the future since the use of highly parallel architectures to evaluate multiple alternatives might be faster than executing this highly specialized knowledge. What is more, this could also save the human cost of acquiring and encoding such knowledge. The acquisition of knowledge

---

[1]Clearly this tree cannot be fully instantiated with the resources available in the universe.

is generally thought to be one of the major obstacles in the way of the more general application of AI systems to real-world problems.

The important thing, for the purpose of this chapter, about problem-solving systems and the problems that they address is that they are structurally different from "conventional" programs. Throughout this chapter the terms "problem-solving" and "AI system" will be used to describe these systems. The term "conventional" will be used to describe existing practice in the supercomputer world. Some of the characteristics that make such a problem different from a conventional programming problem are as follows:

- The problem itself is often ill-defined.
- There is often more than one possible solution. This means that a satisficing[2] rather than an optimal solution is usually the "right" answer. This is quite unlike most conventional programs for which there is one and only one right answer within the margin of error of the system.[3]
- The paths to a solution cannot be predefined in such systems. Possible solution paths must be dynamically generated and tried.
- The structure of such programs differs from conventional programs in three fundamental ways: in their data structures, their control flow, and their control structures.

Data Structure   It is generally the case that the data upon which the system has to operate cannot be encoded simply into an array. This is because such data structures are usually highly complex and often cyclic graphs, which are created dynamically, thus precluding static allocation and optimization.

Control Flow   The solution to the problem is not regular, which is to say that the behavior of the problem solver is typically very data dependent. In a PDE solving program, for instance, the computational demands of the system at any point are well understood. This is because well-defined and well-understood algorithms are used and the computational demands of matrix inversion, for example, are reasonably easy to estimate. This is not the case in AI programs. Apparently trivial changes to the source data can cause huge changes to the computation performed. As an example of this, one might consider the behavior of a chess program when the opponent elects to make an unexpected move. What is more, the code generated for these programs is usually very branchy [17], thus reducing the benefits of fine-grained pipelining.

Control Structures   The knowledge that AI programmers try to encode in their programs is usually functionally different from the knowledge usually encoded in conventional programs. That is to say, it is more likely to be a high-level specification of the intended behavior of the system, as opposed to a set of instructions

---

[2]A solution that is said to be "good enough."

[3]Linear optimization is a notable exception to this. Clearly many programs use heuristics and so the distinction made here is simply one of degree. AI problems are usually composed of a larger proportion of heuristics than conventional programs.

for how to compute the answer. Such details are usually left to the system. For instance, the program might be compiled into a set of assertions and rules in a PROLOG system [5]. The program itself is executed indirectly through a virtual machine which interprets these specifications as its instructions. This results in most of such programs not being amenable either to existing vectorizing algorithms or to the application of well-defined algorithms.[4]

The factors mentioned above result in AI problems not having the properties needed for them to be parallelized by conventional means. This is cause for considerable concern for those who would like to achieve orders of magnitude of speedup for their AI programs.

2.2   Concerns for Supercomputers

On how to trap a lion in a desert [23]: *A topological method*. We observe that a lion has at least the connectivity of the torus. We transport the desert into four-space. It is then possible [27] to carry out such a deformation that the lion can be returned to three-space in a knotted condition. He is then helpless.

Implementors and programmers of supercomputers have traditionally focused on the efficient use of the hardware and the matching of the hardware to the problem. Some examples of these are discussed below.

2.2.1   Where Does Parallelism Come From?

Parallelism in conventional programs is either easy to get or nearly impossible. If the program does a lot of simple operations on arrays whose dependencies and recurrences are simple and can be unraveled, then massive data parallelism[5] can be exploited. It is by this means that vector machines are able to achieve their performance. It is not generally the case that there is, qualitatively speaking, more than one thing happening at any given time. Such programs are parallel in a SIMD sense [11]. If the control flow is too complex to analyze, then the compiler may not be able to unwind the parallelism out of the program.[6]

AI programs are typically short on data parallelism. There are certainly problems which have significant data parallelism but not of the order that one might get in extremely regular, conventional programs. This means that an AI system which hopes for speedup through parallelism must be able to exploit knowledge parallelism. It must be able to execute a significant number of different chunks of the program simul-

---

[4]These interpreters themselves may, however, be implemented using well-understood algorithms or microcode.

[5]Parallelism due to similar operations being performable on independent items of data, for instance, elementwise addition of two arrays.

[6]The Connection Machine® [14] is an example of an experiment to test the contrary hypothesis that SIMD machines are indeed appropriate for AI applications. Connection Machine is a trademark of the Thinking Machines Corporation.

taneously. This is MIMD parallelism. The Poligon system described in Section 3 is designed to exploit this sort of parallelism.[7]

Most high-performance processors today exploit pipeline parallelism in the execution of instructions. Pipeline parallelism is also exploited at a somewhat coarser grain by the new generations of multiprocessor systems such as systolic arrays. It is crucial that any system hoping to exploit parallel hardware effectively should be able to exploit pipeline parallelism. This is, in fact, considerably harder in AI systems because of the irregular structure of the problem. The Poligon system tries wherever it can to exploit pipeline parallelism.

2.2.2   *What Sort of Hardware Should Be Used?*

In order to be able to exploit the parallelism in a program to the best possible degree, there must be an appropriate match between the compiled program and the target hardware. This means that if a speedup of no more that 10–20 is either hoped for or expected, then the program should probably be executed on a shared-memory multiprocessor.[8] If more speedup than this is needed, then a hardware design that will scale better should be used—some form of distributed memory architecture.[9] This could, in practice, have a grain size varying from that of the *Cosmic Cube* [28] to that of the *Connection Machine* [14]. The Poligon system is designed to be matched to run on a multiprocessor, which should scale satisfactorily to the order of hundreds or thousands of processing elements, each element being a highly competent symbolic language processor. This is the pure value-passing *CARE* machine model [3], one of several CARE machine models implemented as part of the same project of which Poligon is a part.

2.2.3   *Compilation*

Vectorizing FORTRAN compilers have been the main implementation language in supercomputing circles for quite some time. There is considerable inertia in the field in this respect. Similarly, AI programmers are in many senses locked into the use of LISP [29] or PROLOG [5] as their implementation languages. Problem-solving systems have traditionally not been very efficiently implemented, even if the underlying implementation language has been. This is because it is expensive in human terms to implement such systems efficiently and their typical life span has not justified this sort of optimization effort. This state of affairs is beginning to change. There is now a demand for highly competent programs using AI techniques being embedded, for

---

[7]MIMD programs typically have a set of implementation difficulties and bugs which are not so frequently seen in SIMD programs. These are caused by having a number of radically different types of program executing, all at different speeds and trying to communicate with one another. This causes data to arrive "out of order" and race conditions. Many of the pitfalls of parallel AI programming mentioned in this chapter are a consequence of this.

[8]Some experiments have shown rather disappointing results here, saying that this is all that can really be hoped for [13].

[9]Recent claims have been made that some shared-memory architectures can scale well [31].

instance, into military hardware. This asks not only for high performance but also for high reliability, maintainability, and modifiability. In their common implementations LISP and PROLOG are not languages which can easily be parallelized in the same way that FORTRAN compilers are.[10] There is, therefore, a need to develop languages not only capable of exploiting the parallelism in forthcoming hardware but also capable of expressing the richness of these complex symbolic programs. On top of these will need to be built highly competent tools and frameworks which will be needed for a satisfactory parallel AI development environment. The Poligon system is a first-cut prototype system developed with the objective of being able to extract parallelism from programs both by the system and by encouraging a clear programming style and problem decomposition methodology, which leads to more parallel programs.

2.3   Concerns for Problem Solvers

The concerns of the implementors of problem-solving systems are quite different from those of supercomputer programmers. Some of these concerns are enumerated below.

2.3.1   Solution Quality

As has been mentioned, AI programs are generally expected to produce a satisficing solution. This has a significant impact on the behavior of the program since paths used to determine heuristic solutions might be very different from those used to find analytic solutions, even if analytic solutions are known.

2.3.2   Search

These heuristic programs are typically characterized by searching a great deal for patterns over a large graph.[11] This large amount of search admits both *And* and *Or* parallelism, in principle. The Poligon system has specific mechanisms to facilitate the efficient execution of such searches.[12]

2.3.3   Coherence

The implementor of an AI program may not be aware of the eventual behavior of a program when implementing it. This is a function of the complex nature of such problems and the fact that the paths to their solutions are not predefined. It is, nevertheless, very important that the program reach a coherent solution, even if just a

---

[10]Implementations of both of these languages have been made with "do-this-bit-in-parallel" constructs [e.g., 12 and 4], and much work is now focusing on the automatic extraction of parallelism in these languages, but as yet no symbolic programming equivalent of a vectorizing FORTRAN compiler has been produced. This is because it is generally not known at compile time whether any given expression is worth evaluating in parallel given the costs of process creation and such-like.

[11]In fact, this graph can be of semi-infinite size and often has to be computed on demand; cf. the game tree for a chess game.

[12]If search dominates the computation, then massively parallel machines such as the Connection Machine [14] may well prove to have the best performance.

satisficing one. It is no good if different parts of the solution space have mutually contradictory local solutions which contribute to the overall solution. Because the knowledge that goes into such systems is usually implemented in distinct chunks, which may know little about the operations performed by other such chunks, there is significant potential for the system getting confused as different subsystems "trample on each others' toes." This means that it is by no means a trivial issue to make sure that a coherent or convergent solution is achieved by problem-solving systems. This problem is exacerbated by the asynchronous behavior which can happen in MIMD parallel systems. The Poligon system is designed to help the programmer arrive at coherent solutions whilst still encouraging parallelism at a fine grain.

2.3.4 Programming

Heuristic programs are typically large and their density is great.[13] This means that their code encapsulates a great deal of knowledge. It is difficult to write such programs for a number of reasons.

- It is difficult to acquire the knowledge that goes into them since this is typically not encoded already in a formal algorithmic way.
- It is difficult to represent the knowledge once it has been acquired. For instance, the programming associated with implementing a statement such as "Control of center is very important during openings" would be considerable.
- Good, clean implementations of such systems need to maintain the logical independence of the knowledge in the system. This is because failure to do so can result in systems that are very brittle when knowledge is executed in new orders or when new knowledge is added. The interconnectedness of knowledge is often difficult to determine when the knowledge is formulated. Clearly, having dependencies between pieces of knowledge could have a significant impact on the amount of parallelism that could be extracted from such a program and on the program's ability to get the "right" answer.

It is therefore a major concern of AI programmers that these programs should be easy to implement, debug, modify, and maintain.

3   POLIGON: A SYSTEM FOR PARALLEL PROBLEM SOLVING

In this section we describe Poligon. Poligon is an attempt to produce a system which addresses the issues mentioned above to support the development of parallel AI systems. It represents, in many ways, an attempt to find an analog for and implement a parallel form of existing AI systems, known as *blackboard systems* [21].

A brief description of the important aspects of blackboard systems will be given and

---

[13]This means that the number of executed machine instructions for each line in the source code is typically very large.

then Poligon itself will be described, structurally, in the way in which it matches its problem domain, and the way in which it is matched to its target hardware.

3.1 Blackboard Systems

Blackboard systems are instances of a particular computational or problem-solving model—the "blackboard" model or metaphor. This metaphor takes as its source the idea of a collection of experts gathered around a blackboard (see Figure 1). Each expert has a specific domain of expertise, which relates to how a part of the problem at hand is to be solved. The experts look at the blackboard for representations of the problem which are of interest to their specific area of expertise. Having found such a piece of information, the expert performs whatever operations are necessary and posts any conclusions on the blackboard. This new representation of part of the solution might itself be of interest to another expert, and so the process continues.

It is clear from this that the sum of the knowledge in the system must be sufficient to connect all of these areas of expertise. With less knowledge than this the problem simply will not be soluble. With more knowledge than this it should be possible to achieve successively higher performance from the system, be it faster solutions or better solutions.

This simple model has considerable intellectual appeal and has been the cause of substantial research. It is often claimed that all of these "experts" should be able to operate simultaneously. The Poligon system represents an attempt to test this assertion.

Figure 1. The blackboard metaphor. The expert Eegar uses encoded knowledge and comes to a startling conclusion.

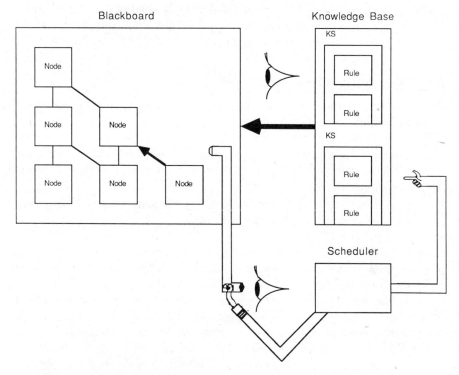

Figure 2. A serial blackboard system. Here, the scheduler notices a modification event and invokes a knowledge source.

Blackboard systems are typically implemented as large data structures—the blackboard—in which are stored the elements of the possible solutions, called *nodes,* which are typically linked together in some way to form a complex graph. There are normally a large number of these nodes representing everything from the input data through intermediate solutions to high-level abstractions of the current state of the solution. Nodes have internal structure, which allows the mapping of names onto values. They are usually made up of a collection of named *slots,* or *fields,* which contain data pertinent to the solution. The knowledge in the system is usually implemented as a collection of pattern–action *rules* collected into groups called *knowledge sources* (*KSs*) [19]. These reside in an area referred to as the *knowledge base* (see Figure 2).

3.1.1   Consistency and Coherence

Reaching a coherent solution (discussed in Section 2.3.3) in a blackboard system is a function of achieving consistency in a number of aspects:

Node Level   The program should create the right number of nodes representing the elements in the solution, and they should be connected together correctly.

Slot Level   The slots in the nodes should contain a respectable representation of the state of that node and its relationship to others.

Rule Execution   When rules are executed, they should do so in an environment
which is internally consistent. This means that any information used in the rule
during its execution should be based on a consistent snapshot of reality.

3.2   A Description of Poligon

Poligon is a framework for the development of blackboard-like applications on a
(simulated) multiprocessor. It consists of

1. a compiler, which compiles a high-level description of the blackboard's structure
   and the knowledge to be applied by the system, to run on a distributed memory
   multiprocessor; and
2. a run time system, which provides a debugging and testing environment for
   Poligon programs as well as run time support.

Both the compiler and the run time system are thoroughly integrated with the
program development environment of Explorer[TM, 14] Lisp machines, the machine on
which the execution of Poligon programs are simulated.

Serial blackboard systems are implemented with the nodes being represented as
records on the blackboard.[15] The knowledge is encoded in knowledge sources. These
are typically compiled into procedures which are invoked by the blackboard system's
kernel. There is some form of scheduler for the knowledge, which invokes one knowledge source after another. The blackboard and the knowledge base both share the same
address space, though they are functionally distinct. Knowledge sources are "invoked"
(executed) as a result of changes in the blackboard placing that change event in a queue
used by the scheduler. The scheduler repeatedly picks a knowledge source which is
interested in the type of event at the end of the queue.

The design of Poligon has been motivated by the idea of trying to eliminate the
bottlenecks that would be experienced if an existing, serial blackboard system were to
be parallelized by the inclusion of do-this-bit-in-parallel constructs.[16] The major
changes from this model are noted below:

- The scheduling queue of a serial system is eliminated altogether in Poligon. This
  means that concurrent attempts to invoke rules are not held up waiting for access
  to this shared data structure.
- Having a knowledge base, which is logically distinct from the blackboard, is no
  longer necessary since there is now nothing to get between them to control the
  application of the knowledge. This allows all knowledge to be attached to those
  nodes that are interested in the knowledge by the compiler (see Figure 3).

[14]Explorer is a trademark of Texas Instruments Incorporated.

[15]These records might well be PASCAL-like records or instances of some class in the native system's
object-oriented package.

[16]The Cage system [1] is an example of a considerably more conservative approach to the parallelizing of
blackboard systems.

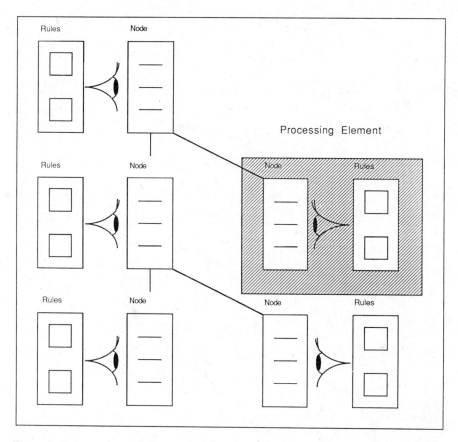

Figure 3. Poligon's blackboard. Nodes are seen linked together being watched by rules, waiting for modification events.

These changes eliminate at one stroke the bottlenecks of the shared scheduler and the knowledge-base-to-blackboard interface. These changes allowed the development of the idea of the "node-as-processor" metaphor for parallel blackboard systems.

Having eliminated the scheduling mechanism, however, one needs some means of determining when a certain piece of knowledge should be invoked. It would be hopelessly inefficient to have all of the knowledge executed all of the time since most of the time it would find itself inapplicable. It was decided that a simple *daemon-driven* approach would be used to avoid this problem. This results in the knowledge being directly sensitive to changes in the blackboard and able to act immediately upon any such changes.

Existing blackboard systems often express the knowledge in their knowledge sources as collections of pattern–action rules. These are normally executed serially, in the lexical order in which they are defined. Poligon, on the other hand, compiles knowledge sources away all together, allowing their constituent rules to be executed in parallel.

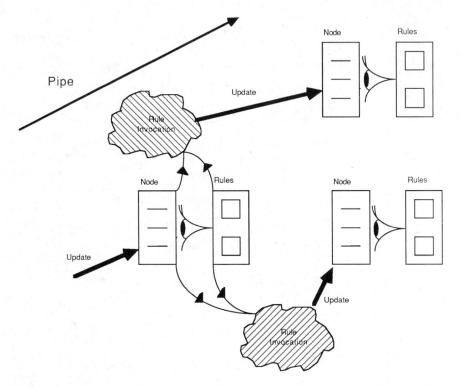

Figure 4. Poligon's execution model. An update to a node triggers concurrent rule invocations, which in turn update other nodes. Pipes are formed as changes to the Blackboard flow from one node to another.

The node-as-processor metaphor is itself a major step away from the normal means of implementing blackboard systems. This, however, is not enough. This would give us data parallelism, resulting from the large number of nodes in the system being able simultaneously to execute rules while still failing to exploit the potential knowledge parallelism. This is because each processing element is a uniprocessor clearly capable of executing at most one rule at a time.[17] Poligon, therefore, goes beyond this simple model to one which would more accurately be called the "rule invocation-as-process" model. This allows the Poligon system to distribute concurrent rule invocations to different processing elements (see Figure 4).

The elimination of serializing components in a blackboard system also eliminates those mechanisms which are normally used to preserve coherency in the solution. Clearly there is a trade-off which can be made between the amount of control- and coherency-preserving mechanisms and the amount of exploitable parallelism. Poligon

---

[17]Each element allows multiple processes, but only one is executed at any time.

is an experiment to explore one extreme of this spectrum. It remains to be seen whether the trade-off made in Poligon results in an overall improvement in system performance.

3.3   How Poligon Matches the Problem Domain

Poligon is not a general-purpose programming language, other than in the *Turing complete* sense [30]. It is specialized to support one computational model, and that computational model, itself, has limitations on its sphere of reasonable applicability. It has been designed with applications such as real-time signal understanding and data fusion in mind, though applications outside this domain are being investigated.

The structure of the problem domain is one that requires the representation of a large number of distinct entities in the solution space. For example, the vocabulary of the problem domain is full of such things as aircraft, radar-emitting platforms, and radar track segments. Poligon provides a rich representation language in which these objects and specializations of them can be expressed. This allows the system to take full advantage of the mutual independence of any of the objects in the solution space to exploit parallelism.

3.4   How Poligon Matches Its Target Hardware

Poligon could, of course, run on any machine in principle. In practice, however, it has been designed with a particular kind of machine model in mind and has been optimized to take advantage of it. This class of target machine, which was briefly described in Section 2.2.2, is exemplified by certain kinds of message-passing, distributed-memory multiprocessors. The grain size of the executable chunks in Poligon programs is designed to suit this model; that is, each chunk represents, ideally, a few function calls. This makes it coarser grained than those systems that want to execute everything that can be in parallel, for instance, data flow machines [10], but it is a lot finer grained than most other concurrent blackboard systems, such as in ref. 18, where each processing element contains a complete Blackboard System.

The target machine model, being of the distributed-memory, message-passing variety including essentially no capability to pass references, strongly discourages shared variables or mutable global data of any sort and encourages a message-passing style of programming. The Poligon language is one in which the programmer is given an abstract view of programming using the blackboard problem-solving model. The Poligon language has no construct for message sending at all, nor has it any primitives by which the user has access to the underlying architecture or topology. It is assumed to be the duty of the Poligon system or the target machine's operating system to look after such concerns. The Poligon compiler compiles its programs into the message-passing primitives of the underlying system. This allows the efficient use of the underlying architecture, whilst leaving the source program uncluttered by concrete details of the target architecture.

Poligon allows only global constants, but not variables, since these can be distributed at program load time.

3.5   What We Have Learned

Truth comes out of error more easily than out of confusion.

—Francis Bacon

Experiments with Poligon are by no means complete, but we have learned quite a bit so far. Some of these lessons are shown below.

- It is very hard to write any program which implements either a framework such as Poligon or an application such as those which have been mounted on Poligon. This is due largely to asynchronous side effects. A system with better formal properties would be less error prone in this respect but might well make less efficient use of the hardware. These difficulties could also be caused by an insufficiency of mechanisms to control coherency in Poligon (see Section 3.1.1).
- In order to produce a reliable program, it is necessary to write code which makes no assumptions about anything that any other part of the system might be doing. Failure to do so results in brittle systems.
- In order to achieve a coherent solution, it was found to be necessary to develop a number of programming methodologies. These will be covered in the same form as they were introduced in Section 3.1.1.

Node Level   The creation of nodes is tricky. Because each element is likely to represent some real-world object, such as an aircraft, it is important either to provide a mechanism for resolving the conflict caused by multiple asynchronous requests to create an element that represents the same thing or to provide a mechanism for managing the creation of nodes. Poligon opts for the latter approach.

Slot Level   The programmer should cause each node to have an idea of how to improve its own idea of the solution—to have goals. In Poligon this is done at a fine grain, with each field of each element in the solution being able to have associated with it functions which enable it to evaluate itself. This state of affairs has been observed in a different manifestation at a larger grain size in [6]. It was found that a good axiom for programming these systems is "Never throw away any data unless you are convinced that you have better data." This is the sort of behavior that is used in the evaluation functions mentioned above.

Rule Execution   Poligon attempts to maintain the smallest critical sections possible. The original implementation of Poligon, in fact, had as its only atomic actions reading a field and writing a field. It was soon found that in order to maintain consistency during rule execution, it had to be possible to read the values from a number of fields simultaneously—taking a snapshot without the subject moving. This, coupled with critical sections for the writing of collections of values, allows confidence that the picture that one sees when taking such a snapshot of a node is consistent, even if not necessarily the most up to date. It is important for a Poligon programmer to be aware that the node of which a snapshot has been taken may well be read from and written to by other rules asynchronously during the invocation of the rule taking the snapshot.

4   EXPERIMENTS

In this section we describe, briefly, a series of experiments being performed by the Advanced Architectures Project [25] at Stanford University on the Poligon system and on Cage [1] and Lamina [8], other systems developed as part of the same project. However, these experiments will be discussed only in the context of the Poligon system.

It would be premature to quote any hard-and-fast performance figures here since we still have much to do in order to understand the results that we are getting. The main purpose of reporting these experiments is to show the lessons that have been learned both from performing the experiments and about the ways in which Poligon behaves.[18]

4.1   The Problem

Each of the systems mentioned above has been used to implement an application called "Elint," a problem in the domain of real-time interpretation of passive radar signal data [2].

The problem is one of receiving reports from radar systems, abstracting these into hypothetical radar-emitting aircraft, and tracking them as they travel through the monitored airspace. These aircraft are themselves abstracted into clusters—perhaps formations—which are themselves tracked. The nature of the radar emissions from the aircraft are interpreted in order to determine the intentions and degree of threat of each of the clusters of emitters.

The Elint application has a number of characteristics which are of significance:

- The system must be able to deal with a continuous data stream. It is not acceptable to wait until all of the data has been read in and then figure out what is going on.
- The application domain is potentially very data parallel. The ability to reason about a large number of aircraft simultaneously is very important. What is more, the aircraft themselves, as objects in the solution space, are quite loosely coupled.
- The application is knowledge poor. This means that the experiments performed were geared primarily to evaluating the performance of these systems with respect to data parallelism, not knowledge parallelism.

4.2   The Purpose of the Experiments

I see no mention of God.

—Napoleon

---

[18]Since this chapter was written many more experiments have been performed and their results published in refs. 7 and 22.

I had no need of that hypothesis.

—Laplace

These experiments have five main objectives:

1. To investigate methods of achieving speedup for expert system applications by mounting them on parallel hardware architectures.[19]
2. To build a number of systems using different computational and problem-solving models and compare their relative performance and thus to deduce an appropriate course for future research. It is therefore imperative that, to the greatest degree possible, each of the systems should implement the same application and should perform the same experiments.
3. To perform experiments on individual systems specialized to investigate the characteristics of each computational model, which might not be shown by the experiments mentioned above and which are not shared by other systems.
4. Having done these experiments, it should be possible to draw some conclusions about the amount of speedup attainable given these architectures. This should help one to conclude whether these architectures are in fact appropriate and efficient for parallel implementation.
5. The implementation of the Elint system in Poligon was intentionally not tuned. This means that it was a copy of the original serial implementation modified only in so far as it was necessary in order to make it solve problems correctly in parallel. The intent was to achieve a reasonable measure of the performance of an average system that might be written by a Poligon user as opposed to a very highly tuned version.

4.3   A Description of the Experiments Performed on Poligon

Deciding exactly which experiments to perform is difficult since there are a very large number of variable factors in the system. Among these are the implementation of the Elint system, the characteristics of the data sets used, and the numerous machine simulation parameters including processor and communications network performance. However, it was decided to freeze most of these and perform a number of experiments, having chosen "reasonable," justifiable values for the frozen parameters. We have, in fact, learned a lot from this process, and this has helped us to design a better set of experiments which are now being performed.

The primary variable factor for these experiments is the data set used to drive the experiment. This data set represents a simulated set of radar observations. These data sets are of finite length. The *length, number of simulated emitters* and *radar observation frequency over time*[20] are the main variable factors in the data sets.

To perform each of these experiments, the simulated rate at which data arrived in the system was fixed at a value which was high enough to prevent data starvation when

---

[19]"Expert systems" are AI systems which attempt explicitly to encode the knowledge of human experts.
[20]Radar system reports per simulated time unit

running the experiment on the largest reasonable processor grid. This meant that the speedup for a grid of size N could be measured simply by dividing the time taken for the grid of size 1 by the time taken by the simulation of the N-sized grid.[21]

It should be noted that these early experiments are open to some criticism as being unrealistic. They represent the speedup for given programs under some fixed conditions. The conditions that are fixed may not be reasonable. For instance, if the program being run was merely a parallel implementation of *Quicksort,* then these would be reasonable experiments. Unfortunately, because the implementations of Elint are intended to be real-time[22] systems, it is not realistic to load the system in this way. The problem-solving behavior of the system is sensitive to machine load. Systems running with smaller numbers of processors will be more heavily loaded. They may, therefore, spend a lot of time queue thrashing.

For this reason it is now known that these experimental results should not be taken at face value. More satisfactory experiments have been devised in which the experiment is run for a given number of processors with the data rate being varied until the latency of the output traces is constant over time. This means that the maximum sustainable data rate without increasing latency in the system's outputs is the preferred measure of the speedup for these systems.

4.3.1   Experiment 1

> The Fusion Plasma requires a temperature of 500 million degrees, but I forget whether that's Centigrade or Absolute.
> —Overheard by Arthur H. Snell, Oak Ridge National Laboratory.

This experiment was intended to be a simple cross-comparison experiment performed by all of the systems. Its data set was a simple and quite small one, which contained observations of sufficient variety to exercise all of the system's required behavior.

The speedup figures produced showed a peak speedup for the system of about 4.5 times for 64 processors, with the speedup trailing off quite sharply. This was disappointing.

One of the problems with this experiment was that the data set was varied in the frequency of input data for the system over time. It was sparse at the beginning, heavy in the middle, and sparse at the end. This resulted in the system being data starved near the beginning of the simulation and then flooded in the middle.

Although such spikes in input data are entirely characteristic of real data, this extra variable factor was thought to be too difficult to factor out in order to arrive at a realistic speedup figure. If the system is lightly loaded, then not much speedup is needed. For

---

[21]Performing experiments in this way was intended to give a baseline set of results of the same form as those derived from the CAOS system's implementation of Elint [26] and of the Lamina implementation of Airtrac, another application [19]. For the reasons mentioned in this section this might not be a good baseline for comparison.

[22]"Real time" is used here in the sense that the system must cope with an unbounded continuous stream of data whilst delivering results reasonably promptly. It is not intended to refer to those real-time systems where guaranteed response times might be required.

this reason all subsequent experiments have been and will be performed on data sets that have a constant frequency of input data.

The most important thing to conclude from this result is that we had much to learn about how to conduct these experiments.

4.3.2   Experiment 2

This experiment was designed to compensate for the variability found in the data set used in experiment 1. The data set had a constant frequency for input data over time.

This experiment showed that the peak speedup had increased to about seven times, which was reached after 16 processors. This result was somewhat better than that from experiment 1, supporting our hypothesis that the shape of the input data was affecting our results. Analysis of the simulator's instrumentation indicated that the limiting factor in the parallelism detected was probably a bottleneck on a particular node representing a cluster of emitters. It also showed that even if all bottlenecks were eliminated so that all pipes were balanced, a major limiting factor in the performance of the system was that there was not enough parallelism at this grain size available in the data set for this system to exploit.

4.3.3   Experiment 3

This experiment was intended to determine how efficiently the simulated hardware architecture was being used and thus show where effort would best be expended to speed up the system if the application could not be changed structurally. To achieve this, experiment 2 (Section 4.3.2) was repeated a number of times, but for each iteration the simulated speed of the processor was varied. This gave speedup figures for processor performances which were two, four, and eight times the speed of the processor simulated in experiment 2.[23] All of the speedup figures produced were then normalized against the case of experiment 2. A significant reduction in the speedup of the system would have indicated that the increasing performance of the processor was swamping the communication hardware, thus indicating that time and effort would better be spent on improving communication performance.

It was found that the normalized speedups matched each other very closely. This is taken to indicate that if such a machine were to be implemented for Poligon programs, effort spent on improving the processor's performance or in optimizing the program would probably be rewarded by close to linear speedup.

4.3.4   Discussion of Experiments: What We Have Learned.

> Experience is the name everyone gives to their mistakes.
> —Oscar Wilde, "Lady Windermere's Fan"

As has already been mentioned, the experiments on these systems are in their infancy. It is essential for the reader to note, therefore, that these results should be taken as

---

[23]For each of these experiments the simulated input data rate was also increased so as to factor out this change.

nothing more than indication of where our research is leading, rather than hard-and-fast statements about the performance of these systems.

We have, however, learned quite a bit in the execution of these experiments. The more important of these lessons are noted below:

- Getting useful speedup out of these systems, at least given the current level of our understanding and methodologies, is very difficult. The speedups shown for the experiments mentioned in this section may, indeed, have been achievable by very careful coding on a uniprocessor. These difficulties are characterized mainly by the difficulty of implementing the program and debugging it and of combating serial components in the processing.

- Problem-solving systems such as the ones mentioned in this chapter are significantly more complex than those programs normally implemented to evaluate experimental parallel hardware. Our difficulty in getting results indicates that there is more to getting useful speedup for real problems than there is to demonstrating speedup for Quicksort programs [e.g., 9].

- The domain of real-time systems is one in which the AI community in general and this project in particular has little experience. This has made implementation of these systems and the analysis of them difficult. The selection of a different field for research, outside that of real-time systems, would have alleviated this problem but would have removed the area of experimentation from an important area of application where it is believed that speedup through parallelism is both necessary and feasible.

- Real-time systems present a set of problems for performance evaluation so great that it is difficult to formulate easily analyzable experiments and draw worthwhile conclusions from them. These problems are caused by the need for continuous data, end effects when the data is bounded in extent, and the difficulty of defining suitable performance measures and Heisenbergian effects; that is, changes in system load during speedup measurement changing the speedup itself.

- Investigation of the amount of "knowledge parallelism" has been limited by the relatively small amount of knowledge available in this area. New applications are being sought in which more knowledge is available. This has concentrated the investigation on the extraction of data parallelism from these systems.

- The data sets for the experiments mentioned above are limited in the amount of data parallelism that can be extracted from them. To add to this problem, the Poligon system is sufficiently difficult to simulate that experiments with significantly larger data sets are probably not feasible.

- The immediate conclusion that one is led to by these results is that a relatively simplistic implementation of a system can lead to speedups on the order of 10 fold. It seems to be possible to get higher speedups from such systems, but at least at present, only by very careful coding and very careful and thorough instrumentation of the running system so that bottlenecks can be eliminated.

- So far, it has not been possible to demonstrate overall speedups of more than ~8 fold using Poligon. The hypothesis that Poligon's implementation of Elint will be able to exploit data parallelism as larger data sets are used remains, as yet, untested, though tentative results from an implementation of Elint in Lamina (~23 fold) and Airtrac in Lamina [19] (~80 fold) give cause for hope, indicating that with larger data sets there definitely is more parallelism to extract.

5 CONCLUSIONS

There is something fascinating about science. One gets such wholesale returns of conjecture out of such a trifling investment of fact.
—Mark Twain, "Life on the Mississippi"

This chapter has introduced the problems associated with attempts to achieve speedup though parallelism for problem-solving systems, systems developed in the AI field. Numerous applications for such systems would benefit greatly from being sped up considerably. Because of their irregular structure, such systems are shown to be difficult to speed up through well-established means.

The Poligon [24] system was described. Poligon is an attempt to create a system which is able to encourage the decomposition of a particular class of problem-solving systems, known as blackboard systems, into a form which can be efficiently executed by it on a distributed-memory, message-passing multiprocessor.

The Poligon system has been implemented and an application called "Elint" has been implemented using it. Lessons learned in the implementation of Poligon and the Elint application are detailed.

Experiments are now being performed on the Elint application, both for the implementation mentioned in Poligon and also for systems called Lamina [8] and Cage[1]. Some preliminary experimental results are shown. Lessons learned from these experiments are described. Some of these are mentioned below:

- It is very difficult to implement both frameworks for concurrent problem-solving and concurrent problem-solving systems themselves. This is due largely to the difficulty of coping with asynchronous events caused largely by these systems being MIMD systems.
- Real-time systems are difficult systems to calibrate for the purposes of experimentation to evaluate speedup.
- Modest speedup has been achieved (~8 fold). Indications of higher performance (~23–80 times) are thought possible through the exploitation of more data parallelism [19].
- The potential for the exploitation of knowledge parallelism has not yet been investigated.
- If these results are supported by further work, they would indicate that large amounts of parallelism at this grain size might not be easily achieved for this type of AI system. Thus, if there is not a lot of knowledge to apply, if there is not a lot of data parallelism available, and if there are not many alternatives to explore in the application, it may be that a software architecture optimized for a distributed-

memory hardware architecture is not appropriate. This does not mean, however, that implementation techniques such as data copying and a message-passing metaphor often used in distributed-memory systems are not appropriate for a shared-memory implementation since they can help to avoid bottlenecks.

Report writing, like motor-car driving and love-making, is one of those activities which every Englishman thinks he can do well without instruction. The results are of course usually abominable.

—Tom Margerison, reviewing *Writing Technical Reports,*
by Bruce M. Cooper in the *Sunday Times,* 3 January 1965

ACKNOWLEDGMENTS

The author gratefully acknowledges the support of the following agencies for this project: DARPA/RADC, under contract number F30602-85-C-0012; NASA, under contract NCC 2-220; and Boeing Computer Services, under contract number W-266875. This chapter originally appeared in the proceedings of the Third International Conference on Supercomputing, May 1988.

REFERENCES

1. N. Aiello, "User-Directed Control of Parallelism; The CAGE System," Technical Report KSL-86-31, Heuristic Programming Project, Department of Computer Science, Stanford University, 1986.

2. H. Brown, E. Schoen, and B. A. Delagi, "An Experiment in Knowledge-Base Signal Understanding Using Parallel Architectures," Technical Report STAN-CS-86-1136, Heuristic Programming Project, Department of Computer Science, Stanford University, 1986.

3. G. T. Byrd and B. A. Delagi, "Considerations for Multiprocessor Topologies," Technical Report KSL-87-07, Heuristic Programming Project, Department of Computer Science, Stanford University, 1987.

4. K. Clark and S. Gregory, "PARLOG: Parallel Programming in Logic, Technical Report Research Report DOC 84/4, Department of Computing, Imperial College of Science and Technology, 1985.

5. W. F. Clocksin and C. S. Mellish, *Programming in PROLOG,* Springer-Verlag, Berlin, 1981.

6. D. D. Corkill and V. R. Lesser, "The Use of Meta-Level Control for Coordination in a Distributed Problem Solving Network," in *Proceedings of the Eighth International Joint Conference on Artificial Intelligence,* William Kaufmann Inc., Los Altos, 1983.

7. B. A. Delagi and N. P. Saraiya, "ELINT in LAMINA: Application of a Concurrent Object Language," Technical Report KSL-88-3, Heuristic Programming Project, Department of Computer Science, Stanford University, 1988.

8. B. A. Delagi, N. P. Saraiya, and G. T. Byrd, "LAMINA: CARE Applications Interface," Technical Report KSL-86-67, Heuristic Programming Project, Department of Computer Science, Stanford University, 1986.

9. J. Deminet, "Experience with Multiprocessor Algorithms," *IEEE Transactions on Computers,* **C-31**(4):278–287, April 1982.

10. J. B. Dennis, "Data Flow Supercomputers," *IEEE Computer,* 48–56, November 1980.

11. M. Flynn, "Some Computer Organizations and their Effectiveness," *IEEE Transactions on Computers,* **C-21**:948–960, 1972.

12. R. P. Gabriel and J. McCarthy, "Queue-based Multi-processing Lisp," in *Proceedings of the ACM Symposium on Lisp and Functional Programming,* August 1984, pp. 25–44.

13. A. Gupta, "Parallelism in Production Systems," Ph.D. Thesis, Department of Computer Science, Carnegie-Mellon University, March 1986.

14. W. D. Hillis, *The Connection Machine,* MIT Press, Cambridge, MA, 1985.

15. D. J. Kuck, R. H. Kuhn, D. A. Padua, B. Leasure, and M. Wolfe, "Dependence Graph and Compiler Optimizations," in *Proceedings of the Eighth ACM Symposium on Principles of Programming Languages,* ACM Press, New York, January 1981.

16. H. T. Kung and C. E. Leiserson, "Systolic Arrays (for VLSI)," in I. S. Duff and G. W. Stewart (Eds.), *Sparse Matrix Proceedings,* Society for Industrial and Applied Mathematics, Philadelphia, 1978, pp. 256–282.

17. G. Lee, C. P. Kruskal, and D. J. Kuck, "An Empirical Study of the Automatic Restructuring on Nonnumerical Programs," *IEEE Transactions on Computers,* 1985.

18. V. R. Lesser and D. D. Corkill, "The Distributed Vehicle Monitoring Testbed: A Tool for Investigation Distributed Problem Solving Networks," *The AI Magazine,* Fall 1983, pp. 15–33.

19. R. T. Nakano and M. Minami, "Experiments with a Knowledge-Based System on a Multiprocessor," Technical Report KSL-87-61, Heuristic Programming Project, Department of Computer Science, Stanford University, 1987.

20. H. P. Nii, "An Introduction to Knowledge Engineering, Blackboard Model, and AGE," Technical Report HPP-80-20, Heuristic Programming Project, Department of Computer Science, Stanford University, March 1980.

21. H. P. Nii, "Blackboard Systems," Technical Report KSL-86-18, Knowledge Systems Laboratory, Computer Science Department, Stanford University, April 1986; *AI Magazine,* **7-2** and **7-3**, 1986.

22. H. P. Nii, N. Aiello, and J. P. Rice, "Experiments on Cage and Poligon: Measuring the Performance of Parallel Blackboard Systems," Technical Report KSL-88-66, Heuristic Programming Project, Department of Computer Science, Stanford University, 1988.

23. H. Petard, "A Contribution to the Mathematical Theory of Big Game Hunting," *American Mathematical Monthly,* **45**:446, 1938.

24. J. P. Rice, "The Poligon User's Manual," Technical Report KSL-86-10, Heuristic Programming Project, Department of Computer Science, Stanford University, 1986.

25. J. P. Rice, "The Advanced Architecture Project," Technical Report KSL-88-71, Heuristic Programming Project, Department of Computer Science, Stanford University, 1988.

26. E. Schoen, "The CAOS System," Technical Report STAN-CS-86-1125, Heuristic Programming Project, Computer Science Department, Stanford University, April 1986.

27. H. Seifert and W. Threfall, Lehrbuch der Topologie, Academic Press, New York, 1934.

28. C. L. Seitz, "The Cosmic Cube," *Communications of the ACM,* **28**:22–33, 1985.

29. G. L. Steele Jr., *Common Lisp,* Digital Press, Burlington, MA, 1984.

30. A. M. Turing," On Computable Numbers, with an Application to the Entscheidungs-

problem," *Proceedings of London Mathematical Society,* **2**(42,43):230–265, 544–546, 1936.

31. A. W. Wilson Jr., "Hierarchical Cache/Bus Architecture for Shared Memory Multi-processors," *Proceedings of the Fourteenth Symposium on Computer Architectures,* IEEE Computer Society Press, Washington, D.C., 1987, pp. 244–252.

PART II
Reasoning by Simulation in Artificial Intelligence Systems

10 Qualitative Reasoning with Causal Models in Diagnosis of Complex Systems

BENJAMIN KUIPERS

Department of Computer Sciences
The University of Texas at Austin
Austin, Texas

1 INTRODUCTION

This chapter describes research that we have been doing in qualitative reasoning. The goal of this work is to understand the role that qualitative reasoning about the structure and behavior of mechanisms might play in medical diagnosis. Although the motivation for this work is medical diagnosis, some of the examples discussed are of simple physical systems, and we anticipate that our results will be applicable to a variety of nonmedical domains.

This chapter discusses the motivation for using qualitative causal models as part of a diagnostic process. The nature of qualitative models is described and an example given of a qualitative model of a relatively simple medical mechanism, the water balance mechanism of the kidney. Finally, in somewhat more detail a recent development that shows promise of solving certain previously open problems in qualitative reasoning is discussed.

2 WHY QUALITATIVE MODELS IN DIAGNOSIS?

The first question is "Why should we not be satisfied with the existing methods for diagnosis in expert systems?" The first generation of expert systems—MYCIN [18], CASNET [19], PIP [16], MDX [2], and INTERNIST-I [13]—represents an impressive accomplishment. The level of performance of these programs in their domain of medicine has been generally comparable to that of expert physicians [6, 20]. Nonetheless, they have not been widely and successfully adapted for daily use.

We must then ask, "Why not?" I would argue that the first-generation systems simply cannot handle the range of unusual cases that are normally encountered in real-world situations. Although these systems may be able to handle the typical and classic cases, there are many less typical cases that experts can handle very straightforwardly using their commonsense knowledge or slightly more specialized *expert common sense* that simply cannot be expressed in the first-generation programs. For example, the first generation of programs describes a disease or fault hypothesis in terms of a set of expected findings, but we sometimes encounter abnormal cases which are idiosyncratic instances of particular diseases or faults. In such cases, it may be quite difficult for a program such as INTERNIST to confirm a diagnosis when the expected features are not seen. In some of our experiments in the medical domain, my collaborator (Dr. J. P. Kassirer of the Tufts University School of Medicine) and I have used a case of nephrotic syndrome in which the patient is a vegetarian and spontaneously on an extremely low-salt diet. The expected finding of edema in this patient is missing, but the physicians we studied were able to discover and explain the discrepancy and complete the diagnosis [12].

Another very common situation, perhaps not statistically as common as single diagnosis but still frequently encountered, is a case in which multiple faults interact in a particular finding [15]. If we see a patient whose blood tests suggest both an acidosis (too much acid in the blood) and an alkalosis (too little acid in the blood) arising from separate processes occurring simultaneously, then depending on the severity of the two problems, the observed serum pH (a measure of blood acidity) could be anything. An expert human physician has no trouble understanding what the problem is. However, the first-generation programs have a great deal of trouble expressing the knowledge that is necessary to understand the interactions between diseases or faults or the unusual context provided by particular cases.

The fundamental problem is that first-generation expert systems do not understand the processes which underlie observable findings. Therefore, they do not understand how the mechanisms in their faulty or diseased states function to produce the observed behaviors. This is because the knowledge in the first generation of programs consists essentially of numerically weighted associations between observations and disease or fault hypotheses.

Figure 1 shows two fragments of knowledge extracted from MYCIN and INTERNIST-I, two programs based in the medical domain. In MYCIN, a rule consists of antecedent clauses, consequent clauses, and a certainty factor. The first antecedent clause tests the state of the problem-solving process, but the remaining clauses test for directly observable characteristics of the patient case. The consequent is an assertion of a certain hypothesis about the identity of the disease. The certainty factor gives us a numerical weight for the association. Similarly, in INTERNIST-I, we have a diagnostic hypothesis, a set of observable findings, and in this case, two separate weights for different aspects of the relation between the findings and the hypothesis. In neither case is there any knowledge of how the mechanisms of the body work.

The CASNET program [19] does contain certain kinds of causal knowledge about how a disease mechanism may work, although not the same kind as will be described here.

3   A MECHANISM EXPLAINS THE OBSERVATIONS

The question now becomes "How should we build programs that *do* understand how the body and other complex systems work, and what should be asked of those

• MYCIN rule

IF: (1) The identity of the organism is not known with certainty, and
(2) The stain of the organism is gramneg, and
(3) The morphology of the organism is rod, and
(4) The aerobicity of the organism is aerobic
THEN: There is strongly suggestive evidence (.8) that the class of the organism is enterobacteriaceae.

• Internist-I manifestation list (partial)

Alcoholic Hepatitis

factor VII proconvertin decreased ... 1 2
LDH blood increased ... 1 3
magnesium blood decreased ... 2 2
prothrombin time increased ... 2 3
SGPT 200 to 600 ... 1 2
SGPT 40 to 199 ... 2 3
SGPT gtr than 600 ... 1 1
liver biopsy bile plugging ... 1 2
liver biopsy fatty metamorphosis ... 2 4
...

Figure 1. Weighted associations in MYCIN and INTERNIST-I.

programs?" We need an explanation, though not necessarily in natural language, that demonstrates how the mechanism behind a hypothesized disease or fault might cause the observed findings [10].

The philosopher Karl Popper defines an explanation in terms of a set of general laws and a set of initial conditions from which we can deduce the observable facts.

To give a **causal explanation** of an event means to deduce a statement which describes it, using as premises of the deduction one or more **universal laws**, together with certain singular statements, the **initial conditions**.

—Karl R. Popper, 1935

Translated to the modeling of a complex mechanism (e.g., the water balance mechanism of the kidneys), an explanation should start with the laws that describe how the mechanism works and a set of facts about its current state and, from that basis, deduce a set of predictions about the behavior of the mechanism over time.

An explanation should also account for the behavior of both the normal as well as the faulty mechanism. We thus want a model which can explain how the normal mechanism responds to normal and abnormal changes in inputs, how a faulty mechanism might produce the observed manifestations, and finally, how different processes and mechanisms can interact. This type of approach is necessary to handle the interactions between separate mechanisms.

Once we can construct such an explanation mechanism or qualitative model, how would we include it in the design of an overall diagnostic program? We would not expect it to simply replace the associational type of diagnostic system. There is a good deal of evidence from psychologists studying physicians that associational reasoning is very important in expert diagnosis [4, 6]. Our view of how causal models of complex

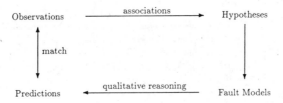

- An associational reasoner proposes diagnostic hypotheses.
- A qualitative reasoner builds models to elaborate and test them.

Figure 2. The hypothesize-and-match problem-solving architecture.

mechanisms should be linked with associational types of reasoning might be characterized as a "hypothesize-and-match" problem-solving architecture (Figure 2) [14].

We start with a set of observations about the state of a system. Using a first-generation associational type of diagnostic system, we propose a set of possible hypotheses, focusing our attention on those that match reasonably well with the observations. The match need not be perfect; possible incorrect matches that an associative system might propose are acceptable because the diagnostic process proceeds to another stage.

Once a diagnostic hypothesis is proposed, we associate with that hypothesis a set of models of the mechanisms involved. These models might include a description of where the fault appears in a mechanism, or they might simply refer to a correctly functioning mechanism that is responding to an unusual environment caused by other factors.

Given a set of relevant mechanism models, we use qualitative reasoning to predict the behavior of the system over time and then match predictions against the observations. Our predictions may also suggest additional observations that should be made.

Through this process of matching predictions with observations, we refute certain hypotheses and elaborate others to produce a more accurate and detailed model of the system's state, filling in parameters that might be otherwise unobservable and predicting the evolution of the system over time.

4   QUALITATIVE SIMULATION

This particular approach to qualitative reasoning is essentially a qualitative abstraction of differential equations. While we need not always start with a differential equation, the abstraction relation (Figure 3) helps us understand the logical status of the qualitative model.

In the real world, physical systems are governed by physical laws, and in an initial situation, they produce actual behavior—something happens. To illustrate this, consider a simple behavior in the context of a gravitational field. If I have a tennis ball in my hand and throw it into the air, it goes up, stops, comes back down, and I catch it.

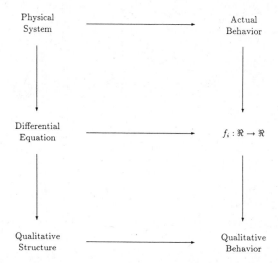

Figure 3. A qualitative model is an abstraction of a differential equation model.

The structure of the system is described by the gravitational field and the initial position and velocity of the ball. The behavior is the ball's trajectory through the air. A physicist describes that physical system in terms of a differential equation, specifying the value of the gravitational constant, the initial velocity, and so forth. The equation is solved in order to obtain a set of functions that describe the way the position and velocity of the ball change over time. The qualitative model is an abstraction of that kind of differential equation, and as I shall discuss, a qualitative description may be constructed even when a differential equation cannot.

The behavioral description, in turn, is a qualitative abstraction of the corresponding continuous functions of time. When I throw the ball up in the air and it comes down, qualitatively I may give a detailed description of that behavior—the ball goes up, it reaches a stopping point, it comes down, and it reaches my hand again. Qualitative reasoning that produces a description at essentially this level of detail is required because this is the level of description that expert humans often use to reason about physical mechanisms.

How are qualitative models to be built and used? Let us take the slightly more complex example of an object oscillating on a spring (Figure 4). The structure of the system is described in terms of the position X, velocity V, and acceleration A of the object (Figure 4a). Derivative constraints state that A is the derivative of V, and V is the derivative of X. The M_0^- constraint is a monotonic function constraint which indicates that there is some (unspecified) monotonically decreasing function $A = M_0^-(X)$. We are not stating that the function is linear: It may be nonlinear, nonsymmetrical, or have other strange properties. We are only stating that there is some (continuously differentiable) monotonic function between those two parameters.

The subscript zero in M_0^- indicates that there are corresponding values, so that $X(t) = 0$ iff $A(t) = 0$. We can write this constraint model as the qualitative differential equation

(a) Structure

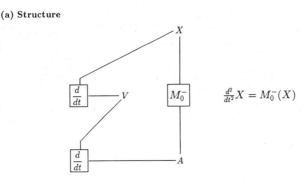

(b) Behavior

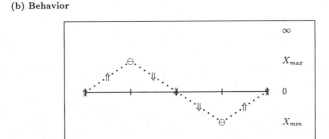

Figure 4. Qualitative structure and behavior of the oscillating spring.

$$\frac{d^2}{dt^2}X = M_0^-(X),$$

which looks very similar to the usual spring equation.

The qualitative behavior (Figure 4b) is described in terms of a quantity space; we plot the qualitative values of X. The value of $X(t)$ is described in terms of qualitative, rather than numerical, values. In this example, the real-number line is described qualitatively as having five landmark values: ∞, X_{max}, 0, X_{min}, and $-\infty$. The magnitude of $X(t)$ at any given point in time is described qualitatively either as being equal to some landmark value or as being in the open interval between two landmarks. There are actually nine possible qualitative magnitudes: five for the landmarks and four for the intervals between them. The time dimension is also described qualitatively in terms of distinguished points and open intervals in time.

The QSIM algorithm for qualitative simulation [8, 9] does not require the maximum and minimum values (X_{max} and X_{min}) to be known in advance. The algorithm determines that the spring cannot go to infinity and creates the landmark values representing the extreme values of X.

Algorithms for qualitative simulation are based on the observation of qualitative transitions (Figure 5). If we assume that variables are changing continuously and that their derivatives are continuous, then if some variable is between two landmark values

(a) Moving toward a limit point

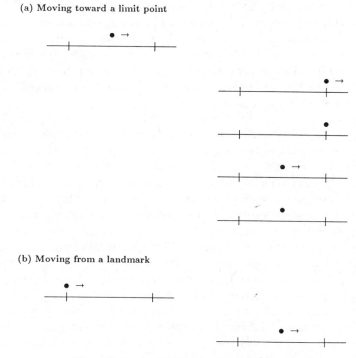

(b) Moving from a landmark

Figure 5. Possible qualitative state transitions.

and increasing, at the next qualitatively distinctive point in time there are four possible states: The variable can be equal to the next landmark and still increasing; it can be equal to that landmark and not increasing, that is, stopped or steady; it may become steady before reaching the landmark; or it may not have reached the landmark and still be increasing (i.e., the value of some *other* variable reached a point of qualitative change). If the variable is currently equal to a landmark value and increasing, there is only one possible future: It must be between the next two landmarks and still increasing. The algorithm determines the possible combinations of those transitions that are consistent with the constraints in the model.

4.1 Qualitative versus Quantitative Models

How can we compare the utility of qualitative versus quantitative models? Much effort has gone into producing quantitative or numerical models of a variety of systems, ranging from the gravitational field, to the kidney, to nuclear power plants. Numerical models are rightly recognized as providing insights into the behavior of a system; qualitative models also have significant advantages. Developing qualitative models to the point where they can be used along with quantitative models may yield the best of both approaches.

First, consider what sort of problems we observe with quantitative models. In trying to make a quantitative numerical simulation of complex systems, we encounter a serious problem: There are many parameter values that are difficult to measure. Furthermore, there are functional relationships between variables that we do not know with complete precision. In order to make a numerical model, we need to make assumptions about those numerical values and the exact shape of those functions or we cannot run the model. And of course, errors in those assumptions can lead to errors in the results provided by the model.

Once we are able to run the model and obtain a numerical description of the behavior, we still do not have a clear notion of what the possible behaviors are and what sort of reliance there is on the initial set of assumptions. The important features of the behavior may be obscured by numerical precision. On the other hand, the big advantage of numerical models is that opposing influences can be specified and balanced. In a numerical simulation of the effect of water intake and water outflow on water balance, the net flow is uniquely determined so the behavior can be predicted uniquely.

The major advantage of a qualitative model over a quantitative model is its capacity to express incomplete states of knowledge. We frequently have incomplete knowledge about the nature of a mechanism. One of the barriers to giving a computer program common sense is that the languages we have to represent knowledge are frequently not capable of expressing incomplete states of knowledge. For example, if all we know about a numerical value is its sign, a numerical simulation requires us to assume an exact numerical value rather than being able to express exactly what we know. The advantage of qualitative models over quantitative models lies in being able to represent incomplete knowledge of functions and values.

Additionally, the qualitatively distinct behaviors of the system may be predicted directly. The design of qualitative reasoning systems is oriented toward predicting the set of qualitatively distinct possible behaviors of a mechanism. Working with qualitative descriptions of quantities, we may not be able to predict the balance between two quantities. If I only know that two opposing quantities are increased, I do not know whether one increases more than the other or whether they increase together. In this case the prediction will branch. Unlike a numerical simulation which predicts a single future, a qualitative simulation may predict multiple possibilities. (I will later discuss a technique for resolving some such branches.)

5   QUALITATIVE MODELS IN MEDICAL PHYSIOLOGY

Now let us turn our attention back to an application area, medicine, and ask how we can use qualitative methods to create a model of an interesting mechanism in the physiology of the kidney, the water balance mechanism. The model of the water balance mechanism has been built to do several things: It can predict the response of the healthy mechanism to a change in the environment; it can express what it means for the mechanism to be defective; and it can predict the response of the defective mechanism to the normal environment or to a change in that environment corresponding to the therapy that a physician may indicate.

Figure 6 is a qualitative description of the structure of the water balance mechanism. There are a number of parameters which are assumed to be constant in the behavior of

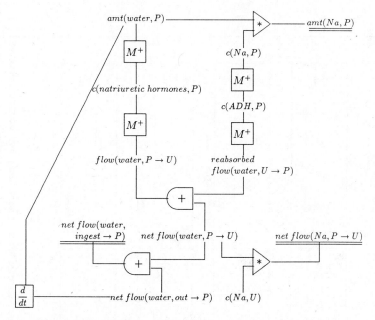

Figure 6. Water balance mechanism: a one-compartment model.

this mechanism: the amount of sodium in the plasma compartment, *amt(Na,P)*; the rate of water ingested into the plasma compartment, *net flow(water, ingest → P)*; and the rate of sodium excretion, *netflow(Na,P → U)*. The principal controlled variable is the amount of water in the plasma compartment, *amt(water,P)*. We see two paths that begin with the amount of water (sometimes called "plasma volume") and control the rate of water excretion from the plasma out into the urine. One path includes the rate of water filtration in the kidney, *flow(water, P → U)*, and the other includes the rate of water reabsorption, *reabsorbedflow(water, U → P)*. The second branch is controlled by the antidiuretic hormone (ADH).

This description captures some of the control paths that participate in the water balance mechanism of the kidney. If I were trying to build a differential equation model to represent this mechanism, I would encounter serious difficulties in that the monotonic functions between the various parameters are not precisely known. For example, even the existence of natriuretic hormones is a recent discovery. However, we do know that these functions exist and are monotonic, so we can reason about them qualitatively even with an incomplete state of knowledge.

5.1 The Normal Mechanism

Let us consider the mechanism's behavior in response to changes to the environment. Figure 7 is an actual screen image of the QSIM algorithm output on a Symbolics LISP machine, and Figure 8 isolates three key parameters from that display. It simulates the response of the water balance mechanism to a sudden increase in the rate of water intake while the amount of sodium remains constant.

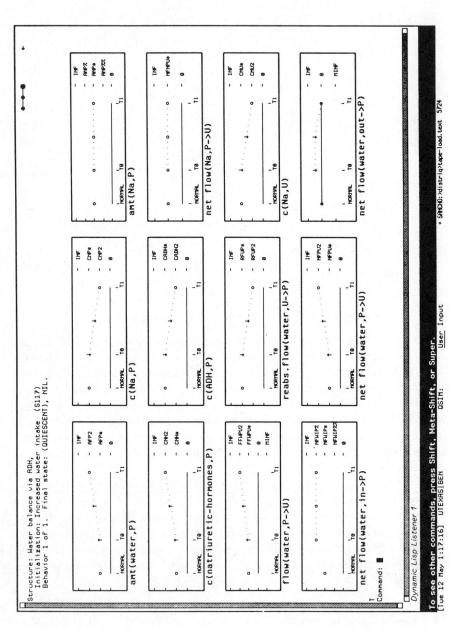

Figure 7. Qualitative behavior of water balance mechanism responding to increased water intake (screen image).

Each qualitative plot shows the normal state of the system to the left of the first time point for reference. At time t_0, the rate of water inflow, *net flow(water, ingest → P)*, is suddenly increased. This puts the body into a nonequilibrium state of positive water balance, as shown by the plot of *net flow(water, out → P)* at the lower right corner of Figure 7. The amount of water in the plasma, *amt(water, P)*, and the rate of excretion, *net flow(water, P → U)*, both increase to compensate for the increased input until the system reaches a new equilibrium state. While the system is moving, we can observe the action of various other parameters, such as the rate of absorption, the level of ADH, and so forth.

5.2   The Defective Mechanism

Figures 7 and 8 showed that in response to a sudden increase in intake, water volume and excretion rate both increased to return the system to equilibrium. In the case of a kidney disorder called SIADH (syndrome of inappropriate secretion of antidiuretic hormone), for some reason external to the mechanism, one of the constraints in the

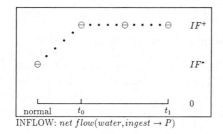

INFLOW: *net flow(water, ingest → P)*

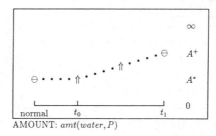

AMOUNT: *amt(water, P)*

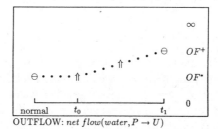

OUTFLOW: *net flow(water, P → U)*

Figure 8. Qualitative behaviors of *inflow*, *amount*, and *outflow* from Figure 7.

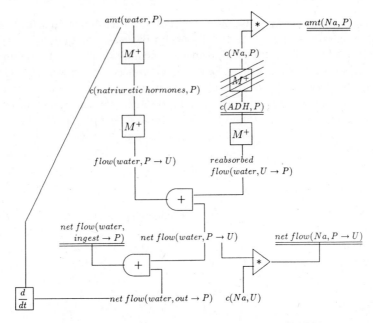

Figure 9. Water balance mechanism with defect: SIADH.

water balance mechanism has been destroyed, and the concentration of ADH is constantly at a very high level regardless of sodium concentration (Figure 9). In fact, this may be happening because of a tumor secreting ADH, but at the level of description of this model, the failure is described simply as loss of the monotonic function constraint between $c(Na, P)$ and $c(ADH, P)$.

We can predict the behavior of this defective mechanism starting with a normal water intake. In Figure 10 the rate of water intake remains constant at its normal value. Because of the defect in the mechanism, its behavior is similar to the response to increased water intake (Figure 8): The amount of water in the plasma goes up to a new higher equilibrium value. We see a different effect, however, in the rate of water excretion. Instead of going up to a higher level and remaining at an elevated level, it falls down to a lower level and then returns to normal, where intake and output are in balance again. Clinically, assuming that sodium intake and excretion are normal, this effect would be observed most effectively by measuring the concentration of the urine rather than its volume. (The sudden decrease below normal results from the assumption that the onset of SIADH is sudden.)

5.3   Response to Therapy

We may also model the effect of therapy on the defective mechanism. The physician, seeing that the patient has an increased plasma volume, may attempt to decrease that volume by prescribing a decreased level of water intake. The prescribed therapy decreases water intake to a level between zero and the normal level.

Figure 11 shows the response to decreased intake. Two reference points are provided to the left of the simulated behavior. The point labeled N is the normal equilibrium state

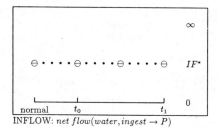

INFLOW: *net flow(water, ingest → P)*

AMOUNT: *amt(water, P)*

OUTFLOW: *net flow(water, P → U)*

Figure 10. Response of water balance mechanism with SIADH to normal water intake.

of the healthy mechanism; the one labeled *S* is the equilibrium state of the defective mechanism with normal intake. Figure 11 shows the intake level decreased below normal and the volume consequently decreased. However, the prediction includes a three-way branch: several possible futures. Having informed the system that the new rate of intake is between zero and the normal value, it predicts three possible outcomes: The plasma volume may decrease but still stay higher than normal; it may decrease precisely back to normal; or it may decrease below normal. The qualitative model has no way to select among these three possibilities.

6 A PROBLEM OF AMBIGUITY AND ITS SOLUTION

What is the source of this ambiguity and how can we understand qualitatively what is happening? The physician looking at this situation recognizes that the decrease in volume is related to the severity of the water restriction. However, the program is not aware of this connection. It only knows that, given a certain set of assumptions, there was a nondeterministic prediction consisting of three possible outcomes. Consider how

$$inflow = (0, IF^*) \implies amount > A^*$$
$$\implies amount = A^*$$
$$\implies amount < A^*$$

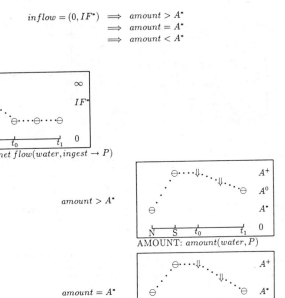

Figure 11. Water balance mechanism with SIADH responds to reduced intake by predicting three-way branch.

the program can draw the conclusion that severity of water restriction accounts for these three possibilities.

The key to the solution is to create an abstraction of the qualitative model with which we began. We began with a relatively complex qualitative model (Figures 6 and 9), but if we focus simply on the rate and amount of inflow, we can say in approximate terms that the equilibrium level of plasma volume increases monotonically with the rate of water intake. (This monotonic function was not in the original model.)

An effective approach for expressing the needed constraint is called *abstraction by time scale* [10, 11]. The water balance mechanism operates over a matter of minutes to reach a new equilibrium, during which the system will pass through nonequilibrium states on its way to a new equilibrium value. At a time scale of hours or days, I may for heuristic purposes treat the change as being instantaneous. At the longer time scale, the relation can be described as a monotonic function; that is, a change in inflow instantly causes a change in amount.

Behavior that takes place at a much longer time scale can be treated as being essentially constant. The amount of sodium in the plasma is controlled by the sodium balance mechanism, which takes place at a much longer time scale. We can use time scale abstraction to capture the relationship between the sodium balance mechanism and the water balance mechanism [11].

We can use the information gained from this abstraction relationship, along with the concept of corresponding values, to solve the problem of our three-way branch. We begin with a monotonic function between *inflow* and *amount*. In the case of the healthy water balance mechanism, we saw that a normal value of *inflow* resulted in a normal *amount*, which establishes a correspondence between these two values, IF^* and A^* in Figure 12 (case 1).

In the case of SIADH, the normal rate of inflow does not correspond to the normal volume but rather corresponds to some higher value, A^+ (Figure 12, case 2). Is there then something that does correspond to the normal value of *amount?* We need to create a new qualitative distinction in this quantity space that represents that amount.

In the graph of Figure 13, the quantity space for *inflow* is plotted along the horizontal axis. The monotonic functions for the normal and the SIADH cases are shown along with their corresponding values. Given a normal value for *inflow*, the corresponding value for *amount* in the SIADH case is higher than in the healthy case, illustrating a qualitative way of stating that one of the monotonic relations has a steeper slope than the other.

Once we have created the two qualitative graphs, we can see that the normal value of *amount*, A^*, must intersect the SIADH curve at some point. That intersection defines a new landmark, IF^-, between zero and the normal rate of *inflow*, which corresponds to the normal level of *amount* (Figure 12, case 3).

1. **Normal water balance**

   $inflow$ $-\infty \cdots 0 \cdots \cdots IF^* \cdots \cdots \infty$

   $amount$ $-\infty \cdots 0 \cdots \cdots A^* \cdots \cdots \infty$

2. **With SIADH, the balance shifts**

   $inflow$ $-\infty \cdots 0 \cdots \cdots IF^* \cdots \cdots \infty$

   $amount$ $-\infty \cdots 0 \cdots A^* \cdots A^+ \cdots \infty$

3. **Create a new landmark:** $IF^- \in (0, IF^*)$.
   Add new corresponding values:

   $inflow$ $-\infty \cdots 0 \cdots IF^- \cdots IF^* \cdots \infty$

   $amount$ $-\infty \cdots 0 \cdots A^* \cdots A^+ \cdots \infty$

4. **The ambiguity is resolved:**

   $inflow = IF^*$ $\implies$ $volume = A^+$
   $inflow = (IF^-, IF^*)$ $\implies$ $volume = (A^*, A^+)$
   $inflow = IF^-$ $\implies$ $volume = A^*$
   $inflow = (0, IF^-)$ $\implies$ $volume = (0, A^*)$

Figure 12. New landmarks and corresponding values for abstracted constraint $amount = M^+(inflow)$ resolve the ambiguity.

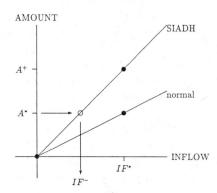

Figure 13. New landmark value IF^- defined by intersection of SIADH curve with *amount* = A^*.

As shown in Figure 12, case 4, this new landmark resolves the ambiguity in Figure 11 by allowing the improved qualitative description of *inflow* to predict which of the three branches is taken. In the SIADH case a normal *inflow* causes a high value for *amount*, and a decreased *inflow* causes a three-way branch. The new landmark between zero and normal *inflow* gives us a correspondence which allows us to eliminate the previous three-way branch. Each of the three qualitative values of *inflow* in $(0, IF^*)$ corresponds to a particular qualitative value of *amount,* and the correspondence is shown between the two quantity spaces.

To illustrate what this might mean in terms of giving a program "common sense," suppose that our program has suggested a relatively severe level of water restriction for a patient with SIADH. Further suppose that even with this level of water restriction the plasma volume is still higher than normal. Without resolving the ambiguous prediction, the program has no idea why the patient's behavior followed one possible path rather than another.

The qualitative reasoning method presented in this section allows it to determine that there is some specific reduced level of *inflow* (the landmark IF^- in Figure 13) that will return *amount* to normal. Since *amount* is now greater than normal, the restricted rate of *inflow* currently imposed on the patient must be in the region (IF^-, IF^*). A further decrease to *inflow* would be required to achieve the normal value for *amount*, and such further reduction may not be clinically desirable. This type of inference permits the computer to exhibit a certain amount of common sense.

7   SUMMARY

In summary, I have argued that qualitative causal models may play a very important role in the diagnosis of complex systems by providing behavioral and structural descriptions of how the system works, which is an important part of domain expertise. I have demonstrated what a qualitative model looks like and how we might construct one for a particular mechanism in medical physiology. I have also shown the results of simulating the behavior of a normal and a defective mechanism and of a defective mechanism with therapy. Motivated by the problem of a branching prediction, I have described the notion of abstraction of these qualitative methods based on time scale and indicated how we can define a new landmark to express a new qualitative distinction. This may be interpreted as giving the program an increased degree of common sense.

ACKNOWLEDGMENTS

This is a revised version of an invited lecture presented at the Fifth Toyobo Biotechnology Foundation Symposium, Tokyo, Japan, August 21–23, 1986. The research reported here was supported in part by the National Science Foundation through grants DCR-8512779 and DCR-8602665 and by the National Library of Medicine through NIH Grants LM 04374 and LM 04515.

REFERENCES

1. R. L. Blum, *Discovery and Representation of Causal Relationships from a Large Time-Oriented Clinical Database: The RX Project,* Lecture Notes in Medical Informatics, Vol. 19, Springer-Verlag, New York, 1982.

2. B. Chandrasekaran, F. Gomez, S. Mittal, and J. Smith, "An Approach to Medical Diagnosis Based on Conceptual Structures," in *Proceedings of the Sixth International Joint Conference on Artificial Intelligence (IJCAI-79),* Stanford University Press, Stanford CA, 1979.

3. R. Davis, "Diagnostic Reasoning Based on Structure and Behavior," *Artificial Intelligence* **24**:347–410, 1984.

4. A. S. Elstein, L. S. Shulman, and S. A. Sprafka., *Medical Problem Solving: An Analysis of Clinical Reasoning,* Harvard University Press, Cambridge, MA, 1978.

5. M. R. Genesereth, "The Use of Design Descriptions in Automated Diagnosis," *Artificial Intelligence* **24**:411–436, 1984.

6. J. P. Kassirer and G. A.. Gorry, "Clinical Problem Solving: A Behavioral Analysis," *Annals of Internal Medicine,* **89**:245–255, 1978.

7. B. J. Kuipers, "Commonsense Reasoning about Causality: Deriving Behavior from Structure," *Artificial Intelligence,* **24**:169–204, 1984.

8. B. J. Kuipers, "The Limits of Qualitative Simulation," in *Proceedings of the Ninth International Joint Conference on Artificial Intelligence (IJCAI-85),* Kaufman, Los Altos, CA, 1985.

9. B. J. Kuipers, "Qualitative Simulation," *Artificial Intelligence,* **29**:289–338, 1986.

10. B. J. Kuipers, "Qualitative Simulation as Causal Explanation," *IEEE Transactions on Systems, Man, and Cybernetics,* **17**:432–444, 1987.

11. B. J. Kuipers, "Abstraction by Time-Scale in Qualitative Simulation," in *Proceedings of the National Conference on Artificial Intelligence (AAAI-87),* Kaufman, Los Altos, CA, 1987, pp. 621–625.

12. B. J. Kuipers and J. P. Kassirer, "Causal Reasoning in Medicine: Analysis of a Protocol," *Cognitive Science,* **8**:363–385, 1984.

13. R. A. Miller, H. E. Pople, Jr., and J. D. Myers, "INTERNIST-I, An Experimental Com-

puter-based Diagnostic Consultant for General Internal Medicine," *The New England Journal of Medicine*, **307**:468–476, 1982.

14. A. Newell, "Artificial Intelligence and the Concept of Mind," in R. C. Schank and K. M. Colby (Eds.), *Computer Models of Thought and Language*, Freeman, San Francisco, 1973.

15. R. S. Patil, P. Szolovits, and W. B. Schwartz, "Causal Understanding of Patient Illness in Medical Diagnosis," in *Proceedings of the Seventh International Joint Conference on Artificial Intelligence (IJCAI-81)*.

16. S. G. Pauker, G. A. Gorry, J. P. Kassirer, and W. B. Schwartz, "Towards the Simulation of Clinical Cognition: Taking a Present Illness by Computer," *American Journal of Medicine*, **60**:981–996, 1976.

17. R. Reiter, "A Theory of Diagnosis from First Principles," *Artificial Intelligence*, **32**:57–95, 1987.

18. E. H. Shortliffe, *Computer-Based Medical Consultations: MYCIN*, Elsevier, New York, 1976.

19. S. M. Weiss, C. A. Kulikowski, S. Amarel, and A. Safir, "A Model-based Method for Computer-aided Medical Decision-making," *Artificial Intelligence*, **11**:145–172, 1978.

20. V. L. Yu, L. M. Fagan, S. M. Wraith, W. J. Clancey, A. C. Scott, J. Hannigan, R. L. Blum, B. G. Buchanan, and S. N. Cohen, "Antimicrobial Selection by a Computer: A Blinded Evaluation by Infectious Disease Experts," *Journal of the American Medical Association*, **242**:1279–1282, 1979.

11 Constructing Qualitative Domain Maps from Quantitative Simulation Models[1]

CHARLES CHIU

Department of Physics and Artificial Intelligence Laboratory
The University of Texas at Austin
Austin, Texas

1 INTRODUCTION

1.1 Qualitative models

Qualitative reasoning has received much attention in the past few years. So far much attention has been directed to *qualitative models*. There are at least two important ingredients in the present qualitative models which are distinctly different from quantitative models.

1. *Sparse Quantity Space*   The quantity space of the parameters in present qualitative models takes on the values of $+, 0, -$ [8, 9, 19], or in a more refined version it also includes additional landmarks [11].

2. *Qualitative Equality in the Constraint Relations*   The equations in these models have been interpreted as equality in sign and in the direction of change. Operators in these equations are to be interpreted as operators of interval arithmetics.[2]

A priori, the sparse quantity space appears to be an attractive framework to reason about the global behavior pattern of a system since the number of behaviors here is guaranteed to be finite. Also the assumption of qualitative equality has been regarded as a welcome feature in commonsense reasoning. On the other hand, in actual applications to some relatively complex systems, qualitative models have been found to be too inconclusive to be useful.

We have been following two approaches to improve the performance of qualitative reasoning on mathematics-based models.

[1]This paper is partially based on ref. 2.

[2]See ref. 17 for an analysis on the properties of operators of present qualitative models.

- One approach is to work within the context of present qualitative models and to introduce additional "filters," which can be motivated, for instance, from expert considerations to "tighten up" qualitative models [4, 7, 13, 14, 19].
- The other approach is to directly abstract qualitative features in quantitative models [3].

This work is a continuation of the second approach.

1.2   Quantitative System with Discrete Behaviors

One way to reason about a quantitative model is to explicitly do quantitative simulations. Here one may organize the output of the simulations by means of a set of qualitative categories and investigate the sensitivity of these categories to the relevant inputs and parameters.

In this work we confine our attention to problems which have a finite number of qualitative behaviors or a finite number of discrete outcomes. A naive example is a check valve in a chemical refinery tank. Suppose the check valve is set at a critical value of, say, 1000 lb/in.^{2} The simulation begins with some amount of catalyst introduced to the tank. It then proceeds with detail chemical reactions and at the end it gives the final pressure in the tank. This pressure is then compared with the critical value, which determines whether the valve should be open or closed.

Suppose our objective is to predict the state of the check valve as a function of the amount of catalyst. For each amount given, one could determine the state of the valve by repeating the entire simulation process. On the other hand, if it is found that there is a monotonic relationship between the pressure and the amount, then a more efficient way to proceed further is to determine the critical amount which leads to the critical pressure. Let us say that this critical amount turns out to be 1 g. From this point on, we only need to compare the amount of catalyst given with 1 g to decide whether the valve should be open or closed.

From this example one may identify several important steps which lead to the prediction of the discrete outcomes.

- *Statement of Critical Condition*   This states the criterion which separates a pair of discrete outcomes. In the check valve example, the critical pressure is at 1000 lb, which separates the "closed" state from the "open" state.
- *Verification of the Monotonicity Relation*   In our example, in order to be able to make use of the approach outlined, it is important to verify that there is a certain monotonicity relation between the two quantities of interest and to determine within what range is this relation satisfied.
- *Determination of the Critical Value of the Independent Variable*   For the example given, this is the critical amount of the catalyst.
- *Prediction of the Discrete Outcome*   This is done through a comparison between the input value of the independent variable and the corresponding critical value.

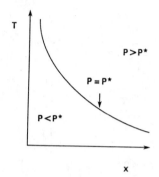

Figure 1. Two monotonic domains of check valve system separated by critical curve.

1.3 Monotonic Domains and the Domain Map

The use of this critical-point approach can be extended to problems having more than one independent variable. For instance, the pressure of the tank can also depend on the temperature. Then the pressure is a function of two independent variables: the catalyst amount x and the temperature T, that is, $P = P(x, T)$. Here in the two-dimensional space of T versus x, the critical pressure P^* of the check valve defines a curve, $P(x, T) = P^*$, which will be referred to as a critical curve. Furthermore, if there are monotonic relationships such as

- for fixed x, $P = M^+(T)$, and
- for fixed T, $P = M^+(x)$,

this critical curve naturally divides this two-dimensional space into two domains; that is, with $P > P^*$ and $P < P^*$. (See Figure 1.) We shall refer to the domains here as the *monotonic domains*, where the variation of the quantity of interest (e.g., P) is a monotonic function of one independent variable while holding the other variable fixed. In defining the term *monotonic domain*, the monotonicity properties of the pair of the independent variables need not be the same. For instance, we can also have a monotonic domain which has an increasing relationship with respect to one variable and a decreasing relationship with respect to the other.

It turns out that monotonic domains are commonplace in many physical systems. In Figure 2, we show several examples of monotonic domains such as in a simple oscillatory system, in two-body head-on collision problems, and in the specification of the Reynolds number in fluid flow and heat flow. The Reynolds number example also illustrates the situation where several independent variables are involved. Here we choose to display the monotonic domains in terms of successive pairs of the independent variables.

The steps outlined in the preceding can also be extended to cases where there are more than one critical conditions. They lead to more domains. We find that the map of these domains is a convenient pictorial representation to display the global behavior

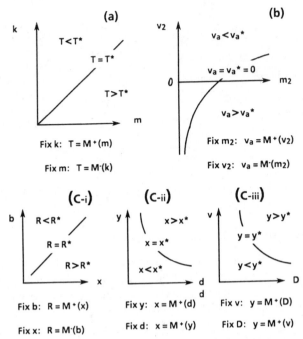

Figure 2. Examples of monotonic domains: (*a*) Mass spring oscillatory system; period: $T = 1/2\pi \, (m/k)^{1/2}$. (*b*) Two-body collision: $v_1 + v_2 \rightarrow v_\alpha + v_\beta$; masses: m_1, m_2, with m_1, v_1 fixed. (*c*) Reynold number in fluid and heat flow; density d, velocity v, diameter D, viscosity b: (i) $R = vDd/b = x/b$, (ii) $x = yd$, and (iii) $y = vD$.

pattern of a model which imitates the expert technique of doing a "back-of-the-envelope" sketch.

Examples of more complex domain maps are the following:

- *Phase Diagrams of Matter*   Here the plot can be, for example, *temperature* versus *volume* at a given *pressure*. The domain labels are *solid, liquid, gas, solid–liquid,* and so on.
- *Geographical Maps*   For instance, consider an altitude map where equal-altitude contours are used to describe a terrain. From this information, one may construct the corresponding domain map. In this domain map, the critical curves may be identified as the local extrema of the altitude and the domain labels are, for example, *uphill, flat,* and *downhill,* defined with respect to some default directions.
- *Phase Portraits of Dynamical Systems*   Here the boundaries of the domain maps are, for example, the asymptotes and the separatrices (see, e.g., refs. 1, 5, 16, and 20).

1.4   Outline of Our Approach

Figure 3 is a schematic illustration of our present work. First we define the quantitative model, which includes the statement of critical conditions. We then follow two

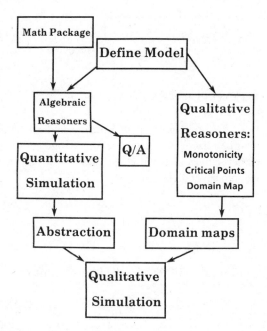

Figure 3. Event simulation approach and domain map approach.

different routes to arrive at "qualitative simulation results." Taking the quantitative route, we first do event-by-event quantitative simulation with the aid of algebraic reasoners. Next is the abstraction step. Here the quantitative results are mapped onto the corresponding discrete categories of qualitative behaviors. This discrete output constitutes the very qualitative simulation results. As shown in the diagram, our algebraic reasoners also support a question-and-answer facility.[3]

The alternative route follows a qualitative approach. Here we qualitatively reason about the quantitative models through the replacement, whenever applicable, of algebraic functions by monotonic functions. Based on the boundary information and the monotonicity property, one constructs the domain map in a two-dimensional space and in turn predicts the qualitative behavior of the system as a function of parameters of interest. This is a generalization of the one-dimensional problem. For the latter case, the landmark information and the monotonicity property lead to the prediction of the qualitative behavior over the one-dimensional parameter space. As an application, we shall show how this map leads to an envisionment tree, which predicts the qualitative behavior pattern of the system.

We shall use the world of a roller coaster similar to de Kleer's [6] to illustrate our approach. Section 2 defines the quantitative model. Section 3 gives a brief discussion on the quantitative simulation and the function of various algebraic reasoners. Section

---

[3]The algebraic reasoners are supported by Macsyma. Our program interfaces with Macsyma at the LISP level. The version of Macsyma we used is in Common LISP, which was translated by William Schelter of the University of Texas in 1984.

4 demonstrates the construction of the qualitative domain map which leads to a semi-quantitative envisionment tree. Section 5 gives a discussion on the related work. Some identities of monotonic functions are given in the Appendix.

2   THE ROLLER COASTER WORLD

Figure 4 shows a typical roller coaster track. A track is made of an arbitrary number of segments. Each pair of adjacent segments are joined together smoothly, with their values and their first derivatives matched at the junction point. The segments can be conveniently divided into several classes.

2.1   The Model

- *Types of Segments*

     Class I: Concave upward segments, for example, S_1, S_3, S_5. Object is moving on the track.

     Class II: Concave downward segments, for example, S_2. Object is again moving on the track.

     Class III: Concave downward segments, for example, S_4. Object is moving beneath the track.

- *Normal Force*   The normal force which an object asserts perpendicularly onto the track is given by (see Figure 5)

$$N = N_g + N_c.$$

N_g is the normal component of the weight mg and is given by

$$N_g = mg \cos \theta.$$

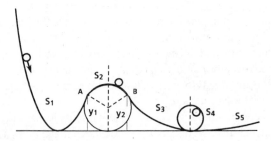

Figure 4. Typical roller coaster model (specifications of roller coaster track for the sample runs given in Figure 8): S_1 is class I segment; junction between segments S_1 and S_2 is at A, where vertical coordinate $y_1 = 1.8R$; segment S_2 is circular arc (class II) with radius R, peak of S_2 at $y = 2R$; junction between S_2 and S_3 at B, where $y_2 = 1.8R$; S_4 is a circular loop (class I and class III) with radius $r = R/2$; S_5 is class I segment.

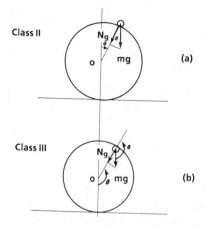

Figure 5. Definitions of circular geometry for (*a*) class II and (*b*) class III.

Here θ is defined in a manner so that $\tan \theta$ corresponds to the local slope of the track defined with respect to the direction of forward motion. For classes I and II, since the object is on the track, N_g is positive; while for class III, since the object is beneath the track, N_g is negative.

N_c is the centrifugal force given by

$$N_c = \pm \frac{mv^2}{r},$$

where r is the local radius of curvature and v the instantaneous velocity of the object. For class II, the centrifugal force is pointing away from the track. It is negative. For classes I and III, it is pointing toward the track and is positive.

Adding up the contributions from the weight and the centrifugal force, one finds that the normal force for class I is always nonnegative, while for classes II and III, the normal force can either be positive or negative.

* *Qualitative Description of Motions* The various cases of motion are shown in Figure 6:

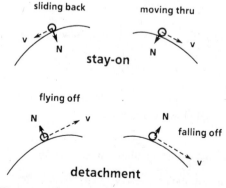

Figure 6. Qualitative descriptions of motion.

"Thru": Here an object moves through an entire segment. Within this segment, $v > 0$ and $N \geq 0$.

"Slide": Here an object slides back within a segment. The sliding back occurs when $v = 0$ and $N \geq 0$.

"Fall" or "fly": Here an object detaches from the track due to the normal force passing from positive to negative. The detachment can either be falling off or flying off. The critical point here is at $N = 0$ with $v > 0$. An abrupt detachment may also occur at the junction due to the discontinuous change of curvature. Here $v > 0$ and the normal force is abruptly changed from a positive value to a negative value.

- *Specification of Geometry* Since a detachment occurs when the normal force becomes negative, this happens only for classes II and III but not for class I. In order to determine the precise circumstance where the point $N = 0$ occurs, one must specify the curvature of the path quantitatively. For the time being we shall assume that class II and III segments are circular arcs. In Section 4, when we come to qualitative reasoning, we shall relax this assumption.

- *Geometric Relations* From Figure 5, one sees that:

for class II

$$y = (1 + \cos \theta)R,$$

for class III

$$y = (1 - \cos \theta)R,$$

for both classes

$$N_g = mg \cos \theta,$$

where $\cos \theta$ is positive for class II and negative for class III.

- *Total Energy* We assume that there is no friction, the total energy of the object can be specified by the initial height, that is, total energy $= mgh$, which is constant throughout the motion.

- *Instantaneous Velocity* At any height y, the velocity square is given by

$$v^2 = 2g(h - y).$$

The physically realizable cases are when $v^2 \geq 0$, so the subsequent object height is always less than or equal to the initial height.

2.2 Total Envisionment of the Roller Coaster Model

Before discussing our simulation work, we pause here to give a bird's eye view of the qualitative and global description of motion. Following the total envisionment scheme of de Kleer [6], we illustrate in Figure 7 the qualitative behavior of the roller coaster of Figure 4 and confine our attention to forward motion only:

- Starting from S_1, if its initial height is too low, the object will slide back; otherwise it will travel through and reach the end of S_1 at A.
- At A, which is also the start of S_2, if the velocity is too high, the corresponding centrifugal force will be too large; in turn the object will fly away. Otherwise it will stay on the track. For the time being, ignore the dotted branch in Figure 7.
- For the stay-on event, along the uphill portion of S_2, there is the possibility of sliding back. Otherwise, the object could either precisely stop at the top or it could pass through the top.
- Along the downhill portion of S_2, the through-going object could subsequently fall off or move through the entire segment. Again ignore the dotted branch.
- For S_3, the object continues to pass through the entire segment.
- For the loop S_4, with the dimension of the track illustrated, the object should traverse through the entire loop. However, if an object begins at rest at different initial heights in S_3, there could also be the possibilities of falling off and sliding back.

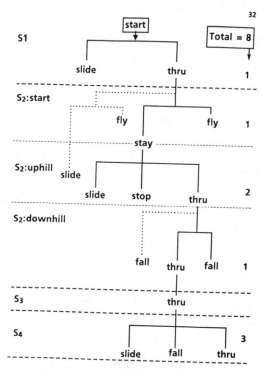

Figure 7. All possible qualitative behaviors predicted by total envisionment tree of de Kleer [6].

3 THE QUANTITATIVE SIMULATOR AND ALGEBRAIC REASONERS

In contrast to the conventional numerical simulation and the qualitative envisionment in de Kleer [6], we do an algebra-based simulation. For simplicity we consider the simulation of forward motion only. This implies that the simulation terminates at "slide," "fall," or "fly" or moves through the entire track.

3.1 The Quantitative Simulator

- When the object is in a given segment of the track, the simulator first instantiates the algebraic expressions of velocity and of the normal forces.
- Then it inspects the instantiated expressions. Based on the properties of the trigonometric functions and inequality relations, it determines the next step for the motion of the object, which can either be slide, or detachment, or moving onto the next segment. For the through-going event, this process iterates repeatedly until the end of the track is reached.
- Along with the simulation, the simulator also prints out a qualitative description of motion. See Figure 8.
- Upon request, the simulator will also provide some local information. More specifically for an object with a local height y, the information provided includes the normal forces N_g, N_c, and N and the instantaneous velocity v. For each parameter, whenever possible, its quantitative value is returned; otherwise its sign is returned.

3.2 Questions and Answers to the Quantitative Model

We now turn to some example quantitative questions for the system:

1. Verify that when the object is moving along the segment S_2, as the object is climbing uphill, the corresponding normal force is increasing.
2. Find the range of the initial height in S_1 such that the object can pass through the entire track.

These questions can always be answered by a brute-force method, that is by doing a number of simulation runs. For instance, for question 1, one can verify the monotonicity relationship empirically by printing out a number of "corresponding values" for the normal force and the object height. For question 2, one can determine the range through trial and error. On the other hand, the answers may also be obtained through algebraic considerations.

We have implemented several algebraic tools for the "question-and-answer" facility. Since it is not the purpose of this chapter to discuss algebraic manipulations in quantitative models, it is sufficient to state the objectives of several tools which we have introduced:

```
Q> (outcome? (stimes 3 R) S1)

Begin in S1 from rest moving to right, initial height:
3*R

Pass through path: S1

Fly away at start of: S2. ******End of run.

Q> (outcome? (stimes 2.4 R) S1)

Begin in S1 from rest moving to right, initial height:
2.4*R

Pass through path: S1

Fly away at start of: S2. ******End of run.

Q> (outcome? (stimes 2.2 R) S1)

Begin in S1 from rest moving to right, initial height:
2.2*R

Pass through path: S1

Pass through path: S2

Pass through path: S3

Pass through path: S4

Pass through path: S5. ******End-of-Track******

Q> (outcome? (stimes 1.8 R) S1)

Begin in S1 from rest moving to right, initial height:
1.8*R

Pass through path: S1

Slide back in: S2 ******End-of-run.

Q> (outcome? (stimes 1.5 R) S1)

Begin in S1 from rest moving to right, initial height:
1.5*R

Slide back in: S1 ******End-of-run.

Q> (outcome? (stimes 0.3 R) S3)

Begin in S3 from rest moving to right, initial height:
0.3*R

Pass through path: S3

Slide back in: S4 ******End-of-run.

Q> (outcome? (stimes 1 R) S3)

Begin in S3 from rest moving to right, initial height:
1*R

Pass through path: S3

Fall off in: S4. ******End-of-run.
```

Figure 8.   Sample simulation runs. Syntax: Q > (Outcome? initial-height path-name).

- *An Algebraic Solver* Given a set of the input data, find the unknown quantity. The program inspects the pattern of input data and rearranges them in a standard form. It then calls the appropriate Macsyma function to solve for the unknown quantity.
- *The Critical-Point Locator* For any given critical event through algebraic manipulations, the program determines the algebraic expression and then the value of the initial height which will lead to the critical event specified.
- *The Monotonicity Verifier* By evaluating the sign of the derivative, it determines the range within which a given function is varying monotonically with respect to the variation of the parameter specified.

The preceding questions and several more questions given in Figure 9 are typical examples which can be answered within our question–answer facility. In the following section we turn to our qualitative domain map approach. Among other things we also return to the previous two questions to see to what extent they can by answered by our qualitative approach.

A list of question categories and sample questions:

1. The $What - is?$ category:

- What is the initial height in S1 if the fall-off occurs at $y = 3R/4$ in S4?
- What is the normal force when the ball begins to slide back at $y = R/3$ in S4?

2. The monotonic function category:

- Verify a negative monotonic function relation between the initial height in S1 and the normal force at the junction between S1 and S2.
- Verify a positive monotonic function relation between the normal force and the height in S2 for a given initial height in S1.

3. Range of initial height category:

- Find the range of the initial height in S1, such that the ball will travel through the entire track.
- Find the range of the initial height in S3, such that the ball will fall off in S4 region before it reaches the height $y = 3R/4$.

Figure 9. Typical questions for question-and-answer session.

4   PATTERN OF QUALITATIVE BEHAVIORS BASED ON DOMAIN MAPS

4.1   Some Preliminaries

4.1.1   A Domain Map for the Description of Global Behavior Pattern

In the approach of event-by-event simulation described in the previous section, our attention was on the behavior of the individual event. In principle it is also of interest, especially in connection with the design of the track, to find out how the behavior pattern of the roller coaster varies as a function of the parameters of the roller coaster. Again one could explore this manually by making a number of simulation runs. The output of the simulation is then relabeled by the corresponding qualitative behaviors.

However, we can also approach this problem with the aid of a domain map. Treating the initial object height and the local object height as two independent variables, we construct qualitative domain maps for the roller coaster system which provide a convenient representation to predict all possible discrete outcomes and to display the effect of variations of track parameters on the behavior pattern.

4.1.2   The Assumption of Quantity Space with Real Numbers

Within the qualitative approach, the real issue is can one abstract qualitative information from a quantitative model so that one can reason qualitatively about the system in question? Most of the qualitative models proposed [e.g., 8, 9, 11, 19] have accomplished this objective to a certain extent.

While being similar in spirit to these models, our approach here has one crucial difference from them. We insist on working within the quantity space of real numbers instead of allowing it to be a discrete space. For instance, consider the relation $f(x, y) = x - y$, where both x and y are positive. The present qualitative models give three-way branchings for the quantity f [e.g., 11]. We also do not have a definite prediction for the sign of f. However, for the boundary defined by $f(x, y) = f^*$, we insist on interpreting it to be a continuous curve instead of a "fuzzy" region implied by the sparse quantity space together with the qualitative equality.

4.1.3   Generalization of Circular Arcs to Monotonic Function Segments

Since we are interested in qualitative conclusions, for the class II and class III segments, we extend the circular forms to monotonic functions. More specifically:

For class II, we assume $R = M_-(y)$. To include the constant-radius case as the limiting case, we also assume the boundary conditions to be the same as those for the circular form; that is,

at $y = R$ the local arc segment is vertical and
at $y = 2R$ it is horizontal.

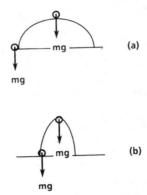

Figure 10. Qualitative shapes for (*a*) class II and (*b*) class III.

For class III, we assume $r = M_-(y)$. Again we include the constant radius as the limiting case and assume the corresponding vertical and horizontal boundary conditions at $y = r$ and $y = 2r$.

Typical generalized segments for class II and class III are illustrated in Figures 10*a* and 10*b*. We proceed now to use the uphill portion of segment S_2 to illustrate the qualitative reasonings involved in the construction of the domain map.

4.2   Inspection on the Monotonicity Relation

To construct the monotonic domain map, we begin with the critical curve and the monotonicity property of the domains:

- *The Monotonic Domain of* v^2 Since $v^2 = 2g(h - y)$, we are interested only in the case where $v^2 > 0$ or $h \geq y$. Again to qualitatively reason about the algebraic expression, we work with the abstractions:

  for fixed y, $v^2 = M_+(h)$, and
  for fixed h, $v^2 = M_-(y)$.

So the domain of v^2 is monotonic. In turn, the domain of v is monotonic also. From the "forward-motion convention" (see the beginning of Section 4), $v \geq 0$. We stress that the algebraic expression of v^2 has been used here only to the extent of abstracting the qualitative monotonic dependence of v^2 on h and on y.

- *The Monotonic Domain of N*

  Monotonicity property of N_g: For the uphill segment of class II, the higher the object the flatter is the slope. So for fixed y, $N_g = $ const, and for fixed h, $N_g = M_+(y)$.
  Monotonicity property of N_c: For the class II segment

$$N_c = -v^2/R.$$

Combining the preceding monotonicity relations for v^2 and the relation $R = M_+(y)$ assumed in Section 4.1,[4] for fixed y, $N_c = -M_+(h) = M_-(h)$, and for fixed h, $N_c = -M_-(y)/M_+(y) = -(M_-(y) * M_-(y)) = -M_-(y) = M_+(y)$.

Monotonicity property of N: From the definition of the normal force $(N = N_g + N_c)$, for fixed y, $N = N_g + N_c = \text{const} + M_-(h) = M_-(h)$, and for fixed h, $N = N_g + N_c = M_+(y) + M_+(y) = M_+(y)$.

Thus in the plot of h versus y, the domain of N is monotonic. Again the algebraic expressions of N_g and N_c have been used here only to the extent of abstracting the corresponding monotonic functional relationships.

4.3   Construction of the Domain Map

The domain map is defined by the kinematic boundaries together with critical curves. This map for the present example the of class II uphill segment is shown in Figure 11a.

- *Boundaries of the Map*

   The critical condition $v = 0$ leads to the boundary $y = h$.

   The upper kinematic limit of this portion of the track leads to the top boundary $y = 2R$.

   The $N = 0$ curve forms the lower boundary of the map.

Notice that the $N = 0$ curve as illustrated is an increasing monotonic function in the plot, since from calculus

$$\left.\frac{dy}{dh}\right|_N = -\frac{dN/dh|_y}{dN/dy|_h} = -\left(\frac{-}{+}\right) = +,$$

where in the second step the monotonicity properties of the normal force derived in Section 4.2 were used.

- *The Interior Line $h = 2R$*   This is the critical line which separates the sliding-back events from through-going events.

4.4   Locations of Critical Points or Landmarks

The *corresponding values* on the $N = 0$ curve as shown in Figure 11a are obtained in following manner:

---

[4]For manipulations of monotonic functions, see identities given in the Appendix.

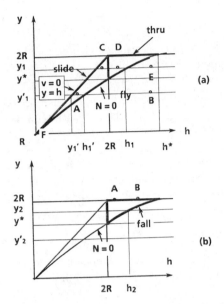

Figure 11. Class II domain maps: (a) map of uphill segment; (b) map of downhill segment.

- The lower endpoint F is at $y = h = R$, where the $v = 0$ and $N = 0$ curves intersect. To verify this, observe that since $h = y$, so $v = 0$, or $N_c = 0$. Also from the boundary condition assumed at $y = R$, $N_g = 0$ (see Figure 10a). So $N = N_g + N_c = 0$.
- The $N = 0$ curve intersects the line $y = 2R$ at $h = h^*$, where $h^* > 2R$. To arrive at this conclusion, we do qualitative reasoning and make use of Figure 12.

    From the assumed boundary condition, as in Figure 10a, for an initial height $h = 2R$, the object will be arriving at the top of S_2 with zero speed. So here at $h = 2R$, the centrifugal force vanishes and $N = N_g = mg$.

    By "exaggeration" [18], at very large initial height (i.e., $h = L$), the centrifugal force is large and negative. In turn the normal force is large and negative (i.e., $N \approx -L$).

    Also $dN/dh|_y < 0$.

These conditions lead to the curve illustrated in Figure 12, which shows that $h^* > 2R$.

- Back to Figure 11a. The local height, where the $N = 0$ curve passes through $h = 2R$, is at $y = y^*$ with $R < y^* < 2R$.

4.5 Prediction of Global Patterns for Different Junction Heights

In Figure 11a, consider the case where the track has a junction height $y_1' < y^*$. Denote the critical or the landmark value of the initial height, which leads to $N = 0$ at this junction, by $h = h_1'$.

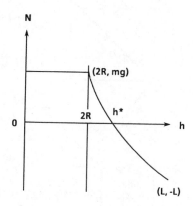

Figure 12. Qualitative reasoning on landmark location h^*.

- An object with its initial height in the range $y_1' \leq h \leq h_1'$ (e.g., point A) will follow the trajectory moving vertically up until it hits the curve $v = 0$; then it slides back.
- An object with $h > h_1'$ (e.g., point B) will fly off abruptly at the junction.

Consider a different junction height where $y_1 > y^*$. Denote the landmark value of the initial height, which leads to $N = 0$ at this junction, by $h = h_1$.

- An object with $h < 2R$ (e.g., point C) will lead to a sliding-back event.
- An object with $2R < h < h_1$ (e.g., point D) will reach the top of S_2 and lead to a through-going event.
- An event with $h > h_1$ (e.g., point E) will fly off at the junction.

4.6   Domain Maps of Other Segments

Similar methods can also be used to construct the domain map and identify the appropriate landmarks leading to different discrete outcomes.

- *Domain Map of Downhill Segment of S_2*   Figure 11b shows the domain map of the downhill segment of S_2. Consider the junction of between the segments S_2 and S_3 in Figure 4.

    First consider the case where the junction height is, say, at $y = y_2 > y^*$. Denote the landmark value of the initial height, which leads to $N = 0$ at this junction, by $h = h_2$: For $h < h_2$ (e.g., point A), it will lead to a through-going event; for h_2 (e.g., point B), it will lead to a falling-off event.

    For junction height $y_2' < y^*$ all events beginning at the top of S_2 will lead to falling-off events.

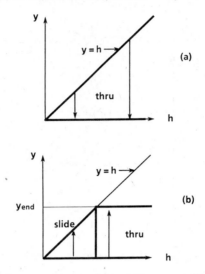

Figure 13. Class I domain maps: (*a*) map of downhill segment; (*b*) map of uphill segment.

- *Domain Map of Class I Segment*

    Figure 13*a* shows the domain map for the class I downhill segment. Here all events correspond to "thru" events.

    Figure 13*b* shows the domain map for the uphill class I segment: For $h \leq y_{end}$ it will lead to sliding-back events. For $h > y_{end}$, it will lead to through-going events.

- *Domain Map of Class III Segment*   Figure 14 shows the domain map of the uphill portion of a loop: Here the upper portion of the loop corresponds to a class III segment. As stated in Section 4.1, the path shape for the class III segment is generalized to include a monotonic function relation $r = M\_(y)$:

    For $h < r$, it will lead to a sliding-back event.

    For $r < h < l^*$, it will lead to a falling-off event.

    For $h > l^*$, it will lead to a through-going event.

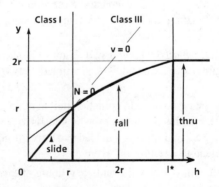

Figure 14. Domain map of loop with class I and class III segments.

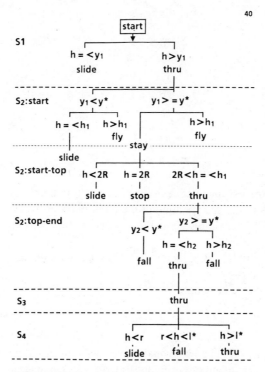

Figure 15. Semi-quantitative envisionment tree.

The set of landmarks introduced through the domain maps can be readily incorporated into the total envisionment tree structure. The envisionment tree with the inclusion of landmarks are illustrated in Figure 15. We shall refer to the tree together with the landmark structure as the semi-quantitative envisionment tree.

4.7   Application of Domain Maps and the Envisionment Tree

Much of the qualitative behavior of the model is contained in the pictorial representation of the domain map. I will illustrate this with the two questions given in Section 3.

- *Monotonic Function Inspection*

    Query: Verify that when the object is moving along the segment S_2, as the object is climbing uphill, the corresponding normal force is increasing.

    Answer: This is the very property of the monotonic domain discussed in Section 4.2; that is, for fixed h, $N = M_+(y)$.

- *Determination of the Range of Initial Height*

    Query: Find the range of the initial height in S_1 such that the object can pass through the entire track.

    Answer: An effective way to determine this range is to backtrack the envisionment tree. Through backtracking, we obtain following set of inequalities:

$$h > l^*,$$

$$h \leq h_2,$$

$$y_2 \geq y^*,$$

$$2R < h \leq h_1$$

$$y_1 \geq y^*,$$

$$h > y_1.$$

Notice that the two inequalities related to junction heights y_1 and y_2 state the requirements in the specification of the track in order to allow events passing through S_2. The remaining inequalities can be written in a compact form:

$$\max(l^*, 2R, y_1) = \max(l^*, 2R) < h \quad \max(h_1, h_2).$$

In the first step we have used

$$y_1 < 2R.$$

This is as far as we can go with qualitative reasoning. To obtain the quantitative results, it requires quantitative inputs. For instance, using the quantitative values of Figure 4, it turns out that

$$l^* = \frac{5}{2}r = \frac{5}{4}R \quad \text{and} \quad h_1 = h_2 = 2.2R.$$

In turn

$$2R < h < 2.2R.$$

4.8   Comments on Implementations

The implementations of our domain map approach proposal can be divided into three parts:

- the construction of the domain map based on the kinematic limits and critical curves,
- abstraction of the semi-quantitative envisionment tree structure from the domain maps, and
- abstraction of inequality constraints implied by the envisionment tree which leads to the specific discrete outcomes.

We defer the development of this program and the extension of the present approach beyond the roller coaster world and those cases of Figure 2 to the future.

5   DISCUSSION

We have presented two approaches to abstract qualitative behaviors. The first is the quantitative approach. Here the system of interest is defined in a quantitative way. One can first determine the quantitative solution and then abstract the qualitative features of the solution. The second is the qualitative approach, which as suggested by the title of this chapter, is our main concern. Our discussion will now concentrate on this second approach.

5.1   Qualitative Reasoning without Invoking Interval Arithmetics

Recently Struss [17] observed that present qualitative models, which are characterized by the sparse quantity space and interval arithmetic operators, do not satisfy the expected associativity. In the last section, we applied qualitative reasonings to quantitative models. The qualitative reasoning there is based on the quantity space of real numbers, where the domain map is defined by continuous curves. Our work demonstrates that within the domain map approach, qualitative reasoning can be carried out without reference to the interval arithmetics. In turn it avoids Struss's criticism.

5.2   De Kleer's Work

Our present work was partially motivated by de Kleer's work [6]. We agree with his general point of view that qualitative global behavior pattern provides an important framework to reason about the behavior of the system. However, de Kleer placed much emphasis on developing qualitative reasoning based on sources other than the physics model itself. More specifically, his total envisionment tree is based on "prephysics envisioning knowledge." At each node of his tree, only possible qualitative behaviors but not landmark information are given.

On the other hand, our semi-quantitative envisionment tree is derived through the application of qualitative reasoning on the domain map, which is abstracted from the original physics model. Furthermore, based on the domain map, the ordinal information of landmark values at each node of the tree has also been deduced.

We are aware of the limitations of quantitative models where the physical system is approximated by a set of mathematical equations. To alleviate some limitations, in Section 4, we considered

- replacement of the mathematical arcs by monotonic function segments and
- the replacement of the algebraic expressions by the corresponding monotonic relations.

This enabled us to reason about algebraic expressions qualitatively without rigidly adhering to the precise mathematical form. Here we are still in the conventional physics.

5.3   Relations to Order-of-Magnitude Approach and Exaggeration Approach

In this work we have paid special attention to problems which are characterized by the existence of monotonic domains. We recall our conclusion on a collision model [3] to illustrate the relationships among the present approaches, the approach of order of magnitude by Raiman [15] and the "exaggeration" approach by Weld [18].

Consider a collision setup. Here the projectile's mass and its initial velocity are fixed, and the target's mass and its initial velocity are treated as two independent variables. We separate the collision events into two categories. After the collision, one category has the projectile recoiled backward, that is, its velocity $v_\alpha < 0$, and the other has the projectile moving forward, that is, $v_\alpha > 0$.

Our domain map result for this case is illustrated in Figure 2b, where the critical curve of $v_\alpha = 0$ separates the forward and backward categories into two monotonic domains. Raiman began with the order-of-magnitude equations directly. He illustrated his implementation with several cases. For each case, his reasoner determines the sign of the projectile final velocity v_α. It turns out that all the unambiguous predictions, on the sign of the projectile, correspond to cases where points in the v_2-versus-m_2 plot in Figure 2b are "far away" from the critical curve. For instance, consider the initial state, where the projectile is moving to the right toward a target, and that the target mass and its speed are both an order of magnitude smaller than the corresponding quantities of the projectile. This point is close to the origin. Raiman's reasoner predicts that after the collision the projectile will continue to travel to the right, that is, $v_\alpha > 0$.

The same conclusion can also be reached through the approach of the "exaggeration" [18]. Here we imagine that the target is essentially massless, and it is initially at rest. Common sense tells us that during the collision, the impact due to the target on the projectile should be negligible. So the projectile is expected to be essentially unperturbed by the collision. In turn its direction of motion should remain unchanged.

One may say that Raiman and in some cases Weld have identified local patches where the final velocity of the projectile is positive and some other local patches where this velocity is negative. This is to be compared to our global picture of Figure 2b, where there is a clear-cut separation between the two monotonic domains. The global picture contains the correlation information between parameters of different events. For instance, if for some event the final projectile happens to be at rest, then for an "adjacent" event where the target mass is slightly increased, our approach predicts that the final projectile will be recoiled backward, that is, $v_\alpha < 0$. On the other hand, when treating the adjacent event as an isolated event, qualitative reasoning, which also includes the order-of-magnitude approach, does not give a definitive sign for v_α.

5.4   Other Related Work

- *Critical Points and Hypersurfaces*   Based on dimensional analysis, Kokar [10] explored the criteria for selecting the appropriate parameter to establish critical points. He pointed out that in the multidimensional parameter space, critical points will appear as a hypersurface. But he did not proceed further. In our present work, we consider the critical curves which are "hypersurfaces" in the two-dimensional space and investigate the ramifications of the domain map defined by these curves and kinematic boundaries.

- *Phase-Space Diagrams*   The domain map approach concerns with a geometric representation of the behavior pattern in terms of maps consisting of boundaries and domains. Besides the present qualitative algebraic approach, other methods have been used to construct the domain maps, especially for complex problems. We look at two methods here, both of which are related to phase-space diagrams.

- *Approximation Method*   Sacks [16] investigated phase diagrams within a piecewise linear approximation. One finds that for sufficiently smooth varying dynamical systems, within the piecewise linear approximation, the asymptotes and the separatrices in the phase diagrams may be determined analytically. In turn, the domain map may also be constructed within the same approximation.

- *Numerical Method*   Yip [20] considered relatively complex phase portraits of nonlinear dynamical systems. Within his work, orbits in a phase-space diagram are generated iteratively through numerical calculations. The partition of the phase space into different domains, or the construction of a domain map, is completed when a consistent set of critical orbits is found.

5.5   Concluding Remarks

Our research in qualitative physics is not concerned with the discovery or the invention of new "wheels" in physics; rather we are interested in the problem of how to "formalize" expert qualitative reasoning so that the program can automate the qualitative reasoning process as much as possible.

In this work we have considered the application of qualitative reasoning through the use of a qualitative domain map. We have given a number of examples to indicate that the domain maps appear to be a common denominator to describe the global behavior pattern of many systems. Within the qualitative reasoning work presented, our approach is mainly based on monotonic function identities and continuity. To our surprise we find that it is possible to do qualitative reasoning without mentioning the fundamental assumptions of present qualitative models, that is, the sparse quantity space and the qualitative equalities of interval arithmetics. We find that we can continue to work within the conventional framework of the quantity space of real numbers and algebraic operators.

We believe that our objective of formalizing and automating expert qualitative reasoning is a tangible goal. This line of approach should have the potential to impact educational and technological applications.

APPENDIX: IDENTITIES FOR THE MONOTONIC FUNCTIONS

- *Definition*   Monotonic functions $M_\pm$ have the property

    1. $M'_+ = dM_+(x) / dx > 0$
    2. $M'_- = dM_-(x) / dx < 0$

- *Identities*[5]

1. $M_+(x) = -M_-(x)$
2. $M_+(x) = \text{const} + M_+(x)$
3. $M_+(x) + M_+(x) = N_+(x)$
4. $M_+(x) \cdot M_+(x) = L_+(x)$ if $M_+, N_+, L_+ > 0$
   Proof: $L = (MN)' = MN' + N'M > 0$. So $L = L_+(x)$.
5. $M_-(x) / N_+(x) = L_-(x)$ if $M_-, L_-, N_+ > 0$
   Proof: $L' = (M / N)' = M' / N - M'N' / N^2 < 0$. So $L = L_-(x)$.

The identities given here satisfy the reflection symmetry, that is, these identities continue to be valid under the interchange of the plus and minus subscripts.

ACKNOWLEDGMENT

I thank Ben Kuipers, Paul Fishwick, and Gordan Novak for discussions. This research was supported in part by the National Science Foundation through grants DCR-8512779 and DCR-8602665.

REFERENCES

1. V. I. Arnold, *Ordinary Differential Equations*, MIT Press, Cambridge, MA, 1973.
2. C. Chiu, "Simulations in a Model-World Based on an Algebraic Approach," Paper presented at the AI and Simulation Workshop, in AAAI-87, Seattle, WA, 1987.
3. C. Chiu, "Qualitative Physics Based on the Quantitative Solution Approach," Draft, Short version presented at AAAI Qualitative Physics Workshop, Champaign, IL, May 1987.
4. C. Chiu, "Higher Order Derivative Constraints and a QSIM-based Total Simulation Scheme," AI Lab, University of Texas, AI TR88-65, 1988.
5. W. Hurewicz, *Lectures on Ordinary Differential Equations*, MIT Press, Cambridge, MA, 1958.
6. J. de Kleer, "Multiple Representations of Knowledge in a Mechanics Problem Solver," *Proceedings of the Fifth International Joint Conference on Artificial Intelligence, IJCAI-1977*, Kaufmann, Los Altos, CA, 1977, p. 299.
7. J. de Kleer and D. G. Bobrow, "Qualitative Reasoning with Higher-Order Derivatives," *Proceedings of the Third National Conference on Artificial Intelligence (AAAI-84)*, Kaufmann, Los Altos, CA, 1984.
8. J. de Kleer and J. S. Brown, "A Qualitative Physics Based on Confluences, *Artificial Intelligence*, **24**:7–83, 1984.

---

[5]See also Kuipers [11] for identities 1, 2 and 3. For clarity we use different symbols to denote those monotonic functions which correspond to different algebraic functions. For qualitative reasoning on monotonic functions, where one is only interested in the sign of the slope of the functions, such distinction is unnecessary.

9. K. D. Forbus, "Qualitative Process Theory," *Artificial Intelligence*, **24**:85–168, 1984

10. M. M. Kokar, "Critical Hypersurfaces and the Quantity Space," *Proceedings of the Sixth National Conference on Artificial Intelligence, AAAI-87,* Kaufmann, Los Altos, CA, 1987, p. 616.

11. B. J. Kuipers, "Common-sense Reasoning about Causality: Deriving Behavior from Structure," *Artificial Intelligence*, **24**:169–204, 1984.

12. B. J. Kuipers, "Qualitative Simulation," *Artificial Intelligence*, **29**:289–338, 1986.

13. B. Kuipers and C. Chiu, "Taming Intractable Branching in Qualitative Simulation," *Proceedings of the Tenth International Joint Conference on Artificial Intelligence, IJCAI-87,* Kaufmann, Los Altos, CA, 1987.

14. W. W. Lee, C. Chiu, and B. Kuipers, "Steps toward Constraining Qualitative Simulation," University of Texas Computer Science TR 87-44, 1987.

15. O. Raiman, "Order of Magnitude Reasoning," *Proceedings of the Fifth National Conference on Artificial Intelligence, AAAI-86,* Kaufmann, Los Altos, CA, 1986, p. 100.

16. E. Sacks, "Piecewise Linear Reasoning," *Proceedings of the Sixth National Conference on Artificial Intelligence, AAAI-87,* Kaufmann, Los Altos, CA, 1987, p. 655.

17. P. Struss, "Problems of Interval-based Qualitative Reasoning, Siemens, ZTIINF.

18. D. Weld, "Comparative Analysis, Presented at the Qualitative Physics workshop, Champaign, IL, May 1987.

19. B. C. Williams, "Qualitative Analysis of MOS Circuits," *Artificial Intelligence*, **24**:281, 1984.

20. K. M. Yip, "Extracting Qualitative Dynamics from Numerical Experiments," *Proceedings of the Sixth National Conference on Artificial Intelligence, AAAI-87,* Kaufmann, Los Altos, CA, 1987, p. 665.

12 Issues in Qualitative Reasoning about Diffusional Processes

SHOSHANA L. HARDT

Department of Computer Science
State University of New York at Buffalo
Buffalo, New York

1 QUALITATIVE PHYSICS

The modeling of qualitative reasoning about everyday-life physical events presents great challenges. In many cases, the knowledge which supports such reasoning processes in people is formulated in yet-to-be-explored fashions and resembles scientific knowledge only abstractly. The knowledge people use to reason so successfully about the many physical events around them is based on their extensive personal experience and is formulated as partial, sometime redundant theories and not always as a unified, logically economical and consistent scientific theory.

The research in the area of qualitative physics lies on strong foundations of existing work in AI, in mathematics, and in physics. The investigation of semi-quantitative methods of analysis which yields useful insight into the behavior of physical systems has been pursued in applied mathematics and in physics for over a century [e.g., 18]. These methods have proven particularly useful in cases where no exact mathematical model exists for a given system but its behavior was cataloged through experimental observations or when the exact mathematical model cannot be solved at the desired level of detail.

The research reported here is based on the hypothesis which is central to many studies in the field of AI [e.g., 19, 22], and which states that problem solving requires critical amounts of knowledge. The problem-solving task involves the interpretation of the problem by constructing relevant conceptualizations, which is guided both by the relevant prior knowledge possessed by the problem solver and by features of the problem and their possible interpretations. When constructed, these conceptualizations support the problem-solving task by providing the necessary inferencing power.

To better understand the form and the content of the knowledge that takes part in the complex inferencing processes involved in qualitative physics, we choose to examine reasoning and problem solving in the domain of diffusional flow processes. The problem-solving task in our domain is characterized as one in which no direct way to solve a given problem is apparent from the problem description. Namely, after the information processor is exposed to a stream of preprocessed features which describe the problem, no direct index to a context can be found such that the whole problem can be solved either directly or analogically. In these latter cases the context provides a way to structure the relevant input features into meaningful components with known behaviors, whereas in our case of interest, such structuring is lacking. As a result, the problem solver has to create this structure dynamically in order to support its problem-solving activity. This dynamic structuring is performed using context-sensitive knowledge and various reasoning mechanisms.

In the following we first review three of the qualitative reasoning inferencing mechanisms that have been developed by researchers in AI to deal with the prediction and the explanation of the behavior of physical systems. We demonstrate the scope of the mechanism by applying them to the simple problem of an ideal spring attached to a block sliding on a friction-free surface. Then we introduce seven problems related to the rates of diffusional flow processes in systems with various source-sink geometric arrangements and review the challenges involved in the modeling of the reasoning processes involved in solving these problems given the current state of the theory of qualitative physics.

2   THE GROWTH OF COMPLEXITY

Building reasoning systems that contain sufficient inferencing power to handle problems of everyday-life physics is still beyond the capabilities of AI theories and technologies. However, progress has been made in understanding the nature of the reasoning processes and the origin of the difficulties in modeling it. Methodologically, one may attempt to gain insight into the workings of a complex system in two ways. On the one hand, one may simplify the system under investigation, model the simplified version, and then try to gradually introduce the missing complexity and reformulate the theory accordingly. On the other hand, one may attack the complex problem directly and, by failures of the model and the theory to capture the complex system, repeatedly modify it. It is of central importance in both approaches that failures of the theories and the models will provide meaningful information that may lead to their improvements.

In this section we first introduce some of the work in AI which deals with inferencing mechanisms for qualitative physics. We demonstrate the mechanisms on a simple physics problem in order to provide the necessary insight into the interplay between the inferencing mechanism and the structure and the content of the knowledge given to the program and its resulting inferencing power. Also, in this section we discuss a way to investigate domains and problems in which these methods cannot be applied.

AI researchers have investigated methods by which applicable qualitative answers can be generated by a computer using knowledge about the structural description of the systems, their potential local and global behaviors, and the processes that generate the behaviors. In the following we discuss the methods of qualitative simulation as presented elsewhere [16], in qualitative process theory [4], and comparative analysis [25]. In this work the structure of the system is described in terms of relations (constraints) between parameters. To give a flavor of the three methods we shall briefly show their application to the simple example of a horizontal spring and block on a friction-free surface shown in Figure 1.

2.1   Qualitative Simulation

Qualitative simulation takes a structural model of a system and qualitatively describes its behavior over time [3, 16]. For the spring-block example the system takes as input the six parameters and their relations, as shown in Table 1. In addition it takes as input the appropriate landmarks. (Here we use the notation used for the qualitative simulation program QSIM described elsewhere [16]. Figure 2 illustrates the output generated by the program QSIM—a description of oscillatory behavior. At every step of the simulation the QSIM algorithm generates a list of all possible behaviors which is then filtered by the constraints to produce a list of behaviors which are consistent with the constraints. In cases where the problem is underconstrained, many nonphysical solutions are produced together with the correct ones. Furthermore, in situations where the process being simulated is complex, the generation of all possible behaviors introduces a great computational burden. These problems may be partially remedied by the introduction of additional knowledge to the program. In the first case, addition of the missing constraints will guarantee the relevance of all the generated behaviors. In the second case, providing the program with knowledge about the time scales involved in the simulated process may drastically reduce the number of possibilities generated (e.g., [7]).

2.2   Qualitative Process Theory

Qualitative process theory [4] provides a representational framework for a certain class of deductions about the physical world. It includes a rich vocabulary to describe the physical world as well as insight into the reasoning tasks. In this theory, physical processes are the mechanisms by which change occurs, and in the spring-block example the spring is modeled as a device, denoted by S, satisfying the constraints on the force given in Table 1. The block is denoted by B. Table 2 illustrates the view structure (VS) and the process structure (PS) for this case [4]. Notice the different vocabulary and scope of this representation as compared with the input and output of the qualitative simulation program shown in Figure 2.

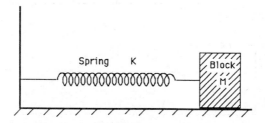

Figure 1.   Ideal spring with constant k attached to block of mass m on friction-free surface.

TABLE 1. Parameters and constraints for spring-block system a[a]

Physical Parameter	Symbol	
Spring constant	k	$-k < 0$
Mass of block	m	$m > 0$
Displacement	x_t	$x_0 < 0$
Velocity	v_t	$DERIV\ (v, x), v_0 = 0$
Acceleration	a	$DERIV\ (a, v)$
Force	F	$MULT\ (F, m, a), MULT\ (F, -k, x_t)$

[a]$MULT$ and $DERIV$ are the multiplication and time-derivative predicates, respectively.

2.3 Comparative Analysis

Comparative analysis [25] involves predicting how the behavior of a system will change if the underlying structure is perturbed and also explaining why it will change. For the spring-block example comparative analysis is used to answer questions such as "What would happen to the period of oscillation if you increase the mass of the block?" Weld [25] implemented, tested, and proved theoretical results about two

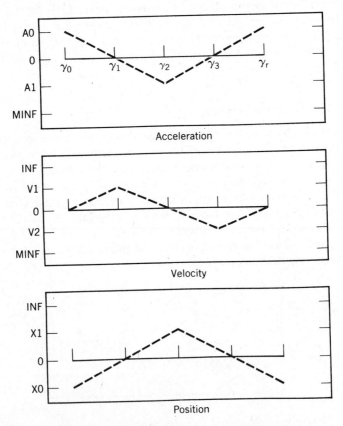

Figure 2. The behavior generated by QSIM [16].

TABLE 2. View structure (VS) and process structure (VP) for the spring-mass problem for one cycle[a]

VS:	{Stretched (S)}
PS:	{Acceleration (B, −1)}
PS:	{Acceleration (B, −1), Motion (B, −1)}
VS:	{Relaxed (S)}
PS:	{Motion (B, −1)}
VS:	{Compressed (S)}
PS:	{Motion (B, −1), Acceleration (B, 1)}
VS:	{Compressed (S)}
PS:	{Acceleration (B, 1)}
VS:	{Compressed (S)}
PS:	{Motion (B, 1)}
VS:	{Relaxed (S)}
PS:	{Motion (B, 1)}
VS:	{Stretched (S)}
PS:	{Motion (B, 1), Acceleration (B, −1)}
VS:	{Stretched (S)}
PS:	{Acceleration (B, −1)}

[a]From ref. 4.

different techniques for solving comparative analysis problems, differential qualitative (DQ) analysis, and exaggeration. The DQ analysis would answer the preceding question as follows: "Since force is inversely proportional to position, the force on the block will remain the same when the mass is increased. But if the block is heavier, then it will not accelerate as fast. And if it does not accelerate as fast, then it will always be going slower and so will take longer to complete a full period (assuming it travels the same distance)." Exaggeration will answer the question in a different manner: "If the mass were infinite, then the block would hardly move at all. So the period would be infinite. Thus if the mass was increased a bit, the period would increase as well."

3 DIFFICULTIES IN MODELING

Difficulties to model qualitative physics inferencing may be caused by the fact that the algorithms involved in this inferencing are complex and do not lend themselves to successful formulation at this point and by the fact that the domain knowledge necessary for the inferencing process is not present in the model in sufficient quantities and in appropriate forms.

3.1 Dependencies between Algorithms and Knowledge

Two important observations can be made at this point based on the the three programs for qualitative simulation and analysis described previously. The first observation is that the robustness of the program's ability to generate behaviors of processes in a given domain depends on the richness of the domain-specific vocabulary which it contains. QSIM is a very general qualitative simulation program and contains abstract knowledge about behaviors. For example, at any given point in the simulation it considers three possible changes in the qualitative values of its variables, namely, they can increase, decrease, or remain steady. The input constraints aid the program at every step to decide which of the three is a possible change. Therefore, the validity of its output depends on the accuracy by which its input describes the structure of the modeled process. A program based on qualitative process theory, on the other hand, may contain explicit knowledge about many aspects of the process being modeled and hence, in principle, is capable of more powerful inferencing. Consequently, this program is less likely to be sensitive to inaccuracy and vagueness of the problem description since it can fill gaps using its own rich domain-specific knowledge. The second observation is that when the knowledge content of the program is represented in a given single form, this form facilitates certain kinds of inferences while making others very difficult. For example, when the program uses knowledge about the structure (the "equations of motion") of a process as the basis of its description of the process, it can generate the behaviors of the process in a relatively straightforward way. However, if it tries to use the knowledge so structured to answer questions which include certain analyses (e.g., comparative analysis), the resulting reasoning algorithm is very complex. The issue of how natural a particular representation is for a certain task has been in existence in all areas of science which are involved in building formal models. However, old as the issue might be, we still do not have a theory of representation which may guide us when we search for the most natural knowledge representation scheme(s) for a certain task. The observation made in the preceding may suggest, however, that for many purposes the redundancy of the knowledge contained in the program may be beneficial in order to maintain the reasoning algorithms sufficiently simple.

3.2 Insufficient Domain Knowledge

In many cases, when the work involves complex domains for which there is no structural description known that can support the required inferences, ontological work has to come before the building and the elaboration of models. This work provides valuable sources of information about the contents of the domains. For example, part of Hayes's [13] work on inferences involved in reasoning about liquids is such a domain ontology, and Hardt [6–8] provided partial ontology for diffusional flow processes. Furthermore, in cases where some structural information is available about the domain in the form of behaviors of simple subsystems, the relations between structural and behavioral aspects of a compound system can in some cases be inferred by the consolidation of the behaviors of its components using composition rules that operate on behaviors [1]. This work indicates the promise in this approach for extending the applicability of reasoning systems in partially specified domains.

4   SEVEN PROBLEMS ABOUT DIFFUSIONAL FLOWS

Problem solving in the domain of diffusional flow processes requires more inferential machinery than is offered by the methods described in the preceding. The formulation of domain knowledge in a way that facilitates inferencing is not straightforward, and the reasoning process seems to involve various cooperating mechanisms. To illustrate this point, consider the following seven problems which deal with rates of diffusional flow processes. Here the problem solver has to estimate diffusion transit times of particles that move randomly between a given release point (source) and accidently hit a preassigned target (sink).

Problem 1   Molecules released from the centers of two cylindrical containers diffuse to and are trapped by the walls (but not the ends) of the containers. Both containers have the same diameter, but in case (b) the height is 10 times greater than in case (a). Compare the transit times (the average time it takes for the molecules to reach the wall).

Problem 2   Molecules released from one spherical surface diffuse to and are trapped by a second concentric, spherical surface. The radius of the inner surface is much less than the radius of the outer surface. Case (a): the molecules are released from the outer surface and diffuse inward. Case (b): the molecules are released from the inner surface and diffuse outward. Compare the transit times.

Problem 3   Molecules released from the surface on the left diffuse to and are trapped by the surface on the right. The molecules are slightly soluble in water and highly soluble in oil. In case (a) they diffuse through the layer of oil before reaching the layer of water. In case (b) the thickness of each layer is unchanged, but the order is reversed so the molecules diffuse first through the water and then the oil. Compare the transit times.

Problem 4   The rates of most enzyme reactions appear to be limited by the time it takes each substrate molecule to diffuse to and "find" the active site. Consider the active site to be positioned behind an "aperture" through which the substrate molecule must diffuse. In case (a) the aperture is a circle with three times greater area than the elliptical aperture in case (b). How rapidly will the substrate molecule "find" site (a) compared to site (b)?

Problem 5   Epithelial cells, as well as cells in many other tissues, appear to communicate with each other by permitting ions and small molecules to diffuse from cell to cell through "gap" junctions. How many gap junctions are needed? That is, how much area must be open between cells to ensure rapid diffusional exchange? In case (a), 0.2%

of the area of contact between cells is open. In case (b), 20% of the area is open. Compare the cell-to-cell diffusion times.

Problem 6   If the rate of diffusional exchange between two cells is strictly limited by the number of gap junctions present, does it matter how they are distributed? For example, if uniformly distributed gap junctions gather together in a cluster, will diffusional exchange be faster, slower, or unchanged?

Problem 7   If the cluster of gap junctions is drawn out into a line, will diffusional exchange be faster, slower, or unchanged?

The estimation of the transit time involves reasoning about features of the diffusion media that may enhance or delay diffusion to the target and about target geometry and position. This domain offers unique problematical advantages. The physical process of diffusion which is characterized by second-order partial differential equations and their initial and boundary conditions does not lend itself to simple mathematical analysis in cases of complicated boundaries. In addition, the nature of the process is such that there is no general way to formulate its dynamical behavior as interaction between fixed components. In an important sense, we are involved in a domain in which there is no clear correspondence between structure and function, and therefore the problem solver has to create a dynamic virtual structure based on the local process dynamics.

An interesting aspect of the preceding seven problems is the counter-intuitiveness of their solutions. Finding out what kinds of heuristics people use to answer the questions and how they fit in the explanations with their reasoning once they find out that they were wrong may provide an important insight into the nature of commonsense reasoning and intuition. Also, it may show how the particular way a problem is formulated biases the problem solver toward certain conceptualizations of the problem. This problem is further enhanced if the questions are posed to people who are not too familiar with technical abstractions. In the following we present some of the observations made on the nature of problem solving in the domain of diffusion when the (human) problem solver does not possess any specialized knowledge about diffusional flows. Most of the reasoning processes observed were based heavily on visualizations and mental simulation through analogies.

5   REASONING AND LACK OF KNOWLEDGE

The reasoning process being investigated appears extremely complex to model. This complexity may be a reflection of the way it is perceived through the existing problem-solving and simulation methods. In order to gain clues into the inferences involved in this process we have collected protocols of problem-solving sessions. Students were given the preceding set of seven problems in diffusion and were asked to make judgments concerning relative transit times. Most of the students had a little background in physics, and hence their reasoning was mostly based on their knowledge of everyday-life (naive) physics [12]. Since naive physics, which is based mostly on experience with inertial movements, does not in many cases provide the right guidance when it comes to problems in diffusion which is driven by random movements, most of the answers given by the students are wrong. However, in the collection of data we were interested in particular in the naive physics mental models and reasoning strategies involved in the reasoning process (see related research in refs. 5 and 14). The following are the highlights of the study.

5.1   The Importance of the Distance Traveled

The theme throughout the responses is the importance of distance traveled. In general, if distance traveled in the presented cases was judged to be equal, then transit times were also judged to be the same. If the distance traveled was longer in one case, then the transit time was reported as longer in that case. For example, in the case of problem 1, students who answered "the same in both" judged that distance traveled would be the same. The basis for this judgment seems to be: (i) The motion along the horizontal and vertical axes is independent. Since the horizontal distance is the same in both, the transit times must also be the same. (ii) Molecules travel only to the walls. One student wrote, "the molecules will take the shortest path which is the same for both." This idea of directed motion is likely to be based on everyday experience. The motion most familiar to us is directed motion. For example, one does not drive randomly in the hope of reaching his destination by chance. Students who responded "longer in (b)" believed that the molecules in the taller cylinder might travel longer. The distance from the center of the cylinder to a point on the wall near an end is longer in case (b) than in case (a). When averaged over all molecules, some students believed that those traveling to the extreme ends of the taller cylinder will bring up the transit time for that case.

5.2   The Influence of the Target Size

A significant number of students assumed that the accessibility of the target has a great impact on the diffusion transit time. For example, in problem 2 they answered "longer in (a)," assuming that the center target is smaller and therefore more difficult to hit. This reasoning may also be based on experience, which indicates that it is easier to hit a bigger target (like the outer sphere) than a smaller one (like the inner sphere). Although most of our experience with targets is based on directed motion (i.e., we generally aim at a target), the rule "bigger targets are easier to hit" seems applicable to the domain of random motion as well. One student drew the following analogy drawn from experience in answering question 5: "I'm reminded of people waiting at a gate. The wider it is, more people get through. That is, assuming that lots of ions want to go from one cell to the next."

5.3   The Effect of Inhomogeneous Media

In problem 3 the majority of students responding answered "the same in both." Their reasoning was based on the assumptions that (i) the same amounts of the same materials are traveled through in each case, (ii) the distance is the same in each case, and (iii) the order in which of the substances traveled through does not affect the diffusion rate. One response included an analogy to a familiar situation: "Liken the molecules to a man wading through water (the water) and then running through the sand (the oil). Reverse the order and still the times in the race should be the same, discounting exhaustion." People that concluded otherwise were generally concerned about the molecule's speed in each substance and how its travel through that substance would affect the rest of its trip. For example, one respondent wrote, "Since going through oil first will slow the molecule down for the rest of its trip, I think that it will take longer if it goes through oil first." The answers to question 3 also provide insight into the way the responders think about solubility. Comments about the molecule being more soluble in oil were varied, indicating the fact that this concept is less universal: (1) The molecules would accelerate faster if traveling through the highly soluble oil and then decelerate in water; (2) molecules that are highly soluble will tend to stay in a much confined place, or not move around as much; (3) they will be able to travel faster in the oil before they get to the water; and (4) the density of oil is greater than the density of water so molecules travel more slowly in oil.

5.4   Assumptions, Background Knowledge, and Mental Simulations

Each student who participated in this quiz has a unique set of experiences and beliefs which affect the interpretation of the problems, the judgment of the relative importance of several factors, and the ultimate answers to the questions. Several explanations referenced information that does not appear in the statement of the problem. Why and how was this information added? In problem 1, for example, students differed in their explanation of what happens to molecules when they reach an end of a cylinder. One student reasoned: "When the molecules are released from the center of the container, they will either reach a wall or diffuse through the top or bottom. Within the larger container less molecules will be lost with respect to (a) because there is more surface interior area of (b) to receive the diffused molecules" Another stated: "The average molecule in (a) would have to bounce off the top and bottom a few times before reaching the side. The average molecule in (b) would have a direct route to the side." Another person assumed the existence pressure in answering problem 2: "Being that the pressure is greater toward the middle of the sphere as compared to the outer part, the particle will be forced faster outward than inward." Notice that the problem does not mention pressure. This is information added by the student and used in solving the problem.

These answers, like many answers already mentioned, indicate the vivid visualization of the process by the problem solver. The latter creates what seems like a clear simulation of the diffusing particles. This simulation does not seem to involve strict overall boundary and initial conditions but instead seems to capture the essential aspects of the process which are needed in order to produce an answer.

Most of the reasoning protocols documented show a heavy use of analogies as a source of inferences. However, as already mentioned, since the analogies were mostly based on everyday-life physics which involved inertia, they usually provided the wrong answer. In the following we summarize the domain-specific heuristics that support reasoning about the problems presented in the quiz.

6 THE ESSENTIALS OF DIFFUSION SPEEDS

The domain of diffusional flows resembles the domain of everyday-life physical events only superficially. In order to be able to successfully reason about these flow processes, one must possess knowledge about the domain which is structured around the domain's unique abstractions. One of the distinguishing factors between reasoning by domain experts and reasoning by novices is that the former reasoning processes are driven knowledge which is organized around the appropriate abstractions so that no cross-contextual analogies which are prone to misconceptions are needed [e.g., 15, 20, 21].

In order to uncover some of the abstractions involved in the domain of diffusion, we have formulated the following eleven relations which are sufficient to answer the seven diffusion problems presented. The relations are tailored specifically to aid answering these problems and therefore may serve as an indicator for the content of the knowledge required and not necessarily of its granularity. Namely, many of these relations may represent a compiled version of reasoning chain built out of "smaller" relations, and the latter may have to be spelled out explicitly in order to answer other problems in the domain.

For readability we present the relation in the form of production rules with considerable amount of "syntactic sugar," for example, variable names (prefixed by '?') and predicate names are suggestive of their meaning. In all the eleven relations the following is true:

```
(and (is-region ?a) (is-region ?b) (is-homogeneous ?a)
(is-homogeneous ?b) (is-particle ?p) (is-position ?x)
(is-position ?y) (is-source ?source) (is-target ?target)
(is-time ?t) (is-time ?ta) (is-time ?tb) (is-time ?ti)
(is-interface ?interface))
```

Relation 1   Range of Influence   This relation states that the range of influence of a target is proportional to the elongation of the target:

```
IF (and (is-target ?s1) (is-target ?s2) (greater (long-
linear-dimension of ?s1) (long-linear-dimension of
?s2)))

THEN (greater (range-of-influence of ?s1) (range-of-
influence of ?s2))
```

Relation 2   Effectiveness   This relation states that the approachability of the target is proportional to its range of influence:

```
IF (and (is-target ?s1) (is-target ?s2) (greater
(range-of-influence of ?s1) (range-of-influence of
?s2)))
```

```
THEN (greater (approachability of ?s1) (approachability
of ?s2))
```

Relation 3   Approach Time   This relation states that the transit time to a target is inversely proportional to its approachability:

```
IF (and (is-target ?s1) (is-target ?s2) (is-particle ?p)
(is-position ?x) (greater (approachability of ?s1)
(approachability of ?s2)))
```

```
THEN (greater (transit-time of ?p from ?x to ?s2)
(transit-time of ?p from ?x to ?s1))
```

Relation 4   Target Overlap   This relation states that an addition of a target in between two targets with overlapping ranges of influence does not change the cluster's combined range of influence. In addition, this range of influence equals that of a single target with a long linear dimension equal to the distance between the two targets:

```
IF (and (is-target ?s1) (is-target ?s2) (is-target ?s3)
(is-target ?s4) (in-between ?s3 ?s2 ?s1) (equal (long-
linear-dimension ?s4) (distance of ?s1 from ?s2))
(greater (plus (range-of-influence of ?s1) (range-of-
influence of ?s2)) (distance of ?s1 from ?s2)))
```

```
THEN (and (equal (range-of-influence of ?s1 and ?s2)
(range-of-influence of ?s1 and ?s2 and ?s3)) (equal
(range-of-influence of ?s1 and ?s2) (range-of-influence
of ?s4)) )
```

Relation 5   Range of Nonoverlapping Targets   This relation states that the combined effect of nonoverlapping targets is the sum of their individual effects:

```
IF (and (is-target ?s1) (is-target ?s2) (greater
(distance of ?s1 from ?s2) (plus (range-of-influence of
?s1) (range-of-influence of ?s2)))
```

```
THEN (equal (range-of-influence of ?s1 and ?s2) (plus
(range-of-influence of ?s1) (range-of-influence of
?s2)))
```

Relation 6   Magnitude   This relation states that the range of influence is equal (approximately) to three times the long linear dimension of the target:

```
IF (equal (range-of-influence of ?s) ?x)

THEN (equal ?x (times 3 (long-linear-dimension of ?s)))
```

Relation 7   Symmetry   This relation states that the transit time between two points in an homogeneous space is independent of the direction of the motion:

```
IF (equal (transit-time of ?p from (?x in ?a) to (?y in
?a)) ?t)

THEN (equal (transit-time of ?p from (?y in ?a) to (?x
in ?a)) ?t)
```

Relation 8   Accessibility   This relation states that the transit time is inversely proportional to the accessibility of the target:

```
IF (greater (accessibility of ?p to ?a) (accessibility
of ?p to ?b))

THEN (greater (duration of ?p at ?a) (duration of ?p at
?b))
```

Relation 9   Interference   This relation states that the time spent going back and forth before being captured by a target in one region is inversely proportional to the duration spent at that region:

```
IF (greater (duration of ?p at ?a) (duration of ?p at
?b))

THEN (greater (interference-time of ?p from (?source in
?a) to (?target in ?b))(interference-time of ?p from
(?source in ?b) to (?target in ?a)))
```

Relation 10   Time Decomposition   This relation states that the transit time across two regions is the sum of the times to cross each region separately plus the interference time:

```
IF (and (equal (transit-time of ?p from (?source in ?a)
to (?interface in ?a)) ?ta)

(equal (transit-time of ?p from (?interface in ?b) to
(?target in ?b)) ?tb)

(equal (interference-time of ?p from (?source in ?a) to
(?target in ?b)) ?ta))
```

```
THEN (equal (transit-time from (?source in ?a) to
(?target in ?b)) (plus ?ta ?tb ?ti))
```

Relation 11   Affinity   Given that all geometric parameters are the same for the two regions, this relation states that the accessibility of a region to a particle is proportional to its affinity to that region. Affinity may be set by the chemical nature of the diffusion medium. For example, a certain diffusing particle may have a high affinity to oil, and then using relation 11 we conclude that a target which is placed in the oil will have higher accessibility. However, notice that accessibility may be determined by many other parameters such as the existence of an obstacle:

```
IF (greater (affinity of ?p to ?a) (affinity of ?p to
?b))
```

```
THEN (greater (accessibility of ?p to ?a) (accessibility
of ?p to ?b))
```

Answering the seven quiz problems involves building the appropriate reasoning chains using these relations. Figure 3 illustrates the reasoning chains that can provide

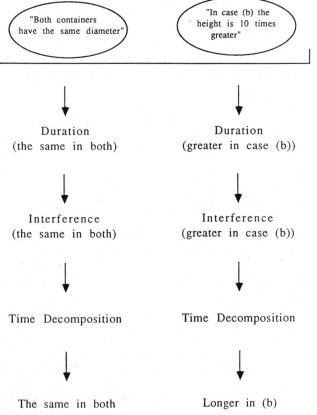

Figure 3. Reasoning chains that can provide answers to problem 1.

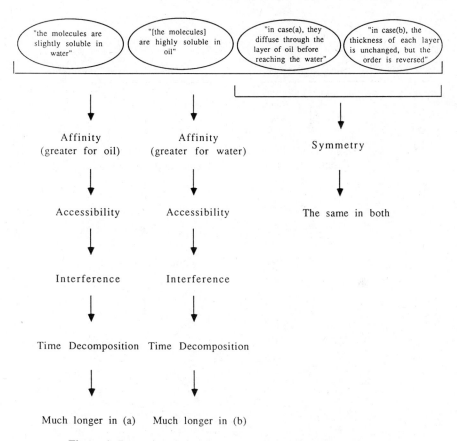

Figure 4. Reasoning chains that can provide answers to problem 1.

answers to problem 1. There are two chains possible depending on the property of the situation which is judged as most important. The chain on the left provides the right answer. Figure 4 illustrates the reasoning chains that may be built after the interpretation of problem 3. Here, again, the correct answer depends on the correct interpretation of the problems and the correct assessment of the importance of the various features mentioned. The right answer is shown on the left. The middle chain leads to the wrong answer because of a misinterpretation of the concept of solubility as related to affinity. The chain on the right places centrality to the distance traveled and therefore yields the wrong answer. Figure 5 illustrates the reasoning chain for problem 5. Figure 6 illustrates the reasoning chain for problems 6 (left) and 7 (right).

7   PROBLEM PERSPECTIVE AND DECOMPOSITION

One of the major reasons behind formulating relations in the domain is to disclose effective primitive vocabulary for each level of description. From the work it became apparent that concepts such as accessibility, range of influence, long linear dimension, interference, time decomposition, overlap, duration, and interference time provide

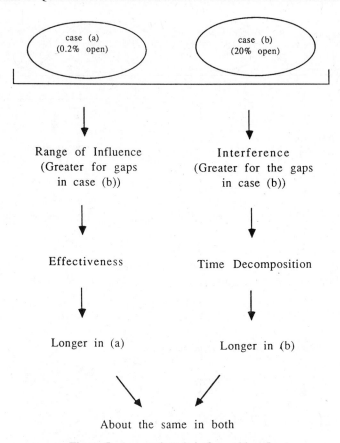

Figure 5. A reasoning chain for problem 5.

structure to the problem and play a major role in knowledge organization.

However, it is important to note that these concepts are very high level and that there is a great conceptual gap between them and the problem description in each case. For example, the range of influence of the target can be defined as that region in space where particles are most likely to find the target. In order to solve problem 4, for example, one should only know that the range of influence is determined by the long linear dimension of the target and not by its area. From this observation one deduces that the a particle will find the elongated target (b) faster. As will be shown later, reasoning about the range of influence can also be used effectively in other problems.

If we now examine the preceding reasoning process, it becomes apparent that the concept of the range of influence has its power in providing a structure to the diffusion space. In effect, it divides this space into a region where the diffusional drift toward the target is fast and a region where it is slow. It should be noted that this concept is part of a conceptual framework that looks at diffusion as a flow process, ignoring details of the individual particle's behavior with the benefit of computational economy. Since this framework can be reduced to and explained by the detailed dynamics of the individual particle's random walk, it is used essentially with no loss of relevant details. For instance, to explain why the transit time is determined by the linear dimension of

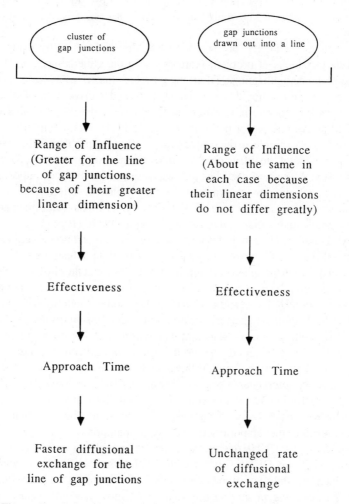

Figure 6. A reasoning chain for problems 6 (left) and problem 7 (right).

the target and not by its area, we can argue thus that an elongated target reduces the search space in its vicinity (range of influence) to two dimensions and a randomly moving particle on the average gets to the target faster in two dimensions than in three.

8 PROBLEM INTERPRETATION AND REASONING

The vocabulary around which the domain knowledge is organized has to be sufficiently abstract in order to be reasonably useful (see a discussion in ref. 12) for solving problems in the domain. Consequently, most problem-solving tasks involve a process of problem interpretation which, in a sense, provides a translation between the vocabulary used to express the problem and the domain vocabulary used for reasoning.

This translation process is dependent on the state of knowledge of the problem solver, and as we saw, lack of knowledge may result in serious misinterpretations of the problem.

One way to model the problem interpretation process is by using a feature recognizer that looks at problem features and groups them successively to form meaningful conceptualizations. Of all the possible clusters which can be computed, only the relevant ones should be singled out and used to drive the reasoning process. In this processing scheme, the reasoning process described in the previous sections can be viewed as the one performed after the preliminary interpretation is completed successfully. For example, in the simple case presented by problem 3, the system is told about the division of the diffusion space into two meaningful regions, the oil and the water. Ideally, the system itself has to infer that the preceding decomposition of the diffusion space is the most relevant one for the problem description.

To further investigate this type of problem solving, we have designed and studied the knowledge organization and reasoning scheme DUNE [10, 11].

DUNE is made out of modules and contains domain and processing knowledge. Each module in DUNE represents a possible cluster of input features and each feature may have a different weight in determining the relevance of the cluster to the problem. Each module can run concurrently with other modules and communicate with them. Each module in DUNE can run concurrently with other modules and communicate with them. A module may perform a variety of operations on its data, and its actions are based on both its internal state and its environment. For the segmentation step, DUNE is used as a collection of top-down processors, and it is now capable of distinguishing between the shapes involved in the diffusion problems and derive some of the necessary inferences discussed. From this end, we view the computations involved in reasoning as composed of steps of parallel feature aggregations. Since some features cannot be computed before others, the sequential element in the process is a direct result of the temporal sequence of computations.

To illustrate how DUNE operates as a qualitative problem solver, we will examine in the following how DUNE solves problem 2. For the sake of brevity and of clarity we introduce here only a portion of the database. Furthermore, we have simplified the demons participating in solving problem 2 and show only the aspects which are relevant for this problem.

In the following some of the participating demons are introduced. The first demon is the demon which is capable of detecting a situation in which the diffusion transit time between the source and the target is longer than some base case. This demon bases its judgment on particular features (criteria), and each feature has its value toward the total confidence of this demon. For example, the line

```
(2 ((longer-source-target-distance 30) (same-target-
accessibility 0)) 70)
```

denotes that two of the features are needed and when they are both present 70 is added to the demon confidence value. In this case, if only the first feature exists, 30 is added to the confidence value of the demon. (The 70 is regarded here as a bonus added in addition to the contributions of the individual features.) A theoretical discussion of this probabilistic technique is given elsewhere [11]. The line

```
(higher-interference 95)
```

signifies that when a situation of higher interference is encountered, 95 is added to the current confidence value of the demon. When a demon accumulates a confidence of 90, it broadcasts its name and the latter is treated as a new feature by the rest of the demons. The other demons shown next follow a similar description. Not shown in this example are inhibitory features between demons which cause the removal of demons from the computation:

```
(defdem      'longer-transit-time
             '((criteria (
             (2 ((longer-source-target-distance 30)
             (same-target-accessibility 0)) 70)
             (higher-interference 95)
             (lower-target-accessibility 95)))))

(defdem      'lower-target-accessibility
             '((criteria (
             (smaller-target-size 95)
             (hidden-target 95)
             (target-dimensionality-effect 95)
             (lower-solubility-target-phase 95)))))

(defdem      'smaller-target-size
             '((criteria (
             (smaller-target-area 20)
             (smaller-target-linear-dimension 100)))))

(defdem      'smaller-target-linear-dimension
             '((criteria (
             (source-surrounding-target 95)))))

(defdem      'hidden-target
             '((criteria (
             (obstacle-near-target 90)))))

(defdem      'obstacle-near-target
             '((criteria (
             (on-source-target-path-obstacle 90)))))
```

The demon's computational features may be viewed from different perspectives. For example, their behavior is somewhat similar to that of production rules in a production system where the left side of the rules (the demon's criteria list) contains an activation pattern and the right side (the demon's name) contains a simple atomic expression. Another way to view the demons is as a special case of a neural net where nodes (demons' names and criteria) are connected through excitation and inhibition links with different weights. Each node has a strength (confidence) during the computation which is based on features seen so far.

Investigations related to the discovery of the appropriate vocabulary for low-level structural features and the clustering of these features reveal processing strategies similar to the those employed in vision research, especially in the field of high-level vision, as in the use of visual routines [23] during visual perception. These perceptual demons are capable of noticing such situations as smaller target area, smaller target linear dimension, obstacle near target, and source surrounding target.

In the following we present an example in which DUNE solves problem 2 which was introduced earlier using the demons presented previously and a few other system demons that perform management tasks. The only user input in this case is the fact the source is surrounding the target. The rest is done spontaneously by the system. First the demon smaller-target-linear-dimension grabs the feature source-surrounding-target which was given by the user, as is denoted by the line

```
Message- (feature user 1 source-surrounding-target)
```

and as a result gains a confidence value of 95 which enables it to broadcast the feature smaller-target-linear-dimension as is denoted by the lines

```
Message- (feature smaller-target-linear-dimension 1.1
smaller-target-linear-dimension)
```

This new finding is treated by the collection of demons as a new feature and hence is grabbed by the demon smaller-target-size which as a result has a confidence value of 100. After this fact is broadcast, the demon lower-target-accessibility gains a confidence value of 95 which results in the activation of the demon longer-transit-time with confidence of 95. At this point the processing stops. The following demonstrates the full processing protocol:

```
Message- (feature user 1 source-surrounding-target)
```

DEMON	STATE	CONF
smaller-target-linear-dimension	ALIVE	95
obstacle-near-target	ALIVE	0
hidden-target	ALIVE	0
smaller-target-size	ALIVE	0
lower-target-accessibility	ALIVE	0
longer-transit-time	ALIVE	0

```
Message- (feature smaller-target-linear-dimension 1.1
smaller-target-linear-dimension)
```

```
DEMON                                    STATE      CONF
smaller-target-linear-dimension          ALIVE      95
obstacle-near-target                     ALIVE      0
hidden-target                            ALIVE      0
smaller-target-size                      ALIVE      100
lower-target-accessibility               ALIVE      0
longer-transit-time                      ALIVE      0


Message- (feature smaller-target-size 1.2 smaller-
target-size)
DEMON                                    STATE      CONF
smaller-target-linear-dimension          ALIVE      95
obstacle-near-target                     ALIVE      0
hidden-target                            ALIVE      0
smaller-target-size                      ALIVE      100
lower-target-accessibility               ALIVE      95
longer-transit-time                      ALIVE      0


Message- (feature lower-target-accessibility 1.3 lower-
target-accessibility)
DEMON                                    STATE      CONF
smaller-target-linear-dimension          ALIVE      95
obstacle-near-target                     ALIVE      0
hidden-target                            ALIVE      0
smaller-target-size                      ALIVE      100
lower-target-accessibility               ALIVE      95
longer-transit-time                      ALIVE      95


Message- (feature longer-transit-time 1.4 longer-
transit-time)

Please give a distinctive feature of the situation.
(type 'done' to end, and 'ask' for a question) -> done
```

Notice that at the end of the problem-solving session the system contains a record of all the activated demons. This pattern of activity which captures the trace of the problem-solving steps is then used to store the solution to the problem. The automatic indexing scheme used to store the solution so that future similar problem-solving sessions can activate it is denoted a "soft" indexing scheme and is reported in Hardt [9].

9   DISCUSSION

To enhance the power of qualitative analysis, reasoning, and simulation theories and programs, we need to elaborate and integrate various qualitative problem-solving methods discovered and developed in the fields of AI, simulation, mathematics, and physics for the purpose of modeling, predicting, and explaining the behaviors of physical systems. (In addition to the work discussed so far see discussions in refs. 2, 24, 26, and 27.) Each of the methods offers a different outlook on the dynamic system and its components and therefore involves its own vocabulary, relations, and control structures. The benefits of the work will include new theoretical insight into problem-solving architecture as well as theoretical tools to improve the performance of the systems. In addition, it will improve understanding of the partial intuitive methods used so successfully in mathematics and physics by making more explicit the reasoning that leads us to a solution.

ACKNOWLEDGMENT

This research was supported in part by the National Science Foundation under grant number MCS-8305249.

REFERENCES

1. T. Bylander and B. Chandrasekaran, "Understanding Behavior Using Consolidation," in *Proceedings of the Ninth IJCAI , Los Angeles CA,* Morgan Kaufmann, San Mateo, CA, pp. 450–454, 1985.

2. B. Chandrasekaran, "Generic Tasks in Knowledge-Based Reasoning: High-Level Building Blocks for Expert System Design," *IEEE Expert,* **3**:23–30, 1986.

3. J. De Kleer and J. S. Brown, "A Qualitative Physics Based on Confluences." *Artificial Intelligence,* **24**:7–83, 1984.

4. K. D. Forbus, "Qualitative Process Theory," *Artificial Intelligence,* **24**:85–168, 1984.

5. D. Gentner and D. R. Gentner, "Flowing Waters or Teeming Crowds: Mental Models of Electricity, in D. Gentner and A. L. Stevens (Eds.), *Mental Models.* Lawrence Erlbaum, Hillsdale, NJ, 1983, pp. 101–129.

6. S. L. Hardt, "Pace of Diffusion Through Membranes," *Journal of Membrane Biology,* **48**: 299–330, 1979.

7. S. L. Hardt, "Naive Physics and the Physics of Diffusion. Or: When Intuition Fails," Research Report number 211, Department of Computer Science University at Buffalo, 1984.

8. S. L. Hardt, in S. Levin (Ed.), *Diffusion in Structured Media,* Lecture Notes in Biomathematics, Springer-Verlag.

9. S. L. Hardt, "A "Soft" Indexing Method for Case Memory," in E. Rissland and J. King (Eds.), *Proceedings of the AAAI Workshop on Case Based Reasoning, Minneapolis, MN,* 1988.

10. S. L. Hardt, D. MacFadden, M. Johnson, T. Thomas and S. Wroblewski, "The DUNE Shell Manual: Version 1," Research Report 12–86, Department of Computer Science, State University of New York at Buffalo, 1986.

11. S. L. Hardt and G. L. Sicherman, in J. F. Lemmer (Ed.), *A Computational Model for*

Flexible Evaluation. Uncertainty in Artificial Intelligence, Vol. 2. North-Holland, Amsterdam, 1987.

12. P. Hayes, "The Naive Physics Manifesto," in J. R. Hobbs and and R. C. Moore (Eds.), *Formal Theories of the Commonsense World,* Ablex, Norwood, NJ, pp. 1–36, 1985.

13. P. Hayes, "The Ontology for Liquids," in J. R. Hobbs and R. C. Moore (Eds.), *Formal Theories of the Commonsense World,* Ablex, Norwood, NJ, pp. 71–108, 1985.

14. M. K. Kaiser, J. Jonides and J. Alexander, "Intuitive Reasoning about Abstract and Familiar Physical Problems," *Memory and Cognition*, **14**:308–312, 1986.

15. J. L. Kolodner, *Retrieval and Organizational Strategies in Conceptual Memory: A Computer Model*, Lawrence Erlbaum, Hillsdale, NJ, 1984.

16. B. J. Kuipers, "Qualitative Simulation," *Artificial Intelligence*, **29**:289–338, 1986.

17. B. J. Kuipers, "Abstraction by Time Scale in Qualitative Simulation," *Proceedings of AAAI87, Seattle WA., 1987,* Morgan Kaufmann, San Mateo, CA, pp. 621–625.

18. C. C. Lin and L. A. Segel, *Mathematics Applied to Deterministic Problems in the Natural Sciences.* Macmillan, New York, 1974.

19. A. Newell, "The Knowledge Level," *Artificial Intelligence*, **18**:87–127, 1982.

20. R. E. Nisbett, G. T. Fong, D. R. Lehman and P. W. Cheng, "Teaching Reasoning," *Science*, **238**:625–631, 1987.

21. C. K. Riesbeck, "Knowledge Reorganization and Reasoning Style," in M. J. Coombs (Ed.), *Developments in Expert Systems*, Academic, New York, 1984, pp. 159–175.

22. R. C. Schank, *Dynamic Memory. A Theory of Reminding and Learning in Computers and People.* Cambridge University Press, Cambridge, 1982.

23. S. Ullman, "Visual Routines," in S. Pinker (Ed.), *Visual Cognition,* Bradford Books, MIT Press, Cambridge, MA, 1985.

24. D. S. Weld, "The Use of Aggregation in Causal Simulation," *Artificial Intelligence*, **30**: 1–34, 1986.

25. D. S. Weld, "Comparative Analysis," *Proceedings of the Tenth IJCAI. Milano, Italy,* 1987, pp. 959–965.

26. L. E. Widman, "Semi-Quantitative 'Close Enough' Systems Dynamics Models: An Alternative to Qualitative Simulation," Chapter 6, this book.

27. B. P. Zeigler and T. I. Oren, "Multifacetted, Multiparadigm Modelling Perspectives: Tools for the 90's," in J. Wilson, J. Henrikson, and S. Roberts (Eds.), *Winter Simulation Conference. ACM, Washington DC, 1986,* IEEE Publications, pp. 460–463.

PART III
Applying Artificial Intelligence to Enrich Simulation

13 The Role of Causal and Noncausal Constraints in Steady-State Qualitative Modeling

OLAYIWOLA O. OYELEYE and MARK A. KRAMER

Department of Chemical Engineering
Massachusetts Institute of Technology
Cambridge, Massachusetts

1 INTRODUCTION

The traditional cornerstones of physical systems modeling are mathematical conservation laws, constitutive relationships, and correlations. Numerical solutions to these equations have significant predictive value and may be interpreted to recognize important events or provide an explanation for the behavior of the system [10]. Human cognition, however, operates at a level of abstraction where qualitative reasoning supplements or supplants numerical processing. Within certain limits, humans employing "physical insight," scientific principles, and/or experience can predict the qualitative behavior of physical systems without resort to detailed numerical analysis.

The current generation of expert systems that emulate the problem-solving ability of humans generally do not exploit the underlying principles of the problem domain. Consequently, these systems often fail when confronted with an unfamiliar problem [6]. This has stimulated research on formal methods of qualitative modeling [1]. Where qualitative models suffice, there may be great economies in avoiding theoretical developments, exhaustive collection of data, and the long computer times associated with conventional numerical simulation. However, qualitative reasoning is fundamentally underspecified and prone to the production of multiple solutions. The primary objective of this chapter is to address the question of multiplicity in qualitative modeling and to identify the elements of steady-state qualitative models that are necessary to minimize spurious interpretations.

As chemical engineers, the systems of primary interest to us are continuous processes, characterized by continuous inflows and outflows of mass and energy, with state variables that are continuous real-valued functions of time. Often these processes are designed to operate at steady state, that is, the process state variables are time invariant. Qualitative simulation in this context entails predicting qualitative changes that may occur in continuous systems due to external disturbances or malfunctions. When a continuous system at steady state is perturbed, state variables change during the transient and ultimately may attain a new steady state. In this chapter, we do not attempt to predict the process behavior during the transient; we focus only on the ultimate (long-time) response of processes to malfunctions. This information is useful in malfunction diagnosis, and other applications may be found in areas such as process control, planning, and design analysis.

Previously, several qualitative simulation methods for continuous systems have been proposed, including qualitative physics methods based on confluences [4], deep-level mechanism models [16], qualitative differential equations [10, 12], and qualitative process theory [7]. All of these methods formulate qualitative models in terms of constraints derived from the physical structure of the system, differing primarily in the way the constraints are derived. In this chapter, constraints are derived from the conventional differential and algebraic equation description of the process. Qualitative behavior is determined by constraint satisfaction as described elsewhere [14]. The state description produced by the constraints is the ultimate direction of change of variables from the initial steady state, represented as $(+, 0, -)$, corresponding to higher than, equal to, or lower than the initial steady-state value.

The loss of numerical information in qualitative modeling potentially leads to multiple solutions (interpretations) of system behavior [4]. Some of these interpretations may be real and valid for some member of the qualitative class of the system while others may be spurious and not exhibited by any quantitative realization of the system's qualitative class. (Systems that differ only in quantitative aspects but have an identical qualitative representation are considered members of the same qualitative class.) Ideally, interpretations produced by a qualitative model should include interpretations for all members of the system's qualitative class (completeness) and be realized by a quantitative realization of the class (realizability). Kuipers [11] has proven that qualitative models in general cannot be guaranteed to exclude spurious interpretations.

Therefore, a major challenge in qualitative modeling is elimination of spurious interpretations. We address this problem by highlighting the role of noncausal and causal constraints in Sections 2 and 3, respectively. An example of qualitative simulation of a complex chemical reactor system is presented in Section 4. Although our examples are drawn from chemical engineering, the elements of our theory are domain independent and can be applied to qualitative modeling of continuous systems in other domains.

2 SIMULATION OF STEADY STATES BY CONFLUENCES

Quantitative mathematical models of continuous systems consist of sets of simultaneous algebraic and differential equations. In the steady-state limit, these models can be reduced to algebraic equation models by eliminating time derivatives and by discretization or lumping of spatial dimensions. Disturbances and faults can be represented by parametric perturbation of the steady-state equations. In this section, we show how the algebraic equations describing the perturbed steady state provide qualitative constraints on the ultimate direction of change of system variables.

2.1 Local Steady-State Constraints

The quantitative model describing a system at steady state can be expressed as a set of n independent nonlinear equations

$$\mathbf{f(x, u, p)} = \mathbf{0}, \qquad (\mathbf{u} = \mathbf{u}_0, \quad \mathbf{p} = \mathbf{p}_0, \quad \text{at} \quad t = 0), \tag{1}$$

where $\mathbf{x}$ is a vector of n independent state variables and $\mathbf{u}$ and $\mathbf{p}$ are vectors of externally specified variables (inputs) and system parameters, respectively. Because of the possibility of algebraic manipulation, this set of equations is not unique. However, in formulating the model, the modeler usually writes equations that refer to particular units or subsystems so that each equation is *local* and does not involve variables in non-adjacent subsystems.

For a finite perturbation from the initial steady state, the change in the system can be expressed as

$$\int \frac{\partial \mathbf{f}}{\partial \mathbf{x}} \cdot d\mathbf{x} + \int \frac{\partial \mathbf{f}}{\partial \mathbf{u}} \cdot d\mathbf{u} + \int \frac{\partial \mathbf{f}}{\partial \mathbf{p}} \cdot d\mathbf{p} = \mathbf{0}, \tag{2}$$

where the lower and upper limits of integration are the initial and final steady states, respectively. Applying the mean value theorem, Equation (2) becomes

$$\frac{\partial \bar{\mathbf{f}}}{\partial \mathbf{x}} \cdot \Delta \mathbf{x} + \frac{\partial \bar{\mathbf{f}}}{\partial \mathbf{u}} \cdot \Delta \mathbf{u} + \frac{\partial \bar{\mathbf{f}}}{\partial \mathbf{p}} \cdot \Delta \mathbf{p} = \mathbf{0}, \tag{3}$$

where $\partial \bar{\mathbf{f}} / \partial \mathbf{i}$ is the mean value of the partial derivative along the integration path. Steady-state confluences can be derived by qualitative translation of Equation (3):

$$\left[\frac{\partial \bar{\mathbf{f}}}{\partial \mathbf{x}} \cdot \Delta \mathbf{x} \right] + \left[\frac{\partial \bar{\mathbf{f}}}{\partial \mathbf{u}} \cdot \Delta \mathbf{u} \right] + \left[\frac{\partial \bar{\mathbf{f}}}{\partial \mathbf{p}} \cdot \Delta \mathbf{p} \right] = \mathbf{0}. \tag{4a}$$

The square brackets represent the qualitative value (sign) of the argument. The operations of qualitative algebra are defined in Table 1. Note that addition of quantities of opposite sign results in ambiguity since relative magnitudes are not known. Under the rules of qualitative algebra, Equation (4a) is equivalent to

$$\left[\frac{\partial \bar{\mathbf{f}}}{\partial \mathbf{x}} \right] \cdot [\Delta \mathbf{x}] + \left[\frac{\partial \bar{\mathbf{f}}}{\partial \mathbf{u}} \right] \cdot [\Delta \mathbf{u}] + \left[\frac{\partial \bar{\mathbf{f}}}{\partial \mathbf{p}} \right] \cdot [\Delta \mathbf{p}] = \mathbf{0}. \tag{4b}$$

TABLE 1. Tables of Qualitative Operations

[dY]	\[dX\] +	\[dX\] 0	\[dX\] -	\[dX\] ?
	\[dX\] + \[dY\]			
+	+	+	?	?
0	+	0	-	?
-	?	-	-	?
?	?	?	?	?
	\[dX\] − \[dY\]			
+	?	-	-	?
0	+	0	-	?
-	+	+	?	?
?	?	?	?	?
	\[dX\] · \[dY\]			
+	+	0	-	?
0	0	0	0	0
-	-	0	+	?
?	?	0	?	?
	δ(\[dX\])			
	0	+	0	+ or 0

In order to maintain consistency with the notation of de Kleer and Brown [4], Equation (4b) is rewritten as

$$\left[\frac{\partial \mathbf{f}}{\partial \mathbf{x}}\right] \cdot [d\mathbf{x}] + \left[\frac{\partial \mathbf{f}}{\partial \mathbf{u}}\right] \cdot [d\mathbf{u}] + \left[\frac{\partial \mathbf{f}}{\partial \mathbf{p}}\right] \cdot [d\mathbf{p}] = 0, \qquad (4c)$$

where the differential d refers to a total macroscopic rather than an infinitesimal change in a quantity.

Equation (4c) is a set of equations that are sums of products of parameter–variable relationships (partial derivatives) and differential quantities, also known as "mixed" confluences [4]. These can be converted to a set of "pure" confluences (a simple sum of differential quantities) by assigning fixed signs to the partial derivatives. This is done by defining a set of inequality constraints **C** under which the partial derivatives in Equation (2) possess the same signs as at the initial state. Usually, the signs of the partial derivatives are determined from ordinal relationships. For example, state variable and physical parameter values are usually positive; the heating stream temperature is normally higher than the cooling stream temperature at points along a heat exchanger. Within **C**, the average values of the derivatives along the path of integration must have the same sign as the partial derivative at the initial state. The ranges of state variables and parameter values which satisfy these inequalities define the range of the validity of the "pure" confluences, that is, the scope of the system's qualitative class.

During a transient, the inequality conditions **C** defining the qualitative class can be violated, leading to a transition between qualitative regimes. Typical qualitative transitions are phase changes, flow reversals, and controller saturation. The problem of identifying potential class transitions has been addressed elsewhere [4, 7, 10, 20]. At best these analyses provide a partial ordering but do not determine which transitions actually occur since this determination usually requires numerical information. In this work, it will be assumed that transitions between qualitative regimes do not occur unless otherwise indicated.

The functional relationships in Equation (1) do not have to be completely specified in order to derive confluences. For example, the equation which describes the flow of liquid for all classes of control valves is

$$F = f^{+}(V, \ |P_I - P_O|) \cdot (P_I - P_O) \ / \ |P_I - P_O| \tag{5}$$

where f^{+} is an unspecified monotonically increasing function of the valve stem position V and the absolute pressure difference $|P_I - P_O|$. For forward flow, $(P_I > P_O)$, the confluence derived from this equation, independent of the exact nature of f^{+}, is

$$[dF] = [dP_I] - [dP_O] + [dV]. \tag{6}$$

Equation (6) states that a positive change in flowrate cannot occur without either a positive change in inlet pressure or valve stem position or a negative change in outlet pressure. This confluence is a logical constraint on the behavior of the valve and not an indication of causality. Causality cannot be construed from this equation, as increased flow would not cause opening of the valve, but could result in increased downstream pressure.

The set of confluences [Equation (4c)] forms a set of inherently simultaneous qualitative equations. A constraint satisfaction technique is used to find solutions to the system [3, 14]. All qualitative patterns of variables that satisfy every confluence in the set are feasible solutions. In testing a confluence, appearance of the ambiguous value, (?), automatically satisfies the confluence. The consequence of this ambiguity is that a set of n independent confluences in n unknowns is not guaranteed to yield a unique solution. If ambiguities cannot be resolved within a set of confluences, multiple solutions result. The set of values $(+, 0, -)$ do not form an algebraic group under qualitative algebraic operations. Therefore, there is no general theory for prediction of solution uniqueness or multiplicity.

2.2   Resolving Ambiguity with Latent Constraints

In cases where multiple solutions result, some of the solutions to the system of independent confluences may be spurious while others may be genuine and occur for certain quantitative realizations of the system. In this section, a procedure for deriving additional noncausal confluences which reduce the number of spurious solutions is outlined.

Qualitative arithmetic in general requires more equations than unknowns to generate unique solutions. Thus, it is usually necessary to begin with an *overspecified* set of quantitative equations to get a fully determined set of confluences. Latent constraints are additional confluences derived from redundant quantitative equations. These redundant equations are derived by algebraic manipulation of the independent equation set [Equation (1)]. As a general rule, redundant equations containing no more, but preferably fewer, nonzero variables than the independent equations from which they are derived are less likely to yield ambiguity and thus are most useful in eliminating spurious solutions.

The potential number of latent confluences that can be derived via algebraic manipulation increases at least exponentially, $O(2^n)$, with the number of variables [14]. Confluences involving one unknown (i.e., the analytical solution set) are included in the potential set of redundant equations. Thus, if an analytical solution to the system exists, the redundant set of noncausal, steady-state confluences is theoretically able to provide the ultimate qualitative response from all (stable and unstable) steady states without other solutions. However, because of analytical complexities and the large number of potential latent confluences, a heuristic approach to deriving latent constraints is needed.

Although the heuristics used to derive latent confluences may be domain dependent, the following heuristics have been employed to guide the search for useful latent constraints in several domains:

(a) *Global Balances for Conserved Quantities* Because of the ambiguity of qualitative arithmetic, qualitative balances for conserved fundamental quantities around subsystems do not necessarily assure conservation of the quantities in the combined system. Examples of these quantities are total mass, species mass, energy, and electric current. Equations (10a) and (10b) are latent confluences of this type.

(b) *Compatibility Relationships* These confluences derive from equating driving forces around loops for potential driven flows. Confluences derived from Kirchhoff's voltage law and pressure compatibility relationships in bypass or recycle loops [Equation (10c)] are examples of this type.

(c) *Balances from Bilinear Conservation Relationships* In several domains, conserved fundamental quantities (e.g., energy) are expressed as products of extensive (mass or volume) and intensive variables (e.g., temperature). Eliminating one of the extensive variables (by using an extensive variable balance) from bilinear conservation equations around the subsystem often results in useful confluences [Equation (9c)]. Confluences derived from redundant component balances (m species plus an overall balance) in systems with m components [Equation (B.36)] are also examples of this type.

(d) *Elimination of Groups of Variables* Characteristic groupings of variables often occur in equations. Elimination of these groups can result in useful latent confluences, especially when the resulting equation contains fewer variables than one of the original equations. Equation (B.37), which is obtained by eliminating the reaction rate term from the reactant mass balance and reactor energy balance in the example of Section 4, is an example of this type.

As yet we have no general method of determining, a priori, how many and which latent confluences are required to eliminate all spurious solutions. In our experience, where a unique qualitative solution is obtained, the number of noncausal latent confluences [types (a) through (d) above] required to eliminate all spurious solutions is less than the number of independent equations.

2.3   Trade-off between Modularity and Multiplicity

Strategies (a) and (b) for deriving latent constraints reveal a very important limitation in qualitative modeling, involving modularity. Modularity is the property that the behavior of a system can be deduced from the behavior of the components of the system. In conventional modeling, the ability to divide a system into its component subsystems has been an extremely useful concept that has led to among other things the creation of modular simulation programs. A similar property is desired in qualitative modeling. However, in general, confluences related to subsystems do not yield unambiguously the global behavior of the system.

In the subsequent example, it will be seen that satisfaction of qualitative mass (energy) balances on subsystems does not automatically result in satisfaction of the mass (energy) balances of the combined system. Similarly, qualitative pressure drop relations at the local or subsystem level do not guarantee pressure compatibility at the global level across recycle or bypass loops. Omission of "global" latent constraints of types (a) and (b) can result in generation of spurious interpretations of system behavior. Therefore, in qualitative modeling, there is a trade-off between modularity and solution multiplicity.

2.4   Example of Simulation Using Confluences

Figure 1 shows a countercurrent heat exchanger with a bypass on the hot stream to control the cold-stream outlet temperature. Boundary pressures, inlet temperatures,

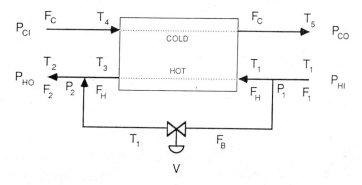

Figure 1. Schematic of countercurrent heat exchanger with bypass.

and valve stem position are externally specified. Fluid physical properties are assumed constant. This system can be modeled with 10 state variables (see the notation section at the end of the chapter) using the equations listed in Appendix A.

The local (basic) steady-state confluences derived from the equations in Appendix A are

$$[dF_C] = [dP_{CI}] - [dP_{CO}], \tag{7a}$$

$$[dF_1] = [dP_{HI}] - [dP_1], \tag{7b}$$

$$[dF_H] = [dP_1] - [dP_2], \tag{7c}$$

$$[dF_B] = [dV] + [dP_1] - [dP_2], \tag{7d}$$

$$[dF_2] = [dP_2] - [dP_{HO}], \tag{7e}$$

$$[dF_1] = [dF_H] + [dF_B], \tag{7f}$$

$$[dF_2] = [dF_H] + [dF_B], \tag{7g}$$

$$[dF_C] + [dT_5] - [dT_4] = [dF_H] + [dT_1] - [dT_3], \tag{7h}$$

$$[dF_B] + [dT_1] + [dF_H] + [dT_3] = [dF_2] + [dT_2]. \tag{7i}$$

No confluence is derived from Equation (A.1i) because the sign of the partial derivative with respect to T_4 cannot be uniquely determined from empirical ordinal relationships.

An increase in valve stem position (opening the valve) implies

$$[dV] = (+), \qquad [dU] = (0), \tag{8a}$$

$$[dP_{HI}] = [dP_{HO}] = [dP_{CI}] = [dP_{CO}] = [dT_1] = [dT_4] = (0). \tag{8b}$$

The combined system of confluences [Equations (7)–(8)], although derived from a set of equations that has a unique solution in the quantitative domain, has 105 solutions.

To reduce this solution set, three additional local latent confluences can be derived from Equations (A.1a)–(A.1j). These are

$$[dT_3] = [dF_H] - [dF_C] + [dT_1] + [dT_4] - [dU], \tag{9a}$$

$$[dT_5] = [dF_H] - [dF_C] + [dT_1] + [dT_4] + [dU], \tag{9b}$$

from explicit solutions for the heat exchanger outlet temperatures [Equations (A.2a) and (A.2b)], and

$$[dF_B] + [dT_1] + [dT_3] = [dF_H] + [dT_2] \tag{9c}$$

from a redundant energy balance about node 2 in the bypass loop [Equation (A.2c)]. There are 21 solutions (interpretations 7–27 in Table 2) to the basic and local latent confluences, Equations (7)–(9).

Three global latent confluences can also be derived for this system. These are

$$[dF_1] = [dF_2] \tag{10a}$$

from an overall mass balance [Equation (A.3a)],

$$[dF_C] + [dT_5] - [dT_4] = [dF_1] + [dT_1] - [dT_2] \tag{10b}$$

from an overall energy balance (eq. A.3b), and

$$[dF_B] = [dF_H] + [dV] \tag{10c}$$

from the pressure compatibility relationship around the bypass loop [Equation (A.3c)]. Combining these global latent confluences with the basic confluences of Equations (7) and (8) results in seven solutions (interpretations 1–7) in Table 2.

TABLE 2. Solutions to Confluences of Heat Exchanger with Bypass for Increase in Valve Stem Position

Interpretation	F_1	F_2	F_B	F_C	F_H	P_1	P_2	T_2	T_3	T_5
1	+	+	+	0	−	−	+	+	+	−
2	+	+	+	0	−	−	+	+	0	−
3	+	+	+	0	−	−	+	+	−	0
4	+	+	+	0	−	−	+	−	−	+
5	+	+	+	0	−	−	+	0	−	+
6	+	+	+	0	−	−	+	+	−	+
7	+	+	+	0	−	−	+	+	−	−
8	+	−	−	0	+	−	−	−	+	+
9	+	−	−	0	+	−	−	0	+	+
10	+	−	−	0	+	−	−	+	+	+
11	+	+	+	0	−	−	+	−	−	−
12	+	+	+	0	−	−	+	0	−	−
13	+	0	+	0	−	−	0	0	−	−
14	+	0	+	0	−	−	0	−	−	−
15	+	0	+	0	−	−	0	+	−	−
16	+	−	+	0	−	−	−	−	−	−
17	+	−	+	0	−	−	−	0	−	−
18	+	−	+	0	−	−	−	+	−	−
19	0	+	+	0	−	0	+	−	−	−
20	0	+	+	0	−	0	+	0	−	−
21	0	+	+	0	−	0	+	+	−	−
22	−	+	−	0	+	+	+	−	+	+
23	−	+	−	0	+	+	+	0	+	+
24	−	+	−	0	+	+	+	+	+	+
25	−	+	+	0	−	+	+	−	−	−
26	−	+	+	0	−	+	+	0	−	−
27	−	+	+	0	−	+	+	+	−	−

Interpretation 7 is the only solution that satisfies all the confluences. This solution is the only possible behavior of the system and is valid for all numerical realizations of parameter values. Thus, redundant noncausal constraints derived from both local and global considerations are necessary to provide the ultimate qualitative response of systems.

3 USE OF CAUSAL INFORMATION IN STEADY-STATE SIMULATION

In this section, we show how a model of the system derived from causal considerations provides additional constraints that eliminate spurious solutions in qualitative modeling. Constraints from the causal model (the extended signed directed graph, ESDG) eliminate qualitative solutions corresponding to the response from unstable steady states, which are included in the set of solutions derived from the basic and latent noncausal confluences. This approach is purely topological and differs from that of Iwasaki and Simon [9], who use dynamic stability criteria (which may be difficult to derive) to eliminate solutions from unstable steady states.

3.1 Representation of Causality by the ESDG

Causality is the principle that effects must be propagated locally within the topology of a system. Using causal information to predict ultimate process response involves predicting initial behavior combined with knowledge about variables that exhibit inverse or compensatory response. Inverse response occurs when the initial and ultimate direction of a change of a variable are opposite. Compensatory response is exhibited if the variable returns to its initial value after all transients have died out.

Local causal interactions are represented by the single-stage signed directed graph (SDG) [8]. The SDG consists of nodes, symbolizing variables, and signed directed branches that represent the immediate local causal relationships between variables. The branch signs + and − indicate whether the cause-and-effect variables tend to change in the same or in opposite directions. The model of causality used in this work is the ESDG, which is derived from the SDG and the global causal topology of the system. The ESDG differs from the SDG in that it includes additional nonphysical feed-forward paths that serve to explain inverse and compensatory response due to negative feedback.

Rules for deriving branches of the SDG from quantitative algebraic and dynamic differential equations describing the system are discussed in detail elsewhere [8, 14, 15] and only a summary is presented here. For the equation,

$$\frac{dx_i}{dt} = f_i(\mathbf{x}, \mathbf{u}, \mathbf{p}) \tag{11}$$

causality proceeds from the right to the left side of the equation. The sign of the SDG branch β_{ij} originating at x_j and ending at x_i is determined by the sign of the first nonzero partial derivative $\partial^n f_i / \partial x_j^n$ ($i \neq j$) evaluated at the (unperturbed) steady state. When branch signs cannot be uniquely determined from ordinal relationships among sub-expressions of partial derivatives, possible dual influences are represented by parallel branches with opposite signs.

Algebraic equations relating state variables do not represent a causal model of the system, and thus the direction of causality among variables cannot be determined unambiguously based solely on the structure of the equation. In order to determine this directionality, knowledge about the origin of the equation, the underlying processes, and context must be utilized. To disambiguate the treatment of algebraic equations, Palowitch [15] classifies algebraic equations into four categories: driving force equations, balance equations, functional relationships, and equalities. For each category, a standard set of procedures are presented that specify the causal arcs.

Propagating the signs of disturbances from the perturbation in acyclic pathways of the SDG provides the initial response of the system with a minimum number of spurious interpretations [14]. However, this excludes the ultimate response of systems in which variables exhibit inverse or compensatory response due to negative causal feedback. These variables are defined as *inverse* or *compensatory* variables, respectively. Knowledge about inverse or compensatory variables is required to deduce the ultimate response of the system.

The following definitions are useful. A *path* from an initial to a terminal node is a directed alternating ordered sequence of nodes and branches that can be traced in the SDG. A *cycle* is a path in which the initial and terminal nodes are the same and all other nodes in the path are traversed exactly once. Conversely, an *acyclic* path is one where all (including the initial and terminal) nodes appear once. A *loop* is a path with the same initial and terminal nodes in which each branch is traversed only once. The *complementary subsystem* to an acyclic path is the subsystem that is obtained if all variables in the acyclic path (including initial and terminal nodes) are eliminated. A *strongly connected component* (SCC) of the SDG is a subgraph of the SDG for which a path exists from every node u to every node v (and from v to u) in the SCC; and the SCC is not a proper subgraph of any other SCC. A *disturbance* node to a SCC is an adjacent node just causally upstream of (but not located in) the SCC.

Using these definitions, inverse or compensatory variables can be identified by a global topological analysis of the SDG and diagonal elements of the linearized system matrix in the state-space representation of the system (self-cycles are not usually depicted in the SDG). In order to identify these variables, it is sufficient to consider the response of variables in strongly connected components to perturbations in their respective disturbance variables. For stable systems, the necessary conditions for a variable in a SCC to display inverse response due to negative feedback to perturbations in a disturbance variable [14] are as follows:

1. The variable is located in a negative-feedback loop.
2a. The complementary subsystem to at least one of the acyclic paths from the disturbance variable to the variable has a positive causal feedback cycle or a positive self-cycle.

For compensatory response, the necessary conditions are 1 and

2b.   The complementary subsystem to each acyclic path from the disturbance
variable has a zero self-cycle (integrating effects).

These conditions are necessary but not sufficient, as variable(s) in a member of the system's qualitative class will not exhibit inverse or compensatory response due to negative feedback if the SDG does not have the preceding features. The sufficient conditions are numerical [14]. In the absence of specific numerical information, variable(s) in a quantitative realization of the class may exhibit these behaviors.

The conditions are best illustrated with examples.

Example 1   The SDG of an irreversible $(A \rightarrow B)$ exothermic reaction taking place in a continuous stirred-tank reactor (CSTR) is shown in Figure 2a. Tank level (reactor liquid volume) is assumed to be constant. For a highly exothermic reaction, the diagonal element (self-cycle, normally not shown in the SDG) corresponding to T in the system matrix could be positive. The strongly connected components of the SDG are (C_A, T), (C_{AO}), (F), (T_O), and (T_C). Of the SCCs only (C_A, T) contain variables $(C_A$ and $T)$ in a negative-feedback loop. With respect to the SCC input (disturbance node) here are two acyclic paths to each of C_A and T. The complementary subsystems to the acyclic paths from F to C_A are (T) and ϕ, respectively (ϕ is the null system). Subsystem (T) contains a positive cycle and thus C_A may be an inverse variable with respect to perturbations in F. The complementary subsystems to the acyclic paths from F to T are (C_A) and ϕ. Neither of the subsystems contains a positive cycle; therefore, T is not an inverse variable with respect to perturbations in F. Similarly, only C_A may be an inverse variable to perturbations in C_{AO}. There are no inverse variables with respect to perturbations in either T_O or T_C.

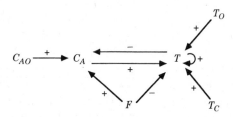

Figure 2a. SDG for CSTR.

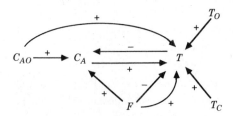

Figure 2b. ESDG for CSTR.

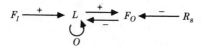

Figure 3a. SDG for tank.

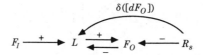

Figure 3b. ESDG for tank.

Example 2   Figure 3a shows the SDG of a tank with one inlet and one outlet stream. The diagonal element (normally not shown in the SDG) corresponding to L in the system matrix is zero. Thus, L behaves as an integrator. Here, F_O and L are located in a negative feedback loop. For a perturbation in R_s (resistance in outlet stream), there is one acyclic path from R_s to each of these variables. The complementary subsystem to the acyclic path from R_s to F_O, subsystem (L), has integrating effects. Thus F_O is the only possible compensatory variable with respect to perturbations in R_s. This is consistent with the actual response of outlet flow to a partial blockage (increase in flow resistance) in the outlet stream. Similarly, it is deduced that there are no compensatory variables when F_I is perturbed.

The ESDG is constructed by adding nonphysical branches to the SDG that account for the behavior of inverse and compensatory variables. An ESDG branch is constructed for each series of adjacent inverse (compensatory) variables on an acyclic path from the disturbance variable. These branches begin at the node immediately upstream of the series of inverse (compensatory) variables in the acyclic path from the disturbance variable and end at the noninverse (noncompensatory) variable immediately downstream of the series of inverse (compensatory) variables [14]. The sign of each additional branch is the product of the signs of the branches in the acyclic path between the origin and termination of the ESDG branch. The ESDG for the CSTR and tank are shown in Figures 2b and 3b, respectively. Transmission of disturbances by the nonphysical branch $\delta([dF_O])$ from R_s to L in Figure 3b is permitted only when F_O is normal (0). The δ "qualitative Dirac delta" function (Table 1) prevents prediction of inverse response by L to changes in R_s.

Propagating disturbances in acyclic pathways of the ESDG provides the ultimate response of the system.

3.2 Derivation of Confluences from the ESDG

The ESDG, presented initially as a graph, can be represented as an equivalent set of confluences. These confluences derive from two sources: local balances around nodes of the ESDG and the global topology of the ESDG [14]. Conversion of the ESDG to

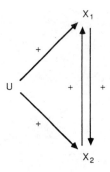

Figure 4. ESDG of system with positive-feedback loop.

confluences provides a convenient uniform representation for both causal and non-causal constraints.

A necessary condition for a steady state to be consistent with the ESDG is that the sign of each node must be the qualitative sum of its inputs. Mathematically, this condition can be expressed by *nodal balances* around each ESDG node:

$$[dx_j] = [\beta_{j1}] \cdot [dx_{i1}] + [\beta_{j2}] \cdot [dx_{i2}] + \cdots + [\beta_{jm}] \cdot [dx_{im}], \tag{12}$$

where x_{ik} ($k = 1, \ldots, m$) are inputs to node x_j and $[\beta_{jk}]$ is the sign of the branch from x_{ik} to x_j.

In systems with positive-feedback loops (PFBLs), the nodal balances admit certain spurious solutions associated with (unstable) self-excitation of the PFBL. Consider the ESDG of Figure 4. When the system is unperturbed, the nodal balances for the system are

$$[du] = [0], \tag{13a}$$

$$[dx_1] = [dx_2] + [du], \tag{13b}$$

$$[dx_2] = [dx_1] + [du]. \tag{13c}$$

The solutions to Equations (13a)–(13c) are shown in Table 3. In order to eliminate these spurious solutions, an additional topological confluence

$$[dx_1] = [du] \quad \text{or} \quad [dx_2] = [du] \tag{14a}$$

is required. This confluence is equivalent to the condition that the feedback loop must have an external input to sustain a signal. It is readily shown that this confluence is equivalent to

$$\delta([dx_1] - [du]) + \delta([dx_2] - [du]) = [+]. \tag{14b}$$

In general, to eliminate these solutions, additional global topological confluences of the form

TABLE 3. Solutions to Nodal Balances of Equations (13)

Solution	u	x_1	x_2
1	0	+	+
2	0	−	−

$$\delta([dx_{j1}] - [\beta_{j1}] \cdot [dx_{i1}]) + \cdots + \delta([dx_{jm}] - [\beta_{jm}] \cdot [dx_{im}]) = [+], \tag{15}$$

where x_{ik} ($k = 1, 2, \ldots, m$) are inputs to nodes x_{jk} within the loop, are required for each positive-feedback loop. Together, Equations (12)–(15) are necessary and sufficient conditions for steady-state consistency with the ESDG.

In summary, global causal topology is used in two ways in deriving confluences from causal information. First, global topology provides necessary conditions for inverse and compensatory variables, which lead to the addition of nonphysical branches to form the ESDG. These branches ensure that the ultimate response of the system is not excluded in cases of inverse and compensatory response. Second, global topological confluences are derived from the PFBLs of the ESDG, which eliminate spurious solutions.

3.3 Eliminating Unstable Steady-State Solutions

Confluences derived from noncausal considerations admit solutions which correspond to the response from unstable steady states. The following example illustrates the use of causal confluences in eliminating these spurious solutions.

Consider an isothermal, irreversible, autocatalytic reaction ($A \to B$), with rate expression

$$r_A = k_r C_A C_B^2 \tag{16}$$

taking place in a CSTR with constant space velocity. The dynamic process equations are

$$\frac{dC_A}{dt} = \frac{F(C_{AO} - C_A)}{V} - k_r C_A C_B^2, \tag{17a}$$

$$\frac{dC_B}{dt} = k_r C_A C_B^2 - \frac{FC_B}{V}. \tag{17b}$$

For this system, $C_{AO} > C_A$. The basic and latent non-causal confluences are

$$[dC_A] + [dC_B] = [dC_{AO}], \tag{18a}$$

$$[dC_A] + [dC_B] = 0. \tag{18b}$$

TABLE 4. Solutions to Noncausal Confluences of Autocatalytic Reaction

Solution	C_{AO}	C_A	C_B
1	+	−	+
2	+	+	−

The solutions to these confluences for an increase in C_{AO} are listed in Table 4. These solutions correspond to the ultimate response from the two steady-state solutions of Equations (17) for $C_{AO}^2 > 4F/k_rV$:

$$C_{AS} = \tfrac{1}{2}(C_{AO} \pm (C_{AO}^2 - 4F/k_rV)^{1/2}). \qquad (19)$$

The second steady state [invoking the plus sign in Equation (19)] is unstable. Thus, the latter solution in Table 4 is spurious and cannot be observed in a physical system.

The ESDG for this system is shown in Figure 5. The nonphysical branch between C_{AO} and C_B is non-physical, accounting for possible inverse response of C_A to changes in C_{AO} is constructed according to the procedure in Section 3.1. Nodal balances for the ESDG yield the following confluences:

$$[dC_A] = [dC_{AO}] - [dC_B], \qquad (20a)$$

$$[dC_B] = [dC_A] + [dC_{AO}]. \qquad (20b)$$

The first of these is the same as Equation (18a). However, Equation (20b) is a new latent constraint which eliminates the latter solution in Table 4. The response from the stable steady state is the only one that satisfies both noncausal confluences and confluences derived from causality.

3.4 Partial Dynamic Information from the ESDG

Confluences derived from causal and noncausal considerations provide the ultimate response of the system to perturbations but do not give a causal account of the response. Partial dynamic information on the order of deviations during the transient can be inferred from the ESDG. The basic premise is that deviations of variables which are upstream in the path from the perturbation must precede deviations of downstream

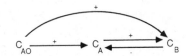

Figure 5. ESDG for autocatalytic reaction.

variables. A complete ordering of deviations is possible in purely serial causal networks. In parallel paths and feedback loops (where inverse response, compensatory response, or oscillatory behavior may be displayed), this order cannot always be determined without information about time delays in the branches of the ESDG, which may be changed by occurrence of faults or disturbances. Specific ordering of deviations requires further research.

4 QUALITATIVE FAULT SIMULATION OF A CHEMICAL REACTOR SYSTEM

To demonstrate the use of both causal and noncausal confluences in determining the steady-state qualitative behavior of continuous process systems, we consider the process shown in Figure 6. An irreversible exothermic reaction ($A \rightarrow mB$) with rate expression

$$r_A = k_r C_A^n, \qquad n > 0, \tag{21}$$

takes place in a CSTR. To provide temperature control, part of the reactor outlet stream is recycled to the reactor through a heat exchanger. The recycle flowrate is controlled, and residence time in the reactor is controlled by maintaining the level of reactants in the reactor. Constant boundary pressures of all input and output streams and constant physical properties are assumed. The objective is to determine the ultimate system response to various faults and disturbances.

This process has several interesting interactions between control loops and many multiple causal pathways with opposing tendencies between variables, tending to generate a great deal of ambiguity. The system can also attain multiple steady states in the absence of temperature control.

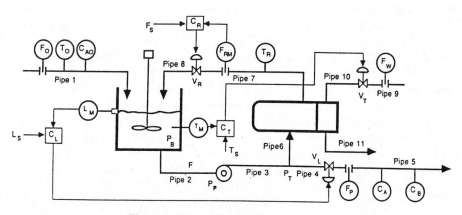

Figure 6. Schematic of CSTR with recycle.

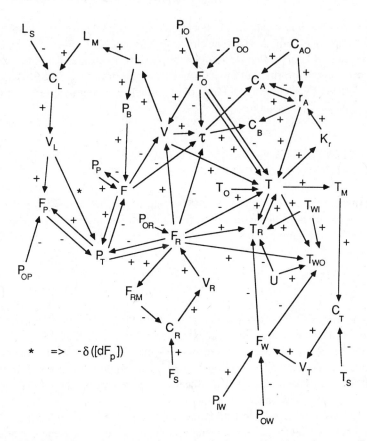

Figure 7. ESDG for CSTR with recycle (for nonphysical control loop branches—see Table 5.)

The system can be modeled by as many as 166 independent state variables, but by eliminating obvious equalities and introducing definitions for three parameters, 27 unknowns (24 variables) result. By using empirical ordinal relationships, 26 basic confluences can be derived for the system. Noncausal confluences (under fault-free conditions) and conditions at which they are valid are presented in Appendix B. Confluences (B.10), (B.11), (B.30), and (B.31) are valid when the reactor outlet flowrate F is greater than the recycle flowrate F_R. Similarly, (B.37) and (B.38) are valid when the reactor temperature T is higher than the recycle stream temperature (T_R). These conditions are violated only in the extreme cases of reverse flow in the product stream or the cooling system acting as a heat source, respectively. Transitions between qualitative regimes due to violation of these conditions will not occur for most faults. Depending on fault magnitudes, perfect control of controlled variables may be maintained or the control loop may become saturated at the new steady state. Control loop saturation will be allowed, and the relevant controller confluences (B.19), (B.22), and (B.25), account for these possible transitions. The only other transitions that may occur are to regimes where process equations are no longer valid, such as boiling. Thus, the assumption of no transitions between qualitative regimes (except for control loop saturation) described in Section 2.1 is not very limiting.

The ESDG for the system is shown in Figure 7. Positive branches between C_{A0} and r_A and F_0 and T are nonphysical feed-forward paths which explain possible inverse response of reactant concentration to changes in feed concentration and flowrate, respectively. The nonphysical conditional branch between V_L and P_T, $\delta([dF_p])$, is dependent on the value of F_p and accounts for the compensatory response of product flowrate to changes in the level control valve stem position. Nonphysical branches that explain compensatory response in control loops (not shown in Figure 7) are listed in Table 5. All other branches of the ESDG represent local causal relationships of the SDG of the process. Nodal balances and global topological confluences for positive-feedback loops (under fault-free conditions) derived from the ESDG are presented in Appendix C.

Selected faults and disturbances for this system are listed in Table 6. These faults are modeled by a qualitative change in one or more of the process inputs or parameters or by modifying the appropriate confluences. Because of the existence of multiple steady states and multiple causal pathways (with opposing tendencies), this process presents a significant challenge for qualitative modeling. For example, if the recycle flowmeter F_{RM} is stuck high, the recycle flow controller C_R in Figure 7 will send a signal to the control valve V_R to reduce recycle flowrate F_R. This decrease in F_R is propagated to any

TABLE 5. ESDG Branches for Control Loops

Controlled Variable	Initial Node	Branch Sign	Terminal Node
F_R	P_{OR}	$+\delta([dF_{RM}])$	C_R
F_R	P_T	$-\delta([dF_{RM}])$	C_R
L	F_0	$+\delta([dL_M])$	C_L
L	P_{OP}	$+\delta([dL_M])$	C_L
L	F	$-\delta([dL_M])$	C_L
L	F	$+\delta([dL_M])$	C_L
L	F_R	$+\delta([dL_M])$	C_L
L	F_R	$-\delta([dL_M])$	C_L
L	P_{OR}	$-\delta([dL_M])$	C_L
L	P_P	$-\delta([dL_M])$	C_L
L	V_R	$+\delta([dL_M])$	C_L
T	F_0	$-\delta([dT_M])$	C_T
T	F_R	$+\delta([dT_M])$	C_T
T	F_R	$-\delta([dT_M])$	C_T
T	P_{IW}	$-\delta([dT_M])$	C_T
T	P_{OW}	$+\delta([dT_M])$	C_T
T	r_A	$+\delta([dT_M])$	C_T
T	T_0	$+\delta([dT_M])$	C_T
T	T_{WI}	$+\delta([dT_M])$	C_T
T	U	$-\delta([dT_M])$	C_T

TABLE 6. Selected Faults for CSTR with Recycle

Number	Fault
1	Normal operation
2	Pipe 1 partially blocked
3	Pipe 6 partially blocked
4	Feed concentration high
5	Recycle flow set point high
6	Fouled heat exchanger
7	Deactivated catalyst
8	Temperature control valve stuck high
9	Leak in reactor
10	Recycle flowmeter stuck high

of five variables (P_T, V, τ, T, and T_R). Changes in these variables are then propagated to other variables in the system, with the different choices of possible causal pathways resulting in ambiguity.

Table 7 shows the number of observable qualitative steady-state solutions for the set of measured variables given in Table 8 for these faults when using

(i)   causal confluences derived from the ESDG,

(ii)   confluences derived from a "basic" set of 27 equations in 27 unknowns,

(iii)   the combination of confluences from (i) and (ii), and

(iv)   noncausal latent confluences in addition to those in (iii).

Combining constraints from causal and noncausal sources reduces the number of solutions obtained with the ESDG by up to a factor of 2–3. Adding latent process constraints leads to further reductions of up to an order of magnitude. The overall

TABLE 7. Number of Valid Solutions Obtained by Utilizing Confluences from Various Sources

Fault	Causal Case	Local Noncausal Case (ii)	Causal and Local Noncausal Case (iii)	Local, Latent, and Causal Case (iv)
1	1	279	1	1
2	1079	984	481	141
3	501	1359	192	13
4	12	287	10	10
5	501	4869	192	13
6	2	279	2	2
7	4	281	4	3
8	1	279	1	1
9	984	1080	178	35
10	309	1215	138	9

reduction in the number of solutions obtained between cases (i) and (iv) is up to a factor of 35 and between cases (ii) and (iv) up to a factor of 370. Thus, combining causal and noncausal confluences significantly reduces ambiguity. However, it cannot be proven (without further analysis, possibly numerical) that all solutions obtained for case (iv) are realizable [11].

4.1 Using Knowledge about Functioning Control Loops to Reduce Ambiguity

The function of an engineered system is the purpose for which the system was designed. A priori knowledge of the function of the system can be used to reduce the ambiguity in qualitative modeling [2, 3]. In chemical process systems, feedback control loops attempt to maintain values of important variables within acceptable ranges, thus playing an important role in determining system behavior. Control loops are designed to achieve their function in the presence of most expected disturbances. Thus, in many situations, zero deviation of the controlled variable is maintained after all transients have died out. Exceptions occur when the disturbance magnitude is large enough to cause loop saturation or when the fault prevents loop operation, as in the case where an element of the control loop is stuck at a fixed position (zero-gain events).

The results of applying confluences [in case (iv) of Section 4] with the additional constraint of control loop functionality (except for zero-gain events) are shown in Table 8. From Table 8, it can be seen that confluences produce one solution for most faults. The fault that produces multiple solutions is associated with a decrease in feed rate to the reactor. The steady-state balances for the system are

$$F = F_0 + F_R, \tag{22}$$

$$FC_A = F_0 C_{A0} + F_R C_A - k_r A L C_A^n, \tag{23}$$

$$\rho C_p F T = \rho C_p F_0 T_0 + \rho C_p F_R T_R + k_r A L C_A^n. \tag{24}$$

TABLE 8. Results of Qualitative Fault Simulation (Perfect Control)

Fault	F_O	T_O	C_{AO}	F_W	T_M	L_M	F_{RM}	T_R	C_T	C_L	C_R	F_P	C_A	C_B
1	0	0	0	0	0	0	0	0	0	0	0	0	0	0
2	–	0	0	+/0/–	0	0	0	+/0/–	+/0/–	–	–	–	–	+
3	0	0	0	0	0	0	0	0	0	0	+	0	0	0
4	0	0	+	+	0	0	0	–	+	0	0	0	+	+
5	0	0	0	–	0	0	+	+	–	+	+	0	0	0
6	0	0	0	+	0	0	0	0	+	0	0	0	0	0
7	0	0	0	–	0	0	0	+	–	0	0	0	+	–
8	0	0	0	+	–	0	0	–	–	0	0	0	+	–
9	0	0	0	0	0	0	0	0	0	–	–	–	0	0
10	0	0	0	+	+	0	+	–	+	–	–	0	–	+

Noting that the steady-state values of C_{A0}, F_R, L, T, and T_0 are unchanged after fault initiation, a differential analysis yields

$$dT_R = \frac{\left[\rho C_p(T - T_0) - \dfrac{k_r AL(-\Delta H_R)\, nC_A^{n-1}\,(C_{AO} - C_A)}{F_0 + k_r ALnC_A^{n-1}} \right] dF_0}{\rho C_p F_R} \qquad (25)$$

The sign of the coefficient of dF_0 in Equation (25) is ambiguous (for the stable system) and may be positive or negative depending on the values of process variables and parameters. Thus, all solutions in Table 8 are realizable.

Caution is required when using a priori knowledge about a system's function to deduce behavior. In certain applications, such as in predicting system behavior to unintended disturbances and changes in system structure (fault simulation), the system may not achieve its intended function. However, if the intended function is achieved, knowledge about function significantly reduces ambiguity. In our experience, spurious solutions have never been produced by causal and noncausal confluences, with the additional constraints of functioning control loops, for all examples we have tried in the chemical engineering domain.

5   DISCUSSION

In this chapter, it was demonstrated that multiple (quantitatively redundant) sources of information are necessary to model the steady-state qualitative behavior of continuous systems. These sources are summarized in Table 9. In one dimension, they can be classified as noncausal or causal; in the other, as local or global. Constraints derived from these sources are required to minimize the ambiguity inherent in qualitative modeling.

Noncausal latent confluences were derived through "heuristic" algebraic manipulation of basic constraints. Latent confluences correspond to a partial analytic solution of the system and therefore reduce the number of qualitative solutions. However, qualitative solutions corresponding to responses from unstable steady states are admitted by noncausal confluences. Causal confluences eliminate some of these

TABLE 9. Information Sources Required for Steady-State Qualitative Modeling

	Noncausal	Causal
Local	Basic confluences, latent confluences	Local causal relationships (SDG)
Global	Latent confluences	Knowledge of inverse and compensatory variables, global topological confluences (PFBL)

spurious solutions (unstable steady states) and also provide constraints which may be difficult to derive through algebraic manipulation. Combining constraints from these various sources theoretically eliminates all spurious solutions in systems where analytic steady-state solutions exist.

Since global information is required in steady-state qualitative modeling, there is an inherent trade-off between modularity and solution multiplicity. Therefore, computer programs using steady-state qualitative models need to store both local causal and noncausal models. Additionally, the ability to generate global confluences corresponding to particular system topographies from these models is required. Care is required in generating these global confluences since they are dependent on the validity of the relevant local models.

However, there are limitations in using the steady-state qualitative models. Dynamic effects were ignored, and it was assumed that the same qualitative constraints were also applicable at the new steady state. This assumption is violated when transitions across qualitative regimes occur and could lead to the exclusion of the steady-state solution. Furthermore, solving the models by a constraint satisfaction technique does not give a causal account of system behavior (which is useful in providing explanations). Future work is directed at developing representations (similar to those in ref. 12) to incorporate dynamic effects and identifying the elements of dynamic qualitative models that are necessary to eliminate spurious interpretations.

Qualitative constraints do not express a system's function. Where the intended function is achieved, knowledge about the system's function can be used to reduce ambiguity. Additionally, reasoning about function can facilitate understanding of system behavior. In complex systems, human experts tend to reason about the functionality of subsystems in relation to overall system function before reasoning in more detail using knowledge about physical structure at the subsystem level [18]. The need for hierarchical representations has been recognized and is a subject of current research by others [5, 19].

Our qualitative models have another drawback in that they are incompatible with quantitative information. This information may be available and could be necessary when solving particular problems. The order-of-magnitude formalisms [13, 17] are partial solutions to this problem in that they extend qualitative modeling by utilizing knowledge of relative magnitudes of quantities in addition to their signs in making inferences. Representations that introduce more quantitative information and retain qualitative relationships when numerical information is not required or unavailable are ultimately desirable.

APPENDIX A: STEADY-STATE EQUATIONS FOR HEAT EXCHANGER WITH BYPASS

Local (Basic) Equations

$$F_C = k_c (P_{CI} - P_{CO})^{1/2}, \qquad \text{(A.1a)}$$

$$F_1 = k_1 (P_{HI} - P_1)^{1/2}, \qquad \text{(A.1b)}$$

$$F_H = k_h(P_1 - P_2)^{1/2}, \tag{A.1c}$$

$$F_B = k_b f^+(V)(P_1 - P_2)^{1/2}, \tag{A.1d}$$

$$F_2 = k_2(P_2 - P_{HO})^{1/2}, \tag{A.1e}$$

$$F_1 = F_H + F_B, \tag{A.1f}$$

$$F_2 = F_H + F_B, \tag{A.1g}$$

$$\rho C_p F_c(T_5 - T_4) = \rho C_p F_H(T_1 - T_3), \tag{A.1h}$$

$$\rho C_p F_c(T_5 - T_4) = \frac{UA_c\{(T_1 - T_5) - (T_3 - T_4)\}}{ln\{(T_1 - T_5)/(T_3 - T_4)\}}, \tag{A.1i}$$

$$\rho C_p(F_B T_1 + F_H T_3) = \rho C_p F_2 T_2. \tag{A.1j}$$

Local (Latent) Equations

$$T_3 = \{T_1(1 - \alpha) + T_4(e^\gamma - 1)\}/(e^\gamma - \alpha), \tag{A.2a}$$

$$T_5 = \{\alpha T_1(e^\gamma - 1) + e^\gamma T_4(1 - \alpha)\}/(e^\gamma - \alpha), \tag{A.2b}$$

where

$$\alpha = \rho C_p F_H/\rho C_p F_C; \qquad \alpha \neq 1$$

$$\gamma = UA_c(1 - \alpha)/\rho C_p F_H; \qquad \gamma \neq 0,$$

$$\rho C_p F_B(T_1 - T_2) = \rho C_p F_H(T_2 - T_3) \tag{A.2c}$$

Global (Latent) Equations

$$F_1 = F_2, \tag{A.3a}$$

$$\rho C_p F_c(T_5 - T_4) = \rho C_p F_1(T_1 - T_2), \tag{A.3b}$$

$$k_h F_B = k_b f^+(V)F_H,$$

APPENDIX B: NONCAUSAL CONFLUENCES FOR CONTINUOUS STIRRED-TANK REACTOR WITH RECYCLE

Basic Confluences

$$[dF_0] = [dP_{I0}] - [dP_{00}], \tag{B.1}$$

$$[dF] = [dP_B] + [dP_p] - [dP_T], \tag{B.2}$$

$$[dF_P] = [dV_L] + [dP_T] - [dP_{OP}], \tag{B.3}$$

$$[dF_R] = [dV_R] + [dP_T] - [dP_{OR}], \tag{B.4}$$

$$[dF_W] = [dV_T] + [dP_{IW}] - [dP_{OW}], \tag{B.5}$$

$$[dF] = [dF_R] + [dF_P], \tag{B.6}$$

$$[dF] = [dF_0] + [dF_R], \tag{B.7}$$

$$[dL] = [dV], \tag{B.8}$$

$$[dP_B] = [dL], \tag{B.9}$$

$$[dC_{A0}] + [dF_0] + [dF_R] = [dr_A] + [dV] + [dC_A] + [dF]; \qquad F > F_R, \tag{B.10}$$

$$[dF] + [dC_B] = [dr_A] + [dV] + [dF_R]; \qquad F > F_R, \tag{B.11}$$

$$[dF] + [dT] = [dF_0] + [dT_0] + [dF_R] + [dT_R] + [dr_A] + [dV], \tag{B.12}$$

$$[dr_A] = [dk_r] + [dC_A], \tag{B.13}$$

$$[dk_r] = [dT], \tag{B.14}$$

$$[dV] = [dF_0] + [d\tau], \tag{B.15}$$

$$[dP_p] + [dF] = 0, \tag{B.16}$$

$$[dF_R] + [dT] + [dT_{W1}] = [dF_W] + [dT_{WO}] + [dT_R], \tag{B.17}$$

$$[dL_M] = [dL], \tag{B.18}$$

$$[dL_M] = [dL_S] \quad \text{or} \quad [dC_L] = [dL_M] - [dL_S] \quad \text{for} \quad [dL_M] \neq [dL_S],$$

equivalent to

$$[dL_M] = [dL_S] + ([dC_L] + [dL_S]) \cdot \delta\{\delta([dL_M] - [dL_S])\}, \qquad \text{(B.19)}$$

$$[dV_L] = [dC_L], \qquad \text{(B.20)}$$

$$[dT_M] = [dT], \qquad \text{(B.21)}$$

$$[dT_M] = [dT_S] \quad \text{or} \quad [dC_T] = [dT_M] - [dT_S] \quad \text{for} \quad [dT_M] \neq [dT_S],$$

equivalent to

$$[dT_M] = [dT_S] + ([dC_T] + [dT_S]) \cdot \delta\{\delta([dT_M] - [dT_S])\}, \qquad \text{(B.22)}$$

$$[dV_T] = [dC_T], \qquad \text{(B.23)}$$

$$[dF_{RM}] = [dF_R], \qquad \text{(B.24)}$$

$$[dF_{RM}] = [dF_S] \quad \text{or} \quad [dC_R] = [dF_S] - [dF_{RM}] \quad \text{for} \quad [dF_{RM}] \neq [dF_S],$$

equivalent to

$$[dF_{RM}] = [dF_S] + ([dF_S] - [dC_R]) \cdot \delta\{\delta([dF_{RM}] - [dF_S])\}, \qquad \text{(B.25)}$$

$$[dV_R] = [dC_R]. \qquad \text{(B.26)}$$

Latent Confluences

$$[dF_O] = [dF_P], \qquad \text{(B.27)}$$

$$[dP_P] + [dP_B] + [dV_R] = [dF] + [dF_R] + [dP_{OR}], \qquad \text{(B.28)}$$

$$[dr_A] = [dT] + [dC_A], \qquad \text{(B.29)}$$

$$[dF_O] + [dC_{AO}] + [dF_R] = [dF] + [dT] + [dC_A] + [dV] ;$$

$$nA_0e^{-Ea/RT}VC_A^{n-1} + F > F_R, \qquad \text{(B.30)}$$

$$[dF_R] + [dT] + [dV] + [dC_A] = [dF] + [dC_B] ; \qquad F > F_R, \qquad \text{(B.31)}$$

$$[dF_O] + [dC_{AO}] = [dT] + [dV] + [dC_A], \qquad \text{(B.32)}$$

$$[dF_O] + [dC_B] = [dT] + [dV] + [dC_A], \qquad \text{(B.33)}$$

$$[dF_O] + [dC_{AO}] = [dr_A] + [dV] + [dC_A], \tag{B.34}$$

$$[dF_O] + [dC_B] = [dr_A] + [dV], \tag{B.35}$$

$$[dC_{AO}] = [dC_A] + [dC_B], \tag{B.36}$$

$$[dF_R] + [dT] + [dC_A] = [dF_O] + [dC_{AO}] + [dT_O] + [dT_R]; \qquad T > T_R, \tag{B.37}$$

$$[dF_R] + [dT] = [dF_O] + [dC_B] + [dT_O] + [dT_R]; \qquad T > T_R, \tag{B.38}$$

$$[dT_{LM}] + [dT_{WO}] + [dT_{WI}] = [dT] + [dT_R], \tag{B.39}$$

$$[dF_W] + [dT_{WO}] = [dU] + [dT_{WI}] + [dT_{LM}], \tag{B.40}$$

$$[dF_R] + [dT] = [dU] + [dT_{LM}] + [dT_R], \tag{B.41}$$

$$[dH_L] + [dT_{WI}] = [dF_W] + [dT_{WO}], \tag{B.42}$$

$$[dH_L] + [dT_R] = [dF_R] + [dT], \tag{B.43}$$

$$[dH_L] = [dT_{LM}] + [dU], \tag{B.44}$$

$$[dH_L] + [dT_{WI}] = [dU] + [dF_W] + [dF_R] + [dT], \tag{B.45}$$

$$[dH_g] = [dr_A] + [dV], \tag{B.46}$$

$$[dH_g] = [dF_O] + [dC_B], \tag{B.47}$$

$$[dH_T] + [dT_O] = [dF_O] + [dT], \tag{B.48}$$

$$[dH_g] = [dH_L] + [dH_T]. \tag{B.49}$$

APPENDIX C: CONFLUENCES DERIVED FROM THE ESDG[1]

$$[dC_A] = [dC_{AO}] - [dr_A] - [d\tau], \qquad\qquad † \quad (C.1)$$

$$[dC_B] = [dr_A] + [d\tau], \qquad\qquad † \quad (C.2)$$

$$[dC_L] = [dL_M] - [dL_S] +$$

$$\delta([dL_M]) \cdot ([dF_O] + [dF_R] + [dF] + [dP_{OP}]$$

$$+ [dV_R] - [dF] - [dF_R] - [dP_{OR}] - [dP_P]), \qquad † \quad (C.3)$$

[1]Daggers indicate additional confluences provided by ESDG.

$$[dC_R] = [dF_s] - [dF_{RM}] + \delta([dF_{RM}]) \cdot ([dP_{OR}] - [dP_T]), \qquad \dagger \quad \text{(C.4)}$$

$$[dC_T] = [dT_M] - [dT_S] +$$

$$\delta([dT_M]) \cdot ([dF_R] + [dT_{WI}] + [dr_A] + [dT_O] + [dV]$$

$$+ [dP_{OW}] - [dU] - [dP_{IW}] - [dF_O] - [dF_R]), \qquad \dagger \quad \text{(C.5)}$$

$$[dF] = [dP_B] + [dP_P] - [dP_T], \qquad \text{(C.6)}$$

$$[dF_O] = [dP_{IO}] - [dP_{OO}], \qquad \text{(C.7)}$$

$$[dF_P] = [dV_L] + [dP_T] - [dP_{OP}], \qquad \text{(C.8)}$$

$$[dF_R] = [dV_R] + [dP_T] - [dP_{OR}], \qquad \text{(C.9)}$$

$$[dF_{RM}] = [dF_R], \qquad \text{(C.10)}$$

$$[dF_W] = [dV_T] + [dP_{IW}] - [dP_{OW}], \qquad \text{(C.11)}$$

$$[dk_r] = [dT], \qquad \text{(C.12)}$$

$$[dL] = [dV], \qquad \text{(C.13)}$$

$$[dL_M] = [dL], \qquad \text{(C.14)}$$

$$[dP_B] = [dL], \qquad \text{(C.15)}$$

$$[dP_P] = -[dF], \qquad \text{(C.16)}$$

$$[dP_T] = [dF] - [dF_P] - [dF_R] - \delta([dF_P]) \cdot [dV_L], \qquad \dagger \quad \text{(C.17)}$$

$$[dr_A] = [dC_A] + [dC_{AO}] + [dk_r], \qquad \dagger \quad \text{(C.18)}$$

$$[dT] = [dF_O] + [dV] + [dT_O] + [dT_R] + [dr_A] - [dF_O] - [dF_R], \qquad \dagger \quad \text{(C.19)}$$

$$[dT_M] = [dT], \qquad \text{(C.20)}$$

$$[dT_R] = [dT] + [dT_{WI}] + [dF_R] - [dF_W] - [dU], \qquad \dagger \quad \text{(C.21)}$$

$$[dT_{WO}] = [dT] + [dT_{WI}] + [dU] + [dF_R] - [dF_W], \qquad \dagger \quad \text{(C.22)}$$

$$[d\tau] = [dV] - [dF] - [dF_O] - [dF_R], \qquad \dagger \quad \text{(C.23)}$$

$$[dV] = [dF_O] - [dF] - [dF_R],$$ †   (C.24)

$$[dV_L] = [dC_L],$$ (C.25)

$$[dV_R] = [dC_R],$$ (C.26)

$$[dV_T] = [dC_T],$$ (C.27)

$$[dT] = [dT_O] + [dr_A] + [dV] - [dF_O] - [dF_R] \quad \text{or}$$

$$[dT_R] = [dF_R] + [dT_{WI}] - [dF_W] - [dU],$$ †   (C.28)

$$[dT] = [dT_O] + [dT_R] + [dV] - [dF_O] - [dF_R] \quad \text{or}$$

$$[dr_A] = [dC_{AO}] + [dC_A],$$ †   (C.29)

$$[dT] = [dT_O] + [dV] - [dF_O] - [dF_R] \quad \text{or}$$

$$[dT_R] = [dF_R] + [dT_{WI}] - [dF_W] - [dU] \quad \text{or} \quad [dr_A] = [dC_{AO}] + [dC_A],$$ †   (C.30)

$$[dV] = [dF_O] \quad \text{or} \quad [dF] = [dP_P] \quad \text{or} \quad [dP_T] = -[dF_P] - \delta([dF_P]) \cdot [dV_L] \quad \text{or}$$

$$[dF_R] = [dV_R] - [dP_{OR}].$$ †   (C.31)

NOTATION

A	chemical species
A, A_c	reactor cross-sectional and heat exchange area
A_0	Arrhenius frequency factor
B	chemical species
C_A, C_B	concentration of A, B in reactor
C_{AO}	feed concentration of A
C_L, C_R, C_T	controller output signals
C_p	specific heat capacity
E_a	activation energy
f^+, f^-	strictly monotonic increasing and decreasing functions
F	liquid flowrate
F, F_0, F_p	reactor outlet, feed, and product flowrates
F_R, F_{RM}, F_S	recycle flowrate, measurement, and set point

F_W	cooling water flowrate
H_g	heat generated due to reaction
H_L	heat load in heat exchanger
H_T	sensible heat change from feed stream to product stream
k, k_I, k_p	constants
k_1, k_2, k_r	reaction rate constants
L, L_M, L_S	reactor level, level measurement, and set point
m	stoichiometric coefficient
n	order of reaction
O	order of magnitude
p	system parameter
P_1, P_2, P_T	pressure at node
P_B	reactor base pressure
P_p	pump head
R	gas constant
r_A	reaction rate
R_s	flow resistance in conduit
T, T_0, T_R	reactor, feed, and recycle stream temperatures
T_{LM}	logarithmic mean temperature difference
T_M, T_S	reactor temperature measurement and set point
T_{WI}, T_{WO}	cooling water inlet and outlet temperatures
u	system input variable
U	heat transfer coefficient
V	volume of reacting mixture
V_L, V_R, V_T	valve stem positions
x	state variable

GREEK SYMBOLS

β	branch in SDG (ESDG)
δ	qualitative Dirac delta function
ΔH_R	heat of reaction
ρ	liquid density
τ	residence time
$[\ ]$	sign of expression
$|\ |$	absolute value of expression
$\cdot$	qualitative multiplication

SUBSCRIPTS

B	bypass stream
C	cold (cooling) stream

H	hot stream
I	inlet
$i, j, k, \ldots$	dummy variables
O	outlet
P	product stream
R	recycle stream
S	steady-state value
W	cooling water stream

REFERENCES

1. D. G. Bobrow, (Ed.), *Qualitative Reasoning about Physical Systems*, MIT Press, Cambridge, MA, 1985.

2. J. de Kleer, "The Origin and Resolution of Ambiguities in Causal Arguments," *Proceedings of the Sixth International Joint Conference on Artificial Intelligence*, Kaufmann, Los Altos, CA, pp. 197–203, 1979.

3. J. de Kleer, "How Circuits Work," *Artificial Intelligence*, **24**:205–280, 1984.

4. J. de Kleer and J. S. Brown, "A Qualitative Physics Based on Confluences," *Artificial Intelligence*, **24**:7–83, 1984.

5. F. E. Finch and M. A. Kramer, "Narrowing Diagnostic Focus Using Functional Decomposition," *AIChE Journal*, **34**:25–36, 1988.

6. P. K. Fink, "Control and Integration of Diverse Knowledge in a Diagnostic Expert System," *Proceedings of the Ninth International Joint Conference on Artificial Intelligence*, Kaufmann, Los Altos, CA, pp. 426–431, 1985.

7. D. F. Forbus, "Qualitative Process Theory," *Artificial Intelligence*, **24**:85–168, 1984.

8. M. Iri, K. Aoki, E. O'Shima, and H. Matsuyama, "An Algorithm for Diagnosis of System Failures in the Chemical Process," *Computers and Chemical Engineering*, **3**:489–493, 1979.

9. Y. Iwasaki and H. A. Simon, "Causality in Device Behavior," *Artificial Intelligence*, **29**:3–32, 1986.

10. B. J. Kuipers, "Common Sense Reasoning about Causality: Deriving Behavior from Structure," *Artificial Intelligence*, **24**:169–203, 1984.

11. B. J. Kuipers, "The Limits of Qualitative Simulation," *Proceedings of the Ninth International Joint Conference on Artificial Intelligence*, Kaufmann, Los Altos, CA, pp. 626–630, 1987.

12. B. J. Kuipers, "Qualitative Simulation," *Artificial Intelligence*, **29**:289–338, 1986.

13. M. L. Mavrovouniotis and G. Stephanopoulos, "Reasoning with Orders of Magnitude and Approximate Relations," *Proceedings of the Sixth National Conference on Artificial Intelligence, (AAAI–87)*, Morgan Kaufmann, Los Altos, CA, pp. 626–630, 1987.

14. O. O. Oyeleye and M. A. Kramer, "Qualitative Simulation of Chemical Process Systems: Steady State Analysis," *AIChE Journal*, **34**:1441–1454, 1988.

15. B. L. Palowitch, Sc.D. Thesis, MIT, Cambridge, MA, 1987.

16. J. Y. Pan, "Qualitative Reasoning with Deep-Level Mechanism Models for Diagnoses of Mechanism Failures," *Proceedings of the IEEE First Conference on Artificial Intelligence Applications,* IEEE Computer Society Press, Washington, DC, pp. 295–301, 1987.

17. O. Raiman, "Order of Magnitude Reasoning," *Proceedings of the Fifth National Conference on Artificial Intelligence,* Morgan Kaufmann, Los Altos, CA, pp. 100–104, 1987.

18. J. Rasmussen, "The Role of Hierarchical Knowledge Representation in Decision Making and System Management," *IEEE Trans. Sys. Man. Cyber.,* **SMC–15**:234, 1985.

19. S. K. Shum and J. F. Davis, "An Expert System for Diagnosing Process Plant Malfunctions," *IFAC Workshop on Fault Detection and Safety in Chemical Plants,* Kyoto, Japan, pp. 116–120, 1986.

20. B. C. Williams, "Qualitative Analysis of MOS Circuits," *Artificial Intelligence,* **24**:281–346, 1984.

14 The Role of Artificial Intelligence in Discrete-Event Simulation

ROBERT M. O'KEEFE

Department of Decision Sciences and Engineering Systems
Rensselaer Polytechnic Institute
Troy, New York

1 INTRODUCTION: SIMULATION OF THE DISCRETE-EVENT KIND

Traditionally, simulation model building has consisted of three paradigms: Monte Carlo, discrete-event, and continuous simulation. In *Monte Carlo simulation,* or *distribution sampling* as it is sometimes now called, the distribution of a particular variable is obtained via a random sampling experiment. Whereas Monte Carlo simulation is a simulation of a static system, discrete-event and continuous simulation are typically used to model dynamic systems which change over time. *Discrete-event simulation* "concerns the modelling of a system as it evolves over time by a representation in which the state variables change only at a countable number of points in time" [29, p. 4], whereas in *continuous simulation* "state variables change continuously with respect to time" [29, p. 46].

While these paradigms were originally quite distinct, recent years have witnessed a considerable merger such that Monte Carlo simulation is now seen as a simplification of discrete-event simulation, and many languages and packages for discrete-event simulation (e.g., SLAM II [41]) allow part of a model to be described as continuous. While here, *simulation* will be used to refer to discrete-event simulation, it should be noted that not only do other types of model-building simulation exist, but what is discussed here is of relevance to all types.

Further, within discrete-event simulation, there has been some distinction between those that view simulation as a *complex programming task* and those that view simulation as an extension of *statistical model building*. This has reached textbook status—for instance, see Kreutzer [28] on simulation as programming and Law and Kelton [29] on simulation as statistical model building. Increasingly, simulation is being seen as an investigative tool, often for the initial anaylsis of poorly understood systems, and thus the statistical aspect of simulation is seen by some as less important. When considering the rolę of artificial intelligence (AI) in simulation, this dichotomy is of some importance and will be alluded to as necessary.

1.1   Some History

Discrete-event simulation dates back to the late 1950s. Tocher, working at United Steels in England, produced what is probably the first specialized simulation programming language (SPL), GSP (the General Simulation Program) [56], and later what is undoubtedly the first textbook on simulation [55]. This period also saw the development of GPSS (the General Purpose Simulation System) at IBM and SIMSCRIPT at the Rand Corporation. Versions of both are still in regular use; GPSS is certainly the most used SPL in the world. The cost of computing and the short word length of available computers (making accurate numeric computing difficult) placed a considerable burden on those pursuing simulation studies.

The 1960s saw the consolidation of simulation as both a research topic and an applied technique, particularly the statistical aspects of simulation. Efficient means of random number generation, random variate generation, and analysis via multiple replications of a simulation were developed. Tool kits of routines for use with a common procedural language, for instance, the FORTRAN routines GASP [42] and the ALGOL-60 routines SIMON [24], were developed. SIMULA [3] was developed at the Norwegian Computing Centre. Now recognized as the first object-oriented language and providing much of the ground work for SMALLTALK [17], the indirect effect of SIMULA on knowledge representation in AI has been considerable.

The late 1960s and early 1970s saw some emphasis on software rather than statistics, particularly software that eased the programming task. Program generators were developed [32] where the user responds to a serious of questions regarding the system under study, following which a simulation program is automatically generated. Network analysis programs, for instance, Q-GERT [43], allow a system to be described by a graph, which can be reduced to data for input to a generic simulator.

In 1976, Hurrion published his thesis on *Visual Interactive Simulation* (VIS), and the seminal simulator SEE-WHY was developed at British Leyland Systems Ltd. (now part of Istel Ltd.) [13]. Since then, the use of visual iconic pictures in simulation, or *animation* as it is called in the United States, coupled with user interaction of the running model has dominated simulation. The majority of simulation software now provides some animation component, and it is estimated that, in the United Kingdom at least, simulation studies without an animation component are few and far between. In the late 1970s, simulation seized upon microcomputers as both hosts for animation and providers of near-zero marginal computing cost [8]. Replications can now be run as necessary when necessary, at least for small to medium-sized simulations.

Finally, perhaps less obviously but of considerable importance, the late 1970s and early 1980s witnessed a reappraisal of the theoretical basis of simulation; for instance, see Nance [35]. Rather like knowledge representation in AI, the lack of a clear theoretical underpinning has made analysis of methodology and comparison between different approaches and the languages that embody them difficult.

While some appreciation of the history of simulation is important so as to follow some of the arguments presented later, the prime reason for this history lesson is to place the effect of AI in simulation in perspective. It is the author's contention that the late 1980s will be seen as the time when AI was combined with simulation so as to produce methods for doing simulation and associated software tools that are far superior (by any criteria) than those in present use.

2   THE PROMISE OF AI IN SIMULATION

The recent and considerable interest given to AI within simulation—for instance, see Kerckhoffs et al. [26]—is driven by two separate concerns: first, the desire to make simulation methods easier to use and more widely available and, second, the need to model increasingly complex systems, particularly systems that include some element of human decision making. These are, of course, to some extent mutual goals since if the process of simulation is easier, then more complex models can be constructed within limitations of budget and time.

2.1   The Desire to Make Simulation Methods Easier to Use

There is a need to make simulation easier (in the sense of more rapid and correct development and analysis of models) for both the simulation developer and the simulation user. Shannon [52] estimates that acquiring essential simulation skills requires a year of study plus two years of practice. The need for both programming and statistical skills and the dichotomy between the proponents of simulation as programming or statistics, discussed in the preceding, means that all too often developers are either simulation programmers with inadequate knowledge of statistical analysis or statisticians to whom programming is a difficult art.

Increasingly, simulations are being handed directly to users, who then undertake all analysis as and when they see fit, or "users" are developing models for themselves, using some of the types of software tool already discussed. In some organizations, considerable effort is being applied to generic model building, where a user can tailor a generic simulation as appropriate without help from a simulation specialist. Thus there is a need to provide some kind of intelligent interface for users that not only makes access to all the facilities of the model quick and easy but also shields the user from a lack of experience, particularly in the area of statistical analysis.

2.2   The Need to Model Increasingly Complex Systems

Despite the success of simulation and its increasing use in a large number of application areas, it has proved inadequate in modeling complex systems which include some element of human decision making. A good example is military applications, such as battle management, where much autonomous decision making happens throughout the management of the system, often based on uncertain information. In production control, decisions such as what to make next can be made by human operators, line managers, and so on. As pointed out by Evans [11] and Grant [18], simulation has only been effective when "what shall we do next" can be reduced to some simple rule that can be easily embodied in the simulation, for example, "always work on the queueing item with shortest processing time." The ability to make complex decisions based on the state of the system plus some plan of action is difficult, if not impossible, using conventional simulation methods and tools.

Hurrion's *visual interactive simulation*, discussed in the preceding, is one solution to this problem. The decision maker sits in front of a display of the running simulation, and all complex decisions are referred to him or her. The user can interact at will to make decisions that are normally made when managing the real system. But visual interactive simulation has a number of drawbacks, not the least being the need to interest the decision maker in 'playing' with the simulation. The limited sample that is given by interaction with a few runs and the difficulty in analyzing the effect of interactions both make experimentation difficult [2]. Typically visual interactive simulation is successful where the interacting decision maker has to make some global decision regarding the system, and really only needs an overall feel for performance; it is less effective when, for instance, being used to design specific decision rules.

Many systems, however, now have "decision rules" programmed into them, and the simulation developer wishing to simulate the system must somehow incorporate them into the simulation. A good example is *flexible manufacturing systems,* where control of the system can be complex, with manufacturing cells making autonomous decisions. Simulation is necessary so as to simulate the behavior of the system under different intelligent control and management regimes, be they human or otherwise. Typically, the major part of the simulation might be the programmed knowledge.

The rest of this chapter concentrates on these two demands for applying AI to simulation. Section 3 considers a number of research attempts which aim to make simulation "easier." Section 4 reviews the present state of combining AI and simulation so as to simulate systems which include some knowledge representation and decision making, which has come to be called knowledge-based simulation. Section 5 is devoted to PROSS, a knowledge-based simulator developed by the author, which uses PROLOG as a base language. This is followed by some discussion on the future of AI in simulation and a dicussion of some unsolved problems.

3   USING AI TO MAKE SIMULATION EASIER

3.1   Intelligent Front Ends

An *intelligent front end* (IFE) [5] is an expert system that sits between a package and the user, generating the necessary instructions or code to use the package following a dialogue with the user and interpreting results from the package and explaining them. Given the large investment in existing simulation packages, this is an obvious path to follow for those interested in making simulation easier. Recently a number of high-quality front ends for existing packages have appeared—for instance, (Stanwood et al., [53]) is a front end for SLAM—yet they typically assume knowledge of the package and thus (in effect) simply speed up development. Simulation program program generators, such as DRAFT [32], already perform some of the functions of IFEs, although they do not actually execute the simulation and interpret the results.

While there is little agreement on what exactly constitutes an IFE, useful "intelligence" includes

1. dialogue handling (a natural-language interface or at least user-directed free format input);
2. some "model" of the user so that the system adjusts its requirements of the user given evidence that the user is inexperienced, experienced, or whatever;
3. a model of the target package so that some decisions can be taken by the IFE rather than referred to the user; and
4. some facilities to explain results to the user.

Some program generators include elements of 3; for instance, CAPS [6] can recognize when a simple model is amenable to queueing theory and reports steady-state values rather than generating a simulation. Haddock's generator for SIMAN models of manufacturing systems [19] automatically executes a model, performing a steady-state analysis where appropriate. Few include 1 and 2. One exception is ECO [34], which generates ecological systems dynamics models in FORTRAN. The ability to include 4 will depend quite considerably on work in generating explanations of simulations, for example, that of Helman and Bahuguna [22].

3.1.1 Natural-Language Understanding Systems

Doukidis and Paul [9] have developed a *natural-language understanding system* (NLUS) for extracting model specifications based on activity cycle diagrams. An activity cycle diagram is a connected graph containing a complete cycle, composed of queues and activities, for every type of entity in the system.

Essentially, the user can specify sentences representing behavior in a model, and the software builds up a description of the system, prompting the user for further information as necessary. For example, given the input,

```
THE CAT SAT ON THE MAT
```

their system assumes that CAT is a dominant entity in the system (in network terms, a transaction) and that MAT is another entity, required by CAT for the activity SITTING (actually, NLUS would probably call the activity SATING, but that is irrelevant here). The system would then prompt the user with questions like

```
"What does a CAT do after SITTING ?"
```

and thus build up an activity cycle description for CAT. The result of the consultation is a language-independent description of the system, which can be used to generate the skeleton of a model.

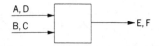

Figure 1. Work flow through a facility.

3.2   Machine Learning

An alternative to the IFE approach is to circumvent the model-building process using ideas from *machine learning* such that a simulation can be automatically generated from some representation of the observable state of the system. Simple machine-learning algorithms can be applied. For instance, induction can be used to automatically generate conditional events, represented as rules, from a set of examples. An example is shown here using the ID3 algorithm developed by Quinlan [44], which is available in a number of commercially available packages, including EXPERT-EASE from Intelligent Terminals Ltd.

Consider the production facility shown in Figure 1, where materials called A, B, C, and D flow in, and these are combined to make E and F. Given the set of example states that can exist at the facility, a conditional event for production at the facility can be induced. Table 1 shows these states. Production depends upon which material is available on the incoming lines. These are shown as Boolean attributes; the ID3 algorithm can also handle integer and other scalar types. This table was presented to

TABLE 1. Input to Induction Algorithm[a]

Aon1	Don1	Bon2	Con2	Result
n	n	n	n	nothing
n	n	n	y	nothing
n	n	y	n	nothing
n	n	y	y	nothing
n	y	n	n	nothing
n	y	n	y	f
n	y	y	n	nothing
n	y	y	y	f
y	n	n	n	nothing
y	n	n	y	nothing
y	n	y	n	nothing
y	n	y	y	e
y	y	n	n	nothing
y	y	n	y	f
y	y	y	n	nothing
y	y	y	y	e

[a]Aon1 means *material A on line 1*; *nothing* shows that no production is possible.

the package EXPERT-EASE, and the resultant rule (shown in EXPERT-EASE format) was produced

```
Con2
        yes: Don1
                yes: Aon1
                        yes: Bon2
                                yes: e
                                no: f
                        no: f
                no: Aon1
                        yes: Bon2
                                yes: e
                                no: nothing
                        no: nothing
        no: nothing
```

This is rather obtuse since the algorithm does not condense the rule tree by using Boolean combinations. If this is done, and the situations where production is not possible (i.e., the activity cannot be started) are removed, the following conditional event is obtained:

if Con2 *then*
    if Don1 *then*
        if Aon1 *and* Bon2 *then* <e>
                        else <f>
    else
    if Aon1 *and* Bon2 *then* <e>

where the parts in brackets will result in an activity starting and require the scheduling of the appropriate event. Hence, it can be seen that A, B, and C combine to make E, C, and D combine to make F, and production of E always takes preference over production of F.

The ID3 algorithm is flawed. The choice of attributes from which the rule is induced is crucial; the preceding event is useless if the order of the raw materials in line is important. It requires a complete set of examples and cannot handle contradictions or uncertainty. This event is not even the most computationally efficient since a better rule is

if Con2 *then*
    if Bon2 *and* Aon1 *then* <e>
    else
    if Don1 *then* <f>

However, advances are being made which overcome a number of these problems [21].

Despite this, induction as practiced in the preceding is a useful aid to devising conditional events with complex queue priority rules where the details of what happens are not obvious. Advances in induction methods and the resultant algorithms may mean that much of the logic of a discrete simulation can be automatically generated, although it is uncertain if generation of an entire complex simulation will ever be possible.

3.3 Advisory Systems

The technology for building simple *expert advisory systems* is now well developed. The are a vast number of so-called shells, and the literature has reached textbook status (e.g., see ref. 25). Perhaps the most obvious means of making simulation easier is by capturing the expert knowledge of simulationists in expert systems, which are then made available for the less expert simulation developer and user.

The dichotomy between statistical and computational knowledge has already been mentioned. Essentially, when developing a simulation and conducting experiments with it, the simulation practitioner uses four types of knowledge:

1. knowledge about the domain in which the model is built, for example, manu-facturing or health care;
2. knowledge about statistics—how to interpret results, what measurements are appropriate, and so on;
3. knowledge of the language or package used to implement the simulation; and
4. knowledge of the way in which the simulation (and hence the real system) behaves.

Many inexperienced simulation users will have good domain knowledge, particularly if the simulation has been constructed for use in their own environment. What they will lack is knowledge of types 2–4. The author has constructed a pilot expert system, called TRANS, which attempts to suggest appropriate experiments to perform with a simulation model solely employing type 4 knowledge. It is oriented toward transaction flow models and thus can be used with the types of models constructed in GPSS, Q-GERT, or the like.

The system is based upon exploring an objective. At present the system provides three possible objectives, namely, increase resource utilization, decrease resource utili-zation, or reduce transaction throughput time. The system suggests model parameters that are worth investigating; hopefully the user's focus of attention will be shifted, so that useful experiments or important parameters are not overlooked. Part of an example session with the system is shown in Figure 2, where the user is exploring the objective of increasing the utilization of a resource.

The system is written in a commercially available shell called ES/P Advisor. The shell itself is written in PROLOG and like PROLOG is founded on logic. It is designed for advisory systems that produce text as opposed to probabilistic systems that use uncertain knowledge, accumulate user estimates, and produce certainty factors for a number of hypotheses (the classic example of this type of system being Prospector [10]). As with many available shells, a system is constructed by programming a knowledge base in a knowledge representation language. A standard run time mechanism then drives the compiled knowledge base, performing backward-chaining deduction. Although Figure 2 shows the consultation proceeding line by line, the run time mechanism of ES/P Advisor is highly interactive, providing menu options that allow the user to request further explanation, to inquire why a question is being asked, to halt the consultation and store it, to recap on advice given, and to do a number of other useful tasks.

What is the name of the resource ? *mechanic*

Does mechanic serve only one activity ? *n*

Do other resource(s) cooperate with mechanic in
serving an activity ? *y*

What is the name of this activity ? *repair*

Do any of these cooperating resource(s) serve any
activity other than repair ? *y*

Do any of these cooperating resource(s) cycle ? *y*

Cooperating resources may be held up elsewhere
Advice: look at any cooperating resources that cycle, and see
            if waiting times are excessive

Is there a priority rule for the order in which
activities are served by mechanic ?

    (1) There is no priority rule
    (2) Activities are served at random as necessary
    (3) Activities are served in a predefined sequence

Enter the number of the relevant entry : *3*

Mechanic may be held up in its cycle
Advice: see if waiting times for mechanic are excessive
            in any part of its cycle

Is the utilization rate of any cooperating resource(s)
higher that the rate for mechanic ? *y*

Utilization of mechanic may be bound by cooperating resource(s)
at one or more activities
Advice: increase provision of cooperating resource(s) with
            higher utilization rates

Figure 2. Consultation with TRANS advisory system investigating objective of increasing resource utilization (user responses are in italics).

In producing expert systems where terminology is varied, and even sometimes conflicting, there is a considerable need for the system to explain technical terms [20]. Here each consultation is preceded with a preamble explaining terminology, not shown in Figure 2. Note that the terminology here is oriented toward systems viewed as a number of activity cycles, as is common in the United Kingdom. The knowledge base could be quite easily tailored, by hand, to a particular domain, with all simulation terminology altered appropriately. However, what is really needed is a capability to tailor the domain-independent advice as desired given the particular domain and simulation software. These problems are discussed at length elsewhere [37].

If an advisory system is developed for use with a specific package, then neither terminology nor any other variable aspect of simulation methodology is a problem since the system and user share the the approach to simulation inherent in that package. A good example of this is the advisory system presented by Hill and Roberts [23], which advises on detecting errors in INSIGHT models.

3.4 Automatic Analysis

Simulation is a purely *descriptive* tool. A valid simulation simply provides a vehicle for appropriate experimentation. Designing experiments, executing them, and analyzing results is one of the most difficult parts of the simulation process. It can be labor intensive and error prone. Hence automation of this task would be a big step toward making simulation easier. The automation of the process of experimenting with a simulation so as to optimize or find some prescribed function or goal is called *automatic analysis.*

Applying AI-based inference to a simulation model is an obvious first step in the development of automatic analysis methods. Often a simulation study can be specified as a goal, for example, "find the best possible production schedule." Thus, at least in theory, goal-directed search can be applied to the analysis such that the model can be given an overall goal and automatically generate and analyze experiments as necessary so as to achieve this goal. Whether or not any real progress can be made with this idea is debatable. In many simulation studies undertaken, the goal of experimentation (i.e., the decision maker's goal) is unknown, or it is simply impossible to represent it. Further, the application of heuristics to automatic analysis, for instance, surface response techniques, has been previously attempted with little success.

Among the various knowledge-based simulation tools, the developers of KBS [46] have placed considerable emphasis on automatic analysis. Baskaran and Reddy [1] describe a method of automatic analysis where the simulation monitors the relationship between events. For instance, when a specific event occurs, certain parameters may be measured. This can be useful for tracing the outcome of specific happenings.

4 THE EMERGENCE OF KNOWLEDGE-BASED SIMULATION

Knowledge-based simulation seems to have two definitions. As originally conceived at the RAND corporation [27], it can be narrowly defined as simulating over time the effects of the interaction between different sets of knowledge. More recently, it has been applied to any simulation, or simulation tool, where traditional simulation methods can be integrated with some means of knowledge representation. Although much of the work under this broader definition is, perhaps, best called something else (e.g., *knowledge-assisted simulation*), the phrase knowledge-based simulation has stuck and will be used here in its wider sense.

The emergence of knowledge-based simulation has been facilitated by a convergence of the representation methods employed in AI and simulation. As discussed in Section 2.1, the object-oriented approach which first appeared in SIMULA has, in various forms, become the doyen of knowledge representation in AI. Similarly, it has been realized that a number of attempts at representation in simulation were, in fact, early attempts at rule-based representation. In particular, the world view known as *activity scanning* [38] requires the expression of a model as a set of conditional events expressed as rules. O'Keefe [36] gives the example of a single-server, single-queue system, which can be completely defined by the three rules

if transaction in queue
    and
    server idle
then make server busy,
    remove transaction from queue,
    schedule the time to end service.
if time to end service
then make server idle,
    destroy transaction.
if transaction arrives
then add transaction to queue,
    schedule the arrival of another transaction.

Therefore, it is quite easy to develop a simulation in a simple rule-oriented language using activity scanning. A good example of this is provided by Bruno et al. [4], who present a production simulation programmed in OPS5.

In developing knowledge-based simulations and knowledge-based simulation tools, rather different approaches have been taken by the AI and simulation communities. The objectives in combining AI and simulation are somewhat different. The distinction between an *AI approach* and a *simulation approach* to knowledge-based simulation is useful for discussing the state of the art.

4.1 The AI Approach

AI workers increasingly have a need to include simulation in the systems they develop, so that, for example, the effects of a decision can be extrapolated over time or an expert system can use a model of a system to aid with reasoning. Thus most knowledge-based simulation coming from the AI community has concentrated on grafting a simulation capability onto existing AI methods and tools.

Early knowledge-based simulation tools were developed on top of AI languages. ROSS [30] was built in LISP, and BLOBS [33] employs POPLOG.

A more sensible alternative, where available, is to use an environment running on a dedicated LISP machine. Thus all facilities available to the knowledge engineer in the environment are available to the simulationist. A system can be developed using the available object-oriented facilities, rule-based programming, interface tools, and so on. Some examples are

1. SimKit, a product of Intellicorp, developed using the Knowledge Engineering Environment (KEE) [12];
2. the Knowledge-Based Simulation system (KBS) [46], developed at Carnegie-Mellon, which uses the facilities of Knowledge Craft; and
3. ROSS, recently reimplemented on top of ART [31].

Alternatively, a simulation can be developed by directly using a tool kit, for instance, see Stefik et al. [54] on LOOPS.

4.2   The Simulation Approach

Within the simulation community, it is realized that the present range of software tools, many of which are underpinned by FORTRAN (e.g., a number of SPLs are translated into FORTRAN), are inadequate for describing complex decision making. The knowledge-based simulation coming from the simulation community has been driven by the need to model increasingly complex systems, as discussed in Section 2.2, and has concentrated on adding complex decision mechanisms to existing simulation methods.

Due to the inadequacy of the procedural languages previously used, those in the simulation community attempting knowledge-based simulation have also employed a relevant AI language. However, the typical approach here is to implement a well-understood method or world view for programming a simulation and then integrate it with some facilities for knowledge representation. This approach is exemplified by T-PROLOG [15, 16]. Here, the programmer uses discrete-event facilities which are based upon SIMULA but can do anything that is possible in PROLOG. PROSS, presented in what follows, is similar, although the simulation facilities are based upon GPSS. However, in PROSS, unlike T-PROLOG, the simulation is kept separate from any knowledge and knowledge-based inference programmed in PROLOG.

A very different alternative, with much appeal to those that are inmates of existing simulation packages, is to entirely separate the simulation and any knowledge base employed by the simulation. An example is given by Flitman and Hurrion [14], where the FORTRAN simulation and the PROLOG knowledge base that is interrogated by the simulation even reside on different machines.

4.3   A Conclusion

At present, the two approaches provide an interesting contrast. In particular,

AI approaches have made better use of available AI methods, software, and hardware, whereas

simulation approaches have used a sounder methodological base (i.e., a well-understood world view) for developing simulations.

This difference is neatly backed up by an anecdote. At the 1986 AAAI workshop on simulation, a speaker from a well-known AI laboratory presented a beautifully engineered knowledge-based simulation that employed very advanced AI software and hardware. The speaker commented that time was advanced by a fixed amount and problems were encountered due to the fact that results were different depending upon the size of this time increment. It transpired that the speaker did not fully understand the problems inherent in synchronous time advance and had no idea how to develop a next-event time-advance mechanism.

All future attempts at knowledge-based simulation will undoubtedly learn from both communities, and the weaknesses of each will be mitigated. It is the author's opinion that the most interesting knowledge-based simulation package at present in SIMYON [49, 50]. Based upon a hybrid AI language called CAYENE that provides elements of object-oriented, logic, and functional programming, SIMYON employs the network world view descended from Q-GERT. Thus the programmer has considerable knowledge representation facilities available from within a well-understood simulation framework.

5   THE PROLOG SIMULATION SYSTEM: PROSS

PROSS is based upon an implementation of GPSS within PROLOG. Any AI modeling that can be programmed in PROLOG can be integrated with a simulation model; PROSS is thus a knowledge-based simulation tool developed using the *simulation approach* previously discussed.

PROSS is written in HC-PROLOG [47], which uses a syntax similar to LISP and thus rather different from standard Edinburgh PROLOG [7]. Random variate generation and statistics collection routines have been implemented by linking into HC-PROLOG the relevant facilities of the Pascal routines Pascal_SIM [39].

GPSS was the first *process description* simulation language. In the process description approach, the sequence of activities for each type of object in the system is mapped out. If objects with different descriptions can communicate, the approach is called *process interaction*. Recent years have seen process description approaches dominate discrete simulation. In addition to GPSS, both SIMSCRIPT II.5 [48] and SLAM II [41] all provide some variation of process description as the main representation vehicle. Process description is generally easier to comprehend than the other approaches and is a natural method of representing behavior that is well defined, procedural, and task oriented (e.g., do A, do B, do C, and then do A again). In comparison with process description, rules are a better method of representing behavior that is less well defined or is best captured declaratively (e.g., if X then do A, if Y then do B, if Z then do C).

Development of PROSS aims to allow the programmer the advantages of representing both processes in GPSS and rules and goals in PROLOG. In GPSS, *transaction flow* through a process is represented as a number of blocks. At each block, a transaction is either admitted or refused entry. If admitted, the block can either delay the transaction or pass it to another block (frequently the sequential block). In PROSS, a block can be a PROLOG goal; if the goal is unsuccessful, the transaction is refused entry, and the goal must be attempted again.

To illustrate the essential simulation capabilities of PROSS, a model of a variation of the classic barber shop problem [51], generally the first GPSS model presented in any GPSS textbook or course, is presented. This is followed by some discussion of a more relevant and realistic example: the simulation of an intelligent scheduling system.

5.1   The Barber Shop Example

Figure 3 shows a PROSS program, with comments, for an extension of the barber shop problem. A single barber serves one queue that contains two types of customer, those requiring a cut and shave and those requiring a cut only, and cut-only customers have priority in the queue. The program is invoked by making *replication* the top-level goal in the PROLOG interpreter.

Those familiar with GPSS will notice considerable similarities:

(a) separate process descriptions for each transaction type,

(b) the use of a timer segment and a run termination counter,

(c) the blocks *generate, advance, priority,* and *terminate,* and

(d) statistics collection queues, with entry and exit provided by the *queue* and *depart* blocks.

However, a number of deviations from GPSS have been included, mainly to facilitate efficient implementation in PROLOG and avoid some historic oddities in GPSS:

(a) The arrival of subsequent transactions is handled by an *arrival* block.

(b) Both GPSS facilities and storages have been replaced by a resource type (which must be declared).

(c) Using resources is provided by the blocks *acquire* and *release.*

(d) The simulation clock is real (in most implementations of GPSS it is integer).

(e) A number of run control blocks have been added concerned with tracing, printing statistics, and so on.

```
(( resources         (joe) ));      ; joe is a resource
(( size              joe 1 ));      ; there is 1 joe
(( cut_and_shave *process_id        (
   ( 1 generate 1 )                 ; generate 1 transaction
   ( 2 arrival       negexp 10 1 )  ; generate future arrival
   ( 3 queue         forjoe )       ; join statistics collection
                                      queue
   ( 4 priority      0 )            ; set priority to 0
   ( 5 acquire       joe 1 )        ; try to acquire barber
   ( 6 advance       negexp 5 2 )   ; delay due to distribution
   ( 7 release       joe 1 )        ; free the barber
   ( 8 depart        forjoe )       ; leave the statistics collection
                                      queue
   ( 9 terminate     ) )            ; leave the simulation
   ));
(( cut_only *process_id (
   ( 1 generate      1 )
   ( 2 arrival       negexp 10 2 )
   ( 3 queue         forjoe )
   ( 4 priority      50 )
   ( 5 acquire       joe 1 )
   ( 6 advance       negexp 5 2 )
   ( 7 release       joe 1 )
   ( 8 depart        forjoe )
   ( 9 terminate ) )
   ));
(( timer *process_id (             ; timer segment
   ( 1 generate 1 )                ; generate 1 transaction
   ( 2 advance constant 10 )       ; delay for 10 time units
   ( 3 arrival constant 0 )        ; generate another
   ( 4 terminate 1 ))              ; leave the simulation, reduce
                                     counter

   ));
((replication) :-
   (trace on)                      ; put trace on
   (start (cut_and_shave           ; specify process segment and
          cut_only timer) 1 )      ; start run-in period
   (statistics)                    ; print statistics
   (reset)                         ; clear statistics
   (start 10 )
   (statistics)
   );
```

Figure 3. Extended barber shop simulation in PROSS.

5.2   The Scheduling Example

Figure 4 shows some code from an intelligent scheduling example. A single process description for material of *type1* is shown (Figure 4*a*) along with the process description for the scheduler (Figure 4*b*) and one of the associated scheduling rules (Figure 4*c*).

Material arrives due to an inter-arrival distribution and queues for one of a number of different machine types. Material is modeled as transactions, with a different process description for each material type and machines. Only one machine can be working at any one time, and a scheduler determines which material is processed next. After processing on the machine, which involves a time delay, the material leaves the system.

```
((type1 *process_id (
   ( 1 generate 1 )              ;generate a transaction
   ( 2 arrival  negexp 10 2.0 )  ;schedule the arrival of another
   ( 3 talk     scheduler a )    ;talk to the scheduler
   ( 4 acquire  machineA 1 )     ;try to acquire a machineA
   ( 5 advance  negexp 11 15.0 ) ;time delay
   ( 6 release  machineA 1 )     ;release the machine
   ( 7 talk     scheduler b )    ;talk to the scheduler
   ( 8 terminate ) )
)) ;
```

(a)

```
((scheduler *process_id (
   ( 1 generate 1 )       ;generate the scheduler
   ( 2 schedule )         ;schedule using process rules
   ( 3 talk    *any b )   ;talk to any material at point b
   ( 4 transfer 2 )       ;do it again
)) ;
```

(b)

```
((schedule *ptype *pid *blno)  :-
   (get_length (machineA) *length) ;get length of queue for
                                   ;machineAs
   (> (*length 5))                 ;length greater than 5 ?
   (talk *ptype *pid *blno         ;talk to type1 material
         (type1 a))                ;at point a
) ;
((schedule *ptype *pid *blno) :-
   (suspend *ptype *pid *blno)   ;suspend the process
) ;
```

(c)

Figure 4. Excerpts from scheduling example: (*a*) process description for type 1 material; (*b*) process description for scheduler; (*c*) example of scheduling rule.

The scheduler is modeled as a process description with a number of associated rules that model the scheduling heuristics. The process description for the scheduler is simply *do a schedule, wait to talk to the finished material, and do it again*. Note that any desired flexibility, for instance, an ability for the scheduler to alter operations following the unexpected, must be programmed at the rule level.

The single rule shown in Figure 4(c) results in material of type1 getting a machineA resource if the queue for machineA exceeds 5. (Note that resources are global, so transactions with other process descriptions could be queueing for a machineA.) If the first version of the rule can succeed, then the first transaction of type1 is reactivated via the message-passing facility talk, which sends a message to the first transaction queueing for a message at the relevant point. The content of the message is empty in this example, so the result of talking is that each transaction resumes its process.

PROLOG will attempt all goals with the appropriate clause head, in the order they appear, until one succeeds. In this example, a version of the rule that suspends the process can always succeed. Typically, an associated rule may reference other clauses, and backward chaining of subgoals will occur as appropriate.

It is important to note that if the scheduling heuristics changed or the scheduling constraints changed (e.g., more than one machine can be working at any time but only certain combinations of machine types), then only the rules need changing. The process descriptions are still valid models of the materials behavior. Further, the size and number of the rules is irrelevant. The process descriptions are adequate whether there is one rule (as in Figure 4) or hundreds.

6   CONCLUSIONS

The application of AI to discrete-event simulation is an exciting area of research. To those that have developed them and those that use them, hybrid symbolic knowledge-based simulation systems, which combine various knowledge representation methods and inference mechanisms with an established simulation method, appear to be a significant advance over existing simulation tools. They allow the simulation of systems that involve some elements of human decision making, modeled as heuristic reasoning, and provide an environment conducive to rapid valid development.

Intelligent front ends provide an opportunity for the development of new interfaces to existing packages, languages, and models that are better and more accessible than, for instance, the present range of program generators. Coupled with the appearance of appropriate advisory systems, domain experts, with limited experience using simulation, can expect to have the full power of simulation modeling and analysis at their fingertips in the not too distant future.

Despite the tremendous promise, however, there are a number of problems which need to be overcome if the synergy of AI and discrete simulation is to provide lasting benefits.

First, there is a tendency for AI to redefine methodology (less charitable commentators would say "reinvent the wheel"). The established body of knowledge in simulation about how to relate time and state should be acknowledged and in many instances followed. For instance, anyone foolish enough to consider a redefinition of time-based relationships are well advised to look at Nance [35]. Where deviations are scientifically appropriate, explanations must be given: For example, many working in continuous simulation are scornful of qualitative simulation, not seeing the need to "replace" differential equations; few working in qualitative simulation feel compelled to explain their work to this important audience.

Second, it must not be forgotten that the prime problem in trying to model many systems is their inherent stochastic nature. Discrete simulation, in many instances, is still statistical model building, where the viability of the results is more a function of the careful design and analysis of experiments than the power of the underlying simulation package. Modeling more complex systems may in fact make this situation worse since the present range of accepted statistical techniques appears increasingly inadequate for analyzing simulations that include the ability to dynamically alter the experimental configuration.

Third, those simulationists who are still struggling with FORTRAN (and despite recent trends, it is probable that the majority of simulations are still written from scratch in FORTRAN) or any other procedural algorithmic language must be convinced of the advantages of using a symbolic language. Use of expensive work stations and software to build trivial simulation models with "gee-whiz" graphics may not be the best way to go about this. Models which are complex in nature are normally also complex in scope, incorporating hundreds of activities and thousands of entities and requiring very long run times for valid results. These so-called industrial-strength models are beyond the range of many of the present LISP or PROLOG simulation tools (they are certainly beyond the range of PROSS).

Fourth, the drive towards making simulations easier to do must be accompanied by the development of methods that safeguard the misuse of models. It is already possible for a naive user to build a relatively complex model interactively and then make invalid inferences from limited analysis. If the analyst is taken out of the *development* part of the cycle, then the skills of the analyst must be somehow available to the user in the *analysis* part of the cycle.

What is required by the comunity of simulation model builders is solid practical proof of exceptional achievement. As yet, there is no regularly used or commercially available intelligent front end or advisory expert system in simulation (not counting program generators), only a number of specific examples. More importantly, knowledge-based simulation needs to prove its worth. In much the same way as practitioners have recently used visual interactive simulation to study systems that could not be successfully studied by batch simulation and have used animation to portray the results of a simulation where previously textual reports were ignored by clients, so must knowledge-based simulation prove to be successful where modeling complex problems with conventional simulation languages has proved difficult.

ACKNOWLEDGMENTS

Some of this work was done at the University of Kent at Canterbury, England, and was supported by a grant from the United Kingdom Science and Engineering Research Council. PROSS was developed at the Department of Computer Science, Virginia Tech, with help from Dr. John Roach.

REFERENCES

1. V. Baskaran and R. Reddy, "An Introspective Environment for Knowledge Based Simulation," in S. Shepard, U. Pooch and C. D. Pegden (Eds.), *Proceedings of the 1984 Winter Simulation Conference,* IEEE Computer Society, Piscataway, NJ, 1984, pp. 645–651.

2. P. C. Bell and R. M. O'Keefe, "Visual Interactive Simulation—History, Recent Developments and Major Issues," *Simulation* **49**:109–116, 1987.

3. G. M. Birtwistle, O.-J. Dahl, B. Myhrhaug, and K. Nygaard, *SIMULA Begin,* Chartwell-Brant, Bromley, England,1979.

4. G. Bruno, A. Elia, and P. Laface, "A Rule-Based System to Schedule Production," *Computer,* **19**(7):32–40, 1986.

5. A. Bundy, "Intelligent Front Ends," in M. Bramer (Ed.), *Research and Development in Expert Systems,* Cambridge University Press, Cambridge, United Kingdom, 1985, pp. 193–204.

6. A. T. Clementson, "ECSL," in *Proceedings of the 1978 UKSC Conference on Computer Simulation,* IPC Press, Guildford, England, 1978, pp. 174–180.

7. W. F. Clocksin and C. S. Mellish, *Programming in Prolog,* Springer-Verlag, Berlin, 1984.

8. J. G. Crookes, "Simulation in 1981," *European Journal of Operational Research,* **9**:1–7, 1982.

9. G. Doukidis and R. Paul, "Research into Expert Systems to Aid Simulation Model Formulation," *Journal of the Operational Research Society,* **36**:319–325, 1985.

10. R. Duda, J. Gaschnig, and P. Hart, "Model Design in the Prospector Consulatant System for Mineral Exploration," in D. Michie (Ed.), *Expert Systems in the Microelectronic Age,* Edinburgh University Press, 1979, pp. 153–167.

11. J. B. Evans, "Simulation and Intelligence," Technical report TR-A5-84, Centre of Computer Studies and Applications, University of Hong Kong, 1980.

12. W. S. Faught, "Applications of AI in Engineering," *Computer,* **19**(7):1–27, 1986.

13. E. Fiddy, J. G. Bright, and R. D Hurrion, "SEE-WHY: Interactive Simulation on the Screen," in *Proceedings of the Institute of Mechanical Engineers,* **293-81**:167–172, 1981.

14. A. M. Flitman and R. D. Hurrion, "Linking Discrete-Event Simulation Models with Expert Systems," *Journal of the Operational Research Society,* **38**:723–733, 1987.

15. I. Futo and T. Gergely, "A Logic Simulation Language," *Transactions of the Society for Computer Simulation,* **3**(4):319–336, 1987.

16. I. Futo and J. Szeredi, "A Discrete Simulation System Based on Artificial Intelligence Techniques," in A. Javor (Ed.), *Discrete Simulation and Related Fields,* North-Holland, Amsterdam, 1982, pp. 135–150.

17. A. Goldberg and D. Robson, *SMALLTALK-80: The Language and Its Implementation,* Addison-Wesley, Reading, MA, 1983.

18. T. Grant, "Lessons for OR from AI: A Scheduling Case Study," *Journal of the Operational Research Society,* **27**:4–57, 1986.

19. J. Haddock, "An Expert System Framework Based on a Simulation Generator," *Simulation* **48**:45–53, 1987.

20. D. J. Hand, "Statistical Expert Systems: Necessary Attributes," *Journal of Applied Statistics,* **12**(1):19–28, 1985.

21. A. E. Hart, "Experience in the Use of an Inductive System in Knowledge Engineering," in M. Bramer (Ed.), *Research and Developments in Expert Systems*, Cambridge University Press, Cambridge, United Kingdom, 1984, pp. 117–126.

22. D. H. Helman and A. Bahuguna, "Explanation Systems for Computer Simulations," in J. R. Wilson, J. O. Henriksen and S. D. Roberts (Eds.), *Proceedings of the 1986 Winter Simulation Conference*, IEEE Computer Society, Piscataway, NJ, 1986, pp. 453–459.

23. T. R. Hill and S. D. Roberts, "A Prototype Knowledge-Based Simulation Support System," *Simulation*, **48**:152–161, 1987.

24. P. R. Hills, "SIMON—A Computer Simulation Language in Algol 60," in S. Hollingdale, (Ed.), *Digital Simulation in Operational Research*, English Universities Press, London, 1965.

25. P. Jackson, *Introduction to Expert Systems*, Addison-Wesley, Reading, MA, 1986.

26. E. J. H. Kerckhoffs, G. C. Vansteenkiste and B. P. Zeigler (Eds.), *Artificial Intelligence Applied to Simulation*, The Society for Computer Simulation, La Jolla, CA, 1987.

27. P. Klahr and W. S. Faught, "Knowledge-Based Simulation," in *Proceedings of the First Annual National Conference on AI*, AAAI, Palo Alto, CA, 1980, pp. 181–183.

28. W. Kreutzer, *System Simulation: Programming Styles and Languages*, Addison-Wesley, Reading, MA, 1986.

29. A. Law and D. Kelton, *Simulation Modelling and Analysis*, McGraw Hill, New York, 1982.

30. D. J. McArthur, P. Klahr and S. Narain, "ROSS: An Object-Oriented Language for Constructing Simulations," in P. Klahr and D. Waterman (Eds.), *Expert Systems Techniques, Tools, and Applications*, Addison-Wesley, Reading, MA, 1986, pp. 70–94.

31. M. McFall and P. Klahr, "Simulation with Rules and Objects," in J. R. Wilson, J. O. Henriksen and S. D. Roberts (Eds.), *Proceedings of the 1986 Winter Simulation Conference*, IEEE Computer Society, Piscataway, NJ, 1986, pp. 470–473.

32. S. C. Mathewson, "The Application of Program Generator Software and Its Extensions to Discrete Event Simulation Modeling," *IIE Transactions*, **16**:3–18, 1984.

33. S. Middleton and R. Zanconato, "BLOBS: an Object-Orientated Language for Simulation and Reasoning," in E. J. H. Kerckhoffs, G. C. Vansteenkiste and B. P. Zeigler (Eds.), *Artificial Intelligence Applied to Simulation*, The Society for Computer Simulation, San Diego, CA, 1986, pp. 130–135.

34. R. Muetzelfeldt, A. Bundy, M. Uschold and D. Robertson, "ECO—An Intelligent Front End for Ecological Modelling," in E. J. H. Kerckhoffs, G. C. Vansteenkiste and B. P. Zeigler (Eds.), *Artificial Intelligence Applied to Simulation*, The Society for Computer Simulation, San Diego, CA, 1986, pp. 67–70.

35. R. E. Nance, "The Time and State Relationships in Simulation Modeling," *Communications of the ACM*, **24**:173–179, 1981.

36. R. M. O'Keefe, "Simulation and Expert Systems: a Taxonomy and Some Examples," *Simulation*, **46**:10–16, 1986.

37. R. M. O'Keefe, "Advisory Systems in Simulation," in E. J. H. Kerckhoffs, G. C. Vansteenkiste and B.P. Zeigler (Eds.), *Artificial Intelligence Applied to Simulation*, The Society for Computer Simulation, San Diego, CA, 1986, pp. 73–78.

38. R. M. O'Keefe, "The Three-Phase Approach: A Comment on Strategy-Related Characteristics of Discrete-Event Languages and Models," *Simulation*, **47**:208–210, 1986.

39. R. M. O'Keefe and R. M. Davies, "Visual Discrete Simulation with Pascal_SIM," in

J. W. Wilson, J. O. Henriksen and S. D. Roberts (Eds.), *Proceedings of the 1986 Winter Simulation Conference,* IEEE Computer Society, Piscataway, NJ, 1986, pp. 517–525.

40. R. M. O'Keefe and J. W. Roach, "Artificial Intelligence Approaches to Simulation," *Journal of the Operational Research Society,* **38**:713–722, 1987.

41. A. A. B. Pritsker, *Introduction to Simulation and SLAM II,* Halsted Press, New York, 1984.

42. A. A. B. Pritsker and P. J. Kiviat, *Simulation with GASP II,* Prentice-Hall, Englewood Cliffs, NJ, 1969.

43. A. A. B. Pritsker and C. E. Sigal, *Management Decision Making—a Network Simulation Approach,* Prentice-Hall, Englewood Cliffs, NJ, 1983.

44. J. R. Quinlan, "Discovering Rules by Induction from Large Collections of Samples," in D. Michie (Ed.), *Expert Systems in the Microelectronic Age,* Edinburgh University Press, 1979, pp. 168–201.

45. R. Rajagopalan, "Qualitative Modelling and Simulation—a Survey," in E. J. H. Kerck-hoffs, G. C. Vansteenkiste and B. P. Zeigler (Eds.), *Artificial Intelligence Applied to Simulation,* The Society for Computer Simulation, San Diego, CA, 1986, pp. 9–26.

46. Y. V. R. Reddy, M. S. Fox, and N. Husain, "The Knowledge-Based Simulation System," *IEEE Software,* **3**:26–37, 1986.

47. J. Roach and G. Fowler, "Virginia Tech Prolog/Lisp: A Dual Interpreter Implementation," in *Proceedings of the 18th Hawaii International Conference on System Sciences,* IEEE Computer Society, Piscataway, NJ, 1985, pp. 88–92.

48. E. C. Russell, *Building Simulation Models with SIMSCRIPT II.5,* CACI, Los Angeles, CA, 1983.

49. S. Ruiz-Mier and J. Talavage, "A Hybrid Paradigm for Modeling of Complex Systems," *Simulation,* **48**(4):135–141, 1987.

50. S. Ruiz-Mier, J. Talavage and D. Ben-Arieh, "Towards a Knowledge-Based Network Simulation Environment," in D. Gantz, G. Blais and S. Soloman (Eds.), *Proceedings of the 1985 Winter Simulation Conference,* IEEE Computer Society, Piscataway, NJ, 1985, pp. 232–236.

51. T. J. Schriber, *Simulation Using GPSS,* Wiley, New York, 1974.

52. R. E. Shannon, "Intelligent Simulation Environments," in P. A. Luker and H. H. Adelsberger (Eds.), *Intelligent Simulation Environments,* Society for Computer Simulation, La Jolla, CA, 1986, pp. 150–156.

53. K. L. Stanwood, L. N. Waller and G. C. Marr, "System Iconic Modeling Facility," in J. W. Wilson, J. O. Henriksen and S. D. Roberts (Eds.), *Proceedings of the 1986 Winter Simulation Conference,* IEEE Computer Society, Piscataway, NJ, 531–536.

54. M. J. Stefik, D. G. Bobrow and K. M. Kahn, "Integrating Access-Orientated Programming into a Multiparadigm Environment," *IEEE Software,* **3**:10–18, 1986.

55. K. D. Tocher, *The Art of Simulation,* English Universities Press, London, 1962.

56. K. D. Tocher, "Some Techniques of Model Building," *Proceedings of the IBM Scientific Computing Symposium on Simulation Models and Gaming,* IBM, White Plains, NY, 1966, pp. 119–155.

15 A Hybrid Paradigm for Modeling of Complex Systems

SERGIO RUIZ-MIER[1] and JOSEPH TALAVAGE
Center for Intelligent Manufacturing Systems
Purdue University
West Lafayette, Indiana

1 INTRODUCTION

Simulation modeling has traditionally been a pragmatic science concerned with providing solutions to real-world problems. On the other hand, research in artificial intelligence has mostly dealt with some of the oldest philosophical questions such as the nature of knowledge and intelligence and with the possibility of programming computers so that they might come to behave with flexibility, common sense, self-awareness, and other human characteristics. Yet, it is apparent that these two disciplines share two fundamental concepts; namely, the concept of a real-world system and the concept of its representation in the form of a model.

A system can be defined to be a collection of entities, (i.e., people, machines, and particles) which interact together thereby generating behavioral data. Specifically, a real system is just a part of the real world which is of interest. A model is a representation of a system developed for the purpose of studying that system.

Ideally, a model should not only accurately represent reality, it should also be simple and easy to manipulate. Yet, because most real systems exhibit very complex behavior, the requirement of a strict conformity between abstract representation and fact often implies the construction of complex, highly detailed models. The modeler is then faced with the problem of finding a modeling methodology that is powerful enough to represent the complex behavior.

Various methodologies for Simulation Modeling were introduced in the 1960s and 1970s which aimed to make modeling a more natural process. One of these, the discrete event approach to systems modeling [13], is a commonly used paradigm which has formed the basis for other powerful methodologies, in particular, the network approach to modeling. The network modeling approach provides the modeler with simple yet powerful concepts which can be used to capture the significant aspects of the system to be modeled. Current simulation languages such as GPSS [10], Slam II [19], Siman

---

[1]Present address: P. O. Box 1615, La Paz, Bolivia.

[18], and INS [22] include this idea and provide a set of constructs (e.g., Arrival, Activity, Waiting, Routing, and Departure) for model building.

Current network modeling methodologies, though advanced, lack explicit concepts for the representation of complex behavior such as decision making. Artificial intelligence research, because of its emphasis on knowledge representation, has provided several techniques which can be successfully applied to the modeling of decision-making behavior. In particular, two methodologies which have been widely used for the representation of knowledge are object-oriented programming [27] and logic programming [14].

2   OBJECT-ORIENTED PROGRAMMING

Many of the ideas behind object-oriented programming have roots going back to SIMULA [5] and the subsequently developed SMALLTALK [9] language. Object-oriented approaches are also related to a line of work in artificial intelligence on the theory of frames [15] and their implementation in knowledge representation languages (such as FRL [21] and KRL [2]) to the work on message passing as in ACTORS [11] and inheritance as in FLAVORS [29].

In an object-oriented system, an object is defined as a symbol associated with a unique database of properties and operations which represent the object. Objects communicate with each other by the passing of messages. A message is a request for an object to carry out one of its operations.

One of the key features of object-oriented systems is the organization of objects into hierarchical classes in which subclasses inherit properties from their superclasses. This method of knowledge organization permits the representation of knowledge in a way which minimizes redundancy and eases data specification.

Another key feature of object-oriented systems is that messages specify only which operation should be performed, not how the operation should be performed. This ensures program modularity and provides a natural paradigm for representing the information transfer inherent in real-world decision hierarchies.

3   LOGIC PROGRAMMING

The roots of logic programming can be traced to the early work in automatic theorem proving and artificial intelligence.

The credit for the introduction of logic programming goes mainly to Kowalski [12] and Colmerauer [4], who proposed the fundamental idea that first-order logic, or at least substantial subsets of it, can be used as a programming language. This idea was revolutionary because logic had only been used as a specification or declarative language in computer science. Kowalski showed that logic has a procedural interpretation, which makes it effective as a programming language where logic clauses are regarded as procedure definitions and as procedure calls. The implementation of this idea was possible thanks to the publication of the landmark paper by Robinson [23], which introduced resolution, an inference rule particularly well suited to automation on a computer. The best known example of a logic programming language is PROLOG [3].

TABLE 1. Characteristics of Some Programming Paradigms

Object oriented	Distributed processing, hierarchical structure, low redundancy of data.
Logic oriented	Declarative, goal oriented, relational, pattern-matching driven
Discrete event	Event oriented, good for modeling dynamic systems

4 MODELING COMPLEX SYSTEMS

As we noted before, the modeling of systems displaying complex behavior such as real-world decision making requires a flexible and powerful modeling paradigm. The paradigm should not only provide concepts for the representation of dynamic behavior (as in the discrete-event approach) and allow for the handling of information transfer in hierarchies (as in object-oriented programming), it should also have explicit constructs for the representation of deductive decision making (as in logic programming). These desired characteristics are summarized in Table 1.

A hybrid methodology unifying the concepts of object-oriented programming, logic programming, and the discrete-event approach to systems modeling should provide a very convenient vehicle for representing complex systems.

Unification of some of these programming paradigms has been attempted before. Object-oriented, message-passing systems have already been used in conjunction with the discrete-event approach; for example, starting with SIMULA [5] and later ROSS [16] and KBS [20].

Approaches using logic programming and discrete-event modeling have also been attempted. In reference 17 the author describes a methodology by which simulation models should be constructed by means of a condition specification language. This language is based on the idea of representing behavior as a set of condition–action pairs (CAPs) which are analogous to the logic clauses of logic programming systems. The fact that discrete-event simulation models can be completely described by means of CAPs or logic clauses is very important. It means among other things that simulation models and intelligent systems can be described within the same framework. This unifying concept provides the basis for TS-PROLOG [8], which was developed as a logic-theoretic basis for logic simulation. In a TS-PROLOG simulation model, everything is described in terms of clauses, which are contained in a database, and control is by means of a resolution theorem prover.

An approach for the unification of logic programming and object-oriented programming is presented elsewhere [26], where objects are represented as logic clauses and communication between objects is through shared logic variables.

The approach to modeling complex behavior which we outline in this chapter has been implemented as a toplevel of CAYENE [24].

5 CAYENE

CAYENE is a member of the class of programming languages known as hybrid AI systems and is based on the idea of unifying the object-oriented, logic, and discrete-event programming paradigms by defining an environment in which objects (logic programs) communicate with other objects by sending messages (well-formed formu-

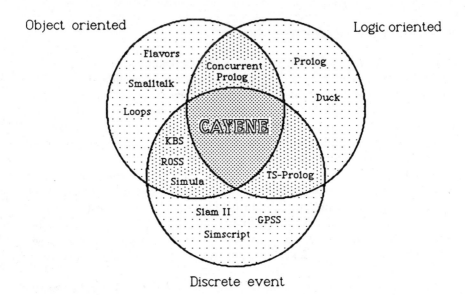

Figure 1. Programming approaches.

las of a logic) at some specific time (through an event file). Within this context, messages are goals to be satisfied by the use of an inference mechanism and the logic clauses (rules) that are local to the target object. Figure 1 shows the relationship between CAYENE and other programming paradigms.

CAYENE consists of a logic language, procedures for describing objects and hierarchies of objects, procedures for the handling of messages (including an event file to provide temporal delay of message delivery), a backward-chaining inference mechanism based on the resolution principle, and pattern-matching routines.

CAYENE's Functional Logic Language (FLL) is similar to PROLOG but more general. While PROLOG clauses are constructed from predicates which map terms (such as variables and constants) into TRUE or FALSE, FLL clauses are constructed from LISP functions which map terms into terms; this allows us to define the value of a goal as the value of its last subgoal. As a consequence, FLL clauses need not specify dummy variables in order to retrieve the value of a computation. For example, the PROLOG definition of "factorial" given elsewhere [28],

```
factorial(0,1).
factorial(N,F) :- N1 is N - 1,
factorial(N1,F1),
F is N * F1.
```

could be translated into FLL keeping the dummy variables. (Terms in FLL starting with a question mark denote variables).

```
(Factorial 0 1)

(Factorial ?N ?F) <==
(bind ?N1 (- N 1))
            (Factorial ?N1 ?F1)
            (bind ?F (* ?N ?F1))
```

However, the following definition, which makes use of the functional orientation of FLL and does not need dummy variables, is more natural.

```
(Factorial 0 ) <== 1
(Factorial ?N) <== (* ?N(Factorial (- ?N 1)))
```

Notice that FLL imposes no restriction as to which functions can be subgoals. Factorial could therefore also be defined by the single rule

```
(Factorial ?N) <== (if (equal ?N 0) 1 (* ?N (Factorial
(- ?N 1))))
```

which is equivalent to the LISP definition of factorial given in reference 30.

```
(defun Factorial (N)
(if (equal N 0) 1 (* N (Factorial (- N 1)))))
```

At the top level, CAYENE is structured as a hierarchy of objects. Objects are defined using the function (defob...). For example, the object PUMA could be defined as follows:

```
defob PUMA
        :properties:
        (a_kind_of  'ROBOT)
        (make       'Unimation)
        (X 3)
        (Y 5)
        (Z 2)
        :rules:
        (Move_gripper ?X ?Y ?Z) <== (place 'X (+ >X ?X))
                                    (place 'Y (+ >Y ?Y))
                                    (place 'Z (+ >Z ?Z)) )
```

This will define an object called PUMA as a subclass of the object ROBOT with the properties "make", "X", "Y", "Z" which represent respectively the manufacturer of the robot and the X, Y, Z coordinates of the robot gripper.

It also defines a behavior (Move_gripper) for the object which updates the coordinates of the gripper if it receives a message to do so. This is accomplished via the function (place...) which replaces the contents of properties, and (look...), which retrieves the value of a property. (>prop and (look prop) are equivalent. The > notation is provided for added perspicuity. The single quote prevents evaluation.

CAYENE also provides explicit functions for message manipulation. The function (send...), which has the form

```
(send <object> <message> )
```

specifies an event where <message> is a goal to be satisfied using the backward-chaining inference mechanism and the knowledge base (the set of rules) associated with object <object>. The function evaluates to the value which satisfies the goal. The more general function (send_at ...) which has the form

```
(send_at <time> <object> <message> )
```

files a "(send <object> <message>)" event at time <time> in the event file.

Finally, top-level control in CAYENE is started by the function (run), which sequentially evaluates the events in the event file and updates the current time variable TNOW.

6   SIMYON

SIMYON [25, 7] is an experimental network simulation environment embedded in CAYENE. Its purpose is to provide explicit concepts for the representation of complex behavior of real-world systems.

SIMYON is implemented by defining a library of CAYENE objects analogous to the "blocks" of network simulation languages and thus providing building blocks for modeling.

For example, SIMYON class object CREATE is analogous to the CREATE node in SLAM II [19] or the GENERATE node in GPSS [10] and is partially defined as follows;

```
(defob CREATE
   :properties:
   (a_kind_of NODE)
   (time_bet_creations (query))
   (time_to_start 0)
   (next_node (query))
   (transaction_name TRANS)
   .
   .
   . more properties
   :rules:
   (Start) <==
      (send_at >time_to_start MYSELF ' (Next_arrival)) :
```

```
(Next_arrival) <==
  (send_at TNOW >next_node (newsym >transaction_name))
  (send_at (+ TNOW >time_bet_creation) MYSELF
  '(Next_arrival))
  .
  .
  .
  . more rules .
```

This defines an object called CREATE as a subclass of the object NODE giving it various properties and rules. Notice the use of the function (query) as the value of some properties. This function is known as a "demon" and is evaluated if there is an attempt to retrieve the value of the property. So, for example, if >next_node is evaluated, then (query) will be evaluated. This prompts a one-time request to the user to provide a value for the property in question.

The two rules define two behaviors of the object. The first one specifies what actions are to be taken if the object receives a message matching (Start); the second specifies what actions are to be taken if the object receives a message matching (Next_arrival).

In the case of the event

```
(send 'CREATE '(Start))
```

CAYENE will attempt to match the goal (the message) to the head (what appears at the left of the <==) of one of the clauses. Since this matches the head of the first clause, CAYENE will attempt to satisfy the subgoal, which in this case happens to be

```
(send_at >time_to_start MYSELF '(Next_arrival))
```

This will send the message (Next_arrival) to the object CREATE at time zero. Upon arrival of the message (Next_arrival) to CREATE, the two subgoals of the second clause will be attempted, prompting the passage of two more messages which represent sending that transaction into the system and then scheduling the arrival of the next transaction.

The SIMYON library contains over 20 predefined objects, including ACTIVITY, WAIT, TERMINATE, BRANCH, QUEUE, RESOURCE, ASSIGN, ACCUMULATE, GATE, COLLECT, and others. SIMYON models are then constructed by making instances of the predefined SIMYON objects thereby describing a network. An example for the classic bank teller problem follows:

```
(model TELLER
        (Arrival CREATE)
        (Wait_for_service WAIT)
        (Service ACTIVITY)
        (Departure TERMINATE))
```

When SIMYON evaluates this expression, it creates instances of the objects CREATE, WAIT, ACTIVITY, and TERMINATE. Although it is true that the instances have no values in their properties (except the ones with default), they do have demons so it is possible to complete the model by telling SIMYON

```
(simulate TELLER 100)
```

which will prompt SIMYON to start the simulation. As soon as the value of a property is needed but not defined, the demon is evaluated and the user gets a message of the type

```
What is the value of property <prop> for object <obj> ?
```

When the values of all needed properties have been specified, the model will run to termination, in this case, when the global current time variable TNOW becomes greater than 100.

7   COMPLEX ROUTING IN A MANUFACTURING CELL

Up to now we have seen how SIMYON behaves at the top level as a network simulation language. Yet the real power of SIMYON lies in its ability to represent complex behavior such as decision making. Consider a case of complex routing in a manufacturing environment.

In this example parts arrive to a manufacturing cell and are scheduled by a human operator which relies on general knowledge about the system. This knowledge is most easily represented as a set of rules that the scheduler applies as needed.

At the highest level of abstraction the scheduler knows that

```
(Move part P to machine M)
        (a machine M is found)
IF      (machine M is available)
        (machine M can process part P)
        (M's queue is not full)
```

Yet the operator does not explicitly know if these conditions are true. Conditions such as (machine M is available) usually depend on other conditions which themselves might depend on further conditions.

At a lower level the scheduler might also know that for all machines in the shop

```
        (machine M is available)
IF      (machine M is not overloaded)
        (machine M is not down)
```

and that

```
        (machine M is down)
IF
        (maintenance for M is from T1 to T2)
        ( T1 < TNOW < T2 )
```

or

```
          (machine M is down)
IF
          (machine M needs repairs)
```

Therefore, in trying to satisfy the goal (Move part P to machine M), subgoals such as (machine M is available) and (machine is not down) have to be satisfied first.

This rule representation of the operators knowledge is implicitly structured as an AND/OR tree with the root of the tree being the topmost goal (Move part P to machine M) and the leaves of the tree being the known facts about the system.

It should be noted at this point that from the scheduler's perspective it is not really important to know why a machine needs repairs. What is important to know is that if that is the case, the scheduler can INFER that the machine is down. The reason why a machine needs a repair is not relevant (in this context) to the scheduling problem.

It is quite possible that in trying to find out if a certain machine needs a repair, control may access that machine's database and use other rules of thumb to do so. For example, the operator at machine M1 might know that for that specific machine

```
          (the machine needs repairs)
IF
          (the output rate is less than 13 parts per hour)
          (the noise level is greater than 30dB)
```

Since this knowledge pertains to machine M1 it should be part of that machine's database.

Representation of this knowledge in SIMYON is straightforward. We define the object SCHEDULE as follows:

```
(defob SCHEDULE
    :properties:
    (machines (M1 M2 M3 ..... Mn))
    :rules:
    (Move ?Part ?Mach) <==
        (find ?Mach)
        (Available ?Mach)
        (can_process ?Mach ?Part)
        (not (full (queue ?Mach)))
        (send_at TNOW ?Mach ?Part)
    :
    (Available ?Mach) <==
        (not (overloaded ?Mach))
        (not (Down ?Mach))
    :
    (Down ?Mach) <==
        (maintenance ?Mach ?T1 ?T2)
        (lessp ?T1 TNOW ?T2)
    :
```

```
(Down ?Mach) <==
    (needs_repair ?Mach)
 .

 .

.other rules )
```

and the object M1 as

```
(defob M1
    :properties:
    (a_kind_of MACHINE)
    (queue Q1)
    (operator Operator1)
    (output_rate (/ ?Num_parts ?Time))
    (noise_level (sample_detector ?Det_1))
    :rules:
    (Needs_repair) <==
        (lessp >output_rate 13)
        (lessp 30 >noise_level)
     .

     .

. other rules )
```

It is easy to imagine how this idea can be expanded to encompass a very large knowledge base with support knowledge maintained at the machine level, resource level, transaction level, and so on. Rules of thumb pertaining to all machines could be located in a generic object class called MACHINE, rules related to all resources in the class RESOURCE, and so forth. Access to all the knowledge could then be supported by defining (needs <Object1>.....) in the appropriate objects.

One of the advantages of this representation schema is that changes to the knowledge base such as addition or deletion of rules and assertions which might affect model behavior are simple to perform. For example, if operator 1 convinces the plant manager that he or she needs to take a 5-min coffee break at 10:00 every day, this could be added to the model by simply inserting the rule

```
(Busy Operator1) <== (lessp 120 TNOW 125)
```

(assuming the day begins at 8:00 and the time unit is 1 min). A change of this type might require significant changes to the model if it would have been represented using current network simulation languages.

8 MODELING ADAPTIVE SYSTEMS

In this example we are concerned with the modeling of a flexible manufacturing system (FMS) that operates via an adaptive heuristic for the allocation of the automated guided-vehicle (AGV) resources. In this automated manufacturing environment, each vehicle uses its own "conceptualization" of the facility layout to determine which action to take (as far as its routing is concerned) by keeping track of its own history with respect to routing and selectively updating this data. (By contrast, state-of-the-art AGVs use a table-lookup method to decide their route [1].)

The automated facility used to demonstrate this adaptive methodology (as shown in Figure 2) is a simplified version of an FMS as described in Dupont-Gatelman [6].

Parts to be machined enter the system through an input buffer and are transported from operation to operation by AGVs. Control is determined by the demand for AGV resources. For example, when a part needs to be routed to a certain machine, it signals the pool of AGVs that it needs to be moved. One of the AGVs will pick up the job and determine which track path it should take in order to minimize the travel time. The actual paths are determined using the A* search algorithm and the AGVs view of the plant (e.g., its perspective represented by weights assigned to each branch of the network).

In the case of blocking at some specific branch, the AGV will modify its picture of the system by decreasing the likelihood of taking that branch again in the future (by increasing the weight of that branch). This type of distributed behavior is reminiscent of the type of behaviors displayed by taxi drivers in big cities.

The AGV can then be modeled by the following object.

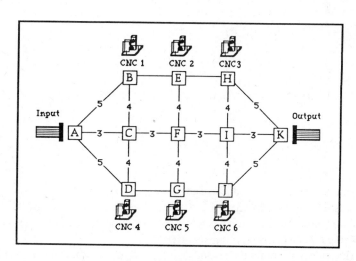

IMS

Figure 2. Modeling adaptive systems.

```
(defob AGV
  :properties:
  (status 'idle)
  (load 'empty)
  (current_pos 'A)
  (distances ((AB 5) (AC 3) (AD 5) (BC 4) (CD 4) (BE 3)
      (CF 3) (DG 3) (EF 4) (FG 4) (EH 3) (FI 3)
      (GJ 3) (HI 4) (IJ 4) (HK 5) (IK 3) (JK 5)))
  (weights ((AB 1) (AC 1) (AD 1) (BC 1) (CD 1) (BE 1)
      (CF 1) (DG 1) (EF 1) (FG 1) (EH 1) (FI 1)
      (GJ 1) (HI 1) (IJ 1) (HJ 1) (IK 1) (JK 1)))
  :rules:
  (Pick_Up ?Part ?Node) <==
      (equal 'idle >status)
      (place 'load ?Part)
      (Take_route (Find_route >current_pos ?Node))
  :
  (Take_route ?Route) <==
      (cond ((send (first ?Route) '(Are_you_blocked))
          (Add_weight (first ?Route))
          (enqueue MYSELF (queue (first ?Route))))
        (t
          (Move_through (first ?Route))
          (Take_route (rest ?Route))))
  :
  (Find_route ?From ?To) <==
      (A* ?From ?To >distances >weights)
  :
  (Add_weight ?Branch) <==
      (replace 'weights ?Branch (+ >weights.?Branch 1))
  :
  (Move_through ?Branch) <==
      (send_at TNOW ?Branch '(AGV MYSELF))
  :
  :
  :
  : other rules )
```

The generic object AGV as defined here has five properties denoting its status, load, current position, and perspective of the system which is represented by the distances between nodes and the subjective weights for each branch (initially one). The object also has five rules which determine its behavior.

The first rule determines the response to a (Pick_Up ...) message. It makes use of two other rules: Find_route, which finds a route using the A* algorithm, and Take_route, which recursively traverses the route list.

Adaptation of a particular agv (an instance of AGV) to its environment is accomplished by selectively updating its view of the system through the use of the Add_weight rule when blockings are encountered.

This approach to adaptation is numerical. Yet, the language poses no restrictions as to how individual objects are modified; this implies that "rule-learning" systems can be implemented by the selective updating of rules as opposed to just numerical parameters. CAYENE provides special rule-handling functions for this purpose.

It is interesting to note that this representation of the AGV is very flexible and will allow for easy changes to its structure. For example, if someone suggests to modify the adaptive heuristic so that it not only reacts to blocked branches but also reacts to free branches by lowering their weight, this can be accomplished by the addition of the term

```
(Sub_weight (first ?Route))
```

in the Take_route rule before the Move_through term and the addition of the rule

```
(Sub_weight ?Branch) <==
    (replace 'weights ?Branch (- >weights.?Branch 1))
```

to the rule set. This AGV object implements a sort of primitive "learning/forgetting" strategy.

9   CONCLUSION

A critical need of current network simulation languages is the capability to represent complex decisions in an efficient and maintainable way. Simulation languages such as the SIMYON language discussed here can provide the ease of use characteristic of network languages and at the same time incorporate user-specified decision processes in a complex and flexible format. For example, the decisions of a human expert could be represented by a rule-based expert system which would be completely compatible with the remaining network representation of the model.

The flexibility of SIMYON extends beyond its representation abilities. Simulation itself is a framework in which to perform experimentation. Yet the use of simulation in an experimentation environment calls for considerable judgment with regard to critical analysis of simulation output. Again, an expert system to control the experimentation aspects of simulation could be incorporated into the SIMYON language. Similar remarks could be made about employment of expert systems to facilitate modeling. Thus a language framework like SIMYON becomes more than just a simulation language. It really becomes a problem-solving language for a fairly broad domain of problems.

REFERENCES

1. W. P. Adams, "Current Industry AGV Control Strategies," Material Handling Focus Proceedings, Atlanta, GA, September 1986.

2. D. G. Bobrow and T. Winograd, "An Overview or KRL: A Knowledge Representation Language," Cognitive Science, 1(1):3–46, 1977.

3. W. F. Clocksin and C. S. Mellish, Programming in PROLOG, 2nd Ed., Springer-Verlag, Berlin, 1984.

4. A. Colmerauer, H. Kanoui, R. Pasero, and P. Roussel, "Un Systeme de Communication Homme-Machine en Francais," Groupe de Recherche en Intelligence Artificielle, Universite d'Aix-Marseille, France, 1983.

5. O. J. Dahl, and K. Nygaard, "SIMULA—An ALGOL-Based Simulation Language," Communications of the ACM, 9(9): September 1966.

6. C. Dupont-Gateland, "A Survey of Flexible Manufacturing Systems," Journal of Manufacturing Systems, 1(1):1–16, 1982.

7. P. Floss, S. Ruiz-Mier, and J. Talavage, "The SIMYON Manual," Research Memorandum, Engineering Research Center for Intelligent Manufacturing Systems, Purdue University, Fall 1986.

8. I. Futo and T. Gergely, *A Logical Approach to Simulation: TS-PROLOG,* Springer-Verlag, Berlin, 1983.

9. A. Goldberg and D. Robson, SMALLTALK-80: The Language and Its Implementation, Addison-Wesley, Reading, MA, 1983.

10. GPSS/360 User's Manual, IBM 420-03261.

11. C. Hewitt, "Viewing Control Structures as Patterns of Passing Messages," Artificial Intelligence, 8:323–364, 1977.

12. R. A. Kowalski, "Predicate Logic as a Programming Language," IFIP 74, pp. 569–574.

13. A. M. Law and W. D. Kelton, *Simulation Modeling and Analysis,* McGraw-Hill, New York, 1982.

14. J. W. Lloyd, *Foundations of Logic Programming,* Springer-Verlag, Berlin, 1984.

15. M. Minsky, "A Framework for Representing Knowledge," in P. Winston (Ed.), The Psychology of Computer Vision, McGraw-Hill, New York, 1975, pp. 211–277.

16. D. McArthur, P. Klahr, and S. Narain, "The ROSS Language Manual," RAND Note, September 1985.

17. M. Overstreet, "Model Specification and Analysis for Discrete Event Simulation," Ph.D. Dissertation, Virginia Polytechnic Institute and State University, 1982.

18. C. Pegden, "Introduction to SIMAN," Systems Modeling Corporation, 1982.

19. A. Pritsker, *Introduction to Simulation and SLAM II,* 2nd Ed., Halsted, 1984.

20. Y. Reddy and M. Fox, "KBS: An Artificial Intelligence Approach to Flexible Simulation," TR CMU-R1-82-1, Robotics Institute, Carnegie-Mellon University, 1982.

21. B. R. Roberts and I. P. Goldstein, "The FRL Primer," Massachusetts Institute of Technology, Memo 408, July 1977.

22. S. Roberts, ."Simulation Modeling and Analysis with INSIGHT," Regenstrief Institute, Indianapolis, 1983.

23. J. A. Robinson, "A Machine-Oriented Logic Based on the Resolution Principle," *JACM* 12(1):23-41, January 1965.

24. S. Ruiz-Mier, P. Floss, and J. Talavage, "The CAYENE Manual," Research Memorandum, Engineering Research Center for Intelligent Manufacturing Systems, Purdue University, Fall 1986.

25. S. Ruiz-Mier and J. Talavage, "Towards a Knowledge-Based Network Simulation Environment," Proceedings of the Winter Simulation Conference '85, San Francisco, CA, December 1985.

26. E. Shapiro and A. Takeuchi, "Object-Oriented Programming in Concurrent Prolog," *New Generation Computing,* **1**:25–48, 1983.

27. M. Stefik and D. G. Bobrow, "Object-Oriented Programming: Themes and Variations," *AI Magazine,* **6**(4), Winter 1986.

28. L. Sterling and E. Shapiro, *The Art of Prolog,* MIT Press, Cambridge, MA, 1986.

29. D. Weinreb and D. Moon, "Lisp Machine Manual," Symbolics Inc.

30. P. H. Winston and B. K. P. Horn, *LISP,* 2nd Ed., Addison-Wesley, Reading, MA, 1984.

16 An Incremental Object-Oriented Language for Continuous Simulation Models

PERTTI LOUNAMAA
Nokia Corporation Research Center
Helsinki, Finland

1 INTRODUCTION

The integration of artificial intelligence (AI) and simulation techniques, or symbolic and numeric computing in general, has become the focus of substantial effort in the past few years, the first workshop results being published in 1986 [7]. One of the central questions has become the role of shallow versus deep coupling of these techniques [6]. Shallow coupling refers to clearly separated tasks of the symbolic versus the numeric parts of the system, each treating the other as a black box. Intelligent user interfaces to complex simulation packages are typical examples of shallow coupling [5, 11, 16]. One of the main roles of an advanced front end is to provide a high-level language for the specification of simulation models. Such specifications are then transformed into input files, in the form of program statements, for a traditional simulator. These files are further compiled, linked, and executed by traditional simulator technology.

This kind of shallow coupling causes problems:

1. With smaller models compilation and linking takes more time than the execution itself, thus increasing the edit–execute–re-edit cycle time for the model developer.

2. Any analysis at execution time, such as debugging and tracing, takes place in the lower-level language. These tools are usually developed for programmers and not for simulationists, making them often unusable for all practical purposes.

3. The simulation tool is predefined, leading to limited alternatives in control and data structures.

The first problem not only reduces the productivity, but more seriously, discourages experimental innovative modeling. The second problem may render the whole approach close to useless because debugging requires the user to work with the lower-level code anyway.

397

Whereas the first two problems are more of a technical nature, the third problem may severely restrict the applicability of the approach.

Most AI-based front ends, for simulators as well as other numerical software, are developed in LISP. Thus a way to avoid these problems is to do the simulation in LISP. The limitation with this alternative has been that LISP code has been relatively slow in executing numerical expressions. Recent developments in LISP compiler technology as well as decreasing hardware costs have, however, resulted in LISP environments that execute essentially as efficiently as FORTRAN code in standard architectures.

These developments have made simulation in LISP an attractive alternative, providing new technologies:

(i) high-level specification languages using concepts such as objects and inheritance,

(ii) direct translation of specifications to flexible control and data structure implementations, and

(iii) advanced LISP programming environments including incremental compilation and efficient execution and good debugging and tracing facilities.

Using this approach leads to the intimate "deep" coupling of symbolic and numeric techniques, resulting in benefits such as the reduction in turnaround time between model definition and execution, interrupt and model state examination facilities, and ability to call tailored reasoning facilities during simulation [10].

In this chapter an incremental object-oriented language for describing difference and differential-equation-based simulation models is presented. Object-oriented LISP-based simulation modeling as a research area is motivated. Then completed research and current research goals are discussed. The main part of the chapter, the language definition, follows. After presenting the language syntax, some implementation and execution details are presented, a simple example model is formulated in the language, and language design trade-offs are considered. The chapter concludes with a short comparison to related research, a discussion on areas for future research, and some comments on the relevance of the work.

2 MOTIVATION FOR RESEARCH

The research is motivated by the belief that our understanding of and ability to analyze complex dynamic phenomena can be improved by providing tools that support explorative and experimental simulation modeling. With current methodologies models are time consuming to build and test, the modeling languages require unnatural and complex formalizations of a problem. In order to overcome these problems a methodology is needed that consists of an easily communicable language for describing models, tools for interactively executing these descriptions, and various ways to summarize the results. This means that an integrated modeling environment is needed which is based upon a high-level language enabling incremental changes to models.

The previously discussed symbolic computing techniques are the best technological basis for reaching this goal.

3   SIMULATION AND EXPERT ENVIRONMENT

In earlier work we explored the usefulness of AI in the development of integrated modeling environments by creating a prototype of a LISP-based environment, SEE (the Simulation and Expert Environment) [8, 10] and by applying it to a few dynamic decision-making problems [9]. In this work two methodologies were emphasized: rule-based reasoning and object-oriented programming [15].

SEE is a set of MACLISP functions that allows the user to describe a problem by both a high-level object-oriented simulation approach and a rule-based approach. The object-oriented language GLISP [12] was used with minor modifications. The inference engine that was developed in the research is similar to MRS [3]. Simulation facilities, such as repeated execution, noise generation, storage of results to files, transformation of files for plotting, and analysis of parametric simulation results, are part of the SEE software. LISP expressions may be used as an interactive query language for analyzing subsets of stored parametric simulation results. Extensive tracing capabilities beyond those provided by MACLISP are included in SEE.

4   CURRENT RESEARCH GOALS

The development of SEE clarified the problems and potential benefits of LISP-based simulation modeling environments. The two main benefits achieved using LISP programming environments are the ability to provide an integrated set of tools and a high-level modeling language. The limitations of SEE can also be classified into these categories.

SEE was developed in a time-sharing environment with no advanced user interface capabilities. The next-generation simulation tools should be implemented in a LISP programming environment on engineering work stations, which have a rich set of user interface functions such as multiple windows, mouse control, and dynamic pop-up menus. This user interface technology combined with relational database technology to store models and computational results forms a much stronger basis for developing an integrated user-friendly environment.

The second limitation of SEE resulted from the use of a general object-oriented language (GLISP). A more powerful and useful language can be defined by exploiting the properties of dynamic simulation models. The key issue is then to clearly identify the unique semantic properties of the model types of interest and exploit these features in the language definition.

This approach of defining high-level languages is fundamental in applying LISP-based techniques to solving complex problems. Thus results obtained by taking this approach should be of interest both to simulationists and to those interested in applying this same approach to other types of problems.

5   AN OBJECT-ORIENTED MODELING LANGUAGE

In this section SLICL (Simulation Language in Common LISP), an object-oriented modeling language for describing models consisting of difference equations, is presented. It is based on the currently standard version of LISP, Common LISP [14]. The language can be applied also for differential equations, but some of the details of the language and its implementation do change. Ways to select numerical integration rules, step sizes, and so on, are natural parts of these changes.

5.1   Domain of the Language

The fundamental idea on which SLICL is based is that it is used to describe problems in a mathematically well-defined domain. This domain restriction is exploited extensively both in the syntax and the semantics of the language.

Let $x(t)$, $y(t)$, and p denote state variable, dependent variable, and parameter vectors, respectively. Then the difference equation models are of the form

$$x(t + 1) = f(x(t), y(t), p), \tag{1}$$

$$y(t) = g(x(t), y(t), p). \tag{2}$$

The equations defined by (2) are restricted to be nonsimultaneous such that they can be solved in one pass without iteration. That is, the dependencies between the dependent variables have to be acyclic, in particular, the right side of the equation that determines the value of a specific y variable cannot contain the variable itself. Dependent variables are used for collecting output information, defining closed-loop control variables, and storing values of intermediate calculations. Mathematically one could implement a model by just using state variables, but the use of dependent variables makes both the modeling more convenient and the computations more efficient.

5.2   Structure of Language and Syntax Rules

In an object-oriented language, mathematical concepts such as variables, parameters, and equations are collected into object classes. Variables are indexed by creating instances of object classes that contain variables.

An important feature of the language that directly follows from the object-oriented approach is that mathematical models can be considered as sets of object instances. These sets are given structure by defining model classes, which are used to reduce unnecessary recompilations. Concrete models are instances of model classes. Using this approach, one never needs to define the order in which the equations are calculated. One just defines the mathematical nature of the problem, and the executable model is automatically generated.

For purposes of convenience and reusability mathematical equations can be described separately from object class definitions. Logically, however, an equation is always associated to some object class.

Typically variables and parameters are organized into object classes such that variables used in an equation belong to the same object instance. References to variables not belonging to the same object instance requires explicit object references. Because all object references have to be within the same model, the references are bound to object instances when creating model instances.

SLICL is implemented by the LISP macros

defsimobject, for defining object classes;

defrule, for defining equations separately; and

defmodel, for defining model classes.

The defmodel macro generates two LISP functions:

make-model, for creating model instances; and

link-model, for linking object instances to references.

These are created separately for each model class.

The syntax of the macros is represented in a modified form of BNF (Backus–Naur form):

1. <x> means that x is optional.
2. x:: = y1
   y2
   means that y_1 and y_2 are alternative definitions of the symbol x.
3. The symbol * means that the expression to the left of * can be repeated arbitrarily many times.
4. Capitalized words and parentheses are terminal symbols.

5.3   Defining Object Classes

The macro defsimobject is used to define object classes:

```
DEFSIMOBJECT class-name (superclass-name*)
            <:STATE-VARIABLES (state-var-spec*)>
            <:DEPENDENT-VARIABLES (inter-var-spec*)>
            <:PARAMETERS (parameter-spec*)>
            <:OBJECT-REFERENCES ((name class-name)*)>
```

in which the specifications are

```
state-var-spec::= name
                (name <rule> <:INIT value> <:STEP step>)

inter-var-spec::= name
                (name rule)
```

```
parameter-spec::= name
                  (name value*)

name::= symbol<%symbol>

rule::= (function-name arg*)
        (vector-op object-set-ref vrule)

arg::= <object-ref!>data-name
       rule

vector-op::= PRODUCT
             SUM

vrule::= (function-name varg*)
         (vector-op object-set-ref vrule)

varg::= <object-ref!>data-name
        <object-ref!>parameter-name!element-ref
        vrule
```

Class-name and superclass-name refer to object classes. Function-name refers to any Common LISP function. Object-ref refers to an object reference defined in object-references. Data-name refers either to a variable or a parameter. Parameter-name refers to a parameter. Object-set-ref refers to a set of objects defined in object-references. Element-ref refers to an element in object-set-ref and its name is identical to the name of object-set-ref except for the last letter *s*. All numeric values are real numbers except step, which is an integer.

Class-name defines the name of the object class being defined.

The list following the class name contains the names of the classes from which the current class inherits slot definitions.

As an example, assume that the object class porsche is a subclass of sportscars and luxury-goods and that sportscars is a subclass of cars and recreational-vehicles:

```
(defsimobject sportscars (cars recreational-vehicles) ..)


(defsimobject porsche (sportscars luxury-goods) ..)
```

The object class definition is structured into four categories: state variables, dependent variables, parameters, and object references, which have corresponding key words. Each category contains a list of slot specifications.

A slot specification is either just the name of the slot or a list in which the first element is the name, and the other elements are information related to that slot.

Slot names are either symbols or of the form symbol%symbol, where the first and latter symbol are alternative names. This is for the purpose of allowing convenient shorthands for slot names in mathematical expressions. The longer names are needed, for example, when storing results to files.

State variable specifications contain the state equation, a default initial value, defined by the key word :init, and a frequency control parameter defined by the key word :step. The internal data structure for state variables contains four facets: value, new-value, init, and step. The init facet is given the value 0.0 if the keyword :init is not given. The step facet is used to control the frequency at which the value of a state variable is updated. For example, if step = 2, the variable is updated every second time period. The default value for step is 1.

The dependent variables are variables that have a direct functional dependency on either the state variables or other dependent variables. The only user-given information related to a dependent variable is the functional dependency defined with a rule. The dependencies may not form cycles. Dependent variables and parameters have one internal facet containing the value of the slot.

A parameter can be given a default value. In most cases, though, parameters are given their values when the object instances are created. Parameters can be vector valued to allow for a convenient representation of state matrices.

For example, a simple linear dynamic system $x(t + 1) = Ax(t) + b$ can be represented by defining one object class with one variable x, one parameter vector a, and two scalar parameters b and $my\text{-}a$. The parameter $my\text{-}a$ is needed for storing the variable's impact on itself, the diagonal element in the state matrix. Each instance of the object class would then define one element of the x and b vectors and a row in the state matrix.

The class definition would look as follows:

```
(defsimobject linear-system-equation ()
     :state-variables
     ((x :init 0.0))
     :parameters  (my-a a (b 0.0)))
```

Object references are defined with the :object-references key word. Since object references are references to object instances, only the name by which a specific object instance will be referenced is defined at object class definition time. To allow for compilation of rules at class definition time, also the class of the other object that will be referenced has to be given. The object references can either be to a single other object instance or to a set of instances, in which case the object reference has to end with the letter *s*.

The class definition of linear-system-equation would be changed to

```
(defsimobject linear-system-equation ()
     :state-variables
       ((x :init 0.0))
     :parameters
       (my-a a (b 0.0))
```

```
:object-references
  ((others linear-system-equation)))
```

expressing that a reference to another object belonging to the class linear-system-equation will be used in the equations.

5.4 Representation of Equations

Difference equations are represented by rules that are limited LISP expressions: lists beginning with a function name or a vector operation. In the previous case the remaining elements have to be either lists or data references. In the latter case, the expressions begin with the word *product* or the word *sum*, the second element is a set reference over which the product or sum is done, and the last element is a rule expression that is executed for each element in the set. The set consists of object instances defined in the object reference section by an object reference definition ending with the letter *s*.

It would be easy to change the mathematical notation from the reverse polish notation of LISP to a more familiar one, but both the language syntax definition and the implementation is simpler with RPN. A problem of using a standard notation is that mixing LISP code into the rules makes them confusing. In practice, for more complex modeling problems, one wants to use Common LISP code in the rules, and therefore it is better to stick to one notation consistently. The alternative is to define a more complete own language with all the normal programming constructs such as assignment, conditional statements, and iteration.

Data references are either names of variables or parameters of the object class itself or expressions of the form object-ref!data-name. The object reference has to be defined in the current object class definition or inherited from superclasses. The variable name has to be a variable (or parameter) of the object class of the object reference in question. The object-ref!data-name construct is needed to access data of objects other than the one to which the rule is defined.

The parameter-name!element-ref construct is needed to access elements of parameter vectors. The vectors are indexed by other object references. Thus the length of each vector has to correspond to the number of object instances in an object reference set. This construct is only meaningful when used in the lexical scope of a SUM or PRODUCT statement. The element-ref refers to an element in the set defined by object-set-ref. An element-ref or an object-ref referring to an object instance in an object-set-ref has to have the same name except the last letter *s*.

As an example of a rule definition, in the case of the simple linear dynamic system the state equation would be defined as

```
(+ (* my-a x) (sum others (* a!other other!x) b).
```

At this point the language does not support vector operations that return vectors, which would allow the use of vectorized variables. This is contrary to the object-oriented philosophy of the language, since in the object-oriented paradigm variables should be indexed and addressed by object instances as shown previously. In complex applications it may be necessary to have vectorized variables belonging to more abstract types of objects for conciseness purposes. This extension should be considered in the future.

The macro

```
DEFRULE reference object-class (arg*) rule

reference::= variable-name
             function-name
```

is needed to allow the definition of rules separately from the class definition. The BNF of the nonterminal symbol rule is the same for defrule and for defsimobject.

When the rule to calculate a variable in an object class is representationally complex, it is more convenient to define the rule separately and not directly in the defsimobject-based definition of the object class. Defrule makes this possible. In case the same rule is used in calculating several variable values or used as a common subexpression in different variable rules, the rule is given a unique name, function-name, instead of the variable name. This allows the definition of mathematical calculations common to several variables, with the representational conveniences achieved in the defsimobject rule definitions. The same rule can be used by several object classes via inheritance.

The second benefit of using defrule, avoiding recompilation, is due to implementation details. For each variable in an object class a LISP function is generated that calculates the value of the variable. If defrule is used, then only this one function is recompiled when changing the rule, instead of recompiling all rules defined in defsimobject, when the object class definition is changed.

The preceding linear system equation could be defined by

```
(defrule x linear-system-equation ()
    (+ (* my-a x) (sum others (* a!other other!x) b))).
```

5.5   Defining Models

The logical structure of a model is defined via defmodel:

```
DEFMODEL class-name (superclass-name*) (slot-spec)*

slot-spec::= object-label :CLASS objectclass-name
```

The defmodel class-name is the name of the defined model class. Essentially the model class is a list of object references. Each object reference consists of an object label and the name of the allowed class for the object to which the label will refer. A functionally similar language could be obtained without using the defmodel macro, but it would be somewhat more complicated to implement and would cause substantially more evaluation and compilation during each model instance creation. Furthermore, defmodel is a useful conceptual tool for the modeler.

For example, a two-dimensional dynamic system could be defined by

```
(defmodel 2dim-linear-system ()
         (eq1 :class linear-system-equation)
         (eq2 :class linear-system-equation))
```

The defmodel macro could easily be extended to allow hierarchical modeling as in SIMPLEX-MDL [2]. Another more powerful way, however, is to define abstract object classes, which, for example, aggregate the values of variables of object instances of other object classes. This approach is demonstrated in the example in Section 7.

5.6   Creating Model Instances

Modeling starts by defining object classes and model classes. Concrete executable models are obtained by making instances of these classes. Object instances are created simultaneously when creating a model instance.

The internal data structure of both objects and models is based on Common LISP structures. Thus instances of objects and models are created by the standard structure instance creation facilities. To initialize the values of parameters and vectors, one has to access the slots of structures directly. For example, to create a simple linear dynamic system with two equations, one could proceed as follows:

```
(setq *current-model*
  (make-2d-linear-system
    (eq1 (make-linear-system-equation
      (x-init 0.0)
      (b 0.5)
      (my-a 1.0)
      (a 0.5))))
    (eq2 (make-linear-system-equation
      (x-init 0.0)
      (b -0.5)
      (my-a 1.0)
      (a -0.5))))))
```

Linking the object references in a model instance is quite inconvenient if one uses directly the Common LISP structure access functions. Therefore, to make the linking convenient, the defmodel macro creates a function

```
LINK-class-name model-instance link-specs*

link-specs::= :object-label '(link*)

link::= :object-reference (object-label*)
```

where the class-name is the class name of the defined model. The object-label key word is an object label defined by defmodel. Similarly, the object reference key word is an object reference of the allowed object class.

Since link-class-name is a function, the arguments for the object label key words have to be quoted.

The link-class-name function sorts the dependent variables of the linked object instances such that those which occur on the right side of an equation are calculated before the variable on the left side. Based on the sorting result, the link-class-name function generates the appropriate code that efficiently executes the calculations in the right order.

The linear dynamic system model could be linked as follows:

```
(link-2d-linear-system *current-model*
        :eq1 '(:others (list eq2))
        :eq2 '(:others (list eq1))
)
```

An alternative to the link-class-name functions is to have an own model instance creation function that first calls the structure instance creation functions and then calls the link-class-name function. This function would not require the user to explicitly make the object instances and would make the initialization of parameter vectors simpler. The use of an own instance creation function is illustrated at the end of Section 7.

6   IMPLEMENTATION AND EXECUTION OF MODELS

Rules are transformed to LISP functions. For each object class three general functions are defined that execute the state equations, initialize the state variables, and move the new state variable values to the old values.

For each model class, the three corresponding functions are defined that call the corresponding object level functions for each object reference in the model class.

The models are executed by calling the function sim with no arguments. The function sim executes the model instance stored in the global variable *current-model* the desired number of times. The desired number of executions is stored in the global variable *max-time*. Alternatively, one can define an own function stop-simulation that returns nil if the simulation should continue and non-nil if the simulation should stop. Sim calls this function each time period. During initialization of the model instance sim creates and compiles a function that it repeatedly calls during simulation.

The important point of the preceding data structure selections and function generations is that during simulation no garbage is created and all calculations are done by direct function calls to compiled functions, making the simulation essentially as efficient as a corresponding FORTRAN model.

Furthermore, the executed model is automatically created by just defining the rules to be simulated. An important detail of this automatic creation is that the execution of the rules is done in the right order in terms of functional dependencies among the variables.

A prototype version of SLICL, lacking inheritance and some other minor features, has been implemented in Common LISP. An initial differential equation version of the language has been successfully tested in analog circuit simulation, improving the system response time compared to a FORTRAN-based simulator when doing explorative simulations with alternative small designs.

7   AN EXAMPLE MODEL IN THE LANGUAGE

To illustrate the use of the preceding language, a simple dynamic decision-making problem is described. There is a company with two divisions. The divisions sell substitute products, which quantity is denoted by q_1 and q_2. The price of each product is determined via a linear demand curve:

$$p_1 = 1 - aq_1 - bq_2, \qquad p_2 = 1 - aq_2 - bq_1,$$

with two unknown parameters a and b. Let us assume that the quantities are determined by maximizing company profits given the division managers' estimates of the two parameters a and b. The prediction errors between observed and estimated prices are attributed to the two parameters according to the parameter s that lies between 0 and 1. The estimates of a and b are assumed to be updated according to a linear learning curve. These four estimates are the state variables of the model.

The model corporate-dm-process is defined by

```
(defmodel corporate-dm-process ()
   (manager1 :class manager)
   (manager2 :class manager)
   (company  :class simple-company))
```

and has no supermodels.

The object class simple-company is defined, without superobjects, by

```
(defsimobject simple-company ()
   :dependent-variables
   ((profit (sum managers manager!profit)))
   :object-references
   ((managers manager)
   )).
```

The definition of the manager object class is, without superobjects,

```
(defsimobject manager ()
  :state-variables
    ((a-estimate%a-e (+ a-e (* l s (/ (- e-p o-p)
      sales)))))
             :init 2.0)
    (b-estimate%b-e :init 0.5))
  :dependent-variables
    (sales
    (deterministic-price%d-p (linear-demand-curve    a b))
    (observed-price%o-p
      (* d-p (+ 1.0 (rand-evenly -0.5 0.5 0.001))))
    (profit (* o-p sales))
    (estimated-price%e-p (linear-demand-curve a-e
      b-e))))
  :parameters
    ((impact-of-own-sales%a    0.5)
    (impact-of-other-sales%b 0.5)
    (attribution-factor%s    0.5)
    (learning-rate%l        0.3))
  :object-references
    ((other manager)))
```

The function (rand-evenly low high inc) returns a number that is evenly distributed between low and high with accuracy inc.

In the definition of the manager object three functions were used:

```
(defrule linear-demand-curve manager (a b)
   (- 1.0 (* a sales) (* b other!sales)))

(defrule sales manager ()
   (/ (- (* 2.0 other!a-e) (+ b-e other!b-e))))
      (- (* 4.0 a-e other!a-e)) 4.0)))

(defrule b-estimate manager ()
   (+ b-e (* l (- 1.0 s) (/ (- e-p o-p) other!sales))))
```

The first rule is defined separately because it is used to calculate the value of two different variables. The mathematical derivation of these rules is irrelevant for current purposes, the important point is how parameters and variables of the object itself and of other objects are referenced.

Finally, the object instances are made and linked:

```
(setq *current-model* (make-corporate-dm-process
                       :manager1 (make-manager)
                       :manager2 (make-manager)
                       :company (make-simple-company)))
```

```
(link-corporate-dm-process *current-model*
        :manager1 '(:other manager2)
        :manager2 '(:other manager1)
        :company  '(:managers manager1 manager2))
```

An own instance creation function might behave as follows:

```
(setq *current-model* (create-corporate-dm-process
        :manager1 '(:other manager2)
        :manager2 '(:other manager1)
        :company  '(:managers manager1 manager2)))
```

8   LANGUAGE DESIGN TRADE-OFFS

In SLICL as already defined, all object class references are binding. One cannot arbitrarily mix various classes in the same model. Removing the requirement for defining classes from defmodel and from object-references in defsimobject would eliminate the need to define new classes just because some other class has changed.

The classes could instead be bound when creating model instances by the own instance creation function. For example, instead of the expression given in Section 7 one could have

```
(setq *current-model* (create-corporate-dm-process
  :manager1 '(manager :other manager2)
  :manager2 '(manager :other manager1)
  :company  '(simple-company :managers manager1
    manager2)))
```

The problem with this approach is that essentially all code generation can only take place after a model instance is created, making model instance creation a relatively heavy operation. This defeats the incrementality goals of the language. Incrementality could be retained if run time class identification would be allowed, which in turn would make execution slower. Here a clear trade-off exists among conflicting language design goals: reuse of code, incremental compilation, and efficiency. The fairly obvious solution is to strictly stick to the efficiency criteria and to generate the code as early as possible. If a class has been defined in object references, then that class should be used to generate code; otherwise the code generation would wait for model instance creation.

A fourth language design goal, reliability of code, has been almost entirely neglected in SLICL because of another goal, minimality of expression. For example, by requiring class definitions both in the object reference section and when creating model instances, their consistency could be verified. It is important to note, however, that a major reliability issue, data typing, has been implicitly solved by using knowledge of the application domain: all variables and parameters are required to be real numbers.

9   RELATED AND FUTURE RESEARCH

The SLICL language resembles SIMPLEX-MDL [2]. The compilation and linking process is fundamentally different because of using C as the result code by SIMPLEX. Thus, for example, when changing a single equation, all information related to an object class has to be recompiled and relinked. The price that SLICL has to pay for incremental compilation and no linking time is the use of the LISP image during execution and in particular the use of the symbol table.

During execution, the notions of object classes, instances, and their relationships is not exploited in SIMPLEX. For example, each time period all trigger conditions of if–then and on–do format have to be executed instead of only those that contain variables that have changed. In LISP-based systems selective execution is a standard computational focusing strategy achieved, for example, by so-called demons [15]. In SIMPLEX-MDL, object instances are linked by defining for each link a variable that copies the desired value from the other object. In SLICL, the value of the other object's variable is directly referenced, saving in data structure size. Inheritance is not used in SIMPLEX. SIMPLEX provides ideas for further development of SLICL to the discrete-event case [1].

Another related effort is the structured modeling technique [4], which aims at a more general modeling language. The corresponding generalization of SLICL remains a topic for future efforts, but object orientation including inheritance provides a more modern basis for a general modeling language than the techniques of data typing and acyclic nets used in structured modeling.

SLICL provides a high-level specification methodology for simulation models but is still not the optimal way to represent mathematical models. In a complete modeling environment the user should operate via a graphic interface that supports the rapid definition of models via pop-up menus, mouse operations, and symbolic editors. A language of the nature discussed in the preceding allows the textual representation of the studied model, which is relevant for documentation purposes. The language also gives the syntactical specification of what the graphical user interface should be able to manipulate. The software G2 marketed by Gensym Corporation contains such interface techniques to define differential equation models. Although the G2 software is specialized to process control applications, it illustrates many of the desirable features of an environment integrating simulation and AI techniques.

Tracing and debugging are important facilities provided by a good LISP environment and can be used as such productively at the LISP code level. Higher-level and more specialized tracing can be easily achieved, as has been shown in earlier work [10]. Although the existing LISP environments already provide good facilities, more effort could be invested in providing a closer link between the higher-level language and a debugger.

In summary, the main areas of future efforts are the development support tools needed in an integrated simulation environment [13] and the generalization of the language to the discrete-event case and other modeling areas. An important area of further effort is also the development of model and object libraries for various application areas, such as analog circuits.

10 RELEVANCE OF OBTAINED RESULTS

The observation, which forms the basis of this chapter, is that one can perform simulation efficiently in LISP if sufficiently sophisticated compilers are used and if the models are formulated in a way that makes efficient execution possible. Considerations are the relative high cost of the more sophisticated compilers and the large memory requirements of LISP environments.

Performing simulation in LISP opens the door to many possibilities for intimately linking symbolic and numeric computing. In this chapter the emphasis has been on developing a language for defining simulation models that

allow compact nonredundant formulation of models,

use object orientation to support modularity and reusability,

lead to minimal recompilation when redefining models, and

result in as efficient code as possible with no run time garbage collection.

Some limitations of the current language and its implementation are minimal error checking, use of reverse polish notation, and lack of its own debugger.

The most relevant point to be made is that object-oriented, compact, and incremental languages are an important technology in improving productivity of simulation modeling.

In what kind of applications is this technology relevant? The final answer can only be obtained empirically, but the basic characteristics are obvious:

The technology is applicable to any simulation problem, classical (analog circuits) or new (robotics).

Compactness of representation is most useful when the models are large.

Object orientation is most useful when the problems can be organized by objects and the problems are complex.

Inheritance is most useful when a large number of structurally slightly varying formulations have to be analyzed.

Incremental recompilation is most useful when alternative formulations of the models are explored.

Efficiency is most useful when numerically accurate, parametric or probabilistic results are desired.

As discussed in the previous section, even a good language is just the starting point; the supporting environment is what makes the final difference. LISP programming environments provide a state-of-the-art basis for developing these supporting environments.

REFERENCES

1. P. Eschenbacher, "An Approach to Transaction-Oriented Modelling Based on System Theory," in H. Adelsberger and F. Broeckx (Eds.), *Proceedings of the European Simulation Multiconference, Ghent, Belgium,* Simulations Councils, Inc., 1987.

2. P. Eschenbacher and B. Schmidt, "The Model Description Language SIMPLEX-MDL," in *Proceedings of the European Simulation Multiconference 1987.*

3. M. R. Genesereth, "An Overview of MRS for AI Experts," Department of Computer Science, Stanford University, 1982.

4. A. Geoffrion, "Structured Modeling," *Management Science,* **33**(3):547–588, 1987.

5. T. Ketonen, P. Lounamaa, and J. Nurminen, "An Analog CAD System Combining Knowledge-Based Techniques with Optimization and Simulation," in J. S. Gero (Ed.), *Artificial Intelligence in Engineering Design,* Elsevier, Amsterdam, 1988.

6. C. Kitzmiller and J. Kowalik, "Coupling Symbolic and Numeric Computing in Knowledge-Based Systems," *AI Magazine,* **8**(2), 1987.

7. J. Kowalik, *Coupling Symbolic and Numeric Computing in Expert Systems,* North-Holland, Amsterdam, 1986.

8. P. H. Lounamaa, "Models of Multi-Agent Behavior: A Simulation and Expert Environment Approach," Ph.D. Dissertation, Stanford University, 1985.

9. P. Lounamaa and J. March, "Adaptive Coordination of A Learning Team," *Management Science,* **33**(1):107–123, 1987.

10. P. Lounamaa and E. Tse, "The Simulation and Expert Environment," in J. Kowalik (Ed.), *Coupling Symbolic and Numerical Computing in Expert Systems,* North-Holland, Amsterdam, 1986.

11. P. Nolan and J. Fegan, "An AI Based Program Generator for Discrete Event Simulation," in *Proceedings of the European Simulation Multiconference 1987.*

12. G. Novak, "GLISP User's Manual," Department of Computer Science, Stanford University, 1982.

13. T. J. Schriber, "The Nature and Role of Simulation in the Design of Manufacturing Systems," in *Proceedings of the European Simulation Multiconference 1987.*

14. G. L. Steele, *Common LISP, The Language,* Digital Press, 1984.

15. P. H. Winston and B. R. Horn, *LISP,* Addison-Wesley, Reading, MA, 1984.

16. B. Zeigler, "DEVS-Scheme: A LISP-based Environment for Hierarchical, Modular Discrete Event Models," Technical Report, AIS-2, CERL Laboratory, Department of Electrical and Computer Engineering, University of Arizona, Tucson, AZ.

17 A Hierarchical Framework for Learning Control

KURT M. BERGER[1] and KENNETH A. LOPARO
Department of Systems Engineering
and
Center for Automation and Intelligent Systems Research
Case Western Reserve University
Cleveland, Ohio

1 INTRODUCTION

A theme throughout the book is that the integration of quantitative and qualitative information is necessary for more complete understanding and reasoning about complex and uncertain systems. In many control design situations, a detailed mathematical model of the system is not available and process knowledge may be available in many different forms, for example, simplified mathematical models which are valid only over limited operating ranges and heuristic rules which attempt to describe observed system behavior. Integrating these various forms of information into a control system in a systematic way is a difficult task.

In this chapter we propose a hierarchical control framework to accomplish the integration task. Hierarchical control theory is concerned with complex interconnected systems which have many inputs and outputs. The design of control procedures is difficult because of the complexity and large information-processing requirements. The hierarchical control theory approach is based on (1) decomposition of the complex overall control problem into simpler, more easily handled subproblems and (2) coordination of the subproblems to satisfy control objectives and constraints. Controllers are arranged on multiple levels according to three basic criteria: (1) functional decomposition, (2) plant decomposition, and (3) temporal decomposition [60].

A functional control hierarchy with four control levels (direct, optimizing, adaptive, and self-organizing) is shown in Figure 1. Each control level provides set points or updates parameters to the level immediately below it. A temporal ordering is induced with lower levels operating in shorter time frames. This approach, also known as the multilayer concept, was introduced by Lefkowitz [60] in 1966.

[1] Present address: Charles Stark Draper Laboratory, Inc., 555 Technology Square, Cambridge, Massachusetts 02139.

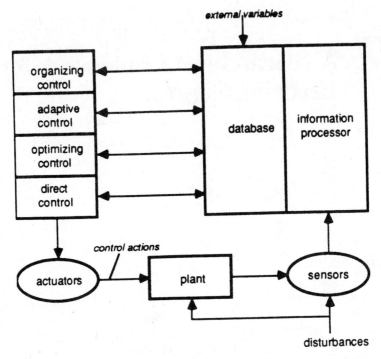

Figure 1. Functional control hierarchy.

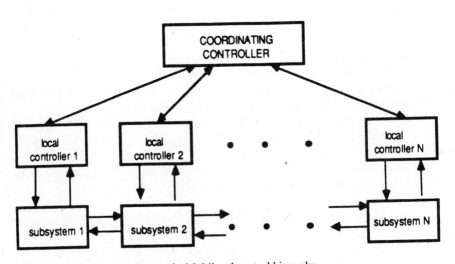

Figure 2. Multilevel control hierarchy.

The multilevel (plant decomposition) approach was first introduced by Mesarovic et al. [61] and is shown in Figure 2. Here the plant is partitioned into subsystems, where each subsystem has its own (first-level) controller to satisfy local objectives and constraints. Decomposition of the control problem into a number of subproblems of reduced dimension simplifies the analysis and may reduce the computational effort. The coordination (second-level) controller influences the first-level controllers to compensate for subsystem interactions to satisfy overall objectives. Two common methods for coordinating the subsystems are the goal coordination method and the interaction prediction method [61].

In a temporal control hierarchy (Figure 3), the control problem is partitioned into subproblems based on the different time scales associated with the different control functions to be performed. Such factors as the degree of uncertainty in the decision-making, model form, and information flow requirements affect the organization of a temporal hierarchy.

The hierarchical control framework directly addresses the complexity issue and is ideally suited for the integration of qualitative and quantitative procedures for control. In particular, the functional or temporal multilayer hierarchy provides for the implementation of algorithmic procedures at the lowest level operating in real time, and the incorporation of reasoning systems at the higher levels where more computational resources and time are available. To deal with the incompleteness of process knowledge and the uncertainty in the environment, learning needs to be incorporated into the hierarchical control system.

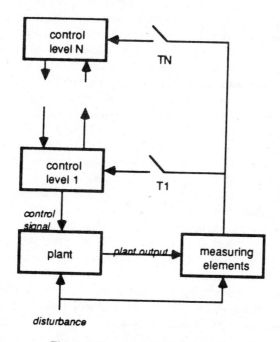

Figure 3. Temporal control hierarchy.

The term "intelligent control" (or "cognitive control") often refers to a control system which can learn, reason, and make judgments. Two research areas that can be considered to be subsidiary to the general field of intelligent control are learning control and expert control.

Learning control methods operate with unknown or incompletely known information about the system dynamics and disturbances and attempt to change the control scheme during system operation; this can be accomplished with or without external supervision. If the desired system output is known (external supervision), the adaptation or learning is based on the error between the desired and actual system outputs. In unsupervised learning/adaptation, two approaches exist to guide the learning. In the first approach all possible answers are considered while in the second a performance measure is used to direct the learning process. Learning control methods attempt to utilize past experiences and thus exhibit a gradual improvement in controller performance. Thus, learning controllers can recognize past control situations, group similar control situations into classes, and learn which control strategies for a particular control situation are more appropriate. Some learning control techniques can operate with as little information as a failure signal and no a priori system model [6].

Surveys of learning control methods (essentially those based on pattern recognition techniques) were given in papers by Fu [9] and Saridis [24]. Some of the learning methods applied to control are (1) trainable controllers (using pattern classifiers), (2) reinforcement learning control, (3) stochastic automata, (4) stochastic approximation, and (5) Bayesian learning.

A trainable controller in the form of a linear pattern classifier has been implemented by Widrow and Smith [30] to realize the switching surface of a "bang-bang" control strategy resulting from the formulation of a minimum-time control problem. The inputs to this controller are the states of the system to be controlled (assumed available) and the output is the control action $u(t)$. Thus the state space is partitioned into the various control situations where two different control laws apply ($u = 1$ or $u = -1$). The learning is supervised by a trainer who applies different control situations and updates the controller weights based on the error between the actual and desired controller outputs (known).

Reinforcement learning can be defined as "the process by which the response probability of a system to a stimulus is strengthened by a reward or weakened by a penalty" [24]. Fu et al. [12, 29] applied reinforcement learning to an optimal control problem. The state space is first subdivided into a set of control situations and a subgoal is assigned to each control situation. The idea is that if each subgoal is optimized, by the learning of an appropriate control action for that situation from a set U of possible actions, then the overall performance measure will be optimized. In order to learn which control action to choose, a set of probabilities for each control situation (one for each possible control) is constantly updated by a linear reinforcement scheme and the control with the maximum probability is chosen when the system is in the appropriate control situation. The learning here is not done with external supervision; rather it is directed by the systems' performance ("learning with a critic").

Michie and Chambers [18] employed a similar approach with their famous "boxes" system. The problem they addressed is to balance a pole on a cart without failure (cart out of bounds or pole too far from vertical) with only knowledge of the system's state or a failure signal using two control actions (force left or force right). The state space is quantized into boxes and a control action for each box is chosen based on the longest lifetime estimates (left or right) which are reinforced upon system failure. The boxes system does not continuously use the state information for reinforcement, only the failure information.

Barto, Sutton, and Anderson [6] attack the same control problem as in reference 18 using neuronlike elements in a reinforcement learning scheme. Two components are working together for learning, the associate search element (ASE) and the adaptive critic element (ACE); they show that the ASE by itself operates essentially like the boxes system with similar results. However, the ACE goes farther by using the state information to keep track of, for each control situation, a prediction or expectation of future reinforcement (reward or punishment) that it sends to the ASE when the control situation is encountered. Thus, learning occurs constantly and not just upon failure. A fully predicted failure will generate no punishment. However, when the control situation changes from one with a low prediction of failure to one with a high prediction of failure, recently made control actions are punished. Thus the system learns which boxes (control situations) are "safe" and which are "dangerous" and rewards itself for moving from any box to a safer one and punishes itself for the opposite. It should be noted that this system performed well in simulation and learned to control the cart-pole system relatively quickly.

If the control space and the state space are finite sets, as in the reinforcement learning described earlier, Fu and McMurtry [17] proposed that the controller could be implemented by a finite-state machine. Here again the output of the controller for a particular control situation is chosen from the control set $U = \{u^1, \dots u^M\}$ such that it has the highest expected probability of success. The probabilities are calculated through a transition equation for a stochastic automaton. McLaren [16] extended the algorithm to allow for a growing number of control actions for each control situation.

A stochastic approximation approach to learning has been developed by Tsypkin [28] and Nikolic and Fu [21] to analyze an unknown process and select controls for "optimal" performance. Given an instantaneous performance cost, it is desired to find the control which minimizes the overall performance cost for a previously given input–output (I/O) pair. The controls are chosen from a finite set of controls U. Similar to the previously described reinforcement learning, the control with the highest probability of minimizing the performance cost is chosen. Here, however, there are no subgoals for each control situation. Rather, there is only one set of probabilities used to select the next control action.

Expert systems applied to real-time control [39] have considerable potential, especially at the higher levels of the control hierarchy. Expert or knowledge-based systems are computer programs which differ from conventional data-processing systems because of at least three key features: symbolic knowledge representations, symbolic inference, and heuristic search. Essentially expert systems reason over a (perhaps incomplete) knowledge base consisting of facts, rules of thumb (heuristics), and other knowledge using either forward chaining or backward chaining or both and provide explanations for inferred conclusions. An ideal expert system used for system control must "repeatedly interpret the current situation, predict the future, diagnose the causes of anticipated problems, formulate a remedial plan, and monitor its execution to insure success." [38] Very few expert systems, however, have been used for real-time, on-line control. Most are used as aids for static, off-line design or consultation. Problems which have been successfully addressed by non-real-time expert systems include medical diagnosis, computer configuration, and financial consultation, and such systems are widely known and well documented.

Knowledge-based systems used for real-time control must overcome the tremendous "cognitive load" [39] associated with such complex control problems. Laffey et al. [39] list 10 critical problems faced by knowledge-based controllers in real-time settings: (1) nonmonotonicity of sensor data, (2) continuous operation, (3) occurrence of asynchronous events, (4) interfacing to external environments, (5) uncertain/missing data, (6) high-performance (speed) requirements, (7) temporal reasoning requirements, (8) focusing of attention, (9) guaranteed response times, and (10) integration with procedural components. Primarily, the controller must be able to process a large volume of (perhaps) conflicting, quickly changing data at high speeds while maintaining stability and handling unexpected critical events.

Despite the immense challenge posed by the above-described control problems, several applications of knowledge-based systems to real-time process control problems have been investigated. Most of these systems have been designed with chemical process or nuclear reactor plants in mind. Notable systems include CEALMON, COOKER, FALCON, ESCORT, and the MCM system [39]. Additionally, Fortin, Romey, and Bristol [35] have designed a process control expert system (EXACT) employing heuristics and pattern recognition techniques to tune a process controller, while Litt [40] implemented a similar system to tune a PID controller based on transient response recognition. Moreover, many expert system "shells" exist for creating expert systems for real-time applications. However, only Picon [41] and G2 [39] were built explicitly for real-time process monitoring and control.

Finally, fuzzy-set theory and decision-making schemata are two additional tools which have been investigated as potentially useful for the control of complex and uncertain systems. Fuzzy-set theory, originally developed by Zadeh [53], is useful for handling process uncertainties that are not described quantitatively. Saridis and Stephanou [52] have implemented a fuzzy automaton as a coordinator (decision maker) in a three-level control system. Decision-making schemata have been used by Saridis, Lee, and Graham [51] for the intelligent control of a prosthetic arm.

In conclusion, the problem of control design for complex and uncertain systems presents a real challenge. In many instances, current control synthesis methodologies cannot completely satisfy all the required performance objectives. AI methodologies provide an opportunity to augment algorithmic, analytical, model-based approaches to achieve overall control structures with a broader range of applicability.

In the remainder of this chapter we outline a framework and general methodology for controller design and operation to deal with complexity and uncertainty. Such an approach, however, is aimed at complementing, rather than competing with, current methods. In this context, hierarchical control, learning control, and expert control are the most relevant areas. For example, the functional hierarchy provides an appropriate control framework through its functional decomposition and commensurate temporal ordering of control tasks. Expert systems can provide reasoning capabilities and explanations and can incorporate nonquantifiable information into the control hierarchy while learning systems can discover control strategies and reduce model uncertainty.

2   A HIERARCHICAL INTELLIGENT CONTROL FRAMEWORK

2.1   Introduction

In this section we present a hierarchical intelligent control framework to address the problems of control for complex and uncertain dynamical systems. First we present a general problem statement and the essential elements of an effective controller for such problems. Next, an outline of applicable paradigms from the fields of artificial intelligence (learning automata, qualitative reasoning, and expert systems) and hierarchical control theory are presented. Finally, the proposed four-level hierarchical intelligent control system is described in detail.

2.2   Problem Statement

The control problem can be simply stated. *Given* a priori information about the system—for example, an approximate mathematical model of the system or a higher level description of the system operation, a performance objective, operational constraints, a collection of sensors which monitor the system outputs, and a set of inputs which are to be used to regulate the system—*determine* a sequence of system inputs which realizes the desired level of performance of the system.

The following information is known:

the process inputs,

the process outputs,

a global performance index which quantifies the long-term performance objectives, and

an instantaneous performance index which establishes short-term goals which are commensurate with the desired long term behavior.

The following information may be known or partially known:

process delay and/or an estimate of the input delay,

the form/structure of a model of the system, and

the statistical properties of the disturbances.

The following information is not known:

an exact model of the system, and

the exact nature of the process disturbances.

2.3   Controller Requirements

A controller for such a complex and uncertain system should satisfy the following requirements: (1) be able to handle time-varying (and otherwise unknown) process dynamics (including perhaps unknown input delay, process delay, etc.), (2) be insensitive to unmodelled/unknown process and measurement disturbances, (3) adapt continually to changing system requirements, (4) be able to achieve the desired level of system performance, (5) maintain real-time stability, and (6) incorporate nonquantifiable (heuristic) process information.

2.4   Useful Intelligent Control Tools

Various elements or tools from the field of artificial intelligence have been and are being recognized as potentially useful for improved system control. (Resulting controllers are said to employ "intelligent control" techniques.) Specifically, expert or automated reasoning systems, learning automata, and qualitative modelling/simulation techniques have recently received considerable attention. A major objective is to integrate such methodologies with conventional control methods. In particular, ideas from areas such as hierarchical control, optimal and stochastic control, and dual control are all suitable to address the general control problems we are considering given that appropriate mathematical models can be formulated.

The advantages and potential usefulness of the following four methodologies are described: (1) a multilevel/hierarchical framework, (2) learning automata, (3) expert/reasoning systems, and (4) qualitative reasoning/simulation. A hierarchical intelligent control framework, which integrates these components, will then be proposed and described in detail.

2.4.1   Hierarchical Structures

The three major hierarchical control schemes are functional decomposition, plant decomposition, and temporal decomposition. All are potentially useful, and all three methods can be thought of as establishing a temporal decomposition—a useful feature since the more difficult control tasks (which require more time and involve more uncertainty) can be handled by the higher layers where more time and presumably more computational resources are available. In addition, the functional (multilayer) hierarchy provides a natural division of labor based on functionality. Such a functional division can be used to reduce the total cost of performing complex decision and control tasks. In complex and uncertain situations it is necessary to coordinate the performance of different tasks such as learning, planning, optimizing, and other time-consuming functions; a hierarchical control framework is an ideal setting for implementation and coordination of such tasks.

2.4.2   Stochastic Learning Automata

In the face of unknown process dynamics, unknown process disturbances, and changing system requirements, the need for learning is paramount. In many instances, experienced operators can outperform conventional model-based controllers through the effective use of control rules learned from operating experience without detailed mathematical knowledge of the process dynamics. Learning has been studied by psychologists and computer scientists for many years. The learning methods which are applicable to our control problem are classified as unsupervised "learning with a critic." This type of learning can be viewed as a trial-and-error interaction with the process (environment). Trainable controllers may not be practical since applying exhaustive training situations with known desired responses is often not possible. Bayesian learning, which has found considerable application in the control of stochastic systems, requires certain a priori information which is often not available.

Learning automata, defined as stochastic automata that can improve their performance while operating in a random environment, are useful for the control of uncertain processes. Formally, a stochastic automaton is defined as a sextuple $\{X, W, Y, p, A, G\}$ where:

> X = input set,
> $\Omega = \{\Omega_1, \ldots, \Omega_s\}$ = set of internal states,
> $Y = \{y_1, \ldots, y_r\}$ = set of output actions,
> p = state probability vector $\{p_1(n), \ldots, p_s(n)\}^{\mathrm{T}}$, T denotes transpose,
> A = reinforcement scheme: $p(n) \to p(n + 1)$,
> $G: \Omega \to Y$ (output function).

For our purposes we let $r = s$ and make G an identity mapping (causing internal states and output actions to be synonymous). A learning automaton then is a stochastic automaton operating with feedback from a random environment.

Learning automata can be distinguished based on many different criteria. For a general discussion of learning automata refer to Narendra and Thathachar [20] and Narendra and Lakshmivarahan [19].

The performance of any learning automaton is affected by three independent factors: (1) the rate at which the environment changes with time, (2) the speed of response of the automaton, and (3) the ease with which the automaton parameters can be changed [19]. For instance, in a nonstationary environment the automaton must be able to discover (with a high probability) the most appropriate action. However, the classical problem of speed versus accuracy is also faced here. One can increase the speed of convergence of a reinforcement scheme by changing the values of its parameters, but this can lead to an increase of the probability of convergence to an undesired action [20]. Another potential problem is the effect that initial action probability values have on the asymptotic behavior of learning automaton. Expedient reinforcement algorithms, however, are insensitive to this initial condition. Again, in nonstationary environments, the initial probability values are a relatively minor consideration.

2.4.3   Expert Systems

Expert systems and other types of automated reasoning systems can enhance problem-solving tasks by integrating heuristics, adding the ability to reason over uncertainty and conflict, and incorporating nonquantifiable information. In essence, an expert system is a software tool for intelligent decision making which is especially useful in dealing with incomplete problem descriptions and large amounts of complex knowledge. The distinctive features which contribute to their usefulness in the control field are the representation of knowledge through situation-implies-action(s) rules and symbolic representations, heuristics used as knowledge rules or as search criteria, and the separation of the inference engine (logic) from the knowledge (data). In addition, the incorporation of confidence factors, belief functions, Shafer–Dempster theory, fuzzy-set theory, and other methods of coping with uncertainty into expert-reasoning systems results in the added ability of expert systems to make judgments. Finally, being able to explain and justify a line of reasoning is a very useful feature of expert systems, both in on-line operation and in off-line knowledge base development.

Expert or knowledge-based systems have been shown to be able to solve (although off-line) difficult design, planning, diagnostic, optimization, and classification problems. With respect to a functional hierarchical framework, then, expert systems would seem potentially very useful at the higher levels where such tasks need to be performed. One drawback to expert systems in real-time control is that they are relatively slow, an attribute that makes them even more appropriate, however, in the higher levels of a control hierarchy.

2.4.4 Qualitative Simulation

Qualitative modeling or simulation systems have received much attention recently by many researchers including Bobrow [55], DeKleer [56], Forbus [57], Kuipers [58], and Williams [59]. Given a representation of the process structure (in terms of a set of qualitative functions and physical constraints) and an initial state, such systems can provide a qualitative description of future (prediction) and past (explanation) behavior. The key point is that it is done qualitatively; a variable's value and perhaps its rate of change are specified within regions (e.g., +, −, or 0). In addition, distinguished time points and landmark values for a variable can be inferred and continuously updated [58]. In essence, key elements of the process behavior are extracted.

The dominant paradigm for qualitative simulation is "generate and test." A directed graph of possible future states (an envisionment [57]) is determined from the causal model and the initial state. Then, branches of the graph are pruned based on the physical constraints of the process and a consistent "global interpretation" is determined. Although convenient to work with, qualitative simulations inherently forfeit some accuracy and knowledge of the process behavior. A further drawback of such systems is their strong dependence on an a priori causal model of the process. The potential uses of qualitative simulations, if such drawbacks are not inhibitory, are for improving diagnostics, fault identification, explanations, and predictions.

2.5 Hierarchical Intelligent Controller

A block diagram of the hierarchical intelligent control system that we propose for the control of complex, uncertain processes is given in Figure 4. A detailed functional description of each of the components of this controller follows. The timing and flow of control throughout the system will also be described. In Section 3, preliminary

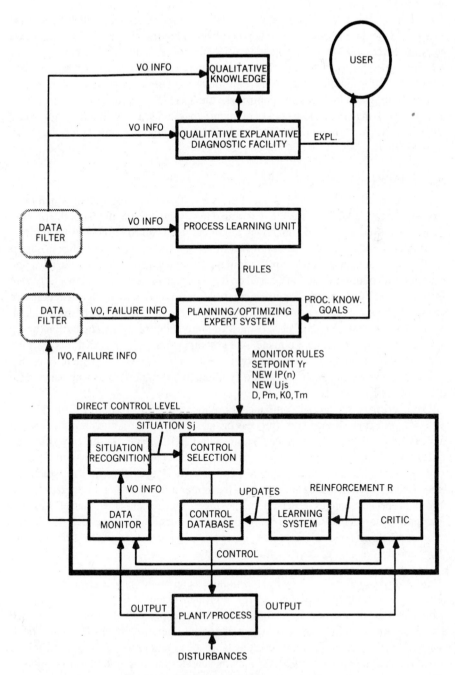

Figure 4. Hierarchical intelligent controller.

results of implementing the controller in software for the problem of controlling an inverted pendulum (pole balancing) will be reported. No specific process is assumed in the following discussion.

The hierarchical intelligent controller we propose consists of four fundamental levels: (1) the direct control level, (2) the planning/optimizing level, (3) the process learning level, and (4) the diagnostic/explanative level. Additionally, data filters or monitors operate on data to be exchanged between control levels to facilitate the usage of such I/O information by the various control levels. The process/plant is shown to be a single unit which includes any controllers, such as PID, which are implemented on the process. It may in fact also consist of many subsystems, and each subsystem would then have its own "direct controller" with a coordinating unit completing the direct control level.

2.5.1   Direct Control Level

The direct control level can be thought of as a feedback control system which must operate (and maintain stability) in real time. However, since the model of the process is assumed to be completely unknown, the direct level controller is in fact a learning controller. In other words, the control action $u^*(n)$ sent to the process has not been predetermined. Instead, the control action must be chosen cognitively from a discrete and finite set of possible actions, based on the interpreted control situation and system performance. Furthermore, the direct controller must learn which control actions are most suitable for every control situation. In essence, a map from the control situation space S to the control action space U must be learned during system operation (based on a reinforcement evaluation made by a system critic). Note also that this learning process is never-ending since new control situations may be encountered and the process dynamics and disturbances are assumed to be unknown and time varying (in the worst case).

Four primary functional components comprise the direct control level: (1) the process performance evaluator (process critic), (2) the control situation recognition unit (CSR), (3) the reinforcement learning unit (RLU), and (4) the control action selection unit (CSU). In addition, a data monitor prescreens I/O information from the process to detect any failure, emergency, or critical operating modes which are specified a priori. In this case the system may enter a reduced level of operation with the appropriate changes reflected in the process critic and the control situation recognition unit or may take an appropriate predetermined special action. Each component of the direct control layer will be described in what follows in terms of functionality and the data structures which it manipulates.

Data Monitor   The direct level data monitor screens the process I/O information every T_m seconds (the data scan time) for significant changes. Based on the interpretation of the data the monitor determines what control responses will be taken. Primarily, the data monitor's function is to detect abnormal operating modes through model-based detection schemes, "fault detection heuristics," and/or recognizing prespecified conditions. Typical problems would include actuator failures, output sensor failures, and other situations which necessitate a fundamental change in controller operation, although not necessarily as a result of past control actions. In the event of a failure mode, the planning/optimizing expert system at the next level is informed prompting the following actions: (1) a new instantaneous performance measure is selected from a preestablished set and (2) control situations in the control-situations data structure are merged as necessary to account for the reduced level of operation. For example, if a sensor fails, its output data is ignored in the information vector and similar situation vectors (of reduced dimension) are merged. Additionally, the learning (updating probabilities) is suspended and restarted when the new operating mode is entered. This action is necessary because our assumption is that past control actions are not responsible for component failures, a new performance evaluation function is being used, and new control situations may have arisen. Thus, learning should be temporarily suspended.

If the data monitor detects an emergency situation, one which is serious enough to require the user's attention, no autonomous action is attempted. The user and perhaps a higher control level are informed of the situation and are responsible for corrective action (e.g., a restart control sequence). Moreover, the diagnosis of the cause of any anomalies is not attempted at the direct control level but is deferred to the highest control level (qualitative explanative/diagnostic) where more time is available.

The third and final condition detectable by the data monitor is a critical condition defined as a control situation that requires special predetermined controller action. For example, critical conditions may be defined in situations that are typically encountered before an emergency state occurs. Thus the special control actions taken in critical conditions form a "safety net," protecting the system from undesirable states.

If the data passes the failure, emergency, and critical mode tests, the process is assumed to be in a normal operating mode and the direct controller cycle consisting of control recognition, control selection, performance evaluation, and control learning is triggered. Necessarily, these four control functions must all be performed before the next process data scan (in less than T_m seconds). Note that the data monitor must also store enough past I/O information to form a control situation (see the next section). In other words, the data monitor maintains in memory a window of I/O information which shifts every T_m seconds.

Structurally, the data monitor is a small, quick expert system, possibly augmented with a detection algorithm, whose knowledge base contains two types of rules: (1) domain-specific heuristics about failure modes and critical conditions and (2) "first principles" (rules of physics such as energy or material conservation rules). The latter rules are used to check sensor readings for their validity based on "common sense" while the heuristics represent less exact methods of detecting system problems. Together the rules in the data monitor knowledge base implement the functions described in the preceding with their conclusions being driven by process I/O data. Ideally, the data monitor rules are arranged hierarchically (e.g., in frames) based on context. In this way only relevant rules are employed in a given situation resulting in more efficient data monitoring.

Control Situation Recognition   Once the determination has been made that the process is not in a failure, emergency, or critical mode, the primary task is to infer the current control situation. The control situation recognition unit (CSR) determines in what region of the information space S the information vector is located. An information vector $I(k)$ consists of the following set of values: $\{u(k-d), \ldots, u(k-d-k_0), y(k), \ldots, y(k-k_0), y_r(k)\}$ (where d is process input *deadtime*, u are the inputs, y are the outputs, and y_r is the set point). This data can be augmented using information from measurable disturbances, if available. Note that k_0, determining the memory content in the control situation, is an adjustable parameter and should be a function of the total process delay. In some instances the inputs may be neglected in favor of a reduced situation space.

The CSR dynamically uses a classification metric to group the $I(k)$ vectors into overlapping control situations $\{S_1, \ldots, S_j, \ldots\}$. Initially, however, no control situations exist. The first measurement vector $I(1)$ becomes the initial point of a region representing control situation S_1 and is entered into the control-situations data structure. A subsequent measurement vector $I(k)$ and an existing vector X (representing a control situation S) are in the same situation if $m(S, I(k)) < D$, where m is the classification metric and $D > 0$ is a parameter. Otherwise, the new measurement vector $I(k)$ is established as the initial point of a new situation. If a measurement vector is within tolerance D of two vectors (situations), it is considered a member of the closest situation. The tolerance parameter D is not static and is updated through the reasoning efforts of the planning/optimizing (P/O) expert system.

Functionally, then, the CSR can be thought of as a pattern classifier which accepts as input the vector $I(k)$ (pattern) and returns as output the corresponding control situation S_j (class). As a side effect the CSR dynamically reproportions the information space S based on incoming measurement vectors. (Note also that when a new situation is discovered, provision is made for it in the control database to be discussed.)

Based on user preference and knowledge of the process the preceding tolerance measure may be weighted based on the recency of the process measurements or more heavily on outputs versus the inputs. At an extreme, the most recent outputs would be deemed the most important in defining a control situation and would have smaller associated thresholds. In the default case, all elements in the measurement vector $I(k)$ are treated as equally important. Obviously, many threshold vector variations are possible, the actual choice being the user's responsibility.

Another possible variation in determining how control situations are organized is to employ a mapping $H : I(k) \to I'(k)$ which converts a measurement vector $I(k)$ into a transformed vector $I'(k)$ (perhaps of lower dimension) to be classified. Based on the user's knowledge of the process, such a mapping could greatly simplify the situation classification effort. (Refer to Section 3 for an example.)

Here we also recognize two options with respect to the size and shape of the control situation sets. Waltz and Fu [29] and Kahne and Fu [13] have suggested, respectively, subdividing situation sets and consolidating situation sets under certain conditions.

In the first scheme subsets are formed with $D' < D$ in a manner similar to the original classification within control situations for which a single preferred control action could not be found. The triggering criteria for forming subsets is the oscillation of the control probabilities (see the next section) between two or more different control actions.

In contrast, if the control choice for a number of control situations is the same with a high probability (above a certain threshold), these situations may be consolidated into one situation. One advantage of this method is the reduction in the number of situations resulting in a more efficient controller.

The preceding actions of the CSR are bypassed if a critical condition which has been "prerecognized" by the data monitor occurs. The output of the CSR in this case is just the critical condition indicator which it received from the data monitor.

Control Selection   Before the control selection decision is made, the finite, discrete set of admissible candidate control actions $U_j(n) = \{u^1, \ldots, u^{M_j}\}$ for each situation S_j must be determined. At any control decision time n, the control set $U_j(n)$ for situation S_j can be any of the $2^M - 1$ subsets of a master set of controls $U = \{u^1, \ldots, u^M\}$ ($M \geq M_j$, for all j). Necessarily, this quantization of the control action space must be based on any and all a priori knowledge of the process. The actual control set $U_j(n)$ is determined by the reasoning of the P/O expert system and can be dynamically expanded or reduced during on-line operation. Initially, however, each new situation is assigned a control set $U_j(0) = U_0 = \{u^1, \ldots, u^{M_0}\}$, where U_0 is a (carefully) predetermined subset of U. Predictably, the general performance of the process is very much dependent on the choice of possible controls. The control values u^i can be, for example, direct inputs to the process (set points) controller parameters for a fixed control structure (like PID) or "indicators" referring to the implementation of a specific control algorithm (adaptive control).

For the purpose of control selection, the following control database is required. (See the section on data structures.) With each control situation S_j we associate a set of probabilities $\{P_{1j}, \ldots, P_{ij}, \ldots, P_{Mj}\}$, one for each possible control in the set U, whose values sum to one. In other words, the control input u^i has probability of "success" $P_{ij}(n)$ in control situation S_j at the nth control selection time. Initially, for M_0 possible control actions, each $P_{ij}(0)$ is set to $1/M_0$ for all i such that $u^i \notin U_0$; thereafter the values are updated by the reinforcement learning unit. Note that for those $u^i \in U_0$, $P_{ij}(0) = 0$, although these probabilities can become nonzero as they are included in $U_j(n)$. Once included in $U_j(n)$, all $P_{ij}(n)$ can only approach zero asymptotically. (See the section on the reinforcement learning unit.)

The control selection rule is then very simple (for situation S_j at time n):

$$u^*(n) = \begin{cases} u^i : \overline{P}_{ij}(n-1) = \max_k \overline{P}_{kj}(n-1) & \text{if any } \overline{P}_{kj}(n-1) > p_m, \\ \text{random } (u^k \in U_j) & \text{otherwise,} \end{cases}$$

where $\overline{P}_{ij}(n)$ represents $P_{ij}(n)$ normalized over the set $U_j(n)$. That is, for a given situation, choose the control in $U_j(n)$ with the highest probability of success if that probability is greater than a threshold $p_m (0 \leq p_m < 1)$; otherwise select a control action at random. Having a threshold "encourages" the controller to explore different control possibilities in each situation. In terms of I/O, the input to the CSU is the situation description S_j, while the output (via the control database) is the control action $u^*(n)$ sent to the process.

After making a control decision the CSU records its action by placing an entry on the eligibility list which assures that the learning cycle will later change the control database based on the consequences of the current control action. Specifically, the following five values are stored for every control decision: t_{ij} (time the decision was made), S_j (situation in which the decision was made), u^i (control chosen), $U_j(t_{ij})$ (control set chosen from), and e_{ij} (eligibility score). The calculation of the eligibility score is described in the section on the reinforcement learning unit.

Again, in a critical situation, the preceding selection rule is bypassed and the correct action is looked up in the special actions table which was provided a priori by the user. This table may expand during on-line operation if a higher level deduces the correct action for a previously encountered emergency situation, in which case the emergency situation becomes a (planned for) critical situation.

Process Critic   In order to update the control probabilities, the RLU needs a criterion to guide its learning. The learning criterion is the feedback reinforcement $r(n)$ it receives from the process critic. Here $r(n)$ is a number between +1 (largest reward) and −1 (largest punishment). Based on the input $u(n)$, output $y(n)$, and set point $y_r(n)$, (and perhaps past values) the critic first evaluates an instantaneous performance index which is commensurate with the global performance index, both of which must be defined a priori. The instantaneous performance evaluation is translated into a reinforcement value, $-1 \leq r(n) \leq +1$ (based on relative performance), which is sent by the process critic to be used by the RLU. The rule for determining $r(n)$ is given where $[IP_l, IP_u]$ determines the allowable range of the instantaneous performance measure $IP(n)$:

$$r(n) = \begin{cases} +1 & \text{if } IP(n) \leq IP_l, \\ -1 & \text{if } IP(n) \geq IP_u, \\ (-2/\Delta IP)IP(n) + 1 & \text{otherwise, } \Delta IP = IP_u - IP_l. \end{cases}$$

However, in the event of the occurrence of a failure or emergency operating mode, the critic must use alternative criteria to judge the system. Again, the evaluation functions used in these situations must be given.

Reinforcement Learning Unit   The purpose of the reinforcement learning unit (RLU) is to change the probabilities in the control database to properly reflect the experiential control learning that has occurred. By changing the probabilities associated with the various control actions for a given control situation, the RLU rewards and punishes control actions for past performance and determines which controls should be "given a chance" in the future.

The obvious difficulty with a reinforcement formula is the "credit assignment" problem, that is, how to determine which in a series of control actions (on a complex plant with uncertain input delay and delayed reinforcement) deserves credit or blame for the overall performance of the system (and how much). In order to address this difficulty, we associate an eligibility function $e_{ij}(t)$, or "forgetting factor," with each control decision as it occurs. Such an eligibility function is based on the assumption that a control action applied at time t should be most responsible for the control performance at time $t + T_d$ (T_d is total process delay including input delay) with its responsibility

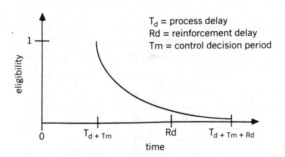

Figure 5. Eligibility function.

decaying thereafter towards zero. In our implementation, the eligibility e_{ij} for each control action u^i taken in a control situation S_j is given by the following function (Figure 5) which assumes that u^i was chosen for S_j at time N and the current time is t:

$$e_{ij}(t) = \begin{cases} e^{\{-4\,(t-N-T_d\,-T_m)/R_d\}} & \text{if } t \geq N + T_d + T_m, \\ 0 & \text{otherwise.} \end{cases}$$

where R_d is the reinforcement delay (time between reinforcements), T_m is time between control decisions, and T_d is an estimate of the process delay. Note that in our design the process scan period (T_m) is equal to the the time between control decisions (since a control decision is made after every process measurement). This may not always be the case and the value of T_m used in the eligibility function should reflect the elapsed time between control decisions. Moreover, we are assuming in our design that $T_m = R_d$ which again may not always be the case.

For every situation S_j which has an associated control with positive eligibility, then, the probabilities are changed for each of the M_j possible controls in that situation (in $U_j(n)$) such that the sum of the changes is equal to zero. A list referred to as the eligibility list (see the next section) keeps track of all the control action–control situation pairs (S_j, u^i) with positive eligibility in order of decreasing eligibility. For every pair, the following value is first calculated: $Z_j(n) = \alpha |r(n)| e_{ij}$, where $r(n) \in [-1, 1]$ is the external reinforcement from the critic and α, $0 \leq \alpha \leq 1$, is a parameter affecting the rate of learning. The following linear reinforcement scheme, a modified symmetric L_{r-p} linear reward–penalty scheme, is proposed:

Case 1 $r(n) > 0$ (rewarding reinforcement):
$\bar{P}_{ij}(n + 1) = \{1 - Z_j(n)\}\bar{P}_{ij}(n) + Z_j(n)$ for i: (S_j, u^i) is eligible,
$\bar{P}_{kj}(n + 1) = \{1 - Z_j(n)\}\bar{P}_{kj}(n)$ for $k \neq i = 1, \dots, M_j$.

Case 2 $r(n) < 0$ (punishing reinforcement):
$\bar{P}_{ij}(n + 1) = \{1 - Z_j(n)\}\bar{P}_{ij}(n)$ for i : (S_j, u^i) is eligible,
$\bar{P}_{kj}(n + 1) = \{1 - Z_j(n)\}\bar{P}_{kj}(n) + Z_j(n)/(M_j - 1)$ for $k \neq i = 1, \dots, M_j$.

Case 3 $r(n)=0$ (no reinforcement):
$P_{ij}(n + 1) = P_{ij}(n)$ for $i = 1, \dots, M_j$.

Note that all $P_{ij}(n)$ corresponding to the $u^i \in U_j(n)(i = 1, \ldots, M_j)$ are first normalized (to $\bar{P}_{ij}(n)$), the reinforcements are made, and the $\bar{P}_{ij}(n + 1)$ are then unnormalized. In other words, only those $P_{ij}(n)$ corresponding to those control actions in $U_j(n)$ are reinforced; all other probabilities $P_{kj}(n)$ (all k such that $u^k \notin U_j$) do not change.

Data Structures Four primary data structures are employed at the direct control level: (1) the control database, (2) the control situations data structure, (3) the eligibility list, and (4) the special-actions table.

The index into the control probabilities database is the control situation S_j. For each situation, a set of probabilities $\{P_{1j}(n), \ldots P_{Mj}(n)\}$ is maintained—one element for each control action. A new entry into this database occurs following the discovery of each new control situation, and all values in the database are updated during every reinforcement cycle.

The index into the control situations table is again the control situation S_j. Associated with each situation is a collection of previous information vectors which characterize the situation S_j. The CSR unit then uses this data structure to classify incoming information and will expand the table as new situations arise.

The eligibility list is a queue of situation–action pairs (S_j, u^i) which have recently occurred and is arranged in decreasing order of positive eligibility $e_{ij}(n)$. Essentially, this is an evolving record of those past actions which are responsible (and to what degree) for the present control performance and is therefore of great use to the RLU. Specifically, the following five values are recorded for each entry on the eligibility list: (1) time the action occurred t_{ij}, (2) situation S_j, (3) chosen control u^i, (4) the control set chosen from $U_j(t_{ij})$, and (5) eligibility e_{ij}.

The special-actions table contains the control actions to be taken when the various critical conditions are encountered. The index into the table is the critical condition indicator which specifies which control is to be used.

Timing and Control Flow In discussing the timing and flow of the control of action in the direct level controller, three fundamental functions are involved: (1) initialization (see the next section), (2) data monitoring, and (3) control selection and learning. After system initialization, the controller scans the process outputs every T_m seconds (T_m is the sampling period). At the kth scan, one of three resulting actions (taking less than T_m seconds each) will occur before the $(k + 1)$th scan (see Figure 6). First, if key measurements indicate a failure mode, the P/O expert system is informed and the CSR and process critic are reorganized to account for the failure and maintain controller operation, albeit in a modified form. However, if the data monitor detects a critical condition in the process output (but not an emergency mode), a special control recognition and selection cycle and the normal learning cycle occurs (see what follows). Finally, if neither of the preceding conditions are met, the normal control and learning cycles are executed.

After exiting the data monitor, control is passed to the CSR which classifies the control situation (first checking to see if it is in a new situation) and forwards its results to the CSU which then uses its selection rule to choose the nth control action $u^*(n)$. The CSU also records its control decision on the eligibility list as described. Meanwhile,

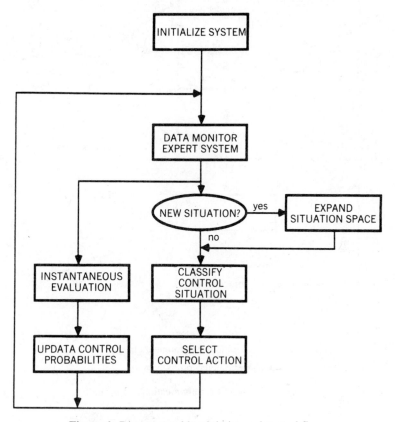

Figure 6. Direct control level timing and control flow.

the process critic has evaluated the process performance (calculated $r(n)$) and the RLU has updated the control database and the eligibility list. With less than T_m seconds having elapsed, control is passed back to the data monitor, which proceeds with the $(k + 1)$th output scan. Refer to Figure 7.

Initialization Actions   The following actions must be performed before the direct level controller can begin operation:

1. Given the dimension of the control space and all a priori knowledge of the process (if any), the finite, discrete set of initial possible control actions $U = \{u^1, \ldots , u^M\}$ must be enumerated. (Thus M must be chosen.)
2. Based on knowledge of the sensors, actuators, and other critical process components, failure operating modes must be listed and the means of detecting these failure modes must be known.

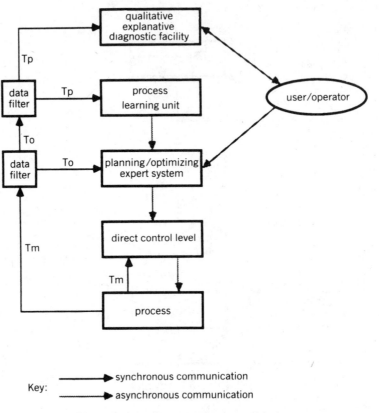

Figure 7. Overall communication and timing.

3. A global performance index and an instantaneous performance index must be available for use by the critic (as well as the range for reinforcement). Furthermore, the adjustments to this index for the failure modes enumerated in need to be determined.

4. Initial values of the following parameters used in the direct control level must be determined:

T_m = data monitor sample time,
D = tolerance defining control situation,
α = learning rate parameter,
k_0 = number of past I/O included in a control situation,
T_d = total process delay estimate,
d = input deadtime estimate,
p_m = probability value above which control actions are not selected in random manner.

Effects of Changing Direct Control Level Parameters   The direct control level parameters that can be adjusted by the P/O expert system are α, p_m, T_d, D, k_0, and T_m. Here we analyze the effects that changes in these parameters have on the performance of the direct control level relative to its control goal and learning objective. Obviously, the control performance hinges upon many complex and interrelated factors: our discussion is only preliminary.

The parameters α and p_m have a direct bearing on the probabilities $P_{ij}(n)$ associated with control actions in various situations. Higher values of α place more importance on the control action reinforcement $r(n)$ and cause the learning rate to increase (probabilities change faster). The opposite is also true. The parameter T_d affects the accuracy of the learning which takes place because it directly affects the assignment of eligibility (responsibility) to control situation–action pairs. An accurate estimate of T_d is very important. A very high or low estimate results in all eligible control choices being rewarded or punished by inaccurate amounts. The purpose of the threshold parameter p_m is to ensure that the control selection is not biased toward "early-reinforced" control actions. Such a threshold encourages the controller to explore different choices, not "locking" itself into one action. Thus p_m is a measure of how sure the controller must be in order to select a control action based on its probability score (which is related to past performance). In other words, the higher the value of p_m, the more accurate the controller will ultimately be (having tried more controls). The obvious trade-off is the cost associated with random control selections that occurred because of a high value of p_m.

Changing the parameters D and k_0 will affect the size and dimension of process control situations. The value of k_0 should be related to the (estimated) total process delay and has an obvious direct effect on the control space dimension. Beyond these simple relationships, however, these parameters directly affect the control performance because they determine the "resolution" in the subdividing of the control space. In other words, since we are grouping control points into sets and choosing one control action for the whole set, the control choice made in response to a particular information vector $I(k)$ is at best an approximation (being made with the whole situation in mind). Thus, any parameters (D, k_0) determining the size of the situations will affect the appropriateness of any control action.

The scan time T_m determines how often the control selection and learning cycles occur. The limit is necessarily once every T_m seconds. Thus the ability of the process to properly follow a trajectory (for instance) is greatly affected by the value of the parameter T_m. Moreover, since learning control rules is dependent upon making control decisions (and receiving reinforcing evaluations), this parameter will directly affect how quickly the direct controller learns. The remainder of this section briefly describes the function of the other levels of the control hierarchy.

2.5.2   Planning/Optimizing Expert System

The purpose of the planning/optimizing expert system (P/O ES) is to optimize the effectiveness and efficiency of the direct control level (DCL). These goals are accomplished by changing (based on current operating conditions) the values of parameters used by the DCL $(k_0, T_m, p_m, D, d, T_d, \alpha)$. Moreover, the P/O ES can also provide new values of the performance indices to the DCL prompted by changing higher-level considerations and the occurrence of failure modes and critical conditions. Furthermore, the control sets U_j (for situations S_j, $j = 1, 2, \ldots$) used by the DCL can be modified for more effective control by the P/O ES.

The knowledge base of the P/O ES contains situation-implies-action rules which are driven by the following data: (1) specifications of control objectives and constraints; (2) failure/emergency conditions indicators from the DCL; (3) summarized values of past inputs, outputs, and performance evaluation; and (4) DCL data structures (control probabilities, eligibilities, situation definitions, etc.). The consequents of the rules in this knowledge base contain "actions" about the following: (1) new values for goals, (2) new values of DCL parameters, (3) new admissible control sets U_j, and (4) new constraints on the outputs for the data monitor ES. Obviously, these rules are domain specific. Moreover, if an exact relationship between the conclusions and the triggering data were known, an expert system would not be needed. As it stands, most of the preceding rules will be heuristical in nature, based on inexact operator knowledge. Finally, the rules should be designed with parameters that can be easily modified by the process learning unit, making the knowledge base dynamic. However, it is advantageous that the structure of the knowledge base remain constant.

The P/O ES is the only interface to the direct controller and adjusts the DCL as a human operator might adjust the controller of a complex plant. Viewed differently, the P/O ES implements the parameter changes that the process learning unit learns. In implementing these changes, the P/O ES sends new parameter values to the data monitor ES which also uses new information learned by the process learning unit.

2.5.3   Process Learning Unit

The purpose of the Process Learning Unit (PLU) is to learn constraints on the process inputs and outputs and to learn aspects of the process I/O mapping. This information, once learned, is incorporated into the knowledge bases of the P/O ES and the data monitor ES by adjusting existing rules (not by adding new rules). In this way the PLU, which has the luxury of a longer operating time horizon, can enhance the performance of the lower control levels through learning. Again, because of process uncertainties and fluctuations, this task will never be completed.

Internally, the PLU is envisaged to consist of several learning automata operating in parallel, one for each variable whose value is to be adjusted. Such variables include the allowable minimum and maximum values of each process input (control), the allowable minimum and maximum values of each process output, and estimates of the process delay (T_d), the input delay (d), the process order, and so on. Thus the outputs of the PLU represent "better" values of these variables chosen from a predetermined set of possibilities. Quite naturally, the critical and most elusive components of the PLU are the performance criteria or measures which guide the learning of each and every automaton. These performance indices (corresponding to "higher level goals" such as stability) must be determined carefully.

In comparing the PLU to the DCL, we note that both contain learning automata employing a linear reinforcement scheme. However, for the direct controller, the CSR determines from which automaton (one for each situation) the output (control) is selected. Moreover, the eligibility list determines which automata are reinforced (have their probabilities changed). In contrast, for the PLU, the outputs of all automata are selected as the current values of the variables used by the lower control levels. Moreover, all automata are "eligible" for reinforcement when it occurs. However, in all other respects, the PLU and DCL, as sets of learning automata, operate in a similar fashion.

Preferred parameter values determined by the PLU are meaningless unless they can be incorporated into the P/O ES and the data monitor ES knowledge bases. Thus these knowledge bases must be designed to be updated by the values the PLU learns. Specifically, the data monitor ES must make use of learned constraints on process outputs in detecting alarm conditions and failure modes. Likewise the P/O ES must use new constraints on the controls and better estimates of process characteristics (T_d, d, ...) to change the admissible control sets U_j and to update DCL parameters (α, D, k_0, ...). Thus the learned PLU parameter values should themselves be parameters (not data) in the rules used by the lower-level expert systems.

2.5.4   Qualitative Explanative Diagnostic System

The qualitative explanative diagnostic system (QED) is situated at the highest level of the hierarchy and is responsible for providing explanations to the user regarding process behavior in general and process failures in particular. To accomplish this task, the QED makes extensive use of a qualitative model of the process which is driven by filtered I/O process data. This qualitative model embodies all of the causal knowledge which the user has about the process.

The QED operates in two modes in response to two separate prompts: (1) a user inquiry and (2) the occurrence of a process failure. In the first case the QED simply uses the qualitative model to trace an explanation of the user's question. In the latter case, the QED first proposes a heuristic to explain the failure and then checks it against the qualitative model for validity. Based on this consistency check, the diagnostic heuristic is modified using learning rules. Thus a set of diagnostic heuristics is developed during controller operation.

2.5.5   Overall Timing and Communication

In considering the timing and communication protocols of the proposed hierarchical controller during operation, the interactions of five components must be examined: the DCL, the P/O ES, the PLU, the QED facility, and the user or operator. First, the direct controller can be considered to be operating (in real time) largely autonomously with the primary goal of maintaining instantaneous performance objectives. The higher levels of the hierarchy then (including the user) can be thought of as operating "in the background," taking more time and communicating with the DCL asynchronously (when they have produced pertinent results). Moreover, the direct controller's timing is not interrupted by changes to its internal structure—all of which are performed by the P/O ES. Similarly, the user interacts with the higher levels on an asynchronous, as-necessary schedule (Figure 6).

In contrast, process I/O data is sent to the four different controller levels on a synchronous schedule with the frequency being higher at the lower levels. Specifically, the DCL receives I/O feedback every T_m seconds, the P/O ES receives (filtered) data every T_0 seconds, and both the PLU and QED facility receive the same (filtered) process information every T_p seconds.

3   SIMULATION RESULTS

3.1   Introduction

In this section we discuss the preliminary testing of the direct control level of the proposed hierarchical intelligent control system. The classic pole-balancing problem was chosen as a suitable test-bed to examine the learning abilities of the DCL. More specifically, our goals were (1) to show that the controller could learn, and (2) to examine its sensitivity to the choice of the control set U and the initial state of the cart-pole system. At this time it is not possible to compare our results with other pole-balancing systems because of such factors as the frequency of reinforcement, the quality of external reinforcement, and the reinforcement delay make any such comparisons impossible. Moreover, we depart substantially from previous systems which relied exclusively upon a failure signal as the source of external reinforcement; solving the temporal credit assignment problem is not the main focus of our work. Our approach is to endow the critic with as much qualitative heuristic knowledge of the process dynamics as possible. As a consequence, the learning may then become technically less "unsupervised." With this in mind, the following subsections discuss the cart-pole process, the learning controller, the simulation experiments, and our initial results.

3.2   Simulation Results

3.2.1   Cart–Pole Process

Key principles of the proposed direct level controller were tested on an inherently unstable, multi output dynamic system: the cart–pole balancing problem. The system has been used as a test-bed for analyzing control techniques, including learning control, by many researchers and was deemed a manageable problem for the scope of this work. A thorough testing of the direct controller would require a more complex and uncertain system and is left for future work.

The system consists of a pole hinged to a wheeled cart that is constrained to move in a straight line (in one dimension) on a bounded track. The pole is constrained to one rotational degree of freedom. The state of the system at any time is given by four variables $\theta(t)$ (pole angle from vertical), $\dot{\theta}(t)$ (angular velocity of pole), $x(t)$ (position of cart from the center of the track), and $\dot{x}(t)$ (velocity of the cart). The units are radians, radians per seconds, meters, and meters per seconds, respectively. The input to the system is a *bidirectional force* with a prespecified magnitude which is applied to the cart. The objective is to balance the pole and to keep the cart "in bounds." Specifically, a failure is defined as either $|\theta| > 12$ degrees or $|x| > 2.4$ meters and the ideal goal is to maintain the state as close to $(0, 0, 0, 0)$ as possible.

A simulation of the process was developed using the Euler integration method (with a step size of 0.1 sec); a dynamic model of the system is given by Equations 1 and 2 where $F(t)$ is the input force, m_c is the mass of the cart, m is the mass of the pole, and l is the half-pole length [1]. Parameter values used for the cart–pole simulation are the same as those given elsewhere [1, 6]: $g = -9.8$ m/sec², $m_c = 1.0$ kg, $m = 0.1$ kg, $l = 0.5$ m. The frictionless version of the system was simulated, making it more difficult to control:

$$\ddot{\theta}(t) = \frac{g \sin \theta + \cos \theta \{-F(t) - ml\theta^2 \sin \theta\} / \{m + m_c\}}{4l/3 - ml\cos^2\theta/(m + m_c)} \tag{1}$$

$$\ddot{x}(t) = \frac{[F(t) + ml\{\theta^2 \sin \theta - \cos \theta\}]}{m + m_c} \tag{2}$$

3.2.2 Controller

The DCL described previously incorporates many parameters, variables, and functions which must be chosen before on-line operation. For the testing of the pole-balancing system, the following values and functions were needed: (1) the admissible control set U, (2) a performance evaluation function (critic), (3) the situation classification scheme and associated parameters D and k_0, (4) the threshold parameter p_m, and (5) the learning rate parameter α.

The admissible control set was varied between $U = \{-10, 10\}$, $U = \{-15, 15\}$, and $U = \{-10, 0, 10\}$ newtons (as described below) and no control subsets $U_j(n)$ were considered for our tests. Each new situation had two or three possible control actions each being equally probable.

A transformation of the four state variables of the system was employed to simplify the problem. Specifically, the two cart position variables were converted into one: $x_a(t) = \dot{x}(t) + x\Delta t$.

The process critic is the key component of our direct level controller and ultimately determines the speed and accuracy of the learned control strategy. Many critics are possible based on the level of process knowledge available. For these simulations our goal was not to select the most knowledgeable critic and indeed both more and less "informed" evaluations could have been chosen. The goal of the critic is to provide a reinforcement score $r(n) \in [-1, +1]$ for updating control probabilities, based on the relative performance of the system. For the cart–pole system we abandoned the formal intermediate step of calculating an instantaneous performance index, $IP(n)$, at the n-th sample time, and then converting to a reinforcement $r(n)$ based on user-set limits of IP. Such an approach could have been implemented with some embellishments of the critic. Such additions are unnecessary however, the controller employed in the simulations is based on the following three-rule heuristic critic:

1. if $\{x(n) > 2.0$ and $\dot{x}(n) < \dot{x}(n-1)\}$ then $r(n) = .5$ else $r(n) = -.5$
2. if $\{x(n) < -2.0$ and $\dot{x}(n) > \dot{x}(n-1)\}$ then $r(n) = .5$ else $r(n) = -.5$
3. if $\{[\theta(n-1) > 0$ and $\dot{\theta}(n-1) > 0$ and $\dot{\theta}(n) < \dot{\theta}(n-1)]$ or $[\theta(n-1) < 0$ and $\dot{\theta}(n-1) < 0$ and $\dot{\theta}(n) > \dot{\theta}(n-1)]$ or $[\theta(n-1) < 0$ and $\dot{\theta}(n-1) > 0$ and

$|\dot{\theta}(n) - \dot{\theta}(n - 1)| < 10$ degrees/sec] or $[\theta(n - 1) > 0$ and $\dot{\theta}(n - 1) < 0$ and $|\dot{\theta}(n) - \dot{\theta}(n - 1)| < 10$ degrees/sec]} then $r(n) = .5$ else $r(n) = -.5$

Measurement vectors $[\dot{\theta}(n), \theta(n), x_{la}(n)]^T$ are grouped into situations based on a tolerance vector D with components 25, 6, and 1.2. If all components of a new measurement vector X are within the range of the corresponding threshold of an existing situation vector $S_j(\|X - S_j\| < D)$ then the new vector is classified as being in that situation. Otherwise the new vector defines a new situation. Moreover, all vectors in a given situation are of the same sign (each component). This was done to distinguish situations whose components have opposite signs. Obviously, having a single control for such a situation would lead to poorer overall performance. The parameter k_0 was chosen to be zero and the input and setpoint were not included in a situation vector because (1) the setpoint did not change, (2) the input deadtime was zero, and (3) a lower-dimensional measurement space was desired. No situation consolidation or division mechanism was implemented.

The threshold parameter p_m which affects the randomness of control decisions was set after some experimentation to 0.65. With only two or three possible controls, being at least twice as sure about one control versus the others was viewed as a sufficient criteria for its selection.

The learning parameter α was set to 0.9, placing a large importance on external reinforcement and causing the probabilities to converge fairly rapidly, two conditions which were deemed desirable.

3.2.3   Experiments

Six different pole-balancing experiments were obtained by varying the control set U and the system reset (initial) state. The control set had three different values ($\{-10, 10\}$, $\{-15, 15\}$, and $\{-10, 0, 10\}$) while the reset state was either $\{0, 0, 0, 0\}$ or $\{R(\theta), 0, 0, 0\}$ where $R(\theta)$ (initial pole angle) is a random value between -3 and 3 degrees. For each experiment a *trial* consisted of a series of control actions (50 per second) on the cart until the cart or pole were out of range indicating a failure. The system was then reset and the process was repeated. The average number of control steps until failure for the first 25 failures (averaged over 5 runs) was recorded for each experiment. However, if a trial reached 60 seconds of control it was halted and the next trial was started. The results are described below.

3.2.4   Results

Figure 8 summarizes the results of the six pole balancing experiments. Scenarios 1–3 correspond to a random reset of the pole angle and reflect relatively disappointing performance regardless of which control set U was chosen. For the dynamics of the cart–pole process, it appears that the controller on average cannot overcome certain undesirable initial states, at least not within the first 25 failures. The last three scenarios (4–6) correspond to a zero reset state, as in the work of Barto et al., and in order $U = \{-15, 15\}$, $U = \{-10, 10\}$, and $U = \{-10, 0, 10\}$. The last scenario, which resulted in the best performance, would have been even better had the trials not been stopped

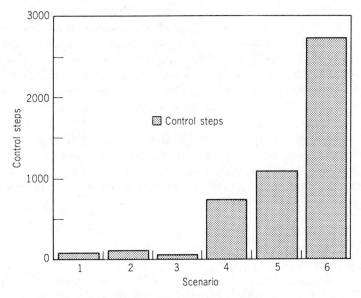

Figure 8. Experimental results.

after 60 seconds of control. With other factors being equal (and a zero reset state), Figure 8 illustrates the substantial effect that the control set U has on the learning abilities of our direct level controller. While changing from $U = \{-15, 15\}$ to $U = \{-10, 10\}$ did improve performance, adding zero force as a control option had a much greater effect on performance. Overall, the results demonstrate the importance of a method of selecting the appropriate control set for a given problem and the sensitivity of the performance to the initial state. The sensitivity of the initial state used in learning to controller robustness is an issue which prevents generalization about the value of an initial system state and requires further investigation.

4 CONCLUSIONS

The results reported in this work, although preliminary, are encouraging and support the validity of the direct control level approach. Much, however, needs to be learned about what classification schemes, instantaneous performance indices, control sets, parameter values, etc., should be used for particular control problems and how sensitive the system performance is to which schemes and values are chosen. However, some heuristics can be offered from our experience with the pole-balancing problem. First, the more often external reinforcement is supplied the faster learning occurs. Secondly, the instantaneous performance index is a very important factor in determining if learning will be possible or accurate. Thirdly, a situation classification scheme should distinguish between vectors which contain components on both sides of critical boundaries (positive and negative, for example) regardless of what those boundaries are determined to be. The vector components for which this consideration is most important is domain-dependent and is something a domain expert may know. In addition, the number of control situations should be kept as small as possible and should be related to the cardinality of the control set. Fourth, the choice of the control set U has a vital effect on control performance. Indeed control sets could be chosen which make basic performance (stability, for instance) impossible. Finally, the choice of the parameter p_m should depend on the number of possible controls M, generally being higher for smaller values of M.

While our success at the direct control level is encouraging, the implementation of the three higher levels will provide a substantial opportunity for even better performance. Moreover, the overall performance will be improved when the controller is endowed with fault-diagnosis abilities, predictive abilities, and so on, provided by the higher levels.

ACKNOWLEDGMENTS

This work was supported by NASA Lewis Research Center, contract NAG-3-788. Thanks also to J. Litt and C. Lorenzo of NASA LeRC and L. E. Widman for valuable comments regarding this work.

REFERENCES

Learning Control

1. C. W. Anderson, "Strategy Learning With Multilayer Connectionist Representations," in *Proceedings of the Fourth International Workshop on Machine Learning, Irvine, CA,* 1987, pp. 103–114.

2. A. G. Barto, "Adaptive Neural Networks for Learning Control: Some Computational Experiments," in *Proceedings, IEEE Workshop on Intelligent Control 1985, Troy, NY,* 1986, pp. 170–175.

3. A. G. Barto, "Learning by Statistical Cooperation of Self-Interested Neuron-Like Computing Elements," *Human Neurobiology,* 4:229–256.

4. A. G. Barto and P. Anandan, "Pattern-Recognizing Stochastic Learning Automata," *IEEE Transactions on Systems, Man, and Cybernetics,* **SMC-15**:360–375, 1985

5. A. G. Barto and R. S. Sutton, "Landmark Learning: an Illustration of Associative Search," *Biological Cybernetics,* **42**:1–8, 1981.

6. A. G. Barto, R. S. Sutton, and C. W. Anderson, "Neuronlike Adaptive Elements That Can Solve Difficult Learning Control Problems," *IEEE Transactions on Systems, Man, and Cybernetics,* **SMC-13** (5), September/October 1983.

7. P. Bock, "The Emergence of Artificial Intelligence: Learning to Learn," *AI Magazine,* pp. 180–190, Fall 1985.

8. E. Ceanga, C. Vasiliu, and S. Bumbaru, "Learning Systems with Control Situations

9. K. S. Fu, "Learning Control Systems—Review and Outlook," *IEEE Transactions on*

Pattern Analysis and Machine Intelligence, **PAMI-8** (3), May 1986 (reprint).

10. K. S. Fu, "Stochastic Automata as Models of Learning Systems," in J. Tou (Ed.), *Computer and Information Sciences II,* Academic, New York, 1967, pp. 177–191.

11. R. A. Jarvis, "Adaptive Global Search in a Time-Variant Environment Using a Probabilistic Automaton with Pattern Recognition Supervision," *IEEE Transactions on Systems, Science, and Cybernetics,* **SSC-6**(3): 209–217, 1970.

12. L.E. Jones III and K. S. Fu, "On the Selection of Subgoals and the Use of A Priori Information in Learning Control Systems," *Automatica,* **5,** November 1969.

13. S. J. Kahne and K. S. Fu, "Learning System Heuristics," *IEEE Transactions on Automatic Control,* (correspondence), **AC-11**:611–612, July 1966.

14. J. D. Lambert and M. D. Levine, "A Two-Stage Learning Control System," *IEEE Transactions on Automatic Control,* **AC-15**(3):351–354, 1970.

15. P. Langley, "Learning to Search: From Weak Methods to Domain-Specific Heuristics," *Cognitive Science,* **9**:217–260, 1985.

16. R. W. McLaren, "Application of a Continuous-Valued Control Algorithm to On-line Optimization of Stochastic Control Systems," in *Proceedings of NEC,* Vol. 25, 1969.

17. G. J. McMurtry, "A Variable Structure Automaton Used as a Multimodel Searching Technique," *IEEE Transactions on Automatic Control,* **AC-11**:379–387, July 1966.

18. D. Michie and R. A. Chambers, "BOXES: An Experiment in Adaptive Control," in E. Dole and D. Michie (Eds.), *Machine Intelligence,* Vol. 2, Oliver and Boyd, Edinburgh, 1968, pp. 127–152.

19. K. S. Narendra and S. Lakshmivarahan, "Learning Automata —A Critique," *Journal of Cybernetics and Information Science,* **1**:53–65, 1977.

20. K. S. Narendra and M. A. L. Thathachar, "Learning Automata—A Survey," *IEEE Transactions on Systems, Man, and Cybernetics,* **SMC-5**(4):323–334, 1974.

21. Z. J. Nikolic and K. S. Fu, "An Algorithm for Learning Without External Supervision and its Application to Learning Control Systems," *IEEE Transactions on Automatic Control,* **AC-11**:414–422, July 1966.

22. M. J. Pazzani, "Refining the Knowledge Base of a Diagnostic Expert System: An Application of Failure-Driven Learning," *Proceedings of the 1986 AAAI Conference on Artificial Intelligence, Philadelphia,* 1986, pp. 1029–1035.

23. J. S. Riordon, "An Adaptive Automaton Controller for Discrete-Time Markov Processes," *Automatica,* **5**:721–730, 1969.

24. G. N. Saridis, "Application of Pattern Recognition Methods to Control Systems," *IEEE Transactions on Automatic Control,* **AC-26**(3), June 1981.

25. G. N. Saridis and T. K. Dao, "A Learning Approach to the Parameter Adaptive S.O.C. Problem," *Automatica,* **8**(5):589–597, 1972.

26. R. S. Sutton, "Temporal Credit Assignment in Reinforcement Learning," Ph.D. Dissertation, University of Massachusetts-Amherst, Amherst, MA, 1984.

27. M. A. L. Thathachar and B. R. Harita, "Learning Automata with Changing Number of Actions," *IEEE Transactions on Systems, Man, and Cybernetics,* **SMC-17** (6):1095–1100, 1987.

28. Y. Tsypkin, *Adaptation and Learning in Automatic Control,* Z. J. Nikoloc, (Trans.), Academica, New York, 1971.

29. M. D. Waltz and K. S. Fu, "A Heuristic Approach to Reinforcement Learning Control

Systems," *IEEE Transactions on Automatic Control,* **AC-10:**390–398, October 1965.

30. B. Widrow and F. W. Smith, "Pattern Recognizing Control Systems," in J. Tou and R. Wilcox (Eds.), *Computer and Information Sciences,* Spartan, Washington, DC, 1964.

Expert Control

31. K. J. Astrom, "Auto-Tuning, Adaptation, and Expert Control," in *Proceedings of the 1985 American Control Conference,* Vol. 3, Boston, MA, 1985, pp. 1514–1519.

32. J. D. Birdwell, J. R. B. Cockett, and J. R. Gabriel, "Domains of Artificial Intelligence Relevant to Systems," in *Proceedings of the 1986 American Control Conference, Seattle, WA,* 1986, pp. 1153–1157.

33. M. H. Davies, "Artificial Intelligence in On-line Control Applications—An Air Traffic Control Example," in *International Conference on Advances in C³ Systems: Theory and Applications,* 1985, pp. 224–233.

34. K. DeJong, "Intelligent Control: Integrating Artificial Intelligence and Control Theory," *Proceedings of Trends and Applications 1983, Automating Intelligent Behavior, Gaithersburg, MD,* 1983, pp. 158–161.

35. D. A. Fortin, T. B. Rooney, and E. H. Bristol, "Of Christmas Trees and Sweaty Palms," in *Proceedings of the Ninth Annual Advanced Control Conference, West Lafeyette, IN,* 1983, pp. 49–54.

36. K. K. Gidwani, "The Role of Artificial Intelligence Systems in Process Control," in *Proceedings of the 1985 American Control Conference, Boston, MA,* pp. 881–884.

37. A. Guha and M. Dudziak, "Knowledge-Based Controllers for Autonomous Systems," in *Proceedings, IEEE Workshop on Intelligent Control 1985, Troy, NY,* 1986, pp. 134–138.

38. F. Hayes-Roth, D. A. Waterman, and D. B. Lenat, *Building Expert Systems,* Addison-Wesley, Reading, MA, 1983.

39. T. Laffey, et al., "Real-Time Knowledge-Based Systems," *AI Magazine,* **9**(1):27–45, 1988.

40. J. Litt, "Adaptive Control Using Pattern Recognition: An Expert System Approach," M.S. Thesis, Case Western Reserve University, Cleveland, OH, 1985.

41. E. Lusk and R. Stratton, "Automated Reasoning in Man-Machine Control Systems," in *Proceedings of the Ninth Annual Advanced Control Conference, West Lafeyette, IN,* 1983, pp. 41-44.

42. R. L. Moore, "Expert Systems in Process Control," *Proceedings of the Controls West Conference,* 1985, pp. 203–207.

43. R. S. Shirley, "Some Lessons Learned Using Expert Systems for Process Control," *IEEE Control Systems Magazine,* **7**(6):11–15, December 1987.

44. B. G. Silverman, "Distributed Inference and Fusion Algorithms for Real-Time Supervisory Controller Positions," *IEEE Transactions on Systems, Man, and Cybernetics,* **SMC-17**(2):230–239, 1987.

Intelligent Control

45. J. R. Crosscope and R. D. Bonnell, "An Integrated Intelligent Controller Employing Both Conceptual and Procedural Knowledge," in *Proceedings, IEEE Symposium on Intelligent Control 1987,* Philadelphia, PA, 1987, pp. 416–422.

46. R. R. Gawronski, "Learning, Hierarchy, and Parallel Processing as a Tool for the Improvement of Control Quality," in *Proceedings, IEEE Workshop on Intelligent Control 1985,* Troy, NY, 1986, pp. 158–169.

47. M. M. Gupta, "Toward the Realization of Intelligent Machines," in *Proceedings, IEEE Workshop on Intelligent Control 1985*, Troy, NY, 1986, pp. 145–149.

48. T. L. Johnson, "Hierarchical Intelligent Control and Computers of the Fifth Generation," in *Proceedings, IEEE Workshop on Intelligent Control 1985*, Troy, NY, 1986, pp. 196–197.

49. S. Lee and M. H. Kim, "Cognitive Control of Dynamic Systems," in *Proceedings, IEEE Symposium on Intelligent Control 1987*, Philadelphia, PA, 1987, pp. 455–460.

50. J. M. Mendel and J. J. Zapalac, "The Application of Techniques of Artificial Intelligence to Control System Design," in C. T. Leondes (Ed.), *Advances in Control Systems*, Academic, New York, 1968, pp. 1–93.

51. G. Saridis and G. Lee, "An Integrated Syntactic Approach and Suboptimal Control for Manipulators and Prosthetic Arms," in *Proceedings, 18th Conference on Decision and Control 1979, Ft. Lauderdale*, December 1979.

52. G. N. Saridis and H. E. Stephanou, "A Hierarchical Approach to the Control of a Prosthetic Arm," *IEEE Transactions on Systems, Man, and Cybernetics*, **SMC-7**:407-420, June 1977.

53. L. A. Zadeh, "Outline of a New Approach to the Analysis of Complex Systems and Decision Processes," *IEEE Transactions on Systems, Man, and Cybernetics*, **SMC-3**:28–44, 1973.

Qualitative Reasoning

54. J. F. Allen, "Maintaining Knowledge About Temporal Intervals," *Communications of the ACM*, **26**(11):832–843, 1983.

55. D. Bobrow (Ed.), *Qualitative Reasoning About Physical Systems*, MIT Press, Cambridge, MA, 1985.

56. J. DeKleer and J. S. Brown, "A Qualitative Physics Based on Confluences," *Artificial Intelligence*, **24**:7–83, 1984.

57. K. D. Forbus, "Interpreting Measurements of Physical Systems," in *Proceedings of the 1986 AAAI Conference on Artificial Intelligence, Philadelphia, PA*, 1986, pp. 113–117.

58. B. Kuipers, "Qualitative Simulation," *Artificial Intelligence*, **29**:289–338, 1986.

59. B. C. Williams, "Doing Time: Putting Qualitative Reasoning on Firmer Ground," in *Proceedings of the 1986 AAAI Conference on Artificial Intelligence, Philadelphia, PA*, 1986, pp. 105–112.

Hierarchical Control Background

60. I. Lefkowitz, "Multilevel Concept for Systems Engineering," *Transactions of the ASME*, **88**(2), 1966.

61. M. Mesarovic, D. Macko, and Y. Takahara, *Theory of Hierarchical Multilevel Systems*, Academic, New York, 1970.

18 Knowledge-Based Simulation: An Artificial Intelligence Approach to System Modeling and Automating the Simulation Life Cycle

MARK S. FOX, NIZWER HUSAIN,[1] MALCOLM McROBERTS,[2] and Y. V. REDDY[3]

Intelligent Systems Laboratory
The Robotics Institute
Carnegie Mellon University
Pittsburgh, Pennsylvania

1 INTRODUCTION

Industry has been slow in adopting simulation as a means for analyzing complex decision problems. One reason is that the complexity of the modeling language and differences between simulation modeling concepts and the system to be modeled make model building a difficult and time-consuming task. Early work in *knowledge-based simulation* [7,10,12,16] has attempted to alleviate this problem by using artificial intelligence (AI) knowledge representation techniques, such as frames, to represent the objects and their relationships, and rules, to represent the procedural behaviors of the objects,[4] to create simulation models which are

- explicit,
- understandable,

[1]Present address: Intellicorp, 1975 El Camino Real West, Mountainview, California 94040-2216.

[2]Present address: Technical Services Company, Kennedy Space Division, McDonnell Douglas Astronautics Company, P. O. Box 21233, Cocoa Beach, Florida 32815.

[3]Co-affiliation: Artificial Intelligence Laboratory, Department of Statistics and Computer Science, West Virginia University, Morgantown, West Virginia 26506.

[4]Confusion exists around the use of a knowledge engineering tool to perform simulation and the use of knowledge representation. In the former, the powerful graphic facilities provided by the tool and the underlying work station provide a rich and powerful interface which does not necessarily have any AI content.

- modifiable, and
- self-explanatory.

By using a frame language to represent domain concepts, such as object structure, and goals, there is a one-to-one correspondence between the domain and the simulation model.[5] Second, by using rules to represent object behavior, the specification and modification of the behaviors become easier. Lastly, explanation techniques developed around rule-based systems provide the basis for explaining event behaviors.

While the AI approach has reduced the difficulty of model building somewhat, more widespread use of simulation technology will not be achieved until the time it takes to perform the activities in the simulation life cycle,

- problem formulation,
- modeling building,
- data acquisition,
- model translation,
- verification,
- validation,
- experiment planning,
- experimentation, and
- analysis of results

is reduced, while at the same time the quality of the results are enhanced. The barrier to achieving these goals is the lack of available expertise both in simulation theories and techniques and the domain of application. This lack of expertise results in

- inaccurate and incomplete models,
- poor experiment designs,
- poor analysis, and
- few ideas of how to alter the model to maximize the simulation goals.

The representation and utilization of expertise has been one of the more important contributions of AI. Consequently, AI knowledge engineering tools, such as Knowledge Craft [8], provide an excellent environment for constructing a knowledge-based simulation tool for supporting and managing the simulation life cycle and applying expertise at each stage of the cycle.

---

[5]There is another confusion between the concepts of objects such as in Simula/object-oriented programming and knowledge representation. Knowledge representation, in addition to being able to represent objects and their procedural behavior [8, 18] focuses on the relations among objects and the deductions supported by them [1]. Even more so, knowledge representation research is directed toward the development of a clear, concise, and consistent semantics for the representation of knowledge. Consequently, standard representations have been developed for a number of domains such as factory scheduling [3] and project management [20].

In this chapter, we describe the knowledge-based simulation system KBS. KBS has been a testbed for exploring the concept of AI in simulation. Since 1980, we have been exploring issues such as:

- Using an object-oriented approach to model representation where objects have a one-to-one correspondence with domain objects, and the objects have methods which define their behavior. This provides flexibility in creating and altering entities and their behavior without altering the simulation model interpreter [4].
- Extending the object-oriented representation with concepts from semantic networks in order to provide a standard semantics for representing entities and their relationships [19].
- Representing an object's behavior (i.e., events) in the form of rules which are easily understood by the user [18].
- Combining menus and graphics to provide interactive model building.
- Verifying models by using logic programming to specify verification axioms.
- Providing the capability to reduce a model's complexity through the use of abstraction mechanisms so that a model can be represented at multiple levels of abstraction. The user specifies the level of simulation and the system automatically configures the model [11].
- Focusing the gathering and analysis of simulation data according to goals specified by the user [17, 22].
- Enhancing the user's understanding of a model's dynamic behavior by providing a variety of simulation monitoring facilities, including stepping, tracing, and the display of inter-event and intra-event communications; providing interrupts and checkpoints to suspend a simulation run in order to investigate entities; recording checkpoints so as to explore the effect of alternate decisions while preserving the option of restoring the system to any one of the several checkpointed model states.
- Rating simulation results according to the goals provided by the user.
- Heuristic (i.e., rule-based) analysis of simulation data and the specification of refinements to the model in order to better satisfy the predefined goals.
- Automatic rule refinement using causal path analysis to determine the degree to which variation of a given effect is determined by each particular cause in the model, achieved by combining the qualitative knowledge regarding causal relations with the quantitative knowledge furnished by correlation and regression.
- Managing the simulation life cycle by means of a goal-directed rule system which examines the performance of a scenario with the help of diagnosis/modification rules which can suggest model modifications that may realize a simulation goal, thereby transforming simulations from being descriptive systems to prescriptive systems.

Section 2 describes the distribution domain which will be used as the primary example throughout the chapter. Section 3 describes the KBS methodologies for representing, creating, and verifying models. Section 4 describes goal acquisition, model instrumentation, simulation execution, and data gathering. Section 5 describes how KBS learns rule refinements from simulation data. Section 6 describes the overall goal-directed architecture of KBS. Lastly, we conclude in Section 7.

2   CORPORATE DISTRIBUTION DOMAIN

In a large manufacturing organization the corporate distribution system plays an important role in assuring adequate market penetration and retention for its products. This is accomplished by keeping transportation and warehousing costs low and facilitating an aggressive pricing policy. In addition, it should provide a good level of service to its customers and resellers by providing products on time while not requiring a high level of customer inventory. In order to achieve this, the corporate distribution system should simultaneously deal with a number of mutually conflicting policies. For example, if a reseller is required to carry a high inventory level to minimize stockouts, it will reduce the cost of transportation but will exact a penalty on the reseller's ability to be competitive, which may result in loss of market share for the corporation. In order to deal with issues such as this, a corporate distribution system needs a tool to aid in decision making. Even though many analytical techniques for dealing with multiechelon inventory systems do exist, we chose a simulation approach so that we can effectively incorporate many idiosyncratic policies that are normally part of complex distribution management systems. The following provides a more detailed description of the distribution system.

A manufacturer produces a number of products which consist of a large number of components and subassemblies some of which are produced by the manufacturer at widely distributed locations while others are purchased from vendors located world-wide. These components and subassemblies are transported to a number of *distribution centers* where they are stocked. Each distribution center serves *customers* located in its assigned area. The customer may be a *reseller* or special customer who can deal with the distribution center or the *corporate business unit* directly. Customer requests are processed by the business unit or the distribution center, which results in shipment of products or components to be merged at the customer site. The distribution centers in turn depend on manufacturing centers and vendors to supply components and products to replenish their stock. This problem is further complicated by factors such as seasonal demands, varying lead times to build or expand manufacturing facilities, need to maintain uniform production levels, contractual agreements with vendors, effects of weather and labor problems on transportation schedules, and a myriad of other problems. It can be easily seen that the corporate distribution problem puts tremendous demands on managers at all levels who are faced with decision making which has far reaching effects on the entire corporation.

Consider some of the decisions faced by managers at various levels in the corporate distribution system (CDS). The primary objectives of simulating a CDS is to be able answer questions similar to the following:

- Where should we locate manufacturing plants for various components and what should their capacities be?
- For a given forecasted demand and its geographic distribution where should we locate distribution centers and what should their capacities be?

- Should the products be merged at distribution centers or at customer sites?
- What is the effect of transportation modes and schedules on customer stockouts and satisfaction?
- What is the overall effect of a delay in vendor shipment of some key components?
- Do we have enough manufacturing and distribution capacity to meet an antici-pated increase in demand for products?
- What is the effect of consolidation of manufacturing and distribution facilities?
- What is the effect of a proposed order-handling procedure on the corporation?

This list illustrates the enormous complexity of the distribution domain and suggests the need for tools to aid in decision making at a number of levels. For example, low inventories can economize inventory carrying costs but lost sales resulting from frequent stockouts can reduce total profits. Because of this, the tool must inherently be able to deal with conflicting goals. The KBS approach to simulation will make it possible to deal with such issues.

A simplified model of a corporate distribution network is shown in Figure 1. (See [15] for the earlier work upon which this model is derived.)

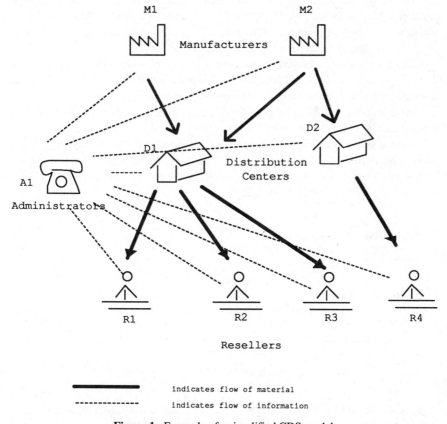

Figure 1. Example of a simplified CDS model.

3 MODEL BUILDING

The acquisition, representation, and verification of simulation models probably consumes the majority of the time spent in the simulation life cycle. The following describes how we have applied AI to increase the quality of models and decrease the time it takes to build them.

3.1 Model Representation

It is our belief that the greater the cognitive distance between an expert's description of a system and the descriptions directly supported by a simulation language, the greater the difficulty there is in constructing the simulation model. Consequently, we have strived in KBS to support the construction of models which closely match the way the expert views the system.

The approach taken in KBS to represent models is based on AI knowledge representation techniques [4, 12–14]. The representation is a frame-based semantic network, which supports the representation of objects, their attributes, structure and procedural behaviors, relations among objects, goals, and constraints. Models are constructed by first building a set of prototypical objects which are standard within a particular domain. In the case of distribution management, some standard objects are resellers, distribution centers, and manufacturing sites. A specific model is built by instantiating these prototypes and connecting them via relations.

Objects in KBS are represented as *schemata*.[6] A schema is represented as in Figure 2, with opening double braces followed by a schema name (printed in bold font) and a set of slot-value pairs and finally terminated by closing double braces.

The **pittsburgh-reseller** schema defines a retail sales store containing two stock items a and b. It also defines who the manager is, its sales region, and its address.

In addition to values, each slot may have a set of associated facets or *metainformation* (printed in italics). The *range* facet restricts the type of values that may fill the slot. The *default* facet defines the value of the slot if it is not present. The range facet restricts the types of values taken on by a slot.

```
{{pittsburgh-reseller
  INSTANCE: reseller
  STOCK: stock-a stock-b
    range: (type instance stock)
  REGION: Allegheny
  MANAGER: Ramana Reddy
  ADDRESS: 123 Easy St.
  REORDER-PROCEDURE: Reorder-rule-1
```

Figure 2. Example of a reseller schema.

---

[6]Early versions of KBS were built on top of SRL [5], a knowledge engineering tool; subsequent versions have been implemented in Knowledge Craft's representation language CRL [8].

The **stock-a** schema defines the status of the in-stock part a and what has been ordered due to the part falling below its reorder point:

```
{{stock-a
   INSTANCE: stock
   PART: a
   ON-HAND:138
   ON-ORDER:{{INSTANCE:stock-order
      PART:a
      AMOUNT:200
      SOURCE: pittsburgh
      DATE-ORDERED: 1 aug 87
      DATE-DUE: 15 aug 87}}
   MIN-STOCK: 200
   RE-ORDER-AMOUNT: 500}}
```

An important aspect of CRL is that schemata may form networks. Each slot in a schema may act as a relation tying the schema to others. The schema may *inherit* slots and their values along these relations. For example, **pittsburgh-reseller** is related to **reseller** by the INSTANCE relation. It inherits its standard slots from **reseller,** but their values are defined locally.

The procedural behaviors of an object, such as the reorder procedures for **pittsburgh-reseller,** are defined by a slot which names the procedure and by the values of the slots which define the actual behavior. Values can be LISP procedures or rules. A rule provides a means of specifying procedural knowledge which is easier to comprehend by the model builder. For example, the REORDER-PROCEDURE for the **pittsburgh-reseller** has its behavior defined by the following rule:

```
{{reorder-rule-1
   INSTANCE: rule
   IF: (less-than stock.on-hand stock.min-on-hand)
   THEN: (send-message :to stock.source
         :message reorder
         :part stock.part
         :amount stock.reorder-amount)
      (create-reorder-record stock)}}
```

The rule reorders a part when the on-hand stock is below the reorder point by sending a message to the object which is the source of the part for the reseller.

Knowledge Craft provides the model builder with a graphical interface for defining new schemata and slots (Figure 3), and to define the inheritance semantics of slots which act as relations. This includes defining what information (slots and their values) is inherited, not inherited, and altered when inherited. This feature will be useful in establishing special relationships between modeling entities that deal with restricted access to information and automatic elaboration of requested information. For a comprehensive treatment of this concept consult Knowledge Craft [8].

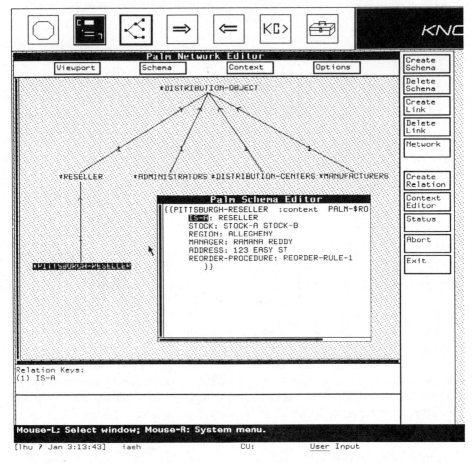

Figure 3. Knowledge Craft representation building interface.

3.2 Model Acquisition

Two philosophies exist for the acquisition of simulation models: a domain-independent view where the interface utilizes simulation concepts as the constructs to be described versus a domain-dependent view where domain-specific concepts are the constructs to be described. Experience has shown [6] that domain-specific knowledge acquisition systems provide a powerful means of acquiring models.

The philosophy taken in our work on knowledge-based simulation has been to develop a set of domain-specific interfaces. With the availability of powerful knowledge engineering tools on work stations with good graphic displays, the door has been opened for the development of rich interfaces. For example, a descendant of the KBS work at Carnegie Mellon University is the Simulation Craft system developed at Carnegie Group [5]. In Figure 4 there is an example of a multiwindow interface which contains a window for process planning and another for facility layout.

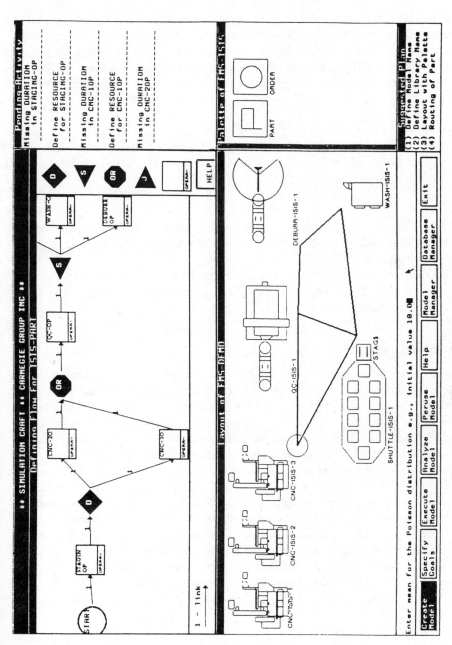

Figure 4. Process plan and facility layout interface.

455

3.3 Consistency and Completeness

A recurring problem in simulation systems, including KBS, is maintaining model *consistency* and *completeness*. We found that much time is wasted discovering errors and holes in the model. To deal with this problem, we use the logic programming facility of Knowledge Craft to specify completeness and consistency rules.

A consistency constraint relating resellers and distribution centers may be specified as:

```
(for-all 'reseller '(VIEWED-AS instance reseller)
  '(there-exists 'dc '(VIEWED-AS instance distribution-
  center)
      '(and (reseller.SUPPLIED-BY = dc)
            (dc.SUPPLIES = reseller))))
```

This constraint may be interpreted as: for all resellers there should exist schemata of the type **distribution-center** such that the schemata have consistent values for the slots SUPPLIED-BY and SUPPLIES.

For each constraint, KBS evaluates it and reports whether it was satisfied or whether it failed. In case of a constraint failure the interpreter provides a trace facility to determine the source of failure.

3.4 Model Reduction

The model we developed of a corporate distribution system was large in terms of the number of facilities and complex in terms of decision processes and levels of detail. In working with the distribution analysts, we found that the entire model was not necessary to answer every question. Instead, a question required a version of the model which is reduced in either breadth or depth. In particular, when focusing on a particular region's distribution logic, only abstractions of other regions were required. Consequently, it was necessary to introduce a mechanism for abstracting selective portions of the model. These alterations can be performed automatically provided the model builder has created a knowledge framework for the task. These simplifications result in faster running models, increased model understanding, and simplified analysis.

Model simplification techniques fall into two main categories, static and dynamic. In static techniques both model structure and model parameters are altered; however, the event behaviors remain unchanged. Since only static aspects of the model are affected, these are called static techniques. Dynamic techniques, on the other hand, alter a model's dynamic processes. This means redefining some of the event behaviors.

3.4.1 Static Abstraction

There are two types of static abstraction, equivalent node aggregation and data class aggregation. Equivalent node aggregation combines several nodes into a single node of the same type. This new node must be in some sense the sum of the original nodes. This will result in information that is unique to the individual nodes being lost, but if

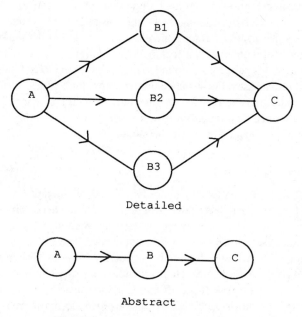

Detailed

Abstract

Figure 5. Equivalent node aggregation.

the new node's parameters are adjusted correctly, then the new node will be functionally similar to the old group. In this manner the rest of the model is not affected. For
example, in Figure 5 individual resellers in a region may be grouped together to form
a regional reseller. The corresponding schema that describe this kind of aggregation is
shown in Figure 6.

```
{{equivalent-node-aggregation
  IS-A: model-abstraction
  TYPE: reseller
    comment: type of node to aggregate
  SUPERNODE: regional-reseller
    comment: single node replaces subnodes when abstracted
  SUBNODES: reseller1 reseller2 reseller3
    comment: set of nodes present at detail level
  AVERAGE-SLOTS: lost-sale-percentage
    comment: aggregate slots filled by averaging
  UNION SLOTS: (order-weeks aggregate-weekly-demand)
      (inventory aggregate-inventory)
      (operating-days)
    comment: aggregate slots filled by summation
  SELECT: (select-node-aggregation)
  DESELECT: (deselect-node-aggregation)}}
```

Figure 6. Example of equivalent node aggregation.

In data class aggregation objects are grouped into classes, and all references to the members are replaced by references to the class. This of course throws away information about variations among the class members, but it should increase the overall efficiency and not greatly affect model execution.

An example of this concept as applied to the distribution model would be to group all items sold into classes. For instance, in the computer business different types of personal computers may be grouped together into a broad class referred to as PC. This would greatly reduce the amount of data needed to track inventory levels for each separate type of personal computer in the model.

3.4.2   Dynamic Abstraction

Dynamic abstraction attempts to simplify simulation models by analyzing the stimulus–response event behavior of one or more nodes and to construct a single node with a stimulus–response behavior which is statistically similar. This technique can be used to combine nodes of the same or different classes. The collection of statistics on event behavior can be achieved by either constructing stimulus–response frames or by postprocessing information gleaned from model introspection. However, purely statistical information on events is difficult to use because event parameters cannot readily be abstracted, and in such cases the abstracted model may become inconsistent. A full treatment of abstraction techniques as used in KBS is provided elsewhere [11].

4   MODEL SIMULATION

In KBS, simulation is viewed as being composed of a sequence of *experiments,* where each experiment measures how well a *scenario* (i.e., an altered version of the original model) optimizes one or more *goals*. The process of simulation begins first with the specification of a set of goals which result in the instrumentation of a scenario in order to gather data. The scenario is then executed interactively with an animated display. The scenario is then rated as to how well it has optimized the goals. The rest of this section provides a detailed description of the process.

4.1   Goal Specification and Instrumentation

The primary purpose for constructing a simulation is to verify a hypothesis or optimize one or more features of a system. Optimization can occur if we are able to measure the performance of a scenario. We introduce the concept of rating a scenario as a method of measuring the goodness or badness of simulation results, for example, if the goal is to utilize machines to their maximum (100%) and if in a given simulation the average utilization of machines is 90% and when confronted with the question "have we reached the goal?" we would like to give a better answer than no. To rate scenarios more smoothly, we chose a continuous scale of rating from -1 to $+1$, -1 meaning the results are far from the goal and $+1$ to indicate the goal has been completely satisfied. Since goals are often complex and may be composed of conflicting subgoals, we therefore describe here an approach to specification of goals of a simulation as a composite of a set of constraints[7] on the performance of various entities of the system being modeled.

Following are the steps involved in the construction and evaluation of goals:

- Represent each organizational *goal* as composed of a set of constraints.
- Select and attach instruments to gather data.
- Specify procedures for computing the performance measures from the raw data collected.
- Execute the simulation for the given scenario.
- Evaluate each constraint by computing a coefficient of constraint satisfaction, which may be positive, to indicate reaching the desired goal, or negative, indicating falling short of the desired goal.
- Evaluate the scenario by computing a coefficient of goal satisfaction as a weighted average of constraint satisfaction coefficients.

4.1.1   Goal Representation

A goal is an aggregation of subgoals which we call *constraints*. A goal is evaluated as a weighted sum of the individual subgoal constraint satisfaction coefficients. (Weights are specified by the model builder.) Figure 7 shows an example goal which when evaluated yields a RATING which is a measure of the desirability of the given scenario.

```
{{inet-pc-goal1
  INSTANCE: KBS-goal
  RATING: 0.35
    comment: a goodness or badness indicator
  CONTRIBUTING CONSTRAINTS: order-fill-rate inventory-turns
        inventory-investment order-cycle-time distribution-
        cost
    comment: the individual goal constraints
  STATUS: inactive
    comment: whether active or inactive
  GRAPH: goal-report-kiviat
    comment: a kiviat graph displays rating
  EVALUATION-SCHEDULE: every-quarter
    comment: governs when to evaluate goal
  GOAL-SCHEDULER: scheduler
    comment: interprets evaluation schedule
  EVAL-FN: eval-KBS-goal
    comment: goal evaluation function
  REPORT-FN: display-evaluated-goal
    comment: function to display goal state}}
```

Figure 7. Composite goal schema.

[7]Constraints are an inherent part of all organizational models. For a detailed treatment of constraints refer to Fox [2].

```
{{order-fill-rate
   INSTANCE: goal-constraint
   CONSTRAINED-BY: order-fill-rate-spec
      comment: specification for constraint
   CONTEXT: order-fill-rate-precondition
   comment: decides if constraint applies
   IMPORTANCE: 0.25
      comment: relative importance of constraint
   RATING: 0.8
      comment: a goodness or badness indicator
   VALUE: 40000
      comment: unrated raw value of constraint}}
```

Figure 8. Constraint schema.

```
{{order-fill-rate-spec
   INSTANCE: goal-constraint-spec
   APPLY: interpolate-linear-graph
   CONSTRAINT-SPEC-OF: order-fill-rate
   UTILITY-GRAPH: (100 -1.0) (10000 0.0) (60000 1.0)
   INSTRUMENTS: measure-orders-filled}}
```

Figure 9. Constraint schema.

This rating is derived by combining the ratings of individual CONTRIBUTING-CON-STRAINTS of the goal:

- order-fill-rate,
- inventory-turns,
- inventory-investment,
- order-cycle-time, and
- distribution-cost.

Other slots in the **goal** schema specify the procedure for evaluation and display of the results. Figures 8 and 9 show the representation of a constraint. The slot CON-STRAINED-BY of the **constraint** schema contains the details of the instrumentation needed to evaluate a constraint.

4.1.2   Instruments

The task of data collection is concerned with recording the changes in the value of a parameter. This can be accomplished by constantly monitoring the parameter and recording every change or by sampling. The former yields greater accuracy albeit with greater computational overhead, whereas the latter approach may be satisfactory in many cases, and thus the selection of the data collection method is subjective. In the KBS environment the monitoring is accomplished by attaching *demons* to slots, whereas sampling is done by scheduling data collection events or as a separate action during the execution of regular events. Since the data collection in KBS is analogous to physical measurements (using measuring instruments), the notion of an *instrument* (Figure 10) is introduced.

An instrument in KBS may be viewed as a probe attached to a schema representing an entity in the model and collects specified data whenever that schema is acted upon in some way. For example, if we are interested in studying inventory levels, we may attach an inventory measurement instrument which is activated whenever inventory levels change (Figure 11). Whenever the instrument is activated, it may simply record the value of the simulation clock and the inventory level. This information is stored within the instrument itself (Figure 12) and can be formatted in a variety of ways using a *report generator* associated with the instrument. For example if we are interested in the time-dependent behavior of inventory, we may subject the data collected to an analysis by a *time-series analyzer*. On the other hand, if we are only interested in the minimum inventory, we can subject the same data to analysis by a *descriptive statistics analyzer*.

```
{{KBS-instrument
   IS-A: instrument
   PURPOSE:
   INSTRUMENT-TYPE:
      range: (OR data-collection data-display)
   INSTRUMENT-MODE:
      restriction: (OR demon event scheduled)
   SLOT-TO-DEPOSIT:
      comment: slot value to be monitored or the event slot when this
      will be executed as one of the event actions
   SCHEMA-TYPE:
      comment: the names of generic schemata to which this instrument
      applies
   INSTRUMENT-SCHEDULE:
      comment: event schedule for scheduled instrument
      restriction: (TYPE is-a event-schedule)
   DATA:
   ACTION:
      comment: the data collection or display function
   ATTACHMENT-FUNCTION:
      comment: the attachment procedure}}
```

Figure 10. KBS instrument schema.

```
{{xa50-inventory-instrument
    INSTANCE: KBS-instrument
    INSTRUMENT-TYPE: data-collection
    INSTRUMENT-MODE: demon
    SLOT-TO-DEPOSIT: on-hand
    SCHEMA-TYPE:xa50-inventory
    DATA: xa50-inventory-on-hand-data }}
```

Figure 11. Inventory instrument schema.

```
{{xa50-inventory-on-hand-data
    INSTANCE: set-data
    SCHEMA-SET: set of xa50 inventory schemata derived
    from the instrument
    SLOT: on-hand
    ANALYSIS: descriptive-status
    DATA: to be filled by the instrument}}
```

Figure 12. Inventory data schema.

```
{{inet-pc-goal1
    INSTANCE: KBS-goal
    CONTRIBUTING-CONSTRAINTS: satisfy-customer
    economize-distribution
    EVALUATION-SCHEDULE: daily-at-midnight }}
```

Figure 13. Example of CDS goal.

```
{{satisfy-customer
    INSTANCE: goal-constraint
    CONSTRAINED-BY:  satisfy-customer-spec
    IMPORTANCE:  0.70 }}
```

Figure 14. Retailer satisfaction goal constraint.

```
{{economize-distribution
    INSTANCE: goal-constraint
    IMPORTANCE: 0.30
    CONTEXT: economize-distribution-precon
    CONSTRAINED-BY: economize-distribution-spec}}
```

Figure 15. Distribution cost reduction goal constraint.

```
{{satisfy-customer-spec
    INSTANCE: goal-constraint-spec
    APPLY: eval-customer-satisfaction
    UTILITY: stockouts-utility-graph
    INSTRUMENTS: measure-stockouts measure-total-orders }}
```

Figure 16. Specifications for customer satisfaction constraint.

```
{{economize-distribution-spec
   INSTANCE: goal-constraint-spec
   APPLY: eval-distribution-costs
   UTILITY: distribution-utility-graph
   INSTRUMENTS: measure-manf-cost measure-distribution-costs }}
```

Figure 17. Specifications for distribution goal constraint.

```
{{ measure-stockouts
   INSTANCE: KBS-instrument
   INSTRUMENT-TYPE: data-collection
   INSTRUMENT-MODE: event
   ACTION: extract-stockout-info
   SLOT-TO-DEPOSIT: back-orders
   SCHEMA-TYPE:  }}
```

Figure 18. Instrument to measure stockouts.

```
{{measure-total-orders
   INSTANCE: KBS-instrument
   INSTRUMENT-TYPE: data-collection
   INSTRUMENT-MODE: event
   ACTION: sum-up-total-orders}}
```

Figure 19. Instrument to measure total orders.

Once an instrument schema is defined, it is attached to an appropriate part of the model, which, when executed, results in the collection of the specified data which can be subjected to analysis. Instruments and data schemata are specified manually.

4.1.3   An Example of Scenario Rating

In this section we illustrate the procedure for rating a scenario via an example from the CDS model (Figure 13). Consider a composite organizational goal to increase customer satisfaction while keeping the distribution overheads low. This goal may be broken down into two subgoals:

- Customer stockouts should not exceed 5% of orders.
- Distribution cost per unit sold should not exceed 10% of the cost of manufacturing.

The corporate goal specified by the schema **inet-pc-goal1** is a composite of two organizational goal constraints: **satisfy-customer** and **economize-distribution**. These are shown in Figures 14 and 15, respectively. Each goal constraint is assigned an importance rating based on the role it plays in the overall corporate plan. Each goal constraint schema points to a constraint specification schema which specifies a utility function and the needed data collection instruments. Figures 16 and 17 show the constraint specifications for the **satisfy-customer** and **economize-distribution** constraints. In order to evaluate the goal constraint **satisfy-customer,** we need to measure the total orders filled as well as the number of stockouts. This is accomplished

```
{{measure-distribution-costs
   INSTANCE: KBS-instrument
   INSTRUMENT-TYPE: data-collection
   INSTRUMENT-MODE: event
   ACTION: compute-distribution-costs}}
```

Figure 20. Instrument to measure distribution costs.

```
{{measure-manf-costs
   INSTANCE: KBS-instrument
   INSTRUMENT-TYPE: data-collection
   INSTRUMENT-MODE: event
   ACTION: compute-manf-costs}}
```

Figure 21. Instrument to measure manufacturing costs.

```
{{KBS-run-spec
   RUN-DISPLAY: kbs-run-display
     comment: the display which is active during the run
   EVENT-TRACE: t
     comment: if event trace is posted to the display
   SYSTEM-STATS: t
     comment: if system stats are needed
   SYSTEM-STAT-FREQUENCY: 20
     comment: tells how often system statistics are updated
   START-TIME: "12 Sept 1985"
     comment: start time for each experiment
   STOP-TIME: "25 Sept 1985"
     comment: stop time for each experiment }}
```

Figure 22. The run specification.

by depositing the instruments **measure-stockouts** and **measure-total-orders,** shown in Figures 18 and 19, respectively.

The data needed to evaluate the **economize-distribution** goal constraint is collected by depositing the instruments **measure-distribution-costs** and **measure-manf-costs**, shown in Figures 20 and 21, respectively.

The instrument action functions will be tailored to extract the desired information and update the "data" in the instrument. Note that instrument data may also be directly available in the schema to which it is attached.

Having defined the goal, its constraints, and the instruments, it is then connected to the model. When a goal is connected, the relevant instruments are automatically attached to the model. The actual evaluation of the goal is an event scheduled to occur at some future date according to the EVALUATION-SCHEDULE, at which time the EVAL-FN is executed. However, it may also be evaluated manually at any time as desired.

A goal evaluation function (e.g., eval-KBS-goal) will normally retrieve the CON-TRIBUTING–CONSTRAINTS of the organizational goal. For each constraint if the *context* of the *constraint* applies, then the constraint is evaluated by the function in the APPLY slot to compute a *rating*. This rating weighted by the *importance* of the constraint contributes to the overall "rating" of the organizational goal. If the goal is evaluated more than once, it should be possible to observe the direction and decide how good or how bad the organization is doing.

4.2   Experiment Specification

Execution of the model consists of simulation runs. Each run of a model is an experiment. KBS defines schemata which contain all the information needed to conduct a series of experiments on models. At the end of each experiment, KBS may optionally "fire" a rule base which may suggest changes that need to be made to the model in the next experiment.

In Figure 22 **KBS-run-spec** specifies the profile for a simple run. RUN–DISPLAY governs what is going to be shown on screen during model execution. If the user is interested in the execution, a trace of model EVENT–TRACE is activated, and in addition, if system statistics such as events per second of CPU time are needed, SYSTEM–STAT is turned on. START–TIME and STOP–TIME refer to the simulation clock. Note that if there are no events in the calendar or if a terminating condition is met, the experiment may stop before the clock reaches STOP–TIME.

```
{{KBS-expert-run-spec
   INITIALIZATION: initialize-run
   LEARNING-REQUESTED: no
      comment: if introspection is requested
      range: (or yes no)
   RATING-REQUESTED: no
      comment: if scenario rating is to be done, implies goals need
      to be connected
      range: (or yes no)
   LEARNED-DATABASE: nil
      comment: name of file to save learned information
   RULES-REQUESTED: yes
      comment: if automatic diagnosis is required
      range: (or yes no)
   EXPERIMENTS-TO-BE-DONE: e4
      restriction: (TYPE instance KBS-experiment)
   COMPLETED-EXPERIMENTS: e1 e2
   RULE-SET: bottleneck-diagnosis
      comment: specifies rule set to use in diagnosis
   ITERATION-LIMIT: 8
      comment: number of experiments before the expert system gives up
   CURRENT-ITERATION: 3
      comment: the current run number
   BASE-CONTEXT: kbs-start-context
      comment: context where the base model resides, experimental
      contexts are children of it}}
```

Figure 23. Expert system run specification.

```
{{e3
    INSTANCE: KBS-experiment
    EXPERIMENTAL-CONTEXT: kbs-experiment-context3
        comment: context for this experiment, child of base-context
    MODEL-CHANGES: e4-change-spec
        comment: provides a description of the model for this experiment.
            The base-model is altered accordingly
    .....
    ITERATION: 3
        comment: the iteration this experiment corresponds to }}
```

Figure 24. Specification of an experiment.

```
{ event24
    INSTANCE: event-notice
    FOCUS: pittsburgh-reseller
        comment: focus of event, the entity
    EVENT: order-arrival
        comment: event-slot in event-schema
    TIME: "21 April 1985 11:00:00"
        comment: time of execution
    PRE-ACTION: nil
        comment: action to take before event execution
    POST-ACTION: nil
        comment: action to take after event execution
    EVENT-PARAMETER: order10
        comment: event parameters
    RUN-EVENT: run-event
        comment: method to execute event    }}
```

Figure 25. An example Event Notice.

Figure 23 shows the execution profile needed to conduct a series of experiments. It specifies options for model introspection (LEARNING–REQUESTED), goal-directed scenario rating (RATING–REQUESTED), automatic diagnosis and correction of model parameters through rule-based analysis (RULES–REQUESTED, RULE–SET, ITERATION–LIMIT), and management of related experiments (INITIALIZATION EXPERIMENTS–TO–BE–DONE,COMPLETED–EXPERIMENTS, BASE–CONTEXT).

The **KBS-experiment** schema in Figure 24 describes individual experiments. The slot MODEL–CHANGES is filled with a set of "change specs," which describe the changes that need to be performed on the model before the start of each experiment. In addition there are slots (not shown) whose values reflect the status of that experiment.

KBS supports a feature rarely found in traditional simulation environments. It is the ability to conduct a series of experiments without human intervention. The important point to note is that individual experiments are not disjoint but are improvements on past experiments, where the improvements are automatically achieved by rule bases detailing the diagnosis/correction heuristics. In order to work correctly, the rules must allow for reasoning between several model scenarios. Management of alternate scenarios in KBS is possible by creating a context tree where each context is devoted to a scenario.

4.3   Simulation Execution

In discrete-event simulation the system changes state at discrete points in time. Running the model simply consists of executing the next imminent event from the calendar of events until there are no more events to execute or some halting criteria are satisfied. Each event notice in the calendar specifies the name of the event, its focus, the time, and any parameters that should be available at the execution time. In the example event notice (see Figure 25) an event "order-arrival" is to occur on "21 April 1985" at 11:00:00 AM simulated time and is focused around **pittsburgh-reseller**. The execution of this event is accomplished by the following steps:

- The simulation clock is advanced to "21 April 1985 11:00:00."
- The value of the slot ORDER–ARRIVAL of the schema **pittsburgh-reseller** is extracted.
- Each item found in the list of values is interpreted.

The items found in the list of values in the Event slot may be representing a LISP function, a *rule*, or an *instrument* which are designed to collect data, display some text, or produce graphic side effects. Simulation proceeds by successively executing event notices until a prespecified terminating condition is met.

4.3.1   Checkpoints and Interrupts

Checkpoints are used in KBS to save the state of a model *during the experiment* along with run time system information such as the simulation clock, the calendar, and other global variable bindings. Checkpoints are also implemented through the use of contexts. Before the experiment is initialized, a new context *kbs-run-context-n,* which is a child of the experiment context, is created to protect that experiment from getting "corrupted" by subsequent modifications. After the "prime event" (i.e., the event that sets the simulation in motion) another context *kbs-run-context-n+1,* a child of *kbs-run-context-n,* is spawned. In addition, the user may interrupt the simulation any number of times to *checkpoint* the model. This facility allows the user to backtrack to some previous point in execution to compare the differences between progressive scenarios. We refer to checkpoints as snapshots of models *within* the same experiment. Checkpoints are useful when comparing different scenarios in a single experiment.

4.3.2   Tracing

A simulation analyst often follows hunches when debugging simulation models. This style of debugging is different from stepping instruction by instruction, which can be frustrating if, for instance, the analyst is only interested in events focused around **pittsburgh-reseller**. In tracing with graphics, the user fills in a *trace specification,* and

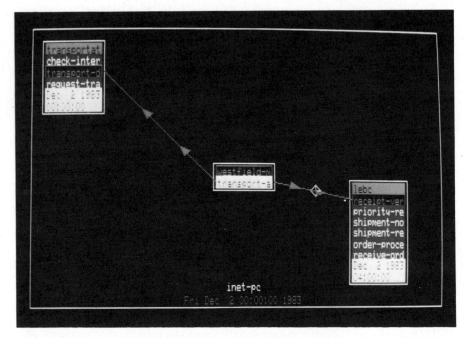

Figure 26. Tracing with graphics in actual runs.

the system traces only under conditions declared in the schema. For example, it is possible to selectively observe **pittsburgh-reseller:** *order-arrival* when *scheduling,* in which case all other events are deemed uninteresting and will not feature in the trace. It is also possible by default to trace everything.

In Figure 26 we show a photograph displaying the event-to-event interaction in the CDS model. The rectangle in the center shows the focus of the current event, "westfield-manufacturing" scheduling two other events focused around "lebc" and "transportation." In practice, we found this to be a powerful feature because it makes the modeler understand the internal workings of the model, thus improving one's confidence in the results of the model.

4.3.3   Stepping

In tracing we saw how events are displayed while they execute. However, due to the limitations of the screen or due to the unavailability of a graphics device, it is useful to have a *stepping* capability. As events are executed, they change values of attributes, and such state changes are observed step by step in a window dedicated to stepping. A *step* command is all that is needed to switch on this kind of trace. Stepping is similar to tracing everything but without the use of graphics. Attribute value bindings are also shown here because information is displayed textually. To summarize the difference between tracing and stepping, it is easier to detect event attribute chains in tracing, but it is not possible to observe individual event parameters, which is better done by stepping.

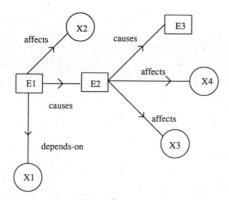

Figure 27. Event tracks.

4.3.4 Event Tracking

The automatic analysis of simulation data (Section 5) requires the recording of event sequences and their interaction with entities and their attributes.

For example, Figure 27 is an example of an event track which includes events E_i and attributes X_j. If we declare that X_1 *causes* E_1 because E_1 *depends on* X_1, then the system can automatically deduce that X_1 indirectly affects X_4, thus tracing a causal path from X_1 to X_4.[8]

Event tracks are stored as metainformation attached to slots which define event behaviors and attributes which are accessed or affected by events.

4.3.5 Simulation Animation

Graphic animation is sometimes the most effective way to represent the dynamics of a simulation. In very large models the screen may not be large enough to display all the information at once to all audiences. In such cases several views of the model may be presented just as is done in perusal. Here, in addition to intelligent use of changing icons and colors, special effects such as flashing and lifelike movement may be shown.

Figure 28 shows the use of changing colors of icons, and animation can be used to effectively communicate the performance of a model scenario.

4.3.6 Report Generation

In KBS, performance data is collected by "instrumenting" the model. The data thus collected is stored in the instrument itself or in some other schema. This data has to be summarized and presented before it can be of any use. These summary reports themselves can be generated by using *report instruments* that are attached to event

---

[8]There is an important limitation in the automatic detection of cause–effect chains when the attributes are included. The system can only detect how an event affects an attribute and not vice-versa. For example, the system is capable of detecting the fact that the inventory is reduced when the event "sell-goods" is executed. But another fact that the reduction in inventory has the effect of causing the event "order-for-goods" goes unnoticed. However since the value of "inventory" is accessed during the event "order-for-goods," for automatic tracing we may make the assumption that *accesses* implies *depends-on*.

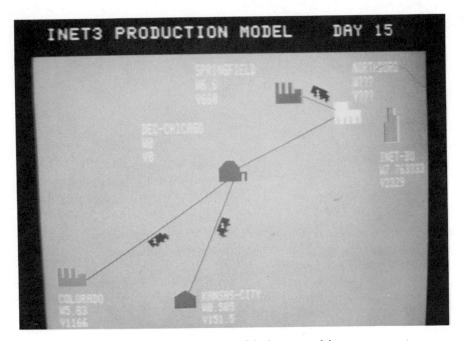

Figure 28. Animation of the inet-pc model.

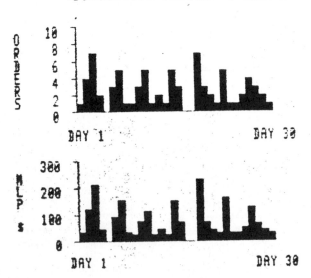

Figure 29. Example of business graphics.

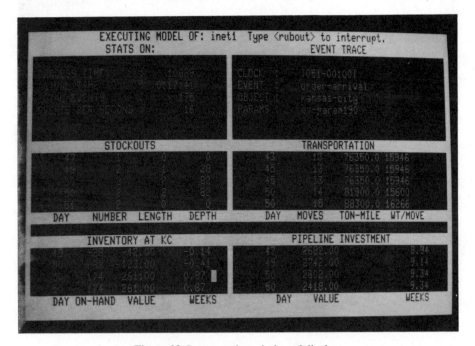

Figure 30. Reports using windowed displays.

slots. As the events are executed, appropriate reports also appear as those instruments are executed. This can take the form of a *textual report* or *graphic side effect* which updates the display screen.

Figure 29 is a typical bar chart produced by KBS. Figure 30 shows how a summary report can be displayed using multiple windows.

4.4   Experiment Rating

The **inet-pc-goal1** discussed in the example on rating scenarios was actually implemented on a model of a distribution network. After a few days of simulated time the goal was evaluated and reported.

Figure 31 shows a goal evaluation report produced by KBS for the CDS model.

This result indicates that customer satisfaction was "bad" because it was rated negatively (–0.9) but the distribution costs were economical and were rated at 0.8, which is "good." However, the overall goal rating is still unsatisfactory because of its negative rating:

$$\text{Overall goal rating}$$
$$= \text{wt. avg. of individual constraint ratings}$$
$$= [0.3 \times 0.8 + 0.7 \times (-0.9)]/(0.3 + 0.7) = -0.39.$$

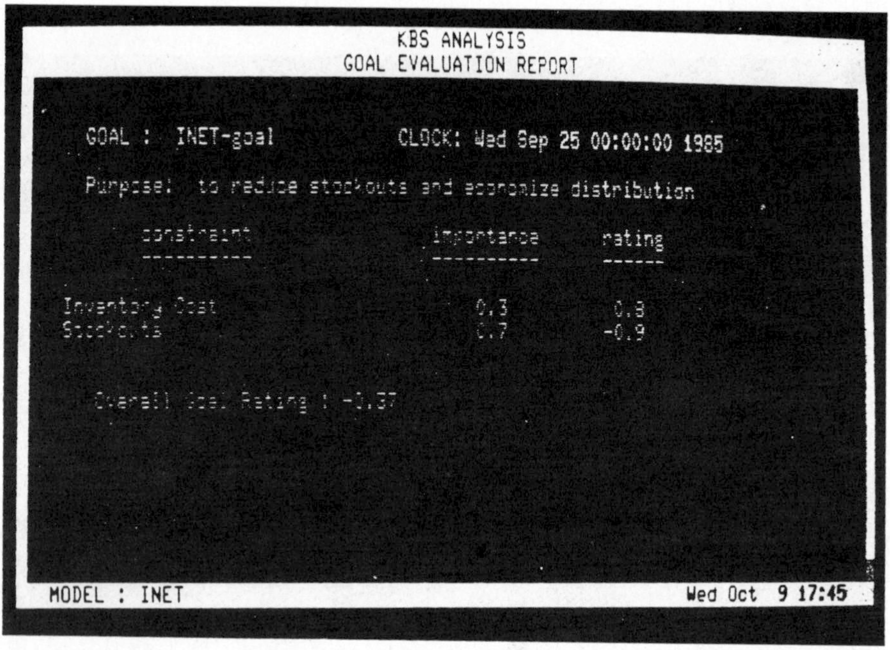

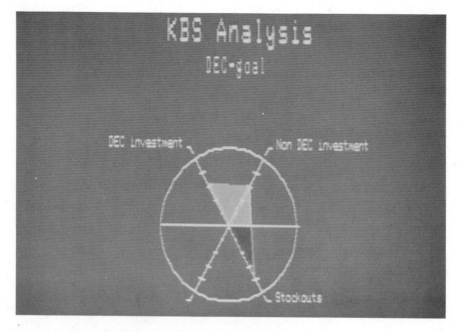

Figure 31. Example of goal evaluation.

Figure 32. Complex goals viewed graphically.

It has been shown in detail how goals, constraints, and instruments work in harmony to rate model scenarios. This means we can collect data from a model run, define and connect goals to the model, and be able to tell how good the model is behaving with respect to the organizational goals. The instruments, goals, and constraints are constructed manually but data collection and reporting are done automatically.

When goals are more complex, they may be viewed graphically with the help of a Kiviat chart like the one shown in Figure 32.

In Kiviat graphs all performance parameters that are good when they assume large values are plotted above the X axis while the performance parameters which are bad when they are large are plotted below the X axis. The shape derived by connecting these parameters can quickly present a view that shows whether the current scenario is good or bad (bad scenarios have large areas below the X axis).

5 AUTOMATIC ANALYSIS OF DATA

A major goal of our research in KBS has been to use knowledge to automate the analysis of data generated by simulation experiments and to suggest ways in which the model can be altered to further optimize the goals and constraints. One method is to use an expert systems approach where a set of experts are interviewed in order to identify and codify their expertise. We believe this is an important first step; any knowledge not widely available to the simulation community at large, which can be made available as part of the simulation system, can have an important impact. An example of this approach can be found in Simulation Craft [5], where expertise is used to identify and correct bottleneck situations. In Figure 33, the report window (upper left) defines the goals to be satisfied by the experiment (e.g., cost, machine breakdown, resource utilization), the exception window (lower right) identifies the constraint deviations (e.g., poor utilization of machines), and the suggestions window (lower left) recommends a change to the model to maximize the goals (add more machines).

In KBS, we have extended this approach. Recognizing that many of the systems which the user wishes to model are quite complex and possibly unique, the amount of available expertise may be limited. Though general rules which describe the causal relations among variables may exist, they may be too general to capture the details of the particular system being modeled. Our approach takes rule-based expertise as a starting point. By analyzing data gathered by event tracking using a procedure known as path analysis, we are able to learn refinements for the rule set.

5.1 Learning Rules Using Path Analysis

Path analysis was originally introduced by Wright [21, 23, 24] as a method of analysis by which the qualitative knowledge that we have regarding causal relations may be combined with the quantitative knowledge of the degree of relationship furnished by correlation and regression. In other words it is a method of measuring the direct influence along each separate causal path in a causal network of variables in a system and thus of finding the degree to which variation of a given effect is determined by each

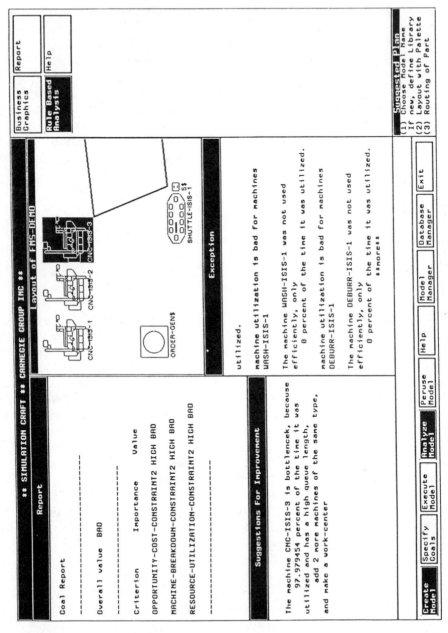

Figure 33. Simulation craft analysis and treatment.

474

particular cause. It must be emphasized that the method of path coefficients is not intended to accomplish the impossible task of deducing causal relations from the values of the correlation coefficients. However, in cases in which the causal relations are uncertain, the method can be used to find the logical consequences of any particular hypothesis.

In KBS, path analysis is used to refine the heuristic knowledge provided by an expert. In particular, it is used to elaborate the simple causal relations normally found in rules to include interactions among variables found "buried" in the model and to refine the degree to which variables are causally related. In other words, KBS performs a type of learning where heuristic knowledge is refined based upon the outcome of simulation experiments. The following outlines the tasks in the learning process:

- A rule is proposed by the domain expert.
- The causal assumptions on which the rule is based are validated against the running model. Validation implies detection of causal chains in KBS models. The rule may need to be modified if the initial causal assumptions were either erroneous or insufficient.
- Alternate causal structures are then proposed and automatically analyzed. The most appropriate causal structure is chosen and the results summarized to yield an equation that reflects the sensitivity of the output parameter with respect to the controllable input parameters. Thus path analysis is used to find the degree to which variation of a given effect is determined by each particular cause in the system being modeled.
- The sensitivity information is used to quantitatively refine the rules.

5.2 A Detailed Example

In the CDS domain several areas for analysis were isolated, namely, inventory policy, capacity planning, topology planning, and operational planning. Of these, inventory planning has been singled out for path analysis mainly because the topic is familiar and numbers are easier to relate to. A typical example will best illustrate the series of steps that are taken to arrive at a refined rule starting from a more general rule proposed by the domain expert.

Example of a diagnosis/correction rule:

IF The Goal is to minimize Stockouts and Average-Inventory is Low and Stockouts are High and Production Rates can be monitored

THEN Increase Production Rate

To be specific, the rule must refer to actual instances of objects in the model, and we proceed with the inet-pc model of the CDS domain shown in Figure 1.

By concentrating on manufacturer M_1 and distribution center D_1 the rule becomes a bit more specific, expressed as:

IF   The Goal is to minimize *D1:stockouts* and

D1: avg-inventory is Low and *D1: stockouts* are High

and *M1:production rate* can be altered

THEN   Increase *M1: production rate*

Drawing upon the CDS model *D1:stockouts* (percentage of orders not filled) is an output parameter and *M1:production-rate* is an input parameter. A few causal structures, as shown in Figure 34, are then proposed which attempt to include the variables in the rule causally connected to each other along different paths.

We first verify with the help of event tracking whether *D1:avg-inventory*, *D1:stockouts*, and *M1:production-rate* are indeed causally connected to each other. For example in Figure 34*b* we must verify whether *M1:production-rate* is connected via an events chain to *D1:stockouts* and *D1:avg-inventory*, and similarly if *D1:avg-inventory* is connected to *D1:stockouts*. The causal chain connecting *M1:production-rate* to *D1:stockouts* is shown in Figure 35.

As can be seen from Figure 36 the causal assumptions for Figures 34*a–d* are valid.

Figure 34*a* is purposely included to show the naive approach which would be taken in the absence of path analysis by ignoring the intermediate variable *D1:avg-inventory*. It must be stressed here that the search algorithm used to discover causal paths can find all paths existing between two model variables given time and resources but currently it returns with the first path found. Thus the causal chain in Figure 35 is not the only

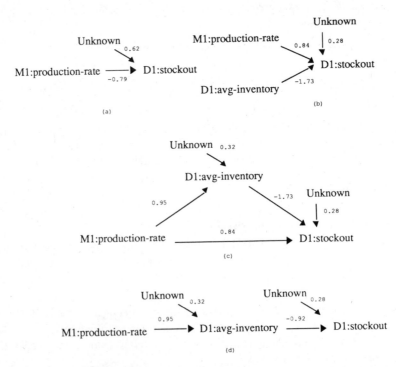

Figure 34. Causal hypotheses in inet-pc model.

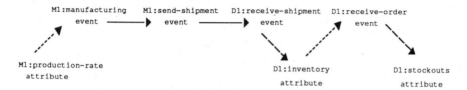

Figure 35. Causal chain derived from event tracking.

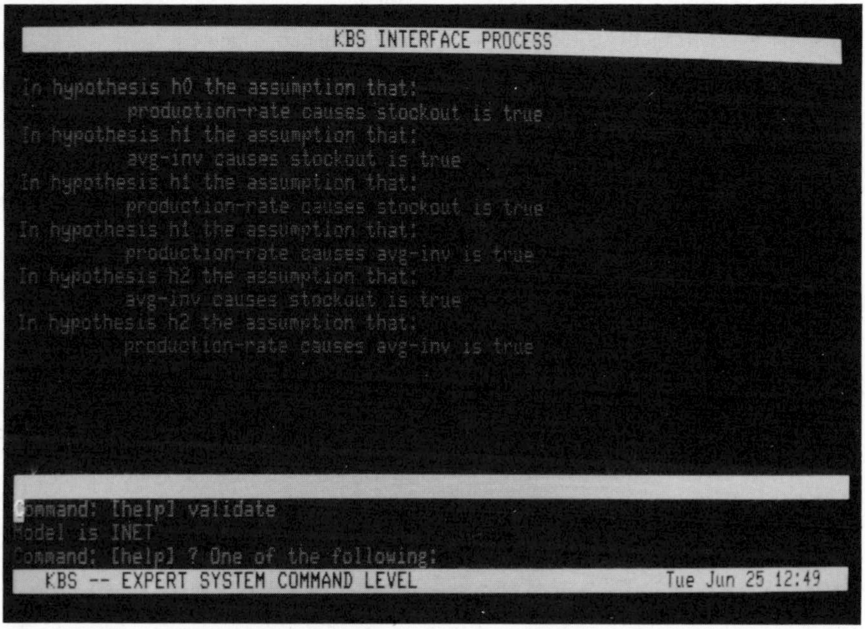

![KBS INTERFACE PROCESS screen showing hypothesis validation text]

Figure 36. Validating hypotheses.

possible path between *M1:production-rate* and *D1:stockouts,* and it would be wrong to place great faith in that path and recommend that the correct causal structure from the several alternatives in Figure 34 is (*d*). [9]

A series of experiments are then designed to measure *D1:avg-inventory* and *D1:stockouts* while changing *M1:production-rate,* and results of these experiments are shown in Figure 37.

Using the preceding results, all alternate causal structures (hypotheses) Figure 34*a* – *d* are subjected to path analysis and the coefficients in the path diagrams are computed. Example schemata from the causal structure representing hypothesis **h1** are shown in Figures 38-41.

---

[9]It is a coincidence that in this example it turns out that it is the most appropriate hypothesis.

Experiment	M1:production rate	D1:stockouts	D1:avg-inventory
1	30	48.592	11.41
2	50	48.449	14.24
3	60	48.470	13.66
4	70	48.290	14.47
5	80	48.205	17.30
6	100	48.122	15.90
7	120	48.248	17.99
8	140	48.152	19.54
9	160	44.256	25.09
10	180	41.264	28.68

Figure 37. Results of experiments on inet-pc model.

```
{{h1
  INSTANCE: causal-network
  MODEL-NAME: inet-pc
    comment: model for which causal analysis is being conducted
  NODES: stockouts1 inventory1 production-rate1
    comment: a set of model variables to be studied
  PATHS: inventory1-stockouts1 production-rate1-to-stockouts1
  production-rate1-to-inventory1
    comment: a set of computed causal paths in the network
  ANALYZE-PATHS: do-path-analysis
    comment: a method for conducting path analysis   }}
```

Figure 38. An example causal hypothesis.

Figure 42 shows the linear regression equations derived from various hypotheses (the schemata for **h1** are shown in Figures 38–41). The residual (unknown) influence on D1:stockouts 0.62 in (*a*) is higher than that in (*b*), (*c*), and (*d*), which is 0.28, thus suggesting that hypothesis (*a*) should be dropped from further consideration. From among (*b*), (*c*), and (*d*) we reject (*b*) and (*c*) because the path coefficient from M1:*production-rate* to D1:*stockout* is positive, leading us to incorrectly believe that increasing production rate results in an increase in stockouts. Thus the most appropriate hypothesis is Figure 34*d*, and from the unstandardized path equations we derive the sensitivity information necessary to improve the rule:

The regression equations:

$$D1:stockouts = -0.418\, D1:avg\text{-}inventory + 54.65,$$

$$D1:avg\text{-}inventory = 0.102\, M1:production\text{-}rate + 7.693.$$

```
{{stockouts1
  INSTANCE: causal-node
  NODE-OF: h1
    comment: causal network this node belongs to
  CAUSES: nil
    comment: nodes caused by this node
  CAUSED BY: inventory1 production-rate1
    comment: nodes which cause this node
  DATA: stockout
    comment: data schema which contains observations and in
      formation for mapping data in the model to data suitable for
      causal analysis
  PATH-EQN: 39.629 - 0.837 production-rate1
    comment: symbolic equation relating this node to all the input
      nodes on which it directly or indirectly depends on, an
      input node is a model variable which can be altered
  REGR-EQN: 48.62 - 0.45 inventory1 + 0.0167 production-rate1
    comment: symbolic equation relating this node to immediately
      preceding nodes on which it directly depends
  RESIDUE:0.116
    comment: unknown component expressed as a standardized path
      coefficient }}
```

Figure 39. An example causal node.

```
{{inventory1-to-stockouts1
  INSTANCE: causal-path
  FROM-NODE: inventory1
    comment: causing node in the path
  TO-NODE: stockouts1
    comment: effect node in the path
  PATH-COEFFICIENT: -1.152
    comment: standardized path coefficient    }}
```

Figure 40. An example causal path.

```
{{stockout
  INSTANCE: model-variable
  OBSERVATIONS: 36.37 31.95 22.87 25.44
    comment: a list of values of the translated model variable,
      one for each experiment
  ACTUAL-VARIABLES: (D1 total-orders) (D1 back-orders)
  TRANSLATE-RESULTS: extract-stockouts
    comment: a message to fill up the observations slot from the
      results of experiments
  MODEL-NAME: inet-pc
  comment: name of model from where data is to be extracted }}
```

Figure 41. The model variable schema.

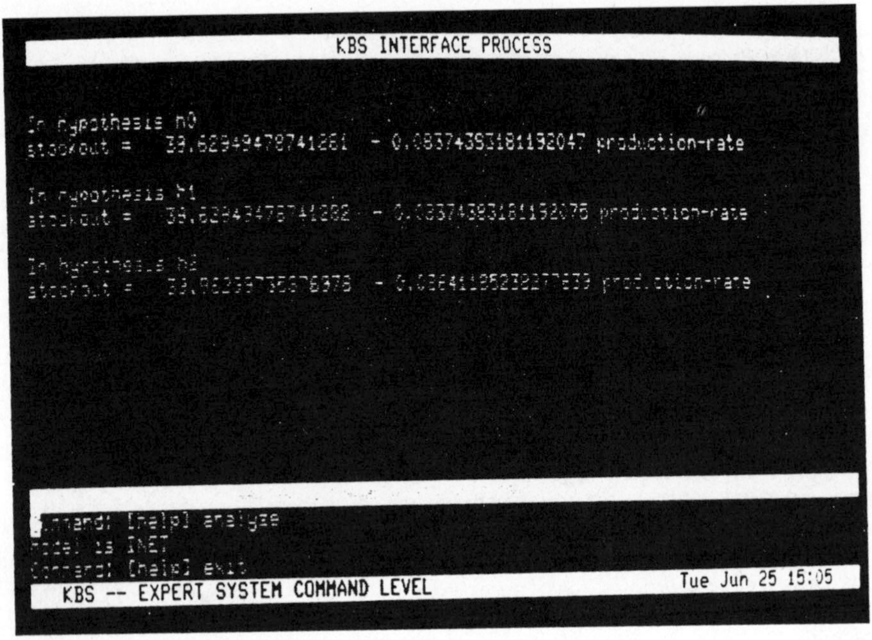

Figure 42. Analyzing hypotheses.

Summarized path analysis:

$$D1:stockouts = -0.0428 \, M1:production\text{-}rate + 51.44.$$

Sensitivity:

$$\delta(D1:stockouts)/\delta(M1:production\text{-}rate) = -0.0428,$$

$$\delta(M1:production\text{-}rate)/\delta(D1:stockouts) = -23.382.$$

Without path analysis we would have assumed

$$D1:stockouts = -0.038 \, M1:production\text{-}rate + 51.$$

Getting back to the rule, a possible refinement may be

IF The goal is to keep *D1:stockouts* below 40% AND
 D1:avg-inventory < 30 AND
 D1:stockouts are in the range 40–50% AND
 M1:production-rate can be altered
THEN *M1:production-rate* = *M1:production-rate* + 23.38 (*D1:stockouts* – 40).

As seen, in simple cases causal path analysis reduces to ordinary linear regression, and by substituting in the value of the input (causing) variable into the regressed equation, we can predict the expected value of the output (caused) variable. However, in a more complicated case such as that of Figure 34*d*, a causal correction is applied to the regression coefficients before predictions can be made. For a detailed treatment on the subject of path analysis refer to the literature [9, 21, 23, 24].

6   AUTOMATING THE SIMULATION LIFE CYCLE

An important component of a knowledge-based simulation system is the reasoning architecture used to manage the simulation life cycle. Both KBS and Simulation Craft [5] use a goal-directed reasoning architecture where each stage of the simulation life cycle is defined as a separate goal with a set of rules which

- identify subtasks to be performed,
- initialize each subtask at the appropriate time,
- identify when the subtask is completed, and
- signal when the entire goal is completed.

In Figure 4, the bottom right window lists the current sequence of subtasks being managed by the system. In addition, unless required subtasks are completed in one stage; the user cannot move on to the next. For example, in Figure 4, the upper right window defines a set of "pending activities" remaining to be completed before the model is complete enough to be simulated.

Figure 43 defines the goal network in KBS. The following outlines the sequence of activities performed by the user:

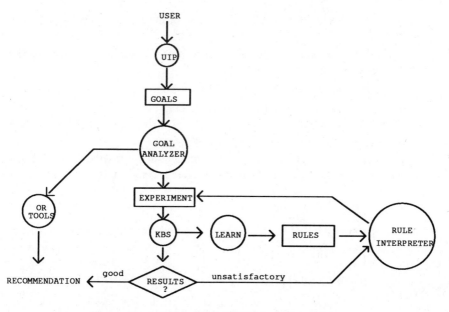

Figure 43. Architecture of a KBS-based expert system.

- The user interface process (UIP) receives a request from the user.
- If it is a simple request for information, the model database is accessed to retrieve the appropriate information.
- If it is a request for a *prescription* (i.e., a goal-oriented request), the request is analyzed by a rule-based *goal analyzer*.
- This analysis may result in invoking an appropriate operations research tool or a specification to conduct a series of experiments or a specification to execute the simulation model in the "learn" mode to detect causal relationships.
- When causal relationships are detected, they may enhance the "domain rule base" which is used in analysis.
- After an experiment is conducted, the results are analyzed. If they are satisfactory with respect to the goal (i.e., a high rating was achieved for that scenario), then a recommendation is made based on the best scenario. If the results are not satisfactory, then the analysis/correction rules are fired, which may generate change specifications for the next experiment to be conducted.

Several types of analyses can be performed by KBS in order to satisfy a specified goal:

- *Static Analysis*   This is used when no time–dependent information plays a role in the analysis.
- *Performance Analysis*   This is used when one of the following is requested:
  - *Rating of a given scenario.*
  - *Analysis:* This is used to detect the causes of unsatisfactory behavior of the model.
  - *Scenario generation:* This is used when a number of scenarios have to be tried before a prescription can be provided.
  - *Trade-off:* This is used when it is necessary to compare several given scenarios.
- *Learning*   If the objective of executing the simulation model is to detect embedded causal relationships, the model is executed in the "learn" mode and subsequently processed by the causal analysis module.
- *Mathematical Analysis*   If the goal analyzer determines that the current request can be satisfied by a mathematical analysis rather than simulation, an appropriate analysis tool will be invoked.

Figure 44 shows a log of the execution of a simulation model which was automatically analyzed resulting in the construction of the improved scenario **kbs-experiment-2.**

The run specifications that produced this analysis are shown being entered by the user in Figure 45.

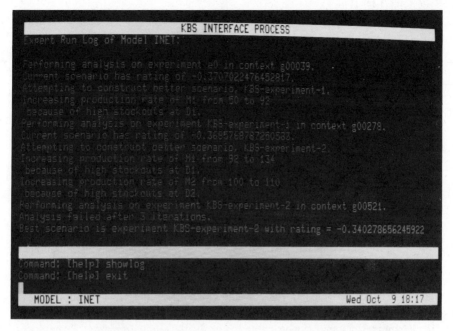

Figure 44. Recommendation from automatic analysis.

```
                        KBS INTERFACE PROCESS
(( INET-expert-run-spec

    learning-requested: ("no")
    rating-requested: ("yes")
    rules-requested: ("yes")
    experiments-to-be-done: ("e0")
    rule-set: ("default-rule-set")
    learned-database: nil
    iteration-limit: (3)
))


Number of experiments before expert system gives up: [5] 3
Is this correct? [yes]
**************Starting run 1 in Context g00039
KBS -- EXPERT SYSTEM COMMAND LEVEL              Wed Oct  9 17:32
```

Figure 45. Simulation run profile.

7 CONCLUSIONS

Since 1980 KBS has been a testbed for experimenting with knowledge-based techniques for model building, execution, and analysis. As such, it has proved invaluable in identifying user needs and testing approaches to solving them. In retrospect, the first step of using a schema representation and a combined object and rule-based programming paradigm for representing simulation knowledge and behavior was perhaps the simplest and most intuitive. It made model creation more easy because models could be built using objects specific to the domain. It also made understanding the model easier. But there is a limit to both the ease of creation and understanding. As models became more complex, the use of simple schema editors did not suffice for creation and perusal. Powerful graphics-based model-building facilities were not explored due to the lack of facilities. By combining good graphics and knowledge-based techniques, such as model verification, interfaces may be constructed to support the building of more complex models.

Perhaps the most important aspect of KBS is its focus on automating the simulation life cycle. First, KBS provides a goal-directed architecture which manages the life cycle enabling the clean interleaving of the reasoning performed by the user and the embedded expertise. Second, KBS provides an automated analysis capability where not only rule-based expertise can identify and recommend corrections for problems, but also rule refinements can be learned by analyzing simulation data. The purpose of performing simulation is to produce data which when analyzed will identify interesting aspects of the model. It is often the case that the data is voluminous and the analyst lacks requisite skills. By embedding knowledge into KBS to automate the analysis, such expertise can be uniformly and consistently applied across many applications.

The ultimate goals of applying knowledge-based systems to simulation should be to reduce the total time in the simulation life cycle and to increase the quality of the results by making available expertise not readily available to the end user. KBS represents a good first step along this path.

ACKNOWLEDGMENTS

The authors thank Digital Equipment Corporation for supporting this and other related research projects in the Intelligent Systems Laboratory. Thanks are also due to Dr. Donald Butcher and Dr. Stanley Wearden for suggesting the use of the path analysis approach to causal analysis.

This research was supported, in part, by Digital Equipment Corporation, Westinghouse Electric Corporation, and the Carnegie Mellon Robotics Institute.

REFERENCES

1. M. S. Fox, "On Inheritance in Knowledge Representation," in *Proceedings of the International Joint Conference on Artificial Intelligence, Los Altos, CA,* 1979.

2. M. S. Fox, "Constraint-Directed Search: A Case Study of Job-Shop Scheduling," Carnegie-Mellon University, Intelligent Systems Laboratory, The Robotics Institute, Technical Report, 1983.

3. M. S. Fox, "Observations on the Role of Constraints in Problem Solving," in *Annual Conference of the Canadian Society for the Computational Studies of Intelligence*, University of Quebec Press, 1986.

4. M. S. Fox and Y. V. Reddy, "Knowledge Representation in Organization Modeling and Simulation: Definition and Interpretation," in *Proceedings of the Thirteenth Annual Pittsburgh Conference on Modeling and Simulation*, University of Pittsburgh School of Engineering, April 1982, pp. 675–683.

5. M. S. Fox, N. Sathi, V. Baskaran, and J. Bouer, "Simulation Craft: An Expert System for Discrete Event Simulation," in *Simulators III: Proceedings of the SCS Simulators Conference*, The Society for Computer Simulation, San Diego, CA, 1986.

6. G. S. Kahn, "From Application Shell to Knowledge Acquisition System," in *Proceedings of the International Joint Conference on Artificial Intelligence*, Kaufmann, Los Altos, CA, 1987, pp. 355–359.

7. P. Klahr and W. S. Fought, "Knowledge-based Simulation," in *Proceedings of the First Annual Conference of the American Association for Artificial Intelligence*, Stanford, CA, 1980, pp. 181–183.

8. Carnegie Group, "Knowledge Craft," Carnegie Group Inc., Pittsburgh, PA, 1985.

9. C. C. Li, *Path Analysis—a primer*, Boxwood Press, Pacific Grove, CA, 1975.

10. D. McArthur and H. Sowizral, "An Object Oriented Language for Constructing Simulations," in *Proceedings of the International Joint Conference on Artificial Intelligence*, Los Altos, CA, 1981.

11. M. McRoberts, M. S. Fox, and N. Husain, "Generating Model Abstraction Scenarios in KBS," in *Artificial Intelligence, Graphics, and Simulation: Proceedings of the 1985 SCS Multiconference*, The Society for Computer Simulation, San Diego, CA, 1985, pp. 29–33.

12. Y. V. Reddy and M. S. Fox, *"KBS: An Artificial Intelligence Approach to Flexible Simulation,"* Technical Report, CMU-RI-TR-82-1, Robotics Institute, Carnegie-Mellon University, Pittsburgh, PA, 1982.

13. Y. V. Reddy and M. S. Fox, "Knowledge Representation in Organization Modeling and Simulation: A Detailed Example," in *Proceedings of the Thirteenth Annual Pittsburgh Conference on Modeling and Simulation*, University of Pittsburgh School of Engineering, April 1982, pp. 685–691.

14. Y. V. Reddy and M. S. Fox, "KBS: A Knowledge Based Simulator—User's Manual," CMU Robotics Institute, Internal Working Document, June 1983.

15. Y. V. Reddy, M. S. Fox, K. Doyle and J. Arnold, "INET: A Knowledge Based Simulation Model of a Corporate Distribution System," in *Proceedings of the IEEE Conference on Trends and Applications*, IEEE, Gaithersburg, MD, May 1983, pp. 109–118.

16. Y. V. Reddy, M. S. Fox, N. Husain, and M. McRoberts, "The Knowledge-Based Simulation System," *IEEE Software*, March 1986, pp. 26–37.

17. Y. V. Reddy, M. S. Fox, and N. Husain, "Automating the Analysis of Simulations in KBS," in *SCS Multiconference on AI, Graphics and Simulation*, January 1985.

18. M. D. Rychener, "PSRL: An SRL-Based Production Rule System—Reference Manual for PSRL Version 1.2," Technical Report, CMU-RI-TR-85-7, Carnegie-Mellon University, The Robotics Institute, Pittsburgh, PA, 1982.

19. A. Sathi, M. S. Fox and M. Greenberg, "Representation of Activity Knowledge for Project Management," *IEEE Transactions on Pattern Analysis and Machine Intelligence,* **PAMI-7**(5) : 531–552, September 1985.

20. A. Sathi, T. E. Morton, and S. Roth, "Callisto: An Intelligent Project Management System," *AI Magazine,* 34–52, 1986.

21. "SPSS Manual," 1978.

22. B. Venkataseshan and Y. V. Reddy, "An Introspective Environment for Knowledge Based Simulation," in *Proceedings of the Winter Simulation Conference,* 1984.

23. S. Wright, "Correlation and Causation," *Journal of Agricultural Research,* 1921.

24. S. Wright, "The Method of Path Coefficients," *Annals of Mathematical Statistics,* 1934.

25. J. Wright and M. S. Fox, "SRL/1.5 User Manual," Technical Report, Carnegie-Mellon University, Intelligent Systems Laboratory, The Robotics Institute, Pittsburgh, PA, 1983.

19 Applications of Explanation in Financial Modeling

DONALD W. KOSY

The Robotics Institute
Carnegie Mellon University
Pittsburgh, Pennsylvania

The purpose of computing is insight, not numbers.

—R. W. Hamming

1 INTRODUCTION[1]

It is February 1974 and as President of the Battery Company you are a little concerned at the results for 1973 that you have just received. Despite a 20% increase in sales over 1972, profits have decreased by 1%.

You feel that the decrease in profit could be due to a combination of three causes: increase in overhead expenses, decrease in contribution (or profit) margins (difference between selling price and direct manufacturing cost), or a change in product mix toward less profitable units. Alternatively, you would like to know how the additional revenues from increased sales were spent. You would like to investigate the cause of the decreased profit using The Information System.

Thus began the statement of a problem that Malhotra gave to a number of managers and management students as part of his investigation into the utility and feasibility of an English language question-answering system to support management [10, 11]. The prototype system that he developed embodied an early version of what have come to be called "financial modeling languages" [7]. Spreadsheet calculators such as Visicalc [2] are simpler systems that also fall into this class. Although they lack a natural-language interface, these systems allow users to display data interactively, aggregate it, compute functions of it (e.g., averages, percentages, and ratios), and define algebraic models that assist in business decision making. Given historical data, the results they produce are similar to the figures that appear on financial reports. An example of a report generated for the Battery Company is shown in Table 1.[2] Given assumed data

---

[1] The first part of this paper was first published in the *Proceedings of AAAI–84* [8].
[2] These data describe only a one-plant, one-product, one-customer version of the original Battery Company. In a later section, we show a two-customer version.

TABLE 1. Financial Model Results for the Battery Company

	1972	1973	1974	1975	1976
Volume	100.00	120.00	132.00	145.20	145.20
Selling price	35.00	35.00	36.40	37.86	39.37
Gross sales	3500.00	4200.00	4804.80	5496.69	5716.56
Labor/unit	9.00	9.00	9.36	9.73	10.12
Material price/unit	8.00	8.00	8.64	9.33	10.08
Material/unit	8.00	8.00	7.34	7.93	8.57
Shipping/unit	2.00	2.00	2.08	2.16	2.25
Unit cost	19.00	19.00	18.78	19.83	20.94
Variable cost	1900.00	2280.00	2479.49	2879.49	3040.42
Indirect cost	285.00	342.00	371.92	431.88	456.06
Production cost	2185.00	2622.00	2851.41	3311.07	3496.49
Gross margin	1315.00	1578.00	1953.39	2185.62	2220.07
Operating expenses	415.00	630.00	720.72	824.50	857.48
Interest expenses	0	0	0	0	0
Depreciation	35.00	35.00	35.00	29.00	29.00
Management salaries	182.00	236.60	246.06	255.91	266.14
Overhead cost	632.00	901.60	1001.78	1109.41	1152.63
Profit	683.00	676.40	951.60	1076.21	1067.45
Contribution margin	16.00	16.00	17.62	18.03	18.43

and expectations about the future, these systems can also generate hypothetical results, or projections, by simulating the effects of activities that might occur in the future. The first two columns in Table 1, for example, show historical data on Battery Company operations and the last three show projections.

However, neither Malhotra's natural-language prototype nor most of the more recent systems allow our president's question to be asked directly, to wit:

Why did profit go down in 1973 even though gross sales went up?

A little reflection on Table 1 may suggest other similar questions:

Why do gross sales go up? in 1975? in 1976?
Why does gross margin go up so little in 1976?
Why is there a peak in profit in 1975?
Why does unit cost go down in 1974?

These questions call for an explanation of results, not just a presentation of them, and the task of explaining results has traditionally been left to human analysts. The purpose of this chapter is to show that, with suitable underlying models, generating such explanations by machine is not difficult and can be quite useful. The technique to be presented was first developed for use in the ROME system, a reason-oriented modeling environment for business planning managers [9]. A modified version has been incorporated into IFPS/PLUS, a financial modeling language offered by Execucom Systems Corp. [6].

2   THE EXPLANATION PROBLEM FOR FINANCIAL MODELS

2.1   Financial Models

A financial model is a representation of the activities of a business in terms of quantitative relationships among financial variables. Financial variables have some economic or accounting significance, and the relationships among them can generally be expressed by formulas and conditional statements. The time span encompassed by the model is normally divided into time periods, and output is generated by computing values for each variable for each period and displaying the values of selected variables on a report.

There are three categories of formulas in a typical model. *Exact formulas* correspond to definitions and equivalences, for example, "sales = volume × selling price" and "beginning inventory(period) = ending inventory(period −1)". *Approximations* are essentially estimating relationships for endogenous variables, which are variables taken to be "internal" to the system of activities being modeled. These formulas are intended to yield the aggregate effect of (very) complex causal processes without actually simulating or even defining those processes. Examples include the use of historically derived ratios to estimate one value from another and the use of cross-sectional regression equations. Finally, *assumptions* are formulas used to estimate values for exogenous (external) variables, such as the price a firm must pay for its raw materials. All the numerous forecasting methods, such as growth rate factors, trend extrapolation, exponential smoothing, and the like, fall into this category. Table 2 shows the formulas used to generate the numbers in Table 1 grouped into the three categories.

Similarly, there are three kinds of input data to a financial model: *actual data, approximation parameters,* and *assumption parameters.* Actual data are historical, factual, nonnegotiable numbers while the parameters are negotiable numbers, estimates, and assumed values. Approximation parameters appear in the approximation formulas and assumption parameters appear in the assumption formulas. Parameters for the Battery Company model are the constants that appear in Table 2.

If we think of a financial model as a kind of "knowledge base" from which we can "infer" (numerical) properties of business activities, we can make an analogy here with backward-chaining rule-based systems like Mycin. The formulas in a model correspond to rules, and evaluating formulas corresponds to drawing conclusions. Rules change the degree of belief in propositions while formulas change the values of variables. The derivation of a value spawns a directed acyclic graph of subderivations much like the goal tree generated by backward chaining. The amount by which belief in a proposition changes can depend on judgmental factors, and the amount of change in a variable can depend on judgmental parameters. Not to push the analogy too far, a rule-based system is much more complicated since it depends on pattern matching and

TABLE 2. Battery Company Model

Definitions

$$\text{Gross sales} = \text{volume} \times \text{selling price}$$
$$\text{Gross margin} = \text{gross sales} - \text{production cost}$$
$$\text{Variable cost} = \text{unit cost} \times \text{volume}$$
$$\text{Unit cost} = \text{labor/unit} + \text{material/unit} + \text{shipping/unit}$$
$$\text{Material/unit} = \text{material price/unit} \times (1 - \text{volume discount})$$
$$\text{Overhead cost} = \text{operating expense} + \text{interest expense} + \text{depreciation} + \text{mgmt salaries}$$
$$\text{Production cost} = \text{variable cost} + \text{indirect cost}$$
$$\text{Profit} = \text{Gross margin} - \text{overhead cost}$$
$$\text{Contribution Margin} = \text{selling price} - \text{unit cost}$$

Approximations

$$\text{Operating expense} = 0.15 \times \text{gross sales}$$
$$\text{Indirect cost} = 0.15 \times \text{variable cost}$$

Assumptions

$$\text{Inflation} = 0.04$$
$$\text{Depreciation}(74) = 35$$
$$\text{Depreciation}(75) = 29$$
$$\text{Depreciation}(76) = 29$$
$$\text{Selling price}(y) = \text{selling price}(y-1) \times (1 + \text{inflation})$$
$$\text{Management salaries}(y) = \text{Management salaries}(y-1) \times (1 + \text{inflation})$$
$$\text{Labor/unit}(y) = \text{labor/unit}(y-1) \times (1 + \text{inflation})$$
$$\text{Material price/unit}(y) = \text{Material price/unit}(y-1) \times 1.08$$
$$\text{Shipping/unit}(y) = \text{shipping/unit}(y-1) \times (1 + \text{inflation})$$
$$\text{Volume discount} = \begin{cases} 0 & \text{if volume} \le 130 \\ 0.15 & \text{if volume} > 130 \end{cases}$$
$$\text{Interest expense} = 0$$
$$\text{Volume}(74) = \text{volume}(73) \times 1.1$$
$$\text{Volume}(75) = \text{volume}(74) \times 1.1$$
$$\text{Volume}(76) = \text{volume}(75)$$

allows for more than one rule to contribute to the degree of belief in a conclusion. Nevertheless, the analogy suggests that the same explanation techniques that are used in Mycin [4] might also work for financial models. The next section shows why these techniques are inadequate for our problem.

2.2 Explanations

The purpose of an explanation is to make clear what is not understood. Depending on their initial level of understanding, users of financial models can benefit from two sorts of explanations. The first sort deals with the model itself and involves showing how it corresponds to reality and why that correspondence is justified. Such an explanation might include, for example, a description of what financial entity some variable represents and a justification for why some approximation was chosen to assign a value to it. The second sort deals with the results of the model and involves showing how those results were derived and why the derivation produces the results observed. In our work on ROME, we have focused primarily on explaining results rather than explaining models.

There are several kinds of results that we might want explained. First, there are the results that are explicit in the output report and are produced directly by formulas. It seems to us that explaining these is simple. For example, to answer a question like *Why is operating expense equal to 724.84 in 1974?* we can imagine nothing better than a display of the associated formula and the values it was used with. In other words, we interpret a *why* question about the value of a variable as a *how* question about its derivation and show the derivation. A more difficult problem arises, however, if the user questions the formula, for example, *But why does operating expense equal 0.15 ×gross sales?* Clearly, such questions could be answered by providing a justification for the formula, or for its parameter values. But notice that this really calls for an explanation of the model: Why did the model builder choose this formula/this parameter value to compute that variable? How to do that goes beyond our present focus.[3] The other kinds of results are all implicit in the report and hinge on *comparisons* the user makes between values. The questions posed in the introduction ask about results of this kind, and answering them involves explaining the difference. We can classify these kinds of results and their associated explanations along several dimensions.

1. *Referent of Comparison*   All questions focus on a particular variable, which is the subject of the question sentence, but the referent it is compared to depends on the question. In a question about change, for example, "Why did gross sales go up in 1973?", the referent is the value the subject variable had in a previous period. In questions of relative magnitude, for example, "Why is depreciation so small?", the referent is the user's expectation for the value of the focus variable. Otherwise, the referent is explicit, for example, "Why is sales of product A greater than sales of product B?" In any case, the result to be explained is the difference between the focus value and the referent.

2. *Implicit Referents*   There are two sources for a user's expectations about values which we will call "local" and "external." Local expectations come from the set of values observed on the report and are essentially local averages. So, for example, we interpret a question like "Why did gross margin go up so little in 1976?" as *Why is the change in gross margin small in 1976 compared to the average change in other periods?* External expectations come from a user's preexisting knowledge of either analogous or prescriptive values. Analogous values include historical norms, industry averages, values observed for competing firms, and the like, while prescriptive values are goals (target values) the user knows to have been set.

---

[3] But see Swartout [13] for a technique that ought to apply if a financial modeler's knowledge could be suitably represented.

3. *Level of Specificity*   A user may phrase his question in terms of mere difference (Why did x change?), direction of difference (Why did x go up?), or magnitude of difference (Why did x go up so much?). An explanation should take these different levels of specificity into account by referring to directions or magnitudes when the user implies he or she desires it.

4. *Interval To Be Covered*   A question may ask about a single difference (Why does x go up in 1974?), several differences (Why does x go up in 1974–1976), or all the differences (Why does x go up?). We interpret the latter questions as calling for a summary explanation that attempts to account for all the differences in the interval using the same factors. If that is not possible, we would like an answer to at least group similar explanations of individual differences into subinterval explanations and to indicate the contrast among the members of the set. Along the same lines, questions about peaks and dips seem to demand an explanation which covers the interval of inflection (at least two time periods) and accounts for the inflection by a single set of factors or by a contrasting set.

5. *Violated Presuppositions*   In general, a user may ask for an explanation of a result either because he or she simply wants to obtain the reason or because there is a reason to believe the contrary and the user wants to resolve the conflict. He or she can highlight the second case, however, by asking a "why not" question or using a contrastive subordinate clause, for example, "Why did profit go down in 1973 even though sales went up?" It is then necessary to infer the presupposed relationship and to show in the answer why it does not hold for the situation at hand.

It may be seen that the major problem in explaining a difference does not lie in determining the difference of interest. Although a small amount of inference may be required to choose an implicit referent, and perhaps somewhat more to determine a presupposition, if these were problematic, one could simply ask the user to select among the possible interpretations. Nor is there a problem in showing the mathematical derivation of a difference. Rather, the problem lies in clarifying that derivation, which is the topic of the next section.

3   AN EXPLANATION PROCEDURE

While it would be truthful to explain a model's results by exhibiting the formulas, the input data, and exclaiming "The math works out that way," it would not be clear. When we asked human analysts to explain model results, they tended to cite only the most important factors involved. What they did in answering specific questions gave us a set of goals for artificial explanations:

- Distinguish the relevant parts of the model from the irrelevant.
- Distinguish the significant effects from the insignificant.
- Translate quantitative information into a qualitative characterization.
- Summarize if the same reason accounts for more than one result.

3.1   General Strategy

To explain a difference Δy, our general strategy is to first find a set of variables A which "account" for it and then to express that information to the user. Suppose, for the sake of simplicity, that we have a direction question—Why did y go up?—so that Δy is the change in variable y. The relevant part of the model is then the formula that computes y, say f; $\Delta y = f(a_2, b_2, c_2, \ldots) - f(a_1, b_1, c_1, \ldots)$ where the subscripts on the arguments denote the two different time periods; and A is a subset of $S = \{a, b, c, \ldots\}$. We first delete from S all variables that did not change since they clearly have no effect on Δy. Call the reduced set S^*.

To determine A, we need to determine the "significance" of each variable in S^* and collect the smallest subset whose joint significance is sufficient to account for Δy. Our initial approach (the obvious one) was to loop through all possible sums of partial derivatives until nearly all of the difference had been accounted for. For example, we would stop with the single variable a if $(\partial f/\partial a) \Delta a$ were approximately equal to Δy. This method turned out not to work because of two fundamental flaws. First, it assumes that the value of $\partial f/\partial a$ is nearly the same at both time points and this was not always true. When $\partial f/\partial a$ changes markedly from period 1 to period 2, there is no clear way of deciding whether it should be evaluated at a_1, or a_2, or perhaps some value in between. Second, it assumes that all the other variables in S remain constant, and this was rarely true. The result was that the preceding test would often fail on a variable that was significant and succeed on one that was not.

So we defined a new measure, called $\varepsilon(X, y)$, to indicate the *effect* of the set of variables in X on y in one context, such as one time period, relative to another. The general definition is

$$\varepsilon(X,y) = y_2 - f(\mathbf{Z}),$$

where the vector $\mathbf{Z}$ contains the values of variables in X evaluated in context 1 and values for the other variables in S evaluated in context 2. If X contains just the variable a, for example, $\varepsilon(X, y) = y_2 - f(a_1, b_2, c_2 \ldots)$. Thus, $f(\mathbf{Z})$ gives the value y_2 *would have* had if all other variables had changed *except* those in X, and $\varepsilon(X, y)$ gives the amount of y_2 contributed by the change in the X variables. Restating this in words, we measure the effect of a variable by what the result would have been without the influence of that variable, leaving all other influences intact.

To assemble the variables in A, variables from S^* are added to X in order of largest absolute effect $|\varepsilon(\{x_i\},y)|$. When the total effect is large enough for some X, we conclude that $X = A$ and Δy is accounted for. The stopping condition we use is

$$1/\theta > \varepsilon(X,y)/\Delta y > \theta,$$

where θ is the fraction of the difference considered large enough to be sufficient. The upper bound is needed when variables not in X counteract the effects of those in X. If the former effects are large enough, they should be included in X and so the test should fail. The value of θ was set empirically to be 0.80. We also associate with each variable x_i in A its relative effect on y, $\alpha_i(y)$, where $\alpha_i(y) = \varepsilon(x_i, y) / \Sigma |\varepsilon(x_j, y)|$.

When *A* is found, we can answer the original question with an explanation. In general, the answer given includes (1) the differences that account for Δy, (2) the formula f, (3) the primary explanatory variable, and (4) a qualification, which expresses counteracting or reinforcing effects. What we do then depends on the specific form of the question and the contents of A, so before discussing that, it will be helpful to look at a specific example.

3.2 Details

Let us consider the first example from the introduction, *Why did profit go down in 1973 even though gross sales went up?* The following describes the processing steps.

1. *Interpreting the Question* As outlined above, it is necessary to determine the focus of the question, referent of comparison, level of specificity, interval to be covered, and presuppositions. The ROME system uses a pattern-matching parser [3] to extract and label the parts of the input sentence and a straightforward set of linguistic tests to make the determinations. For example, the verb or complement of the main clause establishes the type of comparison, and use of a time modifier sets the interval to be covered. If the referent is implicit, we assume the expectation is local unless it is not satisfied by the data displayed, in which case we look for a global expectation. ROME allows the specification of an external expectation for a value, and so we use that if it exists; otherwise we ask the user what referent context he or she has in mind. In the question at hand, the focus is *profit* for the period 1973, the referent is *profit* for period 1972, and the level of specificity is *direction*.

To apply the explanation procedure, the focus and the referent must be comparable. In the present system, this means they must be computed by the same formula so that the difference in value arises from different contexts of evaluation. The contexts allowed are set by internal indices on the variables (e.g., time, plant, product) which range over different instances of entities of the same semantic type. The types are represented as elements in a semantic network using the framestyle language SRL [14]. If the variables are for some reason not comparable, a message is produced giving the reason.

Our treatment of presuppositions has not gone beyond the ad hoc stage. Currently, we just save the variables involved for later use in deciding when to stop the explanation, as described below.

2. *Identifying Significant Effects* Since both gross margin and overhead cost change in the formula for profit, $S^* = \{\text{margin}, \text{overhead}\}$. Working out the calculations gives

$$\varepsilon(\{\text{overhead}\}, \text{profit}) / \Delta\text{profit} = -269.6 / -6.6 = 40.85,$$

$$\varepsilon(\{\text{margin}\}, \text{profit}) / \Delta\text{profit} = 263.0 / -6.6 = -39.85,$$

$$\alpha_{\text{overhead}} = -0.506,$$

$$\alpha_{\text{margin}} = 0.493.$$

Since neither value of ε / Δ passes the significance test, both are needed to explain the difference. The procedure discovers this when it considers $X = \{$overhead, margin$\}$ after determining that $X = \{$overhead$\}$ is insufficient. In the case of a no-change question—Why did y remain constant?—a specialist procedure is invoked which looks for canceling effects, or the absence of change in the terms of the formula, or insignificant changes in those terms.

3. *Characterizing Effects Qualitatively* All the differences for variables in A are translated into direction and magnitude descriptors. The magnitude descriptors are normally percentages since these are more familiar to users than our α values.

4. *Expressing the Answer* The answer generator is template driven, where the templates are just those needed to express formulas, simple comparisons between variables, change, relative significance, reference to change, conjoined noun phrases, and contrast between propositions. The first sentence states either the most significant cause of the difference based on the α values or all the causes if they are positively correlated with the difference. For the question at hand, the first sentence is

Profit went down in 1973 because overhead cost went up and profit = gross margin – overhead cost.

The next sentence expresses the qualification, if any, such as a contrast among counteracting factors, a statment of primary cause, or a statement of additional cause. In this case, the qualification is

Although gross margin went up by 19%, overhead cost went up by 41% and the latter outweighed the former.

5. *Continuing the Explanation* Without the presupposition, the explanation would normally stop at this point with the message *Would you like me to continue?* However, since the answer has not yet mentioned gross sales, it has not yet been related to the presupposition, so we continue down the derivation path that leads to gross sales. The four previous steps yields the following continuation:

Gross margin went up in 1973 primarily because gross sales went up and gross margin = gross sales – production cost. However, the increase in gross sales did not increase gross margin enough to yield an increase in profit given the other factors. Would you like me to continue?

Notice that the qualification is one relevant to the violated presupposition, not the contrast between sales and production cost that would otherwise be generated. It is known that the increase is not enough because gross sales has a positive influence on gross margin and hence on profit but the change in profit was negative.

Continuing one step further will illustrate two final points. Since the presupposition variable has been mentioned, the system returns to the primary path:

Overhead cost went up in 1973 because operating expenses and management salaries went up and overhead cost = operating expenses + interest expenses + depreciation + management salaries. The increase in overhead cost was due largely to the increase in operating expenses. However, the effect of management salaries was also significant to the change in profit.

First, it is important to notice that the last sentence mentions an effect on the initial difference to be explained. It can happen that, while sufficient to explain a local difference, a particular set of variables A is not sufficient to account for a difference higher up in the derivation tree. That is, the higher-level difference would not have been observed without the effect of variables that happen not to be significant to the local difference. Hence, the general strategy described in the preceding section also includes a test for significance with respect to higher-level variables and adds variables to A as required. These secondary "long-distance" effects are important to an accurate explanation and would be missed by a purely local analysis.

Second, the explanation halts at this point since it has reached the leaves of the derivation tree. We define a leaf to be either an input value to the model or a result produced by a formula that refers to the focus variable. The latter case comes from the fact that when a formula is "recursive" in this way, the difference in question is produced by the *values* of the subordinate terms, not differences in those values. We do not continue beyond an explanation of values since there is no clear way of deciding on a single variable to explain next.

4   EXPERIMENTS

The preceding sections have presented an explanation procedure which couples an analytic technique with a natural-language facility in order to explain differences between values of variables. The procedure seems to work well when

- only a few variables out of many account for the difference to be explained,
- the variables form a natural hierarchy via their formulas,
- lower-level variables and their values have a priori meaning to the user, and
- the complexity of the model comes from the depth of the derivation trees, not the complexity of the computations.

These conditions are well met in many financial models, and the procedure can be applied to a number of contrastable situations, such as current versus past, scenario versus scenario, and actual versus budget. The following sections present concrete examples of these applications which we have been experimenting with to determine the power and limitations of the method. For purposes of reference, we will call the procedure ERGO since it is being used as the basis for the ERGO (explaining results generated by others) module of ROME.

TABLE 3. School Board Budget Summary ($1000)[a]

	1983	1982	Difference	%
Administration cost	$635.36	$614.19	$21.17	3.00
Instruction	8,326.56	7,722.45	604.11	7.82
Pupil services	465.52	427.45	38.03	8.90
Health services	152.49	141.08	11.42	8.09
Transportation	1,776.19	1,545.73	230.45	14.91
Plant o&m	2,289.51	2,009.61	279.90	13.93
Fixed charges	2,164.37	1,850.85	313.52	16.94
Food services	30.19	41.26	−11.11	−26.90
Student activities	217.52	208.76	8.75	4.19
Community services	31.62	27.85	3.77	13.54
Capital outlay	127.68	105.14	22.53	21.43
Debt service	1,381.80	1,468.35	−86.55	−5.89
Outgoing transfer	685.64	655.66	29.98	4.57
Budget reserve	25.00	30.00	−5.00	−16.67
Loan payments	125.00	115.00	10.00	8.69
Total	18,434.44	16,963.47	1,470.97	8.67

[a]o&m, operations and maintenance.

4.1   Experiment 1: Budget Comparisons

A budget can be viewed as the output of a very simple sort of financial model in which nearly all the formulas are definitional sums. If a budget report presents past values for expense items as well as current values, it is hard not to wonder why current values differ significantly from those in the past and what changes in circumstances had the greatest effect. ERGO can answer these questions directly.

Table 3 gives a top-level summary of the 1983 budget for a Pittsburgh area school district. Also shown are the corresponding 1982 figures and the amounts by which the 1983 figures increased over 1982. We chose this budget because when it was issued, it was accompanied by a short report containing human-generated explanations of the increases. Hence, it provides a test of whether ERGO's explanations are similar to those of human analysts.

No explanation was given for the top level differences but ERGO's answer is shown below:

> Total went up in 1983 primarily because instruction, fixed charges and plant o&m went up and total = administrative cost + instruction + pupil services + health services + transportation + plant o&m + fixed charges + food services + student activities + community services + capital outlay + debt service + outgoing transfer + budget reserve + loan payments. The increase in total was due largely to the increase in instruction.

When a result is derived from a sum, the effect ε of a subordinate variable is equal to the difference in its value between the focus and referent contexts. Hence, it is easy to see why ERGO selected the three variables with the greatest increase as primary causes of the difference in total.

Note, however, that transportation was not included in this set even though its increase was not much smaller than the increase in plant operations and maintenance. This is due to a threshold effect: transportation was simply not needed to account for a θ of 80% of the increase in total, given the magnitude of the other increases. If θ had been 85%, transportation would have been counted as a significant factor. Now, of course, a user can set threshold θ to be as high as he or she wants, but the question remains as to whether it is misleading to omit mention of an effect when it is actually a close call. In the case of sums, we currently believe that such omissions *are* misleading, so we should continue to bring variables into X even after the θ test has been met until the next effect to be included is appreciably less than the last effect included. However, we have not yet changed the procedure to do this.

The human-produced explanations relate to the lower levels of the budget, and so we will proceed to those. The instruction budget breakdown is shown in Table 4, and the reason the total goes up is shown below:

Why does instruction go up in 1983?

Instruction went up in 1983 primarily because teacher salaries went up and instruction = teacher salaries + nonteacher salaries + books + supplies + library + audio-visual material + other material + training + miscellaneous instruction + contract services. Would you like me to continue? **yes**

Teachers salaries went up in 1983 because average wage went up and teachers salaries = average wage × teacher staff. Although teacher staff went down by 2%, average wage went up by 11% and the latter outweighed the former.

TABLE 4. The Instruction Budget

	1983	1982	Difference
Teacher salaries	6,649.40	6,038.78	610.62
Nonteacher salaries	1,109.43	1,137.21	−27.78
Books	67.96	52.23	15.73
Supplies	241.40	234.20	7.20
Library	44.90	46.10	−1.20
Audio-visual material	19.90	19.19	.71
Other material	11.90	13.30	−1.60
Training	34.45	36.33	−1.88
Miscellaneous instruction	20.54	26.55	−6.01
Contract services	126.68	118.56	8.12
Total instruction	8,326.56	7,722.45	604.11

The corresponding human explanation is

- a new contract with the PSEA is presently being negotiated,
- decrease in teaching staff, and
- salary increases in administration.

Do these explanations agree? Well, they would (partially) if it were known that the new PSEA (teacher union) contract was expected to require higher teacher wage rates. In Helman and Bahuguna [5], this sort of explanation is termed "genetic," meaning that the numeric change is an outcome of an external event and the genesis of that event (i.e., what led up to it) tells why the change occurred. In ERGO, however, there is no way of linking changes in variable values to external events, such as the inception of a new contract with a new wage scale. In general, there is no easy way to express the occurrence of nonnumeric events algebraically, and so they are typically reflected in algebraic models by changes in input values. The system described in reference 5 requires its users to annotate changes in input values with a textual explanation of the change. But, as the authors are quick to point out, such explanations are just text and do not express any analysis done by the system. If there were a good way to link changes in values to a symbolic representation of events and event sequences, then it might be possible to pursue an explanation further. However, this would clearly go beyond the scope of the ERGO procedure, and other explanation techniques would have to be employed.

The last statement in the human explanation is interesting because ERGO's analysis shows it to be wrong. While administrator salaries (i.e., the salaries of school principals and assistant principals) do in fact go up in the 1983 budget, they are part of nonteacher salaries, which in the aggregate go down. Hence, administrator salary increases cannot be a significant component of the increase in instruction cost. Furthermore, if we dig deeper, we find that they are not even a significant part of the change in nonteacher salaries:

Why do nonteacher salaries go down in 1983?

Nonteacher salaries went down in 1983 primarily because aides went down and nonteacher salaries = principals + directors + librarians + aides + secretaries. Although librarians went up by 14% and secretaries went up by 5%, aides went down by 57% and the latter outweighed the former.

Thus we see that the school district is budgeting a substantial reduction in teaching aides, which is offset somewhat by increases for librarians and secretaries, but the increases for administrators are insignificant. Why administrators should be singled out for mention by the human commentator is not something that can be justified by the facts at hand.

The next most important cause of the increase in total budget after instruction costs is fixed charges, which consists of insurance premiums and equipment rentals. The human-produced explanation is uninteresting for our purposes because it only cites rate increases, and there was no data to give to ERGO about these rates. Hence we turn to the third cause, plant o&m increases:

Why does plant o&m go up in 1983?

Plant o&m went up in 1983 primarily because o&m salaries, utilities, equipment replacement, and building equipment went up and plant o&m = o&m salaries + o&m supplies + fuel + utilities + other o&m + site equipment + building equipment + equipment replacement + o&m contracts. Although site equipment went down by 53.5, o&m salaries went up by 119.38, utilities went up by 97.33, equipment replacement went up by 45.17, and building equipment went up by 32.6 and the latter outweighed the former. Would you like me to continue? **no**

Why do utilities go up in 1983?

Utilities went up in 1983 because electricity, water, sewer, and telephone went up and utilities = water + sewer + electricity + telephone. The increase in utilities was due largely to the increase in electricity. Would you like me to continue? **yes**

Electricity went up in 1983 because electricity(1983) = electricity(1982) × [1 + %electricity rate change(1983)] and %electricity rate change(1983) = 0.19.

This may be compared with the following human-generated commentary:

- Salary increases, except for one, are according to Bargaining Agreement.
- Utilities up because of rate increases.

ERGO cites equipment replacement and building equipment because those increases are necessary to offset the effect of site equipment reductions on the overall rise in plant o&m. Otherwise, ERGO mentions the same factors—salaries and utilities—as the human-produced explanation. With regard to utilities, the projected rate increases did happen to appear in the budget, and so their inclusion in the model allowed ERGO to go down to the rate level.

One capability ERGO lacks that would make its explanations more humanlike in the budget domain is the ability to summarize across components of a sum when all the component values are computed by a similar formula and that formula has the same semantic meaning for each component. For instance, the values of the four components of 1983 utilities are obtained by multiplying the 1982 value times a constant factor, and each multiplication represents projected growth. Likewise, aggregate salary values are typically derived from components whose values are obtained by multiplying a wage rate times number of persons. Human analysts recognize this semantic similarity and so can give one explanation that covers a whole class of effects. If ERGO could recognize, or be told, that certain functional forms involving certain types of variables have certain meanings, for example, *basis* × *growth rate* or *price* × *quantity*, it too could make the generalizations that humans make without descending to each component individually. Thus, it could not only state that electricity expenses went up because of a rate increase but also that utility expenses as a class went up because of rate increases. As shown in the preceding commentary, this is what the human analyst did.

4.2   Experiment 2: What-If Cases

A what-if case is a model that differs from a "base case" by changes in input values and/ or changes in formulas. These changes can represent different assumptions about the future environment of a business, or different choices among actions the business might take, or both. The output of a what-if case is then a prediction of the consequences of the different assumptions or choices. The use of what-if cases is the primary means by which simulation models are used to help make planning decisions.

Differences between case results can be explained by asking ERGO questions that specify different cases as focus and referent contexts rather than different columns. The explanation will reveal the path by which a change in input led to a change in output. This path may yield some surprises, particularly if the model contains nonlinear elements such as conditionals or higher-degree polynomials.

As an example, suppose we reduce the assumed volume growth in the Battery Company model from 10 to 5% and call this new model case 1. We would expect projected profit to be less than the base case, which we will call case 0. Running the new model will tell how much of a decrease occurs and explaining the difference will tell why.

The output of case 1 is given in Appendix A. It shows that profit is indeed less in the projected years, 1974–1976, and the explanation for 1974 is as follows:

Why is 1974 profit less in case 1 than in case 0?

Profit was smaller for case 1 primarily because gross margin was smaller and profit = gross margin – overhead cost. Would you like me to continue? **yes**

Gross margin was smaller for case 1 because gross sales was smaller and production cost was larger and gross margin = gross sales–production cost. The difference in gross margin was due largely to the difference in gross sales. Would you like me to continue? **no**

This may be unexpected. How is it that lower volume led to higher production cost? We ask:

Why is 1974 production cost higher in case 1 than in case 0 even though volume is lower?

Production cost was larger for case 1 primarily because variable cost was larger and production cost = variable cost + indirect cost. Would you like me to continue? **yes**

Variable cost was larger for case 1 because unit cost was larger and variable cost = unit cost × volume. Although volume was smaller by 5%, unit cost was larger by 7% and the latter outweighed the former.

Now we see that unit cost is somehow volume dependent. The path ERGO followed was chosen so that it would lead to the volume variable because the initial question expressed a violated presupposition about volume (cf. Section 3). In this case, that path happens to be the same as primary path. Continuing along this path, we get:

> Unit cost was larger for case 1 solely because material/unit was larger and unit cost = labor/unit + material/unit + shipping/unit. Would you like me to continue? **yes**
>
> Material/unit was larger for case 1 solely because volume discount was smaller and material/unit = material price/unit × (1 − volume discount). Would you like me to continue? **yes**
>
> Volume discount was smaller for case 1 solely because volume was smaller and volume discount = vdiscount(volume). vdiscount(v) = (if (< v 130) 0.0 else .15). Would you like me to continue? **yes**
>
> Volume(case 1,1974) is an input item so I can go no further.

It should not be surprising that the difference in profit depends ultimately on the difference in volume since that was the only variable changed. What the explanation procedure adds is how that change propagated out to other variables of interest.

For contrast, consider a second case where instead of reducing volume growth by 5%, we increase unit cost growth by 5%. Output for this case is also shown in Appendix A. As expected, projected profit is reduced and the reason is the increase in unit cost. (The explanation is rather similar to the one just given so we do not show it.) However, profit in case 1 is somewhat smaller than profit in case 2 (707.78 vs. 816.50). Why should this be so when a 5% decrease in volume should have about the same effect on cost as a 5% increase in unit cost? Given what we know about volume discount in case 1, we might suspect that this factor was the cause. To find out, we can ask: Why is 1974 profit lower in case 1 than in case 2? The salient parts of ERGO's explanation are excerpted in the following:

> Profit was smaller in case 1 because gross margin was smaller. Although overhead cost was smaller by 3%, gross margin was smaller by 8% and the latter outweighed the former.
>
> Gross margin was smaller in case 1 because gross sales was smaller. Although production cost was smaller by 3%, gross sales was smaller by 5% and the latter outweighed the former.
>
> Gross sales was smaller in case 1 solely because volume was smaller.

Thus we see that profit was more sensitive to the decrease in gross sales revenue in case 1 than it was to the change in production cost. Production cost was actually lower in case 1 because the effect of lower volume outweighed the increase in unit cost caused by loss of the volume discount. We can conclude that the Battery Company should pay more attention to meeting its initial volume projections than to controlling costs, if it cannot do both.

If we view volume and unit cost as at least partially controllable variables, then the difference in profit between the two cases is a measure of the relative worth of two different courses of action. Explanations can then be viewed as giving reasons why one action leads to a better outcome than another. At least one expert system, the QBKG backgammon program [1], has used a similar sort of procedure to explain the reasons for the actions it recommends. This was possible because the actions were chosen using a quantitative evaluation function and the terms in this function, were defined so as to have a priori meaning to backgammon players.

As formulated, the Battery Company model cannot tell us why profit is more sensitive to volume than to unit cost. The answer is that the contribution margin on a battery is so high that changes in volume are more important than similar percentage changes in unit cost. In the next experiment, we look at a different formulation of the model which shows this effect more clearly.

4.3   Experiment 3: Variance Analysis

Variance analysis is an accounting technique for determining why actual results do not match budget figures. Like the ERGO procedure, it uses an analysis of lower-level differences to identify the causes of higher-level differences. The differences are called "variances" (meaning "variance from the budget"), but unlike ERGO, the amount of difference is expressed in dollars. This amount tells how much of the variance in a top-level variable (profit, revenue, production cost, etc.) was contributed by each lower-level variance independent of all other variances. A variance is called "favorable" if it contributes positively to profit. A variance is called "unfavorable" if it contributes negatively. For example, revenues higher than budgeted produce favorable variances; costs higher than budgeted produce unfavorable variances. (Note that variance analysis in accounting is not the same as analysis of variance in statistics.)

Variances are further divided into two other categories depending on whether they stem from variances in quantity (e.g., number of units sold, amount of raw material used) or variances in price, cost, or contribution margin (contribution margin = unit price–unit cost). The former are called "activity" or "volume" variances and the latter are called "price," "cost," or "efficiency" variances. Variances that do not depend on quantity, such as period costs, are not subdivided. So, in analyzing a variance in gross margin, for instance, the equivalent top-level model formula would be

$$\text{gross margin} = \text{volume} \times \text{contribution margin} - \text{indirect cost}$$

so that the contribution of the three right-hand side variables to gross margin can be contrasted directly.

It is easy to extend variance analysis to situations where a top-level variable is the sum of several lower-level variables, each of which depends on volume and efficiency factors. Such situations include the case of total revenue being the sum of revenues from several products, total profit being the sum of profits from several divisions, total variable cost being the sum of costs for several materials and types of labor, and so on. For each way in which a variable can be disaggregated, one can construct an equivalent volume/efficiency/period cost formula where the efficiency term is the average over

TABLE 5. Top-Level Variances for ABC Company

ABC	Actual	Budget	Variance
Volume	257.00	309.00	−52.00
Selling price	30.38	32.67	−2.29
Gross sales	7,808.15	10,094.52	−2,286.37
Production cost	5,267.87	6,258.30	−990.43
Unit cost	17.92	17.61	.31
Indirect cost	690.88	816.30	−125.42
Operating expense	1,171.22	1,514.18	−342.96
Administrative expense	42.00	42.00	0.0
Selling expense	52.00	52.00	0.0
Depreciation	35.00	35.00	0.0
Overhead cost	1,300.22	1,643.18	−342.96
Profit	1,240.05	2,193.04	−952.99
Contribution margin	12.46	15.06	−2.60

the lower-level components and the other two terms are totals.

To illustrate ERGO's explanation of variances, we define a hypothetical company called ABC which has two distribution channels, wholesale and retail. The same product is distributed via each channel but the wholesale channel involves no shipping charges (goods are picked up at the factory) and the retail operation does some advertising which generates a selling expense. The same production process is used for goods distributed either way (they are made in the same factory). Actual results, budget, and variances for the firm as a whole are shown in Table 5; results for each distribution channel are shown in Appendix B.

There is clearly a shortfall in profit, and the cause would appear to be less gross sales. Is the problem in retail, wholesale, or both?

Why is actual profit(abc) less than in the budget?

Actual profit was smaller because gross margin was smaller and profit = gross margin–overhead cost. Although overhead cost was smaller by 20%, gross margin was smaller by 33% and the latter outweighed the former. Would you like me to continue? **yes**

Actual gross margin was smaller primarily because contribution margin and volume were smaller and gross margin = volume × contribution margin − indirect cost. The decrease in gross margin was due largely to the decrease in contribution margin.

An accountant would say that there was an unfavorable profit variance of $953, a favorable variance of $343 in overhead cost, an unfavorable variance of $1296 in gross margin, an unfavorable volume variance of $783, an unfavorable efficiency variance of $803, and a favorable indirect cost variance of $125.

Actual contribution margin was smaller primarily because selling price was smaller and profit margin = selling price − unit cost.

An accountant would say that there was an unfavorable price variance of $707 and an unfavorable cost variance of $96. Since selling price is an input variable, the explanation must stop here.

However, there remains an interesting question. We would normally expect that lowering the price of a product would lead to higher volume of sales, but the opposite occurred for ABC. Why?

> Actual volume(abc) was smaller because retail volume and wholesale volume were smaller and volume (abc) = volume(retail) + volume(wholesale). The difference in volume(abc) was due largely to the difference in retail volume. Would you like me to continue? **yes**

> Focusing on retail, actual volume was smaller because demand at market price and market price were smaller and volume = demand at market price × (market price / selling price) ^ 2.0. Although selling price was smaller by 10%, demand at market price was smaller by 24% and market price was smaller by 5% and the latter outweighed the former.

The explanation procedure can descend below the volume level here, where it could not with the Battery Company, because ABC uses an explicit market forecasting model to set its budgeted selling price and volume. One formula of this model, shown above, projects ABC's volume as a function of the demand for ABC's product at the market price and the ratio of the market price to ABC's price. At the time the forecast is made, the parameters of this model can only be estimated. After the actual results are in, however, the actual parameter values can be observed (or computed from observables) and these, in turn, can be compared to the estimates to explain why the projection did not match. In this case, ABC's demand fell by 24%. Even though it cut its price, so did everyone else, and it was not enough to make up for the low demand.

The market model contains another formula for estimating ABC's demand as a function of total market demand and ABC's advertising. Therefore, we can descend even further to determine the cause of low ABC demand:

> Actual demand at market-price was smaller because total market and ad effectiveness were smaller and demand at market-price = base demand + (total market - base demand) × %stimulus (selling expense) × ad effectiveness. The difference in demand at market-price was due largely to the difference in total market. Would you like me to continue? **yes**

> Total market(actual) is an input item so I can go no further.

Thus, it appears that ABC faces a declining market for its product, and its advertising is not as effective as hoped. In general, an explanation can be pursued to any depth as long as suitable formulas are provided and enough data is available on-line.

What the ERGO procedure adds to conventional variance analysis is an operational definition of significance. Since it is rare for any actual result to ever exactly equal its budget projection, a variance report for a business will normally show variances in everything. Accounting textbooks suggest a variety of statistical procedures and rules of thumb for deciding which variances are worth examining further. We suggest that the significance of a variance depends on the top-level variable of interest. If one is a high-level manager responsible for a firm's total profit, a large variance in the unit cost for a low volume product is not likely to have a significant effect and so is probably unimportant. On the other hand, if one is the manager responsible for that product, a large variance would be quite important. The explanation procedure takes these different points of view into account automatically by responding differently to questions about different variables.

5 DISCUSSION AND CONCLUSIONS

In today's expert systems, the primary purpose of an explanation facility is to tell the user how the system arrived at its conclusions or why it is asking for certain information. In the future, we might expect systems to be developed that in addition can explain why they made certain recommendations over others. In all three cases, an explanation can be viewed as an attempt to answer the implicit question "Why should I trust these results?"

It should be clear from the previous section that explanations of model results serve a different purpose. They answer the question "What's going on here?" where "here" can refer either to the model or to the world the model represents. Such explanations are useful when an analyst is not fully aware of the factors that affect a given variable or does not realize the relative significance of these factors in the case at hand.

Financial modeling is not the only kind of analysis in which an explanation procedure might be used since there are many other types of quantitative planning tools. The key to using an ERGO-like procedure is to identify something to use as a standard of comparison and then to explain the relevance and significance of variables by reference to this standard. For example, there is currently a project underway in our laboratory to couple explanation with critical path analysis to answer questions about construction schedules [12]. In schedules, the variables of interest are subtask durations, start times, end times, and resource requirements. They are linked by precedence, that is, the need for certain subtasks to be completed before others can begin. To determine why a construction project is behind or ahead of schedule, one should look for subtasks that took more or less time than planned or were delayed or accelerated by resource availability. This is analogous to comparing actual against budgeted figures in the financial domain. To determine why one proposed schedule is better or worse than another, one should look for differences that had the greatest effect on overall project duration and resource loading. This is analogous to explaining what-if cases.

Quantitative models, financial and otherwise, are intended to provide their users with insight into the consequences of quantifiable activities. Automated explanation of the results can enhance that insight by focusing the user's attention on the major factors responsible for those consequences.

APPENDIX A.   What-If Results for the Battery Company

Case 1	1972	1973	1974	1975	1976
Volume	100.00	120.00	126.00	132.30	138.92
Selling price	35	35	36.40	37.86	39.37
Inflation	0.04000	0.04000	0.04000	0.04000	0.04000
Gross sales	3500.00	4200.00	4586.40	5008.35	5469.12
Gross margin	1315.00	1578.00	1676.81	1991.45	2123.98
Production cost	2185.00	2622.00	2909.59	3016.90	3345.14
Variable cost	1900.00	2280.00	2530.08	2623.39	2908.82
Indirect cost	285.00	342.00	379.51	393.51	436.32
Unit cost	19	19	20.08	19.83	20.94
Labor/unit	9	9	9.36	9.73	10.12
Material/unit	8	8	8.64	7.93	8.57
Shipping/unit	2	2	2.08	2.16	2.25
Material price/unit	8	8	8.64	9.33	10.08
Volume discount	0	0	0	0.15000	0.15000
Operating expense	415.00	630.00	687.96	751.25	820.37
Management salaries	182.00	236.60	246.06	255.91	266.14
Depreciation	35.00	35.00	35.00	29.00	29.00
Interest expense	0.0	0.0	0.0	0.0	0.0
Overhead cost	632.00	901.60	969.02	1036.16	1115.51
Profit	683.00	676.40	707.78	955.29	1008.47
Contribution margin	16	16	16.32	18.03	18.43

Case 2	1972	1973	1974	1975	1976
Volume	100.00	120.00	132.00	145.20	145.20
Selling price	35	35	36.40	37.86	39.37
Inflation	0.04000	0.04000	0.04000	0.04000	0.04000
Gross sales	3500.00	4200.00	4804.80	5496.69	5716.56
Gross margin	1315.00	1578.00	1818.29	1864.54	1699.52
Production cost	2185.00	2622.00	2986.51	3632.15	4017.04
Variable cost	1900.00	2280.00	2596.97	3158.39	3493.08
Indirect cost	285.00	342.00	389.55	473.76	523.96
Unit cost	19	19	19.67	21.75	24.06
Labor/unit	9	9	9.81	10.69	11.66
Material/unit	8	8	7.68	8.68	9.81
Shipping/unit	2	2	2.18	2.38	2.59
Material price/unit	8	8	9.04	10.22	11.54
Volume discount	0	0	0.15000	0.15000	0.15000
Operating expense	525.00	630.00	720.72	824.50	857.48
Management salaries	182.00	236.60	246.06	255.91	266.14
Depreciation	35.00	35.00	35.00	29.00	29.00
Interest expense	0	0	0	0	0
Overhead cost	742.00	901.60	1001.78	1109.41	1152.63
Profit	573.00	676.40	816.50	755.13	546.89
Contribution margin	16	16	16.73	16.10	15.31

APPENDIX B.   Wholesale and Retail Results for the ABC Company

	Wholesale			Retail		
	Actual	Budget	Variance	Actual	Budget	Variance
Volume	100.00	120.00	−20.00	157	189.42	−32.42
Selling price	26.35	26.35	0.0	32.95	36.68	−3.73
Gross sales	2635.00	3162.00	−527.00	5173.15	6932.52	−1759.37
Gross margin	739.80	816.00	−76.20	1800.48	3020.22	−1219.74
Production cost	1895.20	2346.00	−450.80	3372.67	3912.30	−539.63
Unit cost	16.48	17.00	−.52	18.84	18.00	.84
Indirect cost	247.20	306.00	−58.80	443.68	510.30	−66.62
Operating expense	395.25	474.30	−79.05	775.97	1039.88	−263.91
Administration expense	14.17	13.16	1.02	27.83	28.84	−1.02
Selling expense	0	0	0	52.00	52.00	0.0
Depreciation	13.62	13.59	0.0264	21.38	21.41	−0.0264
Overhead cost	423.04	501.05	−78.01	877.18	1142.13	−264.95
Profit	316.76	314.95	1.81	923.30	1878.09	−954.79
Contribution margin	9.87	9.35	.52	14.11	18.68	−4.57
Demand at market price	—	—	—	147.89	196.67	−48.78
Market price	—	—	—	33.95	36.00	−2.05
Base demand	—	—	—	60	60	0
Total market	—	—	—	455	600	−455
Ad effectiveness	—	—	—	0.8791	1.0	−0.1209

REFERENCES

1. D. H. Ackley and H. J. Berliner, "The QBKG System: Knowledge Representation for Producing and Explaining Judgements," Computer Science Department, Carnegie-Mellon University, March 1983 (abridged in Berliner and Ackley, "The QBKG System: Generating Explanations from a Non-Discrete Knowledge Representation," *Proceedings of AAAI-82*, Morgan Kaufmann, Los Altos, CA, 1982, pp. 213–216).

2. D. H. Beil, *The Visicalc Book*, Reston, Reston, VA, 1983.

3. W. M. Boggs, J. G. Carbonell, and I. Monarch, "The Dypar-I Tutorial and Reference Manual," Computer Science Department, Carnegie-Mellon University, 1984.

4. R. Davis, *"Applications of Meta Level Knowledge to the Construction, Maintenance and Use of Large Knowledge Bases,"* Ph.D. Thesis, Computer Science Department, Stanford University, July 1976.

5. D. H. Helman and A. Bahuguna, "Explanation Systems for Computer Simulations," in *Proceedings of the 1986 Winter Simulation Conference*, North-Holland, Amsterdam, 1986, pp. 90–114.

6. D. King, "The ERGO Project: A Natural Language Query Facility for Explaining Financial Modeling Results," in *Proceedings of DSS-86*, The Institute for Advancement of Decision Support Systems, San Francisco, CA, 1986, pp. 136–150.

7. R. Klein, "Computer-Based Financial Modeling," *Journal of Systems Management*, **32**: 6–13, 1982.

8. D. W. Kosy, and B. P. Wise, "Self-Explanatory Financial Planning Models," in *Proceedings of AAAI-84,* Morgan Kaufmann, Los Altos, CA, 1984, pp. 176–181.

9. D. W. Kosy, and B. P. Wise, "Overview of ROME: A Reason-Oriented Modeling Environment," in L. F. Pau (Ed.), *Artificial Intelligence in Economics and Management,* Elsevier Science, New York, 1986, pp. 21–30.

10. A. Malhotra, "Design Criteria for a Knowledge-Based English Language System for Management: An Experimental Analysis," Ph.D. Thesis, Sloan School of Management, MIT, Cambridge, MA, 1975.

11. A. Malhotra, "Knowledge-Based English Language Systems for Management Support: An Analysis of Requirements," *Advance Papers of IJCAI-77,* Morgan Kaufmann, Los Altos, CA, 1975, pp. 842–847.

12. S. F. Roth, X. Mesnard, and J. Mattis, "Graphics and Natural Language as Components of Automatic Explanation," presented at the *Workshop on Architectures for Intelligent Interfaces,* sponsored by the American Association for Artificial Intelligence, Monterey, CA, April 1988.

13. W. R. Swartout, "XPLAIN: A System for Creating and Explaining Expert Consulting Programs," *Artificial Intelligence,* **21**:285–325, 1983.

14. M. Wright and M. S. Fox, "SRL/1.5 User Manual," The Robotics Institute, Carnegie-Mellon University, 1982.

20 A Knowledge-Based System for Troubleshooting Real-Time Models

ROBERT PRAGER

CAE Electronics Ltd.
St. Laurent, Quebec, Canada
and
School of Computer Science
McGill University
Montreal, Quebec, Canada

PIERRE BELANGER

Department of Electrical Engineering
McGill University
Montreal, Quebec, Canada

and

RENATO DE MORI

School of Computer Science
McGill University
Montreal, Quebec, Canada
and
Centre de recherche informatique de Montreal
Montreal, Quebec, Canada

1 INTRODUCTION

This chapter describes an on-going program of research into applications of artificial intelligence (AI) in the domain of aerodynamic simulation. One important use of mathematical aerodynamic models is in real-time flight simulators for pilot training. A flight simulator is a reproduction of an aircraft cockpit on a hydraulically powered moving platform, with a visual system to present computer-generated images to a pilot flying the simulator. All the pilot's control movements and other actions are sent to a digital computer which models how the simulated aircraft would respond to the same inputs. Visual, motion, instrument, and control force cues are computed and fed back to the simulator to give the pilot the illusion of actual flight.

A simulation engineer plays two roles in the preparation of a model for real-time simulation. First, the aerodynamic model is designed and coded using available aircraft data. The coded model, called the *flight program,* is one of many programs in the simulator. Second, the engineer must *verify* the fidelity of the model by comparing the performance of the simulator with data recorded during tests of the simulated aircraft. The results of the simulator tests may demonstrate a need to *tune* the model to better simulate the aircraft in some operating regions of the flight envelope. *Troubleshooting* is the combination of two activities: verification and tuning.

The goal of this research is to produce a knowledge-based system (KBS) to assist an engineer in troubleshooting flight programs. An AI system must have a name, this one is called the *Flite system,* which stands for FLight Interactive Troubleshooting Environment. As the research progresses, "interactive" will evolve into "intelligent," but the name will remain the same. The Flite system tunes the flight program and executes it to observe the effects of tuning. The flight program itself is an integral part of the system both as an object being manipulated and as a functional component. Novel methods are proposed for representing and reasoning about the flight program and discrepancies. Original contributions arising from this research are introduced in Section 2 and elaborated in subsequent sections.

The remainder of this section describes the domain and defines some basic terminology. The second section discusses the motivation for this research and the potential role of knowledge-based systems as assistants to simulation engineers. In Section 3 some key issues of the relationship between AI and simulation are discussed. Section 4 describes an approach to two basic problems, interpreting measured signals and controlling experiments. Section 5 describes how expert knowledge is represented in a qualitative model and used to guide troubleshooting. Section 6 is concerned with how the many reasoning components are organized using the blackboard architecture. Finally, some conclusions are presented in Section 7.

1.1   Real-Time Flight Simulation

An aircraft in flight is subject to many forces. Simulating these forces and the motions they cause is the task of the flight program. A flight program is built from aircraft-specific aerodynamic design data, engine data, landing gear data, mass properties data, and an atmosphere model. The aerodynamic data is in the form of dimensionless coefficients which model the forces induced by airflow over different parts of the airframe. There is a separate coefficient to model the forces in each of the three *translational* ($X, Y,$ and Z) axes. The forces cause moments about the three *rotational* ($P, Q,$ and R) axes. Moments are also modeled by individual coefficients. There can be several hundred coefficients, each a function of one or more state variables (Figure 1). The coefficients are represented as tables, containing up to a thousand tabulated points. Coefficients are combined in the *coefficient buildup* (Figure 2) to calculate the total coefficient in each axis. These values are scaled by certain factors (dynamic pressure, wing span, etc.) to give aerodynamic forces and moments. Aerodynamic, thrust, and ground reaction forces and moments are summed to give total forces and moments, from which accelerations and velocities at the center of gravity can be calculated using standard aerodynamic equations.

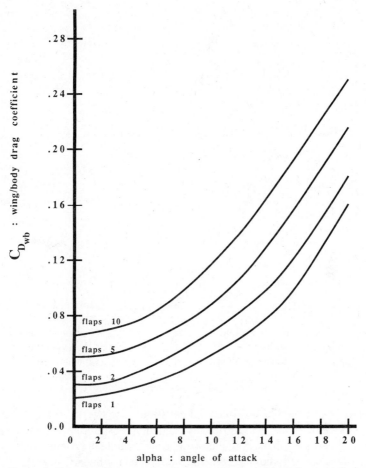

Figure 1. Drag coefficient as function of angle of attack and flap position.

Once the flight program is built, verification can begin. The flight program is tested by comparing *maneuvers* and *experiments*. Maneuvers are performed in the aircraft and the results recorded as time histories. A typical maneuver consists of an initial segment of steady-state motion, a segment with varying pilot inputs and a segment showing the aircraft response. Figure 3 is an example of time histories recorded during a takeoff maneuver. An experiment is an attempt to reproduce, in the simulator, a maneuver performed in the aircraft. Some environmental variables (e.g., air density) may be unknown; in such cases the experiment is performed with default values. A *test* is a pair consisting of a maneuver and an experiment attempting to reproduce that maneuver. During tuning, experiments are repeated, creating a new test each time, until the time histories of the simulator and aircraft match to within certain *tolerances*. A test with such a close match is called *successful* or *acceptable*.

All maneuvers can be divided into segments such that each segment corresponds to a unique *flight regime,* or simply *regime*. An aircraft's motion can be described by 12 time-varying state variables. The regime of the aircraft, or flight program, is modeled

$$C_{D_{basic}} = C_{D_{wb}} + C_{D_{ht}}$$

$$C_{D_{spoilers}} = C_{D_{spl}} \times \delta_{spl} + C_{D_{spr}} \times \delta_{spr}$$

$$C_{D_{ailerons}} = C_{D_{aill}} \times \delta_{aill} + C_{D_{ailr}} \times \delta_{ailr}$$

$$C_{D_{speedbrakes}} = C_{D_{sb}} \times \delta_{sb}$$

$$C_{D_{lateral}} = C_{D_{spoilers}} + C_{D_{ailerons}} + C_{D_{speedbrakes}}$$

$$C_{D_{rudder}} = C_{D_{rud}} \times \delta_{rud}$$

$$C_{D_{gear}} = C_{D_{lg}} \times \delta_{lg}$$

$$C_{D_{thrust}} = C_{D_{sym-thr}} + C_{D_{asym-thr}} \times (thr_l - thr_r)$$

$$C_{D_{total}} = C_{D_{basic}} + C_{D_{lateral}} + C_{D_{rudder}} + C_{D_{gear}} + C_{D_{thrust}}$$

Nomenclature:

wb : wing/body	ht : horizontal tail
δ_{spl} : left spoiler position	δ_{spr} : right spoiler position
δ_{aill} : left aileron position	δ_{ailr} : right aileron position
thr_l : left net thrust	thr_r : right net thrust
δ_{sb} : speedbrakes position	δ_{rud} : rudder position

Figure 2. Drag coefficient buildup.

by a set of first-order linear differential equations (see Section 5.2). The constant coefficients, called *gains,* of the differential equations describe how variations of each state variable affects others. A regime will be an accurate description of the aircraft motion as long as the forces affecting the aircraft change linearly over the described segment. Correct segmentation assures this is true. The division of a maneuver into regimes by segmenting signals is discussed further in Section 4.1. The word "regime" is used for descriptions of motions; "state" is reserved for describing the behavior of the Flite system.

To perform and evaluate an experiment, three types of data are needed: the initial steady-state conditions and the time histories of inputs and outputs. Time histories are considered as *signals* produced by a real-time process—aircraft or simulator—but not processed in real time. Simulator inputs can exactly reproduce the pilot's control inputs as recorded during the maneuver. Comparison of signals allows verification of the transient and dynamic characteristics of the flight program.

The signals of a test can be grouped into pairs of *like signals*. Like signals are two measurements of the same parameter, one from a maneuver and the other from an experiment making up a test. The difference between like signals, which is also a signal, is called a *discrepancy*. A discrepancy in a test is the set of discrepancies between pairs of like signals in the test. Given a discrepancy in a test, one goal of troubleshooting is to *reduce* the discrepancy until an acceptable test is generated. To guide tuning, the engineer tries to identify *deficiencies* in the flight program, where a deficiency is

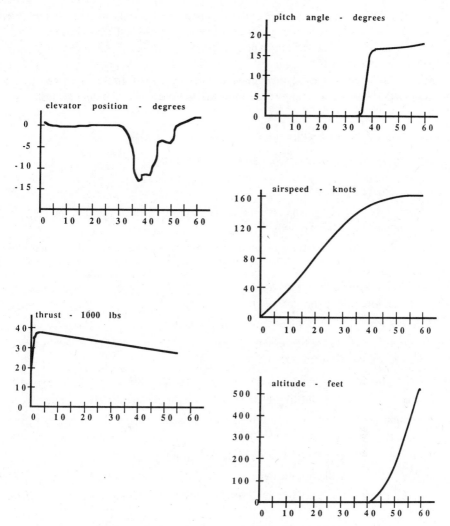

Figure 3. Signals recorded during take-off maneuver.

defined as a coefficient which is inaccurate. Identifying and correcting deficiencies is the second goal of tuning. There is no concept of an absolute *fault* in a coefficient, as in other diagnostic systems; instead deficient coefficients are improved by tuning. Discrepancies are the evidence of deficiencies; as such, detecting and describing discrepancies is a key task.

An engineer who is troubleshooting must be able to identify possible deficiencies from the observed discrepancies and decide how to tune coefficients to improve deficiencies. Another option is to tune the pilot inputs of the experiment to compensate for a deficiency without actually correcting it. This approach produces acceptable tests but may leave some deficiencies uncorrected.

Knowledge about physics, aerodynamics, and the observed discrepancies is used during troubleshooting. Reasoning tends to be qualitative, and the results of reasoning are conjectures about the selection of inputs or coefficients to tune. If tuning a coefficient results in reducing a discrepancy, this is considered as evidence there was a deficiency in that coefficient. In practice, correctly selecting parameters to tune in such a highly dynamic, highly cross-coupled system is very difficult. This is a knowledge-intensive task, with experienced engineers performing much better than beginners. Thus AI technology is a promising approach to automating the task.

1.2 Some Aircraft Terminology

Some aircraft terminology used in this chapter follows:

c.g. Center of gravity.

x-Body Axis An imaginary line along the aircraft fuselage through the c.g.; the component of velocity along the x-body axis is denoted by u.

z-Body Axis An imaginary vertical line perpendicular to the x-body axis and through the c.g.

Lift A force along the z axis.

Drag A force along the x axis.

Dynamic Pressure Force exerted by airflow per unit area.

Pitch Angle The angle between the x axis and the ground, denoted by θ; the rate of change of θ is denoted by q.

Angle of Attack The angle between the x axis and the velocity vector, denoted by α.

Elevator A movable airfoil used to control pitch angle; deflection is denoted by δ_e.

Flaps and *Slats* Movable airfoils on the wings used to change lift–drag characteristics; flap deflection is denoted by δ_f.

Rotation During a takeoff, a large negative elevator input.

Lift-off During a takeoff, the event of leaving contact with the ground.

Ground-effect The boundary layer of the atmosphere within about 120 ft of the ground.

Longitudinal Axes The X, Z, and Q axes—motions in the XZ plane.

Lateral Axes The Y, P, and R axes.

In Figure 3, rotation occurs at 33 sec, lift-off at 42 sec, and the aircraft leaves the ground-effects region at 48 sec. The symbol δ_{lg} denotes landing gear extension.

2 A ROLE FOR KNOWLEDGE-BASED SYSTEMS

2.1 The Demand for Improved Simulation

Recent years have seen numerous improvements in flight simulator technology; for example, in visual systems, computer capacity, and improved modeling of aircraft flight control systems. To achieve the ultimate goal of more effective training through more realistic simulation, aerodynamic models must also continue to improve. Modern simulators are used extensively in airline pilot training programs, largely replacing training in actual aircraft for experienced pilots. This can mean substantial savings to airlines since the operating cost of a simulator is typically one-tenth that of an aircraft. Simulators also permit types of training (e.g., engine failures) that would be dangerous in an aircraft.

Before a simulator can be used for training, it must satisfy strict airline standards and regulatory requirements. In the United States the Federal Aviation Authority certifies training simulators; advanced levels of certification permit greater use of the simulators. Meeting these requirements has placed increased emphasis on objective tests comparing simulator and aircraft performance. In the aerodynamic simulation domain the basic models are well understood, and there is a generally accepted set of maneuvers which are used to evaluate the fidelity of a model. To successfully complete a test can require up to a hundred experiments, comparing results and making small modifications at each repetition. For a particular flight program, troubleshooting can take months of effort.

Certification requires roughly a hundred maneuvers—with different combinations of aircraft weight, airspeed, flap/slat position, and so on—be reproduced. It is accepted that an experiment will not exactly reproduce a maneuver. This is because a complex process is being simulated with a discrete model which cannot include all real-world effects. Furthermore, the checkout data itself may be noisy, there may have been recording errors, or some of the test conditions (e.g., wind conditions) may be unknown.

2.2   A KBS as a Tool for Engineers

The key tasks of a troubleshooting system are illustrated in Figure 4. There are two types of outputs. The first is coefficient modifications to correct deficiencies in the model. The second is an objective proof of the fidelity of the model, namely, the results of experiments which closely match aircraft maneuvers.

Engineers presently troubleshoot using a mixture of physics and heuristics. Decisions about tuning are highly specific to particular tests and discrepancies. Experiential, heuristic knowledge could be represented as rules. This can lead to a system which is brittle and difficult to modify, as discussed by Genesereth [10]. By analyzing sets of rules, it may be possible to discover an underlying structure. Troubleshooting can be based on reasoning about structural knowledge, represented declaratively, rather than on a shorthand or compiled form (rules) of the same knowledge.

For troubleshooting flight programs, it is impractical to create rules for all possible combinations of tests, discrepancies, and deficiencies. Thus the expert's knowledge of the structure of the flight program and the morphology of discrepancies must be represented explicitly. Reasoning about the structure and signals is used to determine the form of the equations making up the regime during a segment. Once the equations are known, the gains of the regime can be estimated from the signals over that segment. Sections 3.1 and 5.2 discuss how the regime is used in troubleshooting. In particular,

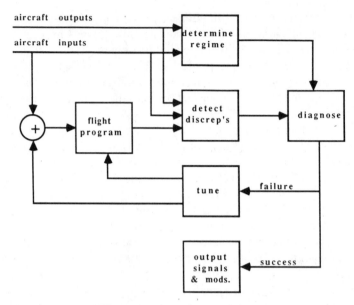

Figure 4. System block diagram.

reasoning about the regime and discrepancies is used to identify deficiencies. Tuning is based on knowledge of the regime and the deficiencies. A discussion of tuning appears in Section 3.2.

The design described in the following sections reflects an idealized view of trouble-shooting. Instead of emulating an engineer's abilities, the system extends them. This is done by providing automated tools for key tasks and integrating them into a system based on a representation of domain knowledge. An important intermediate goal of this research is to provide these tools and representations to practicing engineers in an interactive system.

An interactive system displays a certain synergy: the system maintains the status of troubleshooting while the engineer makes control decisions. Another kind of synergy is that AI techniques are used to improve the quality of simulation while simulation is used to confirm or disprove the results of reasoning.

2.3 Related Research

Two areas of AI research are directly relevant: diagnosis and signal interpretation. As in other research on reasoning about physical systems [1], techniques of constraint propagation [19] are used to model and reason about a system's behavior.

In Davis's approach to diagnosis [4], a model of a device is represented by a hierarchical structure of components and interconnections. The model defines the correct behavior of the device. The goal of diagnosis is to infer faults in an actual device by comparing its input–output behavior to that of the model. Davis considers trou-bleshooting digital circuits. For troubleshooting a flight program, the situation is reversed. Here the model is the subject of diagnosis and the measurements of the device (the aircraft) define the correct behavior. In digital circuits the *adjacency* of components determines their interaction. In a flight program there is no notion of adjacency. The interaction of components is context dependent and must be inferred for every maneuver. Another difference is that measurements of digital circuits are discrete values as opposed to continuous signals. An important problem is transforming signals to an appropriate representation for diagnosis.

To perform diagnosis, two types of measurement interpretation are necessary: interpretation of signals and discrepancies. Forbus proposes a theory for segmentation and interpretation of measurements of physical systems [8]. In this theory a domain-dependent algorithm is used to describe signals as sequences of qualitative values. A segment of a signal is a maximal interval where the qualitative value is unchanged. Within a segment the state of the system is determined by the qualitative values of certain components of the system. The available measurements may not suffice to uniquely determine the state. Interpretation consists of matching sequences of states which are consistent with the measurements against an envisionment (i.e., a space of qualitatively distinct possible behaviors). Constraints and filtering techniques are used to prune the set of candidate interpretations.

Automating troubleshooting requires some advances over Forbus's theory. First, a better qualitative representation based on polynomial approximations is needed to capture a signal's variation over time. Second, the notion of qualitative state is replaced by identification of the regime which, together with the signals, represents the physical behavior during a segment. Third, segmentation is a complex procedure which depends on the accuracy of signal approximations and feedback from regime identification. If the regime does not accurately model a segment, that segment must be split. Forbus's interpretation follows a specific sequence of steps (computing qualitative values, segmentation, identifying states, and matching with envisionment) which is not sufficient for troubleshooting highly complex systems.

A basic assumption in reference 8 is the availability of a total envisionment to prune possible interpretations. An interpretation of discrepancies must identify the deficiencies which caused them. As discussed in the preceding, there is no a priori way to associate deficiencies with discrepancies; thus a total envisionment is impossible.

Two other areas of research have been crucial in the design of the Flite system. Signal interpretation techniques similar to those used in speech understanding research [20] are applied to aircraft and simulator signals. Linear models of dynamic systems and parameter estimation are the basis of identifying regimes. These techniques are used in the state-space approach to control system design [9].

3   THE RELATIONSHIP BETWEEN AI AND SIMULATION TECHNOLOGIES

To design a system which couples two *modes of computation*—symbolic and numeric—the strengths and weaknesses of both must be understood and the interaction between them must be specified. In Section 3.1 troubleshooting is defined as a state-space search problem and the roles of AI and simulation in performing the search are described. Reasoning is used to make choices among alternative branches during search, where branches correspond to hypotheses about deficiencies. Section 3.2 shows how simulation is used to evaluate the outcome of these choices. More details on representations and reasoning techniques are included in Section 5.

3.1   The Qualitative and Quantitative Models

The key to troubleshooting is to make hypotheses about possible deficiencies in the model which could account for observed discrepancies in a test. The correctness of a hypothesis is evaluated by modifying some inputs or coefficients, consistent with the hypothesis, and repeating the experiment. If, in the new test, the discrepancies are reduced, then the hypothesis is considered to be correct.

Coefficients and inputs are referred to collectively as *parameters.* The selection of parameters to modify depends on the test, segment, and discrepancy. For each experiment any subset of the set of coefficients could be modified and simultaneously any of the time-varying inputs could be modified. A portion of the space of maneuvers and modifications is shown in Figure 5 to illustrate the combinatorial explosion possible in troubleshooting. This space is called the *problem space* since it represents all the decisions which need to be made to solve the problem. Some levels of the problem space reflect known groupings, among maneuvers and among coefficients, which are used to determine interactions among subproblems. The problem space is used to generate a *search space,* with internal nodes representing segments, maneuvers, and sets of maneuvers. A terminal node of the search space consists of a subset of the coefficients and inputs appearing below a segment node in the problem space. It represents a hypothesis about which parameters the Flite system needs to modify to reduce discrepancies in that segment. If the tuning is successful, this is considered as evidence of deficiencies in the modified coefficients. Representing inputs and coefficients uniformly as terminal nodes simplifies reasoning.

The result of troubleshooting is a set of terminal nodes of the search space, one for each segment, which specify modifications for any discrepancies in the segment. There may be a hundred or more maneuvers, several hundred coefficients, and hundreds of possible input modifications. Since a solution is a subset of a set of hundreds of parameters, the number of possible solutions is of the form 2^N, where N is some number in the hundreds. Acceptable solutions are those resulting in acceptable tests. There will be many acceptable solutions since the acceptability of tests is determined relative to tolerances and is not unique.

The view of diagnosis as search should now be clear. A diagnosis of discrepancies consists of identifying a set of terminal nodes which, when parameters are modified as indicated, result in acceptable tests.

In order for the Flite system to perform the search, a powerful model of the expert's reasoning is needed. Using this model, intelligent choices can be made, rendering search feasible. There is a trade-off between reasoning and search; time spent in reasoning can only be justified if it reduces search time by a greater amount. This is the case here as the pure search problem is clearly intractable and the evaluation of each terminal node involves performing a simulation which is computationally expensive.

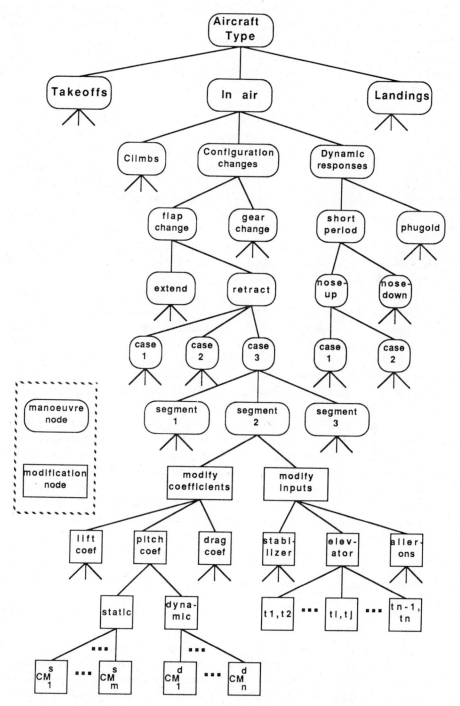

Figure 5. Space of modifications for simulator troubleshooting.

There are two levels at which the aerodynamic model can be understood, the *quantitative* and the *qualitative*. The quantitative model is the flight program. This is a very detailed and complete model but, as pointed out elsewhere [6], too much detail can make diagnostic reasoning more difficult. Furthermore, the quantitative model will necessarily be different for every different flight program.

The qualitative model is the Flite system's guide in its search to identify deficiencies. An important property of the qualitative model is it is independent of the specific aircraft type. The qualitative model is used to make choices at internal nodes of the search space. Each decision focuses diagnosis on simpler subproblems by specifying particular maneuvers and segments or by making assumptions about parameters to modify. With an explicit qualitative model the system can perform a more thorough search than engineers typically do. Thus the Flite system may identify more deficiencies than the engineer and may make better hypotheses about deficiencies.

To guarantee a solution which is consistent and correct for all tests, the qualitative model has *global* and *test-specific* components. A global view is needed since modifications to coefficients have side effects. For example, increasing the landing gear drag coefficient to reduce a discrepancy in one test will increase the drag for other tests. Modifications to pilot inputs have no side effects on other tests.

Inconsistencies can arise if diagnosis incorrectly identifies some coefficients as deficient. Modifying these coefficients can cause unacceptable side effects. To avoid such side effects, coefficients are not modified until enough constraints on modifications are generated to ensure consistency. Since constraints are accumulated from many tests, accumulating constraints is one of the global components. Test-specific reasoning will determine which modifications are needed to reduce discrepancies so that the test is acceptable. These hypothesized modifications become constraints in the global component.

Constraints from different tests on the same coefficient may be contradictory. This can be handled in three ways. First, contradictory constraints cancel each other and a new constraint is generated preventing any modification to the coefficient. Second, if, for some test, no other coefficient (or input) modifications will lead to acceptable results, *compensation* is necessary. This means modifying a coefficient in spite of contradictions and compensating in other tests by modifying other coefficients in the same axis. The third possibility is to interpret contradictory constraints as evidence of a *structural* deficiency (i.e., a new coefficient should be included in the flight program). Structural deficiencies are not currently addressed in this work.

The sequencing of maneuvers for diagnosis is also the responsibility of the global components. Relations between maneuvers and coefficients determine, for each maneuver, which coefficients it can constrain and, for each coefficient, which maneuvers can constrain it. Maneuvers are chosen to generate constraints on any coefficient considered deficient as soon as possible.

The test-specific components are concerned with the regime of each segment of each test. Reasoning about the regime is used to select a set of parameters, P, to modify for a particular segment and discrepancies. If a parameter π corresponds to a coefficient which is hypothesized as deficient, π is included in P. With no evidence of deficiencies, the sensitivity of the experiment to changes in π is considered. A heuristic rule is to modify π if the experiment is sensitive to small changes in π, thereby minimizing side effects on other experiments which are less sensitive to π.

The set P corresponds to a terminal node of the search space. A qualitative solution for P consists of constraints on modifications, as already mentioned. (Full details are in Section 5.) If, after considering other maneuvers, the qualitative solution is found to be consistent, the subproblem can be fully solved by computing exact modifications to elements of P. The subproblem associated with a terminal node is sufficiently simplified that powerful numerical algorithms (Section 3.2) can be applied. Modifications become outputs of the Flite system.

In summary, the search paradigm reduces troubleshooting to a sequence of simplified subproblems. The problem space of Figure 5 shows the decisions to be made during troubleshooting. Decisions at successive levels (e.g., "consider the specific maneuver flap change/retract/case 2") are made by components of the qualitative model. As in Stefik [18], subproblems interact by posting constraints. Constraints influence the order of search since the system tries to find all relevant constraints on a coefficient as soon as possible. Contradictory constraints cause backtracking. Thus the qualitative model uses known relationships from the domain, reasoning about subproblems, and constraint posting to perform an intelligent search.

3.2   Experiments with the Simulator

Experiments are a way of reducing discrepancies by tuning parameters in P. A component of the Flite system, called the *tuning component,* or *tuner,* performs experiments by computing exact modifications to elements of P. The tuner creates an instance of a mathematical optimization problem and calls a numerical algorithm to solve for values of P which minimize discrepancies. The reasoning performed by the tuner is discussed here; the optimization problem is described in Section 4.2.

The tuner has some flexibility in setting up the optimization problem. This flexibility is necessary to satisfy certain design criteria and to deal with the real-time nature of the signals. One criterion is that solutions for P with minimal modifications to coefficients subject to accumulated constraints are preferred. This criteria is justified by the sensitivity heuristic used in determining P. Minimizing modifications also preserves the smoothness of the original coefficient (see also Section 5.3). A second criterion is it may be necessary for some signals to match more closely than their allowed tolerance. Finally, if P specifies modifications to an input, the tuner may have to try modifications at different time points in the segment.

The tuner performs a sequence of experiments until one succeeds (confirming hypothesis P) or a termination criteria is met. The modified parameters are saved, and global reasoning infers effects on other tests. In the event of failure, the tuner has three possible actions. First, to minimize side effects, the tuner initially applies tighter constraints than those allowed by the qualitative model; these could be loosened when experiments fail. Second, the tuner can change the objective function of the optimization problem to force a closer match in some signals. For example, in a takeoff maneuver, just after rotation, it is necessary to have a very close match in pitch angles;

otherwise lift-off can occur at the wrong time. The tuner can repeat experiments, giving greater weight to the pitch angle, until other discrepancies are acceptable.

A possible outcome of the optimization is that an input modification has reduced a discrepancy in a portion of the segment. Then, further modifying the input at different points in the segment can reduce the remaining discrepancy. The tuner specifies input modifications to reduce discrepancies "from left to right." It begins at the earliest point in time in the segment where the discrepancy occurs, modifies inputs there, and proceeds to later points in the segment, always accumulating input modifications. To ensure consistency, the same coefficient modifications must be used for the whole sequence of experiments where input modifications are accumulated.

Any search algorithm needs a way to evaluate terminal nodes. The mathematical formulation of the tuning problem gives a way to decide the correctness of hypothesized deficiencies. If the optimization fails to produce acceptable results, then the hypothesis is considered to be wrong. On the other hand, if optimization does find modifications leading to acceptable results, the hypothesis is confirmed. Thus the combination of AI and optimization is very powerful. Search, using an explicit representation of domain knowledge, leads to optimization problems. Since optimization problems are formulated in an intelligent way, their outcome can be used with confidence to make decisions about hypotheses.

4 METHODS FOR INTERPRETATION AND EXPERIMENTATION

This section focuses on the numerical components of the Flite system. These modules are the flight program itself, the signal interpretation module, and the optimization module discussed in Section 3.2. Signal interpretation is itself composed of submodules for segmentation, approximation, and detecting discrepancies.

4.1 Processing Signals and Discrepancies

A qualitative model needs qualitative descriptions of the objects it describes. The purpose of processing signals is to transform them from a numeric representation (e.g., recorded outputs of the flight program) to a symbolic/qualitative representation.

The basic operations on signals are *segmentation* and *approximation*. Segmentation is the operation of dividing a signal into a small number of adjacent, nonoverlapping intervals. Approximations are polynomials in time, over each segment, which are a representation of signals at an intermediate level of abstraction. The coefficients of these polynomials are easily computed by least-squares algorithms.

Approximations are useful in two ways. First, a polynomial approximation is a way of filtering out noise from signals. Second, an approximation is a convenient representation of a signal's behavior over time and as such is useful for qualitative reasoning. Section 5.2 discusses qualitative representations based on polynomials.

There are two criteria, related to the needs of interpretation and approximation, which segmentation must satisfy. The first criterion can be illustrated by an example. Suppose an aircraft is taking off and the pilot changes rudder position while moving at 30 knots. The heading will not change because the airflow over the rudder does not generate sufficient force. However, moving the rudder once airborne will have an effect. This example illustrates how reasoning about a maneuver depends on the different segments of the maneuver. Division into segments makes it possible to identify different regimes of the aircraft. The second criterion for segmentation is that it must lead to good approximations. Segmentation is a well-known technique in numerical analysis as a step in computing an accurate piecewise approximation to a function over a long interval. These two criteria are combined in a segmentation algorithm with three steps, finding *events,* computing approximations, and *level building.*

An event in a maneuver is an instant when the forces acting on parts of the aircraft change. Typical events are large changes to inputs (e.g., rotation), changes relative to critical values (e.g., lift-off, leaving ground effects), or sign changes of derivatives. Events are found by detecting a specific change in a specific signal. A typical maneuver will have three to five events. A *breakpoint* in a signal is the instant when the changing forces at an event become significant accelerations at the aircraft center of gravity. Since an aircraft is not a rigid body, it takes a small but nonnegligible length of time for the changed forces to be felt at the center of gravity.

Breakpoints are the points used to divide a maneuver into segments. They are located within a small neighborhood (typically 1 or 2 sec long) after an event. If e_1 and e_2 are consecutive events, candidate breakpoints b_1 and b_2 are selected from the neighborhoods about e_1 and e_2, respectively. Polynomial approximations are computed between all possible pairs (b_1, b_2) for all signals. Since b_1 and b_2 are near events, during the interval from b_1 to b_2 the forces acting on the aircraft will change smoothly. Thus higher derivatives of the signal will be nearly zero and low-degree polynomials should be accurate. In practice, with degree 3 polynomials and three or four segments per maneuver, maximum errors are less than $1/2$ unit, or 5%.

A global error for each interval (b_1, b_2) is computed by combining errors of approximations to all signals over (b_1, b_2). Once the errors for all possible segmentations are computed, dynamic programming is used to select the optimum set of breakpoints which minimizes the accumulated global error. This algorithm is based on level building [15], which is used in automatic speech recognition to compare input speech signals with stored references. It is possible to adapt the algorithm to specific maneuvers by assigning different weights to individual signals and segments, but such details are not discussed here.

Level building selects breakpoints in order to give the best possible approximations. After a breakpoint a different polynomial will be more accurate than the one used before the breakpoint. Thus it is reasonable to define the breakpoint to be the point where accelerations at the center of gravity change significantly. These breakpoints then satisfy the criteria of accurate approximations and identification of regime changes.

Discrepancies between a maneuver and an experiment may take two forms, corresponding to differences in the time axis or the ordinal axis of a pair of signals. Time axis errors, called *latency* errors, arise if the delay preceding the response to an input change is different in the simulator from that of an actual aircraft. Both types of discrepancy can be found with the dynamic time warping (DTW) algorithm used in speech recognition [17]. The DTW algorithm is a method of comparing signals which allow nonlinear time distortions. It is used to compare like signals and to report on discrepancies.

Imagine the simulator signal on the x axis of a grid and the aircraft signal on the y axis. At a grid point (x, y), DTW fills in the distance between the simulator point at coordinate x and the aircraft point at coordinate y. The distance metric used is the absolute value of the difference between the points. In practice, to save distance computations, only a window about the diagonal of the grid is considered. The best match between signals is defined as a path through the grid which minimizes the sum of the distances stored at the grid points along the path. The path, which is determined by dynamic programming, gives a mapping between simulator signals and aircraft signals. This mapping is called the *warping function*. Applying the warping function to a simulator signal gives a new, warped signal.

From the warping function, it is possible to detect latency errors by looking, for example, for consecutive simulator points which map to a single aircraft point. This would be observed if a simulator response is more delayed than the aircraft response. If there are no latency errors (or only small ones), the discrepancy is the difference between the aircraft signal and the warped simulator signal. Experimental results with actual aircraft signals and artificially introduced latencies and discrepancies have successfully demonstrated this approach to discrepancy detection.

Some modifications to the basic DTW algorithm have been made for the present application. These involve the restriction to a diagonal window and computing a warping function between multiple pairs of signals. The details are beyond the scope of this chapter.

4.2   Tuning by Optimization

When the tuning component is given a maneuver, it computes values of parameters which minimize the difference between the maneuver and experiment. The other inputs to the tuner are the set of parameters to modify and constraints on allowed modifications.

Since tuning depends on mathematical optimization, it is natural to ask whether the entire troubleshooting problem can be formulated as an optimization problem. The first objection to this approach is sheer size. Simultaneously optimizing hundreds of coefficients over a hundred or more tests, each involving simulation, is a very large numerical problem. An objective function which sums the errors in a hundred or more tests would depend only weakly on specific tests. This would make it difficult to minimize errors in tests which are sensitive to small variations of parameters. A third objection is the problem is inherently underconstrained since the available maneuvers typically do not cover the full range of values of all coefficients. Thus a purely numerical solution may provide a close match between simulator and aircraft for the given maneuvers but not for similar maneuvers. An analogy can be seen with approximating n points by a polynomial of degree n. At the given points the approximation will be exact; in between it is likely to be inaccurate.

Let

$$\dot{x}(t, p) = f(x(t, p), u(t), p)$$

where

f : is a mathematical model of the system,

p : is a parameter whose value is to be determined,

x(t, p) : is the state variable of the system as a function of p,

u(t) : is the input vector (given),

x(0, p) : is the initial condition (given).

Suppose $\hat{x}(t)$ is a response recorded during a maneuver, then

define the error function J(p) by

$$J(p) = \int_{0}^{T} \left[\hat{x}(t) - x(t, p) \right]^2 dt$$

The problem is to find the value of p which minimizes J(p),

subject to the constraint $0 \leq p \leq c$.

Figure 6. Scalar optimization problem.

Optimization techniques can still be very useful when applied to a single test at a time and when reasoning has reduced the parameter space with respect to which the optimization is performed. This is the way engineers actually use optimization techniques on many real-world problems. Within this specific role the definition of an optimization problem is straightforward; see Figure 6. The figure illustrates the problem in the special case where p is a scalar and x and u are scalar functions of time; the generalization to vector functions is also straightforward.

The function f is the flight program, u(t) are the pilot inputs, and the vector p is the parameterization of modifications. It is crucial that the function f in the optimization problem be the flight program itself. This ensures the solution for p which minimizes J(p) maps to an exact modification of a simulator input or coefficient.

The parameters in p can be very general. A simple example is when p includes an increment to a single point in a coefficient's tabular representation. Another parameterization of a modification is an increment to an input u(t) over an interval (t_1, t_2). The generality of p is limited only by the parameterizations the flight program is able to recognize and respond to correctly. Thus as many parameterizations as needed can be coded, at the cost of some programming effort.

In the case where x, u, and p are vectors, the objective function J(p) can be generalized in several ways. First, J(p) can be the sum of the integral square error of several signals. The errors $\hat{x}(t) - x(t, p)$ must all be normalized by dividing by the tolerance for that signal. Finally, each signal can have a weight associated with it and the weights can be time varying.

The outputs of the optimization are the value of J(p), the value of p which minimizes J(p) and the simulator signals x(t, p) obtained with p. If the experiment is still not acceptable these are used by the tuner to formulate a new optimization problem. Otherwise the outputs are returned to the qualitative model.

5   REASONING ABOUT MANEUVERS AND MODELS

This section discusses how the qualitative model is used to make hypotheses about modifications to reduce discrepancies. The role of the qualitative model in diagnosis was discussed in Section 3. The model is qualitative in the following senses: symbolic representations of the data are used; constraint propagation is used for reasoning about values; constraint posting is used to handle interacting subproblems; and an approximate, rather than exact, solution is sought.

The qualitative model has four components which interact to control diagnostic search:

MC-model   A mapping between maneuvers and coefficients.

LDE-model   A model consisting of linear differential equations specific to each segment.

CB-model   A model of the coefficient buildup in a segment.

CCM-model   A model of the constraints on coefficient modifications computed by the LDE-model and the CB-model.

The MC-model and the CCM-model maintain the global view, the LDE-model and the CB-model are test specific. Note that the use of the term "constraint" in two contexts is potentially confusing. In the LDE-model constraints are expressions relating the values of signals, while in the CB-model and CCM-model a constraint restricts the possible values of a quantity. This section uses the term almost exclusively in the latter sense, except in two paragraphs of the description of the LDE-model. A discussion of various types of constraint propagation can be found in the literature [3].

The MC-model is used in the selection of maneuvers on which to work. This corresponds to decisions at the upper levels of Figure 5. When a maneuver is chosen, an initial experiment is run with the simulator using exactly the same inputs and initial conditions as the maneuver. The LDE-model's inputs are signals and discrepancies of a test. Its outputs, the *LDE-solution,* are net changes to coefficients in any of the six axes of motion and approximate input changes. The CB-model takes the net changes in each axis and *posts constraints* (similar to Stefik [18]) on modifications to specific coefficients. The constraints produced by the CB-model are called the *qualitative solution.* The qualitative solution does not specify exact modifications to specific coefficients, but it could be used immediately by the tuner to reduce discrepancies in the segment. However, this would be premature as the numerical solution may be inconsistent with other tests. Qualitative solutions for related maneuvers can be computed before optimization is attempted. It is the role of the CCM-model to combine constraints on modifications proposed by the CB-model to ensure consistency among tests. When constraints from related qualitative solutions are combined, modifications as computed by the tuner will be consistent for those related maneuvers. Thus the

CCM-model actually determines when the tuner is executed for any particular test.

Each component of the qualitative model can be viewed as a description—of objects and relations—and as an executable module reasoning about the described objects and relations. This is consistent with the blackboard model's representation of knowledge as executable *knowledge sources*. Section 6.1 describes the blackboard model and the interaction of knowledge sources through a shared, global database. The remainder of this section discusses the four components of the qualitative model from both points of view.

5.1   From the Global View to Subproblems

The MC-model uses a set of triples of the form

$$\{(M, C, S): M \text{ is a maneuver, } C \text{ is a coefficient, } S \text{ is a segment}\}.$$

The set of maneuvers $\{M\}$ is determined by available aircraft data. Given a maneuver M, the elements (M, C, S) are determined by analysis of the signals of M. An element (M, C, S) is included if C models the forces or moments due to a quantity which changes significantly during segment S of M. The quantities may be

pilot inputs,

dynamic effects due to rates, or

other forces or moments which are functions of changing state variables.

For any (M, C, S), a discrepancy in segment S of a test which includes M is evidence of a deficiency in C. A convenient notation is M *diagnoses* C.

Domain expertise is used to determine which triples to include in the MC-model. For example, rudder coefficients will be included for takeoff maneuvers if the rudder position changes by more than 0.5 degree. Coefficients modeling ground effects will be included for landing maneuvers since ground effects are significant within 120 ft of the ground. These examples are typical of the rules used to determine elements of the MC-model. A rule R_C will specify the conditions when coefficient C is significant. More generally, a rule can specify when a set of related coefficients is significant. If R_C matches the initial conditions of M and signals over segment S, then (M, C, S) is included in the MC-model.

Troubleshooting begins by choosing the aircraft type to work on; this choice also fixes $\{M\}$. The preceding rules are sufficiently general that they can be applied to any $\{M\}$. Thus the MC-model depends on the aircraft type but does not change during troubleshooting.

The MC-model uses two criteria to select a maneuver M for troubleshooting. The first criterion is to chose an M such that M diagnoses as few coefficients C as possible. This helps identify deficiencies earlier since diagnosis is simplified by considering fewer coefficients. Once a deficiency in C is hypothesized, the second criterion is to select all maneuvers which diagnose C. This will generate all constraints on C as soon as possible.

Clearly the MC-model reduces search by restricting diagnosis to those coefficients significant to a maneuver.

5.2   Modeling the Physics of a Maneuver

The LDE-model describes the regime of the aircraft (or simulator) during a segment. The existence of relations between signals implies it is not correct to reason about signals individually since changes to one signal will cause changes in others. For example, an increase in pitch angle to reduce a discrepancy will also increase drag and decrease velocity. In some cases it may be acceptable to correct a discrepancy where velocity is too high by increasing pitch a small amount.

Specifying relations requires simultaneous equations. The equations of the LDE-model are derived by assuming a linear model of the aircraft dynamics, as in Friedland [9]. An important advantage of linearized models is they decouple the longitudinal and lateral axes into disjoint sets of equations. In this section only the longitudinal axes will be considered. The attitude and velocity at the start of a segment define an *operating condition*. The LDE-model consists of the first-order linear differential equations (1) which model the variations in signals relative to the operating condition. In tests with other varying inputs (e.g., flap position or landing gear position) the model includes a term for the input in each equation. In the first equation, g is the gravitational constant; other symbols are defined in Section 1.2.

Coefficients in the LDE-model (e.g., X_u, Z_α, M_q) are called gains. Techniques for estimating gains have been extensively studied, in particular for applications in control systems, [e.g., 7]. Since the true value of a gain is unknown—it may even be time varying—the gains are represented by intervals. An interval is a hypothesis that the true value of the gain lies within certain bounds. Clearly, smaller intervals correspond to better descriptions of the signals.

$$\Delta\dot{u} = X_u\Delta u + X_\alpha\alpha - g\theta + X_e\delta_e,$$

$$\dot{\alpha} = \frac{Z_u}{V}\Delta u + \frac{Z_\alpha}{V}\alpha + q + \frac{Z_e}{V}\delta_e,$$

$$\dot{q} = M_u\Delta u + M_\alpha\alpha + M_q q + M_e\delta_e,$$

$$\dot{\theta} = q.$$

(1)

A qualitative representation for troubleshooting must be able to describe important distinctions between values of variables (gains and signals) and must support appropriate operations to reason about discrepancies. In a representation

gains and signals must be ordered,

gains must be represented as intervals,

it must be possible to represent signal morphologies, and

qualitative values must be precise relative to tolerances.

When discrepancies are close to their tolerances, a *precise* representation is necessary to distinguish between values which are close together. To represent signals which are large relative to tolerances, a less precise representation is adequate. Precision also refers to the ability to describe different morphologies.

Certain operations on gains and signals must be possible:

to combine interval representations of gains;

to multiply a gain and a signal, giving a new signal;

to add or subtract signals, giving a new signal; and

to compare the morphologies of two signals.

There are no formal guidelines to selecting a representation. One approach is to design and test different representations and judge the advantages and disadvantages of each. Three possible representations are

(i)   signals as polynomials with real coefficients, gains as intervals of real numbers;

(ii) signals as sequences of qualitative values, gains as intervals of qualitative values; and

(iii) signals as symbolic descriptions of morphologies, gains as intervals of qualitative values.

Note that signals are represented by polynomial approximations or by qualitative values which are easily derived from polynomials.

Symbolic descriptions of morphologies can vary from simple (e.g., just *constant, ascending,* and *descending*) to complex (e.g., include *peak, oscillation,* and *step input.*) A space of qualitative values, with the required precision, is the set

$$\{0, \pm^z/_8, \pm^z/_4, \pm^z/_2, \pm z, \pm 2z, \pm 4z, \pm 8z\}.$$

For gains, z is taken to be 1. To describe signal magnitudes, z is the tolerance for the signal.

Some criteria used to judge a representation are its precision, the computational cost of operations, the ambiguity introduced by qualitative operations (e.g., what is the sum of morphologies?), and the ability to create new *landmark values.* The need to add landmark values to a qualitative representation is discussed elsewhere [14]. A representation should not be overly precise since it is used in the context of a qualitative model which is itself an abstraction. Artificially precise inferences may be incorrect when interpreted in the quantitative model.

The LDE-model performs two critical roles in the qualitative model. First, it is the component which is used for reasoning about time. Operations on signals are implicitly operations over time intervals. The LDE-model transforms a problem of time-varying signals to a problem of computing nonvarying gains. Second, the LDE-model transforms a problem of multiple, interacting signals into a problem of computing gains in separate axes. These are the two key steps in the reduction of the troubleshooting problem to a form which can be solved by the tuner.

The structure of the LDE-model allows two types of errors and two types of parameters to be handled in a uniform way. Since the LDE-model includes integrators and represents signals over time, it can be used to reason about latency errors as well as ordinal axis errors. Modifications to both inputs and coefficients can be computed with the LDE-model by propagation of qualitative values.

It is common practice to represent the LDE-model as a block diagram (Figure 7). Given this representation, it is natural to use constraint propagation techniques [19] for reasoning. The block diagram is also well suited to an interactive system since it is a familiar structure which can be displayed graphically and directly manipulated by a user. Edges in the diagram are labeled by signals—inputs, state variables, or intermediate results. The gain blocks are labeled by intervals; a label is a hypothesis that the true value of the gain lies within the interval.

Proposed gain modifications depend on the difference between corresponding gains in the LDE-models of a maneuver and experiment. A qualitative model of discrepancies is obtained by subtracting corresponding equations of the two LDE-models. This model describes how discrepancies depend on gains, other signals, and other discrepancies. In particular, an interval bounding the difference between corresponding maneuver and experiment gains can be computed. This interval becomes a bound on any modification to that gain.

Given qualitative descriptions of signals and discrepancies, the LDE-model can make inferences about gain modifications. This can be thought of as applying metarules to the qualitative description as opposed to applying specific rules to particular tests. These rules rank the possible gain modifications according to their contribution to the discrepancies. The LDE-solution is a subset of the gains which is passed to the CB-model. To check the validity of an LDE-solution, a qualitative simulation [14] can be performed using constraint propagation. A subset is chosen to reduce the number of coefficients changed. The interpretation of an LDE-solution is that if the experiment is repeated with coefficients changed in such a way that the new experiment gains equal the maneuver gains, then the discrepancies will be acceptable.

LDE-solutions are not unique, nor do they necessarily fully account for all discrepancies. This is acceptable since tuning inputs can correct some (or some portions of) discrepancies. However, selecting a subset for the LDE-solution means backtracking may be necessary, as explained in the next section.

Some of the rules the LDE-model applies follow. The notation for discrepancies is a prefix D (e.g., $D\dot{\alpha}$ is the discrepancy in $\dot{\alpha}$):

IF a term is small relative to other terms in the same equation, THEN do not modify the gain. For example, if $X_e \delta_e$ is much smaller than $X_\alpha \alpha$, then do not change X_e.

IF a discrepancy in an acceleration is proportional to a discrepancy in another state variable, THEN do not modify gains in the equation for that acceleration. For example, if $D\Delta \dot{u} \approx X_\alpha D\alpha$, then do not change X_u, X_α, X_e.

IF the difference between corresponding maneuver and experiment gains is large, THEN modify that gain.

IF the intervals for corresponding maneuver and experiment gains overlap, THEN do not modify that gain.

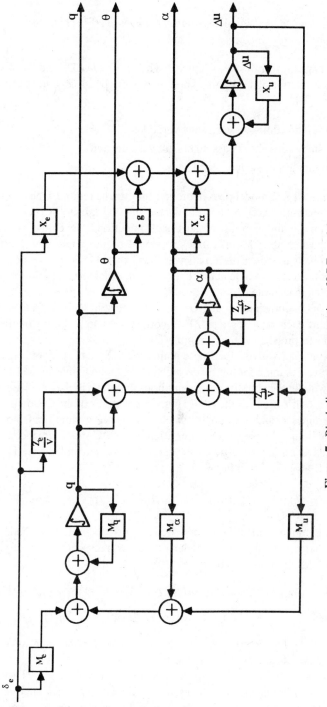

Figure 7. Block diagram representation of LDE-model.

IF a discrepancy and a signal have similar shapes, THEN change the gain on that signal. For example, if $D\dot{q}$ is a peak and δ_e is a trough, change Z_e.

Forces change uniformly over segments. Therefore, the LDE-model should be an accurate representation of the regime. There are various possible sources of inaccuracy in the LDE-model:

nonlinear relationships between state variables,

invalid assumptions about parameters not varying, and

decoupling longitudinal and lateral axes.

An inaccurate LDE-model does not represent the true regime. One simple way to detect such inaccuracies is by examining the interval labels for each gain. Large intervals mean a gain has not been accurately identified; hence the assumption of linearity is questionable. Modifications proposed by reasoning with an inaccurate model are unlikely to reduce discrepancies when experiments are repeated. Thus, if a qualitative solution does not lead the tuner to an acceptable exact solution, the LDE-model could be inaccurate.

One way of handling inaccurate LDE-models is to split segments and create a new LDE-model in each new segment. This corresponds to a failure of the original segmentation to properly identify regime changes. Splitting occurs at maxima or minima of signal derivatives since these points correspond to changes in acceleration and hence forces. A topic for future research is to respond to inaccurate LDE-models by reasoning about the simplifying assumptions upon which they are based.

The gain modifications of the LDE-solution are inputs of the CB-model. The CB-model determines changes to coefficients by creating a simplified model of the coefficient buildup. The coefficients identified in the MC-model are included explicitly. Other, less significant coefficients are grouped in a remainder term. The example of Equation (2) follows from Figure 2:

$$C_D(t) = C_{D_{wb}}(\alpha, \delta_f) + C_{D_{ht}}(\alpha, \delta_e) + C_{D_{lg}}(\alpha, \delta_{lg}) + R_1. \tag{2}$$

To link the CB-model with the LDE-model, each coefficient in the CB-model is written as a constant term and a sum of partial derivatives with respect to time-varying inputs or state variables. Equation (2) becomes:

$$\begin{aligned}
C_D(t) = {} & C_{D_{wb}}^{(0)} + C_{D_{wb}}^{(\alpha)} \alpha(t) + C_{D_{wb}}^{(f)} \delta_f(t) + C_{D_{ht}}^{(0)} + C_{D_{ht}}^{(\alpha)} \alpha(t) \\
& + C_{D_{ht}}^{(e)} \delta_e(t) + C_{D_{lg}}^{(0)} + C_{D_{lg}}^{(\alpha)} \alpha(t) + C_{D_{lg}}^{(lg)} \delta_{lg}(t) + R_2.
\end{aligned} \tag{3}$$

Note that $C_{D_{wb}}^{(0)}$ is the value of $C_{D_{wb}}(\alpha, \delta_f)$ at the start of the segment and $C_{D_{wb}}^{(\alpha)}$ is the partial derivative of $C_{D_{wb}}$ with respect to α.

Now suppose the LDE-solution specifies a modification to gain X_α. The CB-model rescales the bounds on the modification (by known quantities such as dynamic pressure) to the same units as the coefficients and generates the following constraint on coefficient modifications:

$$x_1 \leq \Delta C_{D_{wb}}^{(\alpha)} + \Delta C_{D_{ht}}^{(\alpha)} + \Delta C_{D_{lg}}^{(\alpha)} \leq y_1, \tag{4}$$

where $\Delta C^{(\alpha)}$ denotes a modification to the partial derivative of C with respect to α. A similar constraint is generated for each gain modification in the LDE-solution. The constraint only restricts modifications to coefficients over the range of values of their independent variables as measured in the segment. In the preceding constraint, if $\alpha_1 \leq \alpha \leq \alpha_2$ on the current segment, then only modifications to $C_{D_{wb}}(\alpha, \delta_f)$ over the same range of α are considered.

The CB-model is also used in cases where no discrepancies are found. A close match between aircraft and simulator in a segment implies the coefficients which vary over that segment are accurate. The CB-model generates a constraint, as in (4), but with upper and lower bounds equal to zero, thereby limiting modifications to the coefficients appearing in the constraint.

5.3   Recovering the Global State of Troubleshooting

The final component of the qualitative model, the CCM-model, combines constraints on coefficient modifications generated by the CB-models. The CCM-model maintains a large network of constraints with a structure of dependencies to record which instance of a CB-model (i.e., which test) generated each constraint. There are three important aspects to the CCM-model: representation of constraints, operations on them, and use of constraint information to guide the tuner and the MC-model.

A discussion of different categories of constraint languages and their properties appears elsewhere [3]. The CCM-model can be described using Davis's terminology. First, the CCM-model is concerned with *label inference,* that is, labeling nodes with sets of possible values. In particular, labels are intervals over the underlying qualitative representation. Intervals are used since the common $-1, 0, 1$ labels are too coarse and intervals can represent approximate values of an unknown quantity. The constraints themselves are linear inequalities [e.g., (4)] with unit coefficients. Qualitative arithmetic operations are used to combine inequalities and compute intersections of intervals. Two types of quantities are involved, the partial derivatives which appear in constraints from the CB-model and the actual coefficients which appear in the flight program and are modified by the tuner. All constraints are represented with frames; propagation uses attached demons.

Several operations are performed on constraints: merging (two types), mapping between constraints on the two types of quantities, smoothing, and substituting known values (from the tuner) into constraints. The first type of merging involves a pair of constraints with the same sum of partial derivatives over the same range of independent variables. The merged constraint uses the intersection of the interval labels. For example, in (5), the first two constraints are merged to give the third:

$$x_1 \leq \Delta C_{D_{wb}}^{(\alpha)} + \Delta C_{D_{ht}}^{(\alpha)} + \Delta C_{D_{lg}}^{(\alpha)} \leq y_1,$$

$$x_2 \leq \Delta C_{D_{wb}}^{(\alpha)} + \Delta C_{D_{ht}}^{(\alpha)} + \Delta C_{D_{lg}}^{(\alpha)} \leq y_2, \tag{5}$$

$$\max(x_1, x_2) \leq \Delta C_{D_{wb}}^{(\alpha)} + \Delta C_{D_{ht}}^{(\alpha)} + \Delta C_{D_{lg}}^{(\alpha)} \leq \min(y_1, y_2).$$

Another type of merging is when one sum consists of a subset of the terms of another. The first constraint of (5) merges with

$$x_3 \le \Delta C_{D_{wb}}^{(\alpha)} + \Delta C_{D_{lg}}^{(\alpha)} \le y_3 \tag{6}$$

to give

$$x_4 \le \Delta C_{D_{ht}}^{(\alpha)} \le y_4. \tag{7}$$

where $x_4 = x_1 - y_3$ and $x_4 = y_1 - x_3$. As new constraints are generated by the CB-model, these merging operations will tighten bounds and simplify sums as much as possible.

The constraints considered so far limit changes to derivatives of coefficients. Suppose the constraint (7) is valid over the range $\alpha_1 \le \alpha \le \alpha_2$ and for landing gear position given by $\delta_{lg} = 1$. Then (7) is mapped to a constraint on coefficient value modifications $\Delta C_{D_{lg}}(\alpha_1, 1)$ and $\Delta C_{D_{lg}}(\alpha_2, 1)$.

$$x_4(\alpha_2 - \alpha_1) \le \Delta C_{D_{lg}}(\alpha_2, 1) - \Delta C_{D_{lg}}(\alpha_1, 1) \le y_4(\alpha_2 - \alpha_1). \tag{8}$$

Constraints of this form require complex nodes and a three level representation, Davis [3] discusses the representation and increased inferential power of complex constraints.

Smoothing refers to the creation of new constraints to limit changes in slope on adjacent segments of a coefficient. Continuing the example of (8), suppose $\alpha_3 \ge \alpha_2$. Then a constraint must be generated on $C_{D_{lg}}(\alpha_2, 1)$ to ensure that after modification of $C_{D_{lg}}(\alpha_2, 1)$ the slope of $C_{D_{lg}}(\alpha, \delta_{lg})$ on (α_2, α_3), is (i) not too different from its prior value and, (ii) not too different from the slope on (α_1, α_2).

With successful tuner results, coefficient modifications are determined and the values can be substituted into constraint equations to simplify them. If, for example, $C_{D_{lg}}(\alpha_1, 1) = z_1$ and $C_{D_{lg}}(\alpha_2, 1) = z_2$, then

$$\Delta C_{D_{lg}}^{(\alpha)} = \frac{z_2 - z_1}{\alpha_2 - \alpha_1}. \tag{9}$$

This value can be used to simplify constraints such as (5).

Another type of constraint is a limit imposed by an engineer on individual modifications. For example, an engineer may decide not to allow any coefficient to be modified by more than 10% of its nominal value. Default constraints are built in to the Flite system and the user has graphic tools to display coefficients and constraints and to adjust constraints.

Inconsistencies can occur when constraints from different tests are merged. These are defined as constraints which allow no modification. For example, after the merge of (5) if $y_1 \le x_2$, then there is no consistent modifications of the given coefficients. In such an event the CCM-model identifies the constraints (and their LDE-solutions) which led to the inconsistency by using the dependency records. One or more LDE-solutions will be revised by having the appropriate LDE-model compute a different set of gain modifications. Backtracking continues until the set of LDE-solutions is consistent.

The tuner is also affected by the state of the CCM-model. Its execution is deferred until, for a maneuver M, all coefficients appearing in the qualitative solution for M are constrained and all other maneuvers diagnosing the same coefficients have been analyzed qualitatively. Then M can be optimized by the tuner, with the coefficients of the qualitative solution as parameters and subject to the constraints of the CCM-model. The results of the tuner are substituted into the CCM-model, as in (9).

The CCM-model performs an essential role of a constraint-posting system, combining constraints to defer premature commitment to specific values. Furthermore, by restricting the range of variation of the parameters adjusted by the tuner, the convergence of the numerical solution is improved.

6   IMPLEMENTATION ISSUES

This section discusses some issues which are important in the implementation of the Flite system. A computer system has architectures at many levels. This section is concerned with the highest levels, the objects and operations directly manipulated by system developers and domain experts.

6.1   The Blackboard Model

The blackboard model [16] has become increasingly popular as an architecture for complex AI systems. Adopting the blackboard model allows a system developer to think in terms of individual executable components, called *knowledge sources* (KSs), which communicate via a shared global database, the *blackboard*. The blackboard database is a collection of frames and can be structured as required by the developer. A KS is a generalization of a rule [13], in particular, each KS definition includes preconditions (see what follows) determining when it can be executed. The executable part of a KS can consist of forward- or backward-chaining rules, a LISP function, or a call to a C or FORTRAN routine. Thus KSs are a natural unit of representation for domains requiring hybrid knowledge representation and where much knowledge is procedural.

The blackboard model promotes experimentation with KSs while simplifying problems of interfacing KSs with each other. Such experimentation is essential to support the constant evolution of prototypes typical of AI research projects. The KSs also embody the principles of modular development and information hiding. Only the frames placed on the blackboard affect other KSs; the internal workings of a KS are invisible. For example, in the the LDE-model of a prototype system knowledge for selecting gains to modify may be incomplete. To allow system testing and integration to proceed, a KS stub can be defined which queries the user to make hypotheses about gains. Other KSs will not depend on whether the LDE-solution was generated by queries or automatically.

For this project a simplified version of the BB1 system [13], called BBC-1, has been implemented. In BBC-1 the notion of separate *domain* and *control* KSs has been preserved. Domain KSs perform actions relevant in a particular domain, (e.g., signal interpretation and maintaining constraints). Control KSs are used to sequence the execution of KSs for efficient problem solving. An application designed according to the blackboard model using the facilities provided by BBC-1 is an example of a *blackboard system.*

The generalization of conflict resolution is the set of control decisions used to select a KS for execution at each cycle of the blackboard system. A *blackboard engine* performs the role of an inference engine. A KS is *triggered* when a condition exists which makes it desirable to execute the *action* of that KS. A KS is *invokable* when the preconditions necessary for executing the KS's action are satisfied. The trigger conditions and preconditions are expressed as patterns of blackboard frames. An *executable* KS is both triggered and invokable. *Ratings* are associated with each KS; each rating is a numerical value. A weighted sum of ratings is used to calculate a *priority* for each KS, and the action of the executable KS with the highest priority is performed. Other policies can be defined in the event of ties. Priorities of nonexecutable KSs are calculated in order to plan to achieve preconditions of high-priority, nonexecutable KSs. A system developer can control a blackboard system as little or as much as necessary by defining trigger conditions, preconditions, ratings, and policies.

The many components of the Flite system map in a natural way to one or more KSs, as illustrated in Figure 8. A useful division of the domain blackboard is to consider

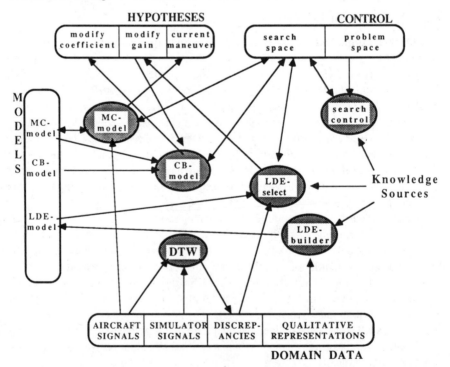

Figure 8. Knowledge sources interacting via blackboard.

separately domain data, models to explain behavior in the domain data, and troubleshooting hypotheses made using the models. The DTW KS maps between different representations of domain data. Two KSs are used for the LDE-model; LDE-builder, which takes signals and produces the gains; and equations of the model and LDE-select, which selects gains to modify. There will be an instance of LDE-builder and LDE-select for each maneuver. Similarly, for each maneuver an instance of CB-model takes significant coefficients from the MC-model and hypothesized gain modifications and returns hypothesized constraints to the blackboard. These constraints satisfy the precondition of the CCM-model KS (not shown), which transforms the constraints and places new constraints on the blackboard for the tuner.

Different KSs use different knowledge representations: the MC-model uses rules, LDE-select uses rules and constraint propagation, and the tuner uses a numerical algorithm. This variety is supported in a blackboard system; other frameworks would restrict module interactions (e.g., explicit procedure calls) or force less appropriate representations (e.g., code all knowledge as rules). Another useful feature of the blackboard model is the ability to change KS selection policies dynamically. For example, if early in troubleshooting both the LDE-model and the CCM-model can execute, the LDE-model is given higher priority. This favors qualitative solutions initially. Later, when many related constraints have been generated, the CCM-model is favored in order to confirm possible deficiencies by combining constraints.

A high-level shell has been developed to provide tools for building blackboard systems. These tools support operations on KSs and other blackboard objects. Tracing and debugging tools are also incorporated in the shell; for example, a syntax checker for production rules has been implemented. The shell allows a developer to interact with BBC-1 at the level of abstraction of components of the blackboard system.

The system BBC-1 has been (and is being) developed using the Knowledge Craft [2] environment running on a VAXstation II/GPX. Knowledge Craft provides important tools [e.g., a frame language (CRL) and a production rule language (CRL-OPS)] and ensures portability to other computers. The KSs and blackboard objects are represented as CRL schemata. Trigger conditions and preconditions are compiled to CRL-OPS rules; actions may be similarly compiled or may be LISP functions. This design uses frames (e.g., for blackboard objects) and rules (e.g., for KS preconditions) in roles where they are most suitable. Careful design of functionality and representations has resulted in a simple blackboard engine consisting of two pages of LISP code.

6.2 Knowledge Source Selection

The system BBC-1 supports three paradigms for allowing a KS to control when another KS is executed. The first is *planning,* in the general sense of a KS consulting a data structure to determine sequences of actions. Diagnostic search is a form of planning since the decisions made at various nodes during search determine when components of the qualitative model are executed. *Backward chaining* of KSs is another form of control. If KS-A is triggered but not invokable, KS-B, a control KS, can increase the priority of any KSs which satisfy the precondition of KS-A. Backward chaining can continue until preconditions are satisfied by existing data or user inputs. Finally, *iteration* of KSs is needed. The control KS-C can evaluate the outputs of KS-D to check if they satisfy some predicate; if not, KS-C can cause KS-D to be reexecuted, possibly with different parameters.

It is up to a developer to design the appropriate control strategies for an application. To control a KS, its trigger condition must be coded to recognize when that KS is required. One type of object on the blackboard can be a *plan* (i.e., a sequence of KSs). The plan contains a pointer indicating the next KS to execute. A KS's trigger condition can be that it is the next KS to be executed as part of a plan. When a KS is part of a plan, it receives a rating equal to the priority of the KS which created the plan, further favoring its execution.

As an example, suppose the MC-model marks a node corresponding to a specific maneuver M.The LDE-builder will have as its trigger condition that a maneuver node is marked. The precondition of LDE-builder will be that the qualitative representation of signals of M is known. Backward chaining from LDE-builder's preconditions and the marked node M will cause a signal interpretation KS's trigger condition to be satisfied—the precondition will be the existence of signals. Once LDE-builder executes and places its outputs on the blackboard, a KS for the CB-model for M becomes invokable; its trigger condition will be the same as LDE-builder's.

The example describes top-down control, executing KSs as they are needed. Bottom-up control is also possible; for example, selection of maneuvers depends on currently hypothesized deficiencies.

Many KSs have a similar structure; when executed in a particular context, they identify a set of options and make a choice. The decisions which must be made correspond to internal nodes in the problem space. The MC-model is an example of a KS of this type. Another example is LDE-select, which must choose specific gains to modify. Using the structured representations and rules described in previous sections, a decision can be reduced to a small number of options. However, even experts find it difficult to explain the reasons for choosing a particular option. This is a serious knowledge acquisition problem. A useful *assistant* system can still be built by depending on the engineer to make difficult choices. Another property of an assistant is it always allows the user to override its decisions. For example, before modifying a coefficient, the engineer's authorization is required.

An assistant system is highly interactive. It must provide tools to let a user get the information needed to make intelligent choices. The user interface must be flexible since, almost by definition, the user's requests cannot be known in advance. For troubleshooting, signals, coefficients, block diagrams, constraints, and possible modifications all need to be displayed.

The interactive assistant has two other important roles. It can be used as a tutoring tool and as a knowledge acquisition tool. Presenting a domain novice with valid options and feedback on the consequences of choices is a good tutorial approach. Observing an expert user's choices and the reasons for them may allow this aspect of domain knowledge to be added to the Flite system. For either class of user the assistant looks after many details, freeing the user to concentrate on the more challenging parts of the task.

To fully automate the system requires further research. Two issues in particular are difficult. These are related to controlling the tuner and the diagnostic search. The tuner's task is to plan a sequence of calls to an optimization program by varying input modifications, constraints and the objective function. This resembles a problem of *reactive planning* [11], where different formulations of the optimization problem correspond to different actions. Planning must be reactive since the outcomes of actions cannot be predicted before performing the actions.

Controlling search during troubleshooting is also difficult due to the sheer size of the problem space, the cost of evaluating terminal nodes, and the fact that a solution is a set of terminal nodes in different parts of the space. The key issue is maintaining dependencies among choices at different levels of the problem space. Assumption-based truth maintenance systems [5] seem to be a promising approach to these problems.

6.3   Current Implementation Status

This chapter has sought to describe an on-going research and development project. Research activities have concentrated on the principles and techniques needed for an intelligent troubleshooting environment. The implementation strategy is composed of short-term and long-term phases. The short-term goal is to build an interactive environment with the basic tools to assist an engineer performing troubleshooting. Important user interface and system integration issues are being addressed during this phase. As research results are tested and proven, they will be incorporated, increasing the intelligence of the Flite system and reducing the reliance on the user.

The blackboard engine is a combination of LISP functions, precoded rules (e.g., to apply control decisions), and rules compiled from KS declarations (e.g., to verify preconditions). The main procedure switches between rule sets which perform specific subtasks; running a set of rules is like a subroutine call. The blackboard shell is an extension of the Knowledge Craft environment and is implemented using the interface building facilities of Knowledge Craft. An object-oriented approach is used to represent tasks, icons, windows, and other elements of the shell. Most objects are manipulated using a mouse and menus; a command window is also available.

One subtask of the blackboard shell is dedicated to the application-specific user interface. Two major components of the user interface have been implemented: packages to display (graphically) signals and coefficients. Taxonomies of signals and coefficients have been built using CRL; these structures are referenced and updated by LISP functions. Functions of the user interface can be initiated by the user or called by knowledge sources. Both packages allow the user to display many individual signals (and/or coefficients), request zooms, plot tolerances, and perform other operations on displays.

All the basic signal processing routines of Section 4.1 have been implemented in C. These routines have been tested on real recorded data and the final, fine-tuned versions have been integrated with the blackboard system. Routines for describing signal morphologies given polynomial approximations have been developed using LISP and C. Identifying the gains of the LDE-model has been formulated as an optimization problem and tested with real signals using routines from available subroutine libraries.

Finally, a program for building networks of constraints and performing propagation has been developed with CRL, to represent the network, and LISP demons for propagation. The program is independent of the representation of signals and gains; a user need only supply functions to perform basic operations in the representation. Experiments to evaluate different representations are being performed using this program.

7   CONCLUSIONS

The research described here combines AI and simulation in a troubleshooting system. Simulation is both the subject of troubleshooting and a critical element in evaluating the hypotheses generated by reasoning. This approach to troubleshooting uses the complementary strengths of the two technologies to tackle difficult real-world problems.

Researchers in AI have studied qualitative reasoning as an approach to understanding devices and physical systems. Much of this research is motivated by the desire to endow computers with the ability to reason about so-called *naive physics* [12]. The investigation of a real-world problem involving time-varying processes shows a need to make physical reasoning less naive. Troubleshooting, in particular, seeks to identify and correct specific deficiencies. The need to take corrective actions with an objective measure of the success of these actions means qualitative solutions in terms of discrete values and directions of change are not sufficient.

Simulation is concerned with modeling process behavior over time. Applying AI to reason about the results of simulation requires a transformation of signals to a qualitative representation. A careful choice of qualitative representations is crucial to interpretation. Interpretation gives insight into the behavior of the modeled process in different operating conditions.

AI techniques for structured representations of domain knowledge are a good approach to constructing useful systems even if those systems are "assistants" rather than "experts." Representing knowledge in familiar ways makes interaction with users much easier. This allows users to play a decision-making role, with the assistant system determining the consequences of decisions and subsequent options.

ACKNOWLEDGMENTS

The work described in this chapter is supported by the Centre de recherche informatique de Montreal (CRIM), in its role of promoting joint university–industry research in computer science.

REFERENCES

1. D. G. Bobrow, (Ed.), *Qualitative Reasoning about Physical Systems,* A Bradford Book, MIT Press, Cambridge, MA, 1985. Reprinted from *Artificial Intelligence: An International Journal,* **24,** 1984.

2. Carnegie Group, "Knowledge Craft 3.1 Reference Manual," Carnegie Group Inc., Pittsburgh, PA, 1987.

3. E. Davis, "Constraint Propagation with Interval Labels," *Artificial Intelligence: An International Journal,* **32**(3): 281–332, 1987.

4. R. Davis, "Diagnostic Reasoning Based on Structure and Behavior," in D. G. Bobrow, (Ed.), *Qualitative Reasoning about Physical Systems,* MIT Press, Cambridge, MA, pp. 347–410, 1985.

5. J. de Kleer, "An Assumption-based TMS," *Artificial Intelligence: An International Journal,* **28**(2):127–162, 1986.

6. J. de Kleer and J. S. Brown, "A Qualitative Physics Based on Confluences," in D. G. Bobrow (Ed.), *Qualitative Reasoning about Physical Systems,* MIT Press, Cambridge, MA, pp. 7–83, 1985.

7. P. Eykhoff, *System Identification,* Wiley, New York, 1974.

8. K. D. Forbus, "Interpreting Observations of Physical Systems," *IEEE Transactions on Systems, Man, and Cybernetics,* **SMC-17**(3):350–359, 1987.

9. B. Friedland, *Control System Design: An Introduction to State-Space Methods,* McGraw-Hill, New York, 1986.

10. M. R. Genesereth, "The Use of Design Descriptions in Automated Diagnosis," in D. G. Bobrow (Ed.), *Qualitative Reasoning about Physical Systems,* MIT Press, Cambridge, MA, pp. 411–436, 1985.

11. M. P. Georgeff and A. L. Lansky, "Reasoning about Actions and Plans," in *Proceedings of the 1986 Workshop,* Morgan Kaufmann, Los Altos, CA, 1987.

12. P. J. Hayes, "The Naive Physics Manifesto," in D. Michie (Ed.), *Expert Systems in the Micro-Electronic Age,* Edinburgh University Press, Edinburgh, pp. 242–270, 1979.

13. B. Hayes-Roth, "A Blackboard Architecture for Control," *Artificial Intelligence: An International Journal,* **26**(3):251–321, 1985.

14. B. J. Kuipers, "Qualitative Simulation," *Artificial Intelligence: An International Journal,* **29**(3):289–338, 1986.

15. C. S. Myers and L. R. Rabiner, "A Level Building Dynamic Time Warping Algorithm for Connected Word Recognition," *IEEE Transactions on Acoustics, Speech and Signal Processing,* **ASSP-29**(2):284–297, 1981.

16. H. P. Nii, "Blackboard Systems," *The AI Magazine,* **7**(3, 4), 1986.

17. H. Sakoe and S. Chiba, "Dynamic Programming Algorithm Optimization for Spoken Word Recognition," *IEEE Transactions on Acoustics, Speech and Signal Processing,* **ASSP-26**(1):43–49, 1978.

18. M. Stefik, "Planning with Constraints (Molgen: Part 1)," *Artificial Intelligence: An International Journal,* **16**(1):111–140, 1981.

19. G. J. Sussman and G. L. Steele, "CONSTRAINTS: A Language for Expressing Almost-Hierarchical Descriptions," *Artificial Intelligence: An International Journal,* **14**(1):1–39, 1980.

20. T. Y. Young and K.-S. Fu, (Eds.), *Handbook of Pattern Recognition and Image Processing,* Academic, New York, 1986.

INDEX